Love the Great Outdoors?

When getting away means getting off the beaten path, visit AAA.com/campgrounds or AAA.com/maps for:

More than 20,000 places to camp across the U.S. and Canada

Complete mapping and travel information to plan your adventure

Look for locations with the trusted mark of approval.

Inspected & Approved

Make the Conn🔗ction

For trip planning and local activities, AAA TourBook guides are just the beginning.

Open the door to a whole lot more on **AAA.com**. Get extra travel insight, more information and online booking.

Find this symbol for places to look, book and save on AAA.com.

Virginia

Published by AAA Publishing
1000 AAA Drive, Heathrow, FL 32746-5063
Copyright AAA 2017, All rights reserved

Advertising Rate and Circulation Information: (407) 444-8280

Printed in the USA by Quad/Graphics

This book is printed on paper certified by third-party standards for sustainably managed forestry and production.

Printed on recyclable paper.
Please recycle whenever possible.

Stock #4679

CONTENTS

Get more travel information at
AAA.com/travelguides

Attractions, hotels, restaurants and other
travel experience information are all
grouped under the alphabetical listing of
the city in which those experiences are
physically located—or the nearest
recognized city.

Virginia

Williamsburg, Jamestown & Yorktown

Featured Information

free to soak it all in

TripAssist travel insurance from Allianz Global Assistance can free you up to make the most of your vacation. Nothing will hold you back knowing that you and your travel plans are safe.

Talk to your AAA Travel Agent today for more information.

relax

Get the credit card with
unlimited rewards.

With a AAA Member Rewards Visa® credit card you can earn **3x points** on qualifying AAA and travel purchases, **2x points** on gas, grocery store and drugstore purchases, **1 point** per $1 on all other purchases. *

There are no spending tiers, no rotating categories, no limit to the points you can earn—and you don't have to enroll. Just make purchases, earn rewards and relax.

Visit any participating AAA branch or AAA.com/creditcard.

The card that gets you there™

AAA Member Rewards

4000 1234 5678 9123
4000
VALID THRU 00/00
CHRIS L MARTIN
VISA
Signature

For information on the rates, fees, other costs and benefits associated with the use of thi credit card, visit the website listed above or your participating AAA branch.
***How You Earn Points:** You earn points when you use your card to make purchases, minu returns, credits and adjustments ("Purchases"). The following transactions are not considere Purchases and will not earn points: Balance Transfers and Cash Advances (each as define in your Credit Card Agreement), fees, interest charges, fraudulent transactions and certai other charges. **1 Point:** Earn 1 point (base point) for every $1 of Purchases charged to th credit card each billing cycle. **2 Points:** Earn 2 points (consisting of 1 bonus point and base point) per $1 for Purchases made with the card at any eligible gas, grocery store c pharmacy retail merchant categories as designated by Bank of America. **3 Points:** Earn points (consisting of 2 bonus points and 1 base point) per $1 for Purchases made with th card through any participating AAA Club when AAA is the merchant of record, or at eligibl retail travel merchant categories as designated by Bank of America. **Points Expiratior** Points expire 5 years after the month they were earned. **Rewards Program Rules:** Progran Rules containing additional details will be sent to you with your new account materials. Othe significant terms apply. Program subject to change.
This credit card program is issued and administered by Bank of America, N.A. Visa and Vis Signature are registered trademarks of Visa International Service Association and are used b the issuer pursuant to license from Visa U.S.A. Inc. AAA is a trademark of American Automobil Association, Inc. ©2017 Bank of America Corporation ©2017 AAA   ARDT8X7

Using Your Guide

AAA TourBook guides are packed with travel insight, maps and listings of places to stay, play, eat and save. For more listings, more details and online booking, visit **AAA.com/travelguides**.

Helping You Make the Connection
Look for this symbol 🌐 throughout the guides for direct links to related content.

A to Z City Listings
Cities and places are listed alphabetically within each state or province. Attractions, hotels and restaurants are listed once — under the city in which they are physically located.

Cities that are considered part of a larger destination city or area have an expanded city header. The header identifies the larger region and cross-references pages that contain shared trip planning resources:

- Destination map – outline map of the cities that comprise a destination city or area
- Attraction spotting map – regional street map marked with attraction locations
- Hotel/restaurant spotting map and index – regional street map numbered with hotel and restaurant locations identified in an accompanying index

Cities that are not considered part of a larger destination city or area but have a significant number of listings may have these resources within the individual city section:

- Attraction spotting map
- Hotel/restaurant spotting map and index

Location Abbreviations
Directions are from the center of town unless otherwise specified, using these highway abbreviations:

Bus. Rte.=business route
CR=county road
FM=farm to market
FR=forest road
Hwy.=Canadian highway
I=interstate highway
LR=legislative route
R.R.=rural route
SR/PR=state or provincial route
US=federal highway

About Listed Establishments
AAA/CAA Inspected & Approved hotels and restaurants are listed on the basis of merit alone after careful evaluation and approval by full-time, professionally trained AAA inspectors. An establishment's decision to advertise in the TourBook guide has no bearing on its evaluation or rating; nor does inclusion of advertising imply AAA endorsement of products and services.

Information in this guide was believed accurate at the time of publication. However, since changes inevitably occur between annual editions, please contact your AAA travel professional, visit **AAA.com/travelguides** or download the free AAA Mobile app to confirm prices and schedules.

Attraction Listing Icons
SAVE AAA Discounts & Rewards® member discount

🔌 Electric vehicle charging station on premises. Domestic station information provided by the U.S. Department of Energy. Canadian station information provided by Plug'n Drive Ontario.

GT Guided Tours available
🏕 Camping facilities
🍽 Food on premises
🎿 Recreational activities
🐾 Pet friendly (Call for restrictions/fees.)
🌳 Picnicking allowed

In select cities only:

🚇 Mass transit station within 1 mile. Icon is followed by station name and AAA/CAA designated station number within listing.

🔻 AAA/CAA travel experts may designate an attraction of exceptional interest and quality as a AAA GEM — a *Great Experience for Members®*. See GEM Attraction Index (listed on CONTENTS page) for a complete list of locations.

Consult the online travel guides at **AAA.com/travelguides** or visit AAA Mobile for additional things to do if you have time.

Hotel Listing Icons
May be preceded by CALL and/or SOME UNITS.

Member Information:

SAVE Member rates: discounted standard room rate or lowest public rate available at time of booking for dates of stay.

6   USING YOUR GUIDE

ECO Eco-certified by government or private organization.

⊞ Electric vehicle charging station on premises. Domestic station information provided by the U.S. Department of Energy. Canadian station information provided by Plug'n Drive Ontario.

⊠ Smoke-free premises

In select cities only:

▦ Mass transit station within 1 mile. Icon is followed by station name and AAA/CAA designated station number within listing.

Services:

✈ Airport transportation

🐾 Pet friendly (Call for restrictions/fees.)

🍴 Restaurant on premises

🍴• Restaurant off premises

🍴 Room service for 2 or more meals

🍸 Full bar

♘ Child care

BIZ Business center

♿ Accessible features (Call property for available services and amenities.)

Activities:

♠ Full-service casino

🏊 Pool

💪 Health club or exercise room on premises

In-Room Amenities:

HS High-speed Internet service

$HS High-speed Internet service (Call property for fees.)

📶 Wireless Internet service

$◐ Wireless Internet service (Call property for fees.)

◈ No wireless Internet service

📽 Pay movies

▮ Refrigerator

▤ Microwave

▣ Coffeemaker

A̸C̸ No air conditioning

📺̸ No TV

☎̸ No telephones

Restaurant Listing Icons

SAVE AAA Discounts & Rewards® member discount

ECO Eco-certified by government or private organization.

⊞ Electric vehicle charging station on premises. Domestic station information provided by the U.S. Department of Energy. Canadian station information provided by Plug'n Drive Ontario.

A̸C̸ No air conditioning

♿ Accessible features (Call property for available services and amenities.)

⊠ Designated smoking section

B Breakfast

L Lunch

D Dinner

24 Open 24 hours

LATE Open after 11 p.m.

🐾 Pet friendly (Call for restrictions/fees.)

In select cities only:

▦ Mass transit station within 1 mile. Icon is followed by station name and AAA/CAA designated station number within listing.

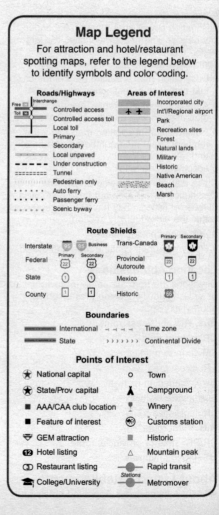

Map Legend

For attraction and hotel/restaurant spotting maps, refer to the legend below to identify symbols and color coding.

Roads/Highways

Free — Interchange
Toll —
Controlled access
Controlled access toll
Local toll
Primary
Secondary
Local unpaved
Under construction
Tunnel
Pedestrian only
Auto ferry
Passenger ferry
Scenic byway

Areas of Interest

Incorporated city
✈ ✈ Int'l/Regional airport
Park
Recreation sites
Forest
Natural lands
Military
Historic
Native American
Beach
Marsh

Route Shields

Interstate 95 95 Business
Federal Primary 22 Secondary 22
State ① ①
County 1 1

Trans-Canada Primary Secondary
Provincial Autoroute 22 22
Mexico 1 1
Historic 66

Boundaries

International
State
Time zone
Continental Divide

Points of Interest

★ National capital
★ State/Prov capital
■ AAA/CAA club location
■ Feature of interest
♦ GEM attraction
⑫ Hotel listing
③ Restaurant listing
🎓 College/University

○ Town
⚲ Campground
🍷 Winery
⊛ Customs station
■ Historic
△ Mountain peak
— Rapid transit
Stations
— Metromover

Understanding the Diamond Ratings

Hotel and restaurant evaluations are unscheduled to ensure our professionally trained inspectors encounter the same experience members do.

- When an establishment is Diamond Rated, it means members can expect a good fit with their needs. The inspector assigns a rating that indicates the type of experience to expect.
- While establishments at high levels must offer increasingly complex personalized services, establishments at every level are subject to the same basic requirements for cleanliness, comfort and hospitality. Learn more at **AAA.com/diamonds**.

Hotels	Restaurants
Budget-oriented, offering basic comfort and hospitality.	Simple, economical food, often quick-serve, in a functional environment.
Affordable, with modestly enhanced facilities, décor and amenities.	Familiar food, often cooked to order, served in casual surroundings.
Distinguished, multifaceted with enhanced physical attributes, amenities and guest comforts.	Trendy cuisine, skillfully prepared and served, with expanded beverage options, in an enhanced setting.

Refined, stylish with upscale physical attributes, extensive amenities and high degree of hospitality, service and attention to detail.	Distinctive fine-dining. Creative preparations, skillfully served, often with wine steward, amid upscale ambience.

Ultimate luxury, sophistication and comfort with extraordinary physical attributes, meticulous personalized service, extensive amenities and impeccable standards of excellence.	Leading-edge cuisine of the finest ingredients, uniquely prepared by an acclaimed chef, served by expert service staff led by maître d' in extraordinary surroundings.

Guest Safety

Inspectors view a sampling of rooms during evaluations and, therefore, AAA/CAA cannot guarantee the presence of working locks and operational fire safety equipment in every guest unit.

Contacting AAA/CAA About the TourBook Guide

Tell us what you think about the content and format of the TourBook guide or about your experience at a listed hotel, restaurant or attraction. If your visit to an attraction, hotel or restaurant listed by AAA/CAA doesn't meet your expectations, please tell us about it **during your visit or within 30 days**. Be sure to save your receipts and other documentation for reference. Or, maybe you'd like to recommend a place you visited and would like AAA inspectors to consider.

Use the easy online form at **AAA.com/tourbookcomments** to send us the details.

Alternatively, you can email your comments to: memberrelations@national.aaa.com or submit them via postal mail to: AAA Member Comments, 1000 AAA Dr., Box 61, Heathrow, FL 32746.

Thomas Jefferson's house at Monticello

Virginia

Entrenched in history and entwined with tradition, Virginia not only embraces its past, but thrives on it. Seven presidential homes, two Colonial capitals, more Civil War battlefields than any other state—only Virginia can offer such a historical legacy.

Climb aboard replicas of wooden ships or visit the ruins of Jamestown and witness archeological digs. Stroll along the streets of Colonial Williamsburg and chat with 18th-century merchants. Discover such Richmond treasures as the Capitol designed by Thomas Jefferson and The Museum of the Confederacy, brimming with Civil War memorabilia. Visit Charlottesville, home of Jefferson's Monticello, and have lunch at Michie Tavern ca. 1784, once an inn for the wayworn.

Alternatively, head for the mountains. The scenery along Skyline Drive and the Blue Ridge Parkway—both meandering, two-lane

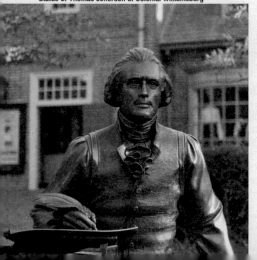

Statue of Thomas Jefferson at Colonial Williamsburg

roads—is breathtaking. If you prefer to have your breath taken in a more jarring way, hop aboard a theme park roller coaster.

Or, experience real-world art in the chambers of caverns in Front Royal, Luray and New Market, where Mother Nature's hands shaped limestone-like molding clay to create striking natural wonders.

Through the Pages of History

In Virginia, you'll find out what life was like when the first permanent English settlers came to North America. Costumed interpreters at Jamestown Settlement demonstrate how the adventurous colonists coped with the hardships of life in the New World.

To get a little closer to the real thing, cruise to the romantic destination of Tangier Island. Life on the largely unspoiled island is a radical departure from the hustle and bustle on the mainland. Residents who live and work along the quaint, narrow streets speak in a lingering Elizabethan dialect and adhere to the customs of a bygone era.

You'll certainly learn about America's past leaders in Virginia—it's the birthplace of eight presidents, including John Tyler and Zachary Taylor. Open to the public are the former residences of George Washington, Thomas Jefferson, James Madison, James Monroe, William Henry Harrison and Woodrow Wilson.

Born at Stratford Hall plantation, Robert E. Lee left footprints all over the state as he led the Confederate Army of Northern Virginia during the Civil War. He chalked up victories at Richmond, capital of the Confederacy, and at Chancellorsville and tasted defeat at Appomattox Court House, the site of his surrender to Gen. Ulysses S. Grant. The Confederate general's body is buried at Lee Chapel on the campus of Washington and Lee University in Lexington.

Southeast of Roanoke, a national monument at Booker T. Washington's birth site pays tribute to the many accomplishments of this freed slave who advised presidents and inspired philanthropists. Founder of the Tuskegee Normal and Industrial Institute in Alabama, Washington helped lay the framework on which the civil rights movement was built.

Recreation

The majestic Allegheny, Appalachian, Blue Ridge and Shenandoah mountains, standing like sentinels over western Virginia, offer a wealth of outdoor opportunities. Scenic Skyline Drive, winding along the crest of the Blue Ridge Mountains, runs the length of Shenandoah National Park and provides the perfect backdrop for bicycling. Crisp autumn days, with trees ablaze with fiery red and yellow leaves, are ideal for two-wheeling it along the 105 miles of twisting roadway. If you're a thrill seeker, try cruising down the mountain bike trails in Mount Rogers National Recreation Area, which boasts Virginia's highest elevation.

Hikers should head to Shenandoah National Park, where more than 500 miles of trails lead through havens abloom in the spring with azaleas, dogwood and mountain laurel.

After an action-packed day of romping through the woods, a night of sound slumber beneath twinkling stars might be just what you need. There are several developed campgrounds available in this pristine wilderness. Additionally, some 535 miles of the Appalachian Trail traverses Virginia, offering numerous opportunities for primitive camping.

Taking to the slopes can be quite rewarding, too. From December to March, you can indulge in skiing and snowboarding at Virginia's four resorts—Bryce Resort in Basye, The Homestead in Hot Springs, Massanutten Resort in McGaheysville and Wintergreen Resort in Wintergreen.

The Tidewater area is a great place for frolicking in the water. Launch your boat, hoist the sails and take to the inviting ocean waters. Shipwrecks off the coast entice experienced scuba divers to explore the mysterious depths.

Swimming, rafting, canoeing and kayaking can be enjoyed in Virginia's many rivers, streams and lakes. Canoe down the remote, tree-lined Shenandoah River or take to the rapids on the James River in downtown Richmond, with the city's skyline towering in the background. The Chesapeake Bay is the perfect backdrop for a day of sailing.

Mountain streams and inland rivers provide the backdrop for excellent freshwater fishing. Several large reservoirs include Lake Anna, Claytor Lake, Smith Mountain Lake, Philpott Reservoir and Kerr Lake. State fish hatcheries help keep the lakes, rivers and streams stocked with trout and bass. Anglers can reel in more than 25 species of fish.

Saltwater fishing is good at Chincoteague and other barrier islands. The Atlantic Ocean is home to such catches as blue marlin, flounder, wahoo, white marlin and yellowfin tuna. The Chesapeake Bay is popular for sport fishing, with some catches weighing in anywhere from 50 to 100 pounds. If the rod and reel are not your style, try scooping up some of the bay's delectable crabs and oysters.

Kayaks sitting on a pier

Historic Timeline

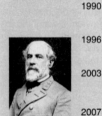

1607	North America's first permanent English colony is founded at Jamestown.
1699	The seat of government is moved to Williamsburg; in 1780, Richmond becomes the capital.
1775	Virginia patriot Patrick Henry makes his famous "Give me liberty or give me death" speech in Richmond.
1781	British general Charles Cornwallis surrenders to Gen. George Washington at Yorktown, ending the Revolutionary War.
1788	Virginia becomes the 10th state in the Union.
1865	Confederate general Robert E. Lee surrenders to Union general Ulysses S. Grant at Appomattox.
1917	Congress commissions a naval station at Hampton Roads, which is today home to numerous military installations.
1990	L. Douglas Wilder becomes the nation's first elected African-American governor.
1996	Archeologists uncover the remains of the original James Fort, abandoned for 3 centuries.
2003	The Lewis and Clark Bicentennial is launched at Monticello, honoring the expedition's Virginian sponsor and leaders.
2007	Queen Elizabeth II arrives in Jamestown to help celebrate its 400th anniversary.

What To Pack

Temperature Averages Maximum/Minimum	JANUARY	FEBRUARY	MARCH	APRIL	MAY	JUNE	JULY	AUGUST	SEPTEMBER	OCTOBER	NOVEMBER	DECEMBER
Arlington	43 / 25	47 / 28	56 / 35	68 / 44	77 / 54	85 / 63	89 / 68	87 / 67	80 / 60	69 / 47	58 / 38	46 / 29
Big Stone Gap	44 / 24	49 / 27	58 / 33	67 / 41	75 / 51	82 / 60	85 / 64	85 / 63	80 / 55	69 / 43	59 / 34	47 / 27
Charlottesville	42 / 25	46 / 27	54 / 35	64 / 44	72 / 54	80 / 63	84 / 67	82 / 65	75 / 57	65 / 46	56 / 37	45 / 28
Norfolk	48 / 33	51 / 35	58 / 41	68 / 49	75 / 58	84 / 67	88 / 72	85 / 71	79 / 65	70 / 54	61 / 45	52 / 36
Richmond	47 / 28	52 / 31	60 / 37	70 / 46	78 / 55	86 / 65	90 / 69	88 / 67	81 / 60	71 / 48	61 / 39	51 / 31
Roanoke	46 / 27	50 / 30	58 / 37	68 / 45	76 / 53	83 / 62	87 / 66	86 / 65	79 / 58	69 / 47	59 / 38	48 / 30

From the records of The Weather Channel Interactive, Inc.

Good Facts To Know

ABOUT THE STATE

POPULATION: 8,001,024.

AREA: 42,775 square miles; ranks 35th.

CAPITAL: Richmond.

HIGHEST POINT: 5,729 ft., Mount Rogers.

LOWEST POINT: Sea level, Atlantic Ocean.

TIME ZONE(S): Eastern. DST.

REGULATIONS

TEEN DRIVING LAWS: Drivers under age 18 are permitted one passenger under age 21 for the first year; no more than three passengers under age 21 after the first year (family members are exempt), unless driving to or from a school activity or accompanied by a passenger age 21 or older. Driving is not permitted daily midnight 1 a.m. The minimum age for an unrestricted driver's license is 18. Phone (800) 435-5137 for more information about Virginia driver's license regulations.

SEAT BELT/CHILD RESTRAINT LAWS: Seat belts are required for driver and front-seat passengers ages 18 and over. Children ages 8-17 are required to be in a child restraint or seat belt; child restraints are required for children under age 8. Rear-facing child restraint devices must be placed in the vehicle's back seat. AAA recommends the use of seat belts and appropriate child restraints for the driver and all passengers.

CELLPHONE RESTRICTIONS: Learner's permit and provisional driver's license holders under age 18 may not operate a cellphone while driving, even if it is equipped with hands-free technology. Text messaging is prohibited while driving.

HELMETS FOR MOTORCYCLISTS: Required for all riders.

RADAR DETECTORS: Not permitted.

MOVE OVER LAW: Driver is required to slow down and vacate the lane nearest stopped police, fire and rescue vehicles using audible or flashing signals. The law also includes tow trucks and road maintenance vehicles.

FIREARMS LAWS: Vary by state and/or county. Contact Firearms Transactions Office, Virginia State Police, P.O. Box 85141, Richmond, VA 23285; phone (804) 674-2292.

HOLIDAYS

HOLIDAYS: Jan. 1 ▪ Lee-Jackson Day, Jan. (Fri. preceding 3rd Mon.) ▪ Martin Luther King Jr. Day, Jan. (3rd Mon.) ▪ Washington's Birthday/Presidents Day, Feb. (3rd Mon.) ▪ Memorial Day, May (last Mon.) ▪ July 4 ▪ Labor Day, Sept. (1st Mon.) ▪ Columbus Day, Oct. (2nd Mon.) ▪ Veterans Day, Nov. 11 ▪ Thanksgiving, Nov. (4th Thurs.) ▪ Christmas, Dec. 25.

MONEY

TAXES: The Virginia statewide sales tax is 5.3 percent, which includes a 1 percent tax levied by city or county governments. Local options also allow admission, lodgings and restaurant taxes of varying increments.

VISITOR INFORMATION

INFORMATION CENTERS: State welcome centers are on US 13S near New Church ▪ on I-64E near Covington ▪ on I-66W near Manassas ▪ on I-81S near Stephenson ▪ on I-81N near Bristol ▪ on I-85N south of Bracey ▪ on I-77 at Lambsburg ▪ on I-77 near Rocky Gap ▪ on I-95N south of Skippers ▪ on I-95S near Fredericksburg ▪ at the Bell Tower on N. Ninth Street in downtown Richmond ▪ and on I-64E in New Kent.

FURTHER INFORMATION FOR VISITORS:
Virginia Tourism Corp.
901 E. Cary St., Suite 900
Richmond, VA 23219
(804) 545-5600
(800) 847-4882

National Park Service
1849 C St. N.W.
Washington, D.C. 20240
(202) 208-3818
(202) 208-6843

NATIONAL FOREST INFORMATION:
George Washington and Jefferson National Forests
5162 Valleypointe Pkwy.
Roanoke, VA 24019
(540) 265-5100
(888) 265-0019

FISHING AND HUNTING REGULATIONS:
Virginia Department of Game & Inland Fisheries
7870 Villa Park Dr.
Henrico, VA 23228
(804) 367-1000
(866) 721-6911

RECREATION INFORMATION:
Virginia State Parks
Department of Conservation & Recreation
600 E. Main St., 24th Floor
Richmond, VA 23219
(804) 786-6124
(800) 933-7275 (reservations)

Virginia Annual Events
Please call ahead to confirm event details.

Visit **AAA.com/travelguides/events** to find
AAA-listed events for every day of the year

JANUARY	FEBRUARY	MARCH
■ Lee-Jackson Day Lexington 540-461-0389 ■ Twelfth Night Virginia Beach 757-385-5100 ■ Ghost Watch / Petersburg 804-733-2400	■ Mid-Atlantic Quilt Festival Hampton 215-862-5828 ■ George Washington's Birthday Celebration Alexandria / 703-838-4242 ■ Richmond Boat Show Richmond 804-337-6479	■ Military Through the Ages Williamsburg 888-593-4682 ■ St. Patrick's Day Parade and Shamrock Festival Roanoke / 540-853-2889 ■ Virginia Festival of the Book / Charlottesville 434-924-3296

APRIL	MAY	JUNE
■ Shenandoah Apple Blossom Festival Winchester 540-662-3863 ■ Dogwood Festival Charlottesville 434-961-9824 ■ Virginia International Tattoo Norfolk / 757-282-2800	■ Roanoke Festival in the Park / Roanoke 540-342-2640 ■ Chesapeake Jubilee Chesapeake 757-482-4848 ■ Memorial Day Ceremonies Arlington 877-907-8585	■ Celebrate Fairfax / Fairfax 703-324-3247 ■ Norfolk Harborfest / Norfolk 757-441-2345 ■ Chautauqua Festival in the Park / Wytheville 276-228-6855

JULY	AUGUST	SEPTEMBER
■ Pony Swim and Auction Chincoteague 757-336-6161 ■ Yorktown Independence Day Celebration / Yorktown 757-890-3500 ■ Independence Day Williamsburg 757-229-1000	■ Discovery Day at Luray Caverns / Luray 540-743-6551 ■ East Coast Surfing Championships Virginia Beach 757-456-1535 ■ Old Fiddler's Convention Galax 276-236-8541	■ Colonial Market and Fair at Mount Vernon Mount Vernon 703-780-2000 ■ Virginia Beach Neptune Festival / Virginia Beach 757-498-0215 ■ Pumpkin Village Fall Festival / Leesburg 703-433-0002

OCTOBER	NOVEMBER	DECEMBER
■ An Occasion for the Arts Williamsburg 757-229-6511 ■ Historic Appomattox Railroad Festival Appomattox 434-352-2338 ■ Yorktown Victory Celebration / Yorktown 757-253-4838	■ Veterans Day Ceremonies Arlington 202-685-2851 ■ Capital of The Confederacy Civil War Show / Richmond 804-649-1861 ■ Foods and Feasts of Colonial Virginia Williamsburg 757-253-4838	■ Dominion GardenFest of Lights / Richmond 804-262-9887 ■ Holidays in the City Norfolk 757-623-1757 ■ Mount Vernon by Candlelight / Mount Vernon 703-780-2000

Downtown Richmond

Mabry Mill, Blue Ridge Parkway

Civil War Cannon

Chincoteague National Wildlife Refuge

USS Wisconsin, Norfolk VA

◤GEM◢ Index: Great Experience for Members

AAA editor's picks of exceptional note

Tomb of the Unknown
Soldier

Susan Constant at
Jamestown, Virginia

Monticello

Great Falls Park

See Orientation map on p. 24 for corresponding grid coordinates, if applicable.
*Indicates the GEM is temporarily closed.

Virginia
Atlas Section

ROADS/HIGHWAYS

- INTERSTATE
- CONTROLLED ACCESS
- CONTROLLED ACCESS TOLL
- TOLL ROAD
- PRIMARY DIVIDED
- PRIMARY UNDIVIDED
- SECONDARY DIVIDED
- SECONDARY UNDIVIDED
- LOCAL DIVIDED
- LOCAL UNDIVIDED
- UNPAVED ROAD
- UNDER CONSTRUCTION
- TUNNEL
- PEDESTRIAN ONLY
- AUTO FERRY
- PASSENGER FERRY
- SCENIC BYWAY
- DISTANCE BETWEEN MARKERS
- EXIT NUMBER-FREE/TOLL
- INTERCHANGE FULL/PARTIAL
- WELCOME/INFORMATION CENTER
- REST AREA/ SERVICE CENTER

BOUNDARIES

- INTERNATIONAL
- STATE
- COUNTY
- TIME ZONE
- CONTINENTAL DIVIDE

ROAD SHIELDS

- INTERSTATE/BUSINESS
- U.S./STATE/COUNTY
- FOREST/INDIAN
- TRANS- CANADA
- PROVINCIAL AUTOROUTE/ KING'S HIGHWAY
- MEXICO
- HISTORIC ROUTE 66
- VT 41 REFERENCE PAGE INDICATOR

AREAS OF INTEREST

- INDIAN
- MILITARY
- PARK
- FOREST
- GRASSLANDS
- HISTORIC
- ✈ INT'L/REGIONAL AIRPORT
- INCORPORATED CITY

POINTS OF INTEREST

- ○ TOWN
- NATIONAL CAPITAL
- STATE/PROVINCIAL CAPITAL
- AAA/CAA CLUB LOCATION
- ■ FEATURE OF INTEREST
- COLLEGE/UNIVERSITY
- CUSTOMS STATION
- HISTORIC
- LIGHTHOUSE
- MONUMENT/MEMORIAL
- STATE/PROVINCIAL PARK
- NATIONAL WILDLIFE REFUGE
- SKI AREA
- SPORTS COMPLEX
- DAM

CITIES/TOWNS are color-coded by size, showing where to find AAA Approved and Diamond rated lodgings or restaurants listed in the AAA TourBook guides and on AAA.com:

- ● Red - major destinations and capitals; many listings
- ● Black - destinations; some listings
- ● Grey - no listings

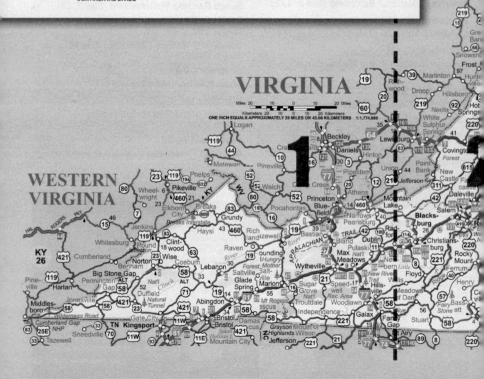

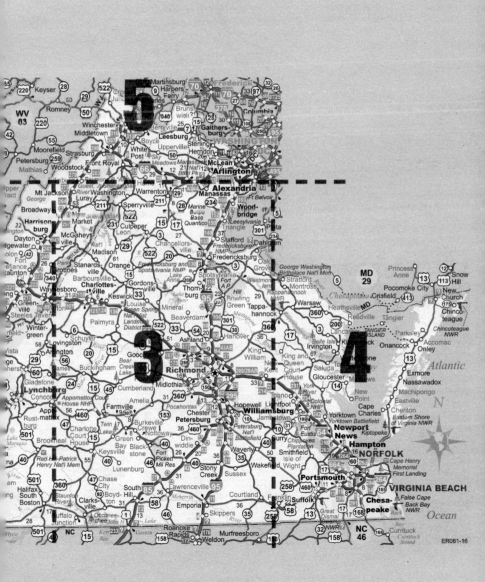

ER061-16

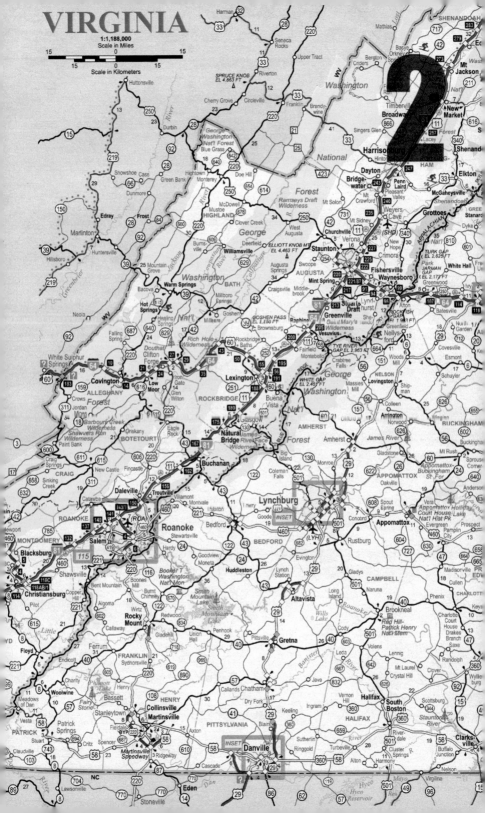

STAY CONNECTED

TO ALL THE THINGS
MEMBERSHIP CAN DO FOR YOU

- member discounts around you
- cheapest gas nearby
- Diamond Rated hotels and restaurants
- travel information and reservations
- roadside assistance

Download today. Connect every day.
AAA.com/mobile | CAA.ca/mobile

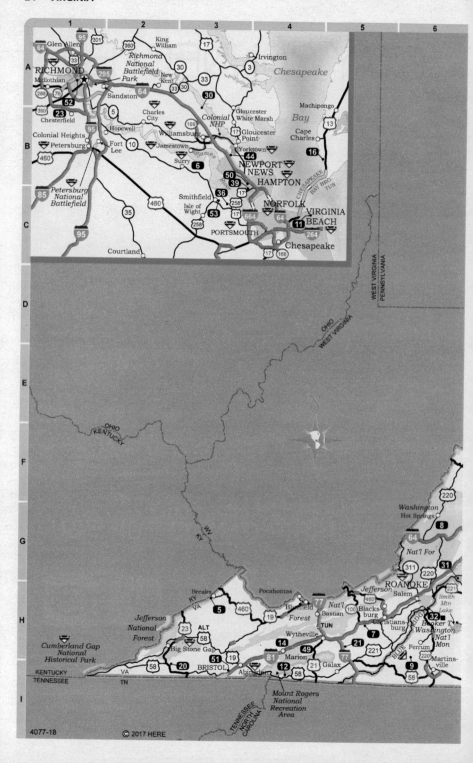

© 2017 HERE

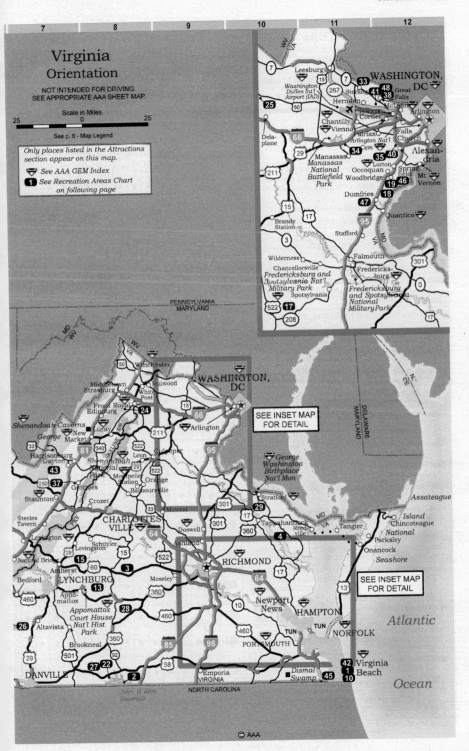

Recreation Areas Chart

The map location numerals in column 2 show an area's location on the preceding map.

Find thousands of places to camp at AAA.com/campgrounds

	MAP LOCATION	CAMPING	PICNICKING	HIKING TRAILS	BOATING	BOAT RAMP	BOAT RENTAL	FISHING	SWIMMING	PET FRIENDLY	BICYCLE TRAILS	WINTER SPORTS	VISITOR CENTER	LODGE/CABINS	FOOD SERVICE
NATIONAL PARKS *(See place listings.)*															
Shenandoah (F-8) 197,439 acres. Western Virginia. Scenic. Bird-watching; horseback riding trails, horse rental.		•	•	•				•		•			•	•	•
NATIONAL FORESTS *(See place listings.)*															
George Washington and Jefferson (F-7) 1,800,000 acres. Western Virginia and eastern edge of West Virginia. Equestrian camping, hunting; horseback riding trails, off-road vehicle trails, shooting ranges.		•	•	•	•	•	•	•	•	•	•	•	•		
NATIONAL RECREATION AREAS *(See place listings.)*															
Mount Rogers (I-4) 200,000 acres in southwestern Virginia.		•	•	•				•	•	•	•	•	•		
NATIONAL SEASHORES *(See place listings.)*															
Assateague Island (G-12) 49,500 acres 8 mi. s. of Ocean City, Md., via SR 611 on Assateague Island.		•	•	•	•			•							
NATIONAL WILDLIFE REFUGES															
Back Bay (I-11) 9,200 acres at 4005 Sandpiper Rd. in Virginia Beach. Bird-watching, canoeing, hunting, kayaking.	❶		•	•				•			•		•		
ARMY CORPS OF ENGINEERS															
John H. Kerr Reservoir (I-8) 106,860 acres off SR 4 near Boydton. Hunting, water skiing.	❷	•	•	•	•	•	•	•	•	•	•		•		
STATE															
Bear Creek Lake (G-8) 329 acres 4.5 mi. w. of Cumberland off US 60. Archery range, beach, horseback riding trails.	❸	•	•	•	•	•	•	•	•	•			•		
Belle Isle (G-10) 892 acres on SR 683 near Litwalton. Historic. Saltwater fishing; horseback riding trails, kayaks, playground.	❹	•	•	•	•	•	•	•					•	•	
Breaks Interstate (E-9) 4,500 acres just w. of Breaks via SR 80. Scenic. Geocaching, pedal boating; water park.	㉕	•	•	•	•	•	•	•	•				•	•	•
Chippokes Plantation (B-3) 1,947 acres on the James River 1.5 mi. e. of Surry via SR 10, then 3 mi. n. on CR 634. Historic. Horseback riding trails.	❻	•	•	•	•	•	•	•	•	•	•		•	•	•
Claytor Lake (H-5) 472 acres 4 mi. s. of Radford via I-81, then 2 mi. s. on SR 660. Nature programs. Beach.	❼	•	•	•	•	•	•	•	•	•			•	•	•
Douthat (G-6) 4,545 acres 6 mi. n. of Clifton Forge on SR 629. Equestrian camping.	❽	•	•	•	•	•	•	•	•	•	•		•	•	•
Fairy Stone (I-6) 4,741 acres 8 mi. w. of Bassett on SR 57. Hunting; horseback riding trails.	❾	•	•	•	•	•	•	•	•	•			•	•	•
False Cape (I-11) 3,844 acres at 4001 Sandpiper Rd. in Virginia Beach. (Accessible only by foot, bicycle, beach transport, tram or boat.) Camping (primitive), fishing (fresh and saltwater); beach.	❿	•	•	•	•			•	•	•	•		•		•
First Landing (C-4) 2,888 acres in Virginia Beach at Cape Henry on Shore Dr. (US 60). Crabbing, fishing (saltwater); beach.	⓫	•	•	•	•			•	•	•	•		•	•	•
Grayson Highlands (I-4) 4,502 acres w. of Volney on US 58. Biking (mountain), cross-country skiing, rock climbing, snowshoeing; equestrian camping, guided canoe trips (seasonal), horseback riding trails, wild pony herd.	⓬	•	•	•				•		•	•	•	•		•
Holliday Lake (H-8) 560 acres 6 mi. n.e. of Appomattox on SR 24, then 4 mi. e. via SR 626/629. Canoeing, kayaking; playgrounds.	⓭	•	•	•	•	•	•	•	•	•			•		•
Hungry Mother (H-4) 3,334 acres 4 mi. n. of Marion on SR 16. Boating (no motors), canoeing, hunting, kayaking; beach, meeting space.	⓮	•	•	•	•	•	•	•	•	•	•		•	•	•
James River (G-7) 1,561 acres on CR 606 near Norwood. Canoeing, equestrian camping, kayaking; bicycle rentals, horseback riding trails.	⓯	•	•	•	•	•	•			•	•			•	
Kiptopeke (B-4) 562 acres 3 mi. n. of the Chesapeake Bay Bridge Tunnel from Virginia Beach on US 13, then w. on SR 704. Bird-watching, crabbing, fishing (saltwater); fishing pier.	⓰	•	•	•	•	•	•		•	•	•		•		

Recreation Areas Chart

The map location numerals in column 2 show an area's location on the preceding map.

🔗 Find thousands of places to camp at AAA.com/campgrounds

	MAP LOCATION	CAMPING	PICNICKING	HIKING TRAILS	BOATING	BOAT RAMP	BOAT RENTAL	FISHING	SWIMMING	PET FRIENDLY	BICYCLE TRAILS	WINTER SPORTS	VISITOR CENTER	LODGE/CABINS	FOOD SERVICE
Lake Anna (D-10) 3,127 acres 25 mi. s.w. of Fredericksburg off SR 208. Hunting; horseback riding trails.	17	•	•	•	•	•		•	•	•	•		•	•	•
Leesylvania (C-12) 543 acres 10.3 mi. s. of Woodbridge off I-95 exit 156 at 2001 Daniel K. Ludwig Dr. Canoeing, kayaking; fitness trail, fishing pier, playground.	18		•	•	•	•	•	•	•	•			•		
Mason Neck (B-12) 1,856 acres 5 mi. n. of Woodbridge on US 1, then 5 mi. e. on SR 242. Bicycle rentals.	19		•	•	•	•	•	•		•	•		•		
Natural Tunnel (I-3) 909 acres .4 mi. s. of Duffield on US 23, then 4.2 mi. e. on Daniel Boone Tr. Swimming (pool); meeting space.	20	•	•	•				•	•	•	•		•		•
New River Trail (H-5) 1,668 acres off I-77 exit 24, then 1.5 mi. n. on US 52 in Wytheville. Historic. Equestrian camping, horseback riding, tubing; canoe rental, guided horseback tours (seasonal), show ring, tower.	21	•	•	•	•	•	•	•	•	•	•		•		•
Occoneechee (I-8) 2,698 acres 1 mi. e. of Clarksville on US 58. Equestrian camping, hunting; archery range, horseback riding trails.	22	•	•	•	•	•	•	•		•	•		•	•	•
Pocahontas (B-1) 8,115 acres 4 mi. s.w. of Chesterfield off SR 655. Hunting; horseback riding trails and show ring.	23	•	•	•	•	•	•	•	•	•	•		•		•
Shenandoah River (E-8) 1,619 acres 8 mi. s. of Front Royal off US 340 at 350 Daughter of Stars Dr. Tubing, zipline tours.	24	•	•	•	•	•		•		•			•	•	
Sky Meadows (A-10) 1,864 acres 5.1 mi. n. of Delaplane off US 17. Scenic. Camping (primitive); guided tours, historic buildings, horseback riding trails.	25	•	•	•				•		•			•		
Smith Mountain Lake (H-7) 1,148 acres 26 mi. s. of Bedford via SR 122 to SR 608 to SR 626. Beach.	26	•	•	•	•	•	•	•	•	•	•		•	•	•
Staunton River (I-8) 2,336 acres 9 mi. s.e. of Scottsburg on SR 344. Horseback riding trails.	27	•	•	•	•	•	•	•		•			•	•	•
Twin Lakes (H-8) 548 acres 3 mi. n.e. of Green Bay off US 360 to SR 613. Horseback riding trails.	28	•	•	•	•	•	•	•	•	•			•	•	•
Westmoreland (G-10) 1,321 acres 6 mi. n.w. of Montross on SR 3. Fishing (saltwater); pool.	29	•	•	•	•	•	•	•	•	•			•	•	•
York River (A-3) 2,531 acres .8 mi. n. of I-64 exit 231B on Croaker Rd., then 2 mi. e. to 5526 Riverview Rd. in Williamsburg. Canoeing, kayaking; horseback riding trails.	30		•	•	•	•	•		•		•		•		
BLUE RIDGE PARKWAY *(See place listing.)*															
Peaks of Otter (G-6) 4,150 acres at Milepost 86.	31	•	•	•	•			•		•			•	•	•
Roanoke Mountain (H-6) 65 acres at Milepost 120.3.	32	•		•						•	•		•		
OTHER															
Algonkian Regional Park (A-11) 838 acres 11 mi. e. of Leesburg and 3 mi. n. of SR 7. Golf, miniature golf; water park.	33		•		•	•		•	•	•					•
Bull Run Regional Park (B-11) 1,563 acres 3 mi. s.w. of Centreville off US 29. Miniature and disc golf, skeet and trap shooting; horseback riding trails, playground.	34	•	•	•				•	•	•	•				•
Burke Lake Park (B-12) 888 acres 6 mi. s.w. of I-495 exit 5W via CR 620, CR 645 and SR 123. Disc golf, miniature golf, golf (18 holes), volleyball; amphitheater, carousel, fitness trail, miniature train, playgrounds.	35	•	•	•	•	•	•		•	•	•		•	•	•
Carrollton Nike Park (C-3) 100 acres 2 mi. n. of Carrollton at 13036 Nike Park Rd. Historic. Athletic fields/courts, fishing pier, historical buildings, playground, skate park.	36		•	•				•		•			•		
Grand Caverns Park (F-7) 99 acres off I-81 exit 235, then 6 mi. e. on SR 256 to 5 Grand Caverns Dr. in Grottoes. Miniature golf; pool.	37		•	•					•						
Great Falls Park (A-12) 800 acres at 9200 Old Dominion Dr. in McLean. Bird-watching, cross-country skiing, horseback riding, kayaking.	38		•	•	•			•		•	•		•	•	•
Huntington Park (B-3) 60 acres at Riverpark Dr. and Mercury Blvd. in Newport News. Tennis; athletic fields, beach, fishing piers, garden, memorials, playground.	39		•		•	•		•	•						•

Recreation Areas Chart

The map location numerals in column 2 show an area's location on the preceding map.

Find thousands of places to camp at AAA.com/campgrounds

	MAP LOCATION	CAMPING	PICNICKING	HIKING TRAILS	BOATING	BOAT RAMP	BOAT RENTAL	FISHING	SWIMMING	PET FRIENDLY	BICYCLE TRAILS	WINTER SPORTS	VISITOR CENTER	LODGE/CABINS	FOOD SERVICE
Lake Accotink Park (B-12) 493 acres 3 mi. from I-495 exit 5E via CR 620 and Heming Ave. Canoeing, miniature golf, volleyball; bike rental, carousel, guided boat tour, playground.	40		•	•	•	•	•	•		•	•	•			
Lake Fairfax Park (A-12) 476 acres 7 mi. w. of I-495 exit 10W via SR 7 and CR 606. Cross-country skiing, tubing; athletic fields, carousel, playground, skate park.	41	•	•	•	•	•	•	•	•	•	•	•			
Little Island Park (I-11) 144 acres at 3820 S. Sandpiper Rd. in Virginia Beach. Canoeing, crabbing, kayaking; athletic courts, beach, equipment rental, fishing pier, playground.	42		•		•	•	•	•	•	•					•
Natural Chimneys Park (F-7) 150 acres .5 mi. n.w. on SR 731 following signs. Swimming (pool).	43	•	•	•				•	•	•	•				
Newport News Park (B-3) 7,711 acres on SR 143, .5 mi. w. of jct. SR 105 in Newport News. Canoeing, disc golf, golf, horseback riding, jogging, sledding; archery range, dog park, playgrounds, skate park.	44	•	•	•	•		•	•		•	•	•	•		•
Northwest River Park (I-11) 763 acres 7.4 mi. s. of Chesapeake on Battlefield Blvd. S. (SR 168), then 3.8 mi. e. on Indian Creek Rd. Bird-watching, canoeing, disc golf (18 holes), kayaking, miniature golf; cabins, garden, horseback riding trails, playground.	45	•	•	•	•		•	•		•	•		•	•	
Pohick Bay Regional Park (B-12) 1,003 acres 1 mi. s.w. of Lorton on US 1, then 3.2 mi. s.e. on Gunston Rd. Golf, miniature golf; horseback riding trails, water park.	46	•	•	•	•	•	•	•	•	•	•			•	
Prince William Forest Park (C-11) 15,000 acres off I-95 exit 150B, then .2 mi. w. to Joplin Rd. (SR 619). Cross-country skiing; exhibits.	47	•	•	•				•		•	•	•	•		
Riverbend Park (A-12) 409 acres 10 mi. w. of I-495 exit 13 via SR 193, CR 603 and Jeffrey Rd. (CR 1268). Nature center.	48		•	•	•	•	•	•		•	•		•		•
Rural Retreat Lake (H-4) 90 acres 4 mi. s.w. of Rural Retreat off I-81 exit 60, 4 mi. e. on CR 749, then 1 mi. s. on CR 677. Bird-watching, disc golf.	49	•	•	•	•	•	•	•	•	•					•
Sandy Bottom Nature Park (B-3) 456 acres off I-64 at 1255 Big Bethel Rd. in Hampton. Camping (primitive); fishing pier, garden, nature center, playground, tower.	50	•	•	•	•		•	•		•	•		•	•	
Sugar Hollow Park (H-3) 400 acres in Bristol off Lee Hwy. via I-81 exit 7. Golf driving range, playground.	51	•	•	•						•	•				
William Byrd Park (A-1) 287 acres at the s. end of Boulevard at Idlewood Ave. in Richmond. Boating (no motors), tennis; amphitheater, dog parks, fitness trail, monuments, pedal boat rides, playground, softball fields.	52		•	•	•		•	•	•	•	•				•
Windsor Castle Park (C-3) 208 acres at 301 Jericho Rd. in Smithfield. Canoeing, kayaking; dog park, fishing pier, historic buildings.	53		•	•		•	•	•		•	•				

ABINGDON (I-3) pop. 8,191, elev. 2,057'
• Restaurants p. 30

Abingdon, one of the oldest English-speaking towns in the Blue Ridge Mountains, was founded in 1778 at the junction of two Native American trails on a site where Daniel Boone had camped some years before.

The Virginia Creeper National Recreation Trail follows one of the traditional footpaths for 34 miles along a former railbed of the Virginia-Carolina Railroad. Beginning in Abingdon, the trail is popular with hikers, bicyclists, runners and horseback riders. A 15-mile section provides an easy hike on winding trails leading to Damascus.

The community's 20-square-block historic district contains many museums, craft shops, art studios, galleries and lodgings housed in 19th-century buildings. The area is a thriving arts community and includes the Arts Depot on Depot Square, which offers changing exhibits. In early August, the ☒ Virginia Highlands Festival offers an antiques market and a variety of art competitions.

Abingdon Convention and Visitors Bureau: 335 Cummings St., Abingdon, VA 24210. **Phone:** (276) 676-2282 or (800) 435-3440.

Self-guiding tours: A brochure detailing a walking tour of Abingdon's historic district is available from the convention and visitors bureau.

Shopping: The Holston Mountain Artisans (214 Park St.) offers regionally made wares; phone (276) 628-7721. The downtown district is known for its antiques and locally owned specialty shops. A farmers market draws crowds on Tuesday afternoons and Saturday mornings, late April through Thanksgiving; on Saturday morning in December; and the first and third Saturday, January 1 to late April.

☒ ☒ **BARTER THEATRE** is off I-81 exit 17 at 127 W. Main St. One of the country's oldest professional regional theaters, the "State Theatre of Virginia" was founded in 1933 on the theory that drama could be bartered for food. During the Depression, Robert Porterfield convinced 22 Broadway actors that it was better to eat in Virginia than to starve in New York. Though cash is now the accepted medium of payment, Porterfield's original theater offered tickets in exchange for milk, ham, chicken and other provisions.

Along with new works, time-honored dramas, comedies and musicals are presented year-round on two stages; spring, summer and fall repertories allow patrons to see four shows in 2 days. **Hours:** Box office open Tues.-Sat. 9-5, Sun. 1-5. Performances are given Tues. and Thurs. at 7:30, Fri.-Sat. at 8, Sun. at 7, with matinees Tues.-Thurs. and Sat. at 2 and Sun. at 3, Feb.-Dec. Show times may vary; phone ahead. **Cost:** Performance tickets $27-$46. Reservations are recommended. **Phone:** (276) 628-3991. ⑪

ALPINE MOTEL   (276)628-3178

Motel
$49-$89

Address: 882 E Main St 24210 **Location:** I-81 exit 19 (US 11), 0.5 mi w. **Facility:** 19 units. 1 story, exterior corridors. **Terms:** cancellation fee imposed. **Featured Amenity: continental breakfast.**

COMFORT INN ABINGDON   (276)676-2222
☒☒ Motel. **Address:** 170 Jonesboro Rd 24210

COMFORT SUITES ABINGDON   (276)698-3040
☒☒☒ Hotel. **Address:** 1093 Ole Berry Dr 24210

COUNTRY INN & SUITES BY CARLSON
(276)676-2829

Hotel
$109-$460

Address: 940 E Main St 24210 **Location:** I-81 exit 19 (US 11), just w. **Facility:** 81 units. 3 stories, interior corridors. **Pool:** outdoor. **Guest Services:** valet and coin laundry. **Featured Amenity: full hot breakfast.**

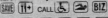
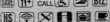

Nestled in the foothills of the Appalachian Mts in beautiful historic Abingdon home of Barter Theater

---

HAMPTON INN ABINGDON   (276)619-4600
☒☒☒ Hotel. **Address:** 340 Commerce Dr 24211

AAA Benefit:
Members save up to 10%!

THE MARTHA WASHINGTON INN & SPA   276/628-3161

Classic Historic Hotel
Rates not provided

Address: 150 W Main St 24210 **Location:** I-81 exit 17, 0.7 mi w on Cummings St, then just n. **Facility:** Built in 1832 as a private home that later served as a women's college, this red-brick Federalist mansion is set amid landscaped grounds. Rooms are richly appointed with wonderful art and furnishings. 63 units. 3 stories, interior corridors. *Bath:* shower only. **Parking:** on-site and valet. **Dining:** Sister's at the Martha, see separate listing. **Pool:** heated indoor. **Activities:** hot tub, miniature golf, tennis, exercise room, spa. **Guest Services:** valet laundry, area transportation.

QUALITY INN & SUITES OF ABINGDON   (276)676-9090
☒☒☒ Hotel. **Address:** 930 E Main St 24210

SUPER 8 MOTEL ABINGDON   276/676-3329
☒ Hotel. **Address:** 298 Town Center Dr 24210

WHITE BIRCHES INN   276/676-2140
▼▼▼ Historic Bed & Breakfast. **Address:** 268 Whites Mill Rd
24210

WHERE TO EAT

BELLA'S   276/628-8101
▼ American. Casual Dining. **Address:** 872 E Main St 24210

MILANO'S ITALIAN CUISINE   276/698-3331
▼▼ Italian. Casual Dining. **Address:** 1060 W Main St 24210

MOON DOG BRICK OVEN   276/525-1655
▼ Pizza. Casual Dining. **Address:** 1099 Ole Berry Dr 24210

THE PEPPERMILL RESTAURANT & LOUNGE   276/623-0530
▼▼ American. Casual Dining. **Address:** 231 W Main St
24210

SISTER'S AT THE MARTHA   276/628-9151
▼▼▼ Regional American. Fine Dining. **Address:** 150 W Main
St 24210

THE TAVERN   276/628-1118
▼▼ American. Casual Dining. **Address:** 222 E Main St 24210

AFTON elev. 1,360'
• Part of Shenandoah National Park area — see
map p. 241

BLUE MOUNTAIN BREWERY   540/456-8020
▼▼ American. Casual Dining. **Address:** 9519 Critzers Shop
Rd 22920

ALEXANDRIA (B-12) pop. 139,966, elev. 20'
• Hotels p. 51 • Restaurants p. 54
• Hotels & Restaurants map & index p. 38, 49

Although an integral part of the Washington, D.C.,
metropolitan area, Alexandria is a distinct city in its
own right. It was established in 1749 by a group of
Scottish merchants and named for John Alexander,
who had purchased the land in 1669. During the
Revolutionary period Alexandria was a principal Colonial port as well as a trade, social and political
center.

George Washington maintained a town house in
Alexandria. During his residence he was elected
vestryman of Christ Church Parish and was a
member of the Masonic Lodge, becoming its
Charter Master in 1788.

Alexandria also was the home of Revolutionary
War general Henry "Light Horse Harry" Lee, and the
boyhood home of his son, Robert E. Lee. During the
Civil War the city was captured and occupied by
Federal forces, which used it as a base of opera-
tions for various Union campaigns in Virginia.

Through careful guardianship and planning, parts
of Alexandria have managed to retain the appearance of another century. Old Town Alexandria, ex-
tending westward from the Potomac River, is the
major historical area (see AAA Walking Tours p. 34).

The city provides a free trolley service along King
Street, with trolley stops every 2 to 3 blocks between
the King Street Metro station and the Potomac River
waterfront. The trolleys depart every 15 minutes
Thurs.-Sat. 10 a.m.-midnight, Sun.-Wed. 10 a.m.-
10:15 p.m. In addition the city's DASH bus system
connects the King Street and Braddock Road Metro

stations with various Old Town locations. The base
fare is $1.60 (exact change only), and under 4 with
adult are free; phone (703) 746-3274 for route and
schedule information.

The Potomac Riverboat Co. offers water taxis
linking Alexandria with the National Mall and
Georgetown in the District of Columbia; Mount
Vernon, Va.; and National Harbor, Md. Phone (877)
511-2628. The cruise ship *Nina's Dandy*, at the foot
of Prince Street, is an enclosed ship offering three-
course luncheon and four-course dinner-dance
cruises on the Potomac River; phone (703)
683-6076 for information and reservations.

The Alexandria Visitor Center, 221 King St., is
staffed by Visit Alexandria employees. Built about
1724 by William Ramsay, a founder and first lord
mayor of Alexandria, the Ramsay House moved to
the site of the current visitors center in 1749. In
1949, the building was reconstructed after a fire destroyed much of the structure, one of the oldest in
Alexandria.

The special events hotline maintained by the Alexandria Department of Recreation, Parks and Cultural Activities provides information about local
music events; phone (703) 746-5592.

Alexandria Visitor Center: 221 King St., Alexandria, VA 22314. **Phone:** (703) 746-3301 or (800)
388-9119.

Self-guiding tours: Among the visitor center's offerings are walking tour brochures and bicycle trail
maps.

Shopping: Old Town Alexandria's streets are lined
with art galleries, antique shops and boutiques. The
main thoroughfare, King Street, features more than
150 independent stores and restaurants as well as
national brands housed in preserved warehouses
and other historic buildings.

Antique enthusiasts looking to expand their collections should do some browsing at Eisenhower
Consignment (4926-C Eisenhower Ave.), The Antique Guild (113 N. Fairfax St.), Silverman Galleries
(110 N. St. Asaph St.) and BW Art, Antiques & Jewelry (108 N. Fayette St.). All are great places to peruse merchandise from yesteryear.

Many of Old Town Alexandria's boutique consignment stores sell high-end pieces by Ralph Lauren,
Max Azria, Milly, Valentino and other designers. Give
Current Boutique (1009 King St.) or Diva Designer
Consignment (116 S. Pitt St.) a try for upmarket
finds sold at a fraction of the usual asking price.
Modern and eclectic fashions also are sold at shops
like Imagine Artwear (1124 King St.) and Lou Lou
(132 King St.).

Old Town is a great source for unique home furnishings as well. Fresh and sophisticated Coco
Blanca (210 S. Union St.) sells everything from
French farmhouse-style lamps to gilded nesting
tables that would fit perfectly in a chic urban loft.

(See maps & indexes p. 38, 49.)

Of course, no shopping trip in Alexandria would be complete without a stop at the Torpedo Factory Art Center *(see attraction listing p. 34)*, an ammunitions plant-turned-visual arts center on Union Street that contains 82 working artists' studios and six art galleries.

Nightlife: There's still plenty to see and do in Alexandria after the city's museums and historical sites shut down for the day. One hot spot, Union Street Public House (121 S. Union St.), calls a renovated Colonial warehouse on the waterfront home. After a long day of sightseeing, it's a chill place to kick back with a cold brew. Phone (703) 548-1785.

Another laid-back option—especially if you're a fan of "The Lord of the Rings" trilogy—is Bilbo Baggins (208 Queen St.). Dine in the upstairs restaurant or head downstairs to the Green Dragon Pub (named after the Hobbits' favorite meeting place) to enjoy a refreshing glass of Shire Spiked Cider or a Gandalf's Cask Manhattan. Phone (703) 683-0300.

Looking for something a tad more sophisticated? Drop in at Society Fair (277 S. Washington St.), where wine is the drink of choice. The bar offers up to 120 varieties, including a few on tap! The drink menu also features wine-based cocktails. Boasting a chic Parisian circus theme, the establishment encompasses a gourmet market and a demonstration kitchen as well. Phone (703) 683-3247.

You'll want to make reservations online for PX (728 King St.), an intimate 1920s-style speakeasy known for its expert mixologists. PX hearkens back to a golden age when ladies dressed to the nines and gents donned jackets. Be sure to look your best before setting out in search of the blue light marking the club's otherwise nondescript "secret" entrance.

Your toes will be tapping at Nick's Night Club (642 S. Pickett St.), where live music performed by country bands gets boot-clad patrons moving on two spacious dance floors. If your line dancing's not up to snuff, don't worry. Lessons are offered most weeknights. Phone (703) 751-8900.

CHRIST CHURCH (Anglican) is at 118 N. Washington St. near Columbus and Cameron sts. Built 1767-73, this Georgian-style brick church, with a Palladian chancel window unusual for its time, is in nearly original condition.

George Washington purchased Pew 60 for 36 pounds and 10 shillings when the church first opened, and he regularly attended services. Robert E. Lee, who also attended services regularly, was confirmed in the church in 1853. The cut-glass chandelier, under the gallery, represents one of the most advanced types of lighting fixtures available in the early 19th century.

Time: Allow 30 minutes minimum. **Hours:** Mon.-Sat. noon-4, Sun. 2-4:30, except during services. Closed holidays and after services. Phone ahead to confirm schedule. **Cost:** Donations. **Phone:** (703) 549-1450. King St-Old Town, 91

GADSBY'S TAVERN MUSEUM, 134 N. Royal St., comprises the original Georgian tavern, built about 1785, and the 1792 City Hotel. The tavern—with its taproom, small dining room and assembly room—and the hotel ballroom were a center for Alexandria's social and political life. Prominent patrons have included George Washington, Thomas Jefferson, James Madison and John Adams. Interpretive programs are offered year-round.

Hours: Tues.-Sat. 10-5, Sun.-Mon. 1-5, Apr.-Oct.; Wed.-Sat. 11-4, Sun. 1-4, rest of year. Tours are available for a fee. Closed Jan. 1, Thanksgiving and Christmas. **Cost:** $5; $3 (ages 5-12). **Phone:** (703) 746-4242. GT King St-Old Town, 91

THE GEORGE WASHINGTON MASONIC NATIONAL MEMORIAL surmounts Shuter's Hill at the w. end of King St. The 333-foot-tall landmark was inspired by the ancient lighthouse at Alexandria, Egypt. The Replica Room contains original furnishings of Alexandria Lodge No. 22, the lodge in Alexandria over which Washington was the first Worshipful Master under Virginia charter.

A colossal bronze statue of our nation's first president greets visitors entering Memorial Hall, a second-floor space that also showcases two murals by distinguished American artist Allyn Cox. The Memorial Theater shelters 16 St. Genevieve gold-veined Missouri marble columns and a Möller pipe organ, along with 14 bronze bas-relief plaques, one for each of the Freemason U.S. presidents.

The structure's three-tier tower includes a research library and The George Washington Museum, which features such relics as a Washington family Bible. Guided tours introduce the symbols and allegory of the fraternal organization and include access to the structure's three-tier tower. Exhibits there include The Family of Freemasonry, which explains the diverse world of the Masonic fraternity. The ninth floor observation deck provides 360-degree views of the Washington, D.C., metropolitan area.

Note: Backpacks and strollers are prohibited. Tickets for a 1-hour guided tour are available on a first-come, first-served basis. **Hours:** Daily 9-5. Guided tours are given daily at 9:30, 11, 1, 2:30 and 4. Library open by appointment. Closed major holidays. **Cost:** First- and second-floor galleries and a guided tour $15; free (ages 0-12). **Phone:** (703) 683-2007. GT King St-Old Town, 91

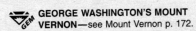 **GEORGE WASHINGTON'S MOUNT VERNON**—see Mount Vernon p. 172.

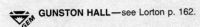 **GUNSTON HALL**—see Lorton p. 162.

LEE-FENDALL HOUSE MUSEUM AND GARDEN, 614 Oronoco St., was built in 1785 by Philip Richard Fendall, an Alexandria civic leader who was the cousin of Henry "Light Horse Harry" Lee, the father of Confederate general Robert E. Lee. The house remained in the family until 1903. Accessible by

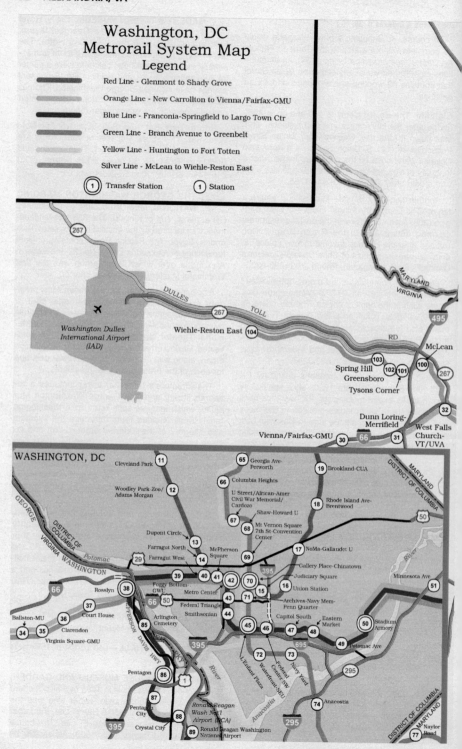

Washington, DC
Metrorail System Map
Legend

— Red Line - Glenmont to Shady Grove

— Orange Line - New Carrollton to Vienna/Fairfax-GMU

— Blue Line - Franconia-Springfield to Largo Town Ctr

— Green Line - Branch Avenue to Greenbelt

— Yellow Line - Huntington to Fort Totten

— Silver Line - McLean to Wiehle-Reston East

(1) Transfer Station   (1) Station

Washington Dulles International Airport (IAD)

Wiehle-Reston East (104)

McLean (100)

Spring Hill (103)
Greensboro (102) (101)
Tysons Corner

Dunn Loring-Merrifield

West Falls Church-VT/UVA (32)

Vienna/Fairfax-GMU (30) (31)

WASHINGTON, DC

Cleveland Park (11)

Woodley Park Zoo/Adams Morgan (12)

Dupont Circle (13)

Farragut North
Farragut West (14)
(29)

McPherson Square

Georgia Ave-Petworth (65)

Columbia Heights (66)

U Street/African-Amer Civil War Memorial/Cardozo

Shaw-Howard U (67)

Mt Vernon Square 7th St-Convention Center (68)

Brookland-CUA (19)

Rhode Island Ave-Brentwood (18)

NoMa-Gallaudet U (17)

Gallery Place-Chinatown

(39) (40) (41) (42) (70)
(69)
Foggy Bottom-GWU
Rosslyn (38)
(66) (50)
Metro Center (15) (71)
(43)
Federal Triangle
Smithsonian (44)

Judiciary Square
Union Station (16)

Archives-Navy Mem-Penn Quarter

Capitol South
Eastern Market

Minnesota Ave

(51)

Ballston-MU (34) (35) (36)
Court House (37)
Clarendon
Virginia Square-GMU

Arlington Cemetery (85)

(45) (46) (47) (48)

Stadium Armory (50)

Potomac Ave (49)

Pentagon (86)

Pentagon City (87)

Crystal City (88)

Ronald Reagan Wash Nat'l Airport (DCA)

(72) (73)
L'Enfant Plaza
Federal Center SW
Waterfront-SEU
Navy Yard

Anacostia (74)

Naylor Road (77)

Ronald Reagan Washington National Airport (89)

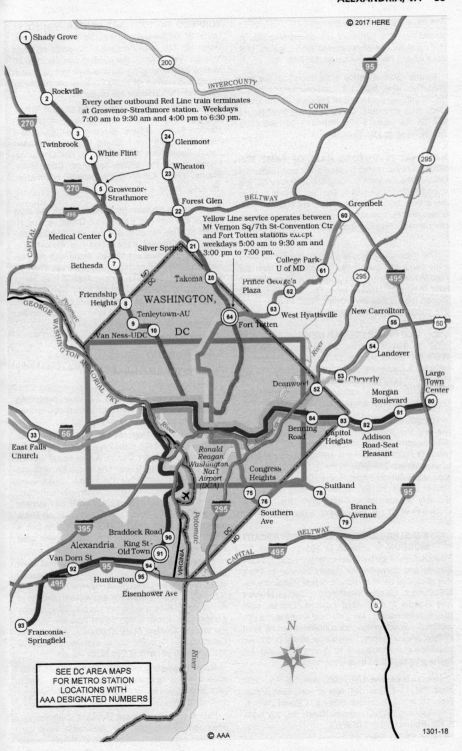

© 2017 HERE

Every other outbound Red Line train terminates at Grosvenor-Strathmore station. Weekdays 7:00 am to 9:30 am and 4:00 pm to 6:30 pm.

Yellow Line service operates between Mt Vernon Sq/7th St-Convention Ctr and Fort Totten stations except weekdays 5:00 am to 9:30 am and 3:00 pm to 7:00 pm.

SEE DC AREA MAPS FOR METRO STATION LOCATIONS WITH AAA DESIGNATED NUMBERS

© AAA

1301-18

(See maps & indexes p. 38, 49.)

guided tour, it is furnished with period antiques, including many Lee possessions. John L. Lewis, U.S. labor leader, owned the house 1937-69.

Hours: Guided house tours depart on the hour Wed.-Sat. 10-4, Sun. 1-4. Last tour begins 1 hour before closing. Closed major holidays. Phone ahead to confirm schedule. **Cost:** Grounds free. House tour $5; $3 (ages 5-17). **Phone:** (703) 548-1789. GT 🏢 King St-Old Town, 91

NATIONAL INVENTORS HALL OF FAME MUSEUM is at the United States Patent and Trademark Office in the Madison Building at 600 Dulany St., just s. of SR 236 (Duke St.). The site pays tribute to more than 500 inventors and their technological achievements. Interactive kiosks and exhibits showcase these influential individuals and their inspirational stories.

The Intellectual Property Power exhibit explains trademarks and patents with installations from the Ford Motor Company and Qualcomm. **Time:** Allow 1 hour minimum. **Hours:** Mon.-Fri. 10-5, Sat. 11-3. Closed federal holidays. **Cost:** Free. **Phone:** (571) 272-0095. 🏢 King St-Old Town, 91

GEM **OLD PRESBYTERIAN MEETING HOUSE** is at 321 S. Fairfax St. between Duke and Wolfe sts. Established in 1772, the meeting house became a gathering place for patriots during the Revolutionary War and was the site of George Washington's funeral sermons in December 1799. During the Civil War it was used briefly as a hospital.

The grave of social and political figure John Carlyle and the Tomb of the Unknown Revolutionary War Soldier are in the churchyard. The old-fashioned gate pews of this still-active church have been retained. The keys to the sanctuary are available at the church office. **Hours:** Office open Mon.-Thurs. 8:30-4:30, Fri. 8:30-1. Phone ahead for worship service times. **Cost:** Donations. **Phone:** (703) 549-6670. 🏢 King St-Old Town, 91

SAVE **STABLER-LEADBEATER APOTHECARY MUSEUM** is entered at 105 S. Fairfax St. Founded in 1792 by Quaker pharmacist Edward Stabler and opened in its current location in 1796, this is said to be Alexandria's oldest mercantile establishment. George Washington, James Monroe and Robert E. Lee were patrons. Old account books, prescriptions, early medical wares and a collection of period apothecary containers can be seen in their original setting. The same family continued operation of the shop until 1933, when it closed due to the effects of the Great Depression.

Hours: Tues.-Sat. 10-5, Sun.-Mon. 1-5, Apr.-Oct.; Wed.-Sat. 11-4, Sun. 1-4, rest of year. Last admission 15 minutes before closing. Closed Jan. 1, Thanksgiving and Christmas. **Cost:** $5; $3 (ages 5-12). **Phone:** (703) 746-3852. 🏢 King St-Old Town, 91

TORPEDO FACTORY ART CENTER is at 105 N. Union St. on the waterfront in Old Town Alexandria. Used for the manufacture of torpedo casings through World War II, the building now contains 82 studios and seven galleries where visitors can watch artists and crafters at work. Purchasable pieces by more than 165 artisans are on display.

The center also includes the Art League School and the Alexandria Archaeology Museum (see attraction listing). **Hours:** Building open daily 10-6 (also Thurs. 6-9 p.m.). Studio hours vary. Closed Jan. 1, Easter, July 4, Thanksgiving and Christmas. Phone ahead to confirm schedule. **Cost:** Free. **Phone:** (703) 838-4565 for general information. 🏢 King St-Old Town, 91

Alexandria Archaeology Museum is on the third floor of the Torpedo Factory Art Center at 105 N. Union St. This museum displays and interprets objects from recent excavations in Alexandria. Hands-on activities are offered, along with the permanent exhibit A Community Digs its Past: The Lee Street Site. The museum's collection has items dating from 13,000 B.C. to the early 20th century. **Hours:** Tues.-Fri. 10-3, Sat. 10-5, Sun. 1-5. Closed Jan. 1, Easter, July 4, Thanksgiving and Christmas. **Cost:** Free. **Phone:** (703) 746-4399. 🏢 King St-Old Town, 91

AAA Walking Tours
Old Town Alexandria
See map p. 36.

This tour of Old Town takes 2-3 hours, depending on your pace and the points of interest you choose to stop and visit along the way.

Served by both Metrorail's Blue and Yellow lines, the King Street Metro station is about a mile west of the Alexandria Visitor Center. A free trolley service connects the King Street Metro station with the Potomac River waterfront; the trolleys depart every 15 minutes Thurs.-Sat. 10 a.m.-midnight, Sun.-Wed. 10 a.m.-10:15 p.m. The city's DASH bus system connects the King Street and Braddock Road Metro stations with various Old Town locations. The fare is $1.60 (exact change only), and under 4 with adult are free.

If street-side parking is at a premium—and it will be on weekdays—there are several parking garages in the area as well. The most convenient is the City Hall garage (during evenings and weekends only) at the corner of King and Fairfax streets. Other nearby garages are across Union Street from the Torpedo Factory Art Center; at 10 Thompson Alley; at the Courthouse, 111 S. Pitt St.; at 418 Cameron St.; at 115 S. Union St.; and at 210 N. St. Asaph St.

Note: In keeping with Old Town's quaint ambience, many of its sidewalks are brick-paved. Watch your step or you'll risk tripping over the occasional protruding paver.

. Few areas offer a more pleasant stroll into another century than Old Town Alexandria. Here visitors can enjoy shady cobblestone streets closely

(See maps & indexes p. 38, 49.)

flanked by 18th- and 19th-century houses with leafy courtyards. Newer buildings emulate the prevailing architectural style, helping to preserve this historic district's charm.

Begin your tour at the visitor center, on the corner of King and Fairfax streets in the historic Ramsay House, then walk east on King Street toward the river. Turn left at Lee Street, and follow Lee to the corner of Cameron Street for a view of Cameron Mews, mews being another word for alley or back street. This Colonial town house development exemplifies Alexandria's approach to new housing in Old Town. Turn left on Cameron Street and walk past the lovely gardens on the southwest corner of Cameron and Lee. These belong to the **Carlyle House.**

John Carlyle, a Scottish merchant and city founder, built this grand Georgian Palladian manor 1751-53. Two years after its completion, Gen. Edward Braddock and five Colonial governors met there to discuss funding a campaign against the French during the French and Indian War. The issue of financing the war later became so contentious that it led to the American Revolution.

Continue west on Cameron, which is one of the city's most interesting shopping streets. The north side of the block between Fairfax and Royal streets has many boutiques and specialty shops. Opposite is the block-long, brick City Hall, and behind it is airy Market Square. The market held here every Saturday morning is reputed to be the nation's oldest.

The neat brick facades facing Cameron Street between Royal and Pitt streets hide Tavern Square, named for **Gadsby's Tavern Museum,** which forms its northeast corner. Made up of two historic buildings—a circa 1785 tavern and the 1792 City Hotel—Gadsby's Tavern prospered due to its location along the main stage route between Williamsburg and Boston. For many years it was a center for social and political life in the city.

Proceed 1 block west on Cameron past George Washington's reconstructed town house, which is the clapboard house on the street's south side. Washington stayed here when business or bad weather prevented him from returning to his Mount Vernon estate. Like many historic homes, it is a private residence not open to the public.

Turn right on tree-lined St. Asaph Street, where the town homes are beautified by landscaped courtyards and pocket gardens. As you cross Princess Street, look left to see a section of restored cobblestone roadway between St. Asaph and Washington streets.

Make a left at Oronoco, and on the right as you approach Washington Street you'll find the boyhood home of Gen. Robert E. Lee, which is a private residence. Lee lived here from age 5 until he left to enroll at West Point when he was 18. Across the street, on the southeast corner of Oronoco and Washington, is the 1785 **Lee-Fendall House Museum and Garden.** Home to generations of Robert E. Lee's relatives, the house contains a variety of items that once belonged to this celebrated Virginia family.

Head south on Washington Street. On the southwest corner of Queen and Washington is the 1797 Lloyd House, one of the city's best examples of late Georgian architecture. Turn left on Cameron; on your left, at 611 Cameron, is a small, red-brick house that once belonged to Revolutionary War hero Gen. Henry "Light Horse Harry" Lee. Due to financial difficulties, Lee was forced to move his family—including young son Robert Edward—to this house from their Stratford Hall plantation in Stratford, Va. The Lees lived here 1810-12; it is currently a private residence.

The peaceful grounds of **Christ Church** occupy the southwest corner of Washington and Cameron. Completed in 1773, the Georgian-style church remains an active house of worship. George Washington was an early parishioner; his original pew is preserved inside. A silver plaque marks the spot where Robert E. Lee was confirmed in 1853.

The church grounds served as Alexandria's cemetery until 1809; its oldest tombstone is dated March 20, 1791. Just inside the wall on Washington Street, a mass grave holds the remains of 34 Confederate soldiers who were reburied here after the Civil War.

Continue south on Washington Street for a block and turn right on King Street. The tower you see ahead of you, west of the walking tour route, is **The George Washington Masonic National Memorial.** Dedicated in 1932, it stands atop Shooter's Hill, which was the site of a Civil War fort. An observation deck on the ninth level offers a fantastic bird's-eye view of Alexandria and the monuments and government buildings of the nation's capital.

Go 2 blocks west and turn left on Alfred Street. The Friendship Firehouse Museum, which by tradition claimed George Washington as a member, is on the west side of Alfred. The Friendship Fire Co. was founded in 1774, and the current building was completed in 1855. Among the historic firefighting equipment inside are leather water buckets, antique fire engines and ceremonial regalia used for parades.

Continue south on Alfred Street, and at the corner turn left onto Prince Street. Walk 2 blocks to the corner of Prince and Washington streets. The bronze Confederate Statue stands within the intersection. Dedicated in 1889, it depicts a Confederate soldier gazing south with head bowed and arms folded across his chest. The memorial, the base of which is inscribed with the names of 100 Confederate dead, marks the spot where more than 700 Alexandrians left the Union-occupied city to fight for the Confederacy.

Adjacent is the two-story, Greek Revival structure known as **The Lyceum** (lie-SEE-um), an interpretive center for the history of Alexandria. Lyceums were early 19th-century organizations that promoted public debates and lectures on a host of topics. Formed in 1834, the Alexandria Lyceum hosted its first programs at a local school. These programs

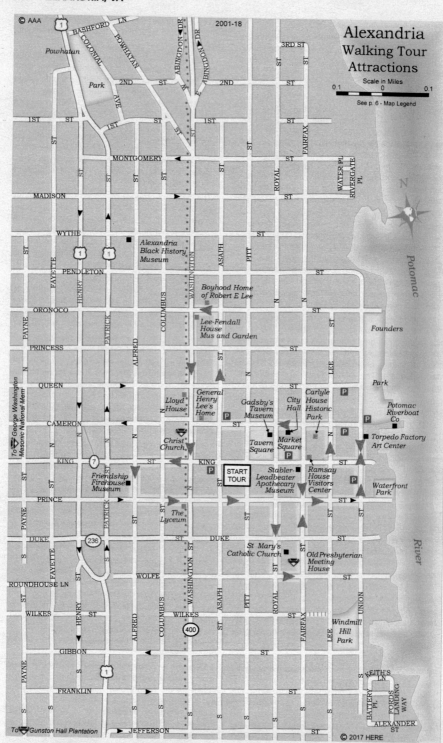

© AAA

BASHFORD LN
COLONIAL
POWHATAN AVE
Powhatan
Park
2ND
2ND
ABINGDON DR
W ABINGDON DR
2001-18
3RD ST

Alexandria
Walking Tour
Attractions

Scale in Miles
0.1   0.1
See p. 6 - Map Legend

1ST
MONTGOMERY
MADISON
WYTHE
Alexandria Black History Museum
PENDLETON
Boyhood Home of Robert E Lee
ORONOCO
Lee-Fendall House Mus and Garden
PRINCESS
QUEEN
CAMERON
General Henry Lee's Home
Lloyd House
Gadsby's Tavern Museum
City Hall
Carlyle House Historic Park
Founders
Park
Potomac Riverboat Co
Torpedo Factory Art Center
Christ Church
Tavern Square
Market Square
To George Washington Masonic National Mem
KING
Friendship Firehouse Museum
START TOUR
Stabler-Leadbeater Apothecary Museum
Ramsay House Visitors Center
Waterfront Park
PRINCE
The Lyceum
DUKE
St Mary's Catholic Church
Old Presbyterian Meeting House
WOLFE
ROUNDHOUSE LN
WILKES
Windmill Hill Park
GIBBON
FRANKLIN
To Gunston Hall Plantation
JEFFERSON
KEITH'S LN
FORDS LANDING WAY
BATTERY PL
ALEXANDER ST

Potomac
River

N

FAIRFAX
WATER PL
RIVERGATE PL
ROYAL
ASAPH
PITT
WASHINGTON
COLUMBUS
ALFRED
PATRICK
HENRY
FAYETTE
PAYNE
LEE
UNION

© 2017 HERE

ALEXANDRIA, VA   37

(See maps & indexes p. 38, 49.)

were so popular that the organization was soon able to fund construction of a grand hall to serve as its headquarters and main venue, which is the building (completed in 1839) you see today. Eventually Alexandrians began applying the organization's name to the hall itself, and it remained the center of the city's intellectual life until the Civil War.

Cross Washington Street, continue east to Royal Street and turn right. The neat, well-maintained homes in this block of Royal are typical restored 18th-century houses, many marked with the oval Early Buildings Survey registry plaque.

Across Duke Street on the east side of Royal is St. Mary's Catholic Church; beyond the church, turn left into what appears to be a small grassy play yard. You are actually approaching the **Old Presbyterian Meeting House** through its churchyard, which contains 18th-century grave markers and the Tomb of the Unknown Revolutionary War Soldier.

Upon reaching the front of the meetinghouse, turn left and proceed 2 blocks, crossing Duke and Prince streets. The **Stabler-Leadbeater Apothecary Museum** is at 105 S. Fairfax St. This former pharmacy operated in this location under the same family from 1796 until the Great Depression forced it to close in 1933. At that time the entire contents were bought at auction by a pharmaceutical association for a museum, which opened in 1939. Inside the shop are wooden boxes hand-lettered with the names of medicinal herbs, along with a huge collection of drug tins and hand-blown bottles.

Return to Prince Street and make a left. Gentry Row, along the 200 block of Prince Street, boasts the Fairfax House, 207 Prince St., and other homes typical of those built by the city's wealthiest inhabitants during the late 1700s. Number 209 next door belonged at one time to George Washington's long-time physician, Dr. James Craik. Another physician of his, Dr. Elisha Cullen Dick, lived at 211 Prince St.

The 1850 Athenaeum (also known as the Old Dominion Bank Building), on the northwest corner of Prince and Lee streets, is an excellent example of Greek Revival architecture. Originally a banking house, the Athenaeum now houses contemporary art shows.

Continue east across Lee Street. You are now walking along Captains' Row, named for sea captain John Harper, who had many of the Federal-style houses built for his numerous children.

Turn left on Union Street and cross King. The **Torpedo Factory Art Center** is on your right. This waterfront facility, constructed in 1918, produced torpedo casings through World War II. For years afterward it was used for storage until someone hit upon the idea for using it to house art studios.

More than 165 artists working in such media as sculpture, photography, painting, printmaking, jewelry, ceramics and glass are represented, and numerous examples of their work are on display. The center also houses the **Alexandria Archaeology Museum**, where you can view items recovered from excavations throughout Alexandria. Most of these are from the late 1600s to the early 1900s, but many prehistoric artifacts are on display as well.

From the Torpedo Factory, return to Ramsay House by making a right on King Street. If your feet are willing, a stroll along this main thoroughfare, which is lined with specialty shops, pubs and ethnic restaurants, can be an enjoyable way to conclude your tour.

Two points of interest on the periphery of the walking tour route are the **Alexandria Black History Museum**, 902 Wythe St., which documents the history of African-Americans in Alexandria and Virginia from 1749 to the present, and the partially restored bastions of **Fort Ward** and its interpretive museum, at 4301 W. Braddock Rd.

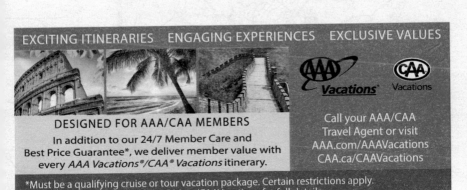

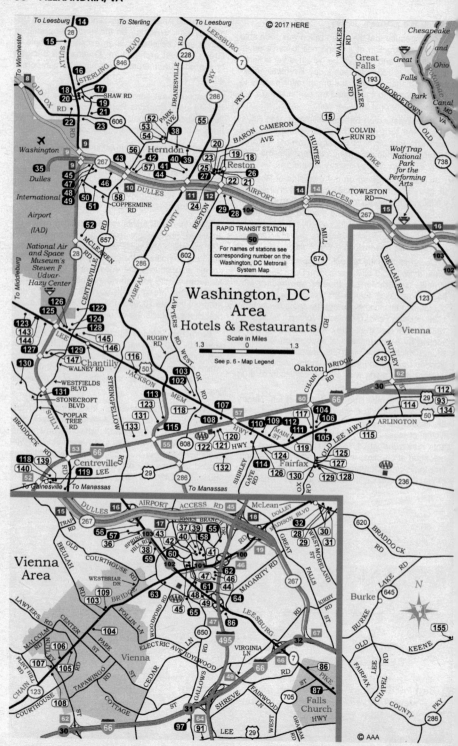

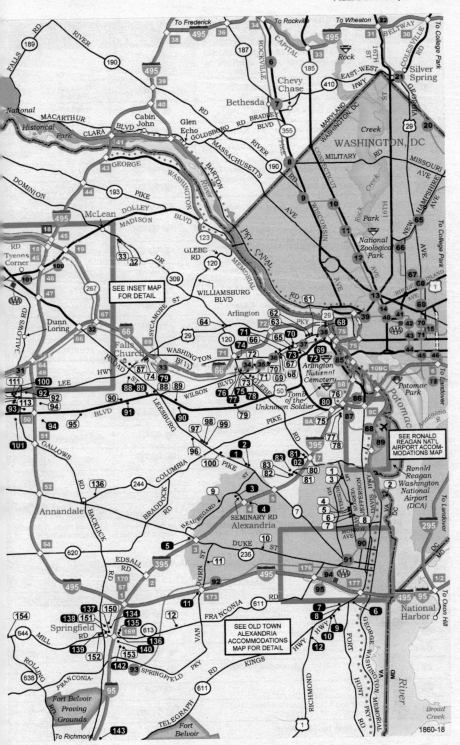

1860-18

✈ Airport Hotels

Map Page	WASHINGTON DULLES INTERNATIONAL (Maximum driving distance from airport: 5.9 mi)	Diamond Rated	Rate Range	Page
50 p. 38	Candlewood Suites Washington Dulles-Herndon, 3.6 mi	◈◈	Rates not provided	152
43 p. 38	Crowne Plaza Dulles Airport, 3.3 mi	◈◈◈	Rates not provided	153
52 p. 38	**Hilton Washington Dulles Airport, 4.4 mi**	◈◈◈	$89-$299 SAVE	153
46 p. 38	Homewood Suites by Hilton Washington-Dulles Airport, 3.7 mi	◈◈◈	$99-$239	153
48 p. 38	**Hyatt Place Herndon/Dulles Airport-East, 4.2 mi**	◈◈◈	$74-$239 SAVE	153
45 p. 38	**Hyatt Regency Dulles, 4.2 mi**	◈◈◈	$75-$319 SAVE	153
47 p. 38	Sheraton Herndon Dulles Airport Hotel, 4.3 mi	◈◈◈	Rates not provided	153
51 p. 38	Staybridge Suites Herndon Dulles, 3.7 mi	◈◈◈	Rates not provided	154
35 p. 38	**Washington Dulles Airport Marriott, on airport property**	◈◈◈	$71-$367 SAVE	154
42 p. 38	**Washington Dulles Marriott Suites, 3.3 mi**	◈◈◈	$79-$414 SAVE	154
49 p. 38	**The Westin Washington Dulles Airport, 4.8 mi**	◈◈◈	$89-$299 SAVE	154
20 p. 38	**Best Western Dulles Airport Inn, 4.4 mi**	◈◈	$79-$189 SAVE	248
21 p. 38	Country Inn & Suites By Carlson, Washington Dulles International Airport, 3.5 mi	◈◈	Rates not provided	248
22 p. 38	Fairfield Inn & Suites by Marriott Dulles Airport, 3.9 mi	◈◈◈	$51-$188	249
17 p. 38	Hampton Inn & Suites by Hilton Dulles Airport, 4.3 mi	◈◈◈	$89-$219	249
19 p. 38	Holiday Inn Washington Dulles International Airport, 4.3 mi	◈◈◈	$79-$199	249
23 p. 38	**Hyatt House Sterling/Dulles Airport North, 3.4 mi**	◈◈◈	$74-$199 SAVE	249
15 p. 38	**Residence Inn by Marriott Dulles Airport Dulles 28 Centre, 5.9 mi**	◈◈◈	$92-$260 SAVE	250
16 p. 38	SpringHill Suites by Marriott Washington Dulles Airport, 4.1 mi	◈◈◈	$67-$207	250
18 p. 38	TownePlace Suites by Marriott at Dulles Airport, 4.2 mi	◈◈	$75-$261	250

Washington, D.C. Area

This index helps you "spot" where approved hotels and restaurants are located on the corresponding detailed maps. Hotel daily rate range is for comparison only. Restaurant price range is a combination of lunch and/or dinner. Turn to the listing page for more information and consult display ads for special promotions.

 For more details, rates and reservations: AAA.com/travelguides/hotels

ALEXANDRIA

Map Page	Hotels	Diamond Rated	Rate Range	Page
1 p. 38	Homewood Suites by Hilton-Alexandria/Pentagon South	◈◈◈	$129-$289	52
2 p. 38	Hampton Inn-Alexandria/Pentagon South	◈◈◈	$109-$269	52
3 p. 38	Hilton Alexandria Mark Center	◈◈◈	$89-$259	52
4 p. 38	**Courtyard by Marriott Alexandria Pentagon South**	◈◈◈	$67-$313 SAVE	51
5 p. 38	Comfort Inn Landmark	◈◈	$99-$199	51
6 p. 38	Hampton Inn & Suites by Hilton Alexandria/Old Town Area-South	◈◈◈	$99-$259	52
7 p. 38	**Budget Host Travelers Motel**	◈◈	$85-$105 SAVE	51

ALEXANDRIA (cont'd)

Map Page	Hotels (cont'd)	Diamond Rated	Rate Range	Page
8 p. 38	**Red Roof PLUS+ Washington DC-Alexandria**	◈◈	$70-$200 SAVE	53
9 p. 38	Holiday Inn Express & Suites Alexandria	◈◈◈	Rates not provided	52
10 p. 38	SpringHill Suites by Marriott Alexandria	◈◈◈	$79-$309	53
11 p. 38	Comfort Inn & Suites Alexandria	◈◈	$99-$189	51
12 p. 38	**Fairfield Inn & Suites by Marriott Alexandria**	◈◈◈	Rates not provided SAVE	52

Map Page	Restaurants	Diamond Rated	Cuisine	Price Range	Page
1 p. 38	RT's Restaurant	◈◈	Regional American	$10-$29	54
2 p. 38	Indigo Landing	◈◈◈	American	$12-$28	54
3 p. 38	Bombay Curry Company	◈◈	Indian	$7-$15	54
4 p. 38	Pork Barrel BBQ	◈	Barbecue	$7-$23	54
5 p. 38	Holy Cow	◈	Burgers	$6-$13	54
6 p. 38	Thai Peppers	◈◈	Thai	$8-$16	55
7 p. 38	Evening Star Café	◈◈	Southern American	$16-$28	54
8 p. 38	Del Ray Cafe	◈◈◈	French	$12-$39	54
9 p. 38	Illusions Thai Cafe	◈◈	Asian	$8-$28	54
10 p. 38	Tempo Restaurant	◈◈	Northern Italian	$14-$27	54
11 p. 38	Thai Lemongrass	◈◈	Thai	$12-$22	54
12 p. 38	Paradiso Ristorante Italiano	◈◈	Italian	$9-$22	54

STERLING

Map Page	Hotels	Diamond Rated	Rate Range	Page
14 p. 38	DoubleTree by Hilton Hotel Sterling - Dulles Airport	◈◈◈	$79-$269	249
15 p. 38	**Residence Inn by Marriott Dulles Airport @ Dulles 28 Centre**	◈◈◈	$92-$260 SAVE	250
16 p. 38	SpringHill Suites by Marriott Washington Dulles Airport	◈◈◈	$67-$207	250
17 p. 38	Hampton Inn & Suites by Hilton Dulles Airport	◈◈◈	$89-$219	249
18 p. 38	TownePlace Suites by Marriott at Dulles Airport	◈◈	$75-$261	250
19 p. 38	Holiday Inn Washington Dulles International Airport	◈◈◈	$79-$199	249
20 p. 38	**Best Western Dulles Airport Inn**	◈◈	$79-$189 SAVE	248
21 p. 38	Country Inn & Suites By Carlson, Washington Dulles International Airport	◈◈	Rates not provided	248
22 p. 38	Fairfield Inn & Suites by Marriott Dulles Airport	◈◈◈	$51-$188	249
23 p. 38	**Hyatt House Sterling/Dulles Airport North** (See ad p. 249.)	◈◈◈	$74-$199 SAVE	249

RESTON

Map Page	Hotels	Diamond Rated	Rate Range	Page
26 p. 38	**Hyatt Regency Reston**	◈◈◈◈	$109-$389 SAVE	191
27 p. 38	Extended Stay America Washington DC-Reston	◈◈	$55-$140	191
28 p. 38	The Westin Reston Heights	◈◈◈	Rates not provided	191
29 p. 38	Sheraton Reston Hotel	◈◈◈	Rates not provided	191

Map Page	Restaurants	Diamond Rated	Cuisine	Price Range	Page
18 p. 38	Neyla Mediterranean Bistro	◈◈	Mediterranean	$13-$30	191

Map Page	Restaurants (cont'd)	Diamond Rated	Cuisine	Price Range	Page
(19) p. 38	Morton's The Steakhouse	◈◈◈	Steak	$25-$95	191
(20) p. 38	Busara	◈◈	Thai	$12-$21	191
(21) p. 38	M & S Grill	◈◈◈	Steak Seafood	$13-$46	191
(22) p. 38	McCormick & Schmick's	◈◈◈	Seafood	$12-$50	191
(23) p. 38	Mon Ami Gabi	◈◈◈	French Steak	$13-$40	191
(24) p. 38	Jackson's Mighty Fine Food & Lucky Lounge	◈◈	American	$12-$27	191
(25) p. 38	PassionFish	◈◈◈	Seafood	$13-$45	191

MCLEAN

Map Page	Hotel	Diamond Rated	Rate Range	Page
(32) p. 38	**Staybridge Suites Tysons McLean Hotel (Washington, D.C. area)**	◈◈◈	Rates not provided (SAVE)	170

Map Page	Restaurants	Diamond Rated	Cuisine	Price Range	Page
(28) p. 38	Pulcinella The Italian Host	◈◈	Southern Italian	$9-$25	170
(29) p. 38	7Spice Fine Indian Cuisine	◈◈	Indian	$10-$22	170
(30) p. 38	The Greek Taverna	◈◈	Greek	$13-$32	170
(31) p. 38	Kazan Restaurant	◈◈◈	Turkish	$10-$30	170
(32) p. 38	Cafe Oggi	◈◈◈	Italian	$10-$31	170
(33) p. 38	Tachibana	◈◈	Japanese Sushi	$9-$42	170

HERNDON

Map Page	Hotels	Diamond Rated	Rate Range	Page
(35) p. 38	**Washington Dulles Airport Marriott**	◈◈◈	$71-$367 (SAVE)	154
(38) p. 38	Fairfield Inn & Suites by Marriott-Dulles Herndon	◈◈◈	$70-$174	153
(39) p. 38	Residence Inn by Marriott-Herndon/Reston	◈◈◈	$68-$256	153
(40) p. 38	**SpringHill Suites by Marriott Herndon-Reston**	◈◈◈	$63-$254 (SAVE)	154
(41) p. 38	**Hyatt House Herndon**	◈◈◈	$79-$269 (SAVE)	153
(42) p. 38	**Washington Dulles Marriott Suites**	◈◈◈	$79-$414 (SAVE)	154
(43) p. 38	Crowne Plaza Dulles Airport	◈◈◈	Rates not provided	153
(44) p. 38	**Courtyard by Marriott/Herndon-Reston**	◈◈◈	$63-$304 (SAVE)	152
(45) p. 38	**Hyatt Regency Dulles**	◈◈◈	$75-$319 (SAVE)	153
(46) p. 38	Homewood Suites by Hilton Washington-Dulles Airport	◈◈◈	$99-$239	153
(47) p. 38	Sheraton Herndon Dulles Airport Hotel	◈◈◈	Rates not provided	153
(48) p. 38	**Hyatt Place Herndon/Dulles Airport-East**	◈◈◈	$74-$239 (SAVE)	153
(49) p. 38	**The Westin Washington Dulles Airport**	◈◈◈	$89-$299 (SAVE)	154
(50) p. 38	Candlewood Suites Washington Dulles-Herndon	◈◈	Rates not provided	152
(51) p. 38	Staybridge Suites Herndon Dulles	◈◈◈	Rates not provided	154
(52) p. 38	**Hilton Washington Dulles Airport**	◈◈◈	$89-$299 (SAVE)	153

Map Page	Restaurants	Diamond Rated	Cuisine	Price Range	Page
(52) p. 38	Russia House Restaurant	◈◈◈	Russian	$15-$31	154
(53) p. 38	Zeffirelli Ristorante Italiano	◈◈◈	Italian	$13-$35	154
(54) p. 38	**Ice House Cafe**	◈◈	American	$9-$30	154

Map Page	Restaurants (cont'd)	Diamond Rated	Cuisine	Price Range	Page
⑤⑤ p. 38	Euro Bistro	◆◆	International	$8-$28	154
⑤⑥ p. 38	Amphora Diner Deluxe	◆◆	American	$10-$25	154
⑤⑦ p. 38	TurCuisine	◆◆	Turkish	$9-$26	154
⑤⑧ p. 38	Stone's Cove Kitbar	◆◆	American	$10-$20	154

TYSONS CORNER

Map Page	Hotels	Diamond Rated	Rate Range	Page
55 p. 38	**Hilton McLean Tysons Corner**	◆◆◆◆	$95-$449 SAVE	254
56 p. 38	**Sheraton Tysons Hotel**	◆◆◆◆	$79-$299 SAVE	254
57 p. 38	**Residence Inn by Marriott-Tysons Corner**	◆◆◆	$63-$294 SAVE	254
58 p. 38	**The Ritz-Carlton, Tysons Corner**	◆◆◆◆◆	Rates not provided SAVE	254
59 p. 38	Embassy Suites Hotel by Hilton Tysons Corner	◆◆◆	$99-$309	253
60 p. 38	**DoubleTree by Hilton McLean Tysons**	◆◆◆	Rates not provided	253
61 p. 38	**Courtyard by Marriott, Tysons Corner**	◆◆◆	$63-$528 SAVE	253
62 p. 38	**Hyatt Regency Tysons Corner Center**	◆◆◆	$99-$459 SAVE	254
63 p. 38	Residence Inn by Marriott Tysons Corner Mall	◆◆◆	$67-$291	254
64 p. 38	**Tysons Corner Marriott Hotel**	◆◆◆	$71-$529 SAVE	254
65 p. 38	Extended Stay America-Washington, DC-Tysons Corner	◆◆	$80-$160	253

Map Page	Restaurants	Diamond Rated	Cuisine	Price Range	Page
㊱ p. 38	Bombay Tandoor	◆◆	Indian	$12-$31	254
㊲ p. 38	P.F. Chang's China Bistro	◆◆◆	Chinese	$10-$27	255
㊳ p. 38	Ruth's Chris Steak House	◆◆◆	Steak	$25-$88	255
㊴ p. 38	Lebanese Taverna	◆◆◆	Lebanese	$11-$27	255
㊵ p. 38	Legal Sea Foods	◆◆◆	Seafood	$11-$45	255
㊶ p. 38	The Palm Restaurant	◆◆◆	American	$15-$100	255
㊷ p. 38	Maggiano's Little Italy	◆◆◆	Italian	$10-$46	255
㊸ p. 38	McCormick & Schmick's	◆◆◆	Seafood	$13-$39	255
㊹ p. 38	Fleming's Prime Steakhouse & Wine Bar	◆◆◆	Steak	$16-$48	255
㊺ p. 38	Da Domenico	◆◆◆	Italian	$12-$35	255
㊻ p. 38	Coastal Flats	◆◆	American	$11-$24	255
㊼ p. 38	La Sandia Mexican Kitchen & Bar	◆◆	Mexican	$12-$22	255
㊽ p. 38	The Capital Grille	◆◆◆	Steak	$18-$54	255
㊾ p. 38	Neisha Thai Cuisine	◆◆	Thai	$10-$18	255

ARLINGTON

Map Page	Hotels	Diamond Rated	Rate Range	Page
68 p. 38	**Courtyard by Marriott-Arlington/Rosslyn**	◆◆◆	$79-$396 SAVE	61
69 p. 38	Red Lion Hotel Rosslyn/Iwo Jima	◆◆	Rates not provided	64
70 p. 38	**Hyatt Place - Arlington**	◆◆◆	$89-$369 SAVE	63
71 p. 38	Residence Inn by Marriott Arlington Courthouse	◆◆◆	$100-$496	64
72 p. 38	**Hilton Garden Inn Arlington/Courthouse Plaza**	◆◆◆	$99-$399 SAVE	62

ARLINGTON (cont'd)

Map Page	Hotels (cont'd)	Diamond Rated	Rate Range	Page
73 p. 38	**Arlington Court Suites Hotel, A Clarion Collection**	◆◆◆	$99-$379 SAVE	60
74 p. 38	**Comfort Inn Ballston**	◆◆◆	$89-$409 SAVE	60
75 p. 38	Hilton Arlington	◆◆◆	Rates not provided	62
76 p. 38	Holiday Inn Arlington at Ballston	◆◆◆	$85-$369	62
77 p. 38	**The Westin Arlington Gateway**	◆◆◆	Rates not provided SAVE	65
78 p. 38	Residence Inn by Marriott Arlington Ballston	◆◆◆	$101-$426	64
79 p. 38	**Econo Lodge-Metro Arlington**	◆◆	$100-$200 SAVE	62
80 p. 38	**Sheraton Pentagon City Hotel**	◆◆◆	$79-$499 SAVE	65
81 p. 38	**Comfort Inn Pentagon City**	◆◆	$119-$204 SAVE	61
82 p. 38	**Best Western Pentagon Hotel-Reagan Airport**	◆◆	$89-$199 SAVE	60
83 p. 38	Hilton Garden Inn Arlington/Shirlington	◆◆◆	$139-$309	62

Map Page	Restaurants	Diamond Rated	Cuisine	Price Range	Page
61 p. 38	Mele Bistro	◆◆	Continental	$11-$39	65
62 p. 38	Guajillo	◆◆	Mexican	$8-$21	65
63 p. 38	Ben's Chili Bowl	◆	Hot Dogs Burgers	$5-$10	65
64 p. 38	Metro 29 Diner	◆◆	American	$9-$30	65
65 p. 38	Fire Works American Pizzeria & Bar	◆◆	Pizza	$10-$21	65
66 p. 38	Mexicali Blues	◆	Mexican	$12-$22	65
67 p. 38	CIRCA at Clarendon	◆◆	Small Plates	$12-$25	65
68 p. 38	Delhi Club	◆◆	Indian	$11-$29	65
69 p. 38	Spider Kelly's	◆◆	American	$6-$16	66
70 p. 38	El Pollo Rico	◆	Peruvian Chicken	$6-$18	65
71 p. 38	Cafe Tirolo	◆	Italian	$7-$13	65
72 p. 38	Rus Uz	◆◆	Russian	$8-$18	65
73 p. 38	Pepita Cantina	◆◆	Mexican Small Plates	$5-$19	65
74 p. 38	La Cote D'or Cafe	◆◆◆	French	$13-$35	65
75 p. 38	Lebanese Taverna	◆◆◆	Lebanese	$11-$29	65
76 p. 38	Sine Irish Pub and Restaurant	◆◆	Irish	$9-$23	66
77 p. 38	Ristorante Murali	◆◆	Italian	$10-$29	65
78 p. 38	Thaiphoon	◆◆	Thai	$10-$16	66
79 p. 38	Crystal Thai Restaurant	◆◆	Thai	$10-$18	65
80 p. 38	T.H.A.I. in Shirlington	◆◆	Thai	$8-$19	66
81 p. 38	Carlyle	◆◆◆	American	$12-$28	65
82 p. 38	Aroma Indian Cuisine	◆◆	Indian	$10-$25	65
83 p. 38	Samuel Beckett's Irish Gastro Pub	◆◆	Irish	$10-$24	65

FALLS CHURCH

Map Page	Hotels	Diamond Rated	Rate Range	Page
86 p. 38	**The Westin Tysons Corner**	◆◆◆	Rates not provided SAVE	107

FALLS CHURCH (cont'd)

Map Page	Hotels (cont'd)	Diamond Rated	Rate Range	Page
87 p. 38	Hilton Garden Inn Falls Church	♦♦♦	$129-$359	106
88 p. 38	TownePlace Suites by Marriott-Falls Church	♦♦	$71-$338	107
89 p. 38	Hampton Inn & Suites by Hilton Falls Church	♦♦♦	Rates not provided	106
90 p. 38	Comfort Inn Arlington Boulevard	♦♦	$109-$169	106
91 p. 38	**Best Western Falls Church Inn**	♦♦	$89-$149 SAVE	106
92 p. 38	Homewood Suites by Hilton-Falls Church	♦♦♦	$139-$309	106
93 p. 38	**Residence Inn by Marriott Fairfax-Merrifield**	♦♦♦	$80-$348 SAVE	107
94 p. 38	**Falls Church Marriott Fairview Park**	♦♦♦	$65-$305 SAVE	106

Map Page	Restaurants	Diamond Rated	Cuisine	Price Range	Page
86 p. 38	Haandi	♦♦	Indian	$12-$22	107
87 p. 38	Argia's	♦♦	Italian	$11-$45	107
88 p. 38	Pistone's Italian Inn	♦♦	Italian	$10-$37	107
89 p. 38	Mark's Duck House	♦♦	Chinese Dim Sum	$8-$25	107
90 p. 38	Present Restaurant	♦♦♦	Vietnamese	$10-$30	107
91 p. 38	Trio Grill	♦♦♦	American	$24-$39	107
92 p. 38	Sea Pearl	♦♦♦	Seafood Sushi	$10-$30	107
93 p. 38	Four Sisters Restaurant	♦♦	Vietnamese	$10-$25	107
94 p. 38	2941 Restaurant	♦♦♦♦	New American	$11-$40	107
95 p. 38	Celebrity Delly	♦♦	Deli	$5-$14	107
96 p. 38	Peking Gourmet Inn	♦♦	Chinese	$12-$45	107
97 p. 38	Rabieng	♦♦	Thai	$9-$27	107
98 p. 38	Duangrat's	♦♦♦	Thai	$10-$33	107
99 p. 38	Raaga	♦♦♦	Indian	$12-$26	107
100 p. 38	City Diner	♦♦	American	$7-$26	107

VIENNA

Map Page	Hotel	Diamond Rated	Rate Range	Page
97 p. 38	**Courtyard by Marriott Dunn Loring Fairfax**	♦♦♦	$68-$318 SAVE	256

Map Page	Restaurants	Diamond Rated	Cuisine	Price Range	Page
103 p. 38	**Ristorante Bonaroti**	♦♦♦	Northern Italian	$15-$31	256
104 p. 38	Cafe Renaissance	♦♦♦	Continental	$14-$42	256
105 p. 38	Tom Yum Thai	♦♦	Thai	$9-$16	256
106 p. 38	Amphora Restaurant	♦♦	American	$9-$25	256
107 p. 38	Istanbul Blue	♦♦	Turkish	$9-$23	256
108 p. 38	Sunflower Vegetarian Restaurant	♦♦	Vegetarian	$8-$13	256
109 p. 38	Clarity	♦♦♦	American	$14-$38	256

FAIRFAX

Map Page	Hotels	Diamond Rated	Rate Range	Page
100 p. 38	**Hyatt House Falls Church/Merrifield**	♦♦♦	$99-$369 SAVE	105
101 p. 38	Extended Stay America Washington DC-Falls Church-Merrifield	♦♦	$75-$140	104
102 p. 38	Hilton Garden Inn Fairfax	♦♦♦	$89-$269	104

FAIRFAX (cont'd)

Map Page	Hotels (cont'd)	Diamond Rated	Rate Range	Page
103 p. 38	Extended Stay America Washington DC-Fairfax	◆◆	$70-$125	104
104 p. 38	**Best Western Fairfax**	◆◆	$80-$160 SAVE	104
105 p. 38	Holiday Inn Express Fairfax	◆◆	Rates not provided	104
106 p. 38	**Residence Inn by Marriott Fairfax City**	◆◆◆	$89-$264 SAVE	105
107 p. 38	**Fairfax Marriott at Fair Oaks**	◆◆◆	$68-$282 SAVE	104
108 p. 38	Extended Stay America-Washington DC-Fairfax-Fair Oaks	◆◆	$55-$125	104
109 p. 38	**Courtyard by Marriott-Fair Oaks**	◆◆◆	$61-$273 SAVE	104
110 p. 38	Candlewood Suites Fairfax-Washington, D.C.	◆◆	Rates not provided	104
111 p. 38	Hampton by Hilton-Fairfax	◆◆◆	$99-$219	104
112 p. 38	Comfort Inn University Center	◆◆	$79-$194	104
113 p. 38	**Residence Inn by Marriott-Fair Lakes**	◆◆◆	$75-$251 SAVE	105
114 p. 38	SpringHill Suites by Marriott Fairfax/Fair Oaks	◆◆◆	$71-$266	105
115 p. 38	**Hyatt Regency Fairfax**	◆◆◆	$69-$259 SAVE	105

Map Page	Restaurants	Diamond Rated	Cuisine	Price Range	Page
111 p. 38	Red Apron	◆	Sandwiches Hot Dogs	$7-$12	106
112 p. 38	True Food Kitchen	◆◆◆	Natural/Organic Vegetarian	$12-$26	106
113 p. 38	Sisters Thai - The Ordinary Cafe	◆◆	Thai	$11-$17	106
114 p. 38	Jaipur Royal Indian Cuisine	◆◆◆	Indian	$12-$20	106
115 p. 38	Arties	◆◆	American	$12-$39	105
116 p. 38	Lebanese Kitchen	◆◆	Lebanese	$7-$16	106
117 p. 38	Bombay Bistro	◆◆	Indian	$10-$20	105
118 p. 38	Chutzpah, A Real New York Deli	◆◆	Deli	$9-$20	105
119 p. 38	Dolce Vita	◆◆	Italian	$7-$31	106
120 p. 38	Ozzie's Good Eats	◆◆	Italian	$13-$39	106
121 p. 38	Coastal Flats	◆◆	American	$11-$30	105
122 p. 38	Ruth's Chris Steak House	◆◆◆	Steak	$33-$80	106
123 p. 38	Blue Iguana	◆◆	American	$8-$27	105
124 p. 38	Arigato Sushi	◆◆	Japanese Sushi	$9-$38	105
125 p. 38	Bollywood Bistro	◆◆	Indian Vegetarian	$10-$22	105
126 p. 38	Pad Thai Restaurant	◆◆	Thai	$8-$16	106
127 p. 38	The Auld Shebeen	◆◆	Irish	$9-$22	105
128 p. 38	Bellissimo Restaurant	◆◆◆	Northern Italian	$11-$33	105
129 p. 38	Sisters Thai-The Living Room Cafe	◆◆	Thai	$9-$16	106
130 p. 38	Villa Mozart	◆◆◆	Northern Italian	$14-$36	106
131 p. 38	Tsunami	◆◆	Japanese Sushi	$8-$38	106
132 p. 38	Mazadar Restaurant	◆◆	Middle Eastern	$10-$23	106
133 p. 38	Tony's New York Pizza	◆	Italian Pizza	$6-$18	106
134 p. 38	Brine	◆◆	Seafood	$12-$32	105

CENTREVILLE

Map Page	Hotels	Diamond Rated	Rate Range	Page
118 p. 38	**SpringHill Suites by Marriott Centreville/Chantilly**	◈◈◈	$63-$216 SAVE	78
119 p. 38	Extended Stay America-Washington DC-Centreville/Manassas	◈◈	$55-$100	78

Map Page	Restaurants	Diamond Rated	Cuisine	Price Range	Page
139 p. 38	My Thai Place	◈◈	Thai	$10-$16	79
140 p. 38	Ciao Wood-Fired Pizza & Osteria	◈◈	Italian Pizza	$9-$39	78

CHANTILLY

Map Page	Hotels	Diamond Rated	Rate Range	Page
122 p. 38	Wingate by Wyndham Dulles Airport-Chantilly	◈◈◈	Rates not provided	80
123 p. 38	Hampton Inn Washington Dulles International Airport South	◈◈◈	$89-$219	80
124 p. 38	Staybridge Suites Hotel Chantilly/Dulles International Airport	◈◈◈	Rates not provided	80
125 p. 38	Fairfield Inn & Suites by Marriott Dulles Airport Chantilly	◈◈	$57-$205	80
126 p. 38	TownePlace Suites by Marriott-Chantilly Dulles South	◈◈	$81-$202	80
127 p. 38	Residence Inn by Marriott Chantilly Dulles South	◈◈◈	$70-$309	80
128 p. 38	**Courtyard by Marriott-Dulles Airport-Chantilly**	◈◈◈	$63-$212 SAVE	79
129 p. 38	Holiday Inn Chantilly-Dulles Expo Center	◈◈◈	Rates not provided	80
130 p. 38	**Westfields Marriott**	◈◈◈	$74-$302 SAVE	80
131 p. 38	**Hyatt Place Chantilly/Dulles Airport-South**	◈◈◈	$64-$199 SAVE	80

Map Page	Restaurants	Diamond Rated	Cuisine	Price Range	Page
143 p. 38	Picante! The Real Taco	◈◈	Mexican	$8-$16	80
144 p. 38	Thai Basil	◈◈	Thai	$8-$20	80
145 p. 38	Sila Thai Cuisine	◈◈	Thai	$8-$18	80
146 p. 38	Otani Japanese Steak House	◈◈	Japanese Sushi	$8-$40	80
147 p. 38	Willard's Real Pit BBQ	◈	Barbecue	$7-$24	80

SPRINGFIELD

Map Page	Hotels	Diamond Rated	Rate Range	Page
134 p. 38	**TownePlace Suites by Marriott Springfield**	◈◈	$89-$263 SAVE	245
135 p. 38	Courtyard by Marriott-Springfield	◈◈◈	$80-$367	244
136 p. 38	**Best Western Springfield**	◈◈	$99-$299 SAVE	244
137 p. 38	Holiday Inn Express Springfield	◈◈◈	Rates not provided	244
138 p. 38	Residence Inn by Marriott Springfield Old Keene Mill	◈◈◈	$160-$401	244
139 p. 38	**Homewood Suites by Hilton Springfield**	◈◈◈	$149-$500 SAVE	244
140 p. 38	Wingate by Wyndham Springfield	◈◈◈	Rates not provided	245
142 p. 38	**Hilton Springfield**	◈◈◈	$119-$199 SAVE	244
143 p. 38	Embassy Suites by Hilton Springfield	◈◈◈	$139-$339	244

Map Page	Restaurants	Diamond Rated	Cuisine	Price Range	Page
150 p. 38	Eleni's Greek Taverna	◈◈	Greek	$9-$20	245
151 p. 38	Mike's American Grill	◈◈	American	$13-$39	245
152 p. 38	Sandwich Republic	◈	Sandwiches	$7-$9	245

Map Page	Restaurants (cont'd)	Diamond Rated	Cuisine	Price Range	Page
(153) p. 38	Maggiano's Little Italy	◈◈◈	Italian	$14-$38	245
(154) p. 38	BGR-The Burger Joint	◈	Burgers	$7-$18	245
(155) p. 38	Monty's Steakhouse	◈◈◈	Steak Seafood	$12-$44	245

GREAT FALLS

Map Page	Restaurant	Diamond Rated	Cuisine	Price Range	Page
(15) p. 38	Dante Ristorante	◈◈◈	Northern Italian	$15-$36	123

ANNANDALE

Map Page	Restaurant	Diamond Rated	Cuisine	Price Range	Page
(136) p. 38	Silverado	◈◈	American	$10-$29	55

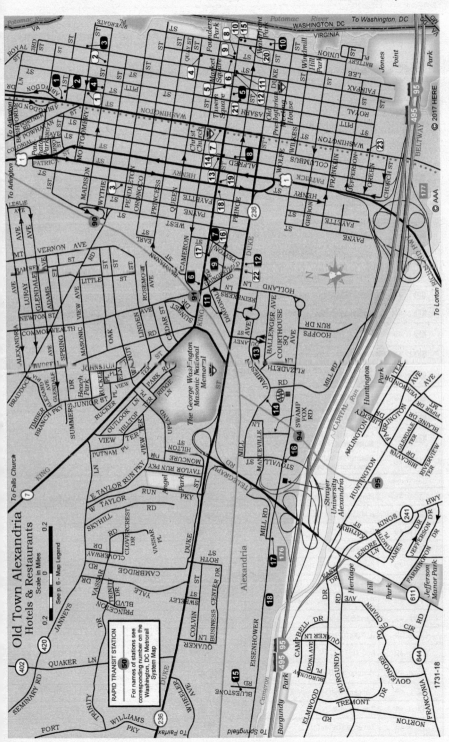

Old Town Alexandria
Hotels & Restaurants

Scale in Miles

See p. 6 - Map Legend

RAPID TRANSIT STATION

50

For names of stations see
corresponding number on the
Washington, DC Metrorail
System Map

© 2017 HERE

© AAA

1731-18

Old Town Alexandria

This index helps you "spot" where approved hotels and restaurants are located on the corresponding detailed maps. Hotel daily rate range is for comparison only. Restaurant price range is a combination of lunch and/or dinner. Turn to the listing page for more information and consult display ads for special promotions.

 For more details, rates and reservations: **AAA.com/travelguides/hotels**

ALEXANDRIA

Map Page	Hotels	Diamond Rated	Rate Range	Page
❶ p. 49	**Old Colony Inn Alexandria**	♦♦	$129-$169 SAVE	53
❷ p. 49	Holiday Inn Hotel & Suites-Alexandria Old Town	♦♦♦	$89-$599	52
❸ p. 49	**Crowne Plaza Old Town Alexandria**	♦♦♦	$89-$499 SAVE	51
❹ p. 49	**Sheraton Suites Old Town Alexandria**	♦♦♦	$99-$389 SAVE	53
❺ p. 49	The Alexandrian, Autograph Collection	♦♦♦	$134-$436	51
❻ p. 49	**Hilton Alexandria Old Town**	♦♦♦	$109-$339 SAVE	52
❼ p. 49	**Kimpton-The Lorien Hotel & Spa**	♦♦♦	Rates not provided SAVE	53
❽ p. 49	Morrison House, Autograph Collection	♦♦♦	$95-$500	53
❾ p. 49	**Hilton Garden Inn Alexandria-Old Town**	♦♦♦	Rates not provided SAVE	52
❿ p. 49	**Hotel Indigo Old Town Alexandria**	♦♦♦	$99-$599 SAVE	53
⓫ p. 49	**Embassy Suites by Hilton Alexandria Old Town**	♦♦♦	$109-$329 SAVE	52
⓬ p. 49	**Residence Inn by Marriott Alexandria-Old Town/Duke St.**	♦♦♦	$82-$370 SAVE	53
⓭ p. 49	**The Westin Alexandria**	♦♦♦	$159-$599 SAVE	54
⓮ p. 49	Residence Inn by Marriott Alexandria Old Town South at Carlyle	♦♦♦	$85-$367	53
⓯ p. 49	Extended Stay America-Washington DC-Alexandria-Eisenhower Ave	♦♦	$80-$145	52
⓰ p. 49	**Holiday Inn Alexandria at Carlyle**	♦♦	$99-$309 SAVE	52
⓱ p. 49	**Courtyard by Marriott-Alexandria Old Town Southwest**	♦♦♦	$120-$300 SAVE	51
⓲ p. 49	**SpringHill Suites by Marriott Alexandria Old Town Southwest**	♦♦♦	$76-$309 SAVE	53

Map Page	Restaurants	Diamond Rated	Cuisine	Price Range	Page
① p. 49	Hank's Pasta Bar	♦♦	Italian	$16-$29	54
② p. 49	a la Lucia	♦♦	Italian	$9-$35	54
③ p. 49	Bastille	♦♦♦	French	$14-$35	54
④ p. 49	Bilbo Baggins	♦♦	International	$11-$24	54
⑤ p. 49	Gadsby's Tavern Restaurant	♦♦	American	$11-$30	54
⑥ p. 49	Two Nineteen Restaurant	♦♦	Creole	$21-$38	55
⑦ p. 49	BGR-The Burger Joint	♦	Burgers	$7-$15	54
⑧ p. 49	Landini Brothers	♦♦	Italian	$11-$41	54
⑨ p. 49	IL PORTO Ristorante	♦♦	Northern Italian	$11-$30	54
⑩ p. 49	Mai Thai	♦♦	Thai	$12-$24	54
⑪ p. 49	Warehouse Bar & Grill	♦♦♦	Regional American	$12-$40	55
⑫ p. 49	Sangjun Thai Restaurant	♦♦	Thai	$10-$19	54
⑬ p. 49	The Majestic	♦♦♦	American	$9-$36	54
⑭ p. 49	**Taverna Cretekou**	♦♦	Greek	$14-$35	54

Map Page	Restaurants (cont'd)	Diamond Rated	Cuisine	Price Range	Page
(15) p. 49	Virtue Feed & Grain	◈◈	American	$12-$38	55
(16) p. 49	Brabo	◈◈◈	French	$26-$38	54
(17) p. 49	Brabo Tasting Room	◈◈	Belgian	$16-$24	54
(18) p. 49	Vermilion	◈◈◈	American	$11-$36	55
(19) p. 49	Hank's Oyster Bar	◈◈	Seafood	$13-$32	54
(20) p. 49	Union Street Public House	◈◈	American	$12-$39	55
(21) p. 49	Restaurant Eve	◈◈◈◈	American	$15-$40	54
(22) p. 49	Laporta's	◈◈◈	American	$10-$33	54
(23) p. 49	Southside 815	◈◈	Southern Comfort Food	$10-$22	54

THE ALEXANDRIAN, AUTOGRAPH COLLECTION
(703)549-6080 **5**
◈◈◈ Hotel. **Address:** 480 King St 22314
AAA Benefit: Members save 5% or more!

BEST WESTERN MOUNT VERNON/FT. BELVOIR
(703)360-1300
◈◈ Hotel $99-$500
AAA Benefit: Members save 10% or more & earn 10% bonus points!
Address: 8751 Richmond Hwy 22309 **Location:** I-95/495 exit 177A, 7 mi s on US 1. **Facility:** 132 units, some efficiencies. 5 stories, interior corridors. **Terms:** 3 day cancellation notice-fee imposed. **Amenities:** safes. **Activities:** exercise room. **Guest Services:** coin laundry.

BUDGET HOST TRAVELERS MOTEL
(703)329-1310 **7**
◈◈ Vintage Motel $85-$105
Address: 5916 Richmond Hwy 22303 **Location:** I-95/495 exit 177A, just s on US 1. Huntington, 95. **Facility:** Near the interstate and a short drive to Old Town, this motel offers at-room parking and some units with a sleeper sofa. Hair dryers and irons are available at the front desk. 29 units. 1 story, exterior corridors. **Guest Services:** area transportation. **Featured Amenity:** continental breakfast.

CANDLEWOOD SUITES ALEXANDRIA-FT. BELVOIR
703/780-1111
◈◈ Extended Stay Hotel. **Address:** 8847 Richmond Hwy 22309

COMFORT INN & SUITES ALEXANDRIA (703)922-9200 **11**
◈◈ Hotel. **Address:** 5716 S Van Dorn St 22310

COMFORT INN LANDMARK (703)642-3422 **5**
◈◈ Hotel. **Address:** 6254 Duke St 22312

COURTYARD BY MARRIOTT-ALEXANDRIA OLD TOWN SOUTHWEST (703)329-2323 **17**
◈◈◈ Hotel $120-$300
COURTYARD Marriott **AAA Benefit:** Members save 5% or more!
Address: 2700 Eisenhower Ave 22314 **Location:** I-95/495 exit 176B, 0.3 mi s. Eisenhower Ave, 94. **Facility:** 178 units. 8 stories, interior corridors. **Terms:** cancellation fee imposed. **Activities:** exercise room. **Guest Services:** valet and coin laundry, boarding pass kiosk, area transportation. **Featured Amenity:** full hot breakfast.
  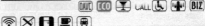

COURTYARD BY MARRIOTT ALEXANDRIA PENTAGON SOUTH (703)751-4510 **4**
◈◈◈ Hotel $67-$313
COURTYARD Marriott **AAA Benefit:** Members save 5% or more!
Address: 4641 Kenmore Ave 22304 **Location:** I-395 exit 4, 0.8 mi s of jct SR 7. **Facility:** 203 units. 11 stories, interior corridors. **Parking:** on-site (fee). **Terms:** cancellation fee imposed. **Pool:** heated indoor. **Activities:** hot tub, exercise room. **Guest Services:** valet and coin laundry, boarding pass kiosk, area transportation.

CROWNE PLAZA OLD TOWN ALEXANDRIA
(703)683-6000 **3**
◈◈◈ Hotel $89-$499
Address: 901 N Fairfax St 22314 **Location:** Between First and Montgomery sts. Located in Old Town. Braddock Road, 90. **Facility:** 254 units. 12 stories, interior corridors. **Parking:** on-site (fee) and valet. **Terms:** cancellation fee imposed. **Activities:** exercise room. **Guest Services:** valet and coin laundry, area transportation.
  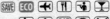 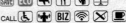

52 ALEXANDRIA, VA

(See maps & indexes p. 38, 49.)

EMBASSY SUITES BY HILTON ALEXANDRIA OLD TOWN (703)684-5900 **11**

Hotel
$109-$329

AAA Benefit: Members save 5% or more!

Address: 1900 Diagonal Rd 22314 **Location:** I-95/495 exit 176B, 0.5 mi n on SR 241 N, then 0.5 mi e on SR 236. Located opposite King Street Metro/Amtrak station; in Old Town. 🚇 King St-Old Town, 91. **Facility:** 288 units, some two bedrooms. 8 stories, interior corridors. **Parking:** on-site (fee). **Terms:** 1-7 night minimum stay, cancellation fee imposed. **Amenities:** safes. **Pool:** heated indoor. **Activities:** hot tub, exercise room. **Guest Services:** valet and coin laundry. **Featured Amenity:** full hot breakfast.

EXTENDED STAY AMERICA-WASHINGTON DC-ALEXANDRIA-EISENHOWER AVE (703)329-3399 **15**
Extended Stay Hotel. **Address:** 200 Bluestone Rd 22304

FAIRFIELD INN & SUITES BY MARRIOTT ALEXANDRIA
703/721-0600 **12**

Hotel
Rates not provided

AAA Benefit: Members save 5% or more!

Address: 6421 Richmond Hwy 22306 **Location:** I-95/495 exit 177A, 1.7 mi s on US 1. Located in a commercial area. **Facility:** 116 units. 4 stories, interior corridors. **Pool:** heated indoor. **Activities:** hot tub, exercise room. **Guest Services:** valet and coin laundry.

HAMPTON INN-ALEXANDRIA/PENTAGON SOUTH (703)671-4800 **2**
Hotel. **Address:** 4800 Leesburg Pike 22302

AAA Benefit: Members save up to 10%!

HAMPTON INN & SUITES BY HILTON ALEXANDRIA/OLD TOWN AREA-SOUTH (703)329-1400 **6**
Hotel. **Address:** 5821 Richmond Hwy 22303

AAA Benefit: Members save up to 10%!

HAMPTON INN & SUITES BY HILTON MT. VERNON-BELVOIR-ALEXANDRIA SOUTH (703)619-7026
Hotel. **Address:** 8843 Richmond Hwy 22309

AAA Benefit: Members save up to 10%!

HILTON ALEXANDRIA MARK CENTER (703)845-1010 **3**
Hotel. **Address:** 5000 Seminary Rd 22311

AAA Benefit: Members save 5% or more!

HILTON ALEXANDRIA OLD TOWN (703)837-0440 **6**

Hotel
$109-$339

AAA Benefit: Members save 5% or more!

Address: 1767 King St 22314 **Location:** I-95/495 exit 176B, 0.5 mi n on SR 241, 0.5 mi e on SR 236, then just ne on Diagonal Rd. Located in Old Town. 🚇 King St-Old Town, 91. **Facility:** 252 units. 7 stories, interior corridors. **Parking:** on-site (fee). **Terms:** check-in 4 pm, 1-7 night minimum stay, cancellation fee imposed. **Amenities:** safes. **Activities:** exercise room. **Guest Services:** valet laundry.

HILTON GARDEN INN ALEXANDRIA-OLD TOWN
703/302-8300 **9**

Hotel
Rates not provided

AAA Benefit: Members save up to 10%!

Address: 1620 Prince St 22314 **Location:** I-95/495 exit 176B, 0.5 mi n on SR 241, 0.7 mi e on SR 236, then just n; jct Dangerfield Rd and Prince St. Located in Old Town. 🚇 King St-Old Town, 91. **Facility:** 109 units. 6 stories, interior corridors. **Parking:** valet only. **Amenities:** safes. **Activities:** exercise room. **Guest Services:** valet and coin laundry.

HOLIDAY INN ALEXANDRIA AT CARLYLE (703)960-2000 **16**

Hotel
$99-$309

Address: 2460 Eisenhower Ave 22314 **Location:** I-95/495 exit 176B to Eisenhower Ave. Located near Old Town. 🚇 Eisenhower Ave, 94. **Facility:** 207 units. 10 stories, interior corridors. **Amenities:** safes. **Pool:** heated indoor. **Activities:** exercise room. **Guest Services:** valet and coin laundry, area transportation.

HOLIDAY INN EXPRESS & SUITES ALEXANDRIA
571/257-9555 **9**
Hotel. **Address:** 6055 Richmond Hwy 22303

HOLIDAY INN HOTEL & SUITES-ALEXANDRIA OLD TOWN (703)548-6300 **2**
Hotel. **Address:** 625 First St 22314

HOMEWOOD SUITES BY HILTON-ALEXANDRIA/PENTAGON SOUTH (703)671-6500 **1**
Extended Stay Hotel. **Address:** 4850 Leesburg Pike 22302

AAA Benefit: Members save up to 10%!

🔗 **Save on travel, shopping and more:**
AAA.com/discounts

(See maps & indexes p. 38, 49.)

HOTEL INDIGO OLD TOWN ALEXANDRIA
(703)721-3800 **10**

Hotel
$99-$599

Address: 220 S Union St 22314 **Location:** Waterfront. Jct Duke St; between Duke and Prince sts. Located in Old Town. **Facility:** 120 units. 5 stories, interior corridors. *Bath:* shower only. **Parking:** valet only. **Terms:** cancellation fee imposed. **Amenities:** safes. **Activities:** exercise room. **Guest Services:** valet laundry.

[icons]

KIMPTON-THE LORIEN HOTEL & SPA
703/894-3434 **7**

Boutique
Contemporary
Hotel
Rates not provided

Address: 1600 King St 22314 **Location:** Between Harvard and Peyton sts. King St-Old Town, 91. **Facility:** In the heart of Old Town, this luxury hotel is tucked back off the main street just blocks from the King Street Metro/Amtrak station. The guest rooms are designed for comfort and relaxation. 107 units. 6 stories, interior corridors. **Parking:** valet only. **Amenities:** safes. **Dining:** Brabo, Brabo Tasting Room, see separate listings. **Activities:** steamroom, bicycles, exercise room, spa. **Guest Services:** valet laundry.

[icons]

MORRISON HOUSE, AUTOGRAPH COLLECTION
(703)838-8000 **8**

Hotel. **Address:** 116 S Alfred St 22314

AAA Benefit:
Members save 5%
or more!

OLD COLONY INN ALEXANDRIA
(703)739-2222 **1**

Hotel
$129-$169

Address: 1101 N Washington St 22314 **Location:** George Washington Memorial Pkwy, jct 2nd St. Located in Old Town. Braddock Road, 90. **Facility:** 49 units. 2 stories (no elevator), interior corridors. **Activities:** exercise room. **Guest Services:** area transportation. **Featured Amenity:** full hot breakfast.

[icons]

RED ROOF PLUS+ WASHINGTON DC-ALEXANDRIA
(703)960-5200 **8**

Hotel
$70-$200

Address: 5975 Richmond Hwy 22303 **Location:** I-95/495 exit 177A, 0.5 mi s on US 1. Huntington, 95. **Facility:** 115 units. 3 stories, exterior corridors. **Amenities:** safes. **Guest Services:** coin laundry.

[icons]

RESIDENCE INN BY MARRIOTT ALEXANDRIA-OLD TOWN/DUKE ST.
(703)548-5474 **12**

Extended Stay
Hotel
$82-$370

Residence Inn Marriott **AAA Benefit:**
Members save 5%
or more!

Address: 1456 Duke St 22314 **Location:** I-95/495 exit 176B, 0.5 mi n on SR 241, then 0.7 mi e on SR 236. Located in Old Town. King St-Old Town, 91. **Facility:** 240 units, some two bedrooms, efficiencies and kitchens. 8 stories, interior corridors. **Parking:** on-site (fee). **Terms:** cancellation fee imposed. **Pool:** heated indoor. **Activities:** exercise room. **Guest Services:** valet and coin laundry, boarding pass kiosk, area transportation. **Featured Amenity:** breakfast buffet.

[icons]

RESIDENCE INN BY MARRIOTT ALEXANDRIA OLD TOWN SOUTH AT CARLYLE
(703)549-1155 **14**

Extended Stay Hotel. **Address:** 2345 Mill Rd 22314

AAA Benefit:
Members save 5%
or more!

SHERATON SUITES OLD TOWN ALEXANDRIA
(703)836-4700 **4**

Hotel
◊◊◊ ◊◊◊◊

Sheraton **AAA Benefit:**
Members save 5%
or more!

Address: 801 N St. Asaph St 22314 **Location:** Just e of Washington St. Located in Old Town. Braddock Road, 90. **Facility:** 247 units. 10 stories, interior corridors. **Parking:** on-site (fee). **Terms:** cancellation fee imposed. **Amenities:** safes. **Pool:** heated indoor. **Activities:** hot tub, exercise room. **Guest Services:** complimentary and valet laundry, rental car service.

[icons]

SPRINGHILL SUITES BY MARRIOTT ALEXANDRIA
(571)481-4441 **10**

Hotel. **Address:** 6065 Richmond Hwy 22303

AAA Benefit:
Members save 5%
or more!

SPRINGHILL SUITES BY MARRIOTT ALEXANDRIA OLD TOWN SOUTHWEST
(703)317-0013 **18**

Hotel
$76-$309

SPRINGHILL SUITES MARRIOTT **AAA Benefit:**
Members save 5%
or more!

Address: 2950 Eisenhower Ave 22314 **Location:** I-95/495 exit 176B, 0.6 mi e. Eisenhower Ave, 94. **Facility:** 155 units. 5 stories, interior corridors. **Terms:** cancellation fee imposed. **Activities:** exercise room. **Guest Services:** valet and coin laundry, area transportation. **Featured Amenity:** breakfast buffet.

[icons]

(See maps & indexes p. 38, 49.)

TOWNEPLACE SUITES BY MARRIOTT ALEXANDRIA-FORT BELVOIR (703)619-6060
▼▼ Extended Stay Hotel. **Address:** 8632 Woodlawn Ct 22309

AAA Benefit: Members save 5% or more!

THE WESTIN ALEXANDRIA (703)253-8600 **13**

Hotel $159-$599

WESTIN HOTELS & RESORTS

AAA Benefit: Members save 5% or more!

Address: 400 Courthouse Square 22314 **Location:** I-95/495 exit 176B, just n on Telegraph Rd (SR 241 N), 0.4 mi e on SR 236, then just s on Dulany St. 🚇 Eisenhower Ave, 94. **Facility:** 319 units. 9 stories, interior corridors. **Parking:** valet only. **Terms:** 3 day cancellation notice-fee imposed. **Amenities:** safes. **Activities:** exercise room, massage. **Guest Services:** valet laundry, area transportation.

[SAVE] 🍴 ♿ 🍽 CALL 📞 📶 [BIZ] [SHS] 🔊 ❌ 📷 🛅 💻 /SOME UNITS 🧳 🚐

WHERE TO EAT

A LA LUCIA 703/836-5123 **2**
▼▼ Italian. Casual Dining. **Address:** 315 Madison St 22314

BASTILLE 703/519-3776 **3**
▼▼▼ French. Casual Dining. **Address:** 606 N Fayette St 22314

BGR-THE BURGER JOINT 703/299-9791 **7**
▼ Burgers. Quick Serve. **Address:** 106 N Washington St 22314

BILBO BAGGINS 703/683-0300 **4**
▼▼ International. Casual Dining. **Address:** 208 Queen St 22314

BOMBAY CURRY COMPANY 703/836-6363 **3**
▼▼ Indian. Casual Dining. **Address:** 2607 Mt. Vernon Ave 22301

BRABO 703/894-3440 **16**
▼▼▼ French. Fine Dining. **Address:** 1600 King St 22314

BRABO TASTING ROOM 703/894-5253 **17**
▼▼ Belgian. Casual Dining. **Address:** 1600 King St 22314

CLYDE'S OF MARK CENTER 703/820-8300
▼▼ American. Casual Dining. **Address:** 1700 N Beauregard St 22311

DEL RAY CAFE 703/717-9151 **8**
▼▼▼ French. Casual Dining. **Address:** 205 E Howell Ave 22301

EVENING STAR CAFÉ 703/549-5051 **7**
▼▼ Southern American. Casual Dining. **Address:** 2000 Mt. Vernon Ave 22301

GADSBY'S TAVERN RESTAURANT 703/548-1288 **5**
▼▼ American. Casual Dining. **Address:** 138 N Royal St 22314

HANK'S OYSTER BAR 703/739-4265 **19**
▼▼▼ Seafood. Casual Dining. **Address:** 1026 King St 22314

HANK'S PASTA BAR 571/312-4117 **1**
▼▼ Italian. Casual Dining. **Address:** 600 Montgomery St 22314

HARD TIMES CAFE 703/837-0050
▼▼ American. Casual Dining. **Address:** 1404 King St 22314

HOLY COW 703/666-8616 **5**
▼ Burgers. Quick Serve. **Address:** 2312 Mt. Vernon Ave 22301

ILLUSIONS THAI CAFE 703/575-1999 **9**
▼▼ Asian. Casual Dining. **Address:** 1472 N Beauregard St 22311

IL PORTO RISTORANTE 703/836-8833 **9**
▼▼ Northern Italian. Casual Dining. **Address:** 121 King St 22314

INDIGO LANDING 703/548-0001 **2**
▼▼▼ American. Casual Dining. **Address:** 1 Marina Dr 22314

KING STREET BLUES 703/836-8800
▼▼ American. Casual Dining. **Address:** 112 N St. Asaph St 22314

LANDINI BROTHERS 703/836-8404 **8**
▼▼ Italian. Fine Dining. **Address:** 115 King St 22314

LAPORTA'S 703/683-6313 **22**
▼▼ American. Casual Dining. **Address:** 1600 Duke St 22314

MAI THAI 703/548-0600 **10**
▼▼ Thai. Casual Dining. **Address:** 6 King St 22314

THE MAJESTIC 703/837-9117 **13**
▼▼▼ American. Casual Dining. **Address:** 911 King St 22314

PARADISO RISTORANTE ITALIANO 703/922-6222 **12**
▼▼ Italian. Casual Dining. **Address:** 6124 Franconia Rd 22310

PORK BARREL BBQ 703/822-5699 **4**
▼ Barbecue. Quick Serve. **Address:** 2312 Mt. Vernon Ave 22301

RESTAURANT EVE 703/706-0450 **21**
▼▼▼ American. Fine Dining. **Address:** 110 S Pitt St 22314

RT'S RESTAURANT 703/684-6010 **1**
▼▼ Regional American. Casual Dining. **Address:** 3804 Mt. Vernon Ave 22305

SANGJUN THAI RESTAURANT 571/312-3377 **12**
▼▼ Thai. Casual Dining. **Address:** 300 King St 22314

SOUTHSIDE 815 703/836-6222 **23**
▼▼ Southern Comfort Food. Casual Dining. **Address:** 815 S Washington St 22314

TAVERNA CRETEKOU 703/548-8688 **14**
▼▼ **Greek Casual Dining** $14-$35

AAA Inspector Notes: The restaurant offers a wide assortment of appetizers—as well as lamb, chicken and seafood dishes—in a Greek tavern setting. The Tuesday-Friday lunch buffet, where diners can sample two or three Greek entrées with salad and soup, is a popular draw. The courtyard terrace is open seasonally and live music is offered on Thursday night. **Features:** full bar, patio dining, Sunday brunch. **Reservations:** suggested, for dinner. **Address:** 818 King St 22314 **Location:** On SR 7, just e of US 1; in Old Town. 🚇 King St-Old Town, 91. **Parking:** street only. [L] [D] [🚐]

TEMPO RESTAURANT 703/370-7900 **10**
▼▼ Northern Italian. Casual Dining. **Address:** 4231 Duke St 22304

THAI LEMONGRASS 703/751-4627 **11**
▼▼ Thai. Casual Dining. **Address:** 506 S Van Dorn St 22304

(See maps & indexes p. 38, 49.)

THAI PEPPERS   703/739-7627 [6]
♥♥ Thai. Casual Dining. **Address:** 2018 Mt. Vernon Ave 22301

TWO NINETEEN RESTAURANT   703/549-1141 [6]
♥♥ Creole. Fine Dining. **Address:** 219 King St 22314

UNION STREET PUBLIC HOUSE   703/548-1785 [20]
♥♥ American. Casual Dining. **Address:** 121 S Union St 22314

VERMILION   703/684-9669 [18]
♥♥♥ American. Fine Dining. **Address:** 1120 King St 22314

VIRTUE FEED & GRAIN   571/970-3669 [15]
♥♥ American. Casual Dining. **Address:** 106 S Union St 22314

WAREHOUSE BAR & GRILL   703/683-6868 [11]
♥♥♥ Regional American. Fine Dining. **Address:** 214 King St 22314

ALTAVISTA (H-7) pop. 3,450, elev. 596'

A relatively young town by Virginia standards, Altavista was founded in 1905 by the Lane brothers. In 1912 the Lane family opened a box plant, today known for its cedar chests and furniture. Steeped in railroad history, the town is part of the Virginia Railway Heritage Trail and the state's Historical Railway Trail.

Altavista Area Chamber of Commerce: 414 Washington St., P.O. Box 606, Altavista, VA 24517. **Phone:** (434) 369-6665.

DAYS INN   434/369-4070
♥♥ Hotel. **Address:** 1557 Main St 24517

QUALITY SUITES ALTAVISTA-LYNCHBURG SOUTH
                            (434)369-4000
♥♥ Hotel. **Address:** 1558 Main St 24517

AMHERST (G-7) pop. 2,231, elev. 761'

Amherst County Chamber of Commerce: 328 Richmond Hwy., Suite A, P.O. Box 560, Amherst, VA 24521. **Phone:** (434) 946-0990.

ANNANDALE pop. 41,008
• Hotels & Restaurants map & index p. 38

SILVERADO   703/354-4560 [136]
♥♥ American. Casual Dining. **Address:** 7052 Columbia Pike 22003

APPOMATTOX (H-7) pop. 1,733, elev. 850'

[SAVE] **THE MUSEUM OF THE CONFEDERACY—APPOMATTOX** is at 159 Horseshoe Rd. This state-of-the-art facility, an extension of The American Civil War Museum in Richmond, offers two permanent exhibitions showcasing Civil War artifacts. The frock coat and sword Gen. Robert E. Lee wore when he surrendered to Gen. Ulysses S. Grant at Appomattox on April 9, 1865, are among the many uniforms and weapons included in the museum's impressive collection. Hands-on displays also

help chronicle the 4-year conflict, as do the photos, letters and diaries of individuals from varying walks of life who were affected by the war.

Many exhibits focus on Lee's Army of Northern Virginia in the months prior to the Appomattox surrender. Other galleries relate the Civil War's aftermath in the defeated South and the Reconstruction period. Temporary exhibitions also are offered. **Time:** Allow 45 minutes minimum. **Hours:** Daily 10-6, Memorial Day-Labor Day; 10-5, rest of year. Closed Jan. 1, Thanksgiving and Christmas. **Cost:** $10; $8.50 (ages 62+); $5 (ages 6-17). **Phone:** (434) 352-5791.

THE BABCOCK HOUSE   (434)352-7532
♥♥♥ Historic Country Inn. **Address:** 250 Oakleigh Ave 24522

SUPER 8   434/352-2339
♥ Motel. **Address:** 7571 Richmond Hwy 24522

WHERE TO EAT

THE BABCOCK HOUSE   434/352-7532
♥♥ Regional American. Casual Dining. **Address:** 250 Oakleigh Ave 24522

APPOMATTOX COURT HOUSE NATIONAL HISTORICAL PARK (H-7)

Three miles northeast of Appomattox on SR 24, Appomattox Court House National Historical Park is a 1,744-acre site. On April 9, 1865, Gen. Robert E. Lee's weakened and outnumbered Confederate Army of Northern Virginia was cut off at Appomattox Court House by Gen. Ulysses S. Grant. The two commanders met in the parlor of a house owned by Wilmer McLean—and the Army of Northern Virginia was surrendered to Grant.

Markers designate Grant's and Lee's headquarters, the site of the last shots fired by the Confederate artillery and infantry, and the road where the arms were laid down.

The courthouse building burned in 1892, and a new one was built at the location of the present town of Appomattox. A speculator razed the McLean House in 1893 with the intention of rebuilding it in Washington, D.C. This project failed and the materials, left exposed to the ravages of decay and souvenir hunters, soon were lost. The McLean House was reconstructed on the original site by the National Park Service.

A village of 27 structures has been restored to its 1865 appearance. Among the buildings open to visitors are Clover Hill Tavern, a county jail, a guest house, Jones Law Office, a kitchen, McLean House, Meeks General Store and Woodson Law Office.

Exterior restorations include Isbell House, Mariah Wright House and Peers House. The reconstructed courthouse serves as a visitor center and has a museum and an auditorium where audiovisual programs are shown every half-hour.

Living-history programs are presented in summer. Costumed interpreters portraying Confederate and Union soldiers and village residents answer visitors' questions. Area information is available at the park visitor center in the reconstructed courthouse and at the visitor information center in the Main Street railroad depot in the town of Appomattox.

The park and buildings are open daily 9-5. Closed Jan. 1, Thanksgiving and Christmas. Phone (434) 352-8987, ext. 226.

ARLINGTON (E-10) pop. 207,627, elev. 236'
• Hotels p. 60 • Restaurants p. 65
• Hotels & Restaurants map & index p. 38, 58

Arlington, on the southwest bank of the Potomac, is a suburb of Washington, D.C. One of the smallest counties in the United States, it covers 25.7 square miles, of which about 4.6 square miles are federal property. Some of the major centers of development (the county contains no incorporated communities) are Ballston, Clarendon, Columbia Pike, Crystal City, Rosslyn and Shirlington.

Shopping: At the Crystal City Metro station there is a collection of underground boutiques, restaurants and clothing stores. The Fashion Centre at Pentagon City (1100 S. Hayes St.), at the Pentagon City Metro station, features Macy's, Nordstrom and more than 150 other stores. Adjacent to the mall is Pentagon Row (1101 S. Joyce St.), an outdoor, mixed-use residential, shopping and dining area. Parking can come at a premium, so the Metro is the best way to get there.

For above-ground shopping, Ballston Common Mall (4238 Wilson Blvd.) offers an indoor array of more than 130 stores, including Macy's.

Nightlife: When D.C. shuts down, Arlington has plenty to keep office workers busy after hours. Sports bar Spider Kelly's (3181 Wilson Blvd.) combines good sandwiches and libations with old-school gaming (everything from shuffleboard and darts to classic video games). Several lounge areas complete with couches give this popular watering hole the feel of a really large, comfortable basement. Phone (703) 312-8888.

Whitlow's on Wilson (2854 Wilson Blvd.) is a longtime hangout that boasts a seasonal rooftop bar and drink and food specials. A word of advice: It's often packed, especially on weekends, and the noise level can be deafening. Phone (703) 276-9693.

For something a little more elegant, head to the Clarendon Ballroom (3185 Wilson Blvd.), a nightclub housed in a classic Art Deco-style building with a huge rooftop pavilion. Phone (703) 469-2244.

The intimate, laid-back IOTA Club & Cafe (2832 Wilson Blvd.) is one of the best places in Arlington to hear live music. Bands lean toward indie rock, and local talent takes to the stage on open mic nights. Phone (703) 522-8340.

MARINE CORPS WAR MEMORIAL stands on a promontory off N. Meade St., adjacent to Arlington National Cemetery. The memorial, commonly referred to as the Iwo Jima Memorial, is a 78-foot, 100-ton portrayal of Joseph Rosenthal's photograph of the raising of the flag on Iwo Jima during World War II. The figures were cast in bronze from a model created by Felix de Weldon. The Sunset Parade, also known as the Iwo Jima Memorial Parade, is a color ceremony featuring the Marine Silent Drill Team, Color Guard, and Drum and Bugle Corps.

Hours: Grounds daily 6 a.m.-midnight. Sunset Parade begins Tues. at 7, June-July; at 6:30, early to mid-Aug. **Cost:** Grounds free. Free bus service to the ceremony runs from the Arlington National Cemetery visitors' parking area. **Phone:** (703) 289-2500, or (202) 433-4073 for parade information.
🚇 Rosslyn, 38

THE PENTAGON, across the Potomac River from Washington, D.C., accessible via I-395, the George Washington Memorial Pkwy., I-66 or US 1, is one of the world's largest office buildings. The five-sided structure, which was completed in 1943 after only 16 months of construction, covers 29 acres and houses branches of the Department of Defense. Tours lasting approximately 1 hour cover nearly 1.5 miles and provide an overview of the Department of Defense. Exhibits showcase military history. The Pentagon Memorial also is on the grounds.

Note: Tours are offered by advance reservation only. Reservations can be made at http://pentagontours.osd.mil. Visitors over age 17 must show a government-issued ID; non-citizens without a government-issued ID must show a passport. Large bags, including camera bags and backpacks, are discouraged. There is no visitor parking at the Pentagon; paid public parking is available at The Fashion Centre at Pentagon City Mall. Photography is not permitted inside or outside of the Pentagon, except for the photo area in the visitor center and at the Pentagon Memorial. **Hours:** Tours are offered Mon.-Fri. 9-3. Closed Federal holidays. **Cost:** Free. **Phone:** (703) 697-1776.
GT 🚇 Pentagon, 86

The Pentagon Memorial is at the s.w. corner of the Pentagon, accessible via I-395, the George Washington Memorial Pkwy., I-66 or US 1. "We claim this ground in remembrance of the events of September 11, 2001." These are the first words inscribed on a marker at the entrance to the memorial that commemorates the lives lost when hijacked American Airlines Flight 77 crashed into the Pentagon at 9:37 a.m., killing 184 people. It was dedicated in 2008, exactly 7 years following 9/11.

The simple yet eloquent design is based on a timeline of ages (the youngest victim was 3 years old; the oldest, 71). Each of the 184 memorial units—narrow, cantilevered stainless steel benches inlaid with granite—is positioned on a gravel field

(See maps & indexes p. 38, 58.)

according to the year the individual was born. Beneath each bench is a rectangular pool of water; throughout the day light is reflected onto the benches.

Each unit also is positioned to distinguish those who were inside the Pentagon from those who were on board Flight 77. Reading the benches inscribed with the names of the 59 passengers and crew, you face the direction of the plane's approach; reading the inscriptions on the benches honoring the 125 military and civilian personnel, you face the Pentagon building.

Sheltering the field of benches are 85 crape myrtle trees. Not dedicated to any one victim, they will eventually grow some 30 feet tall, providing a canopy of shade as well as seasonal summer blooms. Visitors who want to locate a specific memorial bench can look up the name and birth year on the locator stone at the Pentagon Memorial Gateway near the entrance.

A 24-minute audio tour offers a narrative of the 9/11 events that occurred at the Pentagon, Pentagon history and the concept behind the design. To get more out of your experience, download the interactive map from the website.

Photography is permitted only at the memorial site. Food and beverages (except for water) are not permitted. Although public parking is available in a lot off Hayes Street (Mon.-Fri. 5 p.m.-7 a.m., all day Sat.-Sun. and holidays), using Metro is recommended. It's about a 10-minute walk from the Pentagon Metro station exit to the site entrance; there is no shuttle service. **Time:** Allow 30 minutes minimum. **Hours:** Site daily 24 hours, Restrooms open daily 7 a.m.-10 p.m. **Cost:** Free. **Phone:** (703) 697-7351, or (202) 741-1004 for the audio tour. ⊛ Pentagon, 86

THE UNITED STATES AIR FORCE MEMORIAL is at One Air Force Memorial Dr., along the edge of Arlington National Cemetery *(see place listing p. 66)*. Set on a hillside overlooking Washington, D.C., the memorial, designed by James Ingo Freed and dedicated in 2006, honors the men and women who have served in the United States Air Force. The plaza area is dominated by three stainless steel spires rising into the sky. Ranging from 201 feet to 270 feet, the vertical arcs portray the contrails of the Air Force Thunderbirds doing their signature "bomb burst" maneuver.

Additional features of the plaza include two granite inscription walls, one listing Medal of Honor recipients and the other the Air Force's core values; the freestanding Glass Contemplation Wall, etched with a depiction of the "missing man" aerial salute; and the "Honor Guard" sculpture, comprising four 8-foot-tall soldiers standing at attention. The Air Force Band offers free concerts every Friday at 8 p.m. June through August. **Time:** Allow 30 minutes minimum. **Hours:** Daily 9-9. Closed Christmas. **Cost:** Free. **Phone:** (703) 462-4093. ⊛ Pentagon City, 87

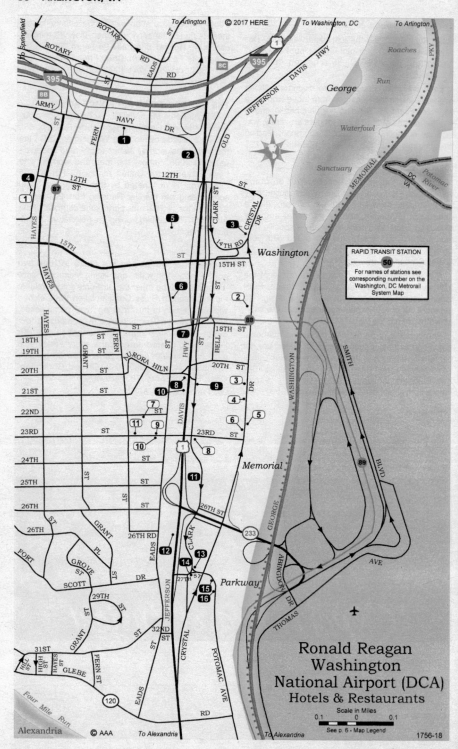

Ronald Reagan
Washington
National Airport (DCA)
Hotels & Restaurants

✈ Airport Hotels

Map Page	RONALD REAGAN WASHINGTON NATIONAL (Maximum driving distance from airport: 3.6 mi)	Diamond Rated	Rate Range	Page
14 p. 58	Courtyard by Marriott Crystal City, 1.9 mi	◆◆◆	$59-$444 SAVE	61
3 p. 58	Crowne Plaza Hotel Washington National Airport, 2.2 mi	◆◆◆	Rates not provided	61
9 p. 58	Crystal City Marriott at Reagan National Airport, 2.0 mi	◆◆◆	$67-$530 SAVE	61
6 p. 58	Crystal Gateway Marriott Hotel, 3.2 mi	◆◆◆	$77-$537 SAVE	61
2 p. 58	DoubleTree by Hilton Washington DC-Crystal City, 3.5 mi	◆◆◆	$96-$469 SAVE	61
5 p. 58	Embassy Suites by Hilton Crystal City-National Airport, 3.3 mi	◆◆◆	$108-$489 SAVE	62
8 p. 58	Hampton Inn & Suites by Hilton Reagan National Airport, 3.3 mi	◆◆◆	$199-$289 SAVE	62
11 p. 58	Hilton Crystal City at Reagan National Airport, 1.9 mi	◆◆◆	$99-$429 SAVE	62
10 p. 58	Hilton Garden Inn Reagan National Airport, 3.4 mi	◆◆◆	$139-$289 SAVE	62
12 p. 58	Holiday Inn National Airport, 1.8 mi	◆◆◆	Rates not provided SAVE	63
13 p. 58	Hyatt Regency Crystal City at Reagan National Airport, 2.1 mi	◆◆◆	$89-$429 SAVE	63
15 p. 58	Renaissance Arlington Capital View Hotel, 2.0 mi	◆◆◆	$75-$491 SAVE	64
16 p. 58	Residence Inn by Marriott Arlington Capital View, 2.0 mi	◆◆◆	$70-$473 SAVE	64
1 p. 58	Residence Inn by Marriott-Pentagon City, 3.3 mi	◆◆◆	$82-$480	64
4 p. 58	The Ritz-Carlton, Pentagon City, 3.6 mi	◆◆◆◆	Rates not provided	64
7 p. 58	The Westin Crystal City, 2.1 mi	◆◆◆	$79-$499	65

Ronald Reagan Washington National Airport

This index helps you "spot" where approved hotels and restaurants are located on the corresponding detailed maps. Hotel daily rate range is for comparison only. Restaurant price range is a combination of lunch and/or dinner. Turn to the listing page for more information and consult display ads for special promotions.

 For more details, rates and reservations: AAA.com/travelguides/hotels

ARLINGTON

Map Page	Hotels	Diamond Rated	Rate Range	Page
1 p. 58	Residence Inn by Marriott-Pentagon City	◆◆◆	$82-$480	64
2 p. 58	DoubleTree by Hilton Washington DC-Crystal City	◆◆◆	$96-$469 SAVE	61
3 p. 58	Crowne Plaza Hotel Washington National Airport	◆◆◆	Rates not provided	61
4 p. 58	The Ritz-Carlton, Pentagon City	◆◆◆◆	Rates not provided	64
5 p. 58	Embassy Suites by Hilton Crystal City-National Airport	◆◆◆	$108-$489 SAVE	62
6 p. 58	Crystal Gateway Marriott Hotel	◆◆◆	$77-$537 SAVE	61
7 p. 58	The Westin Crystal City	◆◆◆	$79-$499	65
8 p. 58	Hampton Inn & Suites by Hilton Reagan National Airport	◆◆◆	$199-$289 SAVE	62
9 p. 58	Crystal City Marriott at Reagan National Airport	◆◆◆	$67-$530 SAVE	61
10 p. 58	Hilton Garden Inn Reagan National Airport	◆◆◆	$139-$289 SAVE	62
11 p. 58	Hilton Crystal City at Reagan National Airport	◆◆◆	$99-$429 SAVE	62

ARLINGTON (cont'd)

Map Page	Hotels (cont'd)	Diamond Rated	Rate Range	Page
🆔 p. 58	Holiday Inn National Airport	▼▼▼	Rates not provided SAVE	63
🆔 p. 58	Hyatt Regency Crystal City at Reagan National Airport	▼▼▼	$89-$429 SAVE	63
🆔 p. 58	Courtyard by Marriott Crystal City	▼▼▼	$59-$444 SAVE	61
🆔 p. 58	Renaissance Arlington Capital View Hotel	▼▼▼	$75-$491 SAVE	64
🆔 p. 58	Residence Inn by Marriott Arlington Capital View	▼▼▼	$70-$473 SAVE	64

Map Page	Restaurants	Diamond Rated	Cuisine	Price Range	Page
① p. 58	fyve Restaurant & Lounge	▼▼▼	New American	$12-$40	65
② p. 58	Morton's The Steakhouse	▼▼▼	Steak	$17-$63	65
③ p. 58	We, The Pizza	▼	Pizza Wings	$3-$20	66
④ p. 58	Good Stuff Eatery	▼	Burgers	$7-$15	65
⑤ p. 58	Ruth's Chris Steak House	▼▼▼	Steak	$25-$88	65
⑥ p. 58	Jaleo	▼▼▼	Spanish Small Plates	$8-$65	65
⑦ p. 58	Athena Pallas	▼▼	Greek	$9-$27	65
⑧ p. 58	Legal Sea Foods	▼▼▼	Seafood	$11-$45	65
⑨ p. 58	Cafe Italia	▼▼	Italian	$10-$25	65
⑩ p. 58	The Portofino Restaurant	▼▼	Northern Italian	$10-$29	65
⑪ p. 58	Urban Thai Restaurant	▼▼	Thai	$9-$16	66

ARLINGTON COURT SUITES HOTEL, A CLARION COLLECTION
(703)524-4000 🟦73

▼▼▼
Extended Stay Hotel
$99-$379

Address: 1200 N Courthouse Rd 22201 **Location:** 1.5 mi sw of Theodore Roosevelt Bridge, just n off US 50. 🅿 Court House, 37. **Facility:** 187 units, some two bedrooms, three bedrooms, efficiencies and kitchens. 10 stories, interior corridors. **Parking:** on-site (fee). **Amenities:** safes. **Activities:** exercise room. **Guest Services:** valet and coin laundry, area transportation. **Featured Amenity:** breakfast buffet.

SAVE 🍴 CALL ♿ 📶 BIZ HS
📶 ✕ 🔒 📺 🚌 / SOME UNITS 🐾 🚌

BEST WESTERN PENTAGON HOTEL-REAGAN AIRPORT
(703)979-4400 🟦82

▼▼▼
Motel
$89-$199

BW **Best Western.** **AAA Benefit:** Members save 10% or more & earn 10% bonus points!

Address: 2480 S Glebe Rd 22206 **Location:** I-395 exit 7B northbound; exit 7 southbound, 3.2 mi s of 14th St Bridge on SR 120. **Facility:** 199 units. 2 stories (no elevator), exterior corridors. **Terms:** cancellation fee imposed. **Amenities:** safes. **Pool:** outdoor. **Activities:** exercise room. **Guest Services:** valet and coin laundry, area transportation.

SAVE 🚫 🚐 BIZ 📶 ✕
📺 / SOME UNITS 🔒 🚌

COMFORT INN BALLSTON
(703)247-3399 🟦74

▼▼
Hotel
$89-$409

Address: 1211 N Glebe Rd 22201 **Location:** I-66 exit 71; jct Glebe Rd (SR 120). Located in Ballston area. 🅿 Ballston-MU, 34. **Facility:** 126 units. 3 stories, interior corridors. **Activities:** exercise room. **Guest Services:** valet laundry, rental car service, area transportation.

SAVE 🍴 BIZ 📶 ✕ 🔒
📺 📺 🚌

(See maps & indexes p. 38, 58.)

COMFORT INN PENTAGON CITY   (703)682-5500 81

Hotel
$119-$204

Address: 2480 S Glebe Rd 22206 **Location:** I-395 exit 7B northbound; exit 7 southbound, 3.2 mi s of 14th St Bridge, on SR 120. **Facility:** 120 units. 7 stories, interior corridors. **Activities:** exercise room. **Guest Services:** valet and coin laundry, area transportation. **Featured Amenity: breakfast buffet.**

COURTYARD BY MARRIOTT-ARLINGTON/ROSSLYN
(703)528-2222 68

Hotel
$79-$396

COURTYARD Marriott
AAA Benefit: Members save 5% or more!

Address: 1533 Clarendon Blvd 22209 **Location:** I-66 exit 73, 0.3 mi s on Fort Myer Dr, 0.3 mi w on Wilson Blvd, just s on N Pierce St, then just e. Located in Rosslyn area. Rosslyn, 38. **Facility:** 162 units. 10 stories, interior corridors. **Parking:** on-site (fee). **Terms:** 3 day cancellation notice-fee imposed. **Activities:** exercise room. **Guest Services:** valet and coin laundry, boarding pass kiosk, area transportation.

COURTYARD BY MARRIOTT CRYSTAL CITY
(703)549-3434 14

Hotel
$59-$444

COURTYARD Marriott
AAA Benefit: Members save 5% or more!

Address: 2899 Jefferson Davis Hwy 22202 **Location:** 2 mi s of 14th St Bridge on US 1; just s of jct SR 233. Located in Crystal City area. Ronald Reagan Washington National Airport, 89. **Facility:** 272 units. 14 stories, interior corridors. **Parking:** on-site (fee). **Terms:** 3 day cancellation notice-fee imposed. **Activities:** exercise room. **Guest Services:** valet and coin laundry, boarding pass kiosk, area transportation. **Featured Amenity: full hot breakfast.**

CROWNE PLAZA HOTEL WASHINGTON NATIONAL AIRPORT
703/416-1600 3

Hotel. **Address:** 1480 Crystal Dr 22202

CRYSTAL CITY MARRIOTT AT REAGAN NATIONAL AIRPORT   (703)413-5500 9

Hotel
$67-$530

MARRIOTT
AAA Benefit: Members save 5% or more!

Address: 1999 Jefferson Davis Hwy 22202 **Location:** US 1, 1.2 mi s of 14th St Bridge; entrance on Bell St. Located in Crystal City area. Crystal City, 88. **Facility:** 345 units. 11 stories, interior corridors. **Parking:** on-site (fee) and valet. **Terms:** check-in 4 pm, 3 day cancellation notice-fee imposed. **Pool:** heated indoor. **Activities:** hot tub, exercise room. **Guest Services:** complimentary and valet laundry, boarding pass kiosk.

CRYSTAL GATEWAY MARRIOTT HOTEL
(703)920-3230 6

Hotel
$77-$537

MARRIOTT
AAA Benefit: Members save 5% or more!

Address: 1700 Jefferson Davis Hwy 22202 **Location:** 1.3 mi s of 14th St Bridge on US 1; entrance just w on S Eads St. Located in Crystal City area. Crystal City, 88. **Facility:** 697 units. 18 stories, interior corridors. **Parking:** on-site (fee) and valet. **Terms:** check-in 4 pm, 3 day cancellation notice-fee imposed. **Amenities:** safes. **Pool:** heated outdoor, heated indoor. **Activities:** hot tub, exercise room. **Guest Services:** complimentary and valet laundry, boarding pass kiosk, rental car service.

DOUBLETREE BY HILTON WASHINGTON DC-CRYSTAL CITY   (703)416-4100 2

Hotel
$96-$469

DOUBLETREE
AAA Benefit: Members save 5% or more!

Address: 300 Army Navy Dr 22202 **Location:** I-395 exit 8C, 1 mi s of 14th St Bridge; jct I-395 and US 1. Located in Crystal City area. Pentagon City, 87. **Facility:** 627 units. 15 stories, interior corridors. **Parking:** on-site (fee) and valet. **Terms:** check-in 4 pm, 1-7 night minimum stay, cancellation fee imposed. **Amenities:** safes. **Dining:** 2 restaurants. **Pool:** heated indoor. **Activities:** exercise room. **Guest Services:** valet laundry, boarding pass kiosk, area transportation.

🔗 **Use the free online TripTik**

Travel Planner at AAA.com/maps

(See maps & indexes p. 38, 58.)

ECONO LODGE-METRO ARLINGTON
(703)538-5300 **79**

Motel
$100-$200

Address: 6800 Lee Hwy 22213 **Location:** I-66 exit 69; jct US 29 (Lee Hwy), SR 237 and Washington Blvd. 🚇 East Falls Church, 33. **Facility:** 47 units, some efficiencies. 3 stories (no elevator), interior corridors. **Guest Services:** coin laundry.

EMBASSY SUITES BY HILTON CRYSTAL CITY-NATIONAL AIRPORT
(703)979-9799 **5**

Hotel
$108-$489

AAA Benefit: Members save 5% or more!

Address: 1300 Jefferson Davis Hwy 22202 **Location:** I-395 exit 8C, 1 mi s of 14th St Bridge, then just s on Eads St; entrance on Eads St. Located in Crystal City area. 🚇 Crystal City, 88. **Facility:** 267 units, some two bedrooms. 11 stories, interior corridors. **Parking:** on-site (fee). **Terms:** check-in 4 pm, 1-7 night minimum stay, cancellation fee imposed. **Amenities:** safes. **Pool:** heated indoor. **Activities:** hot tub, exercise room. **Guest Services:** valet and coin laundry, area transportation. **Featured Amenity:** full hot breakfast.

HAMPTON INN & SUITES BY HILTON REAGAN NATIONAL AIRPORT
(703)418-8181 **8**

Hotel
$199-$289

AAA Benefit: Members save up to 10%!

Address: 2000 Jefferson Davis Hwy 22202 **Location:** I-395 exit 8C, 1.5 mi s of 14th St Bridge on US 1. Located in Crystal City area. 🚇 Crystal City, 88. **Facility:** 161 units. 10 stories, interior corridors. **Parking:** on-site (fee). **Terms:** 1-7 night minimum stay, cancellation fee imposed. **Amenities:** safes. **Pool:** heated indoor. **Activities:** exercise room. **Guest Services:** valet and coin laundry, area transportation. **Featured Amenity:** breakfast buffet.

HILTON ARLINGTON   703/528-6000 **75**
🔹🔹🔹 Hotel. **Address:** 950 N Stafford St 22203

AAA Benefit: Members save 5% or more!

HILTON CRYSTAL CITY AT REAGAN NATIONAL AIRPORT
(703)418-6800 **11**

Hotel
$99-$429

AAA Benefit: Members save 5% or more!

Address: 2399 Jefferson Davis Hwy 22202 **Location:** 1.8 mi s of 14th St Bridge on US 1. Located in Crystal City area. 🚇 Crystal City, 88. **Facility:** 393 units. 14 stories, interior corridors. **Parking:** on-site (fee). **Terms:** 1-7 night minimum stay, cancellation fee imposed. **Amenities:** safes. **Activities:** exercise room. **Guest Services:** valet laundry, area transportation.

HILTON GARDEN INN ARLINGTON/COURTHOUSE PLAZA
(703)528-4444 **72**

Hotel
$99-$399

AAA Benefit: Members save up to 10%!

Address: 1333 N Courthouse Rd 22201 **Location:** 1.5 mi sw of Theodore Roosevelt Bridge, off US 50, then n. 🚇 Court House, 37. **Facility:** 193 units. 8 stories, interior corridors. **Parking:** on-site (fee). **Terms:** 1-7 night minimum stay, cancellation fee imposed. **Activities:** exercise room. **Guest Services:** valet and coin laundry, area transportation.

HILTON GARDEN INN ARLINGTON/SHIRLINGTON
(703)820-0440 **83**
🔹🔹🔹 Hotel. **Address:** 4271 Campbell Ave 22206

AAA Benefit: Members save up to 10%!

HILTON GARDEN INN REAGAN NATIONAL AIRPORT
(703)892-1050 **10**

Hotel
$139-$289

AAA Benefit: Members save up to 10%!

Address: 2020 Jefferson Davis Hwy 22202 **Location:** I-395 exit 8C, 1.5 mi s of 14th St Bridge on US 1. Located in Crystal City area. 🚇 Crystal City, 88. **Facility:** 248 units. 8 stories, interior corridors. **Parking:** on-site (fee). **Terms:** 1-7 night minimum stay, cancellation fee imposed. **Amenities:** safes. **Activities:** exercise room. **Guest Services:** valet and coin laundry, rental car service, area transportation.

HOLIDAY INN ARLINGTON AT BALLSTON   (703)243-9800 **76**
🔹🔹🔹 Hotel. **Address:** 4610 N Fairfax Dr 22203

(See maps & indexes p. 38, 58.)

HOLIDAY INN NATIONAL AIRPORT   703/684-7200   12

◆◆◆
Hotel
Rates not provided

Address: 2650 Jefferson Davis Hwy 22202 **Location:** 2 mi s of 14th St Bridge on US 1; jct SR 233. Located in Crystal City area. ⊕ Ronald Reagan Washington National Airport, 89. **Facility:** 280 units. 17 stories, interior corridors. **Parking:** on-site (fee). **Terms:** check-in 4 pm. **Amenities:** safes. **Dining:** 2 restaurants. **Activities:** exercise room. **Guest Services:** valet and coin laundry, area transportation.

[SAVE] [ECO] 🚗 🍽 📶 ⛉ 🖐
[BIZ] [HS] 📶 ✕ 💻
/SOME UNITS 🛏 🚌

HOLIDAY INN ROSSLYN   703/807-2000
◆◆◆ Hotel. **Address:** 1900 N Fort Myer Dr 22209

HYATT CENTRIC ARLINGTON   (703)525-1234

◆◆◆
Hotel
$89-$459

HYATT CENTRIC

AAA Benefit: Members save 10%!

Address: 1325 Wilson Blvd 22209 **Location:** I-66 exit 73, just sw of Key Bridge. Located in Rosslyn area. ⊕ Rosslyn, 38. **Facility:** 318 units. 15 stories, interior corridors. **Parking:** on-site (fee) and valet. **Terms:** cancellation fee imposed. **Amenities:** safes. **Activities:** exercise room. **Guest Services:** valet laundry.

[SAVE] 🍽 ⛉ 🖐 CALL ♿ 🖐
[BIZ] [HS] 📶 ✕ 💻 🚌

HYATT PLACE - ARLINGTON   (703)243-2494   70

◆◆◆
Hotel
$89-$369

HYATT PLACE®

AAA Benefit: Members save 10%!

Address: 2401 Wilson Blvd 22201 **Location:** Jct Wilson Blvd and N Adams St. ⊕ Court House, 37. **Facility:** 168 units. 8 stories, interior corridors. **Parking:** valet only. **Terms:** cancellation fee imposed. **Activities:** exercise room. **Guest Services:** valet laundry. **Featured Amenity:** full hot breakfast.

[SAVE] 🍽 ⛉ CALL ♿ 🖐 [BIZ]
[HS] 📶 ✕ 💻
/SOME UNITS 🛏 🖨 🚌

HYATT REGENCY CRYSTAL CITY AT REAGAN NATIONAL AIRPORT   (703)418-1234   13

◆◆◆
Hotel
$89-$429

HYATT REGENCY®

AAA Benefit: Members save 10%!

Address: 2700 Jefferson Davis Hwy 22202 **Location:** 2 mi s of 14th St Bridge on US 1; jct SR 233; entrance just e of US 1 on Clark St. Located in Crystal City area. ⊕ Ronald Reagan Washington National Airport, 89. **Facility:** 686 units. 19 stories, interior corridors. **Parking:** valet only. **Terms:** cancellation fee imposed. **Amenities:** safes. **Pool:** heated outdoor. **Activities:** hot tub, exercise room. **Guest Services:** valet laundry, area transportation.

[SAVE] 🚗 🍽 ⛉ ⛉ CALL ♿ 🚗 🖐 [BIZ] [HS]
📶 ✕ 📷 💻 /SOME UNITS 🛏 🖨 🚌

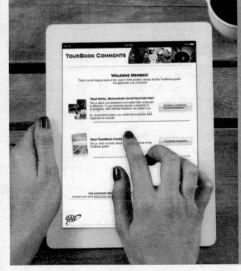

(See maps & indexes p. 38, 58.)

KEY BRIDGE MARRIOTT HOTEL   (703)524-6400

Hotel
$80-$429

AAA Benefit:
Members save 5% or more!

Address: 1401 Lee Hwy 22209 **Location:** I-66 exit 73, just sw of Key Bridge. Located in Rosslyn area. Ⓜ Rosslyn, 38. **Facility:** 583 units. 4-13 stories, interior corridors. **Parking:** on-site (fee). **Terms:** check-in 4 pm, 3 day cancellation notice-fee imposed. **Pool:** heated outdoor, heated indoor. **Activities:** hot tub, exercise room. **Guest Services:** valet and coin laundry, boarding pass kiosk, rental car service.

LE MÉRIDIEN ARLINGTON   (703)351-9170

Hotel
$99-$699

ℒℯ MERIDIEN

AAA Benefit:
Members save 5% or more!

Address: 1121 N 19th St 22209 **Location:** I-66 exit 73, just sw of Key Bridge. Located in Rosslyn area. Ⓜ Rosslyn, 38. **Facility:** 154 units. 12 stories, interior corridors. **Parking:** on-site (fee) and valet. **Terms:** cancellation fee imposed. **Amenities:** safes. **Activities:** exercise room. **Guest Services:** valet laundry.

RED LION HOTEL ROSSLYN/IWO JIMA   703/524-5000 **69**
♦♦ Hotel. **Address:** 1501 Arlington Blvd 22209

RENAISSANCE ARLINGTON CAPITAL VIEW HOTEL   (703)413-1300 **15**

Contemporary
Hotel
$75-$491

R
RENAISSANCE®
HOTELS

AAA Benefit:
Members save 5% or more!

Address: 2800 S Potomac Ave 22202 **Location:** 2 mi s of 14th St Bridge on US 1; just s of jct SR 233. Located in Crystal City area. Ⓜ Ronald Reagan Washington National Airport, 89. **Facility:** 287 units. 14 stories, interior corridors. **Parking:** on-site (fee) and valet. **Terms:** 3 day cancellation notice-fee imposed. **Amenities:** safes. **Activities:** bicycles, exercise room. **Guest Services:** valet and coin laundry, boarding pass kiosk, area transportation.

🅰 **Get member rates and**
reservations at AAA.com/hertz

RESIDENCE INN BY MARRIOTT ARLINGTON BALLSTON
(703)310-1999 **78**
♦♦♦♦ Extended Stay Hotel. **Address:** 650 N Quincy St 22203

AAA Benefit:
Members save 5% or more!

RESIDENCE INN BY MARRIOTT ARLINGTON CAPITAL VIEW   (703)415-1300 **16**

Extended Stay
Hotel
$70-$473

Residence
Inn®
Marriott

AAA Benefit:
Members save 5% or more!

Address: 2850 S Potomac Ave 22202 **Location:** 2 mi s of 14th St Bridge on US 1; just s of jct SR 233. Located in Crystal City area. Ⓜ Ronald Reagan Washington National Airport, 89. **Facility:** 325 units, some efficiencies and kitchens. 14 stories, interior corridors. **Parking:** on-site (fee) and valet. **Terms:** check-in 4 pm, 3 day cancellation notice-fee imposed. **Amenities:** safes. **Guest Services:** valet and coin laundry, boarding pass kiosk, area transportation. **Featured Amenity:** breakfast buffet.

RESIDENCE INN BY MARRIOTT ARLINGTON COURTHOUSE
(703)312-2100 **71**
♦♦♦♦ Extended Stay Hotel. **Address:** 1401 N Adams St 22201

AAA Benefit:
Members save 5% or more!

RESIDENCE INN BY MARRIOTT ARLINGTON ROSSLYN   (703)812-8400

Extended Stay
Hotel
$89-$516

Residence
Inn®
Marriott

AAA Benefit:
Members save 5% or more!

Address: 1651 N Oak St 22209 **Location:** I-66 exit 73, 0.3 mi s on Fort Myer Dr, 0.3 mi w on Wilson Blvd to N Pierce St, then 2 blks e on Clarendon Blvd. Located in Rosslyn area. Ⓜ Rosslyn, 38. **Facility:** 176 units, some two bedrooms, efficiencies and kitchens. 12 stories, interior corridors. **Parking:** on-site (fee). **Terms:** cancellation fee imposed. **Amenities:** safes. **Activities:** exercise room. **Guest Services:** valet and coin laundry. **Featured Amenity:** full hot breakfast.

RESIDENCE INN BY MARRIOTT-PENTAGON CITY
(703)413-6630 **1**
♦♦♦♦ Extended Stay Hotel. **Address:** 550 Army Navy Dr 22202

AAA Benefit:
Members save 5% or more!

THE RITZ-CARLTON, PENTAGON CITY   703/415-5000 **4**
♦♦♦♦♦ Hotel. **Address:** 1250 S Hayes St 22202

AAA Benefit:
Unequaled service at special member savings!

(See maps & indexes p. 38, 58.)

SHERATON PENTAGON CITY HOTEL
(703)521-1900 **80**

Hotel
$79-$499

Sheraton

AAA Benefit:
Members save 5%
or more!

Address: 900 S Orme St 22204 **Location:** I-395 exit 8A; at SR 27 and 244; 1.3 mi s of 14th St Bridge. Near the Pentagon and US Air Force Memorial. Pentagon City, 87. **Facility:** 416 units. 5-16 stories, interior corridors. **Parking:** on-site (fee). **Terms:** cancellation fee imposed. **Amenities:** safes. **Pool:** heated indoor. **Activities:** exercise room. **Guest Services:** valet laundry, area transportation.

THE WESTIN ARLINGTON GATEWAY
703/717-6200 **77**

Hotel
Rates not provided

WESTIN
HOTELS & RESORTS

AAA Benefit:
Members save 5%
or more!

Address: 801 N Glebe Rd 22203 **Location:** I-66 exit 71, just e on Fairfax Dr to Vermont Ave; just n of jct N Glebe Rd (SR 120) and Wilson Blvd. Located in Ballston area. Ballston-MU, 34. **Facility:** 338 units. 15 stories, interior corridors. **Parking:** valet only. **Amenities:** safes. **Pool:** heated indoor. **Activities:** hot tub, exercise room. **Guest Services:** valet laundry.

THE WESTIN CRYSTAL CITY   (703)486-1111 **7**
Hotel. **Address:** 1800 Jefferson Davis Hwy 22202

AAA Benefit:
Members save 5%
or more!

WHERE TO EAT

AROMA INDIAN CUISINE   703/575-8800 **82**
Indian. Casual Dining. **Address:** 4052 Campbell Ave 22206

ATHENA PALLAS   703/521-3870 **7**
Greek. Casual Dining. **Address:** 556 22nd St S 22202

BEN'S CHILI BOWL   571/312-1091 **63**
Hot Dogs Burgers. Quick Serve. **Address:** 1725 Wilson Blvd 22209

CAFE ITALIA   703/521-2565 **9**
Italian. Casual Dining. **Address:** 519 S 23rd St 22202

CAFE TIROLO   703/528-7809 **71**
Italian. Quick Serve. **Address:** 4001 N Fairfax Dr, Suite 16 22203

CAPITOL CITY BREWING COMPANY   703/578-3888
American. Gastropub. **Address:** 4001 Campbell Ave 22206

CARLYLE   703/931-0777 **81**
American. Casual Dining. **Address:** 4000 Campbell Ave 22206

CIRCA AT CLARENDON   703/522-3010 **67**
Small Plates. Casual Dining. **Address:** 3010 Clarendon Blvd 22201

CRYSTAL THAI RESTAURANT   703/522-1311 **79**
Thai. Casual Dining. **Address:** 4819 1st St N 22203

DELHI CLUB   703/527-5666 **68**
Indian. Casual Dining. **Address:** 1135 N Highland St 22201

EL POLLO RICO   703/522-3220 **70**
Peruvian Chicken. Quick Serve. **Address:** 932 N Kenmore St 22201

FIRE WORKS AMERICAN PIZZERIA & BAR
703/527-8700 **65**
Pizza. Casual Dining. **Address:** 2350 Clarendon Blvd 22201

FYVE RESTAURANT & LOUNGE   703/412-2762 **1**
New American. Fine Dining. **Address:** 1250 S Hayes St 22202

GOOD STUFF EATERY   703/415-4663 **4**
Burgers. Quick Serve. **Address:** 2110 Crystal Dr 22202

GUAJILLO   703/807-0840 **62**
Mexican. Casual Dining. **Address:** 1727 Wilson Blvd 22201

JALEO   703/413-8181 **6**
Spanish Small Plates. Casual Dining. **Address:** 2250A Crystal Dr 22202

LA COTE D'OR CAFE   703/538-3033 **74**
French. Fine Dining. **Address:** 6876 Lee Hwy 22213

LEBANESE TAVERNA   703/415-8681 **75**
Lebanese. Casual Dining. **Address:** 1101 S Joyce St, Suite B30 22202

LEGAL SEA FOODS   703/415-1200 **8**
Seafood. Casual Dining. **Address:** 2301 Jefferson Davis Hwy 22202

MELE BISTRO   703/522-5222 **61**
Continental. Casual Dining. **Address:** 1723 Wilson Blvd 22209

METRO 29 DINER   703/528-2464 **64**
American. Casual Dining. **Address:** 4711 Lee Hwy 22207

MEXICALI BLUES   703/812-9352 **66**
Mexican. Casual Dining. **Address:** 2933 Wilson Blvd 22201

MORTON'S THE STEAKHOUSE   703/418-1444 **2**
Steak. Fine Dining. **Address:** 1750 Crystal Dr 22202

PEPITA CANTINA   703/312-0200 **73**
Mexican Small Plates. Casual Dining. **Address:** 4000 Wilson Blvd 22203

THE PORTOFINO RESTAURANT   703/979-8200 **10**
Northern Italian. Fine Dining. **Address:** 526 23rd St S 22202

RISTORANTE MURALI   703/415-0411 **77**
Italian. Casual Dining. **Address:** 1201 S Joyce St 22202

RUS UZ   571/312-4086 **72**
Russian. Casual Dining. **Address:** 1000 N Randolph St 22201

RUTH'S CHRIS STEAK HOUSE   703/979-7275 **5**
Steak. Fine Dining. **Address:** 2231 Crystal Dr, 11th Floor 22202

SAMUEL BECKETT'S IRISH GASTRO PUB
703/379-0122 **83**
Irish. Gastropub. **Address:** 2800 S Randolph St, Suite 110 22206

(See maps & indexes p. 38, 58.)

SILVER DINER   703/812-8600
💓💓 American. Casual Dining. **Address:** 3200 Wilson Blvd 22201

SINE IRISH PUB AND RESTAURANT   703/415-4420 (76)
💓 Irish. Casual Dining. **Address:** 1301 S Joyce St 22202

SPIDER KELLY'S   703/312-8888 (69)
💓💓 American. Casual Dining. **Address:** 3181 Wilson Blvd 22201

T.H.A.I. IN SHIRLINGTON   703/931-3203 (80)
💓💓 Thai. Casual Dining. **Address:** 4029 Campbell Ave 22206

THAIPHOON   703/413-8200 (78)
💓💓 Thai. Casual Dining. **Address:** 1310 S Joyce St, Suite D4 22202

UNCLE JULIO'S   703/528-3131
💓💓 Mexican. Casual Dining. **Address:** 4301 N Fairfax Dr 22203

URBAN THAI RESTAURANT   703/979-0777 (11)
💓💓 Thai. Casual Dining. **Address:** 561 S 23rd St 22202

WE, THE PIZZA   703/415-7992 (3)
💓 Pizza Wings. Quick Serve. **Address:** 2100 Crystal Dr 22202

◤GEM ARLINGTON NATIONAL CEMETERY (B-12)

Directly across the Potomac River west of Washington, Arlington National Cemetery was established in 1864 on the confiscated estate of Robert E. Lee. It is an impressive sight, with seemingly endless rows of simple white headstones. Imposing stones and monuments mark the graves of many individuals and groups.

Among those buried are the original owners of the estate, George Washington Parke Custis and his wife Mary Lee Fitzhugh Custis, in addition to Gen. Omar Bradley, three-time presidential nominee William Jennings Bryan, Rear Adm. Richard E. Byrd, Lt. Gen. Claire L. Chennault, Secretary of State John Foster Dulles, Chief Justice Oliver Wendell Holmes Jr., Sen. Edward M. Kennedy, President John F. Kennedy, Sen. Robert F. Kennedy, engineer Pierre-Charles L'Enfant, heavyweight champion boxer Joe Louis, Gen. George C. Marshall, Medal of Honor recipient Audie Murphy, first lady Jacqueline Kennedy Onassis, Rear Adm. Robert E. Peary, Gen. John J. Pershing, Gen. Hoyt S. Vandenberg and Chief Justice Earl Warren.

The cemetery is open daily 8-7, Apr.-Sept.; 8-5, rest of year. The welcome center is closed on Christmas. Paid parking, available off of Memorial Drive at the welcome center, is $2 per hour. People visiting grave sites of relatives can use a free shuttle service to get around the cemetery. Special vehicle passes are available to the physically impaired, who must show their handicapped placard. For those using public transportation, the closest Metro stop to the cemetery entrance is the Arlington Cemetery station on the Blue Line.

The ANC Explorer app allows visitors to locate graves and other points of interest using a smartphone or web browser. In addition, you can view and download photos, obtain walking directions and self-guiding tour details, and save information. The app is available through the cemetery's website, kiosks in the welcome center and online app stores.

Guided bus tours leave from the welcome center continuously daily 8:30-7, Apr.-Sept.; 8:30-5, rest of year. Arlington National Cemetery Tours Inc. fare is $13.50; $10 (ages 65+); $6.75 (ages 3-11 and active military and veterans with ID); $3.25 (dependents ages 4-12 of active military); free (ages 0-2 and military personnel in uniform). Phone (877) 907-8585 for general visitor information or (703) 979-0747 for Arlington National Cemetery Tours Inc. information.

◤GEM ARLINGTON HOUSE, THE ROBERT E. LEE MEMORIAL, off Sherman Dr. near the center of Arlington National Cemetery, is where young Lee courted and married Mary Anna Randolph Custis; it was their residence 1831-61. Mrs. Lee inherited the property from her father, George Washington Parke Custis, grandson of Martha Washington. He began building the house in 1802 on land purchased by his father, John Parke Custis.

The historic site also is where, in 1861, at the start of the Civil War, Lee chose to resign his commission in the U.S. Army to defend his native state. Union troops would later occupy the house because of its commanding position overlooking the Potomac and the capital. In 1864 the Arlington estate was confiscated on a legal technicality for nonpayment of taxes. After the war George Washington Custis Lee, Lee's eldest son, sued to receive compensation for the seizure of the property. In 1882 the U.S. Supreme Court ruled in his favor, but by then thousands of graves covered the estate. Custis Lee elected to sell everything to the U.S. government for $150,000.

Administered by the National Park Service, the mansion has been restored to its 1861 appearance and contains some of the original Custis and Lee family furnishings. The grand portico faces the river and affords a splendid view of Washington, D.C. Also on the grounds is the Robert E. Lee Museum, which displays exhibits and relics pertaining to the Confederate general.

Note: The Arlington House is closed for renovations until early 2019; phone ahead for updates. **Phone:** (703) 235-1530.
GT 🅿 Arlington Cemetery, 85

CIVIL WAR UNKNOWN MONUMENT is w. of Arlington House off Sherman Dr. in Arlington National Cemetery. The stone and masonry burial vault marks the mass grave of 2,111 unidentified soldiers who died on nearby Virginia battlefields during the Civil War. **Hours:** Daily 8-7, Apr.-Sept.; 8-5, rest of year. **Cost:** Free. **Phone:** (877) 907-8585.
🅿 Arlington Cemetery, 85

CONFEDERATE MEMORIAL, on the w. side of Arlington National Cemetery off McPherson Dr., was erected by the United Daughters of the Confederacy

in 1914 to honor their dead and to symbolize a re-united North and South. The graves of Confederate soldiers and veterans who died in the Washington, D.C., area are arranged in concentric circles around the monument. **Hours:** Daily 8-7, Apr.-Sept.; 8-5, rest of year. **Cost:** Free. **Phone:** (877) 907-8585.
Arlington Cemetery, 85

THE GRAVE OF PRESIDENT JOHN F. KENNEDY is on the slope below Arlington House in Arlington National Cemetery. The site is marked by an eternal flame and excerpts from his inaugural address. Next to it is the grave of his wife, Jacqueline; their infant son Patrick; and an unnamed stillborn daughter.

Near them are the graves of two of his brothers—Sen. Robert F. Kennedy, also the victim of an assassin's bullet, and Sen. Edward M. Kennedy—as well as a memorial marker for Joseph P. Kennedy Jr., Joseph and Rose Kennedy's eldest son who died in World War II. **Hours:** Free. **Phone:** (877) 907-8585.
Arlington Cemetery, 85

THE L'ENFANT MONUMENT is in front of Arlington House in Arlington National Cemetery. Consisting of four white marble slabs, with the upper section supported by six marble posts, the monument marks the site of Pierre-Charles L'Enfant's grave. The French engineer planned the city of Washington; his original plan is depicted on the monument. **Hours:** Daily 8-7, Apr.-Sept.; 8-5, rest of year. **Cost:** Free. **Phone:** (877) 907-8585.
Arlington Cemetery, 85

MAST OF THE BATTLESHIP USS *MAINE* is bordered on two sides by Sigsbee Dr. in Arlington National Cemetery. The battleship was sunk in Havana Harbor on Feb. 15, 1898. The explosion was one of a series of events that led to the beginning of the Spanish-American War. The memorial is surrounded by the graves of the 62 known and 167 unknown men who died in the disaster. **Hours:** Daily 8-7, Apr.-Sept.; 8-5, rest of year. **Cost:** Free. **Phone:** (877) 907-8585. Arlington Cemetery, 85

MEMORIAL AMPHITHEATER, just w. of jct. Memorial and Wilson drs. in Arlington National Cemetery, is an elliptical white marble structure honoring those who have defended the nation. It seats approximately 5,000 people. The Memorial Display Room, between the amphitheater and the Tomb of the Unknown Soldier, contains information about the amphitheater's construction as well as details about the unknown American service members interred at the tomb and the sentinels who guard the monument.

Hours: Grounds daily 8-7, Apr.-Sept.; 8-5, rest of year. Easter service begins at 6 a.m.; Memorial Day and Veterans Day services begin at 11 a.m. **Cost:** Free. **Phone:** (877) 907-8585.
Arlington Cemetery, 85

TOMB OF THE UNKNOWN SOLDIER is s. of Memorial Amphitheater, just w. of jct. Memorial and Wilson drs. in Arlington National Cemetery. Striking in its simplicity, the die piece of Colorado marble on which the sculpture is carved is one of the largest blocks ever quarried. Before carving, it weighed 50 tons. Lying beneath the tomb sarcophagus is the body of an unknown American soldier brought back from France after World War I. In 1958 the remains of unknown American military personnel from World War II and the Korean War were interred in marked crypts at the head of the tomb.

Specially selected members of the Army's 3rd U.S. Infantry Regiment (The Old Guard) guard the tomb 24 hours a day. **Hours:** Grounds daily 8-7, Apr.-Sept.; 8-5, rest of year. During the day the guard is changed every half-hour, Apr.-Sept.; every hour, rest of year. **Cost:** Free. **Phone:** (877) 907-8585. Arlington Cemetery, 85

WOMEN IN MILITARY SERVICE FOR AMERICA MEMORIAL, on Memorial Dr. at the entrance to Arlington National Cemetery, honors women who have served in the nation's defense. The national memorial chronicles their history, beginning with the American Revolution. It includes an education center with exhibits, a theater, the Hall of Honor and an interactive computer kiosk. **Hours:** Daily 8-5. Closed Christmas. **Cost:** Free. **Phone:** (703) 892-2606, ext. 130 or (800) 222-2294.
Arlington Cemetery, 85

ARRINGTON pop. 708

HARMONY HILL BED AND BREAKFAST   434/263-7750
Bed & Breakfast. **Address:** 929 Wilson Hill Rd 22922

ASHBURN pop. 43,511
• Restaurants p. 68

ALOFT DULLES AIRPORT NORTH   (703)723-6969
Contemporary Hotel. **Address:** 22390 Flagstaff Plaza 20148

EMBASSY SUITES HOTEL BY HILTON DULLES-NORTH
          (703)723-5300
Hotel. **Address:** 44610 Waxpool Rd 20147

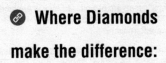

HILTON GARDEN INN DULLES NORTH   (703)723-8989
▼▼▼ Hotel. **Address:** 22400 Flagstaff Plaza 20148

> **AAA Benefit:** Members save up to 10%!

HOMEWOOD SUITES BY HILTON/DULLES NORTH
(703)723-7500
▼▼▼ Extended Stay Hotel. **Address:** 44620 Waxpool Rd 20147

> **AAA Benefit:** Members save up to 10%!

SPRINGHILL SUITES BY MARRIOTT ASHBURN DULLES NORTH   (703)723-9300
▼▼▼ Hotel. **Address:** 20065 Lakeview Center Plaza 20147

> **AAA Benefit:** Members save 5% or more!

WHERE TO EAT

AT KAISER'S   571/291-3981
▼▼ Austrian. Casual Dining. **Address:** 44110 Ashburn Shopping Plaza, Suite 100 20147

BLUE RIDGE GRILL   703/729-0100
▼▼ American. Casual Dining. **Address:** 44065 Ashburn Shopping Plaza 20147

CLYDE'S WILLOW CREEK FARM   571/209-1200
▼▼ American. Casual Dining. **Address:** 42920 Broadlands Blvd 20148

D.C. PRIME   703/840-2099
▼▼▼ Steak Seafood. Casual Dining. **Address:** 20120 Lakeview Center Plaza 20147

FORD'S FISH SHACK   571/918-4092
▼▼ Seafood. Casual Dining. **Address:** 44260 Ice Rink Plaza, Suite 101 20147

OPA! MEZZE GRILL   703/729-2211
▼▼ Greek. Casual Dining. **Address:** 44110 Ashburn Shopping Plaza, Suite 170 20147

THE V EATERY & BREW HOUSE   703/723-6500
▼▼ American. Gastropub. **Address:** 44630 Waxpool Rd 20147

ASHLAND (G-9) pop. 7,225, elev. 221'
- **Hotels & Restaurants map & index p. 212**
- **Part of Richmond area — see map p. 193**

This turn-of-the-20th-century railroad town originally was developed as a resort for Richmond residents. Later, the growing village assumed the name of a Kentucky estate belonging to Henry Clay, a statesman born nearby. When the railroad company gave land to the Methodist Church in 1866, the church moved its Randolph-Macon College to Ashland.

The town has various Victorian houses. Self-guiding walking tours that include outdoor exhibits and historic markers are offered by the Ashland Museum at 105 Hanover Ave.; phone (804) 368-7314 for more information.

Ashland/Hanover Visitor Center: 112 N. Railroad Ave., Ashland, VA 23005. **Phone:** (804) 752-6766 or (800) 897-1479.

▼ **KINGS DOMINION**—see Doswell p. 101.

COUNTRY INN & SUITES BY CARLSON, ASHLAND-HANOVER
804/798-7378 **37**
▼▼▼ Hotel. **Address:** 11600 Lakeridge Pkwy 23005

FAIRFIELD INN & SUITES BY MARRIOTT RICHMOND ASHLAND   (804)412-4800 **36**
▼▼▼ Hotel. **Address:** 11625 Lakeridge Pkwy 23005

> **AAA Benefit:** Members save 5% or more!

HAMPTON INN BY HILTON   (804)752-8444 **32**
▼▼▼ Hotel. **Address:** 705 England St 23005

> **AAA Benefit:** Members save up to 10%!

HOLIDAY INN EXPRESS HOTEL & SUITES
804/752-7889 **31**
▼▼▼ Hotel. **Address:** 107 S Carter Rd 23005

SLEEP INN & SUITES   (804)752-2355 **33**
▼▼▼ Hotel. **Address:** 80 Cottage Green Dr 23005

WHERE TO EAT

THE CABOOSE MARKET & CAFE   804/798-2933 **53**
▼▼ Small Plates. Casual Dining. **Address:** 108 S Railroad Ave 23005

EL AZTECA   804/798-4652 **50**
▼▼ Mexican. Casual Dining. **Address:** 103 N Washington Hwy 23005

HOMEMADES BY SUZANNE   804/798-8331 **51**
▼ Regional American. Casual Dining. **Address:** 102 N Railroad Ave 23005

IRON HORSE RESTAURANT   804/752-6410 **52**
▼▼▼ Regional American. Casual Dining. **Address:** 100 S Railroad Ave 23005

YOKOZUNA SUSHI   804/496-6960 **49**
▼▼ Japanese Sushi. Casual Dining. **Address:** 207 N Washington Hwy 23005

ASSATEAGUE ISLAND NATIONAL SEASHORE (G-12)

Eight miles south of Ocean City, Md., via SR 611, Assateague Island is a narrow 37-mile-long barrier island paralleling the coast of Maryland and Virginia. Assateague Island National Seashore and Assateague State Park manage the Maryland portion of the island, and the Chincoteague National Wildlife Refuge manages the Virginia end. The national seashore encompasses 49,500 acres (19,000 of which are land), including Assateague Island and nearby small islands.

There are two herds of horses on the island, including Chincoteague ponies that eat marsh grass and drink from freshwater ponds. Both herds reportedly are descendants of a 16th-century herd that swam ashore from a sinking Spanish galleon, although a more likely story is that they descended from local farm horses. The island is also a stop-off point during the migration of the once-endangered peregrine falcon and several waterfowl, including the greater snow goose.

General Information and Activities

The National Park Service operates a visitor center with exhibits at the bridge approach to the north end of the island. Allow 30 minutes minimum. Both the National Park Service and the wildlife refuge operate information centers at the southern end.

Boating, crabbing, fishing, swimming and camping opportunities are available. Naturalists conduct kayak trips, campfire talks, guided nature walks and clamming and fishing demonstrations daily mid-June through August. Lifeguard-protected beaches are open in both Maryland and Virginia districts mid-June through Labor Day.

Allow 1 hour minimum to see the island. The Maryland district is open daily 24 hours while the Virginia district is open daily dawn to dusk. Visitor center hours may vary seasonally but are generally open daily 9-5; a limited schedule is offered January-February. Phone to confirm schedule. The visitor center is closed Thanksgiving and Christmas. *See Recreation Areas Chart.*

ADMISSION to the national seashore includes Chincoteague National Wildlife Refuge and is $20 (per private vehicle); free (for persons arriving on foot or bicycle). Permits are valid for 7 days. An annual pass is $40. Admission to Assateague State Park Memorial Day-Labor Day is $6 (per out-of-state visitor); $4 (per Maryland resident with ID). Admission rest of year is $5 (per private out-of-state vehicle); $3 (per private in-state vehicle).

PETS must be restricted at all times, either in vehicles or by leash, and are not allowed in public buildings or on trails. This pet policy varies by area; phone ahead to find out where pets are not allowed. Pets are not permitted in Chincoteague National Wildlife Refuge, even in vehicles.

ADDRESS inquiries to the Superintendent, Assateague Island National Seashore, 7206 National Seashore Ln., Berlin, MD 21811; phone (410) 641-1441 for the national seashore, (757) 336-6122 for Chincoteague National Wildlife Refuge or (410) 641-2120 for Assateague State Park.

ATKINS pop. 1,143

COMFORT INN	(276)783-2144

♦♦ ◊◊
Motel
$85-$171

Address: 5558 Lee Hwy 24311 **Location:** I-81 exit 50, just w, then just n on US 11. **Facility:** 50 units. 2 stories (no elevator), interior corridors. **Activities:** exercise room. **Featured Amenity:** full hot breakfast.

BARBOURSVILLE (F-8) elev. 510'

Among his many interests, Thomas Jefferson hoped to establish vineyards in America to rival those of Europe. He employed an Italian viticulturist to plant vines at Monticello and along the mountain slopes toward Barboursville, but disease killed the vines before they could mature. Jefferson remained convinced that the region was ideal for winemaking. Successful vineyards were re-established here in the 1970s.

In his spare time, Jefferson designed a plantation home for his friend James Barbour, who served as governor of Virginia, U.S. senator and secretary of war. The mansion with its octagonal parlor was completed in 1822. After Barbour's death, a Christmas fire destroyed the estate. The ruins are visible on the grounds of the Barboursville Vineyard.

BASTIAN (H-4) elev. 2,180'

The Wolf Creek Railroad came to Bastian in 1914 to serve a growing logging industry, and the Virginia Hardwood Lumber Mill opened here in 1927. Thanks to the mill, Bastian was the first town in Bland County to receive electricity. During the Great Depression, thousands of young men worked at a model camp established in Bastian by the Civilian Conservation Corps (CCC). The mill and railroad closed after World War II.

SAVE **WOLF CREEK INDIAN VILLAGE & MUSEUM** is off I-77 exit 58, then just n. on US 52 at 6394 N. Scenic Hwy. Interpretive guides conduct hands-on tours of a re-created Native American village that stands near an actual archeological site. Museum displays include excavated artifacts. Walking trails also are on the grounds. **Time:** Allow 1 hour minimum. **Hours:** Mon.-Sat. 9-5, Apr.-Dec. (weather permitting). Last admission 1 hour before closing. Guided tours depart Mon.-Sat. 9-3:30. Phone ahead to confirm schedule. **Cost:** $10; $9 (ages 55+ and veterans with ID); $6 (ages 6-11). **Phone:** (276) 688-3438. GT 🅰️

BEDFORD (H-7) pop. 6,222, elev. 1,004'

Founded as the town of Liberty in 1782, Bedford soon was renamed after the Fourth Duke of Bedford. The town is home to many historic structures, including Avenel, a former 1838 plantation manor house that once welcomed such visitors as Gen. Robert E. Lee and writer Edgar Allan Poe. Tours are available by appointment; phone (540) 586-1814.

Bedford Area Welcome Center: 816 Burks Hill Rd., Bedford, VA 24523. **Phone:** (540) 587-5681 or (877) 447-3257.

Shopping: Held April through October, the Bedford Farmers' Market, downtown on Washington Street, offers fresh fruits and vegetables and homemade wares on Friday mornings and on the first Saturday of the month.

BEDFORD MUSEUM AND GENEALOGICAL LIBRARY is at 201 E. Main St. This former Masonic Lodge built in 1895 houses permanent and changing exhibits related to city and county history, Bedford County Native American artifacts, Civil War relics and local genealogy information. A live bluegrass band plays on Friday nights. **Hours:** Mon.-Fri. 10-5, Sat. 10-3 (extended hours on Sat., Dec.-Jan.). Closed major holidays. Phone ahead to confirm schedule. **Cost:** $5. **Phone:** (540) 586-4520.

THE NATIONAL D-DAY MEMORIAL, 3 Overlord Cir., honors the Allied forces that participated in the invasion of Normandy during World War II. More than 9,000 Allied soldiers were killed or wounded during landing operations on June 6, 1944. The town of Bedford had the highest per capita loss of life on D-Day than any single community in the United States.

The memorial features three plazas and includes an "invasion pool," sculptures and the central 44-foot-tall Overlord Arch, which represents the ultimate victory of the campaign, code-named "Operation Overlord." Volunteer docents are on hand to answer questions, and guided 45-minute walking tours also are offered when staff is available. Tickets, as well as information about guided tours and brochures detailing a self-guiding tour, are available at the Bedford Area Welcome Center, 816 Burks Hill Rd.

Time: Allow 45 minutes minimum. **Hours:** Daily 10-5, Mar.-Nov.; Tues.-Sun. 10-5, rest of year. Last admission 30 minutes before closing. Closed Jan. 1, Thanksgiving, Christmas Eve and Christmas. **Cost:** $10; $8 (active military and veterans with ID); $6 (ages 6-18 and college students with ID). **Phone:** (540) 587-3619, (540) 586-3329 or (800) 351-3329. GT

BIG STONE GAP (H-2) pop. 5,614, elev. 1,334'

Big Stone Gap is at the junction of three forks of the Powell River, which has created a pass through Stone Mountain. This mountain country provided the inspiration and setting for novelist John Fox Jr.'s "The Trail of the Lonesome Pine."

Heart of Appalachia Tourism Authority: 3028 4th Ave., P.O. Box 186, St. Paul, VA 24283. **Phone:** (276) 762-0011.

THE HARRY W. MEADOR JR. COAL MUSEUM is at jct. E. Third St. and Shawnee Ave. In addition to displays about the coal-mining industry, the museum also features collections of medical and dental equipment, cash registers and antique office machines. **Hours:** Wed.-Sat. 10-5, Sun. 1-5; otherwise by appointment. Closed major holidays. Phone ahead to confirm schedule. **Cost:** Free. **Phone:** (276) 523-9209.

JUNE TOLLIVER HOUSE is at 522 Clinton Ave. E. June Tolliver, the heroine of John Fox Jr.'s book "The Trail of the Lonesome Pine," lived in this 1896 house while she attended school. It is furnished in

period and features an 1890s kitchen and local antiques. **Hours:** Guided tours Tues.-Sat. 10-5, Apr. 1 to mid-Dec. Phone ahead to confirm schedule. **Cost:** Donations. **Phone:** (276) 523-4707 or (800) 362-0149. GT

"The Trail of the Lonesome Pine" is performed at the June Tolliver Playhouse at 518 Clinton Ave. Telling the story of a Virginia mountain girl who falls in love with a mining engineer from the East, this production is the state's official historical outdoor drama. Inquire about weather policies. **Hours:** Shows are given Thurs.-Sat. at 8 p.m., late June-late Aug. **Cost:** $18; $15 (ages 55+); $10 (ages 6-12). **Phone:** (276) 523-1235 or (800) 362-0149.

SOUTHWEST VIRGINIA MUSEUM HISTORICAL STATE PARK is at 10 W. First St. near Wood Ave. An 1880s house contains exhibits relating to the exploration and development of southwestern Virginia and the lives of the early settlers of that region.

The first floor of the museum features exhibits about the area's coal and iron ore deposits and their part in the town's "boom and bust" mining past. Second- and third-floor displays offer Victorian and pioneer memorabilia including a quilt exhibit, tools, household furnishings and Native American artifacts.

Hours: Tues.-Thurs. 10-4 (also Mon. 10-4, Memorial Day-Labor Day), Fri. 9-4, Sat. 10-5, Sun. 1-5, Mar.-Dec. Guided tours by appointment. Closed Thanksgiving and Christmas. **Cost:** $5; $3 (ages 6-12). **Phone:** (276) 523-1322. GT

COMFORT INN   (276)523-5911
♥♥♥ Hotel. **Address:** 4609 Aerial Way 24219

BLACKSBURG (H-5) pop. 42,620, elev. 2,135'

Blacksburg originally was founded as the Draper's Meadow Settlement in 1748 by a group of German, English and Scotch-Irish farmers. The settlement was short-lived, however, when only four people survived a 1755 Shawnee Indian attack in what became known as the Draper's Meadow Massacre. In 1798 the present town was established on land donated by William Black.

Huckleberry Trail, a recreational pathway popular with bicyclists, walkers, runners and inline skaters, connects Blacksburg and Christiansburg, a 6-mile distance. The trail winds along the Huckleberry Rail Line, used by Virginia Tech to transport cadets in the early 1900s.

SAVE **HISTORIC SMITHFIELD** is w. off US 460 bypass exit to US 314, on the edge of the Virginia Tech campus at 1000 Smithfield Plantation Rd. This 1774 house was built by noted surveyor and patriot Col. William Preston and named for his wife, Susanna Smith. The original frame house was the birthplace of two Virginia governors and the home of a third. The 1,900-acre farmstead was one of the earliest and largest estates west of the Blue Ridge Mountains. A demonstration kitchen garden and heirloom orchard are on the grounds. Blacksmith demonstrations at an active forge are given during special events.

Hours: Guided tours are given on the hour Mon.-Tues. and Thurs.-Sat. 10-5, Sun. 1-5, early Mar.-first weekend in Dec. Last tour begins 1 hour before closing. **Cost:** $8; $7 (ages 55+ and military with ID); $5 (ages 13-17 and college students with ID); $3 (ages 5-12). **Phone:** (540) 231-3947. GT

COMFORT INN BLACKSBURG (540)951-1500

Hotel
$70-$269

Address: 3705 S Main St 24060 **Location:** 3.5 mi s on US 460; jct US 460 Bypass. **Facility:** 80 units. 4 stories, interior corridors. **Amenities:** safes. **Pool:** heated outdoor. **Guest Services:** valet laundry. **Featured Amenity:** full hot breakfast.

DAYS INN BLACKSBURG 540/951-1330

Hotel. **Address:** 3503 Holiday Ln 24060

HILTON GARDEN INN BLACKSBURG (540)552-5005

Hotel
$109-$189

Hilton Garden Inn
AAA Benefit: Members save up to 10%!

Address: 900 Plantation Rd 24060 **Location:** I-81 exit 118 (US 460 Bypass), 4.1 mi w; follow signs for Virginia Tech. **Facility:** 137 units. 4 stories, interior corridors. **Terms:** 1-7 night minimum stay, cancellation fee imposed. **Pool:** heated indoor. **Activities:** hot tub, exercise room. **Guest Services:** valet and coin laundry. **Featured Amenity:** full hot breakfast.

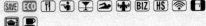

HOLIDAY INN EXPRESS & SUITES (540)552-5636

Hotel. **Address:** 1020 Plantation Rd 24060

HYATT PLACE BLACKSBURG/UNIVERSITY (540)552-7500

Hotel
$89-$269

HYATT PLACE
AAA Benefit: Members save 10%!

Address: 650 University City Blvd 24060 **Location:** I-81 exit 118 (US 460 Bypass); follow signs to Virginia Tech University. **Facility:** 123 units. 6 stories, interior corridors. **Terms:** cancellation fee imposed. **Pool:** heated indoor. **Activities:** exercise room. **Guest Services:** valet and coin laundry.

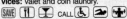
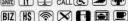

MAIN STREET INN (540)552-6246

Hotel
$119-$299

Address: 205 S Main St 24060 **Location:** Center of downtown. **Facility:** 34 units. 3 stories, interior corridors. *Bath:* shower only. **Terms:** 3 day cancellation notice-fee imposed. **Amenities:** safes. **Featured Amenity:** continental breakfast.

WHERE TO EAT

BOUDREAUX'S CAJUN RESTAURANT 540/961-2330

Cajun. Casual Dining. **Address:** 205 N Main St 24060

ZEPPOLI'S ITALIAN RESTAURANT 540/953-2000

Italian. Casual Dining. **Address:** 810 University City Blvd 24060

BLUEFIELD (H-4) pop. 5,444, elev. 2,369'

Tazewell County Visitor Center: 163 Walnut St., Bluefield, VA 24605. **Phone:** (276) 322-1345 or (800) 588-9401.

COMFORT INN-BLUEFIELD (276)326-3688

Motel
$90-$189

Address: 38769 Governor G C Peery Hwy 24605 **Location:** I-77 exit 1, 2.7 mi nw on SR 52, then 9.7 mi w on US 460. **Facility:** 61 units. 2 stories (no elevator), interior corridors. **Pool:** heated outdoor. **Featured Amenity:** continental breakfast.

BLUE RIDGE PARKWAY (H-6)

The Blue Ridge Parkway connects Shenandoah National Park in Virginia and Great Smoky Mountains National Park in North Carolina and Tennessee. The 469-mile scenic road follows the crest of the Blue Ridge and other ranges at elevations from 649 to 6,047 feet.

The concept for the construction of the parkway began during Franklin D. Roosevelt's administration in the 1930s. The project, in addition to creating a scenic route linking the two new national parks and spurring tourism, was a way to provide jobs for many of those left unemployed during the peak of the Great Depression. Begun in 1935, the dedication of the completed parkway did not take place until 1987, although sections of the road have been enjoyed by travelers for many years.

Free of billboards and with little residential encroachment, the road is tailor-made for leisurely drives. Areas of outstanding scenic interest include Humpback Rocks, Otter Creek, the Peaks of Otter, Roanoke Mountain, Rocky Knob and Smart View in

Virginia; and Doughton Park, E.B. Jeffress Park, Julian Price and Moses H. Cone memorial parks, Linville Falls, Crabtree Falls, Craggy Gardens, Mount Pisgah and Waterrock Knob in North Carolina.

Hiking trails, varying in length from short strolls to the lengthy and strenuous Appalachian Trail, can be reached from many overlooks and parking areas; information can be obtained at parkway visitor centers. During the summer ranger programs and living-history demonstrations at various points along the parkway provide insights into the natural diversity and cultural traditions of the Southern Appalachian region.

Wildflowers are in bloom from mid-May through August; fall foliage is at its peak in October. Pets are prohibited in parkway lodges but are permitted on trails and in campgrounds if leashed. Picnic areas and drinking water are available at intervals along the parkway. Hunting is prohibited.

Many visitor accommodations are open May through October only. Food is available seasonally at Mabry Mill, Mount Pisgah and Peaks of Otter. There are overnight facilities at Peaks of Otter Lodge and lodges at Mount Pisgah. Other accommodations are nearby but off the parkway.

Concrete mileposts help motorists keep track of mileage along the road, beginning at Milepost 0, south of the entrance to Shenandoah National Park, and concluding at Milepost 469, the southern terminus, at Great Smoky Mountains National Park.

The speed limit of 45 mph is enforced. To drive the entire length, plan on 2 to 4 days at an average speed of 35 mph. For additional information contact Blue Ridge Parkway Headquarters, 199 Hemphill Knob Rd., Asheville, NC 28803; phone (828) 348-3400.

The parkway is open all year, but sections of the road may be closed during icy or snowy weather. Most park facilities are closed November through April. Schedules are subject to change.

North Carolina High Country Host Visitor Center: 6370 US 321, Blowing Rock, NC 28605. **Phone:** (828) 264-1299 or (800) 438-7500.

Note: *The points of interest below are listed in order from north to south according to their location to the northern terminus of the parkway at Shenandoah National Park.*

HUMPBACK ROCKS VISITOR CENTER is at Milepost 5.8, 6 mi. s.e. of Afton, Va. The center features an outdoor museum of 1890s farm buildings, including a single-room log cabin. Costumed interpreters provide demonstrations of gardening, basket making and weaving. Three hiking trails are on the grounds. Picnic tables are available. **Time:** Allow 1 hour minimum. **Hours:** Daily 10-5, May-Oct. Demonstrations are typically offered Memorial Day-Labor Day. Phone ahead to confirm schedule. **Cost:** Free. **Phone:** (540) 943-4716. 🅰

JAMES RIVER VISITOR CENTER, at Milepost 63.6, 3 mi. n. of Big Island, Va., chronicles the story of the James River and the Kanawha Canal. A pedestrian walkway crossing the river leads to a restored canal lock. **Hours:** Wed.-Fri. 10-5, Sat.-Sun. 9-5, May-Oct. Phone ahead to confirm schedule. **Cost:** Free. **Phone:** (434) 299-5496. 🅰

PEAKS OF OTTER VISITOR CENTER, at Milepost 86, 10 mi. n.w. of Bedford, Va., houses exhibits about forest ecology and the history of the Peaks of Otter area. Nearby is an 1830s cabin that sheltered early travelers. A 1930s-era historic farm offers living-history demonstrations. Stop by the Nature Center to learn about the plants and animals of the Blue Ridge. Walking trails to the summit of Sharp Top Mountain and around Johnson Farm and Abbott Lake are available. **Time:** Allow 1 hour minimum. **Hours:** Daily 10-5, May-Oct. **Cost:** Free. **Phone:** (540) 586-4496. 🄶🅣

ROCKY KNOB VISITOR CENTER is at Milepost 169, 8 mi. n.e. of Meadows of Dan, Va. The center provides information about the Rocky Knob recreation area, which covers nearly 5,000 acres. **Hours:** Sat.-Sun. 10-5, May-Oct. Phone ahead to confirm schedule. **Cost:** Free. **Phone:** (540) 745-9662.

MABRY MILL is at Milepost 176, just n. of jct. US 58, 1 mi. n.w. of Meadows of Dan, Va. A display of pioneer items includes a blacksmith shop, a gristmill, a sawmill and a sorghum press. **Time:** Allow 1 hour minimum. **Hours:** Daily 10-4, May-Oct. Phone ahead to confirm schedule. **Cost:** Free. **Phone:** (276) 952-2947.

BLUE RIDGE MUSIC CENTER is at Milepost 213, 10 mi. s. of Galax, Va. The natural beauty of the Blue Ridge Parkway is the backdrop for concerts, performances and special events held at this facility. Banjo and fiddle players frequent the main outdoor stage and the center's intimate indoor theater. Local and regional musicians perform in the visitor center breezeway as part of the Midday Mountain Music Program. Evening concerts are offered on weekends. The state-of-the-art Roots of American Music Museum explores the history, development and cultural impact of the music made in this region.

Time: Allow 45 minutes minimum. **Hours:** Daily 10-5 (open later on concert nights), early May-late Oct. Midday Mountain Musicians perform daily noon-4. Mainstage concert schedule varies but is generally Sat. evening, Memorial Day-Labor Day; phone ahead to confirm schedule. **Cost:** Visitor center, museum and Midday Mountain Musicians performances free. Mainstage concerts $10-$30. **Phone:** (276) 236-5309, or (866) 308-2773, ext. 212, for concert tickets. 🍴🅰

CUMBERLAND KNOB, at Milepost 217.5, marks the site where the Civilian Conservation Corps (CCC) began the construction of the Blue Ridge Parkway in 1935. Several interpretive signs describe the history of the parkway and the philosophy behind its design: to build a road that does not detract from the natural landscape's beauty. A small family cemetery, one of more than 75 within the parkway's boundaries, stands nearby.

Two trails begin behind a building that was the parkway's first concession stand. The Cumberland Knob Trail offers an easy half-mile stroll through a forest to a rustic stone shelter. The Gully Creek Trail leads down into a heavily wooded ravine and along—and even through—a picturesque creek with several splashing cascades. It is a strenuous 2.5-mile climb down and back; hikers should allow at least 2 hours for the round-trip.

Note: Due to the often slick, wet rocks along the Gully Creek Trail, sturdy shoes with a nonslip sole are recommended. **Hours:** Open daily May-Oct. Hours vary seasonally. **Cost:** Free. 🅵

BLUE RIDGE MOUNTAIN FRESCOES are at Milepost 259 in Glendale Springs, N.C., 3 mi. n. of the parkway's jct. with SR 16, and in West Jefferson, N.C., following signs from jct. US 221 Bus. Rte. and SR 194. North Carolina artist Benjamin F. Long painted these religious artworks in two Episcopal churches: Holy Trinity in Glendale Springs and St. Mary's in West Jefferson. Prerecorded narratives describe their history. The church frescoes, along with Long's work in six other North Carolina cities, comprise the Benjamin F. Long Fresco Trail. **Time:** Allow 1 hour minimum. **Hours:** Daily 24 hours. **Cost:** Donations. **Phone:** (336) 982-3076 or (828) 298-5330.

E.B. JEFFRESS PARK is at Milepost 272, near Deep Gap, N.C. Named for a prominent North Carolina newspaper publisher and early Blue Ridge Parkway advocate, this roadside park features two trails. The Cascades Trail is a moderate 1-mile loop following Falls Creek through a forest thick with rhododendron and mountain laurel down to two overlooks from which you can watch the creek spill over the rocky sides of the mountain.

The half-mile Tomkins Knob Trail leads through woods to the site of Cool Springs Baptist Church, a historic location of outdoor church gatherings where mountain families once gathered to hear circuit-riding preachers. The picturesque Jesse Brown Cabin nearby, which is visible from the parkway, is where the itinerant preachers would spend the night. This easy trail ends at Tomkins Knob Overlook at Milepost 272.5. **Phone:** (828) 348-3400 for Parkway headquarters. 🅵

MOSES H. CONE MEMORIAL PARK AND PARKWAY CRAFT CENTER is at Milepost 294, 3 mi. w. of Blowing Rock, N.C. The park features 25 miles of trails and panoramic views. The Parkway Craft Center occupies Moses Cone's former manor house and is operated by the Southern Highland Craft Guild. Cone, a wealthy textile manufacturer, built his country estate at the turn of the 20th century. Traditional handmade crafts are available for

purchase and demonstrated throughout the season. **Time:** Allow 30 minutes minimum. **Hours:** Grounds open daily 24 hours. Parkway Craft Center open daily 9-5, Mar. 15-Nov. 30. Closed Thanksgiving. **Cost:** Free. **Phone:** (828) 295-7938.

LINN COVE VIADUCT AND VISITORS CENTER is at Milepost 304.6, 5 mi. n.e. of Linville, N.C. Completed in 1983, the Linn Cove Viaduct is one of the most complicated concrete spans ever built. The quarter-mile bridge skirting the rugged perimeter of Grandfather Mountain was designed for minimal environmental impact. The visitors center exhibits a scale model of this engineering marvel. A hiking trail leads under the viaduct for closer inspection. **Hours:** Daily 10-5, May-Oct. Phone ahead to confirm schedule. **Cost:** Free. **Phone:** (828) 733-1354.

GRANDFATHER MOUNTAIN is 1 mi. s. of jct. US 221 and Blue Ridge Pkwy. Milepost 305. The rugged 5,946-foot peak was named by early pioneers for its profile: When viewed from the north, it resembles a bearded grandfather looking toward the sky.

At the entrance gate you'll receive an audio tour CD narrating the winding 2-mile drive to the summit. The road ends at the Top Shop visitor center, where you'll find several trailheads, including those for strenuous hikes along the ridge into adjacent Grandfather Mountain State Park.

The highlight of a visit to Grandfather Mountain is the Mile High Swinging Bridge, a steel suspension footbridge completed in 1999 that despite the name swings very little, especially compared to its wooden predecessor. Although it stands a mile above sea level, the bridge—accessible by way of stairs behind the Top Shop or an elevator inside the shop—is only 80 feet above the ravine it spans. The views from the bridge as well as the rock outcroppings at either end are spectacular.

Halfway up the mountain is a nature museum, which has several indoor displays and a theater showing nature movies filmed on location. Outside you'll see five native wildlife habitats that are home to black bears, cougars, white-tailed deer, river otters and two bald eagles.

Time: Allow 1 hour, 30 minutes minimum. **Hours:** Daily 9-5 (weather permitting), with extended hours in summer and fall. Last admission 1 hour before closing. Closed Thanksgiving and Christmas. **Cost:** $20; $18 (ages 60+); $9 (ages 4-12). **Phone:** (828) 733-4337 or (800) 468-7325. 🍴 🅵

LINVILLE FALLS RECREATION AREA, at Milepost 316.4, 2 mi. n.w. of Linville Falls, N.C., has three hiking trails that begin at the visitor center. The Erwin's View Trail crosses a bridge over the Linville River, passes through a forest of hemlock and white pine trees, and leads to four overlooks, each offering a different perspective of the falls and gorge. The first has a pretty view of the relatively tranquil cascades of the Upper Falls as well as the narrow slot through which the river churns on its way to the Lower Falls.

The trail climbs to the Chimney View Overlook where you'll have a spectacular view of the 45-foot-tall Lower Falls and the columns of weathered rock that give this overlook its name. Climbing higher, the trail ends at Erwin's View Overlook, which commands a sweeping vista that includes the distant Lower Falls and Linville Gorge. A nearby overlook allows you to peer down into the gorge. The entire 1.6-mile round-trip is moderately difficult mainly due to the elevation gain.

The Plunge Basin Trail, a more strenuous hike than the first, follows the opposite edge of the river .5 miles to the Plunge Basin Overlook, which offers a sidelong view of the Lower Falls as well the pool at the falls' base. The trail descends into the gorge to a second overlook on the rocky river bank for a close-up view of the Plunge Basin. Round-trip Plunge Basin Trail traverses 1.5 miles.

The recreation area's third trail, Dugger's Creek Loop Trail, offers an easy .6-mile out-and-back stroll along a small creek with picturesque falls. Picnicking and fishing are permitted in the campground only. **Time:** Allow 3 hours minimum. **Hours:** Park open daily 24 hours. Visitor center open daily 10-5, May-Oct. **Cost:** Free. **Phone:** (828) 765-1045.

Linville Gorge is a scenic chasm within Linville Falls Recreation Area at Milepost 316.4. Linville Gorge Wilderness, below the falls, is part of Pisgah National Forest and has been set aside for scientific and recreational use. Paths to the falls and to lookouts have been cut through great jungles of rhododendron. Wiseman's View observation point on the west overlooks the gorge.

Note: The wilderness area is reached only by trail or cross-country travel. A few steep trails require moderate to expert hiking skills. **Cost:** Free. **Phone:** (828) 652-2144.

LINVILLE CAVERNS is at Milepost 317 at Linville Falls, N.C., then 4 mi. s. on US 221. In 1822 the spectacle of trout swimming in and out of the mountainside led settlers on a torch-lit expedition inside the caves. Ever since, their discovery has been a source of fascination, and sometimes shelter. During the Civil War, deserting soldiers from both armies sought refuge among the cathedral-like arches, columns and deep passageways.

The underground temperature is a constant 52 F; a jacket and comfortable walking shoes are recommended. **Hours:** Daily 9-6, June 1-Labor Day; daily 9-5, Apr.-May and day after Labor Day-Oct. 31; daily 9-4:30 in Nov. and Mar.; Sat.-Sun. 9-4:30, rest of year. Guided 35-minute tours depart every 10 minutes. **Cost:** Guided tour $8.50; $7.50 (ages 62+); $6.50 (ages 5-12). **Phone:** (828) 756-4171 or (800) 419-0540. [GT]

MUSEUM OF NORTH CAROLINA MINERALS, at Milepost 331 on SR 226, 5 mi. s. of Spruce Pine, N.C., has interactive displays about the region's rocks, gems and minerals. Exhibits also describe the local mining industry. The Mitchell County Chamber of Commerce Visitor Center is inside the museum. **Time:** Allow 30 minutes minimum. **Hours:** Daily 9-5. Closed Jan. 1, Thanksgiving, Christmas Eve and Christmas. Phone ahead to confirm schedule. **Cost:** Free. **Phone:** (828) 765-2761.

CRABTREE FALLS is at Milepost 339.5. The 2.5-mile Crabtree Falls Trail begins from the parking lot of the visitor center and descends steeply nearly a mile through oak and hickory forest to beautiful Crabtree Falls. Tucked away in a forest glade, the falls splash down a 60-foot-high sloping rock face in a twinkling curtain of droplets.

Hikers can complete the loop by way of an easier but longer route that follows Crabtree Creek or return the shorter, steeper path back up the hillside. **Phone:** (828) 298-0398 for the Blue Ridge Parkway information line. [A] [T] [X] [K] [A]

MOUNT MITCHELL STATE PARK is at Milepost 355, near Burnsville, N.C. The park encompasses the 6,684-foot summit of Mount Mitchell, the highest peak east of the Mississippi River, and a portion of its slopes. The mountain was named for Dr. Elisha Mitchell, who fell to his death in 1857 while attempting to prove the accuracy of elevation measurements he had recorded in prior decades.

The 1,996-acre state park offers numerous hiking trails. Guided hikes and interpretive programs are offered seasonally. Facilities include an interpretive center, an observation platform and a museum. In spring and winter check road conditions before visiting. Food is available May-Oct. Parking is available near the summit. **Hours:** Daily 7 a.m.-10 p.m., May-Aug.; 7 a.m.-9 p.m., Sept.-Oct.; 7 a.m.-8 p.m., Mar.-Apr.; 7-6, rest of year. Closed Christmas. **Cost:** Free. **Phone:** (828) 675-4611. [GT] [A] [T] [X] [K] [A]

CRAGGY GARDENS is at Milepost 364.6, 18 mi. n.e. of Asheville, N.C. The Craggy Mountains, at an elevation of 5,500-6,000 feet, are a colorful sight when the rhododendrons bloom around mid-June. Trails and a visitor center are available. **Hours:** Daily 10-5, May-Oct. (weather permitting); Fri.-Sat. 10-5, mid-Apr. to early May. Phone ahead to confirm schedule. **Cost:** Free. **Phone:** (828) 298-0398 for the Blue Ridge Parkway information line or (828) 271-4779. [A]

FOLK ART CENTER is at Milepost 382, 5 mi. n.e. of Asheville, N.C., via I-40 to US 70W exit 55. Operated by the Southern Highland Craft Guild, the center celebrates the tradition of craft work in the southern Appalachian region through demonstrations, special events and changing exhibits of past and present Southern Highlands crafts. A Blue

Ridge Parkway information desk is in the center. **Time:** Allow 30 minutes minimum. **Hours:** Daily 9-6, Apr.-Dec.; 9-5, rest of year. Closed Jan. 1, Thanksgiving and Christmas. **Cost:** Free. **Phone:** (828) 298-7928.

BLUE RIDGE PARKWAY VISITOR CENTER is at 195 Hemphill Knob Rd. (Milepost 384), about 8 mi. e. of downtown Asheville, N.C. Exhibits focus on the cultural heritage and recreational opportunities of western North Carolina and along the Blue Ridge Parkway. The I-Wall, a 22-foot interactive map of the entire parkway, provides multimedia information about points of interest.

"The Blue Ridge Parkway—America's Favorite Journey," a 24-minute film that utilizes panoramic aerial photography and surround sound to give an overall picture of the parkway's construction and the natural history of the Blue Ridge Mountains, is shown in the center's theater. You can hike, too; a 1.2-mile loop trail that starts at the parking lot joins the Mountains-to-Sea Trail. **Time:** Allow 30 minutes minimum. **Hours:** Daily 9-5. Closed Jan. 1, Thanksgiving and Christmas. **Cost:** Free. **Phone:** (828) 298-5330. 🏞

NORTH CAROLINA ARBORETUM is at Milepost 393, 9 mi. s. of Asheville, N.C. Fringed by the Southern Appalachian Mountains, the 434-acre arboretum offers 65 acres of cultivated gardens and 10 miles of forested hiking and biking trails.

The Baker Exhibit Center adjacent to the main parking lot houses temporary exhibitions and the work of regional artists. The center's small greenhouse opens out to the Baker Garden, filled with colorful perennials. From here you can make your way along the Grand Garden Promenade, a broad path through series of meticulously maintained themed gardens.

You'll know you've stepped into the Heritage Garden when you see the rough stone chimney and flagstone patio. It recalls the rustic cabins built by the area's settlers; surrounding it are beds with medicinal herbs and plants once used to make such practical items as brooms and baskets.

The adjacent Quilt Garden also highlights the area's heritage by re-creating traditional quilt block patterns in multihued flowerbeds. You can best enjoy this floral quilt from a raised observation area, which offers a nice view of the other gardens and features a bronze sculpture of Frederick Law Olmsted. Western North Carolina's natural heritage is the subject of the Stream Garden where the focal point is a splashing water channel filled with boulders and lined with decorative shrubs. Benches throughout the gardens offer a welcome place to rest and enjoy the beautiful surroundings.

The promenade ends at the Educational Center Entrance Plaza, where you'll find a pond and tiered waterfalls, container gardens and sculptures, both abstract and realistic. The most prominent is "Oh Great Spirit," a 12-and-a-half-foot-tall, bronze statue of a Native American man with his arms and head raised toward the heavens. Nearby is the entrance to the Bonsai Exhibition Garden, a minimalist series of outdoor rooms dedicated to this centuries-old Japanese art form. Arranged on shelves along the bare, concrete walls are containers of dwarfed trees cultivated to create the illusion of miniature landscapes.

In addition to garden demonstrations, educational programs and guided tours, the arboretum offers cellphone tours, enabling you to dial the numbers on tour stop signs placed at various locations to learn about the arboretum's collections.

Time: Allow 2 hours minimum. **Hours:** Arboretum open daily 8 a.m.-9 p.m., Apr.-Oct.; 8-7, rest of year. Last admission 1 hour before closing. Closed Christmas. Bonsai Exhibition Garden, Educational Center and Baker Exhibit Center open daily 9-5; phone for holiday closures. **Cost:** Arboretum free. **Parking:** $12; $6 (first Tues. of the month). **Phone:** (828) 665-2492. 🕐 🍴 🏞

MOUNT PISGAH is at Milepost 408.6. From the Mount Pisgah parking lot you can hike up to the 5,721-foot summit of the area's namesake mountain for spectacular views of the French Broad River Valley. It's worth the 1.5-mile moderate-to-strenuous hike. A sign at the trailhead explains the origin of the name Pisgah: the Old Testament mountain from which Moses first saw the Promised Land.

Several other trails wind through the wilderness nearby. The 1-mile Buck Spring Trail leads from the Mount Pisgah parking lot to the Pisgah Inn, passing a clearing where George W. Vanderbilt's hunting lodge once stood. It was here in the early 1900s that Vanderbilt, grandson of wealthy industrialist Cornelius Vanderbilt, entertained guests visiting his elegant Biltmore mansion near Asheville.

The 16.3-mile Shut-In Trail, which also begins at the Mount Pisgah parking lot, was originally the road Vanderbilt constructed to connect his estate with the hunting lodge. Frying Pan Trail begins at the picnic area lot and ascends to a fire tower 2 miles away. **Cost:** Free. **Phone:** (828) 235-8228. ⛰ 🍴 🏞

RICHLAND BALSAM, near Milepost 431, 12 mi. n.e. of Balsam, N.C., is the highest point on the parkway, with a peak of 6,410 feet. A 1.5-mile walking trail winds to the summit of Richland Balsam Mountain, passing through a spruce and fir woodland that is native to climates usually found 1,000 miles north. Trail pamphlets describe this plant community, which is a living relic of the last ice age. **Cost:** Free. **Phone:** (828) 298-0398 for the Blue Ridge Parkway information line.

WATERROCK KNOB, at Milepost 451.2, 8 mi. n.w. of Balsam, N.C., commands a 360-degree view of the main ranges of the southern Appalachian Mountains from a 6,292-foot elevation. **Hours:** A visitor information center in the parking area is open daily 10-5, May-Oct. **Cost:** Free. **Phone:** (828) 298-0398 for the Blue Ridge Parkway information line.

WINERIES

- **Chateau Morrisette Winery** is off Black Ridge Rd. (SR 726) between Mileposts 171 and 172, then s.w. on Winery Rd. (SR 777) to 287 Winery Rd. S.W. in Floyd, Va. **Hours:** Mon.-Sat. 10-5 (also Fri.-Sat. 5-6), Sun. 11-5. Tours are given Mon.-Sat. at 11, 1 and 3 (also Fri.-Sat. at 5), Sun. at noon, 2 and 4. Closed Jan. 1, day before Thanksgiving, Thanksgiving, Christmas Eve and Christmas. **Phone:** (540) 593-2865.

GT 🍴 🎁 🍽

BOOKER T. WASHINGTON NATIONAL MONUMENT (H-6)

Booker T. Washington National Monument is 30 miles southeast of Roanoke via US 220 south to Rocky Mount, then north on SR 122. The 239-acre site commemorates Booker T. Washington's first 9 years in slavery by re-creating the environment of his childhood at Burroughs Plantation.

Freed at the end of the Civil War, Booker T. Washington rose from his impoverished childhood to gain international recognition as an educator, advisor to President Theodore Roosevelt, author and orator. He graduated from Hampton Institute in 1875 and received honorary degrees from Harvard University and Dartmouth College. In 1881, the African-American leader became the first principal of Tuskegee Normal and Industrial Institute in Alabama; Washington headed the school until his death in 1915.

A visitor center offers both permanent and traveling exhibits and a 15-minute video presentation about Washington's life. Crops, farm animals and re-creations of 19th-century buildings can be seen from the quarter-mile Plantation Trail. The Jack-O-Lantern Heritage Trail passes through fields and forests. Tours, special events and educational programs are offered. Picnic facilities are available. Allow 1 hour minimum. Daily 9-5. Closed Jan. 1, Thanksgiving and Christmas. Free. Phone (540) 721-2094.

BRANDY STATION (C-10) elev. 350'

Some 17,000 mounted soldiers fought at the Battle of Brandy Station, making it the largest cavalry engagement of the Civil War. On June 9, 1863, Major Gen. J.E.B. Stuart and his cavalry division were screening the northern movement of Confederate troops toward Pennsylvania. Union forces led by Brigadier Gen. Alfred Pleasonton launched a surprise attack near Brandy Station. The daylong battle was considered a draw, but it would mark the high point of the Confederate cavalry in the east. Brandy Station became the opening battle of Gen. Robert E. Lee's Gettysburg Campaign. The town got its name from a stagecoach stop that served brandy.

@ **AAA.com/campgrounds –**
For overnights under the stars

BREAKS (H-3) elev. 1,470'

The town of Breaks is named for one of the longest and deepest gorges east of the Mississippi River, a 5-mile-rift carved by the Big Sandy River through Pine Mountain. Daniel Boone is said to have discovered The Breaks in 1767 while forging trails into Kentucky. Few visitors saw the remote "Grand Canyon of the South" until after World War II, when coal roads were built into the mountains.

BRIDGEWATER pop. 5,644, elev. 1,982'

BOB-A-REA'S	540/828-3433
▽ Italian. Casual Dining. **Address:** 305 N Main St 22812	

FRANCESCO'S RISTORANTE ITALIANO	540/828-3255
▽▽ Italian. Casual Dining. **Address:** 101 N Main St 22812	

SERGIO'S PIZZA	540/828-6651
▽ Pizza. Casual Dining. **Address:** 425 N Main St 22812	

BRISTOL (I-3) pop. 17,835, elev. 1,680'

State Street, Bristol's main thoroughfare, is bisected by the Tennessee/Virginia border. The double yellow lines down the street's center denote the dividing line. Although each side has its own government and city services, together they form an important industrial center that manufactures metal goods, textiles and electronic products.

Evan Shelby, noted for battling Native Americans and founding what became the city of Bristol, built a stockade here in 1776. Daniel Boone and many other distinguished pioneers bartered in Bristol and planned the campaign that defeated the British at the Battle of Kings Mountain in South Carolina.

Congress declared Bristol the Birthplace of Country Music in 1998 because of the 1927 Bristol Sessions recordings that launched the careers of music legends Jimmie Rodgers and The Carter family. Today, Bristol hosts outdoor concerts between May and October and an annual music festival, Bristol Rhythm and Roots Reunion, in September.

The city has a theater, an arts center and a ballet company. Recreational activities on the Tennessee side are provided by Steele Creek Park and South Holston Dam and Lake. Sugar Hollow Park is on the Virginia side. Both Steele Creek and Sugar Hollow parks provide miles of hiking, biking and walking trails. Area lakes and waterways offer opportunities for fishing and boating.

The Bristol Motor Speedway, a half-mile racetrack 5 miles south on US 11E in Tennessee, is on the NASCAR circuit; phone (423) 989-6900. Scenic I-81 passes through Bristol and continues 88 miles south to the I-40 junction.

COURTYARD BY MARRIOTT   (276)591-4400

Hotel
$73-$232

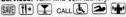
AAA Benefit: Members save 5% or more!

Address: 3169 Linden Dr 24202 **Location:** I-81 exit 7, just w. **Facility:** 175 units. 5 stories, interior corridors. **Terms:** cancellation fee imposed. **Amenities:** video games. **Pool:** heated indoor. **Activities:** hot tub, exercise room. **Guest Services:** valet and coin laundry.

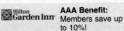

HILTON GARDEN INN   276-644-4000

Hotel
Rates not provided

AAA Benefit: Members save up to 10%!

Address: 121 Village Cir 24201 **Location:** I-81 exit 7, just e. **Facility:** 104 units. 5 stories, interior corridors. **Amenities:** safes. **Pool:** heated indoor. **Activities:** exercise room. **Guest Services:** valet and coin laundry.

HOLIDAY INN HOTEL & SUITES   276/466-4100
▼▼▼ Hotel. **Address:** 3005 Linden Dr 24202

MOTEL 6 #4125   (276)466-6060
▼ Motel. **Address:** 21561 Clear Creek Rd 24202

WHERE TO EAT

ATHENS STEAK HOUSE   276/466-8271
▼▼ Greek Steak. Casual Dining. **Address:** 105 Goodson St 24201

LOS ARCOS RESTAURANT   276/591-3180
▼▼ Mexican Seafood. Casual Dining. **Address:** 3175 Linden Dr 24201

Nearby Tennessee

BRISTOL pop. 26,702, elev. 1,680'

Bristol Convention & Visitors Bureau: 20 Volunteer Pkwy., Bristol, TN 37620. **Phone:** (423) 989-4850.

THE BIRTHPLACE OF COUNTRY MUSIC MUSEUM is at 520 Birthplace of Country Music Way. The Smithsonian-affiliated museum features permanent and rotating exhibits documenting the impact of the 1927 Bristol Sessions recordings on country music. Themed display stations include interactive music-mixing and listening booths and a kiosk honoring Bristol native Tennessee Ernie Ford. Visitors can watch video profiles of important Appalachian musicians and also view signed instruments once owned by Ralph Stanley, Earl Scruggs and Bill Monroe.

A 70-seat theater screens the 14-minute orientation film "Bound for Bristol," while a 13-minute film about the influence of gospel music on the area's musical heritage is shown in a small second-floor chapel. Live performances and educational programming also are offered year-round at the state-of-the-art facility. **Time:** Allow 2 hours minimum. **Hours:** Tues.-Sat. 10-6, Sun. 1-5. Closed Jan. 1, Easter, Thanksgiving and Christmas. **Cost:** $13; $11 (ages 6-17, ages 65+ and students and military with ID). **Phone:** (423) 573-1927. GT

FAIRFIELD INN & SUITES BY MARRIOTT   (423)574-4500
▼▼▼ Hotel. **Address:** 3285 W State St 37620
AAA Benefit: Members save 5% or more!

HAMPTON INN   (423)764-3600
▼▼▼ Hotel. **Address:** 3299 W State St 37620
AAA Benefit: Members save up to 10%!

WHERE TO EAT

FATZ   423/968-4498
▼▼ Regional American. Casual Dining. **Address:** 1175 Volunteer Pkwy 37620

STATE LINE BAR & GRILLE   423/652-0792
▼▼ American. Casual Dining. **Address:** 644 State St 37620

This ends the Bristol section and resumes the alphabetical city listings for Virginia.

BROADWAY pop. 3,691

STRUT'S RESTAURANT & BAR   540/901-9799
▼▼ American. Casual Dining. **Address:** 116 S Main St 22815

BROOKNEAL (H-7) pop. 1,112, elev. 537'

One of the smallest incorporated towns in central Virginia, Brookneal was founded in 1802 upon the marriage of two landowners, John Brook and Sarah Neal. Patrick Henry, the state's first elected governor, had retired to the area in 1794, spending the last 5 years of his life at Red Hill plantation, which he called "the garden spot of the world." Fire destroyed the manor home in 1919.

RED HILL PATRICK HENRY NATIONAL MEMORIAL is 5 mi. e. on SR 40, following signs to 1250 Red Hill Rd. The site preserves the last home and burial place of Patrick Henry, the American patriot who said, "Give me liberty or give me death!" The main building has been reconstructed and contains Henry family furnishings. Henry's grave, his law office, a coachman's cabin, a blacksmith shop, a kitchen, and boxwood and herb gardens can be seen. An orientation and introductory video begin the self-guiding tour at the museum and visitor center.

Hours: Mon.-Sat. 9-5, Sun. 1-5, Apr.-Oct.; Mon.-Sat. 9-4, Sun. 1-4, rest of year. Closed Jan. 1,

Thanksgiving and Christmas. **Cost:** $8; $7 (ages 65+); $6 (military with ID); $4 (ages 6-17 and college students with ID). **Phone:** (434) 376-2044 or (800) 514-7463.

BUCHANAN pop. 1,178

WATTSTULL INN	540/254-1551

Motel
Rates not provided

Address: 130 Arcadia Rd 24066 **Location:** I-81 exit 168, just e on SR 614. Located in a quiet rural area. **Facility:** 25 units. 1 story, exterior corridors. **Pool:** outdoor. **Featured Amenity:** continental breakfast.

BULL RUN—See Manassas National Battlefield Park p. 168.

BURKE pop. 41,055

ANITA'S	703/455-3466

Mexican. Casual Dining. **Address:** 9278 Old Keene Mill Rd 22015

GLORY DAYS GRILL	703/866-1911

American. Casual Dining. **Address:** 9526 Old Keene Mill Rd 22015

CAPE CHARLES (B-4) pop. 1,009, elev. 7'

This planned community on the Eastern Shore was incorporated in 1886. With its deep harbor, Cape Charles served as a railroad terminus for ferries carrying freight and passengers from Little Creek. Development slowed after the last ferry terminal closed in 1950. One of the town founders, Alexander Cassatt, was the brother of impressionist painter Mary Cassatt.

Most of the original town has been preserved as a historic district, with houses reflecting Victorian, Colonial Revival, Craftsman and neoclassic styles. Contemporary residences dot the landscape at the 1,700-acre Bay Creek Resort and Club, 1 Marina Villages Cir., which features a marina as well as golf courses designed by Jack Nicklaus and Arnold Palmer.

EASTERN SHORE OF VIRGINIA NATIONAL WILDLIFE REFUGE is at the tip of the Delmarva Peninsula; a visitor center is at 32205 Seaside Rd. The 2,972-acre refuge protects four habitats: the Chesapeake Bay, barrier islands, salt marshes and upland forests. Songbirds, raptors and monarch butterflies assemble on the peninsula for the fall migration. Fisherman Island, a military installation during World Wars I and II, is home to a variety of shore birds. Wildlife exhibits and a 2.5-mile biking and hiking trail are offered. Another walking trail leads to an observation deck, from which nearby Atlantic Ocean islands can be seen. A 120-ton, 16-inch World War II gun from the USS *Missouri* is located inside the bunker under the observation deck.

Time: Allow 1 hour minimum. **Hours:** Refuge open daily 30 minutes before dawn-30 minutes after dusk. Visitor center open daily 9-4, May-Oct.; Fri.-Sun. 10-2, rest of year. Guided tours of Fisherman Island are offered Sat. at 9, Oct.-Feb. Closed Thanksgiving, Christmas Eve and Christmas. **Cost:** Free. Reservations are required for guided tours. **Parking:** $10 per day for public boat ramp. **Phone:** (757) 331-2760. GT

SHORE STAY SUITES	757/331-4090

Extended Stay Motel. **Address:** 26406 Lankford Hwy 23310

WHERE TO EAT

DEADRISE PIES	757/331-6232

Pizza. Casual Dining. **Address:** 424 Mason Ave 23310

THE OYSTER FARM AT KINGS CREEK	757/331-8660

Seafood. Fine Dining. **Address:** 900 Marina Village Cir 23310

THE SHANTY	757/695-3853

Seafood. Casual Dining. **Address:** 33 Marina Rd 23310

STINGRAY'S RESTAURANT	757/331-1541

Seafood Comfort Food. Casual Dining. **Address:** 26507 Lankford Hwy 23310

CENTREVILLE pop. 71,135
• Hotels & Restaurants map & index p. 38

**EXTENDED STAY AMERICA-WASHINGTON DC-CENTREVILLE/
MANASSAS**   (703)988-9955   **119**

Extended Stay Hotel. **Address:** 5920 Fort Dr 20121

**SPRINGHILL SUITES BY MARRIOTT CENTREVILLE/
CHANTILLY**   (703)815-7800   **118**

Hotel
$63-$216

SPRINGHILL SUITES
MARRIOTT

AAA Benefit: Members save 5% or more!

Address: 5920 Trinity Pkwy 20120 **Location:** I-66 exit 52, just n on US 29. Located in a business area with shopping nearby. **Facility:** 136 units. 4 stories, interior corridors. **Terms:** cancellation fee imposed. **Pool:** heated indoor. **Activities:** hot tub, exercise room. **Guest Services:** valet and coin laundry. **Featured Amenity:** breakfast buffet.

WHERE TO EAT

CIAO WOOD-FIRED PIZZA & OSTERIA	703/543-8955 **140**

Italian Pizza. Casual Dining. **Address:** 14115 St. Germain Dr 20121

GLORY DAYS GRILL	703/266-4100

American. Casual Dining. **Address:** 13850 Braddock Rd 20121

🔖 Booth or table?

AAA.com/travelguides/restaurants

(See map & index p. 38.)

MY THAI PLACE   703/543-6665   (139)

♥♥ Thai. Casual Dining. **Address:** 14245-N Centreville Square 20121

SWEETWATER TAVERN   703/449-1100

♥♥ American. Gastropub. **Address:** 14250 Sweetwater Ln 20121

CHANCELLORSVILLE (C-11) elev. 344'

Twelve miles west of Fredericksburg on SR 3, Chancellorsville Battlefield is part of Fredericksburg and Spotsylvania National Military Park *(see place listing p. 117).*

The battles of Chancellorsville and Salem Church, April 27 through May 6, 1863, were among the most important engagements of the Civil War. The Confederate Army of Northern Virginia, under the command of Gen. Robert E. Lee, numbered approximately 60,000. Maj. Gen. Joseph Hooker directed about 134,000 Union troops.

Hooker crossed the Rappahannock River and entrenched his army along a 6-mile line centered at an inn known as Chancellorsville. Lee sent Gen. Thomas J. "Stonewall" Jackson to attack the right wing of the Union line, driving it back to Chancellorsville. That evening Jackson's own men accidentally shot him; a week later he died of pneumonia.

The next day Lee attacked, forcing Hooker to withdraw. The result was a brilliant victory for the South that sparked Lee's invasion of Pennsylvania.

The Three Battles Visitor Center at Chancellorsville *(see attraction listing p. 118)* offers exhibits and a 22-minute film. A 12-mile, self-guiding driving tour of the battlefield begins near the visitor center parking lot. Another way to tour the battlefield is by following a 3-hour audio tour, available for sale or rent at the visitor center.

The park is open daily dawn-dusk. Visitor center hours vary; phone ahead. Closed Jan. 1, Thanksgiving and Christmas. Walking tours led by park historians are conducted seasonally. Phone (540) 786-2880.

CHANTILLY (B-11) pop. 23,039, elev. 325'

• Restaurants p. 80
• Hotels & Restaurants map & index p. 38

Dulles Regional Chamber of Commerce: 3901 Centerview Dr., Suite S., Chantilly, VA 20151. **Phone:** (571) 323-5300.

NATIONAL AIR AND SPACE MUSEUM'S STEVEN F. UDVAR-HAZY CENTER is at 14390 Air and Space Museum Pkwy., near Washington Dulles International Airport. Part of the Smithsonian, this facility allows the public to see thousands of items from the Smithsonian's air and space collection that are not on loan or displayed at the museum's building on the National Mall in Washington, D.C. Until the center opened in 2003, a majority of these artifacts had never before been on display.

Hundreds of famous air- and spacecraft and thousands of small historic artifacts are displayed, including a supersonic Concorde; the B-29 Superfortress *Enola Gay,* which dropped the first atomic bomb during WWII; *Global Flyer,* the first airplane to be flown solo, nonstop around the globe without refueling; and the Space Shuttle *Discovery.*

Free realistic space shuttle and mission control simulations can be enjoyed. IMAX films are shown on a five-story theater screen, and various immersive flight simulator experiences are offered.

Time: Allow 2 hours minimum. **Hours:** Daily 10-5:30 (also 5:30-6:30, early June-early Sept.). Closed Christmas. **Cost:** Museum free. Fees for IMAX films and flight simulators vary. **Parking:** $15; free most days after 4 p.m. **Phone:** (703) 572-4118, (202) 633-1000 for general Smithsonian information, or (866) 868-7774 for IMAX film information. GT 🍴

SAVE SULLY HISTORIC SITE is on SR 28 about .3 mi. n. of US 50 and 5 mi. s. of the Dulles Toll Rd. at 3650 Historic Sully Way. This house was built in 1794 by Richard Bland Lee, uncle of Robert E. Lee and northern Virginia's first congressman. The restored house is furnished with antiques of the Federal period and appears much as it did 1795-1811. Features include the kitchen/laundry, a smokehouse, a stone dairy, the slave quarters and a flower garden.

Time: Allow 2 hours minimum. **Hours:** Guided 45-minute house tours are offered Wed.-Mon. on the hour 11-4, Mar.-Dec.; 11-3, rest of year. Guided outbuildings and grounds tours are given Wed.-Mon. (weather permitting) at 2, mid-Mar. to mid-Nov.; by appointment rest of year. Closed Jan. 1, Thanksgiving, Christmas Eve and Christmas. Phone ahead to confirm schedule.

Cost: Grounds free except during events. House or outbuildings tour $7; $6 (students with ID); $5 (ages 5-15 and 65+). House and outbuildings tour $9; $8 (students with ID); $7 (ages 5-15 and 65+). **Phone:** (703) 437-1794 or TTY (703) 803-3354. GT 🎨

COURTYARD BY MARRIOTT-DULLES AIRPORT-CHANTILLY   (703)709-7100   (128)

♥♥♥ Hotel $63-$212

COURTYARD Marriott **AAA Benefit:** Members save 5% or more!

Address: 3935 Centerview Dr 20151 **Location:** Jct SR 28, just e on US 50. **Facility:** 149 units. 3 stories, interior corridors. **Terms:** cancellation fee imposed. **Pool:** heated indoor. **Activities:** hot tub, exercise room. **Guest Services:** valet and coin laundry, boarding pass kiosk, area transportation.

/ SOME UNITS 📷

(See map & index p. 38.)

FAIRFIELD INN & SUITES BY MARRIOTT DULLES AIRPORT
CHANTILLY   (703)435-1111   **125**
▼▼ Hotel. **Address:** 3960 Corsair Ct
20151
| | **AAA Benefit:** Members save 5% or more! |

HAMPTON INN WASHINGTON DULLES INTERNATIONAL
AIRPORT SOUTH   (703)818-8200   **123**
▼▼▼ Hotel. **Address:** 4050
Westfax Dr 20151
| | **AAA Benefit:** Members save up to 10%! |

HOLIDAY INN CHANTILLY-DULLES EXPO CENTER
                                            703/815-6060   **129**
▼▼▼ Hotel. **Address:** 4335 Chantilly Shopping Center 20151

HYATT PLACE CHANTILLY/DULLES AIRPORT-SOUTH
                                            (703)961-8160   **131**

▼▼▼
Hotel
$64-$199

❖ HYATT PLACE·

AAA Benefit: Members save 10%!

Address: 4994 Westone Plaza Dr
20151 **Location:** I-66 exit 53, 2 mi in on
SR 28, then just w on Westfields Blvd;
1.7 mi s of jct SR 28 and US 50. Adjacent to shopping plaza. **Facility:** 123
units. 6 stories, interior corridors. **Terms:**
cancellation fee imposed. **Pool:** outdoor.
Activities: exercise room. **Guest Services:** valet laundry, area transportation.
Featured Amenity: full hot breakfast.

SAVE ✈ ▮¶▮ CALL 🖐 🚲 ✚ BIZ 🛜 ✕ 🎥
🖥 🖭 / SOME UNITS 🐾 HS

RESIDENCE INN BY MARRIOTT CHANTILLY DULLES SOUTH
                                            (703)263-7900   **127**
▼▼▼ Extended Stay Hotel. **Address:** 14440 Chantilly Crossing Ln
20151
| | **AAA Benefit:** Members save 5% or more! |

STAYBRIDGE SUITES HOTEL CHANTILLY/DULLES
INTERNATIONAL AIRPORT   703/435-8090   **124**
▼▼▼ Extended Stay Hotel. **Address:** 3860 Centerview Dr
20151

TOWNEPLACE SUITES BY MARRIOTT-CHANTILLY DULLES
SOUTH   (703)709-0453   **126**
▼▼ Extended Stay Hotel. **Address:**
14036 Thunderbolt Pl 20151
| | **AAA Benefit:** Members save 5% or more! |

WESTFIELDS MARRIOTT   (703)818-0300   **130**

▼▼▼
Hotel
$74-$302

Ⓜ
MARRIOTT

AAA Benefit: Members save 5% or more!

Address: 14750 Conference Center Dr
20151 **Location:** I-66 exit 53, 2 mi n on
SR 28, just w on Westfields Blvd, then
0.5 mi n on Stonecraft Blvd; 1.7 mi s of
jct SR 28 and US 50. **Facility:** 336 units.
4 stories, interior corridors. **Parking:** on-site and valet. **Terms:** check-in 4 pm,
cancellation fee imposed. **Amenities:**
safes. **Dining:** 2 restaurants. **Pool:**
heated outdoor, heated indoor. **Activ-
ities:** sauna, hot tub, steamroom, regulation golf, tennis, exercise room. **Guest Services:** valet laundry, boarding pass kiosk,
area transportation.

SAVE ▮¶▮ 🚲 🍽 CALL 🖐 🚲 ✚ BIZ 🛜 ✕
🖭 / SOME UNITS 🖥

WINGATE BY WYNDHAM DULLES AIRPORT-CHANTILLY
                                            571/203-0999   **122**
▼▼▼ Hotel. **Address:** 3940 Centerview Dr 20151

WHERE TO EAT

ANITA'S   703/378-1717
▼▼ Mexican. Casual Dining. **Address:** 13921 Lee Jackson
Memorial Hwy 20151

EGGSPECTATION   703/263-7444
▼▼ Breakfast. Casual Dining. **Address:** 5009 Westone Plaza
Dr 20151

FORD'S FISH SHACK   703/542-7520
▼▼ Seafood. Casual Dining. **Address:** 25031 Riding Plaza,
#150 20152

OTANI JAPANESE STEAK HOUSE   703/802-3400   **146**
▼▼ Japanese Sushi. Casual Dining. **Address:** 13952 Lee
Jackson Memorial Hwy 20151

PICANTE! THE REAL TACO   703/222-2323   **143**
▼▼ Mexican. Casual Dining. **Address:** 14511 Lee Jackson
Memorial Hwy, Suite B 20151

SILA THAI CUISINE   703/488-9829   **145**
▼▼ Thai. Casual Dining. **Address:** 13971 Metrotech Dr 20151

THAI BASIL   703/631-8277   **144**
▼▼ Thai. Casual Dining. **Address:** 14511 Lee
Jackson Memorial Hwy, Suite P 20151

WILLARD'S REAL PIT BBQ   703/488-9970   **147**
▼ Barbecue. Quick Serve. **Address:** 4300 Chantilly Shopping
Center, Unit 1A 20151

CHARLES CITY (B-2) pop. 133, elev. 45'
• **Part of Williamsburg, Jamestown & Yorktown
area — see map p. 273**

Charles City County, settled by the English in
1613, is wedged between the James and Chickahominy rivers. From its very beginning the area has
been tied to America's history. Benjamin Harrison V,
a signer of the Declaration of Independence, and
presidents William Henry Harrison and John Tyler
were born here. Historic plantations *(see individual
attraction listings)* border the James River, on or just
off scenic SR 5, near the Colonial capitals of Williamsburg and Jamestown and convenient to the
later capital, Richmond.

SAVE   **BERKELEY PLANTATION** is 6.5 mi. w. on SR
5, then 1 mi. s. to 12602 Harrison Landing Rd.
The 1726 Georgian mansion is the birthplace of
both Benjamin Harrison V, a signer of the Declaration of Independence, and William Henry Harrison,
ninth U.S. president. "Taps" was composed here
while Gen. George McClellan used Berkeley as a
Civil War headquarters.

The grounds feature five terraces that contain restored boxwood and flower gardens along the
James River. Costumed guides lead tours. **Hours:**
Daily 9:30-4:30, Mar.-Dec.; 10:30-3:30, rest of year.
Closed Thanksgiving and Christmas. **Cost:** $12; $7
(ages 6-16). **Phone:** (804) 829-6018 or (888)
466-6018. **GT**

SHIRLEY PLANTATION is 9.5 mi. w. via SR 5 to 501 Shirley Plantation Rd. Founded in 1613, the plantation has been owned by the Hill and Carter families since 1638 and is purportedly the oldest continuously owned family business in the United States. The present mansion, built in 1723, was the birthplace of Anne Hill Carter and the setting for her marriage to Henry "Light Horse Harry" Lee. In later years their son Gen. Robert E. Lee was a frequent visitor.

Historical interpreters highlight family portraits, silver and furniture—items handed down for 11 generations—on tours of the mansion, which sits on a bluff of the James River. A carved-walnut staircase rises three stories without visible support and is said to be the only one of its kind in America. Self-guiding tours of the plantation grounds, which also includes four brick outbuildings set in a Queen Anne-style courtyard, are available with admission. A stable, smokehouse and dovecote are other original structures included on the grounds tour.

Time: Allow 1 hour minimum. **Hours:** Daily 9:30-4, Apr.-Nov.; 10-4, rest of year. Last house tour begins at closing. Closed Thanksgiving and Christmas. **Cost:** $12.50; $11.50 (ages 60+); $10 (active military, veterans and their spouses with ID); $8.50 (ages 7-16); $8 (military dependents ages 7-16). **Phone:** (804) 829-5121. [GT]

EDGEWOOD PLANTATION BED & BREAKFAST
(804)829-2962
Historic Bed & Breakfast. **Address:** 4800 John Tyler Memorial Hwy 23030

NORTH BEND PLANTATION BED & BREAKFAST
804/829-5176
Historic Bed & Breakfast. **Address:** 12200 Weyanoke Rd 23030

PINEY GROVE AT SOUTHALL'S PLANTATION-1790
(804)829-2480
Historic Bed & Breakfast. **Address:** 16920 Southall Plantation Ln 23030

CHARLOTTESVILLE (G-8) pop. 43,475, elev. 480'
• Hotels p. 87 • Restaurants p. 89
• Hotels & Restaurants map & index p. 85
• Part of Shenandoah National Park area — see map p. 241

No matter where your interests take you, you'll find it easy to visualize Charlottesville's many esteemed former citizens working and playing in this lively settlement in the foothills of the Blue Ridge Mountains. Visitors to the University of Virginia "see" Thomas Jefferson strolling the grounds of the prestigious school he founded and designed. Nearby, outdoor enthusiasts ambling through the Ragged Mountain Natural Area imagine themselves hiking alongside Edgar Allan Poe. (The Gothic writer frequented the dense woods during his 10-month stint as a UVA student in 1826. Unless you're faint-hearted, try reading his short story "A Tale of the Ragged Mountains" before exploring the 980-acre natural area.) Meanwhile, across town, sightseers

reading an interpretive marker on Park Street envision tall, slender James Monroe as he dashes into the old courthouse.

These "ghosts" of Charlottesville are revered by present-day residents. For a few choice tidbits about the fascinating people who helped shape the area, sign up for a guided walking tour. On Thursday and Friday evenings and Saturday mornings from late April to late October, the Albemarle Charlottesville Historical Society offers a tour focusing on the development of the original downtown district; phone (434) 296-1492.

On the east end of Main Street, about 2 blocks south of Charlottesville's historic Court Square, the tree-lined Downtown Pedestrian Mall features more than 150 shops and eateries. (Stop at the lunch counter inside Timberlake's Drug Store, 322 E. Main St., for a refreshing drink from its old-fashioned soda fountain.) The mall also is home to the Sprint Pavilion, which presents outdoor musical events spring through fall, including the free Fridays After Five summer concert series. Phone (434) 245-4910 or (877) 272-8849 for pavilion schedule and ticket information.

Look for the marquee of the Greek Revival-style Paramount on Main Street for year-round entertainment options. While you can still catch classic films in this grand movie palace built in 1931, the restored theater now hosts comedians, dance troupes and bands regularly; phone (434) 979-1333. Known for its innovative theatrical presentations, Live Arts delivers everything from the avant-garde to bold interpretations of classic plays. Shows take place October through July in the 199-seat DownStage theater, off Main Street at 123 E. Water St.; phone (434) 977-4177.

Although there are several leisure activities available on and around the pedestrian mall, a trolley traverses Charlottesville and connects downtown with the UVA campus. The free trolleys operate Mon.-Sat. 6:40 a.m.-midnight, Sun. 8-6; phone (434) 970-3649.

Outdoor enthusiasts don't have to travel far for down-and-dirty fun in the sun. The Ragged Mountain Natural Area off US 29, open daily from 7 a.m. to dusk, features about 4 miles of trails encircling the Ragged Mountain Reservoir. A number of other trails exist in Charlottesville, some connecting parks, schools and other public spaces. Starting at Riverview Park, the multipurpose Rivanna Trail at the end of Chesapeake Street curves 2.3-miles north along the Rivanna River. The placid waterway, which begins approximately 6 miles northeast of Charlottesville and continues 42 miles south and east to Columbia affords additional recreational opportunities, including boating, canoeing, fishing and swimming.

Charlottesville Albemarle Convention and Visitors Bureau: 610 E. Main St., P.O. Box 178, Charlottesville, VA 22902. **Phone:** (434) 293-6789 or (877) 386-1103.

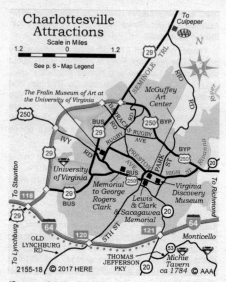

Charlottesville
Attractions
Scale in Miles
1.2   0   1.2
See p. 6 - Map Legend

(See map & index p. 85.)

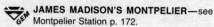

Self-guiding tours: Brochures outlining self-guiding walking tours of Charlottesville's historic downtown and the University of Virginia are available at the convention and visitors bureau.

Shopping: Barracks Road Shopping Center (1117 Emmet St. N.) features some 80 upscale stores. Charlottesville Fashion Square (1600 Rio Rd. E.) has more than 70 stores, including Belk, Eddie Bauer, JCPenney and Sears. Charlottesville's Historic Downtown Pedestrian Mall offers art galleries, restaurants and various specialty shops on and around Main Street. The Shops at Stonefield (1954 Swanson Dr.) draws locals with the latest in luxury movie theaters along with shopping at Trader Joe's, Brooks Brothers and Pier 1 Imports.

JAMES MADISON'S MONTPELIER—see Montpelier Station p. 172.

JAMES MONROE'S HIGHLAND is off I-64 exit 121, .5 mi. s. on SR 20, 3 mi. e. on SR 53, then .5 mi. s. on CR 795. The 535-acre estate once was owned by James Monroe, fifth president of the United States. Thomas Jefferson encouraged Monroe to purchase the land adjoining Monticello to form "a society to our taste" in Albemarle County. Monroe and his family owned the plantation from 1793 until 1826. Today, the estate is owned and operated by William & Mary, Monroe's alma mater.

New discoveries have rewritten the history of the property. Archaeological excavations, tree ring dating and architectural research have determined that the structure once thought to be a wing of Monroe's original house was actually his presidential guest house, built 1818. The same research has identified the remains of Monroe's primary residence; the foundation was recently uncovered

during excavations just east of the 1870s Massey house.

Guests can learn about Monroe's contributions to American democracy through exploration of historic buildings including the guest house, kitchens and outbuildings. Guided tours of the main house, which contains many Monroe possessions, are available daily. Periodic cooking and spinning demonstrations and other activities are offered. The kitchens, overseer's house, slave quarters and farm animals also can be seen. The grounds feature flowering plants, Monroe-era trees and kitchen and vegetable gardens. The boxwood gardens feature a 300-year-old oak tree and a statue of Monroe by Attilio Piccirilli. Rolling hills and mountains views are visible on the horizon.

Photography is not permitted in the interior of the home. **Time:** Allow 2 hours minimum. **Hours:** Daily 9-6, Apr.-Oct.; 11-5, rest of year. Closed Jan. 1, Thanksgiving and Christmas. **Cost:** $14; $12 (ages 60+ and military with ID); $8 (ages 6-11); free (active military with ID and family). Guided tour $14. A combination ticket (Monticello Neighborhood Pass) with Michie Tavern ca. 1784 and Monticello is available. **Phone:** (434) 293-8000. GT

KLUGE-RUHE ABORIGINAL ART COLLECTION OF THE UNIVERSITY OF VIRGINIA, 400 Worrell Dr., features an extensive collection of Australian Aboriginal art. About 35 of the facility's more than 1,800 objects, including paintings, sculpture and artifacts, are on display at any one time. Indigenous artists and scholars visit regularly; phone ahead for schedule. A study center and library is available for research. **Time:** Allow 30 minutes minimum. **Hours:** Tues.-Sat. 10-4, Sun. 1-5. Guided tours are given Sat. at 10:30. **Cost:** Free. **Phone:** (434) 244-0234. GT

McGUFFEY ART CENTER is at 201 Second St. N.W. Housed in a former school building, the center encompasses 23 artist studios, performance space and three exhibition galleries. Works on display include photographs, paintings, ceramics and glass. **Time:** Allow 1 hour minimum. **Hours:** Tues.-Sat. 10-6, Sun. 1-5. Closed Jan. 1, the last 2 weeks in Aug., Thanksgiving and Christmas. **Cost:** Free. **Phone:** (434) 295-7973.

MICHIE TAVERN CA. 1784 is .5 mi. s. of I-64 on SR 20, then 1 mi. e. to 683 Thomas Jefferson Pkwy. Established by Scotsman William Michie in the late 1700s, the tavern once accommodated travelers with food, drink and lodging. In 1927 the inn was moved 17 miles to its present location as part of the 1920s Preservation Movement.

Continuous self-guiding tours of the oldest section of the landmark building include interpretations of period customs and lifestyles with a look at drinking, gaming, dining, sleeping and entertainment.

Hours: Daily 9-5. Closed Jan. 1 and Christmas. **Cost:** Self-guiding tour only $6; $5 (ages 65+ and

(See map & index p. 85.)

military with ID); $2 (ages 6-11). Self-guiding tour with lunch $3. A combination ticket (Monticello Neighborhood Pass) with James Monroe's Highland and Monticello is available. **Phone:** (434) 977-1234.

MONTICELLO is at 931 Thomas Jefferson Pkwy. One of the best documented, best preserved and best studied plantations in North America, Monticello was Thomas Jefferson's home—when he was not serving in public affairs—from 1770 until his death in 1826. Monticello is truly a reflection of Jefferson's innovations and diversity; the domed house contains maps, books, scientific instruments, time-saving inventions and items from Lewis and Clark's journey westward. The Monticello Day Pass includes a guided tour of the first floor, as well as two outdoor tours: a guided Slavery at Monticello tour and a guided Gardens and Grounds tour. Behind-the-Scenes tours take you to the upstairs rooms, including the Dome Room. Other specialized tours are available, including the Hemings Family Tour, Garden Tasting Tour and the evening Sunset Pass.

Jefferson died at Monticello July 4, 1826, exactly 50 years after the adoption of the Declaration of Independence. The plantation was sold at auction to pay his debts. His grave is in the family cemetery on the grounds, which also include dependencies, slave quarters, a garden terrace, an 8-acre fruit orchard and two vineyards.

Note: Bags larger than 11"x15"x6" and photography are not permitted inside the house. Backpacks and large bags must be worn in front of or carried by hand while inside the house.

Time: Allow 3 hours minimum. **Hours:** Open daily 8:30-6, Mar. 1 to mid-Nov.; 10-5, rest of year with extended hours on weekends and holidays. Guided 35-minute tours of the house depart throughout the day. Last tour begins 50 minutes before closing. Gardens and Grounds tours are given daily every hour 10-5, Mar.-Oct. Slavery at Monticello Tour departs daily on the hour 11-4, Apr.-Oct.; at noon and 2, rest of year. Family Friendly Tours are offered several times throughout the day, late Mar.-early Apr. and early June-early Sept. (except July 4); Sat.-Sun. 10-3, in Oct. Holiday hours vary. Closed Christmas. Phone ahead to confirm schedule.

Cost: Monticello Day Pass Mar.-Oct. $28; $9 (ages 5-11). Monticello Day Pass rest of year $20; $9 (ages 5-11). Other tour tickets are available. A combination ticket (Monticello Neighborhood Pass) with James Monroe's Highland and Michie Tavern ca. 1784 is available. **Phone:** (434) 984-9800. GT

David M. Rubenstein Visitor Center and Carl and Hunter Smith Education Center, 931 Thomas Jefferson Pkwy., is the gateway to Monticello. The visitor center comprises five pavilions surrounding a courtyard with gardens, honey locust trees and a scale model of the Monticello plantation. Four exhibit galleries house a variety of items, including artifacts, interpretive panels and interactive displays.

Shown in the Howard and Abby Milstein Theater, "Thomas Jefferson's World," a 15-minute introductory film, reveals Monticello's central role in Jefferson's life. **Time:** Allow 1 hour minimum. **Hours:** Daily 8:30-5, Mar.-Nov.; 10-5, rest of year. Closed Christmas. Phone ahead to confirm schedule. **Cost:** Included with Monticello Day Pass Mar.-Oct. $28; $9 (ages 5-11). Monticello Day Pass rest of year $20; $9 (ages 5-11). Other Monticello tour tickets are available. **Phone:** (434) 984-9822. GT

UNIVERSITY OF VIRGINIA is in the center of town on US 29 and US 250 Bus. Rtes. Thomas Jefferson founded this "academical village" in 1819 and devoted his final years to its design, construction and curriculum. The state university opened in 1825 with 123 students and a hand-picked faculty of American and European scholars.

Seeking to create an environment in which learning infused daily life, Jefferson planned the school with 10 pavilions built around an expansive lawn. Each pavilion contained a professor's home and classrooms, with students' quarters interspersed between the pavilions. At the heart of the campus grounds is the Rotunda, a domed library modeled after the Pantheon in Rome; a highlight is Alexander Galt's 1860 statue of Jefferson made out of Carrara marble. The university design also is considered an outstanding accomplishment in American architecture. Edgar Allan Poe was among the students who attended dinner at Monticello before Jefferson's death in 1826.

Hours: Guided historical tours are given daily at 10, 11 and 2. No tours are given during winter holiday break, spring break or exam periods. Tours given during the academic year include the Rotunda and grounds; in summer, the tour includes the Rotunda only. **Cost:** Free. **Parking:** Available for a fee at the Central Grounds parking lot at Emmet Street and Ivy Road. **Phone:** (434) 924-3239 for guided tour information, or (434) 924-7969 for Rotunda information. GT

The Fralin Museum of Art at the University of Virginia is n. of US 250 (University Ave.) in the Bayly Building at 155 Rugby Rd. First opened in 1935, this fine arts museum displays works from the 15th century through the present with an emphasis on American and European art. Other highlights include pre-Columbian, African, Asian, Native American and Oceanic art. **Time:** Allow 1 hour minimum. **Hours:** Tues.-Sat. 10-5 (also Thurs. 5-7), Sun. noon-5. Closed major holidays. **Cost:** Free. **Phone:** (434) 924-3592.

VIRGINIA DISCOVERY MUSEUM is at the e. end of the downtown pedestrian mall. The museum, geared toward children ages 1-8 and their

(See map & index p. 85.)

families, invites learning through hands-on exhibits and exploratory and imaginative play. Highlights include a STEM (Science, Technology, Engineering and Math) Lab, Literacy Lounge, Construction Zone, Sensory Studio, Creation Station art studio and Sound & Music studio. Also featured are a reconstructed 18th-century pioneer log cabin, an antique children's carousel, a live observation honeybee hive and Little C'ville, which includes mini versions of various locations around town. **Hours:** Mon.-Sat. 10-5. Closed major holidays. **Cost:** $8; free (ages 0-11 months). **Phone:** (434) 977-1025.

WINERIES

- **First Colony Winery** is off I-64 exit 121, 11 mi. s. on SR 20, then 1 mi. w. on CR 720 to 1650 Harris Creek Rd. **Hours:** Mon.-Fri. 10-6, Sat.-Sun. 11-6, mid-Mar. to early Nov.; Mon.-Fri. 11-5, Sat.-Sun. 11-6, rest of year. Closed Jan. 1, Easter, Thanksgiving and Christmas. **Phone:** (434) 979-7105. GT

- **Jefferson Vineyards** is off I-64 exit 121A, .7 mi. s. on SR 20, then 2 mi. e. on SR 53 to 1353 Thomas Jefferson Pkwy. **Hours:** Open daily 11-6. Tours are given at 1 and 2. Closed Jan. 1, Thanksgiving and Christmas. Phone ahead to confirm schedule. **Phone:** (434) 977-3042. GT

- **Trump Winery Tasting Room** 3550 Blenheim Rd. **Hours:** Wed.-Mon. 10-4. Closed Jan. 1, Easter, Thanksgiving and Dec. 24-31. **Phone:** (434) 977-3895.

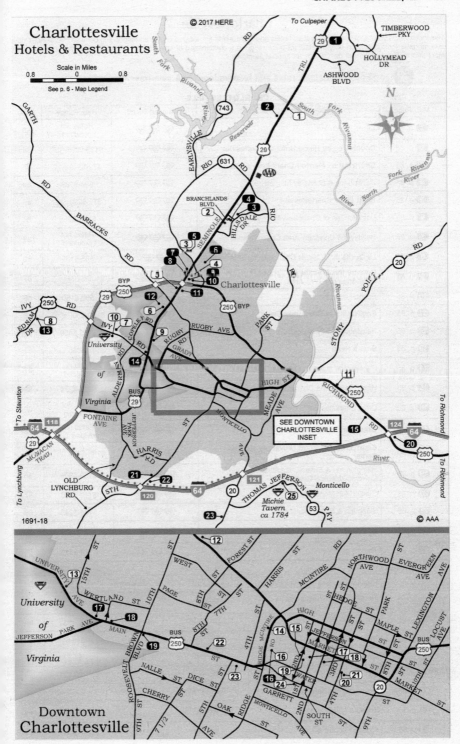

Charlottesville
Hotels & Restaurants

Scale in Miles
0.8   0   0.8

See p. 6 - Map Legend

© 2017 HERE

To Culpeper

TIMBERWOOD PKY

HOLLYMEAD DR

ASHWOOD BLVD

Charlottesville

BRANCHLANDS BLVD

SEE DOWNTOWN CHARLOTTESVILLE INSET

University of Virginia

FONTAINE AVE

To Staunton

To Lynchburg

OLD LYNCHBURG RD

To Richmond

Monticello

Michie Tavern ca 1784

THOMAS JEFFERSON PKY

1691-18

© AAA

Downtown Charlottesville

University of Jefferson Virginia

Charlottesville

This index helps you "spot" where approved hotels and restaurants are located on the corresponding detailed maps. Hotel daily rate range is for comparison only. Restaurant price range is a combination of lunch and/or dinner. Turn to the listing page for more information and consult display ads for special promotions.

 For more details, rates and reservations: AAA.com/travelguides/hotels

CHARLOTTESVILLE

Map Page	Hotels	Diamond Rated	Rate Range	Page
❶ p. 85	Silver Thatch Inn	◈◈◈	Rates not provided	89
❷ p. 85	**DoubleTree by Hilton Hotel Charlottesville**	◈◈◈	$129-$299 (SAVE)	88
❸ p. 85	**Courtyard by Marriott Charlottesville North**	◈◈◈	$79-$349 (SAVE)	87
❹ p. 85	Fairfield Inn & Suites by Marriott	◈◈◈	$85-$289	88
❺ p. 85	**Hyatt Place Charlottesville**	◈◈◈	$79-$299 (SAVE)	89
❻ p. 85	Hampton Inn of Charlottesville	◈◈◈	$139-$285	88
❼ p. 85	Holiday Inn University Area Charlottesville	◈◈◈	Rates not provided	89
❽ p. 85	La Quinta Inn & Suites Charlottesville-UVA Medical	◈◈	$85-$169	89
❾ p. 85	**Country Inn & Suites by Carlson Charlottesville-UVA Area**	◈◈◈	$109-$299 (SAVE)	87
❿ p. 85	Econo Lodge-North	◈◈	$60-$150	88
⓫ p. 85	**English Inn of Charlottesville** *(See ad p. 88.)*	◈◈◈	$100-$300 (SAVE)	88
⓬ p. 85	Residence Inn by Marriott	◈◈◈	$132-$459	89
⓭ p. 85	**Boar's Head**	◈◈◈◈	$145-$865 (SAVE)	87
⓮ p. 85	Cavalier Inn at the University of Virginia	◈◈	Rates not provided	87
⓯ p. 85	Hilton Garden Inn Charlottesville	◈◈◈	$129-$239	88
⓰ p. 85	Omni Charlottesville Hotel	◈◈◈	Rates not provided	89
⓱ p. 85	**Graduate Charlottesville**	◈◈◈	Rates not provided (SAVE)	88
⓲ p. 85	**Courtyard by Marriott University Medical Center**	◈◈◈	$108-$371 (SAVE)	87
⓳ p. 85	Hampton Inn & Suites-Charlottesville at the University Medical Center	◈◈◈	$159-$309	88
⓴ p. 85	Comfort Inn Monticello	◈◈◈	$110-$280	87
㉑ p. 85	Sleep Inn & Suites Monticello	◈◈◈	$100-$249	89
㉒ p. 85	Holiday Inn-Monticello/Charlottesville	◈◈◈	Rates not provided	89
㉓ p. 85	The Inn at Monticello	◈◈	$179-$315	89

Map Page	Restaurants	Diamond Rated	Cuisine	Price Range	Page
① p. 85	Rhett's River Grill and Raw Bar	◈◈	American	$8-$25	89
② p. 85	Flaming Wok & Teppan Yaki Japanese Steak House	◈◈	Chinese	$7-$22	89
③ p. 85	Parallel 38	◈◈◈	Mediterranean	$9-$32	89
④ p. 85	**Aberdeen Barn**	◈◈	Steak	$18-$45	89
⑤ p. 85	Cavalier Diner	◈◈	American	$6-$19	89
⑥ p. 85	Tara Thai	◈◈	Thai	$8-$21	90
⑦ p. 85	The Ivy Inn Restaurant	◈◈◈	American	$20-$40	89
⑧ p. 85	**The Old Mill Room**	◈◈◈◈	Regional American	$20-$50	89
⑨ p. 85	Afghan Kabob Palace	◈◈	Afghan	$10-$24	89

Map Page	Restaurants (cont'd)	Diamond Rated	Cuisine	Price Range	Page
⑩ p. 85	Vivace	♦♦♦	Italian	$12-$30	90
⑪ p. 85	Tip Top Restaurant	♦♦	American	$6-$18	90
⑫ p. 85	Sticks Kebob Shop	♦	American	$6-$15	90
⑬ p. 85	The Virginian	♦♦	American	$6-$20	90
⑭ p. 85	The Shebeen	♦♦	Southern African	$12-$32	89
⑮ p. 85	The Downtown Grille	♦♦♦	American	$19-$44	89
⑯ p. 85	The Pointe Restaurant & Lounge	♦♦♦	Regional American	$12-$35	89
⑰ p. 85	Hamilton's at First and Main	♦♦	American	$10-$30	89
⑱ p. 85	Zo Ca Lo	♦♦♦	Latin American	$10-$31	90
⑲ p. 85	Christian's Pizzeria	♦	Pizza	$5-$16	89
⑳ p. 85	Red Pump Kitchen	♦♦	Northern Italian	$10-$26	89
㉑ p. 85	The Nook	♦♦	American	$6-$22	89
㉒ p. 85	Maya	♦♦	Southern American	$12-$32	89
㉓ p. 85	Orzo	♦♦	Mediterranean	$9-$27	89
㉔ p. 85	South Street Brewery	♦♦	American	$9-$25	89
㉕ p. 85	Michie Tavern ca 1784	♦♦	American	$12-$28	89

BOAR'S HEAD
(434)296-2181 13

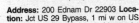
Resort Hotel
$145-$865

Address: 200 Ednam Dr 22903 **Location:** Jct US 29 Bypass, 1 mi w on US 250 (University Ave). Located in a quiet area. **Facility:** On 53 sprawling acres in the Blue Ridge foothills, this country resort offers historic ambience, modern luxurious amenities and a variety of dining options. Rooms offer crown molding and deluxe beds. 175 units. 3 stories, interior/exterior corridors. **Terms:** check-in 4 pm, 7 day cancellation notice-fee imposed, resort fee. **Amenities:** video games, safes. **Dining:** 4 restaurants, also, The Old Mill Room, see separate listing. **Pool:** outdoor. **Activities:** sauna, hot tub, steamroom, fishing, regulation golf, tennis, recreation programs, bicycles, playground, health club, spa. **Guest Services:** valet laundry, area transportation.

CAVALIER INN AT THE UNIVERSITY OF VIRGINIA
434/296-8111 14

♦♦ Hotel. **Address:** 105 N Emmet St 22903

COMFORT INN MONTICELLO
(434)977-3300 20

♦♦♦ Hotel. **Address:** 2097 Inn Dr 22911

COUNTRY INN & SUITES BY CARLSON CHARLOTTESVILLE-UVA AREA
(434)293-4600 9

Hotel
$109-$299

Address: 1600 Emmett St 22901 **Location:** Jct US 250 Bypass, just n on US 29. **Facility:** 87 units. 4 stories, interior corridors. **Terms:** cancellation fee imposed. **Amenities:** safes. **Pool:** heated indoor. **Activities:** exercise room. **Guest Services:** valet and coin laundry.

COURTYARD BY MARRIOTT CHARLOTTESVILLE NORTH
(434)973-7100 3

Hotel
$79-$349

COURTYARD Marriott
AAA Benefit: Members save 5% or more!

Address: 638 Hillsdale Dr 22901 **Location:** US 29 (Emmet St), 1.4 mi n of US 250 Bypass. **Facility:** 150 units. 2-3 stories, interior corridors. **Terms:** cancellation fee imposed. **Pool:** heated indoor. **Activities:** hot tub, exercise room. **Guest Services:** valet and coin laundry.

COURTYARD BY MARRIOTT UNIVERSITY MEDICAL CENTER
(434)977-1700 18

Hotel
$108-$371

COURTYARD Marriott
AAA Benefit: Members save 5% or more!

Address: 1201 W Main St 22903 **Location:** I-64 exit 120, 2 mi n on 5th St, then left. **Facility:** 139 units. 4 stories, interior corridors. **Terms:** cancellation fee imposed. **Amenities:** video games. **Pool:** indoor. **Activities:** hot tub, exercise room. **Guest Services:** valet and coin laundry.

🌐 **For highways, byways and more:**
AAA.com/maps

(See map & index p. 85.)

DOUBLETREE BY HILTON HOTEL CHARLOTTESVILLE
(434)973-2121 **2**

Hotel
$129-$299

DOUBLETREE BY HILTON

AAA Benefit:
Members save 5% or more!

Address: 990 Hilton Heights Rd 22901 **Location:** I-64 exit 118B (US 29/Emmet St), 4 mi n of jct US 250 Bypass. **Facility:** 235 units. 9 stories, interior corridors. **Terms:** 1-7 night minimum stay, cancellation fee imposed. **Amenities:** video games. **Pool:** heated indoor. **Activities:** hot tub, exercise room. **Guest Services:** valet laundry, area transportation.

ECONO LODGE-NORTH   (434)295-3185 **10**
♥♥ Motel. **Address:** 2014 Holiday Dr 22901

ENGLISH INN OF CHARLOTTESVILLE
(434)971-9900 **11**

♥♥♥
Hotel
$100-$300

Address: 2000 Morton Dr 22903 **Location:** US 29 business route, just s of jct US 29 (Emmet St) and 250 Bypass. **Facility:** 106 units, some kitchens. 3 stories, interior corridors. **Terms:** 3 day cancellation notice-fee imposed. **Amenities:** *Some:* safes. **Pool:** heated indoor. **Activities:** sauna, health club. **Guest Services:** valet and coin laundry, area transportation. **Featured Amenity:** breakfast buffet. *(See ad this page.)*

 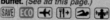

FAIRFIELD INN & SUITES BY MARRIOTT (434)964-9411 **4**
♥♥♥ Hotel. **Address:** 577 Branchlands Blvd 22901

AAA Benefit:
Members save 5% or more!

FOXFIELD INN   434/923-8892
♥♥♥ Bed & Breakfast. **Address:** 2280 Garth Rd 22901

GRADUATE CHARLOTTESVILLE   434/295-4333 **17**

♥♥♥
Hotel
Rates not provided

Address: 1309 W Main St 22903 **Location:** US 29 (Emmet St), 1 mi e on US 250 (University Ave). **Facility:** 134 units. 9 stories, interior corridors. **Parking:** on-site and valet. **Amenities:** video games, safes. **Activities:** bicycles, exercise room. **Guest Services:** coin laundry.

HAMPTON INN & SUITES-CHARLOTTESVILLE AT THE UNIVERSITY MEDICAL CENTER   (434)923-8600 **19**
♥♥♥ Hotel. **Address:** 900 W Main St 22903

AAA Benefit:
Members save up to 10%!

HAMPTON INN OF CHARLOTTESVILLE (434)978-7888 **6**
♥♥♥ Hotel. **Address:** 2035 India Rd 22901

AAA Benefit:
Members save up to 10%!

HILTON GARDEN INN CHARLOTTESVILLE   (434)979-4442 **15**
♥♥♥ Hotel. **Address:** 1793 Richmond Rd 22911

AAA Benefit:
Members save up to 10%!

▼ See AAA listing this page ▼

(See map & index p. 85.)

HOLIDAY INN-MONTICELLO/CHARLOTTESVILLE
434/977-5100   **22**

WWW Hotel. **Address:** 1200 5th St SW 22902

HOLIDAY INN UNIVERSITY AREA CHARLOTTESVILLE
434/977-7700   **7**

WWW Hotel. **Address:** 1901 Emmet St/US 29 S 22901

HYATT PLACE CHARLOTTESVILLE (434)995-5200   **5**

WWWW
Hotel
$79-$299

HYATT PLACE
AAA Benefit: Members save 10%!

Address: 2100 Bond St 22901 **Location:** Jct US 250 Bypass, 0.4 mi n on US 29. **Facility:** 137 units. 6 stories, interior corridors. **Terms:** cancellation fee imposed. **Pool:** heated indoor. **Activities:** exercise room. **Guest Services:** valet and coin laundry, area transportation. **Featured Amenity:** full hot breakfast.

SAVE ⊞ ▥ ⥮ CALL ⅋ ⚓
⊞ BIZ HS ⧉ ⤬ ⊟ ▦

⊞ / SOME UNITS 🛏

THE INN AT MONTICELLO   (434)979-3593   **23**

WWW Historic Bed & Breakfast. **Address:** 1188 Scottsville Rd (Rt 20) 22902

LA QUINTA INN & SUITES CHARLOTTESVILLE-UVA MEDICAL
(434)293-6188   **8**

WWW Hotel. **Address:** 1803 Emmet St 22901

OMNI CHARLOTTESVILLE HOTEL   434/971-5500   **16**

WWW Hotel. **Address:** 212 Ridge McIntire Rd 22903

RESIDENCE INN BY MARRIOTT   (434)923-0300   **12**

WWW Extended Stay Hotel. **Address:** 1111 Millmont St 22903

AAA Benefit:
Members save 5%
or more!

SILVER THATCH INN   434/978-4686   **1**

WWW Historic Country Inn. **Address:** 3001 Hollymead Dr 22911

SLEEP INN & SUITES MONTICELLO   (434)244-9969   **21**

WWW Hotel. **Address:** 1185 5th St 22902

WHERE TO EAT

ABERDEEN BARN   434/296-4630   **4**

WW
Steak
Casual Dining
$18-$45

AAA Inspector Notes: Founded in 1965, the local favorite offers huge portions of quality steaks, prime rib and seafood in a comfortable, club-like atmosphere. Fresh salad, dressing and bread accompany the meals which are served by a friendly, attentive waitstaff. The cheese crock for bread sticks is a favorite among patrons and you will love the old school hot plates. **Features:** full bar. **Reservations:** suggested, Fri & Sat. **Address:** 2018 Holiday Dr 22901 **Location:** I-64 exit 118B (US 29/Emmet St), just n of jct US 250 Bypass, then just e. D

AFGHAN KABOB PALACE   434/245-0095   **9**

WW Afghan. Casual Dining. **Address:** 400 Emmet St N 22903

CAVALIER DINER   434/977-1619   **5**

WW American. Casual Dining. **Address:** 1403 Emmet St 22903

CHRISTIAN'S PIZZERIA   434/977-9688   **19**

W Pizza. Casual Dining. **Address:** 118 N Main St 22902

THE DOWNTOWN GRILLE   434/817-7080   **15**

WWW American. Fine Dining. **Address:** 201 W Main St 22902

FLAMING WOK & TEPPAN YAKI JAPANESE STEAK HOUSE
434/974-6555   **2**

WW Chinese. Casual Dining. **Address:** 1305 Seminole Tr 22901

HAMILTON'S AT FIRST AND MAIN   434/295-6649   **17**

WWW American. Casual Dining. **Address:** 101 W Main St 22902

THE IVY INN RESTAURANT   434/977-1222   **7**

WWW American. Fine Dining. **Address:** 2244 Old Ivy Rd 22903

MAYA   434/979-6292   **22**

WWW Southern American. Casual Dining. **Address:** 633 W Main St 22903

MICHIE TAVERN CA 1784   434/977-1234   **25**

WW
American
Casual Dining
$12-$28

AAA Inspector Notes: Historic. The tavern evokes a bygone age, and diners will be hard-pressed to find a better Colonial-style lunch buffet served in the true Southern tradition. Fried chicken can be enjoyed with a rich array of traditional sides, including stewed tomatoes, black-eyed peas and cornbread. Desserts vary; for a taste, try the peach cobbler. The atmosphere takes its cue from the 200-year-old log cabin setting. Don't miss the walk alongside the mill. **Features:** beer & wine. **Address:** 683 Thomas Jefferson Pkwy 22902 **Location:** I-64 exit 121A, just s on SR 20, then 1 mi e on SR 53. L D

THE NOOK   434/295-6665   **21**

WW American. Casual Dining. **Address:** 415 E Main St 22902

THE OLD MILL ROOM   434/972-2230   **8**

WWW
Regional
American
Fine Dining
$20-$50

AAA Inspector Notes: Historic. An Early American atmosphere pervades the restored gristmill, a city fixture since 1834. Gentle rolling hills surround the restaurant. The menu, which changes slightly each night, showcases local ingredients blended in imaginative ways and with a hint of traditional Southern influence. The staff is pleasant and attentive. Top off the meal with the chocolate shining star. **Features:** full bar. **Reservations:** suggested. Comformal attire. **Address:** Rt 250 W 22903 **Location:** Jct US 29 Bypass, 1 mi w on US 250 (University Ave); in Boar's Head. B L D

ORZO   434/975-6796   **23**

WW Mediterranean. Casual Dining. **Address:** 416 W Main St 22903

PARALLEL 38   434/923-3838   **3**

WWW Mediterranean. Casual Dining. **Address:** 2055 Bond St 22901

THE POINTE RESTAURANT & LOUNGE   434/971-5500   **16**

WWW Regional American. Casual Dining. **Address:** 212 Ridge McIntire Rd 22903

RED PUMP KITCHEN   434/202-6040   **20**

WW Northern Italian. Casual Dining. **Address:** 401 E Main St 22902

RHETT'S RIVER GRILL AND RAW BAR   434/974-7818   **1**

WW American. Casual Dining. **Address:** 2335 Seminole Tr, Suite 100 22901

THE SHEBEEN   434/296-3185   **14**

WW Southern African. Casual Dining. **Address:** 247 Ridge-McIntire Rd 22903

SOUTH STREET BREWERY   434/293-6550   **24**

WW American. Casual Dining. **Address:** 106 W South St 22902

(See map & index p. 85.)

STICKS KEBOB SHOP   434/295-5262 ⑫
🍷 American. Quick Serve. **Address:** 917 Preston Ave 22903

TARA THAI   434/984-9998 ⑥
🍷🍷 Thai. Casual Dining. **Address:** 1107 Emmet St 22903

TIP TOP RESTAURANT   434/244-3424 ⑪
🍷🍷 American. Casual Dining. **Address:** 1420 Richmond Rd 22911

THE VIRGINIAN   434/984-4667 ⑬
🍷🍷 American. Casual Dining. **Address:** 1521 University Ave 22903

VIVACE   434/979-0994 ⑩
🍷🍷🍷 Italian. Fine Dining. **Address:** 2244 Ivy Rd 22903

ZO CA LO   434/977-4944 ⑱
🍷🍷🍷 Latin American. Casual Dining. **Address:** 201 E Main St, Suite E 22902

CHESAPEAKE (C-4) pop. 222,209, elev. 10'
- Hotels & Restaurants map & index p. 134
- Part of Hampton Roads Area — see map p. 124

   Nestled in the southeast corner of the commonwealth in the heart of the Tidewater/Hampton Roads region, Chesapeake was created in 1963 following the merger of Norfolk County and the city of Norfolk. Though relatively new as a city, Chesapeake was one of the first areas explored by Capt. John Smith in the 1600s. During the Revolutionary War, American and British forces clashed here in the Battle of Great Bridge.

   Two branches of the Atlantic Intracoastal Waterway stretch southward from Chesapeake, providing boaters with a choice of two scenic routes to Florida.

   An untamed wilderness is nearby at the Dismal Swamp *(see place listing p. 101)*. Boating access to Lake Drummond in the Great Dismal Swamp National Wildlife Refuge is available at the Chesapeake ramp off US 17 at Ballahack Road and west to the junction of George Washington Highway. Birds and bird-watchers share common ground on the South Chesapeake Loop of the Virginia Birding and Wildlife Trail.

Chesapeake Parks, Recreation & Tourism: 1224 Progressive Dr., Chesapeake, VA 23320. **Phone:** (757) 382-6411 or (888) 889-5551.

Shopping: Chesapeake Square Mall (4200 Portsmouth Blvd.) is anchored by JCPenney. Greenbrier Mall (1401 Greenbrier Pkwy.) includes Dillard's, JCPenney, Macy's and Sears.

ALOFT CHESAPEAKE   (757)410-9562 ㉟
🍷🍷🍷 Contemporary Hotel. **Address:** 1454 Crossways Blvd 23320
AAA Benefit: Members save 5% or more!

CANDLEWOOD SUITES   757/405-3030 ㉘
🍷🍷🍷 Extended Stay Hotel. **Address:** 4809 Market Pl 23321

COMFORT INN & SUITES   (757)673-8585 ㊴
🍷🍷🍷 Hotel. **Address:** 3355 S Military Hwy 23323

COMFORT SUITES   (757)420-1600 ㉝
🍷🍷🍷 Hotel. **Address:** 1550 Crossways Blvd 23320

COURTYARD BY MARRIOTT CHESAPEAKE GREENBRIER   (757)420-1700 ㉙

🍷🍷🍷 **Hotel** **$88-$221**

COURTYARD Marriott
AAA Benefit: Members save 5% or more!

Address: 1562 Crossways Blvd 23320 **Location:** I-64 exit 289B (Greenbrier Pkwy), 0.3 mi s, just w on Jarman Rd (at Crossways Center) to Crossways Blvd, then 0.3 mi n. **Facility:** 90 units. 3 stories, interior corridors. **Terms:** cancellation fee imposed. **Pool:** heated indoor. **Activities:** hot tub, exercise room. **Guest Services:** valet and coin laundry, boarding pass kiosk.

🅂🄰🅅🄴 ECO ⊞ 🍽 🍸 CALL & 🏊 📶 BIZ HS
📶 ✕ 🖥 🖨 / SOME UNITS 🖼

FAIRFIELD INN & SUITES BY MARRIOTT CHESAPEAKE   (757)420-1300 ㉜
🍷🍷🍷 Hotel. **Address:** 1560 Crossways Blvd 23320
AAA Benefit: Members save 5% or more!

FAIRFIELD INN & SUITES BY MARRIOTT CHESAPEAKE SUFFOLK   (757)966-2727 ㉗
🍷🍷🍷 Hotel. **Address:** 2122 Jolliff Rd 23321
AAA Benefit: Members save 5% or more!

HAMPTON INN & SUITES   (757)819-5230 ㊳
🍷🍷🍷 Hotel. **Address:** 1421 N Battlefield Blvd 23320
AAA Benefit: Members save up to 10%!

HAMPTON INN & SUITES CHESAPEAKE SQUARE MALL   (757)465-7000 ㉖
🍷🍷🍷 Hotel. **Address:** 4449 Peek Tr 23321
AAA Benefit: Members save up to 10%!

HAMPTON INN CHESAPEAKE/GREENBRIER   (757)420-1550 ㉔
🍷🍷🍷 Hotel. **Address:** 701A Woodlake Dr 23320
AAA Benefit: Members save up to 10%!

HILTON GARDEN INN-CHESAPEAKE/GREENBRIER   (757)420-1212 ㉚
🍷🍷🍷 Hotel. **Address:** 1565 Crossways Blvd 23320
AAA Benefit: Members save up to 10%!

HOLIDAY INN EXPRESS & SUITES   757/465-2222 ㉕
🍷🍷🍷 Hotel. **Address:** 2436 Gum Rd 23321

HOLIDAY INN EXPRESS CHESAPEAKE-NORFOLK   757/698-4400 ㉑
🍷🍷🍷 Hotel. **Address:** 721 Conference Center Dr 23320

(See map & index p. 134.)

HOMEWOOD SUITES BY HILTON (757)213-0808 **31**
▼▼▼ Extended Stay Hotel. **Address:** 1569 Crossways Blvd 23320
AAA Benefit: Members save up to 10%!

HYATT PLACE-CHESAPEAKE/GREENBRIER
(757)312-0020 **37**

Hotel
$124-$229

♣HYATT PLACE'
AAA Benefit: Members save 10%!

Address: 709 Eden Way N 23320 **Location:** I-64 exit 289B (Greenbrier Pkwy), 1 mi s; in Towne Place at Greenbrier. **Facility:** 119 units. 4 stories, interior corridors. **Terms:** cancellation fee imposed. **Pool:** heated indoor. **Activities:** exercise room. **Guest Services:** valet laundry, area transportation. **Featured Amenity: full hot breakfast.**

RED ROOF INN CHESAPEAKE CONFERENCE CENTER
(757)523-0123 **20**

▼▼▼ **Hotel** **$60-$150**

Address: 724 Woodlake Dr 23320 **Location:** I-64 exit 289A (Greenbrier Pkwy), just n to Woodlake Dr, then just e. **Facility:** 108 units. 2 stories (no elevator), exterior corridors. **Amenities:** safes.

RESIDENCE INN BY MARRIOTT, CHESAPEAKE-GREENBRIER
(757)502-7300 **34**
▼▼▼ Extended Stay Hotel. **Address:** 1500 Crossways Blvd 23320
AAA Benefit: Members save 5% or more!

SPRINGHILL SUITES BY MARRIOTT GREENBRIER
(757)410-9406 **36**
▼▼▼ Hotel. **Address:** 1446 Crossways Blvd 23320
AAA Benefit: Members save 5% or more!

STAYBRIDGE SUITES GREENBRIER 757/420-2525 **23**
▼▼▼ Extended Stay Hotel. **Address:** 709 Woodlake Dr 23320

WINGATE BY WYNDHAM GREENBRIER
757/531-7777 **19**

▼▼▼ **Hotel** **Rates not provided**

Address: 817 Greenbrier Cir 23320 **Location:** I-64 exit 289A (Greenbrier Pkwy), just n. **Facility:** 100 units. 4 stories, interior corridors. **Amenities:** Some: safes. **Pool:** heated indoor. **Activities:** hot tub, exercise room. **Guest Services:** valet and coin laundry. **Featured Amenity: full hot breakfast.**

BAKER'S CRUST 757/547-2787
▼ American. Casual Dining. **Address:** 1244 Greenbrier Pkwy 23320

BERGEY'S BREADBASKET BAKERY & MORE 757/546-9225
▼ Breads/Pastries. Quick Serve. **Address:** 2207 Mt. Pleasant Rd 23322

COURTHOUSE CAFE 757/482-7077 **55**
▼ Regional American. Casual Dining. **Address:** 350 S Battlefield Blvd 23322

CUTLASS GRILLE 757/382-0015 **53**
▼▼ Jamaican. Casual Dining. **Address:** 805 N Battlefield Blvd 23320

THE CUTTING EDGE CAFE 757/389-5754 **46**
▼ Sandwiches. Quick Serve. **Address:** 1434 Sam's Dr, Suite 102 23320

DAIKICHI SUSHI JAPANESE BISTRO 757/549-0200 **48**
▼▼ Japanese Sushi. Casual Dining. **Address:** 1400 N Battlefield Blvd 23320

THE EGG BISTRO 757/410-8515 **54**
▼▼ American. Casual Dining. **Address:** 501 Kempsville Rd 23320

EL LORO MEXICAN RESTAURANTE 757/436-3415 **44**
▼▼ Mexican. Casual Dining. **Address:** 801 Volvo Pkwy, Suites 114-115 23320

THE GOURMET GANG 757/361-0482 **49**
▼ Sandwiches. Quick Serve. **Address:** 109 Volvo Pkwy, Suite 15 23320

INDIA PALACE 757/410-1183 **47**
▼▼ Indian. Casual Dining. **Address:** 1437 Sam's Dr, #124 23320

KERVAN KEBAB HOUSE 757/233-9350 **38**
▼▼ Turkish. Casual Dining. **Address:** 1757 Parkview Dr, Suite B 23320

MAYMAR FILIPINO RESTAURANT 757/548-1731 **52**
▼ Philippine. Quick Serve. **Address:** 805 Battlefield Blvd, Suite 107 23320

OISHI SUSHI 757/382-0011 **51**
▼▼ Japanese Sushi. Casual Dining. **Address:** 817 Botetourt Ct, Suite 105 23320

PHO DALAT 757/233-9995 **40**
▼ Vietnamese. Casual Dining. **Address:** 826 Eden Way N, Suite 140 23320

POLLARD'S CHICKEN 757/482-3200 **56**
▼ Chicken. Quick Serve. **Address:** 717 Battlefield Blvd S 23320

SPAGHETTI EDDIE'S PIZZA CAFE 757/410-5500 **43**
▼▼ Italian Pizza. Casual Dining. **Address:** 733 Eden Way N, Suite 400 23320

STACKED EATERY COMPANY 757/410-4551 **42**
▼ Breakfast Comfort Food. Casual Dining. **Address:** 717 Eden Way N 23320

SURF RIDER CHESAPEAKE 757/549-2626 **41**
▼ Seafood. Casual Dining. **Address:** 725 Eden Way N 23320

TASTE UNLIMITED 757/424-4583
▼ Specialty Sandwiches. Quick Serve. **Address:** 717 N Eden Way, Suite 600 23320

THAI 99 757/543-9116 **39**
▼▼ Thai. Casual Dining. **Address:** 1937 S Military Hwy 23320

(See map & index p. 134.)

VA YAMA SUSHI BAR   757/410-4000   50
▽▽◆ Japanese Sushi. Casual Dining. **Address:** 109 Volvo Pkwy, Suite 8 23320

WARRIOR'S GRILL   757/382-7007   45
▽ Asian. Casual Dining. **Address:** 1437 Sam's Dr, Suite 113 23320

CHESTER pop. 20,987, elev. 174'
- Hotels & Restaurants map & index p. 212
- Part of Richmond area — see map p. 193

COMFORT INN-RICHMOND/CHESTER   (804)751-0000   85
▽▽◆ Hotel. **Address:** 2100 W Hundred Rd 23836

COUNTRY INN & SUITES BY CARLSON   804/751-0080   90
▽▽◆ Hotel. **Address:** 2406 W Hundred Rd 23831

COURTYARD BY MARRIOTT RICHMOND/CHESTER
    (804)414-1010   88
▽▽◆ Hotel. **Address:** 2001 W Hundred Rd 23836

| AAA Benefit: Members save 5% or more! |

FAIRFIELD INN BY MARRIOTT   (804)778-7500   87

Hotel
$77-$163

FAIRFIELD INN & SUITES Marriott

AAA Benefit: Members save 5% or more!

Address: 12400 Redwater Creek Rd 23831 **Location:** I-95 exit 61B, just w of jct SR 10. **Facility:** 115 units. 4 stories, interior corridors. **Terms:** cancellation fee imposed. **Pool:** heated indoor. **Activities:** exercise room. **Guest Services:** valet and coin laundry. **Featured Amenity:** breakfast buffet.

SAVE ⊞ CALL 🚹 🚭 🛏 BIZ

HS 🛜 ⊠ 🎦 🖥 🖨 🖳

/SOME UNITS 🐾

HAMPTON INN   (804)768-8888   84
▽▽◆ Hotel. **Address:** 12610 Chestnut Hill Rd 23836

| AAA Benefit: Members save up to 10%! |

HOLIDAY INN EXPRESS   804/751-0123   89
▽▽◆ Hotel. **Address:** 1911 W Hundred Rd 23836

HOMEWOOD SUITES BY HILTON RICHMOND/CHESTER
    (804)751-0010   91
▽▽◆ Extended Stay Hotel. **Address:** 12810 Old Stage Rd 23836

| AAA Benefit: Members save up to 10%! |

HYATT PLACE RICHMOND/CHESTER
    (804)530-4600   83

Hotel
$89-$199

HYATT PLACE
AAA Benefit: Members save 10%!

Address: 13148 Kingston Ave 23836 **Location:** I-295 exit 15B, just w; I-95 exit 61A, 4.5 mi e; in River's Bend. **Facility:** 120 units. 4 stories, interior corridors. **Terms:** cancellation fee imposed. **Pool:** outdoor. **Activities:** exercise room. **Guest Services:** valet and coin laundry. **Featured Amenity:** full hot breakfast.

SAVE 🖥 ⊞ ⊡ 🍴 🛉 CALL 🚹 🚭

🚹 BIZ HS 🛜 ⊠ 🎦 🖥 🖨 🖳 /SOME UNITS 🐾

QUALITY INN & SUITES   (804)796-5200   86
▽▽◆ Hotel. **Address:** 12711 Old Stage Rd 23836

RESIDENCE INN BY MARRIOTT   (804)530-5501   82
▽▽◆ Extended Stay Hotel. **Address:** 800 Bermuda Hundred Rd 23836

| AAA Benefit: Members save 5% or more! |

WHERE TO EAT

ANTONIO'S RISTORANTE, PIZZERIA & WINE BAR
    804/530-1047   88
▽▽ Italian. Casual Dining. **Address:** 13301 River's Bend Blvd 23831

BROCK'S BAR-B-QUE   804/796-7539   92
▽▽ Barbecue. Casual Dining. **Address:** 11310 Ironbridge Rd 23831

CENTRAL PARK DELI   804/796-9660   90
▽ Deli. Casual Dining. **Address:** 12744 Jefferson Davis Hwy 23831

DIVINE   804/571-6383   85
▽▽ American. Fine Dining. **Address:** 13127 River's Bend Blvd 23836

DON PAPA GRANDE MEXICAN RESTAURANT
    804/796-7988   91
▽▽ Mexican. Casual Dining. **Address:** 12806 Jefferson Davis Hwy 23831

JALAPENOS   804/530-2787   87
▽▽ Mexican. Casual Dining. **Address:** 13130 Kingston Ave 23836

NARITA JAPANESE RESTAURANT   804/530-0013   86
▽▽ Japanese Sushi. Casual Dining. **Address:** 13115 River's Bend Blvd 23836

PEKING RESTAURANT   804/751-9898
▽▽ Chinese. Casual Dining. **Address:** 12730 Jefferson Davis Hwy 23831

SIBLEY'S BAR-B-Q   804/748-3299   89
[fyi] Southern Barbecue. Casual Dining. Under major renovation, scheduled to be completed December 2017. **Last rated:** ▽ **Address:** 12000 Winfree St 23831

CHESTERFIELD (B-1) elev. 209'
- Hotels & Restaurants map & index p. 212
- Part of Richmond area — see map p. 193

A number of the earliest land grants to English colonists lay along the south side of the James River and were recorded in Chesterfield's courthouse. During the American Revolution the courthouse

(See map & index p. 212.)

served as the headquarters for Maj. Gen. Friedrich von Steuben. The importance of this training facility provoked the British—with the aid of Benedict Arnold—to burn the courthouse in 1781.

LA QUINTA INN RICHMOND SOUTH   (804)743-0770 **79**
▼▼▼ Hotel. **Address:** 9040 Pams Ave 23237

SLEEP INN RICHMOND   (804)275-8800 **78**
▼▼▼ Hotel. **Address:** 2321 Willis Rd 23237

CHINCOTEAGUE (G-12) pop. 2,941, elev. 3'
• Hotels p. 94 • Restaurants p. 95

Local legends say that Chincoteague (SHIN-ko-teeg) ponies, an island trademark, are descendants of mine horses that survived the shipwreck of a 16th-century Spanish galleon. Most historians, however, agree that the ponies were brought over by the first English colonists, who turned the herds loose on Assateague and Chincoteague in the late 1600s when the horses began to damage their crops.

Off the Eastern Shore in Chincoteague Bay, the 7-mile-long, 1.5-mile-wide island is connected to the mainland by a causeway and bridges. Assateague Island, which includes Assateague Island National Seashore (see place listing p. 68), shields Chincoteague from the sea. Serpentine waterways, called "guts" by the islanders, punctuate Chincoteague's flat expanses of salt marsh and scrub-pine woods. Duck and goose hunting and deep-sea or channel fishing are excellent.

Chincoteague oysters and clams constitute the island's second-greatest industry, after tourism. The local watermen cultivate oysters and clams on the leased tideflats, or "rocks," surrounding the island and in the inlet. Crabbing is a popular pastime, particularly in the early summer when the blue crabs are out of their hibernation in the Chincoteague Bay mud.

The Pony Swim and Auction, held the last consecutive Wednesday and Thursday in July, probably originated from the colonists' practice of rounding up foals and yearlings to renew their supply of workhorses. On these days the partly wild ponies are rounded up from their home on the southern end of Assateague Island to swim at slack tide (when the tide is changing and there is no movement) across the narrow channel to Chincoteague. Foals are sold at auction; the rest swim back to Assateague. The island's ponies were made famous by Marguerite Henry's book, "Misty of Chincoteague."

The Pony Express, a trolley bus system covering most of the island, offers access to many hotels, restaurants, shops, parks and other points of interest. Schedules and routes vary seasonally; the fare is 25c per ride and correct change is appreciated. Additionally, a 1-hour narrated trolley tour departs from the Community Center, 6155 Community Dr., Tuesday and Thursday at 2 and 3:15, early June-Labor Day (excluding July 30). The fare for the guided trolley tour is $4; $2 (ages 2-12). Phone (757) 336-6519.

Chincoteague Chamber of Commerce: 6733 Maddox Blvd., Chincoteague, VA 23336. **Phone:** (757) 336-6161.

CHINCOTEAGUE PONY CENTRE is at 6417 Carriage Dr. The facility houses Chincoteague ponies that visitors can pet and ride. The Memories of Misty Museum features memorabilia and other items that highlight the pinto horse featured in the 1947 children's novel "Misty of Chincoteague" and the 1961 film "Misty." A pony show is offered nightly in season and showcases the talents of the Chincoteague Pony Drill Team. The skilled animals perform various drills, stunts and maneuvers during the presentation, which lasts approximately one hour.

Hours: Center Mon.-Sat. 9-9, Memorial Day-Labor Day; Fri.-Sat. 9-6, early Apr. to mid-May; otherwise varies. Pony rides are available Mon.-Sat. 9-2 and 4-9. Phone ahead to confirm schedule. **Cost:** Center $5. Pony ride $7. Nighttime pony show $10; $5 (children). **Phone:** (757) 336-2776.

CHINCOTEAGUE NATIONAL WILDLIFE REFUGE occupies the Virginia portion of Assateague Island and several barrier islands along the Atlantic coast. Chincoteague ponies and other wildlife can be observed at the 14,000-acre refuge, which protects beaches, dunes, marshes and maritime forests. Sightings of migratory birds include snow geese, great blue herons, sanderlings, peregrine falcons and bald eagles. A 3.2-mile wildlife trail is open to walkers and bicyclists; vehicles are permitted from 3 p.m. until dusk.

The 5-mile beach at Toms Cove offers surf fishing, shell collecting and swimming. Nesting areas for piping plovers and other shorebirds are closed to public access March 15 through August 31. Information about guided walks, talks, tours of the historic Assateague Lighthouse and a 2-hour Wildlife Bus Trek are available from the Herbert H. Bateman Education Center and the National Park Service Visitor Center at Toms Cove (see attraction listings).

Pets are not permitted. **Hours:** Refuge daily 5 a.m.-10 p.m., May-Sept.; 6 a.m.-8 p.m., Mar.-Apr. and in Oct.; 6-6, rest of year. **Cost:** Entrance pass, valid for 7 days, $20 (per private vehicle); free (for persons arriving on foot or bicycle). **Phone:** (757) 336-6122 for general information, or (757) 336-3696 for tour information. **GT** 🎨

Herbert H. Bateman Education Center, 8231 Beach Rd., houses a variety of exhibits relating to the history of Assateague Island and to the flora and fauna protected by Chincoteague National Wildlife Refuge. Visitors can view mounted animals and walk through re-creations of the island's various habitats. Opened in 2003, the visitor center building uses sustainable and energy-efficient technology as well as recycled materials.

Time: Allow 1 hour minimum. **Hours:** Daily 9-4. Closed Jan. 1 and Christmas. **Cost:** Visitor center free. Chincoteague National Wildlife Refuge entrance pass, valid for 7 days, $20 (per private vehicle); free (for persons arriving on foot or bicycle). **Phone:** (757) 336-6122.

National Park Service Visitor Center at Toms Cove is at 8586 Beach Rd. Focusing on the saltwater environment of Chincoteague National Wildlife Refuge, educational displays include kid-friendly touch tanks filled with marine life. **Time:** Allow 30 minutes minimum. **Hours:** Daily 9-5, Mar.-Nov.; Fri.-Mon. 9-4, rest of year. Closed Thanksgiving and Christmas. **Cost:** Visitor center free. Chincoteague National Wildlife Refuge entrance pass, valid for 7 days, $20 (per private vehicle); free (for persons arriving on foot or bicycle). **Phone:** (757) 336-6577.

MUSEUM OF CHINCOTEAGUE ISLAND is at 7125 Maddox Blvd, at the entrance to the Chincoteague National Wildlife Refuge. Exhibits discuss shipwrecks and the impact of hurricanes on the island as well as the area's Native American and early settler history, seafood industry and wildlife. The horses that inspired the young-adult novel "Misty of Chincoteague" and its sequel, "Stormy, Misty's Foal," are mounted and on display. The collection also includes the first order Fresnel lens from the Assateague Lighthouse.

A scavenger hunt is available. **Time:** Allow 45 minutes minimum. **Hours:** Tues.-Sun. 11-5, Memorial Day-Labor Day; Fri.-Sun. 11-5, day after Easter-day before Memorial Day and day after Labor Day-Thanksgiving. Closed July 4. Phone ahead to confirm schedule. **Cost:** $4; free (ages 0-12). **Phone:** (757) 336-6117.

AMERICAS BEST VALUE INN & SUITES   (757)336-6562

Motel
$50-$225

Address: 6151 Maddox Blvd 23336 **Location:** Just e of Chincoteague Cswy. **Facility:** 23 units, some cottages. 1 story, exterior corridors. **Terms:** 10 day cancellation notice-fee imposed, resort fee. **Pool:** outdoor. **Activities:** picnic facilities.

ASSATEAGUE INN   (757)336-3738

Extended Stay Hotel
$65-$165

Address: 6570 Coachs Ln 23336 **Location:** Waterfront. 0.8 mi e on Maddox Blvd, just s on CR 2102 to Chicken City Rd, follow signs. Located in a wetlands area. **Facility:** 27 units, some kitchens. 2 stories (no elevator), exterior corridors. **Terms:** 2-4 night minimum stay - seasonal and/or weekends, 3 day cancellation notice-fee imposed. **Pool:** outdoor. **Activities:** picnic facilities. **Featured Amenity:** continental breakfast.

BEST WESTERN CHINCOTEAGUE ISLAND
(757)336-6557

Hotel
$79-$319

AAA Benefit: Members save 10% or more & earn 10% bonus points!

Address: 7105 Maddox Blvd 23336 **Location:** 1.5 mi e on Maddox Blvd/Beach Rd; at entrance to Assateague National Seashore. **Facility:** 52 units, some two bedrooms. 3 stories, interior/exterior corridors. **Terms:** cancellation fee imposed. **Pool:** outdoor. **Activities:** bicycles, picnic facilities, exercise room. **Guest Services:** coin laundry.

BIRCHWOOD MOTEL   757/336-6133
Motel. **Address:** 3650 S Main St 23336

COMFORT SUITES   (757)336-3700
Hotel. **Address:** 4195 N Main St 23336

FAIRFIELD INN & SUITES BY MARRIOTT CHINCOTEAGUE ISLAND   (757)336-0043

Hotel
$80-$409

FAIRFIELD INN & SUITES Marriott
AAA Benefit: Members save 5% or more!

Address: 3913 Main St 23336 **Location:** Waterfront. Jct Maddox Blvd and bridge, 1 mi s. **Facility:** 92 units. 3 stories, interior corridors. **Terms:** check-in 4 pm, cancellation fee imposed. **Pool:** heated outdoor. **Activities:** boat dock, fishing, exercise room. **Guest Services:** coin laundry. **Featured Amenity:** continental breakfast.

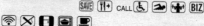

HAMPTON INN & SUITES   (757)336-1616
Hotel. **Address:** 4179 Main St 23336
AAA Benefit: Members save up to 10%!

ISLAND RESORT   (757)336-3141
Hotel. **Address:** 4391 Main St 23336

MARINA BAY HOTEL & SUITES, ASCEND HOTEL COLLECTION MEMBER   757/336-3500
Boutique Hotel. **Address:** 3801 Main St 23336

REFUGE INN   (757)336-5511

Hotel
$89-$415

Address: 7058 Maddox Blvd 23336 **Location:** 1.5 mi e on Maddox Blvd/Beach Rd. **Facility:** 72 units. 2 stories (no elevator), interior corridors. **Terms:** check-in 4 pm, 2 night minimum stay - seasonal and/or weekends, 3 day cancellation notice-fee imposed. **Pool:** heated outdoor, heated indoor. **Activities:** sauna, hot tub, bicycles, exercise room. **Guest Services:** coin laundry. **Featured Amenity:** breakfast buffet.

SEA SHELL MOTEL   757/336-6589
Motel. **Address:** 3720 Willow St 23336

WATERSIDE INN   (757)336-3434
Hotel. **Address:** 3761 S Main St 23336

WHERE TO EAT

AJ'S...ON THE CREEK   757/336-5888
🍷🍷 Seafood. Casual Dining. **Address:** 6585 Maddox Blvd 23336

BILL'S PRIME SEAFOOD & STEAKS   757/336-5831
🍷🍷🍷 Seafood. Casual Dining. **Address:** 4040 Main St 23336

THE CRAB SHACK   757/336-1880
🍷🍷 Seafood. Casual Dining. **Address:** 6560 Maddox Blvd 23336

DON'S SEAFOOD RESTAURANT   757/336-5715
🍷🍷 Seafood. Casual Dining. **Address:** 4113 Main St 23336

ETTA'S CHANNEL SIDE RESTAURANT   757/336-5644
🍷🍷 Seafood. Casual Dining. **Address:** 7452 East Side Rd 23336

THE FARMER'S DAUGHTER
🍷 American. Quick Serve. **Address:** 6700 Maddox St 23336

MR. BALDY'S FAMILY RESTAURANT   757/336-1198
🍷🍷 Seafood. Casual Dining. **Address:** 3441 Ridge Rd 23336

MR. PAUL'S KITCHEN   757/336-0010
🍷🍷 American. Casual Dining. **Address:** 5030 Chicken City Rd 23336

PICO TAQUERIA   757/785-9920
🍷 Mexican. Quick Serve. **Address:** 6382 Maddox Blvd 23336

ROPEWALK - CHINCOTEAGUE   757/336-0512
🍷🍷 Seafood. Casual Dining. **Address:** 6262 Marlin St 23336

SAIGON VILLAGE   757/336-7299
🍷🍷 Vietnamese. Casual Dining. **Address:** 4069 Main St 23336

SEA STAR CAFE   757/336-5442
🍷 Sandwiches. Quick Serve. **Address:** 6429 Maddox Blvd 23336

STEAMERS   757/336-5300
🍷🍷 Seafood. Casual Dining. **Address:** 6251 Maddox Blvd 23336

SUGARBAKER'S   757/336-3712
🍷 Breads/Pastries. Quick Serve. **Address:** 4095 Main St 23336

THE VILLAGE RESTAURANT   757/336-5120
🍷🍷 Seafood. Casual Dining. **Address:** 6576 Maddox Blvd 23336

WOODY'S BEACH BARBECUE   410/430-4429
🍷 Barbecue Chicken. Quick Serve. **Address:** 6700 Maddox Blvd 23336

CHRISTIANSBURG (H-5) pop. 21,041, elev. 2,093'
• Restaurants p. 96

Montgomery County Chamber of Commerce: 1520 N. Franklin St., Christiansburg, VA 24073. **Phone:** (540) 382-3020.

ECONO LODGE   (540)382-6161
Motel $50-$269
Address: 2430 Roanoke St 24073 **Location:** I-81 exit 118, just w on US 11/460. **Facility:** 72 units. 2 stories (no elevator), exterior corridors. **Pool:** outdoor. **Featured Amenity:** continental breakfast.

FAIRFIELD INN & SUITES BY MARRIOTT   (540)381-9596
Hotel $79-$286
AAA Benefit: Members save 5% or more!
Address: 2659 Roanoke St 24073 **Location:** I-81 exit 118C, just e. **Facility:** 87 units. 3 stories, interior corridors. **Terms:** cancellation fee imposed. **Pool:** outdoor. **Activities:** exercise room. **Guest Services:** coin laundry. **Featured Amenity:** breakfast buffet.

HAMPTON INN CHRISTIANSBURG/BLACKSBURG   (540)381-5874
🍷🍷🍷 Hotel. **Address:** 380 Arbor Dr 24073
AAA Benefit: Members save up to 10%!

HOLIDAY INN EXPRESS HOTEL & SUITES CHRISTIANSBURG/BLACKSBURG   (540)382-6500
Hotel $99-$309
Address: 2725 Roanoke St 24073 **Location:** I-81 exit 118C, just e. **Facility:** 74 units. 4 stories, interior corridors. **Pool:** heated indoor. **Activities:** exercise room. **Guest Services:** coin laundry. **Featured Amenity:** breakfast buffet.

HOMEWOOD SUITES BY HILTON CHRISTIANSBURG   540/381-1394
Extended Stay Hotel. Rates not provided
AAA Benefit: Members save up to 10%!
Address: 2657 Roanoke St 24073 **Location:** I-81 exit 118, just e. **Facility:** 82 kitchen units. 4 stories, interior corridors. **Pool:** heated indoor. **Activities:** exercise room. **Guest Services:** coin laundry.

MICROTEL INN & SUITES BY WYNDHAM   540/381-0500
Hotel. Rates not provided
Address: 135 Ponderosa Dr 24073 **Location:** I-81 exit 118B, 3 mi w on US 460, then just n; off Arbor Rd. Located in New River Valley Mall. **Facility:** 86 units. 3 stories, interior corridors. **Activities:** exercise room. **Guest Services:** coin laundry. **Featured Amenity:** continental breakfast.

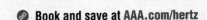
🅗 **Book and save at AAA.com/hertz**

THE OAKS VICTORIAN INN (540)381-1500

Historic Bed & Breakfast
$159-$219

Address: 311 E Main St 24073 **Location:** I-81 exit 114, 2 mi w. **Facility:** Large guest rooms reflect period ambience but offer modern conveniences at this 1893 Queen Anne Victorian inn, where huge oak trees line the grounds. 6 units, some cottages. 3 stories (no elevator), interior corridors. **Terms:** check-in 4 pm, 7 day cancellation notice-fee imposed. **Activities:** hot tub, health club, massage. **Guest Services:** valet laundry. **Featured Amenity:** full hot breakfast.

QUALITY INN (540)382-2055

Motel
$69-$179

Address: 50 Hampton Blvd 24073 **Location:** I-81 exit 118C, just e. **Facility:** 124 units. 2 stories (no elevator), exterior corridors. **Amenities:** safes. **Pool:** outdoor. **Activities:** hot tub, exercise room. **Guest Services:** valet and coin laundry. **Featured Amenity:** full hot breakfast.

WHERE TO EAT

DUE SOUTH BBQ 540/381-2922
Barbecue. Casual Dining. **Address:** 1465 Roanoke St 24073

CHURCHVILLE pop. 194

T-BONE TOOTER RESTAURANT 540/337-6500
American. Casual Dining. **Address:** Rt 250 W 24421

CLARKSVILLE pop. 1,139, elev. 1,468'

MAGNUSON HOTEL ON THE LAKE CLARKSVILLE (434)374-5023

Hotel
$95-$150

Address: 103 Second St 23927 **Location:** US 58 business route, just n; downtown. Located on Buggs Island Lake/John H. Kerr Reservoir. **Facility:** 70 units. 2 stories, interior corridors. **Terms:** 3 day cancellation notice. **Pool:** outdoor. **Featured Amenity:** continental breakfast.

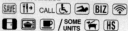

CLIFTON pop. 282

ROSEMARY'S THYME BISTRO 703/502-1084
Mediterranean. Casual Dining. **Address:** 5762 Union Mill Rd 20124

TRATTORIA VILLAGIO 703/543-2030
Italian. Casual Dining. **Address:** 7145 Main St 20124

From simple to spectacular:

AAA.com/travelguides/restaurants

TRUMMER'S ON MAIN 703/266-1623
American. Fine Dining. **Address:** 7134 Main St 20124

CLINTWOOD pop. 1,414, elev. 1,755'

SLEEP INN & SUITES (276)796-1058

Hotel
$92-$119

Address: 5625 Dickenson Hwy 24228 **Location:** Just w on SR 83. **Facility:** 53 units. 4 stories, interior corridors. **Activities:** exercise room. **Guest Services:** coin laundry. **Featured Amenity:** full hot breakfast.

COLLINSVILLE pop. 7,335

QUALITY INN-DUTCH INN HOTEL & CONVENTION CENTER (276)647-3721
Hotel. **Address:** 2360 Virginia Ave 24078

COLONIAL HEIGHTS (B-1) pop. 17,411, elev. 95'
• Hotels & Restaurants map & index p. 219
• Part of Richmond area — see map p. 193

This area gained its name during the Revolutionary War when Colonial forces led by the Marquis de Lafayette established a garrison on the heights above Petersburg. During the Civil War, Gen. Robert E. Lee made this town his headquarters for the siege of 1864. He arrived in June, setting up a post at the estate known as Violet Bank. The falling leaves of autumn exposed his position to the enemy, making it necessary for him to move his encampment elsewhere.

Colonial Heights Chamber of Commerce: 201 Temple Ave., Suite E, Colonial Heights, VA 23834. **Phone:** (804) 526-5872.

CANDLEWOOD SUITES 804/526-0111 **18**
Extended Stay Hotel. **Address:** 15820 Woods Edge Rd 23834

COMFORT INN COLONIAL HEIGHTS (804)324-4644 **17**
Hotel. **Address:** 15720 Woods Edge Rd 23834

COMFORT SUITES SOUTHPARK (804)520-8900 **20**
Hotel. **Address:** 931 South Ave 23834

HAMPTON INN PETERSBURG-SOUTHPARK MALL (804)520-7333 **21**
Hotel. **Address:** 403 E Roslyn Rd 23834

AAA Benefit: Members save up to 10%!

HILTON GARDEN INN-SOUTHPARK (804)520-0600 **19**
Hotel. **Address:** 800 Southpark Blvd 23834

AAA Benefit: Members save up to 10%!

HOLIDAY INN PETERSBURG NORTH-FT LEE 804/520-5880 **22**
Hotel. **Address:** 401 E Roslyn Rd 23834

(See map & index p. 219.)

WHERE TO EAT

KOREANA ORIENTAL RESTAURANT 804/520-8989 (18)
♦♦ Korean. Casual Dining. **Address:** 168 Southgate Square 23834

SAGEBRUSH STEAKHOUSE 804/520-8216
♦♦ Steak. Casual Dining. **Address:** 204 Southgate Square Shopping Center 23834

COLONIAL NATIONAL HISTORICAL PARK (B-3)
• **Part of Williamsburg, Jamestown & Yorktown area — see map p. 273**

On the peninsula between the York and James rivers, Colonial National Historical Park covers 8,600 acres. It embraces the Colonial Parkway, Historic Jamestowne *(see attraction listing p. 156)*, Yorktown Battlefield *(see attraction listing p. 297)* and the Cape Henry Memorial. Park headquarters is in the Yorktown Battlefield Visitor Center on the eastern end of the Colonial Parkway; phone (757) 898-2410.

COLONIAL PARKWAY links Jamestown, Williamsburg and Yorktown. Protected from modern development, this 23-mile scenic highway winds along the James and York rivers, passing through tidal estuaries and pine and hardwood forests.

From the Jamestown Visitor Center the parkway follows the James River before turning inland to Williamsburg, where it tunnels under the restored city. Just beyond the tunnel is the Colonial Williamsburg Visitor Center. Traveling overland, the parkway passes plantation sites along the York River and ends at the Yorktown Battlefield Visitor Center. Turnouts, most with explanatory markers, allow pauses for more detailed observation. The speed limit is 45 mph or as posted; there are no service facilities, and commercial vehicles are not permitted. **Hours:** Daily 24 hours. **Cost:** Free. **Phone:** (757) 856-1240 for recorded information or (757) 898-3400.

COURTLAND (C-2) pop. 1,284, elev. 32'

Originally named Jerusalem, this settlement was founded in 1791 on 10 acres along the Nottoway River. On Aug. 22, 1831, it experienced one of the nation's bloodiest slave revolts, the Nat Turner Rebellion. When the violent 3-day siege ended, more than 150 people were dead. Turner survived the insurrection and escaped but was captured 2 months later and quickly convicted. While awaiting execution Turner told his story to attorney Thomas Gray, who later published the account as "The Confessions of Nat Turner." In 1888 the town's name was changed to Courtland. Today it serves as the county seat for Southampton County.

🔥 **Dreaming of s'mores and starry nights?**
AAA.com/campgrounds

COVINGTON pop. 5,961

MAGNUSON HOTEL COVINGTON (540)962-4951
♦♦ Hotel $90-$143 **Address:** 820 E Madison St 24426 **Location:** I-64 exit 16, just n. **Facility:** 77 units. 2 stories, exterior corridors. **Dining:** Mountain View Restaurant, see separate listing. **Pool:** outdoor. **Activities:** exercise room. **Guest Services:** coin laundry. **Featured Amenity:** full hot breakfast.

WHERE TO EAT

CUCCI'S 540/962-3964
♦♦ Italian. Casual Dining. **Address:** 566 E Madison Ave 24426

MOUNTAIN VIEW RESTAURANT 540/962-4951
♦♦ American. Casual Dining. **Address:** 820 E Madison St 24426

CROZET (G-8) pop. 5,565, elev. 718'

WINERIES
• **White Hall Vineyards** is 8 mi. w. of US 29 on Barracks/Garth Rd., then 1.5 mi. n. w. to 5282 Sugar Ridge Rd. **Hours:** Wed.-Sun. 11-5. Closed major holidays. **Phone:** (434) 823-8615. (GT)

CULPEPER (F-8) pop. 16,379, elev. 423'
• **Hotels p. 98** • **Restaurants p. 98**

It was here in 1749 that 17-year-old George Washington began surveying work for proprietor Thomas Fairfax, 6th Baron Fairfax of Cameron. (The town was officially called Fairfax until it was renamed by the Virginia Assembly in 1870.) In 1775, as the Revolution became imminent, 350 volunteers from Culpeper, Orange and Fauquier counties gathered under an oak tree near present-day Yowell Meadow Park and dubbed themselves the Culpeper Minute Men. Under a flag depicting a coiled rattlesnake with the defiant legends "Liberty or Death" and "Don't tread on me," they would later march to Williamsburg in answer to Gov. Patrick Henry's call to arms.

Situated in the Piedmont River Valley in the state's north-central region, Culpeper County is said to have seen more Civil War activity in the early 1860s than any other area. Among the prominent individuals to fight, camp or headquarter there were Ulysses S. Grant, Robert E. Lee, Thomas J. "Stonewall" Jackson and James Ewell Brown "Jeb" Stuart. Wounded soldiers from the battles of Cedar Mountain, Kelly's Ford and Brandy Station were treated in makeshift hospitals set up in many Culpeper residences, churches and vacant buildings.

It's no wonder that outdoor adventures on Culpeper's sweeping flatlands, bold hills, rushing rivers and tranquil streams often evolve into engaging history lessons. You might feel as if you're floating back into the 18th and 19th centuries while you're canoeing, kayaking, tubing or fishing on the Rappahannock and the Rapidan—both rivers roll through canal-system wreckage, deserted gold mines and historic Civil War battlefields. As you soak up the sights and scents of orchards, vineyards, farmland and the Blue Ridge Mountains on foot or atop a bike or horse, ponder the history of this land.

If you'd like a little guidance as you explore Culpeper at your own pace, pick up some self-guiding walking and driving tour brochures from the visitor center, housed in a circa 1904 train depot. Also helpful are the series of markers that highlight the area's historically significant sites. Plus, you'll notice the past preserved in the commercial district's Italianate, neoclassical and vernacular-style structures while browsing specialty shops, galleries and antique malls; scoping out the perfect café; or enjoying a stroll or drive along Main and Davis streets.

For a more tranquil downtown experience, stop by Culpeper National Cemetery, 305 U.S. Ave., and pay homage to those who lost their lives in the vicinity during the Civil War. Or, unwind in Yowell Meadow Park, at the corner of Blue Ridge and SR 522, where you'll find nature and walking trails, a play area for the kids and a monument honoring the men who vowed to "march at a minute's notice."

Culpeper Tourism Office and Visitor Center: 111 S. Commerce St., Culpeper, VA 22701. **Phone:** (540) 727-0611 or (844) 490-2577.

BEST WESTERN CULPEPER INN (540)825-1253

Hotel
$90-$140

Best Western. **AAA Benefit:** Members save 10% or more & earn 10% bonus points!

Address: 791 Madison Rd 22701 **Location:** Jct US 29, 2 mi s on Main St (US 29 business route). **Facility:** 159 units. 2 stories, exterior corridors. **Terms:** check-in 4 pm, cancellation fee imposed. **Pool:** outdoor. **Activities:** exercise room. **Guest Services:** coin laundry.

[SAVE] [🍴] [🛄] [🍸] [🛶] [🐾] [BIZ]
[HS] [📶] [🛗] [📺] [💻]

FOUNTAIN HALL BED & BREAKFAST (540)825-8300
🦅🦅🦅 Historic Bed & Breakfast. **Address:** 609 S East St 22701

HOLIDAY INN EXPRESS & SUITES (540)825-7444
🦅🦅🦅 Hotel. **Address:** 787 Madison Rd 22701

WHERE TO EAT

FOTI'S RESTAURANT 540/829-8400
🦅🦅🦅 Mediterranean. Fine Dining. **Address:** 110 E Davis St 22701

FROST CAFE 540/829-0344
🦅 American. Casual Dining. **Address:** 101 E Davis St 22701

IT'S ABOUT THYME 540/825-4264
🦅🦅 American. Casual Dining. **Address:** 128 E Davis St 22701

LUCIO 540/829-9788
🦅🦅🦅 Italian. Fine Dining. **Address:** 702 S Main St 22701

PANCHO VILLA MEXICAN RESTAURANT 540/825-5268
🦅🦅 Mexican. Casual Dining. **Address:** 910 S Main St 22701

CUMBERLAND GAP NATIONAL HISTORICAL PARK (I-1)

Elevations in the park range from 1,600 ft. at the Cumberland Gap to 3,513 ft. at White Rocks. Refer to AAA maps for additional elevation information.

At the convergence of Kentucky, Tennessee and Virginia, Cumberland Gap National Historical Park covers 24,000 acres of heavily forested, rugged mountains honoring the historic pass.

The gap provides a natural doorway through the mountains. It was first used by migratory animals as a seasonal thoroughfare, then by Native Americans, whose footpaths followed buffalo and deer trails. The westward movement of settlers seemed barred by the Allegheny ridge until April 1750, when Dr. Thomas Walker discovered the gap while seeking the fabled land to the west, the "Kentucke" of Native American lore.

Daniel Boone passed through with a hunting party in 1769, and in 1775 he blazed the Wilderness Road. From 1775 to 1796 the gap could only be used by those on foot or horseback, and although no wagon passed over it during this period, more than 200,000 people made their way through the gap into Kentucky and beyond.

A strategic point during the Civil War, Cumberland Gap changed hands several times without any major battles. Some of the earthwork fortifications remain.

In the 1990s, the 4,600-foot-long Cumberland Gap Highway Tunnel was built; the project also included rerouting US 25E through the tunnel and the addition of new bridges, highway interchanges and parking areas. Although the final cost of this joint effort led by the National Park Service and the Federal Highway Administration was a staggering $265 million, the construction plan alleviated traffic problems and improved motorist safety while simultaneously restoring the historic appearance of the Cumberland Gap and the Wilderness Road.

General Information and Activities

At an elevation of 2,440 feet, Pinnacle Overlook provides a view into the gap as well as views of the mountain range and parts of three states. It is accessible via a 4-mile paved road from the visitor center. No trailers or vehicles more than 20 feet long are allowed. Shuttle service may be arranged for a small fee when staff is available; reservations are required.

Still a wild area, the park offers approximately 85 miles of hiking trails ranging from relatively easy nature trails to those requiring an overnight trek. Many park features, including Sand Cave, a multicolored sandstone overhang, and White Rocks, a prominent sandstone outcropping, can be reached only by trail. Ridge Trail, a 19-mile-long route offering panoramas of the valley, approaches five primitive campsites, all accessible by foot. The Wilderness Road Campground has 160 campsites, 41 of which have hookups.

Hensley Settlement is a reconstruction of a community that was occupied 1903-51. Reminiscent of a time much earlier than that from which it actually dates, Hensley seems like a community of the late 1700s or early 1800s. The settlement sits atop a mountain in the eastern end of the park. With more than 70 acres of land under cultivation, it has several reconstructed log houses, barns and outbuildings. The site can be reached by an all-day hike or, from mid-May through Oct. 31, via a guided tour that departs the park's visitor center daily. Building interiors may be seen during the 3.5- to 4-hour trip, which includes shuttle transportation to and from the settlement. The cost is $10; $5 (ages 0-12 and senior citizens with an Interagency Senior Pass). Phone (606) 248-2817, ext. 1075, for the shuttle tour schedule; reservations are recommended.

It is not advisable to hike alone; overnight camping requires a permit. Trail guides and other information can be obtained at the visitor center. The visitor center also contains a museum, which chronicles the rich history of the gap. Throughout the year ranger-led programs suitable for the entire family introduce visitors to the historical, cultural and natural aspects of the park; phone for a schedule of events.

The park is open daily. Some parking areas close before dusk. The visitor center at the park entrance is open daily 8-5, Memorial Day-Labor Day; 9-4, rest of year; closed Christmas.

ADMISSION to the park is free.

PETS must be restricted at all times, either in vehicles or by leash, and are not allowed in public buildings.

ADDRESS inquiries to the Superintendent, Cumberland Gap National Historical Park, 91 Bartlett Park Rd., Middlesboro, KY 40965; phone (606) 248-2817.

GAP CAVE is .25 mi. s. of Middlesboro, Ky., on US 25E. Two-hour guided tours of the cave, discovered in 1750, cover a 1.5-mile route and are conducted by lantern light. Rooms and walls are covered with stalactites and stalagmites. Wildlife, including bats and salamanders, can be seen, as can the names of Civil War soldiers carved on the walls.

Note: The guided tour's path includes 183 steps; visitors are advised to wear good walking shoes. No sandals or open-toed shoes are permitted. Due to the threat of white-nose syndrome to bats, visitors should not wear clothing and footwear that has been worn in other caves unless properly decontaminated.

Time: Allow 2 hours minimum. Hours: Tours are given daily at 10, early Apr.-late Nov.; phone ahead for additional tour times. Tickets may be purchased at the park visitor center or at Daniel Boone parking

area 30 minutes in advance of the tour. Reservations are recommended, especially on weekends. **Cost:** $8; $4 (ages 5-12 and senior citizens with an Interagency Senior Pass). Ages 0-4 are not permitted on cave tours. **Phone:** (606) 248-2817. GT

DAHLGREN pop. 2,653

COUNTRY INN & SUITES BY CARLSON	(540)644-1500
♦♦♦ Hotel. **Address:** 4755 James Madison Pkwy 22485	

HAMPTON INN DAHLGREN	(540)625-2333
♦♦♦ Hotel. **Address:** 16450 Commerce Dr 22485	**AAA Benefit:** Members save up to 10%!

DALEVILLE pop. 2,557

SUPER 8 ROANOKE/DALEVILLE	540/992-3000
♦♦ Motel. **Address:** 446 Roanoke Rd 24083	

WHERE TO EAT

THREE LI'L PIGS BARBEQUE	540/966-0166
♦♦ Barbecue. Casual Dining. **Address:** 120 Kingston Dr 24083	

DANVILLE (I-7) pop. 43,055, elev. 565'
• Hotels p. 100 • Restaurants p. 100

Danville was the last capital of the Confederacy; President Jefferson Davis and his cabinet officers moved to the town after the evacuation of Richmond on April 3, 1865. Davis wrote his last proclamation as president in Danville. At the Sutherlin House (now the Danville Museum of Fine Arts & History), 975 Main St., Davis received the news that Gen. Robert E. Lee had surrendered at Appomattox.

Lady Astor, the first female member of the British Parliament, was born as Nancy Witcher Langhorne in Danville in 1879. Her cottage birthplace at 117 Broad St. is open by appointment. Information is available at the visitor center; phone (434) 793-4636.

The railroad accident that inspired the popular folk ballad "Wreck of the Old 97" occurred in the town on Sept. 27, 1903, killing nine people. A commemorative marker is on US 58W.

Reflecting Danville's prosperous tobacco and textile heritage, Millionaires Row Historic District along Main Street boasts fine examples of Victorian and Edwardian residential architecture. A few of these private homes are open to the public during the Holiday Walking Tour held the second weekend in December.

Danville Pittsylvania County Chamber of Commerce: 8653 US 29, P.O. Box 99, Blairs, VA 24527. **Phone:** (434) 836-6990.

Self-guiding tours: Brochures outlining a walking tour of Millionaires Row and a driving tour of Civil War sites as well as area information and maps are available from the chamber of commerce and at the downtown visitor center at 645 River Park Dr.

Shopping: Danville Mall (325 Piedmont Dr.) has more than 70 stores, including Belk, JCPenney and Sears. On Saturday mornings from May through October and Wednesday afternoons July through August, the Danville Farmers' Market (626 Craghead St.) offers fresh produce, baked goods, and arts and crafts.

BEST WESTERN WINDSOR INN & SUITES
(434)483-5000

Hotel
$110-$300

 Best Western.

AAA Benefit: Members save 10% or more & earn 10% bonus points!

Address: 1292 S Boston Rd 24540 **Location:** Jct US 29 Bypass, 0.8 mi e on US 58 Bypass. **Facility:** 74 units. 3 stories, interior corridors. **Terms:** cancellation fee imposed. **Pool:** heated indoor. **Activities:** hot tub, exercise room. **Guest Services:** valet and coin laundry.

COMFORT INN & SUITES
(434)793-2000
♦♦ Hotel. **Address:** 100 Tower Dr 24540

COURTYARD BY MARRIOTT
(434)791-2661
♦♦♦ Hotel. **Address:** 2136 Riverside Dr 24540

AAA Benefit: Members save 5% or more!

HAMPTON INN RIVERSIDE
(434)793-1111
♦♦ Hotel. **Address:** 2130 Riverside Dr 24540

AAA Benefit: Members save up to 10%!

HOLIDAY INN EXPRESS DANVILLE
434/793-4000
♦♦♦ Hotel. **Address:** 2121 Riverside Dr 24540

SLEEP INN & SUITES
(434)793-6090
♦♦♦ Hotel. **Address:** 1483 South Boston Rd 24540

SUPER 8
434/799-5845

Motel
Rates not provided

Address: 2385 Riverside Dr 24541 **Location:** Jct US 29 business route/SR 86, just e on US 58 business route. **Facility:** 57 units. 3 stories, interior corridors. **Amenities:** safes.

WHERE TO EAT

CHECKERED PIG
434/793-7447
♦ Barbecue. Quick Serve. **Address:** 155 Crown Dr 24540

DANVIEW RESTAURANT
434/793-3552
♦ American. Casual Dining. **Address:** 116 Danview Dr 24541

DELL'ANNO'S PIZZA KITCHEN
434/793-1100
♦♦ Pizza. Casual Dining. **Address:** 316 Main St 24541

EL VALLARTA RESTAURANTE MEXICANO
434/799-0506
♦♦ Mexican. Casual Dining. **Address:** 418 Westover Dr 24541

FRANK'S ITALIAN RESTAURANT & PIZZERIA
434/792-6157
♦♦ Italian. Casual Dining. **Address:** 1959 Memorial Dr 24541

JOE & MIMMA'S ITALIAN RESTAURANT
434/799-5763
♦♦ Italian. Casual Dining. **Address:** 3336 Riverside Dr 24541

LONG RIVER CHINESE RESTAURANT
434/799-6770
♦ Chinese. Casual Dining. **Address:** 2835 Riverside Dr 24540

MARY'S DINER
434/836-0132
♦ Southern. Casual Dining. **Address:** 1203 Piney Forest Rd 24540

ME'S BURGERS & BREWS
434/792-0123
♦♦ Burgers. Casual Dining. **Address:** 215 Main St 24541

DAYTON (F-7) pop. 1,530, elev. 1,230'

Daniel Harrison, brother of the founder of the town of Harrisonburg, built his home along Cook's Creek just north of town. The Daniel Harrison House also is known as Fort Harrison due to its solid stone structure with an underground passage to a well and a stockade that once surrounded the home, protecting it from Native American attacks. Visitors can tour the 18th-century home Friday and Saturday afternoons, May through October; phone (540) 879-2280.

THE HERITAGE MUSEUM, HOME OF THE HARRISONBURG-ROCKINGHAM HISTORICAL SOCIETY is at 382 High St. Documents and artifacts of the Shenandoah Valley include a permanent exhibit titled Invincible Spirit: History in the Heart of the Shenandoah. The museum also focuses on one of the area's major historical events, Gen. Thomas J. "Stonewall" Jackson's Valley Campaign of 1862. The exhibit includes an electric map detailing Jackson's campaign.

Displays include Civil War artifacts, documents and photographs as well as folk art encompassing works in ceramics, textiles, wood and metals. A genealogy library also is on-site. **Time:** Allow 30 minutes minimum. **Hours:** Mon.-Sat. 10-5 (also Sun. 1-5, Apr.-Oct.). Closed Jan. 1 and Christmas. Phone ahead to confirm schedule. **Cost:** $8; $7 (ages 65+); free (students with ID). **Phone:** (540) 879-2681.

DAYTON TAVERN
540/908-0029
♦♦ American. Casual Dining. **Address:** 245 Main St 22821

THOMAS HOUSE RESTAURANT
540/879-2181
♦ American. Casual Dining. **Address:** 222 Main St 22821

DELAPLANE (B-10) elev. 460'

On July 19, 1861, Gen. Thomas J. "Stonewall" Jackson marched the new recruits of Virginia's First Brigade toward Delaplane, then known as Piedmont Station. Some 10,000 soldiers boarded freight and cattle cars to reach the first major battle of the Civil War, First Manassas. The use of the railroad for large-scale troop movement marked a new era in military transport. The battle 2 days later was a decisive victory for the South.

DISMAL SWAMP (I-11)

In southeastern Virginia and northeastern North Carolina, the Great Dismal Swamp is characterized by forested peat soils and a dense undergrowth of briars and vines. The 126,000-acre area is threaded by canals and ditches, many of which have grown over to resemble green tunnels.

Col. William Byrd of Virginia surveyed the swamp in 1728 and named it Great Dismal. George Washington explored it in 1763, saw its possibilities as a timber producer and commercial canal and formed a company known as The Adventurers for Draining the Great Dismal Swamp. Much of the refuge was once owned by Washington, Patrick Henry and other prominent Virginians. The original swamp area is believed to have covered more than 1 million acres.

Remnants of an Atlantic white cedar forest still can be found. Commercially valuable trees include cypress, juniper, red maple and yellow poplar; however, the peat soils make lumbering difficult. The Great Dismal Swamp National Wildlife Refuge was established in 1973.

Lake Drummond, a circular lake covering 3,000 acres, is in the heart of the swamp. Its average depth is 6 feet, and the unusually pure water is preserved by the tannic acids from the bark of the cypress, juniper and gum trees. Gnarled cypress trees, moss and the dense growth surrounding the lake give it an eerie, mirrorlike appearance. The coffee-colored lake has a sandy bottom and is unusual in that it is not formed in a basin, but rather on a gently sloping hillside.

Boat access is available via a launch on US 17 at the mouth of the feeder ditch, a 3-mile-long shallow waterway connecting the lake with the Dismal Swamp Canal. To enter the lake, boats must be transported across the Corps of Engineers spillway at the head of the feeder ditch via a small motorized tram (1,000-pound weight limit).

The 22-mile canal, part of the Atlantic Intracoastal Waterway, is the oldest continually operating man-made canal in the country. Locks open four times daily to accommodate yachts and private boats. A wildlife canoe trail provides access for small, portable watercraft. The Dismal Swamp Canal Welcome Center is 3 miles south of the state line at 2356 US 17 in South Mills, N.C. A 4.5-mile paved trail along the canal is open to walkers, bicyclists and bird-watchers. The welcome center is open Mon.-Sat. 9-5. Hours may vary; phone ahead. Phone (252) 771-8333 or (877) 771-8333. Adjacent to the welcome center is Dismal Swamp State Park, which features more than 20 miles of trails, a boardwalk and educational exhibits about the swamp; phone (252) 771-6593 or (252) 771-6582.

GREAT DISMAL SWAMP NATIONAL WILDLIFE REFUGE is in southeastern Virginia and northeastern North Carolina; headquarters is off SR 32 in Suffolk, Va., at 3100 Desert Rd. The refuge preserves more than 112,000 acres of forested wetlands surrounding Lake Drummond. Inhabitants include black bears, white-tailed deer, bobcats, otters and more than 200 recorded species of birds. A birding fest is held in late April.

Visitors to the refuge can hike or bicycle on several miles of unpaved trails. Interpretive boardwalks along the Washington and West ditches traverse a variety of swamp habitats. Boating and fishing are permitted on Lake Drummond. An auto tour route also is available; pick up a self-serve permit at the gate next to the park headquarters. **Hours:** Trails daily dawn-dusk. Refuge headquarters Mon.-Fri. 8-4; closed major holidays. Auto tour daily 7-7, Apr.-Sept.; 7:30-5, rest of year. Closed major holidays. Phone ahead to confirm schedule. **Cost:** Free. Auto tour $5. **Phone:** (757) 986-3705. 🐾 🛆

DOSWELL (G-9) elev. 145'

- Hotels p. 102
- Part of Richmond area — see map p. 193

Originally known as Hanover, the town was the home of James Doswell, a Revolutionary War veteran. His estate, Bullfield, was noted for its winning racehorses. Hanover was renamed in the 1890s in honor of Maj. Thomas Doswell, who returned from the Civil War to open a hotel and continue the family's horse-breeding business.

KINGS DOMINION is .5 mi. e. off I-95 exit 98 at 16000 Theme Park Way. A 300-foot replica of the Eiffel Tower stands at the gates to this 400-acre theme park, which features live shows, thrill and family rides, and a water park. Among 12 roller coasters are Intimidator 305, which soars 305 feet into the air and reaches speeds in excess of 90 mph; Dominator, a floorless coaster; and Flight of Fear, an indoor coaster that runs in total darkness. Boo Blasters on Boo Hill is an interactive, animated ride geared to families. Volcano, The Blast Coaster rockets out of a volcanic crater while Delirium is a spinning pendulum swinging riders back and forth. Planet Snoopy is a nearly 14-acre Peanuts-themed children's area with attractions designed for kids and adults to experience together.

Swimsuits are required at Soak City, where Hurricane Heights, Splash Island, two wave pools and a relaxing lazy river are the main attractions. Dinosaurs Alive! is a 6-acre animatronic dinosaur park featuring 39 life-size dinosaurs that move and roar.

Kennels are available. **Time:** Allow a full day. **Hours:** Parks open daily, Memorial Day-Labor Day. Schedules vary rest of year; phone ahead. **Cost:** (includes Soak City in season) $67; $45 (ages 62+ and under 48 inches tall); free (ages 0-2). Dinosaurs Alive! additional $5. Prices may vary. **Parking:** $15. **Phone:** (804) 876-5000. 🍴

COUNTRY INN & SUITES BY CARLSON   804/612-8450

Hotel
Rates not provided

Address: 16250 International St 23047 **Location:** I-95 exit 98, just e on SR 30. **Facility:** 62 units. 3 stories, interior corridors. **Pool:** heated indoor. **Activities:** hot tub, exercise room. **Guest Services:** coin laundry, area transportation. **Featured Amenity: full hot breakfast.**

LA QUINTA INN & SUITES DOSWELL - KINGS DOMINION
(804)876-6900
Hotel. **Address:** 16280 International St 23047

DUBLIN pop. 2,534

HAMPTON INN
(540)674-5700
Hotel. **Address:** 4420 Cleburne Blvd 24084

> **AAA Benefit:**
> Members save up to 10%!

HOLIDAY INN EXPRESS
540/674-1600
Hotel. **Address:** 4428 Cleburne Blvd 24084

SLEEP INN & SUITES
(540)674-4099

Hotel
$70-$180

Address: 5094 State Park Rd 24084 **Location:** I-81 exit 101, just e. **Facility:** 67 units. 3 stories, interior corridors. **Pool:** heated indoor. **Activities:** hot tub, exercise room. **Guest Services:** coin laundry. **Featured Amenity: full hot breakfast.**

WHERE TO EAT

FATZ
540/674-8046
Regional American. Casual Dining. **Address:** 4586 Alexander Farm Rd 24084

DUMFRIES (C-12) pop. 4,961, elev. 43'

It was from the town of Dumfries in 1800 that the itinerant bookseller and former Anglican priest Parson Mason Locke Weems launched his popular biography "Life of Washington." The highly fictionalized book is best known for its story about young Washington chopping down a cherry tree and confessing to his father, "I cannot tell a lie."

The Weems-Botts Museum, 3944 Cameron St., originally served as Weems' bookshop. The property was later purchased by Benjamin Botts, a prominent defense lawyer who represented politician Aaron Burr in his 1807 treason trial. The museum is the starting point for a guided walking tour of Dumfries; phone (703) 221-2218 for more information.

COMFORT INN DUMFRIES NEAR QUANTICO MAIN GATE NORTH
(703)445-8070
Hotel. **Address:** 16931 Old Stage Rd 22025

HAMPTON INN BY HILTON DUMFRIES/QUANTICO
(703)441-9900
Hotel. **Address:** 16959 Old Stage Rd 22025

> **AAA Benefit:**
> Members save up to 10%!

HOLIDAY INN QUANTICO CENTER - DUMFRIES
703/441-9001
Hotel. **Address:** 3901 Fettler Park Dr 22026

WHERE TO EAT

GIORGIO'S FAMILY RESTAURANT
703/580-8500
Italian. Casual Dining. **Address:** 4394 Kevin Walker Dr 22025

EDINBURG (E-8) pop. 1,041, elev. 807'

Nestled in the Shenandoah Valley, Edinburg was founded by German and Swiss immigrants in the late 18th century. The fertile region became known as the "Breadbasket of the Confederacy" during the Civil War. After his soldiers destroyed barns, livestock and crops across the valley in 1864, Union general Philip Sheridan boasted that the Shenandoah was so bare, "a crow would be well advised to take its own provisions."

Shenandoah County Tourism: 600 N. Main St., Suite 101, Woodstock, VA 22664. **Phone:** (540) 459-6227 or (888) 367-3965.

SAL'S ITALIAN BISTRO
540/984-9300
Italian. Casual Dining. **Address:** 125 S Main St 22824

ELKTON pop. 2,726

EL PASO MEXICAN GRILLE
540/298-8861
Mexican. Casual Dining. **Address:** 245 S Stuart Ave 22827

GOODFELLAS
540/298-1001
Italian. Casual Dining. **Address:** 100 S Stuart Ave 22827

LOG CABIN BARBECUE
540/289-9400
Barbecue. Quick Serve. **Address:** 11672 Spotswood Tr 22827

EMPORIA (I-9) pop. 5,927, elev. 112'

Emporia was founded in 1887 from the merger of the towns of Hicksford and Belfield. While it has a population of less than 6,000, the small community is a busy commercial hub with many restaurants, hotels and stores, thanks to its location at the crossroads of I-95, US 58 and US 301.

COUNTRY INN & SUITES BY CARLSON EMPORIA
434/336-0001
Hotel. **Address:** 107 Sadler Ln 23847

FAIRFIELD INN & SUITES BY MARRIOTT EMPORIA/I-95
(434)348-3800
Hotel. **Address:** 104 W Cloverleaf Dr 23847

> **AAA Benefit:**
> Members save 5% or more!

HAMPTON INN BY HILTON   (434)634-9200

Hotel
$109-$159

AAA Benefit: Members save up to 10%!

Address: 898 Wiggins Rd 23847 **Location:** I-95 exit 11B, just w on US 58. **Facility:** 85 units. 5 stories, interior corridors. **Terms:** 1-7 night minimum stay, cancellation fee imposed. **Pool:** heated indoor. **Activities:** exercise room. **Guest Services:** valet laundry. *(See ad this page.)*

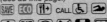
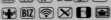

HOLIDAY INN EXPRESS HOTEL & SUITES
(434)336-9999

Hotel
$75-$159

Address: 1350 W Atlantic St 23847 **Location:** I-95 exit 11B, just w on US 58. **Facility:** 78 units. 3 stories, interior corridors. **Terms:** cancellation fee imposed. **Pool:** heated indoor. **Activities:** exercise room. **Guest Services:** coin laundry. **Featured Amenity:** full hot breakfast.

SLEEP INN   (434)348-3900

Hotel
$89-$159

Address: 899 Wiggins Rd 23847 **Location:** I-95 exit 11B, just e on US 58, then just s. **Facility:** 64 units. 4 stories, interior corridors. **Amenities:** safes. **Activities:** exercise room. **Guest Services:** coin laundry. **Featured Amenity:** continental breakfast.

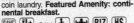

THE BANK BY KAHILL'S   434/336-1232
American. Casual Dining. **Address:** 401 S Main St 23847

LOGAN'S DINER   434/634-5512
Regional American. Casual Dining. **Address:** 414 S Main St 23847

EXMORE pop. 1,460

HAMPTON INN & SUITES BY HILTON EXMORE/EASTERN SHORE   (757)442-7722
Hotel. **Address:** 4129 Lankford Hwy 23350

AAA Benefit: Members save up to 10%!

HOLIDAY INN EXPRESS & SUITES   757/442-5522
Hotel. **Address:** 3446 Lankford Hwy 23350

EL MAGUEY AUTHENTIC MEXICAN RESTAURANT
757/442-0000
Mexican. Casual Dining. **Address:** 2638 Lankford Hwy 23350

EXMORE DINER   757/442-2313
American. Casual Dining. **Address:** 4264 Main St 23350

FAIRFAX (B-12) pop. 22,565, elev. 365'
• Hotels p. 104 • Restaurants p. 105
• Hotels & Restaurants map & index p. 38

Located in prosperous, populous Fairfax County, Fairfax is the site of the original wills of George and Martha Washington; they are housed in the Judicial Center at 4110 Chain Bridge Rd.

Built in 1800, the original Fairfax County Courthouse at 4000 Chain Bridge Rd. has been used continuously except during the Civil War, when Union troops occupied the town and used it as a stable. A

▼ See AAA listing this page ▼

(See map & index p. 38.)

monument to the first Confederate officer killed during the Civil War stands on the courthouse grounds.

Ratcliffe-Allison House (Earp's Ordinary), built in the early 1800s, is on Main Street between University Drive and SR 123. In 1820 it began operating as a post office. The original half of the building reflects specifications that were set by the Virginia Assembly for houses built in 1805. Guided tours of the house are available Sat. 11-2, Apr.-Oct.; phone (703) 385-8414.

🕊 Celebrate Fairfax, a 3-day event occurring in early June, takes place on the grounds of the Fairfax County Government Center, 12000 Government Center Pkwy. The festivities include a carnival, live concerts on eight stages, fireworks, hands-on kids' activities and a petting zoo.

Central Fairfax Chamber of Commerce: 4031 University Dr., Suite 100, Fairfax, VA 22030. **Phone:** (703) 591-2450.

Self-guiding tours: The Fairfax Museum and Visitor Center publishes and distributes an illustrated brochure about local historic buildings and sites.

Shopping: Located at I-66 and US 50, Fair Oaks Mall (11750 Fair Oaks Mall) has more than 200 stores, including JCPenney, Lord & Taylor, Macy's and Sears.

NATIONAL FIREARMS MUSEUM is off I-66 exit 57A, .5 mi. e. on US 50, then .3 mi. n. to 11250 Waples Mill Rd., on the main floor of the National Rifle Association's headquarters. Fifteen galleries of displays feature antique firearms from wars significant in America's history, as well as modern engraved handguns. Life-size dioramas, historical replicas and guns previously belonging to celebrities also are exhibited.

Featured exhibits include Hollywood Guns, the Robert E. Petersen Gallery and the Kentucky Rifle: A Complete Narrative 1750-1850. **Hours:** Daily 9:30-5. Closed Christmas. **Cost:** Free. **Phone:** (703) 267-1600. 🍽

BEST WESTERN FAIRFAX   (703)591-5500   104

AAA Benefit: Members save 10% or more & earn 10% bonus points!

Motel
$80-$160

Address: 3535 Chain Bridge Rd 22030 **Location:** I-66 exit 60, 0.5 mi s on SR 123; jct US 29/50. **Facility:** 127 units. 2-3 stories (no elevator), exterior corridors. **Terms:** 3 day cancellation notice-fee imposed. **Pool:** outdoor. **Activities:** exercise room. **Guest Services:** valet and coin laundry.

CANDLEWOOD SUITES FAIRFAX-WASHINGTON, D.C.
703/359-4490   110

🔶🔶 Extended Stay Hotel. **Address:** 11400 Random Hills Rd 22030

COMFORT INN UNIVERSITY CENTER   (703)591-5900   112

🔶🔶 Hotel. **Address:** 11180 Fairfax Blvd 22030

COURTYARD BY MARRIOTT-FAIR OAKS
(703)273-6161   109

Hotel
$61-$273

COURTYARD Marriott

AAA Benefit: Members save 5% or more!

Address: 11220 Lee Jackson Memorial Hwy 22030 **Location:** I-66 exit 57A, 0.5 mi se on US 50; 0.8 mi nw of jct US 29. **Facility:** 144 units. 3 stories, interior corridors. **Terms:** check-in 4 pm, cancellation fee imposed. **Pool:** heated indoor. **Activities:** exercise room. **Guest Services:** valet and coin laundry, boarding pass kiosk. **Featured Amenity:** full hot breakfast.

EXTENDED STAY AMERICA WASHINGTON DC-FAIRFAX
(703)359-5000   103

🔶🔶 Extended Stay Hotel. **Address:** 3997 Fair Ridge Dr 22033

EXTENDED STAY AMERICA-WASHINGTON DC-FAIRFAX-FAIR OAKS
(703)273-3444   108

🔶🔶 Extended Stay Motel. **Address:** 12104 Monument Dr 22033

EXTENDED STAY AMERICA WASHINGTON DC-FALLS CHURCH-MERRIFIELD
(703)204-0088   101

🔶🔶 Extended Stay Hotel. **Address:** 8281 Willow Oaks Corporate Dr 22031

FAIRFAX MARRIOTT AT FAIR OAKS
(703)352-2525   107

Hotel
$68-$282

MARRIOTT

AAA Benefit: Members save 5% or more!

Address: 11787 Lee Jackson Memorial Hwy 22030 **Location:** I-66 exit 57B, just w on US 50. Adjacent to Fair Oaks Mall. **Facility:** 316 units. 6 stories, interior corridors. **Terms:** check-in 4 pm, cancellation fee imposed. **Activities:** exercise room. **Guest Services:** complimentary and valet laundry.

HAMPTON BY HILTON-FAIRFAX   (703)385-2600   111

🔶🔶🔶 Hotel. **Address:** 10860 Fairfax Blvd 22030

AAA Benefit: Members save up to 10%!

HILTON GARDEN INN FAIRFAX   (703)385-7774   102

🔶🔶🔶 Hotel. **Address:** 3950 Fair Ridge Dr 22033

AAA Benefit: Members save up to 10%!

HOLIDAY INN EXPRESS FAIRFAX   703/359-2888   105

🔶🔶 Hotel. **Address:** 10327 Fairfax Blvd 22030

(See map & index p. 38.)

HYATT HOUSE FALLS CHURCH/MERRIFIELD
(571)327-2277   100

Extended Stay Hotel
$99-$369

AAA Benefit: Members save 10%!

Address: 8296 Glass Alley 22031 **Location:** I-495 exit 50A, just w to SR 650, 0.6 mi n on SR 650, then just w on US 29. Located in Mosaic District, a retail, residential, restaurant, entertainment area. 🚇 Dunn Loring-Merrifield, 31. **Facility:** 148 units, some efficiencies. 7 stories, interior corridors. **Terms:** cancellation fee imposed. **Pool:** heated outdoor. **Activities:** exercise room. **Guest Services:** valet and coin laundry, area transportation. **Featured Amenity:** full hot breakfast.

HYATT REGENCY FAIRFAX   (703)818-1234   115

Hotel
$69-$259

HYATT REGENCY

AAA Benefit: Members save 10%!

Address: 12777 Fair Lakes Cir 22033 **Location:** I-66 exit 55 (SR 286/Fairfax County Pkwy N), just w, then just s. Located near shopping, restaurants and businesses. **Facility:** 316 units. 13 stories, interior corridors. **Terms:** cancellation fee imposed. **Amenities:** safes. **Pool:** heated indoor. **Activities:** hot tub, exercise room. **Guest Services:** complimentary and valet laundry.

  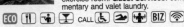

RESIDENCE INN BY MARRIOTT FAIRFAX CITY
(703)267-2525   106

Extended Stay Hotel
$89-$264

Residence Inn Marriott

AAA Benefit: Members save 5% or more!

Address: 3565 Chain Bridge Rd 22030 **Location:** I-66 exit 60, 0.5 mi s on SR 123; jct US 29/50. **Facility:** 155 efficiencies, some two bedrooms. 5 stories, interior corridors. **Terms:** cancellation fee imposed. **Amenities:** safes. **Pool:** heated outdoor. **Activities:** exercise room. **Guest Services:** valet and coin laundry. **Featured Amenity:** breakfast buffet.

🔗 **For complete hotel, dining and attraction listings: AAA.com/travelguides**

RESIDENCE INN BY MARRIOTT-FAIR LAKES
(703)266-4900   113

Extended Stay Hotel
$75-$251

Residence Inn Marriott

AAA Benefit: Members save 5% or more!

Address: 12815 Fair Lakes Pkwy 22033 **Location:** I-66 exit 55 (SR 286/Fairfax County Pkwy N), just w. Located near shopping, restaurants and businesses. **Facility:** 114 units, some two bedrooms, efficiencies and kitchens. 3 stories, interior corridors. **Terms:** cancellation fee imposed. **Pool:** heated outdoor. **Activities:** exercise room. **Guest Services:** valet and coin laundry. **Featured Amenity:** breakfast buffet.

SPRINGHILL SUITES BY MARRIOTT FAIRFAX/FAIR OAKS
(703)691-7880   114

Hotel. **Address:** 11191 Waples Mill Rd 22030

AAA Benefit: Members save 5% or more!

WHERE TO EAT

ANITA'S 703/385-2965
🌮🌮 Mexican. Casual Dining. **Address:** 10880 Lee Hwy 22030

ARIGATO SUSHI 703/352-9338   124
🌮🌮 Japanese Sushi. Casual Dining. **Address:** 11199-A Lee Hwy 22030

ARTIES 703/273-7600   115
🌮🌮 American. Casual Dining. **Address:** 3260 Old Lee Hwy 22030

THE AULD SHEBEEN 703/293-9600   127
🌮🌮 Irish. Casual Dining. **Address:** 3971 Chain Bridge Rd 22030

BELLISSIMO RESTAURANT 703/290-2067   128
🌮🌮🌮 Northern Italian. Fine Dining. **Address:** 10403 Main St 22030

BLUE IGUANA 703/502-8108   123
🌮🌮 American. Casual Dining. **Address:** 12727 Shoppes Ln 22033

BOLLYWOOD BISTRO 703/273-0031   125
🌮🌮 Indian Vegetarian. Casual Dining. **Address:** 3955 Chain Bridge Rd 22030

BOMBAY BISTRO 703/359-5810   117
🌮🌮 Indian. Casual Dining. **Address:** 3570 Chain Bridge Rd 22030

BRINE 703/280-1000   134
🌮🌮 Seafood. Casual Dining. **Address:** 2985 District Ave, Suite 120 22031

CANTINA D'ITALIA 703/631-2752
🌮🌮 Italian. Casual Dining. **Address:** 13015 Fair Lakes Shopping Center 22033

CHUTZPAH, A REAL NEW YORK DELI 703/385-8883   118
🌮🌮 Deli. Quick Serve. **Address:** 12214 Fairfax Towne Center 22033

COASTAL FLATS 571/522-6300   121
🌮🌮 American. Casual Dining. **Address:** 11901 Grand Commons Ave 22030

(See map & index p. 38.)

DOLCE VITA   703/385-1530 (119)
♦♦♦ Italian. Casual Dining. **Address:** 10824 Fairfax Blvd 22030

GLORY DAYS GRILL   703/204-0900
♦♦ American. Casual Dining. **Address:** 3059 Nutley St 22031

HARD TIMES CAFE   703/267-9590
♦♦ American. Casual Dining. **Address:** 4069 Chain Bridge Rd 22030

JAIPUR ROYAL INDIAN CUISINE   703/766-1111 (114)
♦♦♦ Indian. Fine Dining. **Address:** 9401 Lee Hwy, Unit 105 22031

LEBANESE KITCHEN   703/378-5001 (116)
♦♦ Lebanese. Casual Dining. **Address:** 13031 Lee Jackson Memorial Hwy 22033

MAZADAR RESTAURANT   571/432-0101 (132)
♦♦ Middle Eastern. Casual Dining. **Address:** 11725 Lee Hwy 22030

OZZIE'S GOOD EATS   571/321-8000 (120)
♦♦ Italian. Casual Dining. **Address:** 11880 Grand Commons Ave 22030

PAD THAI RESTAURANT   703/591-2525 (126)
♦♦ Thai. Casual Dining. **Address:** 11199 Lee Hwy, Suite E 22030

RED APRON   703/676-3550 (111)
♦ Sandwiches Hot Dogs. Quick Serve. **Address:** 8298 Glass Alley 22031

RUTH'S CHRIS STEAK HOUSE   703/266-1004 (122)
♦♦♦ Steak. Fine Dining. **Address:** 4100 Monument Corner Dr 22030

SILVER DINER   703/359-5941
♦♦ American. Casual Dining. **Address:** 12250 Fair Lakes Pkwy 22033

SISTERS THAI-THE LIVING ROOM CAFE
703/267-9619 (129)
♦♦ Thai. Casual Dining. **Address:** 4004 University Dr 22030

SISTERS THAI - THE ORDINARY CAFE   703/280-0429 (113)
♦♦ Thai. Casual Dining. **Address:** 2985 District Ave 22031

TONY'S NEW YORK PIZZA   703/502-0808 (133)
♦ Italian Pizza. Casual Dining. **Address:** 13087 Fair Lakes Shopping Center 22033

TRUE FOOD KITCHEN   571/326-1616 (112)
♦♦♦ Natural/Organic Vegetarian. Casual Dining. **Address:** 2910 District Ave, Suite 170 22031

TSUNAMI   703/449-8404 (131)
♦♦ Japanese Sushi. Casual Dining. **Address:** 13039 Fair Lakes Shopping Center 22033

VILLA MOZART   703/691-4747 (130)
♦♦♦ Northern Italian. Fine Dining. **Address:** 4009 Chain Bridge Rd 22030

FALLS CHURCH (B-12) pop. 12,332, elev. 364'

• Hotels & Restaurants map & index p. 38

A Fairfax County suburb, Falls Church dates from the mid-1700s and the formation of Truro Parish, for which George Washington was a vestryman 1762-84.

Falls Church Chamber of Commerce: 417 W. Broad St., Suite 205, Falls Church, VA 22046. **Phone:** (703) 532-1050.

BEST WESTERN FALLS CHURCH INN
(703)532-9000 (91)

Hotel
$89-$149

AAA Benefit: Members save 10% or more & earn 10% bonus points!

Address: 6633 Arlington Blvd 22042 **Location:** I-495 exit 50B, 2.6 mi e on US 50. Located in a commercial area. **Facility:** 106 units. 2 stories (no elevator), interior corridors. **Terms:** 3 day cancellation notice-fee imposed. **Amenities:** safes. **Pool:** outdoor. **Activities:** exercise room. **Guest Services:** valet laundry, area transportation.

COMFORT INN ARLINGTON BOULEVARD
(703)534-9100 (90)
♦♦ Hotel. **Address:** 6111 Arlington Blvd 22044

FALLS CHURCH MARRIOTT FAIRVIEW PARK
(703)849-9400 (94)

♦♦♦♦
Hotel
$65-$305

MARRIOTT
AAA Benefit: Members save 5% or more!

Address: 3111 Fairview Park Dr 22042 **Location:** I-495 exit 50B, just se of US 50. Located in a business park setting. **Facility:** 395 units. 15 stories, interior corridors. **Terms:** check-in 4 pm, 3 day cancellation notice-fee imposed. **Pool:** heated outdoor, heated indoor. **Activities:** hot tub, exercise room. **Guest Services:** complimentary and valet laundry, boarding pass kiosk, area transportation.

HAMPTON INN & SUITES BY HILTON FALLS CHURCH
703/538-1000 (89)
♦♦♦ Hotel. **Address:** 6430 Arlington Blvd 22042

AAA Benefit: Members save up to 10%!

HILTON GARDEN INN FALLS CHURCH   (703)237-8700 (87)
♦♦♦ Hotel. **Address:** 706 W Broad St 22046

AAA Benefit: Members save up to 10%!

HOMEWOOD SUITES BY HILTON-FALLS CHURCH
(703)560-6644 (92)
♦♦♦ Extended Stay Hotel. **Address:** 8130 Porter Rd 22042

AAA Benefit: Members save up to 10%!

GET THE APP
AAA.com/mobile • CAA.ca/mobile

(See map & index p. 38.)

RESIDENCE INN BY MARRIOTT FAIRFAX-MERRIFIELD
(703)573-5200   **93**

▼▼▼
Extended Stay Hotel
$80-$348

Residence Inn Marriott

AAA Benefit: Members save 5% or more!

Address: 8125 Gatehouse Rd 22042 **Location:** I-495 exit 50A, just w to SR 650 N. Located in a commercial area. Dunn Loring-Merrifield, 31. **Facility:** 159 units, some two bedrooms, efficiencies and kitchens. 4 stories, interior corridors. **Terms:** cancellation fee imposed. **Pool:** outdoor. **Activities:** hot tub, exercise room. **Guest Services:** valet and coin laundry, boarding pass kiosk, area transportation. **Featured Amenity:** breakfast buffet.

SAVE ▯ CALL ☒ ➔ ☒ BIZ ☎ ☒ ☐ ☐ / SOME UNITS ☒ ☒

TOWNEPLACE SUITES BY MARRIOTT-FALLS CHURCH
(703)237-6172   **88**

▼▼ Extended Stay Hotel. **Address:** 205 Hillwood Ave 22046

AAA Benefit: Members save 5% or more!

THE WESTIN TYSONS CORNER
703/893-1340   **86**

▼▼▼
Hotel
Rates not provided

WESTIN HOTELS & RESORTS

AAA Benefit: Members save 5% or more!

Address: 7801 Leesburg Pike 22043 **Location:** I-495 exit 47B, just e on SR 7. Located in a business area, near shopping malls. Tysons Corner, 101. **Facility:** 407 units. 9-11 stories, interior corridors. **Parking:** on-site (fee) and valet. **Amenities:** safes. **Pool:** heated indoor. **Activities:** hot tub, exercise room. **Guest Services:** valet laundry, area transportation.

SAVE ECO ▯ ☒ ☒ ➔ ☒ BIZ ☒ ☎ ☒ ☒ ☐ / SOME UNITS ☒ ☐ ☒

WHERE TO EAT

2941 RESTAURANT   703/270-1500   **94**
▼▼▼▼ New American. Fine Dining. **Address:** 2941 Fairview Park Dr 22042

ARGIA'S   703/534-1033   **87**
▼▼ Italian. Casual Dining. **Address:** 124 N Washington St 22046

CELEBRITY DELLY   703/573-9002   **55**
▼▼ Deli. Quick Serve. **Address:** 7263-A Arlington Blvd 22042

CITY DINER   703/671-4108   **100**
▼▼ American. Casual Dining. **Address:** 5616 Leesburg Pike 22041

DUANGRAT'S   703/820-5775   **98**
▼▼ Thai. Casual Dining. **Address:** 5878 Leesburg Pike 22041

FOUR SISTERS RESTAURANT   703/539-8566   **93**
▼▼ Vietnamese. Casual Dining. **Address:** 8190 Strawberry Ln, Suite 1 22042

HAANDI   703/533-3501   **86**
▼▼ Indian. Casual Dining. **Address:** 1222 W Broad St 22046

MARK'S DUCK HOUSE   703/532-2125   **89**
▼▼▼ Chinese Dim Sum. Casual Dining. **Address:** 6184-A Arlington Blvd 22044

PEKING GOURMET INN   703/671-8088   **96**
▼▼ Chinese. Casual Dining. **Address:** 6029 Leesburg Pike 22041

PISTONE'S ITALIAN INN   703/533-1885   **88**
▼▼ Italian. Casual Dining. **Address:** 6320 Arlington Blvd 22044

PRESENT RESTAURANT   703/531-1881   **90**
▼▼▼ Vietnamese. Casual Dining. **Address:** 6678 Arlington Blvd 22042

RAAGA   703/998-7000   **99**
▼▼ Indian. Fine Dining. **Address:** 5872 Leesburg Pike 22041

RABIENG   703/671-4222   **97**
▼▼ Thai. Casual Dining. **Address:** 5892 Leesburg Pike 22041

SEA PEARL   703/372-5161   **92**
▼▼▼ Seafood Sushi. Casual Dining. **Address:** 8191 Strawberry Ln, Suite 2 22042

SILVER DINER   703/204-0812
▼▼ American. Casual Dining. **Address:** 8150 Porter Rd 22042

SWEETWATER TAVERN   703/645-8100
▼▼ American. Casual Dining. **Address:** 3066 Gatehouse Plaza 22042

TARA THAI   703/506-9788
▼▼ Thai. Casual Dining. **Address:** 7501-E Leesburg Pike 22043

TRIO GRILL   703/992-0900   **91**
▼▼▼ American. Casual Dining. **Address:** 8100 Lee Hwy 22042

FALMOUTH (C-11) pop. 4,274, elev. 59'

Chartered in 1720, Falmouth once rivaled Fredericksburg in commercial importance. During the Revolution, James Hunter's ironworks ran full tilt to supply the American Army and Navy with such articles as camp kettles, bayonets and anchors. Tapping into Falmouth's thriving industry, resident Basil Gordon became one of America's first millionaires.

Falmouth is now a subdued but charming relic of its past. George Washington reportedly received his primary education in the town. Noted Falmouth natives include Confederate Secretary of War James Alexander Seddon, and Dr. Kate Waller Barrett, a staunch crusader for social reform. Falmouth served as the headquarters for the Federal Army before and after the Battle of Fredericksburg.

SAVE **THE GARI MELCHERS HOME AND STUDIO AT BELMONT** is s.w. of jct. US 1 and US 17N at 224 Washington St. (SR 1001). The 18th-century manor house, set on 27 acres overlooking the Rappahannock River, is preserved as a memorial to its former owner Gari Melchers, an American Impressionist artist who died in 1932. He acquired the house in 1916 as a country retreat. The house is furnished with antiques and art collected by Melchers and his wife. More than 75 of his paintings are displayed in his studio.

When a road trip stalls and you request AAA/CAA assistance, opt to receive text updates. Messages:

- Confirm receipt of your service request

- Alert you when a service vehicle is en route

- Provide the service vehicle's estimated arrival time

Opt in and stay informed.

AAA.com/mobile | CAA.ca/mobile

A visitor center, which doubles as the Stafford County information center, is located in the former carriage house and offers a 12-minute orientation video. Picnic tables are available. Pets are permitted only in designated areas. **Time:** Allow 1 hour minimum. **Hours:** Daily 10-5, Apr.-Oct.; 10-4, rest of year. The last tour departs 30 minutes before closing. Closed Jan. 1, Easter, July 4, Thanksgiving, Christmas Eve, Christmas and Dec. 31. **Cost:** $10; free (ages 0-18 with paying adult, limit two; each additional child $5 each). **Phone:** (540) 654-1015 for the information line, or (540) 654-1844 for the visitor center. 🐾 🎪

FANCY GAP pop. 237

DOE RUN LODGING AT GROUNDHOG MOUNTAIN
276/398-4099
▼▼ Condominium. **Address:** 27 Buck Hollar Rd 24328

FARMVILLE pop. 8,216

HAMPTON INN   (434)392-8826
▼▼▼ Hotel. **Address:** 300 Sun-
chase Blvd 23901

AAA Benefit:
Members save up to 10%!

QUALITY INN   (434)392-8163
▼▼ Hotel. **Address:** 2108 S Main St 23901

WHERE TO EAT

CHARLEY'S WATERFRONT CAFE & WINE BAR   434/392-1566
▼▼ American. Casual Dining. **Address:** 201 B Mill St 23901

MACADO'S   434/392-8077
▼▼ American. Casual Dining. **Address:** 200 E 3rd St 23901

FERRUM (H-6) pop. 2,043, elev. 1,300'

Ferrum College was founded in 1913 by the Woman's Missionary Union of the Methodist Church. Highlighting the region's folk culture, the Blue Ridge Folklife Festival takes place on campus the fourth Saturday in October.

BLUE RIDGE INSTITUTE AND MUSEUM is on SR 40W on the campus of Ferrum College. Preserving the heritage of the Blue Ridge region, the museum houses both permanent and changing exhibits about Blue Ridge folklife. The Blue Ridge Farm Museum, a re-created German-American farm, illustrates early 19th-century life complete with period furnishings and costumed interpreters.

Time: Allow 2 hours minimum. **Hours:** Mon.-Sat. 10-4, Sun. 1-5, mid-May to mid-Aug.; Mon.-Sat. 10-4, rest of year. Closed Thanksgiving, Christmas Eve and Christmas. Hours vary during holiday weeks; phone ahead to confirm schedule. **Cost:** Blue Ridge Institute and Museum galleries free. Farm museum $4. **Phone:** (540) 365-4416.

FISHERSVILLE pop. 7,462

HAMPTON INN WAYNESBORO/STUARTS DRAFT
(540)213-9500
▼▼▼ Hotel. **Address:** 15 Four
Square Ln 22939

AAA Benefit:
Members save up to 10%!

FLINT HILL pop. 209

GRIFFIN TAVERN & RESTAURANT   540/675-3227
▼▼ American. Casual Dining. **Address:** 659 Zachary Taylor Hwy 22627

FLOYD pop. 425, elev. 2,493'

MICKEY G'S BISTRO   540/745-2208
▼▼ Italian. Casual Dining. **Address:** 113 Parkview Rd 24091

THE RESTAURANT AT CHATEAU MORRISETTE
540/593-2865

▼▼▼
**Continental
Fine Dining
$16-$36**

AAA Inspector Notes: Guests can experience elegant dining in a romantic French country atmosphere. The hillside location is scenic and charming. Nicely presented farm-raised catfish, game and seafood dishes grace the menu, as do some heavenly desserts. Patio seating is an option in nice weather. **Features:** beer & wine, patio dining, Sunday brunch. **Reservations:** suggested. **Address:** 287 Winery Rd SW 24091 **Location:** Blue Ridge Parkway; between mileposts 171 and 172, exit w on Black Ridge Rd, just s on CR 777 (Winery Rd), then 0.3 mi s; at winery. L D

TUGGLES GAP RESTAURANT   540/745-3402
▼▼ American. Casual Dining. **Address:** 3351 Parkway Ln S 24091

FORT LEE (B-1) elev. 165'

Fort Lee, 2 miles east of Petersburg, is the only U.S. Army Quartermaster installation and training center in the nation. Formed in 1775, the Quartermaster Corps is a combat support branch responsible for providing food, fuel and field services to army soldiers. On display on the grounds of Fort Lee are tanks, missiles and other items from the U.S. Army Ordnance Training and Heritage Center's collections.

U.S. ARMY QUARTERMASTER MUSEUM is 1 blk. inside the main gate of Fort Lee. The army's oldest logistic branch, the Quartermaster Corps has fed, clothed and equipped American soldiers since 1775. A variety of exhibits portraying the corps' mission are featured, along with presidential flags, Civil War memorabilia, Gen. George S. Patton's jeep, Gen. Dwight D. Eisenhower's uniforms and Gen. Ulysses S. Grant's saddle. **Note:** A photo ID and an oito background check is required for admission to Fort Lee. **Hours:** Mon.-Fri. 10-5, Sat. 11-5. Closed Jan. 1, Thanksgiving and Christmas. **Cost:** Donations. **Phone:** (804) 734-4203.

FREDERICKSBURG (D-11) pop. 24,286, elev. 69'
• Hotels p. 115 • Restaurants p. 116
• Hotels & Restaurants map & index p. 113

Fredericksburg was officially founded and given its present name in 1728, even though settlers had built a fort as early as 1676. Its location in a valley at the

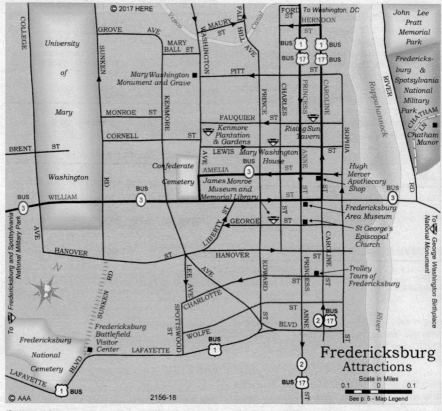

Fredericksburg Attractions

Scale in Miles
0.1   0   0.1

See p. 6 - Map Legend

© 2017 HERE

© AAA   2156-18

(See map & index p. 113.)

head of navigation on the Rappahannock River led to the city's emergence as a prosperous port.

Fredericksburg was George Washington's boyhood home, his mother's last home and the home of his sister, Betty Washington Lewis. James Monroe set up his first law office in the city in 1786.

Between 1861 and 1865 Fredericksburg was an armed camp and the scene of violent battles. By the end of the Civil War it was desolate, its houses torn by shot and shell and the dead buried in its streets.

The Battle of Fredericksburg was fought on Dec. 13, 1862. The Union Army of 142,551 under Gen. Ambrose Everett Burnside camped on Stafford Heights on the north side of the river. The Confederate force of 91,760 under Gen. Robert E. Lee was entrenched west and south of the town.

The Union troops made repeated unsuccessful attacks on the Confederate fortifications, resulting in Burnside's retreat across the river. On the Union side the dead and wounded numbered 12,653; Confederate casualties totaled 5,309.

After the Battle of Chancellorsville the city served as a hospital for the Confederate wounded; it provided a similar service for the Union forces after the Battle of the Wilderness. The Gothic Revival Fredericksburg

Courthouse, erected 1851-52, is still in use today. Its historic documents include the will of Mary Washington. The bell was made by the Paul Revere foundry.

From Fredericksburg SR 3 leads down the historic Northern Neck past such sites as George Washington Birthplace National Monument, Robert E. Lee's birthplace at Stratford and George Washington's mother's birthplace near Lancaster.

Another historic, scenic route is US 17, which follows the Rappahannock River to Tappahannock and Gloucester, crosses the York River to Yorktown and the Colonial Parkway, and continues to Williamsburg.

Fredericksburg Visitor Center: 706 Caroline St., Fredericksburg, VA 22401. **Phone:** (540) 373-1776 or (800) 678-4748.

Self-guiding tours: Brochures and maps outlining self-guiding tours of historic Fredericksburg and the area are available from the visitor center, where a 14-minute orientation film is shown. Brochures, maps and area information also are available at the Spotsylvania County Visitor Center, 4704 Southpoint Pkwy.; phone (800) 678-4748 or (800) 654-4118.

Shopping: Old Town Fredericksburg boasts an array of boutiques, restaurants, art galleries and antiques dealers. At I-95 and SR 3, you'll find the Spotsylvania Mall (137 Spotsylvania Mall Dr.), which

(See map & index p. 113.)

offers more than 120 shops, including Belk, JC-Penney, Macy's and Sears. Across the street from the mall is Central Park (1541 Carl D. Silver Pkwy.), a massive open-air shopping center with restaurants, a movie theater, a handful of specialty stores and such recognizable names as Kirkland's, Kohl's, Lane Bryant, Old Navy, Talbots and Ulta.

INSIDER INFO:
Combination Tickets

The Timeless Ticket to Historic Fredericksburg has no expiration date and includes admission to Fredericksburg area battlefields, the Fredericksburg Area Museum, George Washington's Boyhood Home at Ferry Farm, Hugh Mercer Apothecary Shop, James Monroe Museum and Memorial Library, Kenmore Plantation & Gardens, Mary Washington House, Rising Sun Tavern and The Gari Melchers Home and Studio at Belmont (in Falmouth). The combined admission is $32; free (ages 6-18 with paying adult, limit one per adult; each additional child ages 6-18 is $10).

Another discount option, the Day Pass is valid for a 24-hour period and includes all of the attractions listed above for a combined admission of $16; free (ages 6-18 with paying adult, limit one per adult; each additional child ages 6-18 is $5).

Passes are available at the Fredericksburg or Spotsylvania visitor centers. Phone (000) 678-4748 or (800) 654-4118.

Note: It is a good idea to verify hours and admission fees in advance.

FREDERICKSBURG AREA MUSEUM is at 907 Princess Anne St. The Town Hall, once the center of the city's social, commercial and legal activity, now hosts permanent and changing exhibitions.

The Catherine W. Jones McKann Center features six multimedia exhibits designed to encourage engagement and hands-on learning for all ages. Permanent exhibits interpret the history of both the structure and the region. Temporary and traveling exhibitions reflect the art and artists of the region. **Time:** Allow 30 minutes minimum. **Hours:** Thurs.-Mon. 10-5, Closed Jan. 1, Thanksgiving, Christmas Eve, Christmas and Dec. 31. **Cost:** $5, $4 (ages 65+); $3 (students and teachers with ID); free (ages 0-6). **Phone:** (540) 371-3037.

THE GARI MELCHERS HOME AND STUDIO AT BELMONT—see Falmouth p. 107.

SAVE **HUGH MERCER APOTHECARY SHOP,** at Caroline and Amelia sts., interprets Colonial medical practices in a restored 18th-century building. Living-history presentations and demonstrations with costumed guides discuss once-popular treatments for conditions like "female hysteria" and highlight a variety of medicinal and surgical supplies—from leeches to lancets. A physic garden of medicinal herbs adjoins the building where Dr. Hugh Mercer worked prior to joining the Continental Army as a brigadier general in 1776.

Time: Allow 30 minutes minimum. **Hours:** Mon.-Sat. 9-4, Sun. noon-4, Mar.-Oct.; Mon.-Sat. 11-4, Sun. noon-4, rest of year. Closed Jan. 1, Thanksgiving, Christmas Eve, Christmas and Dec. 31. **Cost:** $7; $3 (ages 6-18). **Phone:** (540) 373-3362 or (800) 678-4748.

GEM SAVE **JAMES MONROE MUSEUM AND MEMORIAL LIBRARY** is at 908 Charles St. Monroe owned this property 1786-92 and probably used it while practicing law as a young attorney in Fredericksburg. The museum contains what is said to be the largest collection of Monroe-related material in the country, including belongings of President and Mrs. Monroe and the Louis XVI furniture they bought in Paris when he was minister to France 1794-97.

The collection includes the desk on which Monroe prepared his 1823 address to Congress, portions of which became known as the Monroe Doctrine. Also displayed are the jewelry and personal effects of Monroe's wife, Elizabeth. A library contains historical manuscripts relating to the president and his era. A bronze bust of the fifth president is in the walled garden.

Hours: Mon.-Sat. 10-5, Sun. 1-5, Mar.-Nov.; Mon.-Sat. 10-4, Sun. 1-4, rest of year. Closed Jan. 1, Thanksgiving, Christmas Eve and Christmas. **Cost:** $6; $5 (ages 65+ and military with ID); $2 (ages 6-17); free (active military with ID and their families Memorial Day-Labor Day). Guided tours $7; $3 (ages 6-17). **Phone:** (540) 654-1043.

GEM **KENMORE PLANTATION & GARDENS** Is at 1201 Washington Ave. Kenmore was the home of Col. Fielding Lewis and his wife, Betty Washington Lewis, sister of George Washington. Built in 1775, this Colonial home is an example of a Georgian manor house. The building was used as a hospital during the Civil War. The house is noted for the elaborate, decorative plasterwork on its ceilings and over its fireplaces.

The Bissell Gallery features an exhibit about the lives of Fielding and Betty Lewis as well as a diorama of Fredericksburg in the late 1700s. There also is an interactive portion of the exhibit for children. The grounds include a wilderness walking trail.

Time: Allow 2 hours minimum. **Hours:** Mon.-Sat. 10-5, Sun. noon-5, Mar.-Oct.; Mon.-Sat. 10-4, Sun. noon-4, Nov.-Dec. Guided house tours daily every 30 minutes. Closed Easter, Thanksgiving, Christmas Eve and Dec. 31. **Cost:** $12; $11 (ages 60+ and military with ID); $6 (ages 6-17). Combination ticket with George Washington's Boyhood Home at Ferry Farm $19; $8.50 (ages 6-17). **Phone:** (540) 373-3381. GT

(See map & index p. 113.)

MARY WASHINGTON HOUSE is at 1200 Charles St. George Washington bought the house in 1772 for his mother, Mary Ball Washington, who lived here until her death in 1789. Washington visited his mother in March 1789 prior to being elected president. He was seeking her blessing on the next phase of his life, which she readily gave. She died a few months later. The home contains some of Mrs. Washington's favorite possessions. Guides are dressed in period costumes.

Hours: Mon.-Sat. 10-4, Sun. noon-4, Mar.-Oct.; Mon.-Sat. 11-4, Sun. noon-4, rest of year. Closed Jan. 1, Thanksgiving, Christmas Eve, Christmas and Dec. 31. Phone ahead to confirm schedule. **Cost:** $7; $3 (ages 6-18); free (ages 0-5 and active military with ID). **Phone:** (540) 373-1569. GT

RISING SUN TAVERN is at 1304 Caroline St. George Washington's youngest brother, Charles, built the landmark in the 1760s as his private residence. It became a tavern in 1793. Costumed "tavern wenches" and male "indentured servants" tell of a typical stay at a Colonial tavern for upper, middle and lower classes. **Hours:** Mon.-Sat. 10-5, Sun. noon-4, Mar.-Oct.; Mon.-Sat. 11-4, Sun. noon-4, rest of year. Closed Jan. 1, Thanksgiving, Christmas Eve, Christmas and Dec. 31. Phone ahead to confirm schedule. **Cost:** $7; $6 (active military with ID); $3 (ages 6-18); free (ages 0-5 and active military with ID). **Phone:** (540) 371-1494.

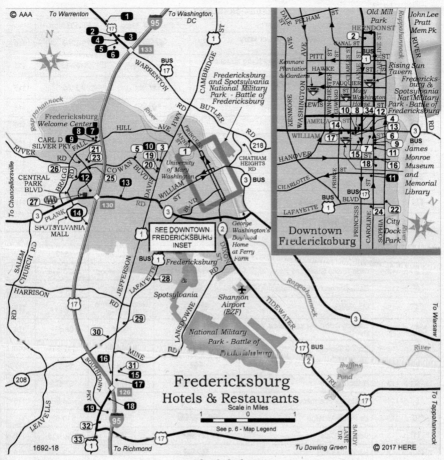

Fredericksburg

This index helps you "spot" where approved hotels and restaurants are located on the corresponding detailed maps. Hotel daily rate range is for comparison only. Restaurant price range is a combination of lunch and/or dinner. Turn to the listing page for more information and consult display ads for special promotions.

For more details, rates and reservations: AAA.com/travelguides/hotels

FREDERICKSBURG

Map Page	Hotels	Diamond Rated	Rate Range	Page
1 this page	Country Inn & Suites By Carlson	◈◈◈	Rates not provided	115
2 this page	Sleep Inn	◈◈	$52-$124	116
3 this page	**Holiday Inn Express & Suites**	◈◈◈	$85-$145 SAVE	116
4 this page	Quality Inn Fredericksburg	◈◈	$72-$103	116
5 this page	Comfort Suites	◈◈◈	$89-$194	115
6 this page	Wingate by Wyndham	◈◈◈	Rates not provided	116
7 this page	Hilton Garden Inn	◈◈◈	$109-$129	115
8 this page	**Homewood Suites by Hilton at Celebrate Virginia**	◈◈◈	Rates not provided SAVE	116
9 this page	**Hampton Inn & Suites at Celebrate Virginia**	◈◈◈	$109-$169 SAVE	115

FREDERICKSBURG (cont'd)

Map Page	Hotels (cont'd)	Diamond Rated	Rate Range	Page
10 p. 113	Hyatt Place Fredericksburg at Mary Washington	◆◆◆	$79-$269 SAVE	116
11 p. 113	Courtyard by Marriott Fredericksburg Historic District	◆◆◆	$109-$229	115
12 p. 113	Fredericksburg Hospitality House Hotel & Conference Center	◆◆	$99-$169 SAVE	115
13 p. 113	Best Western Fredericksburg	◆◆	$79-$150 SAVE	115
14 p. 113	Residence Inn by Marriott	◆◆◆	$110-$283	116
15 p. 113	Hampton Inn & Suites of Fredericksburg South	◆◆◆	$92-$159	115
16 p. 113	Country Inn & Suites By Carlson, Fredericksburg South	◆◆◆	$79-$179	115
17 p. 113	Fairfield Inn & Suites by Marriott	◆◆◆	$83-$159	115
18 p. 113	Candlewood Suites	◆◆◆	Rates not provided SAVE	115
19 p. 113	Comfort Suites Fredericksburg	◆◆◆	$99-$184	115

Map Page	Restaurants	Diamond Rated	Cuisine	Price Range	Page
1 p. 113	Mason-Dixon Cafe	◆◆	American	$18	117
2 p. 113	Olde Towne Steak and Seafood	◆◆	Steak Seafood	$26-$48	117
3 p. 113	Baba Ganoush Mediterranean Grill	◆	Indian	$6-$13	116
4 p. 113	Mercantile	◆◆	Natural/Organic Breakfast	$9-$13	117
5 p. 113	Basilico Italian Market & New York Deli	◆◆	Italian	$8-$11	116
6 p. 113	Cork & Table	◆◆	American	$19-$25	116
7 p. 113	Sprelly	◆	Sandwiches	$5-$10	117
8 p. 113	Bistro Bethem	◆◆◆	American	$7-$28	116
9 p. 113	Goolrick's Pharmacy	◆	American	$4-$7	116
10 p. 113	La Petite Auberge	◆◆◆	French	$10-$31	117
11 p. 113	Bangkok Cafe	◆◆	Thai	$10-$19	116
12 p. 113	Fahrenheit 132	◆◆	Steak	$18-$38	116
13 p. 113	Castiglia's Italian Restaurant & Pizzeria	◆◆	Italian	$10-$17	116
14 p. 113	Kybecca	◆◆	American	$14-$21	117
15 p. 113	Foode	◆◆	Natural/Organic	$7-$24	116
16 p. 113	Sammy T's	◆◆	American	$6-$14	117
17 p. 113	Ristorante Renato	◆◆	Italian	$8-$27	117
18 p. 113	Legume Kitchen & Bar	◆◆	Vegetarian Seafood	$10-$18	117
19 p. 113	Allman's Barbeque	◆	Barbecue	$5-$11	116
20 p. 113	Miso Asian Grill & Sushi Bar	◆◆◆	Asian Sushi	$8-$36	117
21 p. 113	Bonefish Grill	◆◆◆	Seafood	$15-$31	116
22 p. 113	Brock's Riverside Grill	◆◆	American	$6-$28	116
23 p. 113	Peter Chang China Cafe	◆◆	Chinese	$12-$22	117
24 p. 113	The Bavarian Chef	◆◆◆	German	$8-$36	116
25 p. 113	Tito's Diner	◆◆	American	$7-$16	117
26 p. 113	Guru Indian Cuisine	◆◆	Indian	$9-$15	116
27 p. 113	Brother's Pizza	◆	Italian Pizza	$4-$15	116

Map Page	Restaurants (cont'd)	Diamond Rated	Cuisine	Price Range	Page
28 p. 113	El Asador Restaurant	◆◆	Latin American	$7-$17	116
29 p. 113	Garnjana Thai	◆◆	Thai	$8-$21	116
30 p. 113	Fish N' Grill	◆◆	Soul Food Seafood	$7-$19	116
31 p. 113	Pancho Villa Mexican Restaurant	◆◆	Mexican	$5-$14	117
32 p. 113	Kappa Garden Sushi Bistro	◆◆	Japanese	$7-$18	116
33 p. 113	Aubergine Thai	◆◆	Thai	$6-$17	116
34 p. 113	Here & Abroad Bistro & Bakery	◆	Breads/Pastries Sandwiches	$5-$9	116

BEST WESTERN FREDERICKSBURG
(540)371-5050 **13**

Motel
$79-$150

Best Western. AAA Benefit: Members save 10% or more & earn 10% bonus points!

Address: 2205 Plank Rd 22401 **Location:** I-95 exit 130A (US 1), 0.3 mi e. **Facility:** 108 units. 2 stories (no elevator), exterior corridors. **Terms:** cancellation fee imposed. **Pool:** outdoor. **Guest Services:** valet and coin laundry. **Featured Amenity: full hot breakfast.**

CANDLEWOOD SUITES
540/376-7244 **18**

Extended Stay Hotel
Rates not provided

Address: 4821 Crossings Ct 22407 **Location:** I-95 exit 126B northbound; exit 126 southbound, just s on US 1/17 (Jefferson Davis Hwy). **Facility:** 88 efficiencies. 4 stories, interior corridors. **Activities:** exercise room. **Guest Services:** complimentary and valet laundry.

COMFORT SUITES
(540)322-4700 **5**
◆◆◆ Hotel. **Address:** 541 Warrenton Rd 22406

COMFORT SUITES FREDERICKSBURG
(540)891-1112 **19**
◆◆◆ Hotel. **Address:** 4615 Southpoint Pkwy 22407

COUNTRY INN & SUITES BY CARLSON
540/656-2398 **1**
◆◆◆ Hotel. **Address:** 656 Warrenton Rd 22406

COUNTRY INN & SUITES BY CARLSON, FREDERICKSBURG SOUTH
(540)898-1800 **16**
◆◆◆ Hotel. **Address:** 5327 Jefferson Davis Hwy 22408

COURTYARD BY MARRIOTT FREDERICKSBURG HISTORIC DISTRICT
(540)373-8300 **11**
◆◆◆ Hotel. **Address:** 620 Caroline St 22401

AAA Benefit: Members save 5% or more!

FAIRFIELD INN & SUITES BY MARRIOTT
(540)891-9100 **17**
◆◆◆ Hotel. **Address:** 10330 Spotsylvania Ave 22408

AAA Benefit: Members save 5% or more!

FREDERICKSBURG HOSPITALITY HOUSE HOTEL & CONFERENCE CENTER
(540)786-8321 **12**

Hotel
$99-$169

Address: 2801 Plank Rd 22401 **Location:** I-95 exit 130B (SR 3), just e; in Central Park shopping complex. **Facility:** 196 units. 3 stories, interior corridors. **Terms:** cancellation fee imposed. **Dining:** 2 restaurants. **Pool:** outdoor. **Activities:** exercise room. **Guest Services:** valet and coin laundry. **Featured Amenity: continental breakfast.**

HAMPTON INN & SUITES AT CELEBRATE VIRGINIA
(540)786-5530 **9**

Hotel
$109-$169

Hampton AAA Benefit: Members save up to 10%!

Address: 1080 Hospitality Ln 22401 **Location:** I-95 exit 130B (SR 3), just w to Carl D Silver Pkwy, then 2 mi n. Adjacent to Expo Center and Central Park shopping complex. **Facility:** 122 units. 5 stories, interior corridors. **Terms:** 1-7 night minimum stay, cancellation fee imposed. **Pool:** heated outdoor. **Activities:** exercise room. **Guest Services:** valet and coin laundry. **Featured Amenity:** breakfast buffet.

HAMPTON INN & SUITES OF FREDERICKSBURG SOUTH
(540)898-5000 **15**
◆◆◆ Hotel. **Address:** 4800 Market St 22408

AAA Benefit: Members save up to 10%!

HILTON GARDEN INN
(540)548-8822 **7**
◆◆◆ Hotel. **Address:** 1060 Hospitality Ln 22401

AAA Benefit: Members save up to 10%!

(See map & index p. 113.)

HOLIDAY INN EXPRESS & SUITES   (540)479-8000   3

Hotel
$85-$145

Address: 560 Warrenton Rd 22406 **Location:** I-95 exit 133, just nw on US 17. **Facility:** 120 units. 5 stories, interior corridors. **Pool:** outdoor, heated indoor. **Activities:** exercise room. **Guest Services:** valet and coin laundry. **Featured Amenity:** breakfast buffet.

HOMEWOOD SUITES BY HILTON AT CELEBRATE VIRGINIA   540-786-9700   8

Extended Stay Hotel
Rates not provided

HOMEWOOD SUITES BY HILTON

AAA Benefit: Members save up to 10%!

Address: 1040 Hospitality Ln 22401 **Location:** I-95 exit 130B (SR 3), just w to Carl D Silver Pkwy, then 2 mi n. Adjacent to Central Park shopping complex. **Facility:** 124 efficiencies, some two bedrooms. 5 stories, interior corridors. **Terms:** check-in 4 pm. **Pool:** heated outdoor. **Activities:** hot tub, exercise room. **Guest Services:** valet and coin laundry.

HYATT PLACE FREDERICKSBURG AT MARY WASHINGTON   (540)654-3333   10

Hotel
$79-$269

HYATT PLACE

AAA Benefit: Members save 10%!

Address: 1241 Jefferson Davis Hwy 22401 **Location:** On US 1/17; jct College Ave; in Eagle Village. Located across from University of Mary Washington. **Facility:** 93 units. 5 stories, interior corridors. **Terms:** cancellation fee imposed. **Pool:** heated indoor. **Activities:** exercise room. **Guest Services:** valet and coin laundry. **Featured Amenity:** full hot breakfast.

QUALITY INN FREDERICKSBURG   (540)373-0000   4
Motel. **Address:** 543 Warrenton Rd 22406

RESIDENCE INN BY MARRIOTT   (540)786-9222   14
Extended Stay Hotel. **Address:** 60 Towne Centre Blvd 22407

AAA Benefit: Members save 5% or more!

SLEEP INN   (540)372-6868   2
Hotel. **Address:** 595 Warrenton Rd 22406

WINGATE BY WYNDHAM   540-368-8000   6
Hotel. **Address:** 20 Sanford Dr 22406

WHERE TO EAT

ALLMAN'S BARBEQUE   540/373-9881   19
Barbecue. Casual Dining. **Address:** 1299 Jefferson Davis Hwy 22401

AUBERGINE THAI   540/479-4969   33
Thai. Casual Dining. **Address:** 10029 Jefferson Davis Hwy 22407

BABA GANOUSH MEDITERRANEAN GRILL   540/479-1123   3
Indian. Casual Dining. **Address:** 1115 Jefferson Davis Hwy 22401

BANGKOK CAFE   540/373-0745   11
Thai. Casual Dining. **Address:** 825 Caroline St 22401

BASILICO ITALIAN MARKET & NEW YORK DELI   540/370-0355   5
Italian. Quick Serve. **Address:** 2577 Cowan Blvd 22401

THE BAVARIAN CHEF   540/656-2101   24
German. Fine Dining. **Address:** 200 Lafayette Blvd 22401

BISTRO BETHEM   540/371-9999   8
American. Fine Dining. **Address:** 309 William St 22401

BONEFISH GRILL   540/548-1984   21
Seafood. Fine Dining. **Address:** 1779 Carl D Silver Pkwy 22401

BROCK'S RIVERSIDE GRILL   540/370-1820   22
American. Casual Dining. **Address:** 503 Sophia St 22401

BROTHER'S PIZZA   540/548-0400   27
Italian Pizza. Casual Dining. **Address:** 3605 Plank Rd 22407

CASTIGLIA'S ITALIAN RESTAURANT & PIZZERIA   540/373-6650   13
Italian. Casual Dining. **Address:** 324 William St 22401

CORK & TABLE   540/479-1291   6
American. Casual Dining. **Address:** 909 Caroline St 22401

EL ASADOR RESTAURANT   540/898-1556   28
Latin American. Casual Dining. **Address:** 100 Olde Greenwich Dr 22408

FAHRENHEIT 132   540/940-2614   12
Steak. Casual Dining. **Address:** 318 William St 22401

FISH N' GRILL   540/898-8611   30
Soul Food Seafood. Quick Serve. **Address:** 10908 Courthouse Rd, Suite 105 22408

FOODE   540/479-1370   15
Natural/Organic. Casual Dining. **Address:** 900 Princess Anne St 22401

GARNJANA THAI   540/891-0280   29
Thai. Casual Dining. **Address:** 4416 Lafayette Blvd 22408

GOOLRICK'S PHARMACY   540/373-9878   9
American. Quick Serve. **Address:** 901 Caroline St 22401

GURU INDIAN CUISINE   540/548-1011   26
Indian. Casual Dining. **Address:** 1320 Central Park Blvd, Suite 112 22401

HERE & ABROAD BISTRO & BAKERY   540/371-2999   34
Breads/Pastries Sandwiches. Quick Serve. **Address:** 1004 Princess Anne St 22401

KAPPA GARDEN SUSHI BISTRO   540/891-4052   32
Japanese. Casual Dining. **Address:** 10153 Jefferson Davis Hwy 22407

(See map & index p. 113.)

KYBECCA   540/373-3338   (14)
♥♥ American. Casual Dining. **Address:** 400 William St 22401

LA PETITE AUBERGE   540/371-2727   (10)
♥♥♥ French. Fine Dining. **Address:** 311 William St 22401

LEGUME KITCHEN & BAR   540/371-1116   (18)
♥♥ Vegetarian Seafood. Casual Dining. **Address:** 715 Caroline St 22401

MASON-DIXON CAFE   540/371-1950   (1)
♥♥ American. Casual Dining. **Address:** 2100 Princess Anne St 22401

MERCANTILE   540/371-3280   (4)
♥♥ Natural/Organic Breakfast. Casual Dining. **Address:** 205 William St 22401

MISO ASIAN GRILL & SUSHI BAR   540/371-6999   (20)
♥♥♥ Asian Sushi. Fine Dining. **Address:** 1305 Jefferson Davis Hwy 22401

OLDE TOWNE STEAK AND SEAFOOD   540/371-8020   (2)
♥♥ Steak Seafood. Fine Dining. **Address:** 1612 Caroline St 22401

PANCHO VILLA MEXICAN RESTAURANT   540/710-9999   (31)
♥♥ Mexican. Casual Dining. **Address:** 10500 Spotsylvania Ave 22408

PETER CHANG CHINA CAFE   540/786-8988   (23)
♥♥ Chinese. Casual Dining. **Address:** 1771 Carl D. Silver Pkwy 22401

RISTORANTE RENATO   540/371-8228   (17)

♥♥♥

Italian
Fine Dining
$8-$27

AAA Inspector Notes: This classic restaurant has sat in this historic downtown building for at least 20 years. The interior is retro-romantic with a stone hearth and dark woods and a professional bow-tied staff. The menu showcases authentic Northern Italian cuisine with veal and seafood specialties and freshly made pastas such as tortellini, ravioli and gnocchi. Desserts are also homemade including cannoli, cheesecake and spumoni. There is a live classical guitarist on Friday and Saturday nights. **Features:** full bar. **Address:** 422 William St 22401 **Location:** I-95 exit 130A, 2 mi e on SR 3 business route; corner of William and Prince Edward sts; downtown.

SAKURA JAPANESE STEAK AND SEAFOOD HOUSE   540/786-8100
♥♥ Japanese. Casual Dining. **Address:** 4540 Plank Rd 22407

SAMMY T'S   540/371-2008   (16)
♥♥ American. Casual Dining. **Address:** 801 Caroline St 22401

SPRELLY   540/445-0405   (7)
♥ Sandwiches. Quick Serve. **Address:** 920 Caroline St 22401

TITO'S DINER   540/548-3406   (25)
♥♥ American. Casual Dining. **Address:** 1695 Carl D Silver Pkwy 22401

FREDERICKSBURG AND SPOTSYLVANIA NATIONAL MILITARY PARK (D-11)

In and around Fredericksburg, the park covers about 8,400 acres and includes four great battlefields of the Civil War: Chancellorsville *(see place listing p. 79)*, Fredericksburg, Spotsylvania Court House *(see Spotsylvania p. 244)* and the Wilderness *(see place listing p. 272)*.

Due to its strategic location halfway between Richmond and Washington, D.C., Fredericksburg and the surrounding area were of prime military importance to both sides. The intense and continuous fighting resulted in the estimated loss of 65,000 Union soldiers and 40,000 Confederate fighters.

Walking trails from the Fredericksburg Battlefield Visitor Center *(see attraction listing this page)* on US 1 lead to the Sunken Road, Marye's Heights, Fire in the Streets, Lee Hill and the Fredericksburg National Cemetery. The Kirkland Monument honors a 19-year-old Confederate sergeant who risked his life to give water to the wounded and dying of the Union Army. Old Salem Church, which served as a refuge for civilians fleeing the city during the Battle of Fredericksburg, is within the park. The church, also the site of a battle during the Chancellorsville campaign, later was used by the Confederates to tend to the wounded of both sides. Also on the grounds is Ellwood, a house standing in the middle of the Wilderness Battlefield that once served as a hospital for Confederates.

All of the battlefields are in a 17-mile radius of Fredericksburg. Exhibits, paintings, interpretive trails, historic buildings, narrative markers and maps identify Union and Confederate lines and relate the stories of the battles. Roads lead to the battlefields, earthworks and other points of historic interest. Guided walking tours led by park historians are available seasonally; phone ahead to confirm schedule.

The park is open daily dawn-dusk. Visitor center hours vary; phone ahead. Closed Jan. 1, Thanksgiving and Christmas. Park admission is free. Phone (540) 693-3200.

CHATHAM MANOR is .5 mi. e. across the Rappahannock River off SR 212 at 120 Chatham Ln. The 18th-century Georgian mansion served as Union headquarters and a field hospital during the Civil War. From its front terrace, officers had a clear view of the city and points along the river where Northern engineers built pontoon bridges for the Battle of Fredericksburg.

Clara Barton was among those who provided care for wounded soldiers here. A 13-minute film and a museum relate the story of Chatham Manor and the role it played in the war. Gardens and outbuildings also are on the premises. **Hours:** Daily 9-4:30. Closed Jan. 1, Thanksgiving and Christmas. Phone ahead to confirm schedule. **Cost:** Free. **Phone:** (540) 693-3200.

FREDERICKSBURG BATTLEFIELD VISITOR CENTER is at 1013 Lafayette Blvd. (US 1) on the Sunken Road. The center presents a 22-minute film and museum exhibits about the battle that occurred on Dec. 13, 1862. Walking trails lead to the Sunken Road, Marye's Heights and the Fredericksburg National Cemetery. A 5-mile driving tour starts and ends at the center, covering the majority of the battlefield. Historians lead seasonal walking tours along the Sunken Road.

Time: Allow 1 hour minimum. **Hours:** Grounds daily dawn-dusk. Visitor center hours vary. Closed Jan. 1, Thanksgiving and Christmas. Phone ahead to confirm schedule. **Cost:** Park admission free. Film $2; $1 (ages 62+); free (ages 0-9). CD detailing a 3-hour self-guiding tour $12.95 (to purchase); $4.95 (plus $20 deposit to rent). **Phone:** (540) 693-3200. GT

FREDERICKSBURG NATIONAL CEMETERY is on Lafayette Blvd. (US 1) atop Marye's Heights. More than 15,000 U.S. veterans are buried here, the majority of whom are Union soldiers who died in the nearby battles of Fredericksburg, Chancellorsville, Spotsylvania Court House and the Wilderness. More than 80 percent of the soldiers are unknown. The Fredericksburg Battlefield Visitor Center keeps a record of identified soldiers. Pets are not permitted in the cemetery. **Hours:** Grounds daily dawn-dusk. **Cost:** Free. **Phone:** (540) 693-3200.

"STONEWALL" JACKSON SHRINE is 15 mi. s. of Fredericksburg via I-95, US 1 or SR 2, then by CR 606 to Guinea Station. On the night of May 2, 1863, Gen. Thomas J. "Stonewall" Jackson was mistakenly shot by his own men at Chancellorsville; due to his injuries, his left arm had to be amputated. The Confederate general was moved by order of Gen. Robert E. Lee to recover at Fairfield Plantation. With the main house already filled with injured soldiers, Jackson's doctors settled him in the plantation office. The room where he died a week later has been preserved.

Hours: Grounds open daily dawn-dusk. Visitor center hours vary; phone ahead. Closed Jan. 1, Thanksgiving and Christmas. **Cost:** Free. **Phone:** (540) 693-3200.

THREE BATTLES VISITOR CENTER AT CHANCELLORSVILLE is 8 mi. w. of I-95 on SR 3 at 9001 Plank Rd. The center offers a 22-minute film and exhibits about the battles of Chancellorsville, the Wilderness and Spotsylvania Courthouse. A 12-mile driving tour begins at the center with roadside tour markers and informational signs describing the battle. Seasonal walking tours lead to the place where Gen. Thomas J. "Stonewall" Jackson was shot.

Time: Allow 1 hour minimum. **Hours:** Grounds daily dawn-dusk. Visitor center hours vary. Closed Jan. 1, Thanksgiving and Christmas. Phone ahead to confirm schedule. **Cost:** Park admission free. Film $2; $1 (ages 62+); free (ages 0-9). CD detailing a 3-hour self-guiding tour $12.95 (to purchase); $4.95 (to rent, with a $20 down payment). **Phone:** (540) 693-3200. GT

FRONT ROYAL (E-8) pop. 14,440, elev. 565'
• Part of Shenandoah National Park area — see map p. 241

Front Royal began as Lehew Town, a frontier village on the packhorse road to the east. According to local lore, its current name derives from the command by frustrated military officers for unruly troops to "front the royal oak," which once stood in the public square.

Belle Boyd, the Confederate spy who charmed military secrets out of her Union suitors, used Front Royal as one of her most effective bases. On May 15, 1862, Boyd overheard plans that the Union troops were exiting Front Royal, leaving behind a small force. Boyd relayed this information to Gen. Thomas J. "Stonewall" Jackson, and on May 23, Jackson led his troops into town; the Battle of Front Royal ended with the capture of 750 of the 1,000 Union soldiers.

A popular stopping point for visitors bound for the Skyline Drive (see attraction listing p. 242), Front Royal has preserved some of its 19th-century atmosphere on Chester Street, in the historic district. The 1787 Balthis House is the oldest building in town.

Front Royal-Warren County Visitors Center: 414 E. Main St., Front Royal, VA 22630. **Phone:** (540) 635-5788 or (800) 338-2576.

Self-guiding tours: A 10-stop driving tour of the Battle of Front Royal is available at the visitor center, as is information about 1863 and 1864 Civil War actions involving "the Gray Ghost," Col. John S. Mosby, and generals Jubal Early, Philip Sheridan and Ulysses S. Grant. Brochures describing a walking tour of the historic district also are offered.

IVY LODGE MUSEUM is at 101 Chester St. Exhibits in this former private residence include artifacts chronicling the history of Front Royal and Warren County. The lodge is headquarters of the Warren Heritage Society. **Time:** Allow 30 minutes minimum. **Hours:** Daily 10-4, Apr.-Oct.; Mon.-Fri. 10-4, rest of year. Closed major holidays. **Cost:** Free. **Phone:** (540) 636-1446.

SKYLINE CAVERNS are on US 340, approximately 1 mi. s. of the entrance to Skyline Drive and 1.5 mi. s. of jct. SR 55. The caverns contain calcite crystal formations known as anthodites, or cave flowers, found in few caves worldwide. Subterranean streams and cascades are of interest. Indirect illumination is provided. Also offered are the Enchanted Dragon Mirror Maze and a .5-mile tour of the grounds aboard a miniature train (weather permitting).

Hours: Guided cavern tours are given every 15-20 minutes daily 9-6, mid-June through Labor Day; Mon.-Fri. 9-5, Sat.-Sun. 9-6, mid-Mar. to mid-June and day after Labor Day to mid-Nov.; daily 9-4, rest of year. **Cost:** Cavern tour $22; $20 (ages 62+ and military with ID); $11 (ages 7-13). Maze $6; free (ages 0-5). Train ride $6; free (ages 0-2). **Phone:** (540) 635-4545 or (800) 296-4545. GT

WARREN RIFLES CONFEDERATE MUSEUM is at 95 Chester St. The Warren Rifles were an infantry company formed in Front Royal in

1861. The museum houses documents, guns, pictures, letters from Confederate soldiers and personal items of Belle Boyd, the Confederate spy, and Gens. Thomas J. "Stonewall" Jackson, Robert E. Lee and Turner Ashby.

Hours: Mon.-Sat. 9-4, Sun. noon-4, Apr. 15-Nov. 1; by appointment rest of year. **Cost:** $5; free (students and active military with ID). Prices may vary; phone ahead. **Phone:** (540) 636-6982 or (540) 660-0941.

HAMPTON INN/FRONT ROYAL   (540)635-1882
▼▼▼ Hotel. **Address:** 9800 Winchester Rd 22630

AAA Benefit: Members save up to 10%!

HOLIDAY INN & SUITES FRONT ROYAL BLUE RIDGE SHADOWS   540/631-3050
▼▼▼ Hotel. **Address:** 111 Hospitality Dr 22630

WHERE TO EAT

JALISCO MEXICAN RESTAURANT   540/635-7348
▼▼ Mexican. Casual Dining. **Address:** 1303 N Royal Ave 22630

GAINESVILLE pop. 11,481

HAMPTON INN BY HILTON GAINESVILLE/HAYMARKET
     (703)753-1500
▼▼▼▼ Hotel. **Address:** 7300 Atlas Walk Way 20155

AAA Benefit: Members save up to 10%!

WHERE TO EAT

EL TIO TEX-MEX GRILL   703/753-0826
▼▼ Tex-Mex. Casual Dining. **Address:** 7527 Linton Hall Rd 20155

GLORY DAYS GRILL   571/261-1500
▼▼ American. Casual Dining. **Address:** 7581 Somerset Crossing Dr 20155

GRAFTON STREET RESTAURANT & PUB   571/261-9367
▼▼ Irish. Casual Dining. **Address:** 7380 Atlas Walk Way 20155

GALAX (I-5) pop. 7,042, elev. 2,382'

Tucked in the Blue Ridge Mountains on the North Carolina state line, Galax is noted for its pristine beauty. The town is named for the leaf of the galax, a plant indigenous to the area. The terrain is popular with mountain bikers, horseback riders and hikers, while placid rivers and streams draw anglers, canoeists and kayakers.

Every Friday evening at 8, a weekly radio show featuring regional old-time and bluegrass bands is broadcast live on WBRF (98.1 FM) from the historical Rex Theater at 113 E. Grayson St. The shows are open to the public; tickets cost $5 apiece.

City of Galax Tourism: 110 E. Grayson St., Galax, VA 24333. **Phone:** (276) 238-8130 or (888) 217-8823.

GALAX HAMPTON INN   (276)238-4605

▼▼▼ Hotel $109-$399

AAA Benefit: Members save up to 10%!

Address: 205 Cranberry Rd 24333 **Location:** I-77 exit 14, 7 mi se on US 58. **Facility:** 60 units. 4 stories, interior corridors. **Terms:** 1-7 night minimum stay, cancellation fee imposed. **Pool:** heated indoor. **Activities:** hot tub, exercise room. **Guest Services:** coin laundry. **Featured Amenity:** full hot breakfast.

WHERE TO EAT

THE GALAX SMOKEHOUSE   276/236-1000
▼ Barbecue. Casual Dining. **Address:** 101 N Main St 24333

GEORGE WASHINGTON AND JEFFERSON NATIONAL FORESTS (F-7)

Elevations in the forests range from 600 ft near Covington to 5,729 ft. Mount Rogers in the Mount Rogers National Recreation Area. Refer to AAA maps for additional elevation information.

Stretching from Big Stone Gap to Winchester, the George Washington and Jefferson National Forests contain some 1.8 million acres.

The northern end of the forest, known as the George Washington National Forest, extends more than 1 million acres across the Blue Ridge, Massanutten, Shenandoah and Allegheny mountain ranges into West Virginia. Towering over all these ranges is 4,463-foot Elliott Knob, just west of Staunton.

Among the major recreation areas are Brandywine Lake and Todd Lake, respectively west and southwest of Harrisonburg; Elizabeth Furnace, south of Waterlick; Trout Pond, west of Woodstock; Sherando Lake, near Waynesboro; and Lake Moomaw, southwest of Warm Springs.

More than 950 miles of trails wind through the George Washington National Forest leading to scenic views of mountains, valleys and rivers. A portion of the Appalachian Trail traverses the forest, and another trail leads to Crabtree Falls, five cascading waterfalls that are the highest in the Blue Ridge. A 5-mile loop trail winds gradually to the top of Pompey Mountain and Mount Pleasant. Popular because it is not steep, the trail provides scenic vistas of the Blue Ridge Mountains. Also noteworthy is The Highlands Scenic Tour, a 20-mile scenic drive through the mountains along a steep, twisting road.

The southern end of the forest, known as Jefferson National Forest, embraces approximately 710,000 acres in west-central Virginia. Jefferson National Forest has more than 1,100 miles of trails, 500 miles of trout streams, 24 developed campgrounds, 25 picnic areas and six fishing and four swimming lakes, some of which have bathhouses. The Cascades National Recreation Trail is a scenic 4-mile hike leading to a 66-foot waterfall.

Beginning near Wytheville, Big Walker Mountain Scenic Byway winds 16 miles through forested countryside past old farm homesteads, hiking trails, fishing ponds, picnic areas, campgrounds and beautiful mountain vistas. The byway leads up the mountain to Big Walker Lookout, a privately owned attraction featuring a country store and a 100-foot observation tower. The site is open daily 10-5. Closed Thanksgiving and Christmas. Another scenic route, Mount Rogers Scenic Byway, passes through valleys and over mountains rich in the ever-changing colors of leaves and wildflowers.

Nearby are the towns of Abingdon *(see place listing p. 29)*, Big Stone Gap *(see place listing p. 70)*, Blacksburg *(see place listing p. 70)*, Natural Bridge *(see place listing p. 174)*, Roanoke *(see place listing p. 230)*, Winchester *(see place listing p. 291)* and Wytheville *(see place listing p. 294)*.

The main recreation season for George Washington and Jefferson National Forests is April through November. Fees are charged at some sites. For more information contact the Forest Supervisor, 5162 Valleypointe Pkwy., Roanoke, VA 24019; phone (540) 265-5100 or (888) 265-0019. *See Recreation Areas Chart.*

CAVE MOUNTAIN LAKE RECREATION AREA is 8 mi. s.e. of Natural Bridge. The park contains a 7-acre lake with a beach and bathhouse, hiking trails, and tent and trailer camping areas. A scenic drive past Cave Mountain Lake climbs Wildcat Mountain, where it forks; the left spur leads to Sunset Field, where it connects with Blue Ridge Parkway. **Hours:** Daily 6 a.m.-dusk, early Apr.-late Oct. **Cost:** Day-use fee $5 (per private vehicle). Camping $15-$30 (per night). **Phone:** (540) 291-2188.

GEORGE WASHINGTON BIRTHPLACE NATIONAL MONUMENT (F-10)

On the south side of the Potomac River, 38 miles east of Fredericksburg off SR 3 on SR 204, George Washington Birthplace National Monument includes 550 acres and a portion of the old Washington Plantation. John, the first Washington to settle in the area, arrived about 1657. In 1731 his grandson Augustine married Mary Ball of Epping Forest. He brought her to his home on Popes Creek, and there George Washington was born in 1732.

The house, built by Augustine 1722-26, was destroyed by fire on Christmas Day in 1779. Excavations have revealed five original foundations. Since the exact appearance of the original is not known, a memorial house was built to represent an 18th-century plantation home.

Native clay was used to make the bricks for the building, which is furnished with antiques carefully selected to reflect the period of Washington's boyhood. The grounds include a kitchen and garden.

The Colonial Farm interprets some of the farm scenes of young Washington's environment. The heritage breeds, gardens and crops are historical varieties raised by methods common during the colonial period.

Also on the grounds is a cemetery containing the graves of more than 30 members of the family, including George's father, grandfather and great-grandfather. Picnic facilities are available. Grounds open daily 9-5. Visitor center open 9:30-5, Mar.-Dec.; Wed.-Sun. 10-4, rest of year. House open daily 10-4, Mar.-Dec.; Wed.-Sun. 10-4, rest of year. Closed Jan. 1, Thanksgiving and Christmas. Admission free. Phone (804) 224-1732.

GLADE SPRING pop. 1,456

ECONO LODGE GLADE SPRING   (276)429-5191
Motel. **Address:** 33361 Lee Hwy 24340

GLEN ALLEN (A-1) pop. 14,774, elev. 855'
- **Restaurants p. 122**
- **Hotels & Restaurants map & index p. 212**
- **Part of Richmond area — see map p. 193**

First called Mountain Road Crossing, this settlement on the Chickahominy River became known as Glen Allen for an early resident, Benjamin Allen. In 1713, William Sheppard received a land grant for Meadow Farm, which remained in his family until 1993.

ALOFT RICHMOND WEST   (804)433-1888

Contemporary Hotel
$119-$289

 AAA Benefit: Members save 5% or more!

Address: 3939 Duckling Dr 23060 **Location:** I-64 exit 178B, just w on W Broad St; in West Broad Village. **Facility:** 135 units. 5 stories, interior corridors. *Bath:* shower only. **Terms:** cancellation fee imposed. **Amenities:** safes. **Pool:** heated indoor. **Activities:** exercise room. **Guest Services:** valet and coin laundry.

(See map & index p. 212.)

BEST WESTERN PLUS GLEN ALLEN INN
(804)266-3500 **46**

Hotel
$78-$129

Best Western PLUS.

AAA Benefit: Members save 10% or more & earn 10% bonus points!

Address: 8507 Brook Rd 23060 **Location:** I-95 exit 83B, 0.5 mi w to Brook Rd, then just n. **Facility:** 62 units, some efficiencies. 3 stories, interior corridors. **Terms:** 3 day cancellation notice-fee imposed. **Pool:** outdoor. **Activities:** exercise room. **Guest Services:** coin laundry.

CANDLEWOOD SUITES RICHMOND-WEST
804/364-2000 **54**

Extended Stay Hotel **Address:** 4120 Tom Leonard Dr 23060

CANDLEWOOD SUITES VIRGINIA CENTER COMMONS
804/262-2240 **40**

Extended Stay Hotel. **Address:** 10609 Telegraph Rd 23059

COMFORT SUITES-INNSBROOK
(804)217-9200 **51**

Hotel. **Address:** 1051 Innslake Dr 23060

COMFORT SUITES VIRGINIA CENTER COMMONS
(804)262-2000 **41**

Hotel. **Address:** 10601 Telegraph Rd 23059

COURTYARD BY MARRIOTT RICHMOND NORTH/GLEN ALLEN
(804)266-6900 **42**

Hotel. **Address:** 10077 Brook Rd 23059

AAA Benefit: Members save 5% or more!

HAMPTON INN & SUITES RICHMOND VIRGINIA CENTER
(804)261-2266 **43**

Hotel. **Address:** 1101 Technology Park Dr 23059

AAA Benefit: Members save up to 10%!

HAMPTON INN-RICHMOND WEST
(804)747-7777 **53**

Hotel. **Address:** 10800 W Broad St 23060

AAA Benefit: Members save up to 10%!

HILTON GARDEN INN RICHMOND INNSBROOK
(804)521-2900 **52**

Hotel. **Address:** 4050 Cox Rd 23060

AAA Benefit: Members save up to 10%!

HOMEWOOD SUITES BY HILTON RICHMOND WEST END-INNSBROOK
(804)217-8000 **49**

Extended Stay Hotel. **Address:** 4100 Innslake Dr 23060

AAA Benefit: Members save up to 10%!

HYATT PLACE RICHMOND/INNSBROOK
(804)747-9644 **50**

Hotel
$79-$179

HYATT PLACE

AAA Benefit: Members save 10%!

Address: 4100 Cox Rd 23060 **Location:** I-64 exit 178B, 0.5 mi e to Dominion Blvd, then just n. Located in Innsbrook Corporate Center. **Facility:** 124 units. 6 stories, interior corridors. **Terms:** cancellation fee imposed. **Pool:** outdoor. **Activities:** exercise room. **Guest Services:** valet laundry, area transportation. **Featured Amenity:** full hot breakfast.

RICHMOND MARRIOTT SHORT PUMP
(804)965-9500 **48**

Hotel
301-6322

MARRIOTT

AAA Benefit: Members save 5% or more!

Address: 4240 Dominion Blvd 23060 **Location:** I-64 exit 178B, 0.5 mi e to Dominion Blvd, then just n. Located in Innsbrook Corporate Center. **Facility:** 243 units. 6 stories, interior corridors. **Terms:** cancellation fee imposed. **Amenities:** safes. **Pool:** heated indoor. **Activities:** exercise room. **Guest Services:** valet laundry.

SPRINGHILL SUITES BY MARRIOTT
(804)266-9403 **44**

Hotel. **Address:** 9701 Brook Rd 23059

AAA Benefit: Members save 5% or more!

TOWNEPLACE SUITES BY MARRIOTT
(804)747-5253 **47**

Extended Stay Hotel
$67-$207

TOWNEPLACE SUITES MARRIOTT

AAA Benefit: Members save 5% or more!

Address: 4231 Park Place Ct 23060 **Location:** I-64 exit 178B, just e on W Broad St to Cox Rd, then just n to Innslake Dr. Located in Innsbrook Corporate Center. **Facility:** 94 kitchen units, some two bedrooms. 3 stories, interior corridors. **Terms:** cancellation fee imposed. **Pool:** outdoor. **Activities:** exercise room. **Guest Services:** valet and coin laundry.

(See map & index p. 212.)

VIRGINIA CROSSINGS HOTEL & CONFERENCE CENTER
(804)727-1400 **45**

Resort Hotel
$99-$259

Address: 1000 Virginia Center Pkwy 23059 **Location:** I-295 exit 43C, just n on US 1, then 1 mi e. **Facility:** Virginia's Colonial legacy sets the theme in this elegant hotel perched atop a hillside overlooking the rolling fields of the resort's golf course. 183 units. 5 stories, interior corridors. **Terms:** check-in 4 pm, cancellation fee imposed. **Amenities:** video games. **Dining:** 2 restaurants, also, The Glen Restaurant and The Tavern, see separate listing. **Pool:** outdoor. **Activities:** hot tub, regulation golf, lawn sports, trails, exercise room, massage. **Guest Services:** valet laundry.

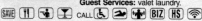

WHERE TO EAT

BURGERWORKS   804/527-2747   **62**
Burgers. Quick Serve. **Address:** 10321 W Broad St 23060

CAPITAL ALE HOUSE   804/780-2537
American. Casual Dining. **Address:** 4024-A Cox Rd 23060

THE GLEN RESTAURANT AND THE TAVERN   804/727-1480   **58**
American. Fine Dining. **Address:** 1000 Virginia Center Pkwy 23059

MAMA CUCINA   804/346-3350   **61**
Italian. Casual Dining. **Address:** 4028 Cox Rd, Suite O 23060

MEXICO RESTAURANT   804/290-0400
Mexican. Casual Dining. **Address:** 4040 Cox Rd, Suite G 23060

NOODLES & DUMPLINGS BY PETER CHANG   804/918-1352   **59**
Chinese Noodles Dim Sum. Quick Serve. **Address:** 11408 W Broad St 23060

PETER CHANG CHINA CAFE   804/364-1688   **60**
Chinese. Casual Dining. **Address:** 11424 W Broad St 23060

PLAZA AZTECA MEXICAN RESTAURANT   804/262-1523   **56**
Mexican. Casual Dining. **Address:** 10099 Brook Rd 23059

TRUE TASTE CHINESE RESTAURANT   804/266-8888   **57**
Chinese. Casual Dining. **Address:** 1090 Virginia Center Pkwy, Suite 102 23059

THE WINE LOFT   804/368-1768   **63**
American. Casual Dining. **Address:** 4035 Whittall Way 23060

GLOUCESTER (A-3) elev. 75'
• Part of Hampton Roads Area — see map p. 124

Gloucester (GLOSS-ter), in Tidewater Virginia, is noted for its many historical landmarks that have remained undisturbed. The 1766 Courthouse, on the Court Green, is enclosed by a brick wall. The Old Debtors Prison dates from the mid-18th century. Several old estates are in this region near Gloucester and near White Marsh *(see place listing p. 271)*. Long Bridge Ordinary, a stagecoach tavern built in 1732, is open during Garden Week in late

April. Dr. Walter Reed, instrumental in the eradication of yellow fever, was born in nearby Belroi.

Gloucester County Chamber of Commerce: 3558 George Washington Memorial Hwy., Hayes, VA 23072. **Phone:** (804) 693-2425.

HAMPTON INN
(804)693-9393

Hotel
$109-$259

AAA Benefit: Members save up to 10%!

Address: 6638 Forest Hill Ave 23061 **Location:** US 17, just s. **Facility:** 84 units. 3 stories, interior corridors. **Terms:** 1-7 night minimum stay, cancellation fee imposed. **Pool:** heated indoor. **Activities:** exercise room. **Guest Services:** valet and coin laundry. **Featured Amenity:** breakfast buffet.

QUALITY INN   (804)695-1900
Hotel. **Address:** 6639 Forest Hill Ave 23061

GLOUCESTER POINT (B-3) pop. 9,402, elev. 36'
• Part of Hampton Roads Area — see map p. 124

Located on the York River, Gloucester Point has been a strategic town throughout its history. The town originally was called Tyndall's Point in honor of an early mapmaker.

VIRGINIA INSTITUTE OF MARINE SCIENCE is off US 17, .8 mi. n. of Coleman Bridge over the York River at 1375 Greate Rd. This research institute and graduate school of William & Mary offers a small visitor center showcasing VIMS' research and aquariums featuring local marine life. Exhibits include a preserved coelacanth. Family programs, tours and lectures are throughout the year.

Hours: Visitor center Mon.-Fri. 9-4:30. Closed Jan. 1, Memorial Day, Thanksgiving, day after Thanksgiving and Christmas Eve-Dec. 31. **Cost:** Free. Reservations are required for most events. **Phone:** (804) 684-7000. **GT**

GOOCHLAND pop. 861
• Part of Richmond area — see map p. 193

TANGLEWOOD ORDINARY COUNTRY RESTAURANT   804/556-3284
Southern Comfort Food. Casual Dining. **Address:** 2210 River Rd W 23102

GORDONSVILLE pop. 1,496, elev. 479'

THE BARBEQUE EXCHANGE   540/832-0227

Barbecue. Quick Serve. **Address:** 102 Martinsburg Ave 22942

GRAFTON
• Part of Williamsburg, Jamestown & Yorktown area — see map p. 273

POP'S DRIVE IN   757/898-6870

American. Quick Serve. **Address:** 6555 George Washington Memorial Hwy 23692

GREAT FALLS (A-12) pop. 15,427, elev. 377'
• Hotels & Restaurants map & index p. 38

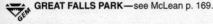

GREAT FALLS PARK—see McLean p. 169.

DANTE RISTORANTE   703/759-3131   (15)

Northern Italian Fine Dining. **Address:** 1148 Walker Rd 22066

L'AUBERGE CHEZ FRANCOIS & JACQUES' BRASSERIE
                                       703/759-3800

French. Fine Dining. **Address:** 332 Springvale Rd 22066

GREENVILLE pop. 832

EDELWEISS RESTAURANT   540/337-1203

German. Casual Dining. **Address:** 19 Edelweiss Ln 24401

GRETNA pop. 1,267

CAMBER INN   434/656-9000

Hotel. **Address:** 200 McBride Ln 24557

GROTTOES (F-7) pop. 2,668, elev. 1,112'
• Part of Shenandoah National Park area — see map p. 241

Known in its early history as Liola and then Shendun, this area was settled around 1735 with a land grant of 60,000 acres on the Shenandoah River. The Grottoes Co. was formed in 1889 to develop the local caves and mineral resources; the enterprise folded 4 years later. The town adopted its present name in 1912.

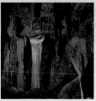

SAVE GRAND CAVERNS PARK is off I-81 exit 235, then 6 mi. e. on SR 256 to 5 Grand Caverns Dr. Said to be the country's oldest show cavern, the Grottoes cave was discovered in 1804 and opened to the public 2 years later. At different times both Union and Gen. Thomas J. "Stonewall" Jackson's Confederate troops visited the Great Cathedral Hall and Grand Ballroom. Signatures of soldiers from both armies are visible on cave walls. Unusual cave formations include calcite shields.

Hiking and biking trails, fishing, swimming and miniature golf are offered. *See Recreation Areas Chart.* **Hours:** Guided cave tours are given daily every 45 minutes 9-5, Apr.-Oct.; on the hour 10-4, rest of year. Phone ahead to confirm schedule. **Cost:** $18; $16 (ages 61+); $11 (ages 6-12). A discount is offered to military and public servants with ID and their children ages 6-12. Prices may vary. **Phone:** (540) 249-5705 or (888) 430-2283.

WOODFIRED OVEN ITALIAN RESTAURANT   540/249-8333

Italian. Casual Dining. **Address:** 75 Augusta Ave 24441

GRUNDY pop. 1,021

COMFORT INN   (276)935-5050

Hotel
$100-$159

Address: 22006 Riverside Dr 24614 **Location:** On US 460 business route, 0.5 mi e. **Facility:** 70 units. 4 stories, interior corridors. **Amenities:** cafes. **Activities:** exercise room. **Guest Services:** coin laundry. **Featured Amenity:** full hot breakfast.

HALIFAX pop. 1,309

MOLASSES GRILL   434/476-6265

American. Fine Dining. **Address:** 63 S Main St 24558

HAMPTON ROADS AREA

If you look at a map of Virginia, you won't find a city called Hampton Roads. Rather the term refers both to the channel through which the James, Elizabeth and Nansemond rivers flow into Chesapeake Bay (and ultimately the Atlantic Ocean) and the Norfolk-Virginia Beach metropolitan area.

So if you locate the cluster of cities around the Hampton Roads harbor in the southeastern corner of Virginia—bingo, you've found the Hampton Roads area.

On the "South Side" of the harbor are the cities of Virginia Beach, Norfolk, Chesapeake, Portsmouth and Suffolk, while the communities of Newport News and Hampton are on the northern "Peninsula." The solution to the challenge of how to best get from one side of the harbor to the other was the creation of the Hampton Roads Bridge-Tunnel, the world's first bridge-tunnel combination, and, later, the Monitor-Merrimac Memorial Bridge-Tunnel. Regardless, traffic backups on summer weekends are common.

So where does this unusual name come from? The most accepted answer is that the Hampton part comes from an English nobleman, the third Earl of Southampton, who was a member of the Virginia Company of London. And Roads refers to the nautical definition of the word, wherein a "road" is a place of deep water where ships can safely anchor.

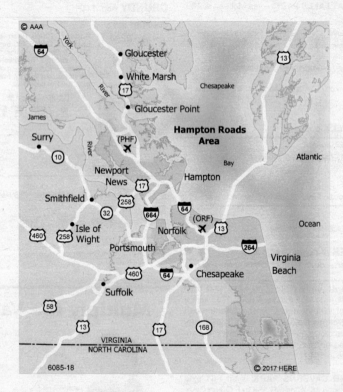

This map shows cities in the Hampton Roads Area where you will find attractions, hotels and restaurants. Cities are listed alphabetically in this book on the following pages.

And ships have been anchoring in these waters for more than 400 years. In fact, the *Susan Constant*, the *Godspeed* and the *Discovery* landed at Cape Henry (the present site of Virginia Beach) in 1607 before heading up the James River and establishing the first permanent English colony in America at Jamestown. This momentous event has come to be known as the "First Landing."

Fast forward a couple of centuries to one of the Civil War's key events—the naval engagement between the CSS *Virginia* (*Merrimac*) and the USS *Monitor*. This first duel between ironclad warships took place in the Hampton Roads harbor, in the waters just off Hampton and Newport News.

It's not surprising then, since Norfolk is blessed with one of the world's finest natural, year-round ice-free harbors, that it also has the world's largest Navy base, home to aircraft carriers, destroyers, frigates, nuclear submarines and amphibious assault ships. In addition to its formidable military presence, shipbuilding, ship repair and the transfer and storage of cargo also are major components of the area's economic base.

Downtown on the waterfront, not far from the Waterside District, is another reminder of the city's naval connection. It's hard to miss Nauticus, Norfolk's waterfront maritime museum; the huge building is painted battleship gray and actually resembles a battleship. And, oh yes, The Battleship *Wisconsin* is docked next to it. The Hampton Roads Naval Museum is on the second floor.

Next to Nauticus is the Half Moone Cruise and Celebration Center where megaships sail off to the Caribbean and Bermuda.

Across the Elizabeth River from Norfolk is the city of Portsmouth. A brief ride on a paddlewheel ferry deposits you right at Portsmouth's Olde Towne Historic District, where you can stroll past centuries-old architectural jewels in a charming residential area.

Hampton Roads' largest city is Virginia Beach, a favorite with vacationers in search of sun, sand, surf and seafood. What more could you expect from an oceanfront destination? How about wide beaches, warm breezes and a 3-mile-long boardwalk that can be traversed via pedal-powered surreys with fringe on top? A favorite photo op along the boardwalk is the 34-foot-tall statue of King Neptune, who seems to be rising from the sea, surrounded by sea life, pointed trident in hand. Be aware, though: The rhythmic sound of the surf is occasionally interrupted by the roar of a Navy jet soaring overhead.

If you prefer being on the water instead of in it, charter boats will take you to just the right spot to hook a marlin, tuna, striped bass, sailfish or wahoo. Or if your idea of seafood comes served with melted butter or tartar sauce, local restaurants offer countless variations of crab, shrimp oyster and fresh-off-the-boat "catch of the day" dishes.

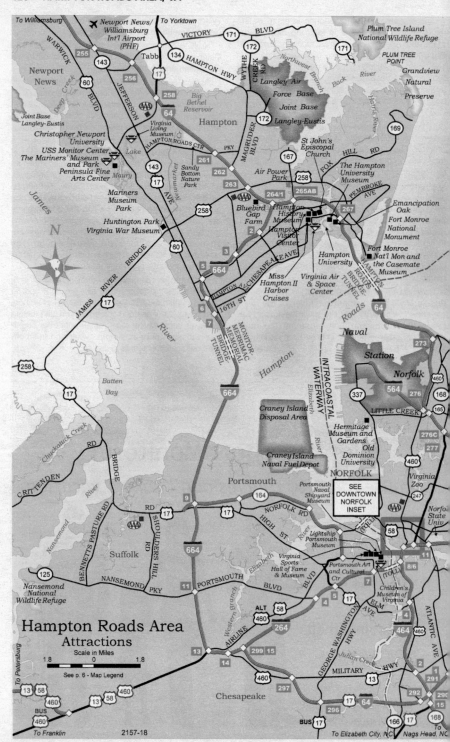

To Williamsburg

To Yorktown

WARWICK
255
143
60
256

Newport News/
Williamsburg
Int'l Airport
(PHF)

Tabb
134

VICTORY   BLVD
171
172
171

HAMPTON HWY

Plum Tree Island
National Wildlife Refuge

PLUM TREE
POINT

Grandview
Natural
Preserve

Newport
News

Deep Creek

JEFFERSON

258

64

Big
Bethel
Reservoir

Hampton

WYTHE
CREEK RD
Langley Air
Force Base

Northwest Branch

Back   River

Joint Base
Langley-Eustis

172

Harris River

169

Joint Base
Langley-Eustis

Christopher Newport
University
USS Monitor Center,
The Mariners' Museum
and Park
Peninsula Fine
Arts Center

Virginia
Living
Museum

HAMPTON ROADS CTR

143

Lake
Maury

17

Newmarket

261

MAGRUDER   BLVD

PKY

167

St John's
Episcopal
Church

258

FOX   HILL   RD

The Hampton
University
Museum

PEMBROKE AVE

Emancipation
Oak

Fort Monroe
National
Monument

James
River

N

Mariners
Museum
Park

Huntington Park
Virginia War Museum

60

Sandy
Bottom
Nature
Park

262

263

258

264/1

265AB

267

Bluebird
Gap
Farm

2

Hampton
History
Museum

Hampton
Visitor
Center

Hampton
University

Fort Monroe
Nat'l Mon and
the Casemate
Museum

JAMES   RIVER   BRIDGE

17

5

3

664

CHESAPEAKE AVE

Miss
Hampton II
Harbor
Cruises

Virginia Air
& Space
Center

HAMPTON

16TH ST

6

7

MONITOR
MERRIMAC
MEMORIAL
BRIDGE
TUNNEL

Hampton   River

Hampton

Roads

Naval

Station
Norfolk

64

273

258

17

Batten
Bay

664

Craney Island
Disposal Area

INTRACOASTAL WATERWAY

Elizabeth   River

337

564

LITTLE CREEK

460
168
165

276

Hermitage
Museum and
Gardens
Old
Dominion
University

276C
277

Chuckatuck Creek

CRITTENDEN

RD

BRIDGE   RD

Craney Island
Naval Fuel Depot

Portsmouth

NORFOLK

460

Virginia
Zoo

Norfolk
State
Univ

BENNETTS PASTURE RD

SHOULDERS HILL   RD

9

17

164

NORFOLK RD

Portsmouth Naval
Shipyard
Museum

SEE
DOWNTOWN
NORFOLK
INSET

247

Nansemond River

Suffolk

RD

17

Lightship
Portsmouth
Museum

HIGH   ST

Elizabeth   River

(TOLL)

58

11

125

NANSEMOND   PKY

664

11

PORTSMOUTH

Virginia
Sports
Hall of Fame
& Museum

Portsmouth Art
and Cultural
Ctr

7

PORTSMOUTH   BLVD

BLVD

Children's
Museum of
Virginia

(TOLL)

8/6

Nansemond
National
Wildlife Refuge

13

Western Branch

AIRLINE

ALT
460

58

264

299   15

GEORGE WASHINGTON HWY

4

17

ELM   AVE

MILITARY   HWY

4

464

460

2

1
291

Hampton Roads Area
Attractions

Scale in Miles

1.8   1.8

See p. 6 - Map Legend

To Petersburg

13

14

460

297

Chesapeake

13

17   64

296

166

17

292

15
168

13   58

460

13   58

460

BUS
460

To Franklin

2157-18

BUS
17

To Elizabeth City, NC

To Nags Head, NC

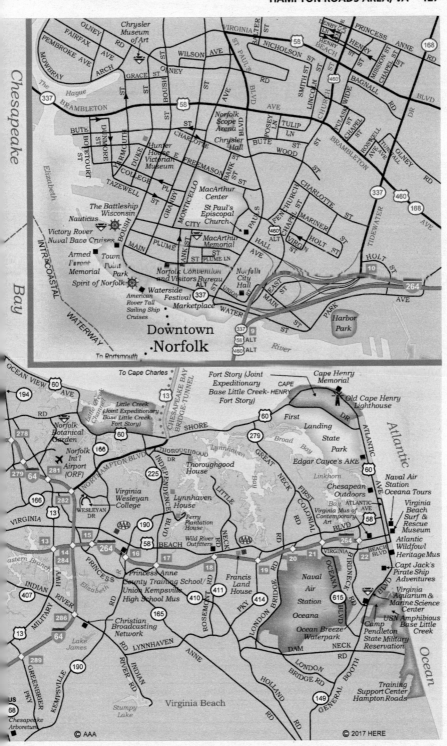

OLNEY
FAIRFAX
AVE
PEMBROKE AVE
MOWBRAY
ARCH
FAIRFAX AVE
Chrysler Museum of Art
WILSON AVE
VIRGINIA
ST
NICHOLSON ST
58
DENBY
LN
PRINCESS
HENRY
ST
ANNE
168
RD

The Hague
337
BRAMBLETON
GRACE ST
ST
OLNEY
BOUSH ST
ST
AVE
ST PAUL'S BLVD
RD
58
SMITH ST
LINCOLN ST
CHURCH ST
HENRY ST
MISSION ST
CHAPEL ST
BEACH
460
BAGNALL RD
WIDE ST
ROSWELL ST
OLNEY RD
TUNSTALL AVE
BLVD

Elizabeth
BUTE
DINMORE ST
BOTETOURT ST
DUKE ST
YARMOUTH ST
ST
Norfolk Scope Arena
BLVD
POSEY ST
TULIP LN
Chrysler Hall
BUTE
WOOD ST
ST
ST
BRAMBLETON AVE
337
460
168
TIDEWATER AVE

TAZEWELL ST
COLLEGE
Hunter House Victorian Museum
CHARLOTTE ST
E FREEMASON ST
BANK ST
ST
CHARLOTTE ST
PENCHURCH ST
CHAPEL ST
MARINER ST
337
460

The Battleship Wisconsin
Nauticus
MONTICELLO
GRANBY ST
MacArthur Center
St Paul's Episcopal Church
PAUL'S
MacArthur Memorial
460 ALT
VIRGIN ST
HOLT ST
HOLT ST

Victory Rover Naval Base Cruises
BOUSH
CITY
PLUME
BANK ST
ST
ST PLUME LN
HALL AVE
264
10

Armed Forces Memorial
Town Point Park
Spirit of Norfolk
MAIN
Norfolk Convention and Visitors Bureau
Norfolk City Hall
UNION ST
EAST MAIN ST
PARK AVE

American Rover Tall Sailing Ship Cruises
Waterside Festival Marketplace
337
WATER ST
337
Harbor Park

Downtown Norfolk
To Portsmouth
58 ALT
460 ALT
9
River

To Cape Charles
194
OCEAN VIEW
60
AVE
RD
13
Little Creek (Joint Expeditionary Base Little Creek- Fort Story)
SHORE
CHESAPEAKE BAY BRIDGE-TUNNEL
Fort Story (Joint Expeditionary Base Little Creek- Fort Story)
CAPE HENRY
Cape Henry Memorial
Old Cape Henry Lighthouse

278
Norfolk Botanical Garden
Norfolk Int'l Airport (ORF)
281
166
80
NORTHAMPTON BLVD
279
THOROUGHGOOD DR
Lynnhaven
GREAT NECK RD
60
First Landing State Park
DR
ATLANTIC
Atlantic

279
64
282
WESLEYAN DR
Virginia Wesleyan College
225
Thoroughgood House
Bay
Broad Bay
Edgar Cayce's ARE
Linkhorn
Chesapean Outdoors
60
Naval Air Station Oceana Tours

166
13
VIRGINIA
190
INDEPENDENCE BLVD
Lynnhaven House
LITTLE NECK RD
Bay
FIRST COLONIAL RD
Virginia Mus of Contemporary Art
ATLANTIC AVE
58
Virginia Beach Surf & Rescue Museum
Atlantic Wildfowl Heritage Mus

15
14
284
58
BEACH
Ferry Plantation House
Wild River Outfitters
264
VIRGINIA BEACH BLVD
BIRDNECK RD
264
22
Capt Jack's Pirate Ship Adventures

264
16
17
18
Princess Anne County Training School/Union Kempsville High School Mus
Francis Land House
19
20
21
OCEANA BLVD
615
Virginia Aquarium & Marine Science Center

INDIAN RIVER RD
407
286
PRINCESS ANNE RD
165
410
411
ROSEMONT RD
LONDON BRIDGE PKY
414
Naval Air Station Oceana
Camp Pendleton State Military Reservation
USN Amphibious Base Little Creek

13
289
64
Lake James
190
Christian Broadcasting Network
LYNNHAVEN
INDIAN RIVER RD
ANNE
Ocean Breeze Waterpark
DAM NECK RD
LONDON BRIDGE RD
GENERAL BOOTH
Ocean

US 66
GREENBRIER PKY
KEMPSVILLE RD
Stumpy Lake
Virginia Beach
HOLLAND RD
149
Training Support Center Hampton Roads

Chesapeake Arboretum
© AAA
© 2017 HERE

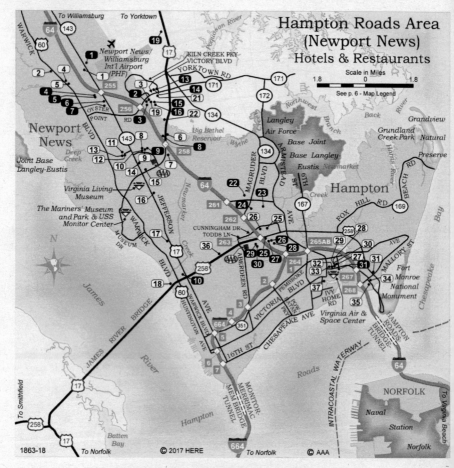

Hampton Roads Area (Newport News) Hotels & Restaurants

See p. 6 - Map Legend

Scale in Miles

© 2017 HERE   © AAA

1863-18

Hampton Roads Area (Newport News)

This index helps you "spot" where approved hotels and restaurants are located on the corresponding detailed maps. Hotel daily rate range is for comparison only. Restaurant price range is a combination of lunch and/or dinner. Turn to the listing page for more information and consult display ads for special promotions.

 For more details, rates and reservations: AAA.com/travelguides/hotels

NEWPORT NEWS

Map Page	Hotels	Diamond Rated	Rate Range	Page
1 this page	Comfort Suites Airport	◈◈◈	$84-$205	177
2 this page	Hampton Inn	◈◈◈	$99-$159	177
3 this page	Hilton Garden Inn	◈◈◈	$109-$169	177
4 this page	Residence Inn by Marriott Newport News Airport	◈◈◈	$89-$251	177
5 this page	Courtyard by Marriott Newport News Airport	◈◈◈	$55-$204	177
6 this page	Hampton Inn & Suites	◈◈◈	$109-$179	177
7 this page	**Best Western Plus Newport News Inn & Suites**	◈◈◈	$79-$199 (SAVE)	177
8 this page	Holiday Inn Express & Suites	◈◈◈	Rates not provided	177
9 this page	**Newport News Marriott at City Center**	◈◈◈	$79-$340 (SAVE)	177

NEWPORT NEWS (cont'd)

Map Page	Hotels (cont'd)	Diamond Rated	Rate Range	Page
10 p. 128	Super 8 Motel Newport News	◆	Rates not provided	177

Map Page	Restaurants	Diamond Rated	Cuisine	Price Range	Page
1 p. 128	Pho 79	◆◆	Vietnamese	$4-$11	178
2 p. 128	La Pena Horeb	◆	Puerto Rican	$8-$15	178
3 p. 128	2nd Street American Bistro	◆◆◆	American	$10-$20	177
4 p. 128	Kyung Sung Korean Restaurant	◆◆	Korean	$8-$25	178
5 p. 128	Balkan Cuisine	◆◆	European	$8-$16	177
6 p. 128	Chic n Fish	◆◆	Korean Chicken	$4-$23	177
7 p. 128	Midtown Eats	◆◆	American	$8-$12	178
8 p. 128	The Lunch Bell	◆◆	American	$4-$12	178
9 p. 128	Aromas	◆	Coffee/Tea Sandwiches	$5-$11	177
10 p. 128	Hayashi Sushi & Grill	◆◆	Japanese	$8-$35	178
11 p. 128	**Fin**	◆◆◆	Seafood	$14-$55	177
12 p. 128	Schlesinger's Chophouse	◆◆◆	Steak	$10-$66	178
13 p. 128	Thaijindesu Thai & Sushi Bar	◆◆	Thai	$9-$25	178
14 p. 128	Al Fresco Ristorante	◆◆	Italian	$11-$24	177
15 p. 128	Harpoon Larry's Fish House & Oyster Bar	◆◆	Seafood	$8-$68	177
16 p. 128	Sage Kitchen at Anderson's Showplace	◆◆	American	$8-$13	178
17 p. 128	Rocky Mount BBQ	◆◆	Southern American	$5-$9	178
18 p. 128	Crab Shack on the James	◆◆	Seafood	$7-$21	177
19 p. 128	Saisaki Asian Bistro & Sushi Bar	◆◆	Japanese Sushi	$8-$16	178

YORKTOWN

Map Page	Hotels	Diamond Rated	Rate Range	Page
13 p. 128	Courtyard by Marriott	◆◆◆	$72-$235	297
14 p. 128	**TownePlace Suites by Marriott**	◆◆	$67-$211 SAVE	297
15 p. 128	Candlewood Suites-Yorktown	◆◆◆	Rates not provided	297
16 p. 128	Staybridge Suites	◆◆◆	Rates not provided	297
19 p. 128	Red Roof Inn Yorktown	◆◆	$60-$120	297

Map Page	Restaurants	Diamond Rated	Cuisine	Price Range	Page
21 p. 128	Food Craft Kitchen & Bar	◆◆	Breakfast Comfort Food	$8-$14	298
22 p. 128	County Grill & Smokehouse	◆◆	Barbecue	$8-$16	298

HAMPTON

Map Page	Hotels	Diamond Rated	Rate Range	Page
22 p. 128	Candlewood Suites	◆◆◆	Rates not provided	148
23 p. 128	**Hampton Inn**	◆◆◆	$89-$220 SAVE	149
24 p. 128	Country Inn & Suites By Carlson	◆◆◆	Rates not provided	148
25 p. 128	Holiday Inn Express Hampton-Coliseum Central	◆◆◆	Rates not provided	149
26 p. 128	**Best Western Hampton Coliseum Inn**	◆◆	$79-$119 SAVE	148

HAMPTON (cont'd)

Map Page	Hotels (cont'd)	Diamond Rated	Rate Range	Page
27 p. 128	Courtyard by Marriott Hampton	◈◈◈	$70-$275	149
28 p. 128	Embassy Suites by Hilton Hampton Roads Hotel, Spa & Convention Center	◈◈◈	$129-$219	149
29 p. 128	Hilton Garden Inn Hampton Coliseum Central	◈◈◈	$89-$229	149
30 p. 128	SpringHill Suites by Marriott	◈◈◈	$63-$206	149
31 p. 128	**Crowne Plaza Hampton Marina Hotel**	◈◈◈	$89-$219 [SAVE]	149

Map Page	Restaurants	Diamond Rated	Cuisine	Price Range	Page
25 p. 128	El Azteca Restaurante Mexicano	◈◈	Mexican	$6-$17	149
26 p. 128	Monsoon	◈◈◈	Indian	$10-$25	149
27 p. 128	La Bodega Hampton	◈	Specialty	$5-$8	149
28 p. 128	Marker 20	◈◈	American	$10-$25	149
29 p. 128	The Taphouse on Queens Way	◈◈	American	$8-$20	149
30 p. 128	Venture Kitchen and Bar	◈◈	Small Plates Pizza	$8-$15	149
31 p. 128	Mama Rosa's	◈◈	Italian	$6-$19	149
32 p. 128	Musasi Japanese Restaurant	◈◈	Japanese Sushi	$9-$20	149
33 p. 128	The Grey Goose	◈◈	American	$5-$10	149
34 p. 128	Mango Mangeaux	◈◈◈	American	$10-$25	149
35 p. 128	The Point at Phoebus	◈◈◈	American	$10-$30	149
36 p. 128	Tommy's Restaurant	◈	Regional American	$3-$10	149
37 p. 128	The Barking Dog	◈	Hot Dogs	$7-$10	149

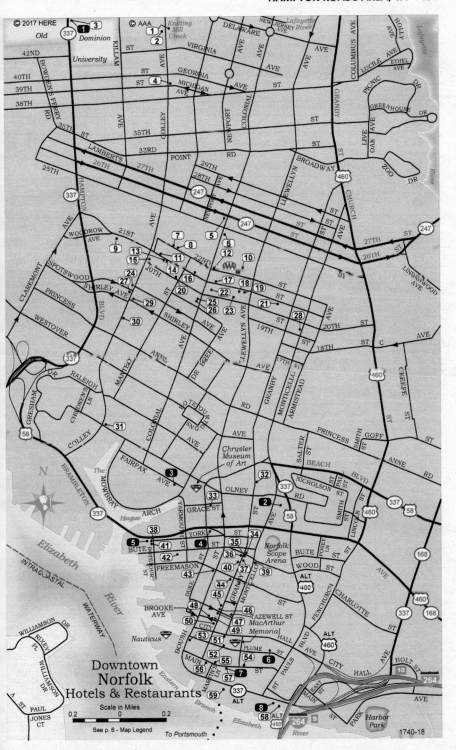

Downtown Norfolk

This index helps you "spot" where approved hotels and restaurants are located on the corresponding detailed maps. Hotel daily rate range is for comparison only. Restaurant price range is a combination of lunch and/or dinner. Turn to the listing page for more information and consult display ads for special promotions.

 For more details, rates and reservations: AAA.com/travelguides/hotels

NORFOLK

Map Page	Hotels	Diamond Rated	Rate Range	Page
1 p. 131	SpringHill Suites by Marriott-ODU	◆◆◆	$104-$246	182
2 p. 131	**Wyndham Garden Norfolk Downtown**	◆◆◆	Rates not provided SAVE	182
3 p. 131	Page House Inn Bed & Breakfast	◆◆◆	Rates not provided	181
4 p. 131	Residence Inn by Marriott Downtown	◆◆◆	$95-$286	181
5 p. 131	Freemason Inn Bed and Breakfast	◆◆◆	Rates not provided	181
6 p. 131	Courtyard by Marriott	◆◆◆	$60-$224	181
7 p. 131	**Norfolk Waterside Marriott**	◆◆◆	$93-$305 SAVE	181
8 p. 131	**Sheraton Norfolk Waterside Hotel**	◆◆◆	$89-$289 SAVE	181

Map Page	Restaurants	Diamond Rated	Cuisine	Price Range	Page
1 p. 131	Shiptown	◆◆◆	Seafood	$16-$40	183
2 p. 131	Cogan's Pizza North	◆◆	Pizza	$8-$20	182
3 p. 131	Recovery Sports Grill	◆◆	American	$9-$15	183
4 p. 131	Fellini's	◆◆	Pizza	$8-$20	182
5 p. 131	Handsome Biscuit	◆	Specialty	$4-$7	183
6 p. 131	Toast	◆◆	Breads/Pastries	$4-$9	184
7 p. 131	La Bella in Ghent	◆◆◆	Italian	$14-$23	183
8 p. 131	Pelon's Baja Grill	◆	Mexican	$7-$13	183
9 p. 131	Streats	◆◆	Small Plates	$9-$14	183
10 p. 131	Mermaid Winery	◆◆	American	$8-$26	183
11 p. 131	Rajput Indian Cuisine	◆◆	Indian	$5-$19	183
12 p. 131	A.W. Shucks Raw Bar & Grill	◆◆	Seafood	$10-$30	182
13 p. 131	Pho 79	◆◆	Vietnamese	$5-$34	183
14 p. 131	Kotobuki	◆◆	Japanese	$10-$27	183
15 p. 131	Luna Maya Cantina	◆◆	Latin American	$12-$28	183
16 p. 131	Katana Japanese Steak House & Sushi	◆	Japanese Steak Sushi	$7-$26	183
17 p. 131	Bardo Edibles & Elixirs	◆◆	Asian Small Plates	$7-$18	182
18 p. 131	Volcano Sushi and China Bistro	◆	Asian Sushi	$8-$18	184
19 p. 131	Supper Southern Morsels	◆◆◆	Southern American	$8-$20	183
20 p. 131	Dog-n-Burger Grille	◆	Burgers Hot Dogs	$4-$19	182
21 p. 131	80/20 Burger Bar	◆◆	Burgers	$9-$14	182
22 p. 131	Kappo Nara Ramen	◆◆	Asian Soup	$12-$13	183
23 p. 131	Jessy's Taco Bistro	◆◆	Mexican	$9-$16	183
24 p. 131	The Green Onion	◆◆◆	American	$9-$34	183
25 p. 131	Cafe Stella	◆◆	Coffee/Tea Natural/Organic	$7-$15	182

Map Page	Restaurants (cont'd)	Diamond Rated	Cuisine	Price Range	Page
26 p. 131	Cogan's Pizza	◆◆	Pizza	$7-$20	182
27 p. 131	Ynot Pizza & Italian Cuisine	◆◆	Italian Pizza	$6-$22	184
28 p. 131	Doumar's Cones & Barbecue	◆	Barbecue Burgers	$2-$5	182
29 p. 131	The Ten Top	◆	American	$8-$15	184
30 p. 131	Colley Cantina	◆◆	Mexican	$6-$14	182
31 p. 131	Press 626	◆◆◆	American	$8-$26	183
32 p. 131	Zeke's Beans & Bowls	◆	Natural/Organic Coffee/Tea	$8-$16	184
33 p. 131	Nouvelle	◆◆◆	New French	$10-$26	183
34 p. 131	Baxter's Sports Lounge	◆◆	American	$7-$20	182
35 p. 131	456 Fish	◆◆◆	Seafood	$15-$37	182
36 p. 131	Leone's	◆◆◆	Italian	$16-$25	183
37 p. 131	Bodega	◆◆	Spanish	$8-$17	182
38 p. 131	Voila Cuisine International	◆◆◆	Continental	$18-$30	184
39 p. 131	Bite Restaurant & Catering	◆◆	American	$8-$13	182
40 p. 131	Field Guide	◆◆	American	$8-$14	182
41 p. 131	Cure Coffeehouse & Brasserie	◆◆	Coffee/Tea Natural/Organic	$7-$10	182
42 p. 131	Omar's Carriage House	◆◆◆	International	$10-$28	183
43 p. 131	Freemason Abbey	◆◆	American	$8-$30	182
44 p. 131	The Grilled Cheese Bistro	◆◆	Sandwiches	$10-$14	183
45 p. 131	Saint Germain	◆◆◆	New American	$20-$30	183
46 p. 131	Luce	◆◆◆	Italian	$15-$24	183
47 p. 131	Granby Street Pizza	◆	Italian Pizza	$7-$11	183
48 p. 131	Byrd & Baldwin Brothers Steakhouse	◆◆◆	Steak	$20-$43	182
49 p. 131	Granby Bistro & Deli	◆◆	Mediterranean	$6-$10	183
50 p. 131	219 American Bistro	◆◆◆	New American	$7-$28	182
51 p. 131	Chartreuse Bistro	◆◆◆	American	$17-$27	182
52 p. 131	3 Way Cafe	◆	Sandwiches	$6-$10	182
53 p. 131	**Todd Jurich's Bistro**	◆◆◆	New American	$9-$42	184
54 p. 131	The Gourmet Gang	◆	Sandwiches	$7-$11	183
55 p. 131	D'Egg Diner	◆	Breakfast Comfort Food	$3-$12	182
56 p. 131	The Lizard Cafe at Prince Books	◆◆	Deli	$6-$9	183
57 p. 131	**Shula's 347**	◆◆◆	Steak	$11-$39	183
58 p. 131	Vintage Kitchen	◆◆◆	Regional American	$9-$32	184
59 p. 131	Guy Fieri's Smokehouse	◆◆	Barbecue	$9-$23	183

Save on travel, shopping, dining and more:

AAA.com/discounts

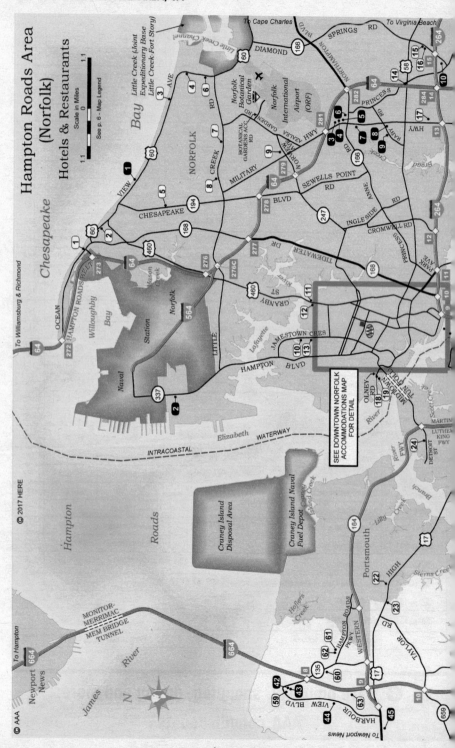

Hampton Roads Area
(Norfolk)

Hotels & Restaurants

Scale in Miles

See p. 6 - Map Legend

© AAA

© 2017 HERE

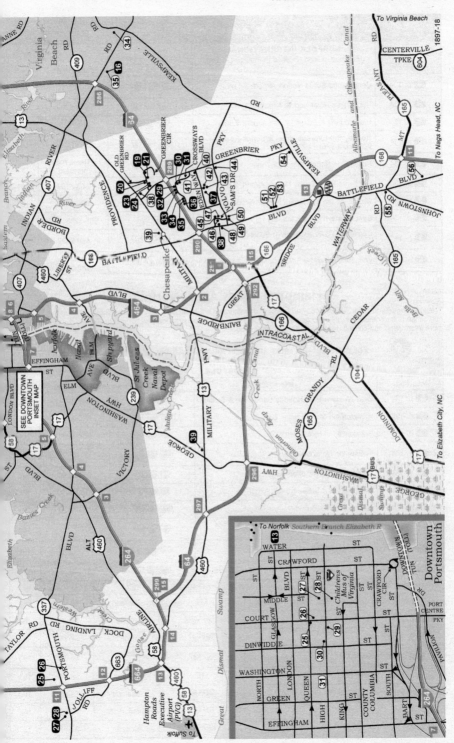

✈ Airport Hotels

Map Page	NORFOLK INTERNATIONAL (Maximum driving distance from airport: 5.1 mi)	Diamond Rated	Rate Range	Page
9 p. 134	Candlewood Suites Norfolk Airport, 3.4 mi	◈◈◈	Rates not provided	181
5 p. 134	DoubleTree Hotel Norfolk Airport, 2.3 mi	◈◈◈	$99-$299	181
6 p. 134	Hampton Inn & Suites Norfolk Airport, 2.5 mi	◈◈◈	$109-$239	181
8 p. 134	**Holiday Inn Express Hotel & Suites-Norfolk Airport, 3.3 mi**	◈◈◈	Rates not provided 〔SAVE〕	181
4 p. 134	Holiday Inn Norfolk Airport, 2.7 mi	◈◈◈	Rates not provided	181
7 p. 134	La Quinta Inn & Suites Norfolk Airport, 2.6 mi	◈◈◈	$63-$109	181
3 p. 134	Residence Inn by Marriott Norfolk Airport, 2.8 mi	◈◈◈	$86-$223	181
4 p. 140	**Best Western Center Inn, 5.1 mi**	◈◈	$65-$259 〔SAVE〕	259
5 p. 140	Comfort Inn & Suites Virginia Beach/Norfolk, 3.3 mi	◈◈◈	$80-$599	261
6 p. 140	Wingate by Wyndham-Norfolk Airport, 3.4 mi	◈◈◈	Rates not provided	266

Hampton Roads Area (Norfolk)

This index helps you "spot" where approved hotels and restaurants are located on the corresponding detailed maps. Hotel daily rate range is for comparison only. Restaurant price range is a combination of lunch and/or dinner. Turn to the listing page for more information and consult display ads for special promotions.

 For more details, rates and reservations: AAA.com/travelguides/hotels

NORFOLK

Map Page	Hotels	Diamond Rated	Rate Range	Page
1 p. 134	**Best Western Plus Holiday Sands Inn & Suites**	◈◈	$79-$259 〔SAVE〕	181
2 p. 134	Hampton Inn Norfolk Naval Base	◈◈◈	$89-$189	181
3 p. 134	Residence Inn by Marriott Norfolk Airport	◈◈◈	$86-$223	181
4 p. 134	Holiday Inn Norfolk Airport	◈◈◈	Rates not provided	181
5 p. 134	DoubleTree Hotel Norfolk Airport	◈◈◈	$99-$299	181
6 p. 134	Hampton Inn & Suites Norfolk Airport	◈◈◈	$109-$239	181
7 p. 134	La Quinta Inn & Suites Norfolk Airport	◈◈◈	$63-$109	181
8 p. 134	**Holiday Inn Express Hotel & Suites-Norfolk Airport**	◈◈◈	Rates not provided 〔SAVE〕	181
9 p. 134	Candlewood Suites Norfolk Airport	◈◈◈	Rates not provided	181
10 p. 134	SpringHill Suites by Marriott Norfolk/VA Beach	◈◈◈	$71-$258	182

Map Page	Restaurants	Diamond Rated	Cuisine	Price Range	Page
① p. 134	Ocean View Fishing Pier Restaurant	◈	Seafood	$8-$20	183
② p. 134	Franco's By the Bay	◈◈	Italian	$8-$20	182
③ p. 134	Razzo	◈◈	Italian	$9-$24	183
④ p. 134	Sandfiddler Cafe	◈◈	Breakfast Comfort Food	$6-$13	183
⑤ p. 134	Pizza Chef	◈	Pizza	$6-$16	183
⑥ p. 134	Capt. Groovy's Grill & Raw Bar	◈◈	Seafood	$8-$27	182
⑦ p. 134	The Azalea Inn	◈◈	Greek Pizza	$9-$25	182
⑧ p. 134	El Azteca Restaurante Mexicano	◈◈	Mexican	$7-$15	182

Map Page	Restaurants (cont'd)	Diamond Rated	Cuisine	Price Range	Page
⑨ p. 134	Franco's Italian Restaurant	▼▼	Italian	$8-$20	182
⑩ p. 134	Chow Restaurant & Bar	▼▼	Southern American	$10-$20	182
⑪ p. 134	Crackers Little Bar Bistro	▼▼▼	New Small Plates	$6-$19	182
⑫ p. 134	Mi Hogar Mexican Restaurant	▼▼	Mexican	$6-$11	183
⑬ p. 134	LeGrand Kitchen	▼▼	New American	$10-$26	183
⑭ p. 134	Cilantro Bangladeshi Bistro	▼	Asian	$6-$12	182
⑮ p. 134	Surf Rider West	▼▼	Seafood	$6-$20	184
⑯ p. 134	The Gourmet Gang	▼	Specialty Sandwiches	$7-$10	182
⑰ p. 134	Ichran Japanese Ramen	▼▼	Japanese Soup	$9-$16	183
⑱ p. 134	The Bakehouse at Chelsea	▼	Breads/Pastries Pizza	$11-$20	182
⑲ p. 134	Tortilla West	▼▼	Mexican	$7-$17	184

PORTSMOUTH

Map Page	Hotel	Diamond Rated	Rate Range	Page
⑬ p. 134	**Renaissance Portsmouth-Norfolk Waterfront**	▼▼▼	$101-$252 (AVL)	190

Map Page	Restaurants	Diamond Rated	Cuisine	Price Range	Page
㉒ p. 134	JoJack's Espresso Bar & Cafe	▼	Coffee/Tea Sandwiches	$8-$11	189
㉓ p. 134	Ono Hawaii BBQ	▼▼	Hawaiian Barbecue	$7-$13	189
㉔ p. 134	Stove	▼▼▼	American	$12-$26	189
㉕ p. 134	Still Worldly Eclectic Tapas	▼▼▼	Small Plates	$7-$19	189
㉖ p. 134	Home Grown	▼▼	Pizza	$9-$16	189
㉗ p. 134	Roger Brown's Restaurant & Sports Bar	▼▼	American	$9-$22	189
㉘ p. 134	Cafe Europa	▼▼▼	Continental	$10-$20	189
㉙ p. 134	**Commodore Theatre**	▼▼	American	$5-$12	189
㉚ p. 134	The Bier Garden	▼▼	German	$7-$20	189
㉛ p. 134	Mannino's Italian Bistro	▼▼	Italian	$10-$30	189

VIRGINIA BEACH

Map Page	Hotel	Diamond Rated	Rate Range	Page
⑯ p. 134	The Founders Inn and Spa	▼▼▼	Rates not provided	263

Map Page	Restaurants	Diamond Rated	Cuisine	Price Range	Page
㉞ p. 134	Pulcinella	▼▼	Italian	$8-$18	268
㉟ p. 134	Swan Terrace	▼▼▼	American	$10-$37	269

CHESAPEAKE

Map Page	Hotels	Diamond Rated	Rate Range	Page
⑲ p. 134	**Wingate by Wyndham Greenbrier**	▼▼▼	Rates not provided (SAVE)	91
⑳ p. 134	**Red Roof Inn Chesapeake Conference Center**	▼▼	$60-$150 (SAVE)	91
㉑ p. 134	Holiday Inn Express Chesapeake-Norfolk	▼▼▼	Rates not provided	90
㉓ p. 134	Staybridge Suites Greenbrier	▼▼▼	Rates not provided	91
㉔ p. 134	Hampton Inn Chesapeake/Greenbrier	▼▼▼	$89-$209	90
㉕ p. 134	Holiday Inn Express & Suites	▼▼▼	Rates not provided	90

CHESAPEAKE (cont'd)

Map Page	Hotels (cont'd)	Diamond Rated	Rate Range	Page
26 p. 134	Hampton Inn & Suites Chesapeake Square Mall	♦♦♦	$93-$149	90
27 p. 134	Fairfield Inn & Suites by Marriott Chesapeake Suffolk	♦♦♦	$70-$229	90
28 p. 134	Candlewood Suites	♦♦♦	Rates not provided	90
29 p. 134	**Courtyard by Marriott Chesapeake Greenbrier**	♦♦♦	$88-$221 SAVE	90
30 p. 134	Hilton Garden Inn-Chesapeake/Greenbrier	♦♦♦	$129-$199	90
31 p. 134	Homewood Suites by Hilton	♦♦♦	$129-$199	91
32 p. 134	Fairfield Inn & Suites by Marriott Chesapeake	♦♦♦	$71-$227	90
33 p. 134	Comfort Suites	♦♦♦	$89-$299	90
34 p. 134	Residence Inn by Marriott, Chesapeake-Greenbrier	♦♦♦	$95-$256	91
35 p. 134	Aloft Chesapeake	♦♦♦	$79-$289	90
36 p. 134	SpringHill Suites by Marriott Greenbrier	♦♦♦	$69-$212	91
37 p. 134	**Hyatt Place-Chesapeake/Greenbrier**	♦♦♦	$124-$229 SAVE	91
38 p. 134	Hampton Inn & Suites	♦♦♦	$79-$309	90
39 p. 134	Comfort Inn & Suites	♦♦♦	$60-$300	90

Map Page	Restaurants	Diamond Rated	Cuisine	Price Range	Page
38 p. 134	Kervan Kebab House	♦♦	Turkish	$6-$9	91
39 p. 134	Thai 99	♦♦	Thai	$7-$15	91
40 p. 134	Pho Dalat	♦♦	Vietnamese	$7-$10	91
41 p. 134	Surf Rider Chesapeake	♦♦	Seafood	$8-$24	91
42 p. 134	Stacked Eatery Company	♦	Breakfast Comfort Food	$7-$12	91
43 p. 134	Spaghetti Eddie's Pizza Cafe	♦♦	Italian Pizza	$8-$13	91
44 p. 134	El Loro Mexican Restaurante	♦♦	Mexican	$6-$13	91
45 p. 134	Warrior's Grill	♦	Asian	$9-$11	92
46 p. 134	The Cutting Edge Cafe	♦	Sandwiches	$6-$10	91
47 p. 134	India Palace	♦♦	Indian	$10-$16	91
48 p. 134	Daikichi Sushi Japanese Bistro	♦♦	Japanese Sushi	$8-$18	91
49 p. 134	The Gourmet Gang	♦	Sandwiches	$7-$9	91
50 p. 134	Va Yama Sushi Bar	♦♦	Japanese Sushi	$8-$20	92
51 p. 134	Oishi Sushi	♦♦	Japanese Sushi	$7-$20	91
52 p. 134	Maymar Filipino Restaurant	♦	Philippine	$4-$10	91
53 p. 134	Cutlass Grille	♦♦	Jamaican	$8-$20	91
54 p. 134	The Egg Bistro	♦	American	$5-$19	91
55 p. 134	Courthouse Cafe	♦♦	Regional American	$9-$28	91
56 p. 134	Pollard's Chicken	♦	Chicken	$4-$9	91

SUFFOLK

Map Page	Hotels	Diamond Rated	Rate Range	Page
42 p. 134	TownePlace Suites by Marriott	♦♦♦	$72-$299	251
43 p. 134	Courtyard by Marriott	♦♦♦	$71-$194	251
44 p. 134	Hilton Garden Inn Chesapeake/Suffolk	♦♦♦	$99-$169	251

SUFFOLK (cont'd)

Map Page	Hotels (cont'd)		Diamond Rated	Rate Range	Page
45 p. 134	**Comfort Suites Suffolk/Chesapeake**		◈◈◈	$84-$179 SAVE	251

Map Page	Restaurants	Diamond Rated	Cuisine	Price Range	Page
59 p. 134	River Stone Chophouse	◈◈◈	Steak Seafood	$28-$47	251
60 p. 134	Nana Sushi	◈◈	Japanese Sushi	$8-$23	251
61 p. 134	Totoy's Filipino Store	◈	Philippine	$6-$17	251
62 p. 134	Bella Napoli Italian Restaurant	◈◈	Italian Pizza	$6-$19	251
63 p. 134	The Egg Bistro	◈◈	Breakfast	$7-$24	251

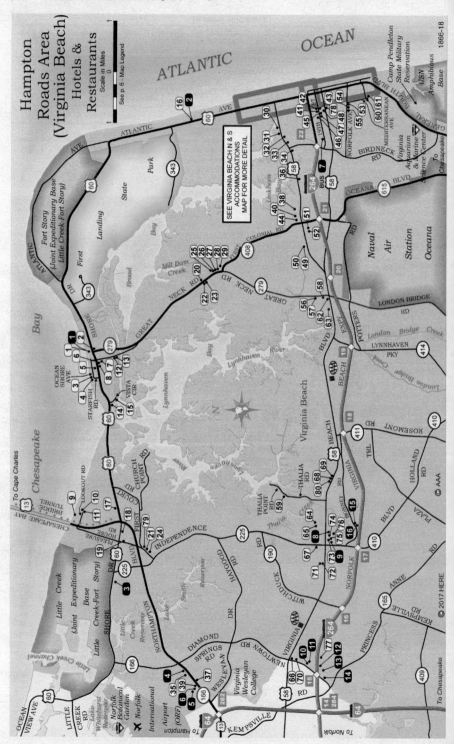

Hampton Roads Area (Virginia Beach) Hotels & Restaurants

See p. 6 - Map Legend

Scale in Miles

SEE VIRGINIA BEACH N & S ACCOMMODATIONS MAP FOR MORE DETAIL.

ATLANTIC OCEAN

1866-18

© 2017 HERE

Hampton Roads Area (Virginia Beach)

This index helps you "spot" where approved hotels and restaurants are located on the corresponding detailed maps. Hotel daily rate range is for comparison only. Restaurant price range is a combination of lunch and/or dinner. Turn to the listing page for more information and consult display ads for special promotions.

 For more details, rates and reservations: AAA.com/travelguides/hotels

VIRGINIA BEACH

Map Page	Hotels	Diamond Rated	Rate Range	Page
1 p. 140	**Virginia Beach Resort Hotel & Conference Center**	◆◆◆	Rates not provided SAVE	266
2 p. 140	Wyndham Virginia Beach Oceanfront	◆◆◆	Rates not provided	266
3 p. 140	**Quality Inn**	◆◆	$72-$149 SAVE	265
4 p. 140	**Best Western Center Inn**	◆◆	$65-$259 SAVE	259
5 p. 140	Comfort Inn & Suites Virginia Beach/Norfolk	◆◆◆	$80-$599	261
6 p. 140	Wingate by Wyndham-Norfolk Airport	◆◆◆	Rates not provided	266
7 p. 140	**DoubleTree by Hilton Hotel Virginia Beach**	◆◆◆	$119-$309 SAVE	262
8 p. 140	Hilton Garden Inn Virginia Beach, Town Center	◆◆◆	$119-$279	264
9 p. 140	**The Westin Virginia Beach Town Center**	◆◆◆	$109-$399 SAVE	266
10 p. 140	**TownePlace Suites by Marriott**	◆◆	$76-$286 SAVE	266
11 p. 140	Homewood Suites by Hilton	◆◆◆	$99-$399	264
12 p. 140	Courtyard by Marriott Virginia Beach Norfolk	◆◆◆	$54-$259	262
13 p. 140	**Holiday Inn Virginia Beach/Norfolk Hotel & Conference Center**	◆◆◆	Rates not provided SAVE	264
14 p. 140	Hampton Inn Norfolk/Virginia Beach	◆◆◆	$99-$219	203
15 p. 140	Candlewood Suites	◆◆◆	Rates not provided	261
16 p. 140	Crowne Plaza Virginia Beach	◆◆◆	Rates not provided	262

Map Page	Restaurants	Diamond Rated	Cuisine	Price Range	Page
1 p. 140	**Tradewinds**	◆◆◆	American	$7-$27	269
2 p. 140	Hot Tuna Bar & Grill	◆◆◆	Seafood	$8-$27	267
3 p. 140	**Lynnhaven Fish House Restaurant**	◆◆◆	Seafood	$11-$33	268
4 p. 140	Pier Cafe	◆◆	Seafood	$9-$17	268
5 p. 140	Dish Restaurant	◆◆	Scandinavian	$6-$16	267
6 p. 140	Bay Local Eatery	◆◆	Breakfast	$6-$20	266
7 p. 140	Citrus	◆◆	Breakfast	$6-$13	267
8 p. 140	Shorebreak Pizza, Sports and Billiards	◆◆	Pizza Wings	$8-$19	269
9 p. 140	Buoy 44 Seafood Grill	◆◆	Seafood	$10-$24	267
10 p. 140	Green Parrot Grille	◆◆	Seafood	$9-$23	267
11 p. 140	Zia Marie	◆◆	Italian	$8-$25	270
12 p. 140	One Fish Two Fish	◆◆◆	Seafood	$22-$34	268
13 p. 140	Il Giardino Ristorante	◆◆◆	Italian	$16-$30	267
14 p. 140	Bubba's Crabhouse & Seafood Restaurant	◆◆	Seafood	$9-$23	267
15 p. 140	Chick's Oyster Bar	◆◆	Seafood	$10-$32	267
16 p. 140	Surf Club Ocean Grille	◆◆◆	Seafood	$9-$29	269

Map Page	Restaurants (cont'd)	Diamond Rated	Cuisine	Price Range	Page
⑰ p. 140	Leaping Lizard Cafe	◆◆◆	American	$7-$20	268
⑱ p. 140	Anchor Allie's Bistro	◆◆	Breakfast Sandwiches	$7-$14	266
⑲ p. 140	Jenna's Mediterranean Deli	◆◆	Mediterranean	$6-$12	268
⑳ p. 140	Coastal Grill	◆◆◆	American	$17-$28	267
㉑ p. 140	Lubo Wine Bar & Cafe	◆◆	American	$8-$23	268
㉒ p. 140	Venuto Italian	◆◆◆	Italian	$15-$24	269
㉓ p. 140	Havana	◆◆	American	$10-$28	267
㉔ p. 140	1608 Crafthouse	◆◆	Southern American	$10-$20	266
㉕ p. 140	Pasta e Pani	◆◆◆	Italian	$15-$28	268
㉖ p. 140	Casby's Kitchen & Tap	◆◆	American	$10-$25	267
㉗ p. 140	Sirena Serious EATalian	◆◆◆	Italian	$12-$22	269
㉘ p. 140	Volcano Sushi Bar	◆◆	Japanese	$10-$32	270
㉙ p. 140	Ynot Italian Restaurant	◆◆	Italian Pizza	$6-$22	270
㉚ p. 140	Eurasia Cafe & Wine Bar	◆◆◆	New American	$10-$30	267
㉛ p. 140	The Heritage Natural Market & Cafe	◆	Vegetarian	$6-$10	267
㉜ p. 140	Beach Pub	◆◆	Seafood	$5-$17	266
㉝ p. 140	La Bella Italia Trattoria	◆◆	Italian	$8-$24	268
㉞ p. 140	Bella Monte Restaurant & Enoteca	◆◆◆	Italian	$12-$30	266
㉟ p. 140	Han Woo Ri	◆◆	Korean	$9-$15	267
㊱ p. 140	Sugar Plum Bakery & Cafe	◆	Breads/Pastries Desserts	$5-$8	269
㊲ p. 140	Aberdeen Barn	◆◆	Steak	$20-$96	266
㊳ p. 140	Cobalt Grille	◆◆◆	American	$9-$35	267
㊴ p. 140	Sakura Sushi Bar & Japanese Restaurant	◆◆	Japanese	$7-$35	269
㊵ p. 140	Fruitive	◆	Natural/Organic Vegan	$8-$15	267
㊶ p. 140	Three Ship Coffee	◆	Coffee/Tea Breads/Pastries	$3-$7	269
㊷ p. 140	Beach Bully Barbeque	◆	Barbecue	$5-$20	266
㊸ p. 140	Java Surf Beach Cafe	◆	Coffee/Tea Sandwiches	$6-$9	268
㊹ p. 140	Baladi Mediterranean Cafe	◆◆	Mediterranean Natural/Organic	$9-$17	266
㊺ p. 140	Croc's 19th Street Bistro	◆◆◆	American	$10-$25	267
㊻ p. 140	**Zoe's**	◆◆◆◆	New American	$20-$40	270
㊼ p. 140	The Stockpot	◆◆	Natural/Organic Soup	$4-$8	269
㊽ p. 140	Mary's Restaurant	◆◆	Breakfast Comfort Food	$5-$10	268
㊾ p. 140	Aldo's Ristorante	◆◆◆	Italian	$11-$41	266
㊿ p. 140	Mizuno Japanese Restaurant	◆◆◆	Japanese	$11-$30	268
(51) p. 140	Guads	◆◆	Mexican	$6-$21	267
(52) p. 140	Pho 79	◆◆	Vietnamese	$8-$20	268
(53) p. 140	Tad's Deli	◆	Deli	$7-$13	269
(54) p. 140	Gringo's Taqueria	◆◆	Mexican	$6-$17	267

Map Page	Restaurants (cont'd)	Diamond Rated	Cuisine	Price Range	Page
⑤⑤ p. 140	Zeke's Beans & Bowls	▽▽	Natural/Organic Vegetarian	$7-$16	270
⑤⑥ p. 140	Warrior's Grill	▽	Mongolian	$8-$12	270
⑤⑦ p. 140	When in Rome Pasta Bar	▽▽	Italian	$16-$24	270
⑤⑧ p. 140	Citrus	▽▽	American	$7-$17	267
⑤⑨ p. 140	Steinhilber's Restaurant	▽▽▽	Seafood	$18-$55	269
⑥⓪ p. 140	**Rockafeller's**	▽▽	Seafood	$10-$33	268
⑥① p. 140	**Rudee's on the Inlet**	▽▽	Seafood	$9-$35	269
⑥② p. 140	Pollard's Chicken	▽	American	$5-$9	268
⑥③ p. 140	Vietnam Garden	▽▽	Vietnamese	$7-$14	269
⑥④ p. 140	Judy's Sichuan Cuisine	▽▽	Chinese	$8-$20	268
⑥⑤ p. 140	El Azteca Mexican Restaurant	▽▽	Mexican	$6-$15	267
⑥⑥ p. 140	Saigon 1 Restaurant	▽▽	Vietnamese	$7-$14	269
⑥⑦ p. 140	Jade Villa Chinese Restaurant	▽▽	Chinese	$7-$20	268
⑥⑧ p. 140	The Route 58 Delicatessen	▽▽	Deli Sandwiches	$10-$18	269
⑥⑨ p. 140	Reginella's Italian Ristorante & Pizzeria	▽▽	Italian	$7-$19	268
⑦⓪ p. 140	Los Cuates Tienda Y Taqueria	▽▽	Mexican	$7-$20	268
⑦① p. 140	Pho 79	▽▽	Vietnamese	$6-$20	268
⑦② p. 140	Peter Chang - Town Center	▽▽	Chinese	$12-$22	268
⑦③ p. 140	Confetti Caffe & Gelato	▽	Sandwiches Desserts	$6-$10	267
⑦④ p. 140	Zushi Japanese Bistro	▽▽▽	Japanese Sushi	$8-$25	270
⑦⑤ p. 140	Sonoma Wine Bar & Bistro	▽▽	American	$10-$39	269
⑦⑥ p. 140	Saffron Indian Bistro	▽▽	Indian	$12-$24	269
⑦⑦ p. 140	Dancing Tomato	▽	Soup Sandwiches	$5-$8	267
⑦⑧ p. 140	Hearth Wood-fired Cuisine & Craft Beer	▽▽	Pizza	$13-$25	267

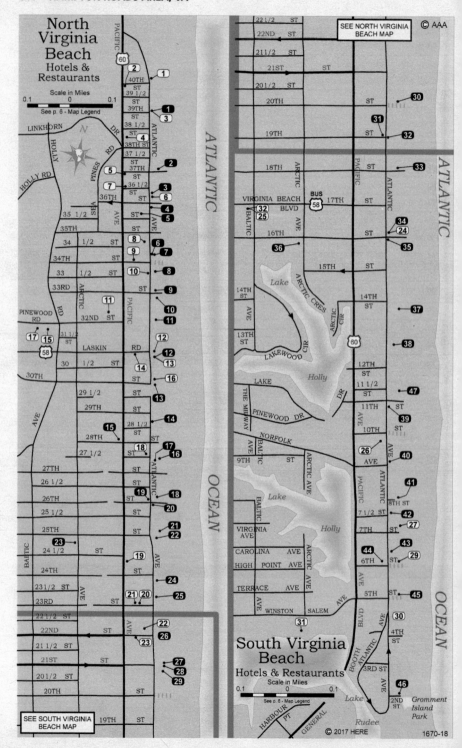

North Virginia Beach
Hotels & Restaurants

Scale in Miles

See p. 6 - Map Legend

SEE SOUTH VIRGINIA BEACH MAP

SEE NORTH VIRGINIA BEACH MAP

© AAA

South Virginia Beach
Hotels & Restaurants

Scale in Miles

See p. 6 - Map Legend

© 2017 HERE

1670-18

Gromment Island Park

Rudee

Hampton Roads Area (Virginia Beach-Beach Area)

This index helps you "spot" where approved hotels and restaurants are located on the corresponding detailed maps. Hotel daily rate range is for comparison only. Restaurant price range is a combination of lunch and/or dinner. Turn to the listing page for more information and consult display ads for special promotions.

 For more details, rates and reservations: AAA.com/travelguides/hotels

VIRGINIA BEACH

Map Page	Hotels	Diamond Rated	Rate Range	Page
1 p. 144	**Holiday Inn & Suites - North Beach**	◆◆◆	Rates not provided (SAVE)	264
2 p. 144	**Courtyard by Marriott-Oceanfront North**	◆◆◆	$79-$437 (SAVE)	261
3 p. 144	**Belvedere Beach Resort**	◆◆	$59-$399 (SAVE)	259
4 p. 144	**Sheraton Virginia Beach Oceanfront Hotel**	◆◆◆	$99-$299 (SAVE)	265
5 p. 144	**Royal Clipper Inn & Suites** *(See ad p. 263.)*	◆◆	$55-$279 (SAVE)	265
6 p. 144	Oceanaire Resort Hotel	◆◆◆	Rates not provided	265
7 p. 144	Oooan Beach Club Resort	◆◆◆	Rates not provided	265
8 p. 144	Hilton Garden Inn Virginia Beach Oceanfront	◆◆◆	Rates not provided	264
9 p. 144	Four Sails Resort Hotel	◆◆◆	$69-$289	263
10 p. 144	Residence Inn by Marriott Virginia Beach Oceanfront	◆◆◆	$112-$468	265
11 p. 144	**Hampton Inn Virginia Beach Oceanfront North**	◆◆◆	$99-$409 (SAVE)	264
12 p. 144	Hilton Virginia Beach Oceanfront	◆◆◆	$119-$569	264
13 p. 144	**The Oceanfront Inn**	◆◆◆	$54-$259 (SAVE)	265
14 p. 144	**Best Western Plus Virginia Beach** *(See ad p. 260.)*	◆◆◆	$73-$300 (SAVE)	260
15 p. 144	**La Quinta Inn & Suites Virginia Beach**	◆◆◆	$59-$259	264
16 p. 144	**Econo Lodge on the Ocean** *(See ad p. 262.)*	◆◆	$59-$319 (SAVE)	263
17 p. 144	**Hyatt House Virginia Beach/Oceanfront**	◆◆◆	$89-$459 (SAVE)	264
18 p. 144	Holiday Inn Express Hotel & Suites Virginia Beach Oceanfront	◆◆◆	Rates not provided	264
19 p. 144	Clarion Inn & Suites	◆◆◆	$79-$399	261
20 p. 144	**Seahawk Motel**	◆◆	$59-$299 (SAVE)	265
21 p. 144	**Courtyard by Marriott-Oceanfront South**	◆◆◆	$84-$459 (SAVE)	262
22 p. 144	**Days Inn Oceanfront**	◆◆	Rates not provided (SAVE)	262
23 p. 144	**Beach Spa Bed and Breakfast**	◆◆◆	Rates not provided (SAVE)	259
24 p. 144	Comfort Suites Beachfront Virginia Beach	◆◆◆	$99-$549	261
25 p. 144	**Ocean Suites** *(See ad p. 263.)*	◆◆	$59-$329 (SAVE)	265
26 p. 144	**Marjac Suites**	◆◆	$49-$650 (SAVE)	265
27 p. 144	**Econo Lodge Oceanfront**	◆◆	$119-$309 (SAVE)	262
28 p. 144	Holiday Inn Oceanside	◆◆◆	Rates not provided	264
29 p. 144	**Comfort Inn & Suites Virginia Beach-Oceanfront**	◆◆◆	$109-$680 (SAVE)	261
30 p. 144	The Capes Ocean Resort	◆◆◆	$90-$425	261
31 p. 144	**19 Atlantic Hotel**	◆◆	$69-$229 (SAVE)	259
32 p. 144	**Fairfield Inn & Suites by Marriott Virginia Beach Oceanfront**	◆◆◆	$78-$447 (SAVE)	263

VIRGINIA BEACH (cont'd)

Map Page	Hotels (cont'd)	Diamond Rated	Rate Range	Page
33 p. 144	Country Inn & Suites By Carlson (Oceanfront)	◆◆◆	Rates not provided	261
34 p. 144	Boardwalk Resort Hotel and Villas	◆◆◆	Rates not provided	260
35 p. 144	**The Breakers Resort Inn** *(See ad p. 261.)*	◆◆◆	Rates not provided (SAVE)	260
36 p. 144	Barclay Cottage Bed & Breakfast	◆◆◆	Rates not provided	259
37 p. 144	**Best Western Plus Sandcastle Beachfront Hotel**	◆◆◆	$89-$359 (SAVE)	260
38 p. 144	**Four Points by Sheraton Virginia Beach Oceanfront** *(See ad p. 263.)*	◆◆◆	$79-$409 (SAVE)	263
39 p. 144	**Hampton Inn Virginia Beach Oceanfront South**	◆◆◆	$109-$409 (SAVE)	264
40 p. 144	SpringHill Suites by Marriott Virginia Beach Oceanfront	◆◆◆	$101-$465	266
41 p. 144	**Barclay Towers**	◆◆◆	$79-$359 (SAVE)	259
42 p. 144	Quality Inn & Suites	◆◆	$59-$519	265
43 p. 144	Ramada On the Beach	◆◆◆	Rates not provided	265
44 p. 144	Turtle Cay Resort	◆◆◆	Rates not provided	266
45 p. 144	Beach Quarters Resort	◆◆◆	Rates not provided	259
46 p. 144	**Schooner Inn**	◆◆	Rates not provided (SAVE)	265
47 p. 144	Surfbreak Oceanfront Hotel - An Ascend Hotel Collection Member	◆◆◆		266

Map Page	Restaurants	Diamond Rated	Cuisine	Price Range	Page
1 p. 144	eat-an american bistro	◆◆◆	New American	$17-$34	267
2 p. 144	Pacifica Little Bar & Bistro	◆◆	New Small Plates	$6-$21	268
3 p. 144	Isle of Capri	◆◆◆	Italian	$15-$25	267
4 p. 144	The Green Cat	◆	Vegan Vegetarian	$6-$10	267
5 p. 144	Sakura Sushi Bar	◆◆	Japanese Sushi	$7-$35	269
6 p. 144	The Belvedere Coffee Shop & Diner	◆	Breakfast Sandwiches	$5-$9	266
7 p. 144	Pelon's Baja Grill	◆	Mexican	$7-$11	268
8 p. 144	Mannino's Italian Bistro Oceanfront	◆◆	Italian	$16-$33	268
9 p. 144	Mayflower Cafe	◆◆	Mediterranean	$5-$23	268
10 p. 144	Big Italy	◆◆	Italian Pizza	$8-$22	266
11 p. 144	Perked Up Coffee Cafe	◆	Coffee/Tea Sandwiches	$5-$8	268
12 p. 144	North Beach Bar & Grill	◆◆	American	$7-$25	268
13 p. 144	Salacia	◆◆◆◆	Steak	$25-$45	269
14 p. 144	Soya Sushi Bar & Bistro	◆◆	Japanese	$11-$35	269
15 p. 144	**Terrapin**	◆◆◆◆	New American	$22-$43	269
16 p. 144	Catch 31 Fish House & Bar	◆◆◆	Seafood	$8-$22	267
17 p. 144	Tempt Restaurant & Lounge	◆◆	American	$10-$23	269
18 p. 144	Cactus Jack's Southwest Grill	◆◆	Southwestern	$10-$33	267
19 p. 144	CP Shuckers Cafe & Raw Bar	◆◆	Seafood	$10-$23	267
20 p. 144	Tautog's	◆◆	Seafood	$7-$27	269

Map Page	Restaurants (cont'd)	Diamond Rated	Cuisine	Price Range	Page
㉑ p. 144	Doc Taylor's	♦♦♦	American	$5-$9	267
㉒ p. 144	Abbey Road Pub & Restaurant	♦♦♦	American	$9-$24	266
㉓ p. 144	Repeal Bourbon & Burgers	♦♦♦	Burgers	$10-$14	268
㉔ p. 144	Rockfish Boardwalk Bar & Sea Grill	♦♦♦	Seafood	$6-$28	268
㉕ p. 144	Commune	♦♦♦	Vegetarian Natural/Organic	$10-$18	267
㉖ p. 144	IL Giardino	♦♦♦♦	Italian	$11-$47	267
㉗ p. 144	Chix Sea Grill and Bar	♦♦♦	American Seafood	$9-$25	267
㉙ p. 144	Mahi Mah's Seafood Restaurant & Sushi Saloon	♦♦♦	Seafood Sushi	$5-$21	268
㉚ p. 144	**Waterman's Surfside Grill**	♦♦♦	Seafood	$8-$33	270
㉛ p. 144	Big Sam's Inlet Cafe & Raw Bar	♦♦♦	Seafood	$7-$33	266
㉜ p. 144	Esoteric Craft Beer and Curated Provisions	♦♦♦♦	New American Small Plates	$12-$31	267
㉟ p. 144	Marchese Italian Market & Cafe	♦	Italian Sandwiches	$8-$13	268
⑧ p. 144	Hair of the Dog Eatery	♦♦	American	$10-$16	267

HAMPTON (H-10) pop. 137,436, elev. 3'

- Hotels p. 148 • Restaurants p. 149
- Hotels & Restaurants map & index p. 128
- Part of Hampton Roads Area — see map p. 124

Settled in 1610, Hampton is the oldest continuously English-speaking settlement still in existence in the nation. In 1619 it was one of the original boroughs in the Virginia Legislature.

One of the first battles of the Revolutionary War in Virginia was fought in Hampton in October 1775. Hampton again was invaded and partially burned by British forces in 1813. The first planned land battle of the Civil War was fought at Big Bethel in Hampton in 1861. In August 1861 the town was burned again, this time by Confederates.

Fort Monroe, now a national monument, was one of the few forts in the South not captured by the Confederates at the outbreak of hostilities. The fortification was an important base in the Chesapeake Bay for the Union Army and Navy during the Civil War. The world's first conflict between two ironclad vessels took place here in 1862 when the Confederate ironclad CSS *Virginia (Merrimac)* attacked the Union fleet and its defending ironclad, the USS *Monitor*. Each failed to pierce the other's armor, but the *Virginia* destroyed two other ships, the *Congress* and the *Cumberland*.

North off SR 134 is Joint Base Langley-Eustis (formerly Langley Air Force Base), headquarters for the 633d Air Base Wing and a number of other Air Force units. The nearby NASA Langley Research Center served as the original training site for the nation's first seven astronauts; the U.S. space program was founded in Hampton and NASA Langley remains active in aeronautical research.

The Hampton area is the center of Virginia's fishing industry. Oysters and Chesapeake Bay blue crabs are of particular importance. Public beach areas include Buckroe Beach, a bayfront park with lifeguards, umbrella rentals, a concert bandstand, a playground and a fishing pier. Grandview Nature Preserve, a 578-acre estuary off Beach Road, is ideal for observing wildlife as well as kayaking, hiking and fishing. Shops, restaurants and museums line Queens Way and the downtown waterfront along Settlers Landing Road, where visitors can watch the traffic of fishing boats, ferries and boat tours that visit Fort Wool. The antique Hampton Carousel, with hand-carved horses and an original band organ, has its own harborside pavilion where rides are offered year-round.

Hampton also caters to sports enthusiasts. The Peninsula Pilots, a Coastal Plain League baseball team, play at War Memorial Stadium, 1889 W. Pembroke Ave., from late May to early August; phone (757) 245-2222.

Hampton Convention & Visitor Bureau: 1919 Commerce Dr., Suite 290, Hampton, VA 23666. **Phone:** (757) 722-1222 or (800) 487-8778.

Area information also is available from the Hampton Visitor Center off I-64 exit 267 at 120 Old Hampton Ln., Hampton, VA 23669; phone (800) 800-2202.

Self-guiding tours: Self-guiding iPod and smartphone tours of downtown Hampton, Hampton University, Fort Monroe, the Virginia Air & Space Center and various historic neighborhoods are available for download through the convention and visitor bureau. In addition, a series of historical markers interpreting 400-plus years of area history are located throughout Hampton, including on the Hampton University campus. A brochure describing a walking tour of the school campus also is available from the Hampton University Museum.

Shopping: In addition to well-tended public greens and bubbling fountains, Peninsula Town Center

(See map & index p. 128.)

(4410 E. Claiborne Sq.) features more than 60 specialty retailers, including such national chains as Chico's, H&M and Victoria's Secret. Anchored by JCPenney, the open-air shopping village is off I-64 exit 263.

BLUEBIRD GAP FARM is at 60 Pine Chapel Rd. between I-64 and Powhatan Pkwy. The 60-acre interactive children's farm has domestic and wild animals and various fowl as well as a display of farm machines, an azalea nature trail and an antique barn. A playground is on the grounds. **Hours:** Daily 9-5. Closed Jan. 1, Thanksgiving and Christmas. **Cost:** Free. **Phone:** (757) 825-4750. 🅰

FORT MONROE NATIONAL MONUMENT AND THE CASEMATE MUSEUM is at 20 Bernard Rd. Named in honor of President James Monroe, the fort was built between 1819 and 1834 and was continuously occupied by the Army 1823-2011. A moat surrounds the structure, which resembles a seven-pointed star.

After the Civil War, Confederate President Jefferson Davis was confined here until 1867. Visitors can view his prison cell at the Casemate Museum, which contains exhibits about the battle between the ironclads and other important events of the Civil War. Coast Artillery memorabilia—including photographs, historic documents and uniforms—is displayed.

Established as the 396th unit in the national park system in 2011, the 565-acre site encompasses more than 150 historic buildings as well as such natural features as 8 miles of waterfront and the Algernon Oak, one of the oldest oaks in the Fort Monroe area. The tree was believed to be growing when the first English colonists arrived in 1607.

In May, Fort Monroe is the site of the "Contraband Decision" Commemoration Series, which encompasses ceremonies, living-history tours and a candlelight procession. Fourth of July festivities at the fort offer family-friendly activities and a fireworks display. Other special events include military band concerts and a summer music series.

Time: Allow 1 hour minimum. **Hours:** Grounds daily dawn-dusk. Museum daily 10:30-4:30, Memorial Day-Labor Day; Tues.-Sun. 10:30-4:30, rest of year. Closed Jan. 1, Easter, Thanksgiving and Christmas Eve, Christmas and Dec. 31. Phone ahead to confirm schedule. **Cost:** Free. **Phone:** (757) 722-3678 for national monument information, or (757) 788-3391 for the museum.
🅶🆃 🅰 ⊠ 🅰

🔗 Discover member savings around the world: AAA.com/discounts

MISS HAMPTON II **HARBOR CRUISES** departs from Hampton Maritime Center on the Hampton waterfront at 710 Settlers Landing Rd. The narrated cruise sails into the Hampton Roads harbor past Blackbeard's Point and Old Point Comfort to Fort Wool, where a guided walking tour of the historic fort is provided. The cruise continues on past the aircraft carriers, guided missile cruisers, destroyers and submarines docked at Norfolk Naval Base.

Time: Allow 3 hours minimum. **Hours:** Cruises depart Tues.-Sat. at 11, Sun. at 2, Apr.-Oct. **Cost:** $27; $25 (ages 60+ and veterans with ID); $17 (ages 6-12); $13.50 (military with ID); free (ages 0-5 and military with ID with purchase of adult ticket). Reservations are recommended. **Phone:** (757) 722-9102 or (888) 757-2628. 🅶🆃

VIRGINIA AIR & SPACE CENTER is off I-64 exit 267, then 1 mi. w. to 600 Settlers Landing Rd. The center features aircraft and spacecraft suspended from a 94-foot ceiling. Adventures in Flight presents interactive exhibits about the Wright Brothers and regional contributions to aviation history. A NASA display includes an Orion spacecraft, the Apollo 12 command module, Solarium (a lunar lander), moon rocks and a Mars meteorite. Also on-site are Space Quest: Exploring the Moon, Mars & Beyond, a gallery featuring hands-on displays; an IMAX theater; and a seven-story observation deck providing panoramic views.

Time: Allow 2 hours minimum. **Hours:** Tues.-Sat. 10-5, Sun. noon-5. Closed Christmas. Phone ahead to confirm schedule. **Cost:** (includes space center and 45-minute IMAX film) $19; $17 (ages 65+); $16 (military with ID); $15.50 (ages 3-18 and students with ID). IMAX only (45-minute film) $9; $8 (ages 65+ and military with ID); $7 (ages 3-18 and students with ID). Special feature IMAX $13.50; $13 (ages 65+ and military with ID); $10.50 (ages 3-18 and students with ID). **Phone:** (757) 727-0900 or (800) 296-0800. 🅶🆃 🍴

BEST WESTERN HAMPTON COLISEUM INN
(757)827-5052 **26**

| ◆◆ Hotel $79-$119 | BW Best Western. | **AAA Benefit:** Members save 10% or more & earn 10% bonus points! |

Address: 1916 Coliseum Dr 23666 **Location:** I-64 exit 263B (Mercury Blvd), just n, then just e. **Facility:** 65 units. 5 stories, interior corridors. **Terms:** cancellation fee imposed. **Pool:** outdoor. **Activities:** exercise room. **Guest Services:** valet and coin laundry.

SAVE 🍴 CALL 🔧 🛫 🏥 BIZ
📶 ⊠ 🔋 🗄 📺 / SOME UNITS HS

CANDLEWOOD SUITES 757/766-8976 **22**
◆◆◆ Extended Stay Hotel. **Address:** 401 Butler Farm Rd 23666

COUNTRY INN & SUITES BY CARLSON 757/224-9994 **24**
◆◆◆ Hotel. **Address:** 1551 Hardy Cash Dr 23666

(See map & index p. 128.)

COURTYARD BY MARRIOTT HAMPTON (757)838-3300 (27)
◆◆◆ Hotel. **Address:** 1917 Coliseum Dr 23666

AAA Benefit:
Members save 5%
or more!

CROWNE PLAZA HAMPTON MARINA HOTEL
(757)727-9700 (31)

Hotel
$89-$219

Address: 700 Settlers Landing Rd 23669 **Location:** Waterfront. I-64 exit 267 (Settlers Landing Rd), 0.5 mi s; downtown. Convenient to Hampton University. **Facility:** 173 units. 9 stories, interior corridors. **Parking:** on-site (fee). **Terms:** check-in 4 pm, cancellation fee imposed. **Pool:** outdoor. **Activities:** exercise room. **Guest Services:** valet laundry.

EMBASSY SUITES BY HILTON HAMPTON ROADS HOTEL, SPA & CONVENTION CENTER (757)827-8200 (28)
◆◆◆ Hotel. **Address:** 1700 Coliseum Dr 23666

AAA Benefit:
Members save 5%
or more!

HAMPTON INN (757)838-1400 (23)

Hotel
$89-$220

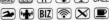

AAA Benefit:
Members save up to 10%!

Address: 3101 Coliseum Dr 23666 **Location:** I-64 exit 262B eastbound; exit 261B (Hampton Roads Center Pkwy) westbound, just e to Coliseum Dr, then just s. Across from Sentara Hampton Hospital. **Facility:** 109 units. 4 stories, interior corridors. **Terms:** 1-7 night minimum stay, cancellation fee imposed. **Pool:** heated indoor. **Activities:** exercise room. **Guest Services:** valet and coin laundry.

HILTON GARDEN INN HAMPTON COLISEUM CENTRAL
(757)310-6323 (29)
◆◆◆ Hotel. **Address:** 1999 Power Plant Pkwy 23666

AAA Benefit:
Members save up to 10%!

HOLIDAY INN EXPRESS HAMPTON-COLISEUM CENTRAL
757/838-8484 (25)
◆◆◆ Hotel. **Address:** 1813 W Mercury Blvd 23666

SPRINGHILL SUITES BY MARRIOTT (757)310-6333 (30)
◆◆◆ Hotel. **Address:** 1997 Power Plant Pkwy 23666

AAA Benefit:
Members save 5%
or more!

WHERE TO EAT

THE BARKING DOG 757/325-8352 (37)
◆ Hot Dogs. Casual Dining. **Address:** 4330 Kecoughtan Rd 23669

EL AZTECA RESTAURANTE MEXICANO 757/838-4063 (25)
◆◆ Mexican. Casual Dining. **Address:** 2040 Coliseum Dr 23666

THE GREY GOOSE 757/723-7978 (33)
◆◆ American. Casual Dining. **Address:** 118 Old Hampton Ln 23669

LA BODEGA HAMPTON 757/722-8466 (27)
◆ Specialty. Quick Serve. **Address:** 22 Wine St 23669

MAMA ROSA'S 757/723-3560 (31)
◆◆ Italian. Casual Dining. **Address:** 617 E Mercury Blvd 23663

MANGO MANGEAUX 757/224-9189 (34)
◆◆◆ American. Fine Dining. **Address:** 33 E Mellon St 23663

MARKER 20 757/726-9410 (28)
◆◆ American. Casual Dining. **Address:** 21 E Queens Way 23669

MONSOON 757/224-1633 (26)
◆◆ Indian. Casual Dining. **Address:** 2150 Allainby Way 23666

MUSASI JAPANESE RESTAURANT 757/728-0298 (32)
◆◆ Japanese Sushi. Casual Dining. **Address:** 49 W Queens Way 23669

THE POINT AT PHOEBUS 757/224-9299 (35)
◆◆◆ American. Gastropub. **Address:** 30 E Mellen St 23663

SURF RIDER GRILL 757/723-9366
◆◆ Seafood. Casual Dining. **Address:** 1 Marina Rd 23669

THE TAPHOUSE ON QUEENS WAY 757/224-5829 (29)
◆◆ American. Casual Dining. **Address:** 17 E Queens Way 23669

TOMMY'S RESTAURANT 757/825-1044 (36)
◆ Regional American. Casual Dining. **Address:** 3406 W Mercury Blvd 23666

VENTURE KITCHEN AND BAR 757/325-8868 (30)
◆◆ Small Plates Pizza. Casual Dining. **Address:** 9 E Queens Way 23666

HARRISONBURG (F-7) pop. 48,914, elev. 1,338'
• Hotels p. 150 • Restaurants p. 151

Harrisonburg was named after founder Thomas Harrison, who settled at the crossroads of a Native American path and the Spotswood Trail about 1739. Supplying lands for municipal expansion, Harrison's two sons followed a tradition set by their father when he donated land to Rockingham County for the erection of a courthouse in 1779.

Gen. Turner Ashby, one of the most respected Confederate officers of the Valley Campaign, fell in battle at Harrisonburg on June 6, 1862, while protecting Gen. Thomas J. "Stonewall" Jackson's approach to Port Republic. The Turner Ashby Monument, 1164 Turner Ashby Ln., memorializes the site of his death. Of Ashby, Jackson wrote, "As a partisan officer, I never knew his superior. His daring proverbial, his powers of endurance almost incredible..."

Harrisonburg lies in the heart of the Shenandoah Valley noted for its deep agrarian roots, vistas, many caverns and prime fishing waters. The cave nearest town is Endless Caverns in New Market (see place listing p. 174), 11 miles north on US 11. The Shenandoah River, Lake Shenandoah and Silver Lake are known for their trout and bass fishing. Developed recreational areas of the George Washington and Jefferson National Forests (see place listing p. 119) are nearby.

A community service project first organized by a group of Girl Scouts, the A Dream Come True Playground welcomes children with and without disabilities. The site's features include colorful slides, climbing walls and the wheelchair-accessible Liberty Swing. The playground, at 1050 Neff Ave. with an entrance on Thomas Bowers Circle, is open daily 8-dusk (weather permitting).

The arts flourish in Harrisonburg. Court Square Theater, on Court Square, opens its doors for various plays, films and concerts; phone (540) 433-9189. An arts complex at James Madison University, The Forbes Center for the Performing Arts, 147 Warsaw Ave., showcases students' musical and dramatic talents; its five venues also host national and international performances. Phone (540) 568-7000.

Self-guiding tours: Brochures, maps, and self-guiding driving tours and walking tours are available from the Hardesty-Higgins House Visitor Center.

Shopping: Valley Mall (1925 E. Market St.) has more than 50 stores, including anchors Belk and JCPenney.

Downtown Harrisonburg features a variety of local, independent stores that sell art, clothing, recreational equipment, vintage-inspired furniture and more. OASIS Fine Art & Craft (103 S. Main St.) sells handcrafted pieces, such as pottery, wearable art and paintings, fashioned by Shenandoah Valley artisans. Started in 1979, Harrisonburg Farmers Market (228 S. Liberty St.) offers a wide selection of high-quality agricultural goods and crafts. The popular downtown market is held Tues. and Sat. 8-1, Apr. 1-Thanksgiving; Sat. 9-1, rest of year.

CANDLEWOOD SUITES HARRISONBURG   540/437-1400
Extended Stay Hotel. **Address:** 1560 Country Club Rd 22802

COMFORT INN   (540)433-6066
Hotel. **Address:** 1440 E Market St 22801

COUNTRY INN & SUITES BY CARLSON   540/433-2400
Hotel. **Address:** 27 Covenant Dr 22801

COURTYARD BY MARRIOTT-HARRISONBURG   (540)432-3031
Hotel. **Address:** 1890 Evelyn Byrd Ave 22801

AAA Benefit: Members save 5% or more!

FAIRFIELD INN & SUITES BY MARRIOTT HARRISONBURG   (540)433-9333
Hotel. **Address:** 1946 Medical Ave 22801

AAA Benefit: Members save 5% or more!

HAMPTON INN/UNIVERSITY AREA   (540)432-1111
Hotel. **Address:** 85 University Blvd 22801

AAA Benefit: Members save up to 10%!

HARRISONBURG ECONO LODGE   (540)433-2576
Motel. **Address:** 1703 E Market St 22801

HARRISONBURG HAMPTON INN SOUTH   (540)437-0090
Hotel. **Address:** 43 Covenant Dr 22801

AAA Benefit: Members save up to 10%!

HOLIDAY INN EXPRESS   540/433-9999
Hotel. **Address:** 3325 S Main St 22801

MICROTEL INN & SUITES BY WYNDHAM   540/437-3777
Hotel. **Address:** 85 Pleasant Valley Rd 22801

RAMADA   540/434-9981
Hotel. **Address:** 91 Pleasant Valley Rd 22801

RESIDENCE INN BY MARRIOTT HARRISONBURG
(540)437-7426

Extended Stay Hotel
$99-$413

Residence Inn Marriott

AAA Benefit: Members save 5% or more!

Address: 1945 Deyerle Ave 22801 **Location:** I-81 exit 245, just e. **Facility:** 108 kitchen units. 3 stories, interior corridors. **Terms:** cancellation fee imposed. **Pool:** heated indoor. **Activities:** hot tub, exercise room. **Guest Services:** valet and coin laundry.

SLEEP INN & SUITES
(540)433-7100

Hotel
$93-$289

Address: 1891 Evelyn Byrd Ave 22801 **Location:** I-81 exit 247A, 0.5 mi e on US 33 to University Blvd, 0.3 mi s to Evelyn Byrd Ave, then just w. **Facility:** 80 units. 4 stories, interior corridors. **Terms:** check-in 4 pm. **Activities:** exercise room. **Guest Services:** coin laundry.

STONEWALL JACKSON INN AND BED & BREAKFAST
540/433-8233

 Historic Bed & Breakfast. **Address:** 547 E Market St 22801

SUPER 8   540/433-8888

Motel
Rates not provided

Address: 3330 S Main St 22801 **Location:** I-81 exit 243, just e, then just s on US 11. Across from truck stop and bus station. **Facility:** 49 units. 3 stories (no elevator), interior corridors. **Featured Amenity:** continental breakfast.

THE VILLAGE INN   (540)434-7355

Hotel
$89-$94

Address: 4979 S Valley Pike 22801 **Location:** I-81 exit 240 southbound, 0.6 mi w on SR 257, then 1.5 mi n on US 11; exit 243 northbound, just w to US 11, then 1.7 mi s. **Facility:** 37 units, some two bedrooms. 1 story, exterior corridors. **Pool:** outdoor. **Activities:** hot tub, playground. **Guest Services:** valet and coin laundry. *(See ad this page.)*

WHERE TO EAT

A BOWL OF GOOD   540/437-9020

 Mediterranean. Quick Serve. **Address:** 831 Mt. Clinton Pike 22802

AGRODOLCE   540/615-5442
Italian. Casual Dining. **Address:** 1647 E Market St 22801

BAR-B-Q RANCH   540/434-3296
Barbecue. Casual Dining. **Address:** 3311 N Valley Pike 22801

BELLA LUNA   540/422-2102
Italian. Casual Dining. **Address:** 80 W Water St 22801

BILLY JACK'S WING & DRAFT SHACK   540/433-1793
Wings. Casual Dining. **Address:** 92 S Main St 22801

BLACK FOREST GERMAN RESTAURANT   540/689-0758
German. Casual Dining. **Address:** 787 E Market St 22801

BLUE STONE INN   540/434-0535
American. Casual Dining. **Address:** 9107 N Valley Pike 22802

BRICKHOUSE TAVERN   540/402-5100
American. Casual Dining. **Address:** 1007 S Main St 22801

BROTHERS ITALIAN FOOD   540/433-1116
Italian Pizza. Casual Dining. **Address:** 1059 S High St 22801

CAPITAL ALE HOUSE   540/564-2537
American. Casual Dining. **Address:** 41-A Court Square 22801

CLEMENTINE   540/801-8881
American. Casual Dining. **Address:** 153 S Main St 22801

▼ See AAA listing this page ▼

CORGAN'S PUBLICK HOUSE   540/564-2674
♦♦ American. Casual Dining. **Address:** 865 Port Republic Rd 22801

EL CHARRO   540/564-0386
♦♦ Mexican. Casual Dining. **Address:** 1570 E Market St 22801

FINNIGAN'S COVE   540/433-9874
♦♦ American. Brewpub. **Address:** 30 W Water St 22801

FRANCO'S   540/564-0105
♦♦ Italian. Casual Dining. **Address:** 225 Burgess Rd 22801

THE GALLEY   540/434-3518
♦ American. Casual Dining. **Address:** 2430 S Main St 22801

GOLDEN CHINA RESTAURANT   540/434-1285
♦ Chinese. Casual Dining. **Address:** 1005 E Market St 22801

GREENS & GRAINS CAFE   540/433-1702
♦ American. Quick Serve. **Address:** 865 Port Republic Rd 22801

IMPERIAL 42 CHINESE RESTAURANT   540/574-0598
♦ Chinese. Casual Dining. **Address:** 1727 S High St 22801

JALAPEÑO   540/433-2469
♦♦ Southwestern. Casual Dining. **Address:** 1039 Port Republic Rd 22801

JESS' LUNCH #2   540/434-8280
♦ American. Casual Dining. **Address:** 1746 E Market St 22801

JIMMY MADISON'S   540/432-1000
♦♦ Southern American. Casual Dining. **Address:** 121 S Main St 22801

LITTLE ITALY PIZZA   540/432-1417
♦ Pizza. Casual Dining. **Address:** 1469 S Main St 22801

LOCAL CHOP & GRILL HOUSE   540/801-0505
♦♦♦ American. Fine Dining. **Address:** 56 W Gay St 22801

MAGNOLIA'S TACOS & TEQUILA BAR   540/217-5816
♦♦ Mexican. Casual Dining. **Address:** 14 E Water St 22801

MR. SATO EXPRESS   540/568-1877
♦ Sushi. Casual Dining. **Address:** 1645 Reservoir St 22801

O'NEILL'S GRILL   540/574-4267
♦♦ American. Casual Dining. **Address:** 221 University Blvd 22801

ORIENTAL CAFE   540/801-8989
♦ Chinese. Casual Dining. **Address:** 563 University Blvd 22801

PANO'S RESTAURANT   540/434-2367
♦♦ American. Casual Dining. **Address:** 3190 S Main St 22801

SKYLINE BUFFET   540/438-8881
♦ American. Casual Dining. **Address:** 233 Burgess Rd 22801

TASTE OF THAI   540/801-8878
♦♦ Thai. Casual Dining. **Address:** 917 S High St 22801

TRADITIONS   540/438-0301
♦♦ American. Casual Dining. **Address:** 625 Mt. Clinton Pike, Suite E 22802

TUTTI GUSTI PIZZERIA   540/434-6177
♦ Pizza. Quick Serve. **Address:** 1326 Hillside Ave 22801

UNION STATION RESTAURANT & BAR   540/437-0042
♦♦ American. Casual Dining. **Address:** 128 W Market St 22802

VIETOPIA VIETNAMESE CUISINE   540/438-0999
♦ Vietnamese. Casual Dining. **Address:** 1015 Port Republic Rd 22801

VITO'S ITALIAN KITCHEN   540/433-1113
♦♦ Italian. Casual Dining. **Address:** 1047 Port Republic Rd 22801

WOOD GRILL BUFFET   540/432-9303
♦ American. Casual Dining. **Address:** 1711 Reservoir St 22801

HERNDON (A-11) pop. 23,292, elev. 358'
• Restaurants p. 154
• Hotels & Restaurants map & index p. 38

Once a quiet vacation town for Washington's elite citizenry and a main stop on the Washington & Old Dominion Railroad, Herndon is in densely developed Fairfax County just 20 miles west of the nation's capital. Maintained by the Herndon Historical Society, the Herndon Depot Museum, 717 Lynn St., has a collection of railroad memorabilia, Civil War information and historic artifacts on loan from local residents. The building served as a train station until 1968.

FRYING PAN FARM PARK is at 2709 West Ox Rd. Rural community history is preserved at this 130-acre park, which contains historic buildings; a carousel; a nature trail; and Kidwell Farm, a 1930s-era working farm. On-site are cows, sheep, goats, pigs, horses, chickens, rabbits, peacocks and a variety of antique farm equipment. Visitors also can learn more about the park's plants and animals on a 20-minute wagon ride.

Time: Allow 1 hour minimum. **Hours:** Grounds daily dawn-dusk (also Thurs. dusk-9 p.m., early June-late Aug. for free concert series). Visitor center Mon.-Sat. 10-4:30, Sun. 11:30-4:30. Kidwell Farm daily 9-5. Wagon rides are offered Mon.-Sat. 10-4, Sun. noon-4, Mar.-Nov. **Cost:** Park admission free. Fees are charged for wagon and carousel rides. **Phone:** (703) 437-9101. 🎟

CANDLEWOOD SUITES WASHINGTON DULLES-HERNDON   703/793-7100 **50**
♦♦ Extended Stay Hotel. **Address:** 13845 Sunrise Valley Dr 20171

COURTYARD BY MARRIOTT/HERNDON-RESTON   (703)478-9400 **44**

♦♦♦
Hotel
$63-$304

COURTYARD Marriott

AAA Benefit: Members save 5% or more!

Address: 533 Herndon Pkwy 20170 **Location:** SR 267 (Dulles Toll Rd) exit 11 (SR 286/Fairfax County Pkwy), just n to Spring St exit, just s to CR 606 (Herndon Pkwy), then 0.3 mi w. Located in office park area. **Facility:** 146 units. 3 stories, interior corridors. **Terms:** cancellation fee imposed. **Pool:** heated indoor. **Activities:** exercise room. **Guest Services:** valet and coin laundry, boarding pass kiosk, area transportation. **Featured Amenity: full hot breakfast.**

(See map & index p. 38.)

CROWNE PLAZA DULLES AIRPORT 703/471-6700 **43**
 Hotel. **Address:** 2200 Centreville Rd 20170

FAIRFIELD INN & SUITES BY MARRIOTT-DULLES HERNDON
(703)478-9777 **38**
 Hotel. **Address:** 485 Elden St 20170

AAA Benefit: Members save 5% or more!

HILTON WASHINGTON DULLES AIRPORT
(703)478-2900 **52**

Hotel
$89-$299

AAA Benefit: Members save 5% or more!

Address: 13869 Park Center Rd 20171 **Location:** SR 267 (Dulles Toll Rd) exit 9, 3 mi s on SR 28; at McLearen Rd (SR 668). Located in a business park area. **Facility:** 449 units. 5 stories, interior corridors. **Terms:** 1-7 night minimum stay, cancellation fee imposed. **Amenities:** safes. **Pool:** outdoor, heated indoor. **Activities:** hot tub, exercise room, spa. **Guest Services:** valet laundry, area transportation.

HOMEWOOD SUITES BY HILTON WASHINGTON-DULLES AIRPORT (703)793-1700 **46**
 Extended Stay Hotel. **Address:** 13460 Sunrise Valley Dr 20171

AAA Benefit: Members save up to 10%!

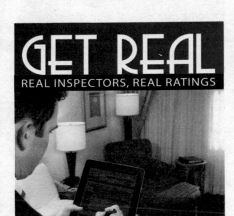

HYATT HOUSE HERNDON (703)437-5000 **41**

Extended Stay Hotel
$79-$269

HYATT house™
AAA Benefit: Members save 10%!

Address: 467 Herndon Pkwy 20170 **Location:** SR 267 (Dulles Toll Rd) exit 11 (SR 286/Fairfax County Pkwy), just n to Spring St exit, just s to CR 606 (Herndon Pkwy), then just w. Located in office park area. **Facility:** 104 units, some two bedrooms, efficiencies and kitchens. 4 stories, interior corridors. **Terms:** cancellation fee imposed. **Pool:** outdoor. **Activities:** exercise room. **Guest Services:** valet and coin laundry, area transportation. **Featured Amenity:** full hot breakfast.

HYATT PLACE HERNDON/DULLES AIRPORT-EAST
(571)643-0905 **48**

Hotel
$74-$239

HYATT PLACE'
AAA Benefit: Members save 10%!

Address: 13711 Sayward Blvd 20171 **Location:** SR 267 (Dulles Toll Rd) exit 9A, 1.1 mi s on SR 28, 0.3 mi e on Frying Pan Rd (CR 608), then 1.2 mi nw on Sunrise Valley Dr. Located near Washington Dulles International Airport, in a business area. **Facility:** 151 units. 6 stories, interior corridors. **Terms:** cancellation fee imposed. **Pool:** heated indoor. **Activities:** exercise room. **Guest Services:** valet and coin laundry, area transportation. **Featured Amenity:** full hot breakfast.

HYATT REGENCY DULLES (703)713-1234 **45**

Hotel
$75-$319

HYATT REGENCY'
AAA Benefit: Members save 10%!

Address: 2300 Dulles Corner Blvd 20171 **Location:** SR 267 (Dulles Toll Rd) exit 9A, 1.1 mi s on SR 28, 0.3 mi e on Frying Pan Rd (CR 608), then 1.2 mi nw on Sunrise Valley Dr. Located near Washington Dulles International Airport. **Facility:** 316 units. 13 stories, interior corridors. **Terms:** cancellation fee imposed. **Pool:** heated indoor. **Activities:** hot tub, exercise room. **Guest Services:** valet laundry, boarding pass kiosk.

RESIDENCE INN BY MARRIOTT-HERNDON/RESTON
(703)435-0044 **39**
 Extended Stay Hotel. **Address:** 315 Elden St 20170

AAA Benefit: Members save 5% or more!

SHERATON HERNDON DULLES AIRPORT HOTEL
571/643-0950 **47**
Hotel. **Address:** 13715 Sayward Blvd 20171

AAA Benefit: Members save 5% or more!

(See map & index p. 38.)

SPRINGHILL SUITES BY MARRIOTT HERNDON-RESTON
(703)435-3100 **40**

Hotel
$63-$254

SPRINGHILL SUITES MARRIOTT **AAA Benefit:** Members save 5% or more!

Address: 138 Spring St 20170 **Location:** SR 267 (Dulles Toll Rd) exit 11 (SR 286/Fairfax County Pkwy), just n to Spring St exit, then just s. Located near retail stores and restaurants. **Facility:** 136 units. 4 stories, interior corridors. **Terms:** cancellation fee imposed. **Activities:** exercise room. **Guest Services:** valet and coin laundry, rental car service, area transportation. **Featured Amenity:** breakfast buffet.

STAYBRIDGE SUITES HERNDON DULLES
703/713-6800 **51**
Extended Stay Hotel. **Address:** 13700 Coppermine Rd 20171

WASHINGTON DULLES AIRPORT MARRIOTT
(703)471-9500 **35**

Hotel
$71-$367

MARRIOTT
AAA Benefit: Members save 5% or more!

Address: 45020 Aviation Dr 20166 **Location:** Waterfront. At Washington Dulles International Airport. **Facility:** 368 units. 3 stories, interior corridors. **Terms:** cancellation fee imposed. **Pool:** outdoor, heated indoor. **Activities:** lawn sports, exercise room. **Guest Services:** valet laundry, boarding pass kiosk.

  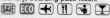

WASHINGTON DULLES MARRIOTT SUITES
(703)709-0400 **42**

Hotel
$79-$414

MARRIOTT
AAA Benefit: Members save 5% or more!

Address: 13101 Worldgate Dr 20170 **Location:** Jct SR 657 and 267 (Dulles Toll Rd) exit 10, just n. Located near Washington Dulles International Airport. **Facility:** 253 units. 11 stories, interior corridors. **Terms:** cancellation fee imposed. **Amenities:** safes. **Pool:** outdoor, heated indoor. **Activities:** hot tub, exercise room. **Guest Services:** complimentary and valet laundry, boarding pass kiosk.

 For exclusive AAA member savings and benefits:

AAA.com/hertz

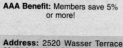

WHERE TO EAT

AMPHORA DINER DELUXE   703/938-3800 **56**
American. Casual Dining. **Address:** 1151 Elden St 20170

ANITA'S   703/481-1441
Mexican. Casual Dining. **Address:** 701 Elden St 20170

CANTINA D'ITALIA   703/318-7171
Italian. Casual Dining. **Address:** 150 Elden St 20170

EURO BISTRO   703/481-8158 **55**
International. Casual Dining. **Address:** 314 Elden St 20170

GLORY DAYS GRILL   703/390-5555
American. Casual Dining. **Address:** 2567 John Milton Dr 20171

ICE HOUSE CAFE   703/437-4500 **54**

American
Casual Dining
$9-$30

AAA Inspector Notes: The focal point of this rustic, lively cafe is an oyster bar that resembles a turn-of-the-20th-century saloon. Signature crab cakes are mixed with scallions and peppers. The chocolate Sheba dessert is decadent. Jazz entertainers perform on weekends. Complimentary parking is available in a lot behind the restaurant. **Features:** full bar, patio dining, happy hour. **Reservations:** suggested, for dinner and weekends. **Address:** 760 Elden St 20170 **Location:** Center. L D

RUSSIA HOUSE RESTAURANT   703/787-8880 **52**
Russian. Fine Dining. **Address:** 724 Pine St 20170

STONE'S COVE KITBAR   703/434-3615 **58**
American. Casual Dining. **Address:** 2403 Centreville Rd 20171

TARA THAI   703/481-8999
Thai. Casual Dining. **Address:** 13021 Worldgate Dr 20170

TURCUISINE   571/323-3330 **57**
Turkish. Casual Dining. **Address:** 13029 Worldgate Dr 20170

ZEFFIRELLI RISTORANTE ITALIANO   703/318-7000 **53**
Italian. Fine Dining. **Address:** 728 Pine St 20170

HILLSVILLE pop. 2,681

COMFORT INN-HILLSVILLE (276)730-9999

Hotel
$99-$219

Address: 151 Farmers Market Dr 24343 **Location:** I-77 exit 14, just sw on US 58, then just s. **Facility:** 73 units. 3 stories, interior corridors. **Pool:** heated indoor. **Activities:** hot tub, exercise room. **Guest Services:** valet laundry. **Featured Amenity:** full hot breakfast.

HAMPTON INN (276)728-2345
♦♦♦ Hotel. **Address:** 90 Farmers Market Rd 24343

AAA Benefit: Members save up to 10%!

HOLIDAY INN EXPRESS 276/728-9100
♦♦♦ Hotel. **Address:** 1094 Carrolton Pike Rd 24343

QUALITY INN (276)728-2120
♦♦♦ Hotel. **Address:** 85 Airport Rd 24343

WHERE TO EAT

PEKING PALACE 276/728-5539
♦♦ Chinese. Casual Dining. **Address:** 2666 Old Galax Pike 24343

HOPEWELL (B-2) pop. 22,591, elev. 5'
• Hotels & Restaurants map & index p, 219

Hopewell is an outgrowth of old City Point, which was founded in 1613 by Sir Thomas Dale. In 1622 the town was wiped out by a Native American attack, and not until the Civil War did the community revive. Its strategic location on the bluffs overlooking the confluence of the James and Appomattox rivers and its deep-water access made City Point an ideal setting for a large Union supply base, which Gen. Ulysses S. Grant transformed into a vast base of operations for his siege of Petersburg. From June 1864 to April 1865, the busy seaport supplied some 100,000 soldiers and served as the nerve center of the Union war effort.

At the close of the Civil War, City Point continued on as a military reservation with the last troops leaving in November 1867. The modern successor to City Point emerged with the building of a dynamite factory by E.I. du Pont on the site of Hopewell Farms in 1912. World War I sparked a boom with the factory manufacturing gun cotton, but that evaporated by 1918, with Hopewell again becoming a quiet village. Diversified industry once more has brought prosperity to this seaport.

GRANT'S HEADQUARTERS AT CITY POINT is at Cedar Ln. and Pecan Ave. Eight miles behind Union lines, City Point served as Gen. Ulysses S. Grant's command post during the siege of Petersburg and was the location of one of the largest supply bases of the Civil War. The unit is part of Petersburg National Battlefield *(see place listing p. 187)*.

The visitor contact station is in a 1763 plantation house owned by the Eppes family for about 215 years. During the siege of Petersburg, the home served as headquarters for Quartermaster General Rufus Ingalls. When Grant arrived on June 15, 1864, he set up a tent on the east lawn. A cabin was later built for Grant, who directed the Union war effort here until April 2, 1865. President Abraham Lincoln visited City Point twice and spent 2 of the last 3 weeks of his life here. **Hours:** Daily 9-5. Closed Jan. 1, Thanksgiving and Christmas. **Cost:** Free. **Phone:** (804) 458-9504 or (804) 732-3531.

BEST WESTERN PLUS HOPEWELL INN (804)452-0025 ⑩

Hotel
$89-$125

Best Western PLUS.

AAA Benefit: Members save 10% or more & earn 10% bonus points!

Address: 3950 Courthouse Rd 23860 **Location:** I-295 exit 9A (SR 36), just e. **Facility:** 60 units, some efficiencies. 3 stories, interior corridors. **Terms:** cancellation fee imposed. **Pool:** outdoor. **Activities:** exercise room. **Guest Services:** coin laundry.

CANDLEWOOD SUITES 804/541-0200 ⑭
♦♦ Extended Stay Hotel. **Address:** 5113 Plaza Dr 23860

FAIRFIELD INN & SUITES BY MARRIOTT (804)458-2600 ⑪
♦♦♦ Hotel. **Address:** 3952 Courthouse Rd 23860

AAA Benefit: Members save 5% or more!

HAMPTON INN-FT LEE (804)452-1000 ⑬
♦♦♦ Hotel. **Address:** 5103 Plaza Dr 23860

AAA Benefit: Members save up to 10%!

STAY OVER SUITES (804)452-1377 ⑫
♦♦♦ Extended Stay Hotel. **Address:** 4115 Old Woodlawn St 23860

WHERE TO EAT

KATCHA THAI RESTAURANT 804/458-2885 ⑮
♦♦ Thai. Casual Dining. **Address:** 5230 Oaklawn Blvd 23860

K&L BARBECUE 804/458-4241 ⑭
♦ Barbecue. Casual Dining. **Address:** 5 Cavalier Square 23860

HOT SPRINGS (G-6) pop. 738, elev. 2,195'
• Hotels p. 156

Hot Springs is in a scenic valley surrounded by forested mountains. The medicinal springs have made it a health resort for generations. Summer and winter sports facilities are available.

Bath County Chamber of Commerce: 120 Old Mill Rd., Warm Springs, VA 24484. Mailing: P.O. Box P.O. Box 718, Hot Springs, VA 24445. **Phone:** (540) 839-5409.

THE OMNI HOMESTEAD RESORT   540/839-1766
♦♦♦ ♦♦♦ Historic Resort Hotel. **Address:** 1766 Homestead Dr
24445

ROSELOE MOTEL   540/839-5373
♦ Motel. **Address:** 10849 Sam Snead Hwy 24445

HUDDLESTON

MARINERS LANDING   540/297-4900
♦♦♦ Vacation Rental Condominium. **Address:** 1217 Graves
Harbor Tr 24104

IRVINGTON (A-3) pop. 432, elev. 30'

At the end of the Northern Neck peninsula between the Rappahannock and Potomac rivers, Irvington long has been associated with Tides Inn, a
golf and water sports resort that has been open
since 1947. Cruises of the Rappahannock and the
coves of Carter's Creek are available.

Irvington Town Office: 235 Steamboat Rd., P.O.
Box 174, Irvington, VA 22480. **Phone:** (804)
438-6230.

STEAMBOAT ERA MUSEUM is at 156 King Carter
Dr. Rotating exhibits detail how steamboats affected
and changed the lives of people living around the
Chesapeake Bay and its tributaries. The golden age
of the steamboat, a period which lasted from about
1813-1937, is related through artifacts, dioramas,
models and historical documents. The museum also
features a large oral history library that includes
video histories from workers, travelers, residents
and others who experienced this era.

Time: Allow 30 minutes minimum. **Hours:** Tues.-
Sat. 10-4, Memorial Day weekend-Labor Day
weekend; Fri.-Sat. 10-4, mid-Apr. through day be-
fore Memorial Day weekend and day after Labor
Day-weekend before Thanksgiving. Otherwise by
appointment. Phone ahead to confirm schedule.
Cost: $5; free (ages 0-12 and active military with
ID). **Phone:** (804) 438-6888.

THE TIDES INN   804/438-5000
♦♦♦ ♦♦♦
**Classic Historic
Resort Hotel
Rates not provided**

Address: 480 King Carter Dr 22480 **Location:** Waterfront. 0.3 mi w of SR 200.
Facility: This gracious riverfront resort
has offered warm Southern hospitality
amid elegant surroundings for more than
60 years. The rooms feature wood plantation shutters and décor reminiscent of
the tropics. 106 units. 4 stories,
interior/exterior corridors. **Terms:**
check-in 4 pm. **Amenities:** safes.
Dining: 3 restaurants, also, The Chesapeake Club, see separate listing, entertainment. **Pool:** outdoor. **Activities:**
marina, fishing, regulation golf, par 3
golf, tennis, recreation programs, bicycles, lawn sports, exercise room, spa.
Guest Services: complimentary and valet laundry, area
transportation.

   CALL
 / SOME UNITS

THE CHESAPEAKE CLUB   804/438-5000
♦♦♦ Regional American. Fine Dining. **Address:** 480 King
Carter Dr 22480

THE LOCAL   804/438-9356
♦ Coffee/Tea Sandwiches. Quick Serve. **Address:** 4437
Irvington Rd 22480

NATE'S TRICK DOG CAFE   804/438-6363
♦♦♦ American. Fine Dining. **Address:** 4357 Irvington Rd
22480

ISLE OF WIGHT (C-3) elev. 60'
• Part of Hampton Roads Area — see map p. 124

Colonists from Jamestown established the Isle of
Wight Plantation on the James River in 1619. Some
of its original settlers may have come from the English island of the same name. Villagers traded
peacefully with the Worrosquoyacke and Nottoway
Indians until 1622, when the Powhatan Confederacy
launched a series of attacks against dozens of
James River settlements. Nearly a third of all Virginia colonists were killed; most local tribes were
driven from their lands in reprisal.

JAMESTOWN (B-3) elev. 5'
• Part of Williamsburg, Jamestown & Yorktown
area — see map p. 273

One hundred and four Englishmen endured a
5-month sea passage to reach the shores of Virginia
in 1607. Sponsored by the Virginia Company of
London, Jamestown was to be England's first permanent colony in the New World and, it was hoped,
a profitable one for its investors. The unfamiliar climate, disease and starvation almost thwarted those
plans; less than a third of the settlers survived the
first year. When tobacco was introduced as a cash
crop around 1613, the colony finally began to
prosper.

HISTORIC JAMESTOWNE, on the western
end of the Colonial Pkwy., preserves the location of America's first permanent English colony,
established here in 1607. Today the 22.5-acre site is
part of Colonial National Historical Park *(see place
listing p. 97).* Archeologists have exposed ruins and
original foundations, revealing the footprint of the
original fort palisades and structures. Nearby, the
ruins of Jamestown's first glass furnace are all that
remain of the colony's dream of a livelihood from
glassmaking.

The site's only surviving 17th-century structure is
the 1690s tower of Jamestown's brick church. Pre-
vious buildings on the site include the church where
the first legislative assembly met in 1619. Earlier
foundations are visible through the glass floor of the
1907 Jamestown Memorial Church.

Foundations of homes, taverns and shops built
after 1620 can be seen in the New Towne section,
which includes the 18th-century Ambler Mansion.
Costumed interpreters lead living-history tours in the

summer, and walking tours lead by rangers or archeologist are available all year (weather permitting). A 5-mile driving tour features interpretive waysides and views of the island's natural environment.

The site is administered jointly by the National Park Service and Preservation Virginia. **Time:** Allow 2 hours minimum. **Hours:** Entrance gate open daily 8:30-4:30, Mar.-Nov.; 8:45-4:30, rest of year. Archeological site and tour road remain open until dusk. Visitor center daily 9-5. Archaearium daily 9:30-5:30, Mar.-Nov.; 9:30-5, rest of year. Closed Jan. 1, Thanksgiving and Christmas. **Cost:** Admission, valid for 7 days, includes Historic Jamestown Visitor Center and Archaearium as well as Yorktown Battlefield and Yorktown Battlefield Visitor Center *(see attraction listings p. 297)* $14; free (ages 0-15 and active military with ID). **Phone:** (757) 856-1250. [GT]

Historic Jamestowne Visitor Center and Archaearium is at 1368 Colonial Pkwy. An immersion theater experience and exhibits portray the story of Historic Jamestowne. The Archaearium museum displays some of the more than 1 million artifacts that have been excavated at the site, including weapons, tools, ceramics and the personal belongings of Jamestown's earliest colonists.

In addition, a walking trail leads to the re-created glasshouse, where costumed interpreters demonstrate early glassblowing techniques. **Hours:** Visitor center daily 9-5. Archaearium daily 9:30-5:30, Mar.-Nov.; 9:30-5, rest of year. Glasshouse 8:30-5. Closed Jan. 1, Thanksgiving and Christmas. **Cost:** Admission, valid for 7 days, includes Historic Jamestowne as well as Yorktown Battlefield and Yorktown Visitor Center *(see attraction listings p. 297)* $14; free (ages 0-15 and active military with ID). **Phone:** (757) 856-1250.

JAMESTOWN SETTLEMENT is on SR 31 next to Historic Jamestowne. This living-history museum was established in 1957 to commemorate the 350th anniversary of Jamestown's founding. An introductory film, "1607: A Nation Takes Root," and galleries displaying 17th-century artifacts trace the first century of the Virginia colony and its origins in England as well as the influence of the Powhatan Indian, English and west-central African cultures in the colony's development.

Costumed historical interpreters provide a glimpse of life during the early 1600s at three outdoor living-history areas. Within the palisade of re-created James Fort are wattle-and-daub buildings, including a church, the governor's house, a storehouse and an armory. Visitors can climb aboard a replica 17th-century sailing vessel on the James River, where the *Discovery, Godspeed* and *Susan Constant* are moored. A Powhatan Indian village, with several houses, a crop field and a ceremonial circle of carved wooden posts, is based on archeological findings and eyewitness accounts of the period.

Time: Allow 2 hours minimum. **Hours:** Museum and outdoor exhibits daily 9-6, June 15-Aug. 15; 9-5, rest of year. Closed Jan. 1 and Christmas. Phone ahead to confirm schedule. **Cost:** $17; $8 (ages 6-12). Combination ticket with American Revolution Museum at Yorktown *(see attraction listing p. 296)* $25.50; $12.25 (ages 6-12). Other combination tickets are available. **Phone:** (757) 253-4838 or (888) 593-4682. [fork/knife icon]

JARRATT

WILSON'S BBQ AND GRILL   434/634-4147
▼▼ Barbecue. Casual Dining. **Address:** 118 Jarratt Ave 23867

JEFFERSON NATIONAL FOREST—See
George Washington and Jefferson National Forests p. 119

KESWICK

KESWICK HALL AND GOLF CLUB   434/979-3440

Resort Hotel
Rates not provided

Address: 701 Club Dr 22947 **Location:** I-64 exit 129, just n. **Facility:** Set in a gorgeous restored mansion amid rolling hills, this small hotel blends European grandeur with Southern charm. The guest rooms are decorated with antiques and baths have heated towel racks. 48 units. 3 stories, interior corridors. **Parking:** on-site and valet. **Terms:** check-in 4 pm. **Amenities:** safes. **Dining:** 3 restaurants, also, Fossett's, see separate listing. **Pool:** heated outdoor, heated indoor. **Activities:** hot tub, fishing, regulation golf, tennis, recreation programs, bicycles, playground, game room, exercise room, spa. **Guest Services:** valet laundry.

[SAVE] [fork/knife] [icon] [icon] CALL [icons] [BIZ] [HS] [wifi]
[icons] / SOME UNITS [icons]

WHERE TO EAT

FOSSETT'S   434/979-3440
▼▼▼
New American Fine Dining
$24-$47

AAA Inspector Notes: Named after Thomas Jefferson's chef at Monticello, the restaurant offers seating in an elegant dining room in a manor home. Surrounded in glass, it offers panoramic views of the rolling fields of the golf course and estate. The menu highlights seasonal local products in creative style, with specialties such as seafood like scallops and hand-crafted fresh pastas, as well as meat and game from local farms and ranches. **Features:** full bar, Sunday brunch. **Reservations:** suggested, weekends. **Address:** 701 Club Dr 22947 **Location:** I-64 exit 129, just n; in Keswick Hall. **Parking:** on-site and valet.

[icon] [B] [D]

KILMARNOCK pop. 1,487

BEST WESTERN KILMARNOCK HOTEL   804/436-1500

Hotel
$69-$159

AAA Benefit: Members save 10% or more & earn 10% bonus points!

Address: 599 N Main St 22482 **Location:** Just n on SR 17. **Facility:** 67 units. 2 stories, interior corridors. **Terms:** cancellation fee imposed. **Amenities:** safes. **Pool:** outdoor. **Activities:** exercise room. **Guest Services:** coin laundry. **Featured Amenity:** full hot breakfast.

WHERE TO EAT

CAR WASH CAFE   804/435-0405
American. Casual Dining. **Address:** 481 N Main St 22482

CHAO PHRAYA SUSHI & THAI GRILL   804/577-4261
Thai Sushi. Casual Dining. **Address:** 45 S Main St 22482

LEE'S RESTAURANT   804/435-1255
Southern Seafood. Casual Dining. **Address:** 30 S Main St 22482

NORTHERN NECK BURGER CO.   804/577-4400
Burgers. Quick Serve. **Address:** 62 Irvington Rd 22482

KING WILLIAM (A-2) pop. 252, elev. 142'

Archeological evidence of the Pamunkey Indians in the area dates back 10,000 years. An English treaty signed by King Charles II in 1677 established articles of peace and a tribal territory that remains in existence today. The Pamunkey Indian Reservation encompasses some 1,200 acres in King William County.

LEBANON pop. 3,424

LEBANON SUPER 8   276/889-1800
Motel. **Address:** 71 Townview Dr 24266

LEESBURG (A-11) pop. 42,616, elev. 313'
• Restaurants p. 160

One of the oldest towns in northern Virginia, Leesburg was an outfitting post during the French and Indian War. In 1758 the House of Burgesses passed a bill authorizing the establishment of a town at that site.

During the War of 1812, when the city of Washington was in flames, 22 wagonloads of U.S. documents, including the Declaration of Independence, the Articles of Confederation, the Constitution, much of George Washington's correspondence, and Congressional and State Department records were brought to Leesburg for safekeeping.

The fourth armed engagement of the Civil War took place northeast of Leesburg at Balls Bluff. On Oct. 21, 1861, Confederate forces inflicted devastating losses upon four Union regiments under the command of Col. Edward D. Baker. Among the injured was a 20-year-old lieutenant from Massachusetts, Oliver Wendell Holmes Jr., who later became chief justice of the U.S. Supreme Court.

The Ball's Bluff National Cemetery is purportedly the smallest in the nation. Surrounding the cemetery is Balls Bluff Battlefield, a regional park with hiking trails and picnicking; phone (703) 737-7800.

Since 1828 a ferry has carried passengers and freight across the quarter-mile-wide Potomac between a point northeast of Leesburg and Whites Ferry, Md. The *Gen. Jubal A. Early* still crosses daily dawn to dusk.

Several of Leesburg's older homes are open to the public during Historic Garden Week in late April. Beginning in late September and running through early November, Pumpkin Village Fall Festival takes place at Leesburg Animal Park. The seasonal event includes a farm-themed children's play area, pony and hay wagon rides, and a pumpkin patch.

Loudoun Convention & Visitors Association: 112-G South St. S.E., Leesburg, VA 20175. **Phone:** (703) 771-2170 or (800) 752-6118.

Self-guiding tours: A walking-tour booklet of Leesburg's historic district is available from the Loudoun Museum.

MORVEN PARK is w. on SR 7 Bus. Rte., then n. on Morven Park Rd. and w. on Old Waterford Rd. The gardens of this 1,000-acre estate surround the Westmoreland Davis Mansion, a restored 1780 residence filled with artifacts from Europe and Asia. In addition, three rooms in the north wing of the mansion house the collection of the Museum of Hounds and Hunting. Morven Park also encompasses the Winmill Carriage Museum, which showcases 40 antique coaches, carriages, sleds and carts; Turkey Hill Farm, the home of the 2015 pardoned White House turkeys; and highland and lowland hiking trails.

Pets on leash are allowed on the grounds only. **Hours:** Grounds daily 8 a.m.-dusk. Park closed Jan.

1, Thanksgiving and Christmas. House tours Thurs.-Mon. noon-5, Memorial Day-Labor Day; Sat.-Sun. noon-5, rest of year. Last tour begins 1 hour before closing. Museum open Sat. noon-5, Feb.-Dec. Museum closed Thanksgiving, Christmas Eve, Christmas and Dec. 31. **Cost:** Grounds free. House tour and museums $10; $5 (ages 6-12). **Phone:** (703) 777-2414. GT 🍴 ㊂

OATLANDS PLANTATION is about 6 mi. s. on US 15 to 20850 Oatlands Plantation Ln. This stately 22-room 1804 mansion combines Federal and Greek Revival styles. The house is furnished with French, English and American art and antiques. Just over 400 of the plantation's original 3,408 acres remain. The grounds retain the original basic design, with more than 4 acres of formal gardens and an 1810 greenhouse. The surrounding fields are the setting for point-to-point races, festivals, dog shows and many other events.

Time: Allow 1 hour minimum. **Hours:** Mon.-Sat. 10-5, Sun. 1-5, Apr.-Dec. Guided 30- to 45-minute tours are given on the hour. Last tour begins 1 hour before closing. Closed Thanksgiving, Christmas Eve, Christmas and Dec. 31. **Cost:** $15; $12 (ages 60+ and active military with ID); $8 (ages 6-16).

Garden and grounds only $10. **Phone:** (703) 777-3174. GT ㊂

BEST WESTERN LEESBURG HOTEL & CONFERENCE CENTER (703)777-9400

Hotel
$99-$169

 Best Western.

AAA Benefit: Members save 10% or more & earn 10% bonus points!

Address: 726 E Market St 20176 **Location:** Off SR 7 business route, just w of jct US 15. Located in a commercial area. **Facility:** 99 units. 2 stories, interior corridors. **Terms:** cancellation fee imposed. **Amenities:** safes. **Pool:** outdoor. **Activities:** exercise room. **Guest Services:** valet and coin laundry, area transportation. **Featured Amenity:** full hot breakfast.

COMFORT SUITES LEESBURG (703)669-1650
Hotel. **Address:** 80 Prosperity Ave OE 20176

HAMPTON INN & SUITES BY HILTON LEESBURG
(703)669-8640
Hotel. **Address:** 117 Fort Evans Rd NE 20176

AAA Benefit: Members save up to 10%!

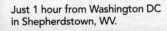

LANSDOWNE RESORT & SPA   703/729-8400

Resort Hotel
Rates not provided

Address: 44050 Woodridge Pkwy 20176 **Location:** SR 7, 3.6 mi w of jct SR 28; 4.4 mi e of jct US 15. **Facility:** In the heart of hunt country, this resort on 476 acres, offers extensive public facilities with world-class golf courses, a variety of pools with water features and a full-service spa. 296 units. 10 stories, interior corridors. **Parking:** on-site and valet. **Terms:** check-in 4 pm. **Amenities:** safes. **Dining:** 4 restaurants. **Pool:** heated outdoor, heated indoor. **Activities:** sauna, hot tub, steamroom, regulation golf, tennis, recreation programs in summer, playground, trails, health club, spa. **Guest Services:** valet laundry, boarding pass kiosk.

(SAVE) 🔌 ✈ 🍴 🛎 ☕ CALL 🚭 🏃 🚐 BIZ
🛜 ✉ 🎦 📖 💻 / SOME UNITS 🐾

≋
LANSDOWNE
RESORT AND SPA

Renewal in VA wine country. Near Wash D.C. Ideal for romantic getaways. Golf, spa & dining options.

WHERE TO EAT

AIYARA THAI RESTAURANT   703/771-1131
♦♦ Thai. Casual Dining. **Address:** 5 Catoctin Cir SE 20175

BLUE RIDGE GRILL   703/669-5505
♦♦ American. Casual Dining. **Address:** 955 Edwards Ferry Rd 20176

FIRE WORKS-WOOD FIRED PIZZA   703/779-8400
♦♦ Pizza. Casual Dining. **Address:** 201 Harrison St 20175

LIGHTFOOT   703/771-2233
♦♦♦ American. Fine Dining. **Address:** 11 N King St 20176

MELT GOURMET CHEESEBURGERS   703/443-2105
♦ Burgers. Quick Serve. **Address:** 525 E Market St, Suite J 20176

TUSCARORA MILL RESTAURANT   703/771-9300
♦♦♦ American. Fine Dining. **Address:** 203 Harrison St SE 20175

LEON (F-8) elev. 560'
• Part of Shenandoah National Park area — see map p. 241

WINERIES
• **Prince Michel Vineyards** is 10 mi. s. on US 29 to 154 Winery Ln. **Hours:** Daily 10-6, Apr.-Dec.; 10-5 (also Sat.-Sun. 5-6), rest of year. Phone ahead to confirm holiday hours. Closed Thanksgiving and Christmas. **Phone:** (800) 800-9463. GT

LEXINGTON (G-7) pop. 7,042, elev. 1,100'
• Restaurants p. 162

Four American generals—George Washington, Robert E. Lee, Thomas J. "Stonewall" Jackson and George C. Marshall—have played major roles in historic Lexington. The two Confederate heroes had homes here and are buried in town.

Of scenic interest is rugged Goshen Pass Natural Area Preserve, 15 miles northwest on SR 39. Here the southwest face of Little North Mountain drops sharply from 3,600 feet to the Maury River, about 1,800 feet below. Rhododendrons, mountain laurels, pines and dogwoods grow profusely along the river and the surrounding mountains. Traversed by stagecoaches in the 19th century, Goshen Pass is enjoyed today for the recreational activities it provides; phone (540) 292-3265.

A 7-mile stretch of railbed between Lexington and Buena Vista has been developed into the Chessie Nature Trail. The trail is designed for pedestrians who enjoy hiking, bird-watching, running, fishing, cross-country skiing and picnicking. The Virginia Horse Center, off SR 39, offers horse shows, workshops and seminars.

Lexington Visitor Center: 106 E. Washington St., Lexington, VA 24450. **Phone:** (540) 463-3777.

Self-guiding tours: A brochure with information about several walking tours is available at the visitor center.

VIRGINIA MILITARY INSTITUTE is off Main St. on Letcher Ave. Founded in 1839, this was the nation's first state-supported military college. On the National Register of Historic Districts, VMI is noted for its military and academic programs; the Barracks is a National Historic Landmark. Alumni include Gen. George C. Marshall, Adm. Richard E. Byrd and Lt. Gen. Lewis B. "Chesty" Puller.

Time: Allow 1 hour minimum. **Hours:** Daily 9-5. Departing from the VMI Museum, cadet-guided post tours are given daily at noon (based on cadet availability). Closed Jan. 1, Thanksgiving and Dec. 23-31. Phone ahead to confirm schedule. **Cost:** Free. **Phone:** (540) 464-7334. GT

George C. Marshall Museum and Library is on the Virginia Military Institute campus at 1600 VMI Parade. The building houses the World War II chief of staff's papers and material relating to U.S. military and diplomatic history through much of the 20th century.

An electric map with narration traces the developments of World War II. Displayed are the Nobel Peace Prize awarded Marshall in 1953 and the Academy Award presented to Gen. Frank McCarthy, the VMI graduate who produced the movie "Patton." **Hours:** Museum Tues.-Sat. 11-4. Library Tues.-Fri. 9-4:30 by appointment. Closed Jan. 1, Thanksgiving and Dec. 24-31. **Cost:** $5; $3 (ages 65+); $2 (students with ID); free (ages 0-12, active military with ID and World War II veterans). **Phone:** (540) 463-2083 for the museum, or (540) 463-7103 for the library.

Jackson Memorial Hall is at 415 Letcher Ave. at the Virginia Military Institute. The cadet assembly hall is dominated by an oil painting depicting the VMI cadet charge at the Battle of New Market. It was painted by Benjamin West Clinedinst, class of 1880. The flags around the hall represent the 26 states in the Union when VMI was founded Nov. 11, 1839. **Time:** Allow 30 minutes minimum. **Hours:** Daily dawn-dusk. Closed Thanksgiving and Christmas break. **Cost:** Free. **Phone:** (540) 464-7334.

VMI Museum is in Jackson Memorial Hall, off Main St. on Letcher Ave. at the Virginia Military Institute. One of the state's oldest museums, it houses items illustrating the history and traditions of the nation's first state military college. Gen. Thomas J. "Stonewall" Jackson's uniform, his bullet-pierced raincoat from Chancellorsville, and the mounted hide of his horse, Little Sorrel, are displayed.

A replica of a barracks room depicts cadet life. Visitors also can view the Henry Stewart Antique Firearms Collection. **Time:** Allow 1 hour minimum. **Hours:** Daily 9-5. Closed Jan. 1, Thanksgiving and Dec. 22-Dec. 31. Phone ahead to confirm schedule. **Cost:** Donations. **Phone:** (540) 464-7334.

WASHINGTON AND LEE UNIVERSITY is at 204 W. Washington St. A white colonnaded building houses the college, which dates from the 1749 founding of Augusta Academy. Later known as Liberty Hall, the academy was endowed by George Washington and renamed Washington Academy in 1796. Gen. Robert E. Lee was president of the college from the end of the Civil War until his death in 1870, after which the university took its present name. **Phone:** (540) 458-8400. 🍴

 Lee Chapel & Museum is at 100 N. Jefferson St. on the historic front campus of Washington and Lee University. Built in 1868 under Gen. Robert E. Lee's supervision, the Victorian-style chapel is the heart of the campus. It preserves Lee's office much as he left it on Sept. 28, 1870, only 2 weeks before his death.

The 1904 Theodore Pine portrait of the Confederate leader and Charles Willson Peale's 1772 portrait of George Washington hang in the chapel. At its far end stands Edward Valentine's recumbent statue of Lee. The general and his family are buried beneath the chapel on the museum level. The museum traces the history of the university, focusing on the heritage of its namesakes.

Time: Allow 1 hour minimum. **Hours:** Mon.-Sat. 9-5, Sun. 1-5, Apr.-Oct.; Mon.-Sat. 9-4, Sun. 1-4, rest of year. Closed Jan. 1, Easter, Thanksgiving-Sat. after Thanksgiving, Dec. 24-31, university holidays and during special events. **Cost:** Donations. **Phone:** (540) 458-8768.

A B&B AT LLEWELLYN LODGE 540/463-3235
👑👑👑 Bed & Breakfast. **Address:** 603 S Main St 24450

BEST WESTERN LEXINGTON INN (540)458-3020

👑👑👑
Motel
$89-$189

🅱🆆 **Best Western.** **AAA Benefit:** Members save 10% or more & earn 10% bonus points!

Address: 850 N Lee Hwy 24450 **Location:** I-64 exit 55, just s on US 11; I-81 exit 191, 1.6 mi w. **Facility:** 72 units. 2 stories (no elevator), exterior corridors. **Terms:** 3 day cancellation notice-fee imposed. **Amenities:** safes. **Activities:** exercise room. **Guest Services:** valet laundry.

BEST WESTERN PLUS INN AT HUNT RIDGE (540)464-1500

Hotel
$109-$269

 Best Western PLUS **AAA Benefit:** Members save 10% or more & earn 10% bonus points!

Address: 25 Willow Spring Rd 24450 **Location:** I-64 exit 55, just n on US 11 to SR 39; I-81 exit 191, 0.6 mi w. **Facility:** 99 units. 3 stories, interior corridors. **Terms:** cancellation fee imposed. **Amenities:** safes. **Activities:** exercise room. **Guest Services:** coin laundry.

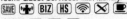

COMFORT INN-VIRGINIA HORSE CENTER (540)463-7311
👑👑 Hotel. **Address:** 62 Comfort Way 24450

COUNTRY INN & SUITES BY CARLSON 540/464-9000

👑👑👑
Hotel
Rates not provided

Address: 875 N Lee Hwy 24450 **Location:** I-81 exit 191, just s on US 11. **Facility:** 66 units. 4 stories, interior corridors. **Pool:** heated indoor. **Activities:** hot tub, exercise room. **Guest Services:** coin laundry. **Featured Amenity:** full hot breakfast.

   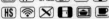

THE GEORGES 540/463-2500
👑👑👑 Historic Hotel. **Address:** 11 N Main St 24450

HAMPTON INN-COL ALTO (540)463-2223
👑👑👑 Hotel. **Address:** 401 E Nelson St 24450

AAA Benefit: Members save up to 10%!

HOLIDAY INN EXPRESS 540/463-7351
👑👑👑 Hotel. **Address:** 880 N Lee Hwy 24450

HOWARD JOHNSON INN 540/463-9181
👑👑 Hotel. **Address:** 2836 N Lee Hwy 24450

MOTEL 6 540/463-7371
👑👑 Motel. **Address:** 65 Econo Ln 24450

QUALITY INN & SUITES (540)463-6400

👑👑👑
Hotel
$79-$219

Address: 2814 N Lee Hwy 24450 **Location:** I-81 exit 195, just sw on US 11. **Facility:** 80 units. 4 stories, interior corridors. **Pool:** heated indoor. **Activities:** exercise room. **Guest Services:** coin laundry. **Featured Amenity:** full hot breakfast.

SLEEP INN & SUITES   (540)463-6000

Hotel
$84-$295

Address: 95 Maury River Rd 24450 **Location:** I-64 exit 55, just n. **Facility:** 71 units. 4 stories, interior corridors. **Pool:** heated indoor. **Activities:** hot tub, exercise room. **Guest Services:** valet and coin laundry. **Featured Amenity:** full hot breakfast.

SAVE ⏱ CALL 🛇 � 👫 BIZ
🛜 ✕ 🔌 🖥 💻
/SOME UNITS 🐾

SUPER 8 LEXINGTON   540/463-7858

Motel
Rates not provided

Address: 1139 N Lee Hwy 24450 **Location:** I-64 exit 55, just n. **Facility:** 50 units. 3 stories (no elevator), interior corridors. **Amenities:** safes. **Featured Amenity: continental breakfast.**

SAVE ⏱ 🛜 🔌 💻
/SOME UNITS 🐾 🖥

WINGATE BY WYNDHAM   540/464-8100
Hotel. **Address:** 1100 N Lee Hwy 24450

WHERE TO EAT

BISTRO ON MAIN   540/464-4888
Southern American. Casual Dining. **Address:** 8 N Main St 24450

DON TEQUILA MEXICAN RESTAURANT   540/463-3289
Mexican. Casual Dining. **Address:** 487 E Nelson St 24450

THE PALMS   540/463-7911
American. Casual Dining. **Address:** 101 W Nelson St 24450

SHERIDAN LIVERY INN RESTAURANT   540/464-1887
American. Casual Dining. **Address:** 35 N Main St 24450

THE SOUTHERN INN RESTAURANT   540/463-3612
American. Casual Dining. **Address:** 37 S Main St 24450

LIGHTFOOT
• **Hotels & Restaurants map & index p. 279**
• **Part of Williamsburg, Jamestown & Yorktown area — see map p. 273**

GREAT WOLF LODGE   757/229-9700   9
Resort Hotel. **Address:** 549 E Rochambeau Dr 23188

HOLIDAY INN EXPRESS WILLIAMSBURG NORTH
757/220-0062   10

Hotel
Rates not provided

Address: 720 Lightfoot Rd 23188 **Location:** I-64 exit 234 (SR 199 E), 0.5 mi s to International Pkwy. **Facility:** 118 units. 5 stories, interior corridors. **Pool:** heated indoor. **Activities:** exercise room. **Guest Services:** valet and coin laundry. **Featured Amenity: full hot breakfast.**

SAVE CALL 🛇 🚙 👫 BIZ 🛜

✕ 🔌 🖥 💻

🅐 **For complete hotel, dining and attraction listings: AAA.com/travelguides**

WHERE TO EAT

FRANCESCO'S RISTORANTE ITALIANO   757/345-0557   24
Italian. Casual Dining. **Address:** 6524 Richmond Rd, Unit D 23188

LA PETITE TEA ROOM   757/565-3422   23
Specialty. Casual Dining. **Address:** 500 Lightfoot Rd 23188

NEW YORK DELI   757/564-9258   22
Deli. Casual Dining. **Address:** 6546 Richmond Rd 23185

PIERCE'S PITT BAR-B-QUE   757/565-2955   20
Barbecue. Quick Serve. **Address:** 447 E Rochambeau Dr 23188

TACO MEXICALI   757/220-3116   21
Mexican. Casual Dining. **Address:** 6572 Richmond Rd 23188

LORTON (B-12) pop. 18,610, elev. 100'

GUNSTON HALL is s. off US 1 via SR 242 to 10709 Gunston Rd. George Mason, the author of the Virginia Declaration of Rights of 1776 and one of the framers of the U.S. Constitution, designed and lived in this 1755 brick Georgian residence. A visitor center offers an 11-minute orientation film called "George Mason and the Bill of Rights."

English architect William Buckland also designed many elements in the home, including a variety of woodcarvings. The English and American furnishings are from the 18th century and earlier. Guided tours are given of the main floor; visitors may take a self-guiding tour of the second-story bedrooms and grounds.

Next to the main house are such reconstructed outbuildings as the kitchen, laundry, dairy, smokehouse and schoolhouse. The 18th-century gardens contain an original English boxwood allée, reconstructed pebble pathways and viewing mounds. Deer and eagle sightings are possible from a nature trail leading to the Potomac River.

Time: Allow 1 hour minimum. **Hours:** Grounds daily 9:30-6. House tours are given every half-hour 9:30-4:30. Closed Jan. 1, Thanksgiving and Christmas. **Cost:** $10; $8 (ages 60+ and military with ID); $5 (ages 6-18). Grounds only pass $5. **Phone:** (703) 550-9220. GT

POHICK CHURCH (Episcopal) is 2 mi. s.w. on US 1 at 9301 Richmond Hwy. This was the Colonial parish church of Mount Vernon, Gunston Hall and Belvoir. George Washington chose the site and served as vestryman for 23 years. George Mason, a vestryman for 37 years, served on the building committee.

During the Civil War the original 1774 interior was torn out by Union troops and the building was used as a stable. The building was restored 1902-17. The old stone baptismal font was found many years later serving as a trough in a nearby farmyard. **Hours:** Mon.-Fri. 9-4:30. Docent-led tours are given the first

Sat. of the month, Sun. after 9 and 11:15 services or by appointment. **Cost:** Donations. **Phone:** (703) 339-6572. GT

GLORY DAYS GRILL   703/372-1770
▼▼ American. Casual Dining. **Address:** 9459 Lorton Market St 22079

LOVINGSTON (G-7) pop. 520, elev. 745'

Lovingston, the county seat for Nelson County, offers a historic district featuring what is said to be the oldest courthouse in continuous use in the state. Farming is a key local industry, particularly the growing of apples and peaches. Area recreational pursuits include hiking, canoeing and fishing.

Nelson County Convention & Visitors Bureau: 8519 Thomas Nelson Hwy., P.O. Box 636, Lovingston, VA 22949. **Phone:** (434) 263-7015 or (888) 662-9400.

LOVINGSTON CAFE   434/263-8000
▼ American. Casual Dining. **Address:** 165 Front St 22949

LOW MOOR pop. 258

OAK TREE INN   540/965-0090
▼▼ Motel. **Address:** 123 Westvaco Rd 24457

WHERE TO EAT

THE CAT AND OWL STEAK AND SEAFOOD HOUSE
      540/862-5808
▼▼ Steak. Casual Dining. **Address:** 110 Karnes Rd 24457

LURAY (F-8) pop. 4,895, elev. 819'
- Hotels p. 165 • Restaurants p. 165
- Part of Shenandoah National Park area — see map p. 241

Luray was settled by a group of German-Swiss at the base of Massanutten Mountain along the South Fork of the Shenandoah River. Laid out in 1812, Luray was close enough to Virginia's untamed wilderness that some of its early homes contained thick stone forts within their walls to guard against the constant threat of Native American attacks. These forts, usually in the basement, were kept supplied with firewood and food and often included a tunnel that connected with a well.

Hiking, fishing and boating can be enjoyed in developed recreational areas of George Washington and Jefferson National Forests (see place listing p. 119) and in Shenandoah National Park (see place listing p. 241), to the east.

Luray-Page County Chamber of Commerce and Visitor Center: 18 Campbell St., Luray, VA 22835. Phone: (540) 743-3915 or (888) 743-3915.

LURAY CAVERNS is at 970 US 211W. Up to 10 stories tall, the massive chambers contain a variety of formations all in beautiful natural color. In the Cathedral Room is the Stalacpipe Organ, which is purportedly the world's largest musical instrument. It uses specially tuned stalactites to produce music of symphonic quality. Hour-long guided tours take visitors along lighted and paved walkways, past towering stone columns and crystal pools.

Hours: Daily 9-7, June 15-Labor Day; daily 9-6, Apr. 1-June 14 and day after Labor Day-Oct. 31; Mon.-Fri. 9-4, Sat.-Sun. 9-5, rest of year. **Cost:** (includes Car and Carriage Caravan and Luray Valley Museum) $27; $23 (ages 62+); $14 (ages 6-12). **Phone:** (540) 743-6551. *(See ad p. 164.)* GT ▦

Car and Carriage Caravan is at 970 US 211W at the entrance to Luray Caverns. The progress of transportation is depicted through carriage and automobile exhibits. Among the more than 140 items on display are an 1892 Benz, a 1904 Cadillac, a 1935 Hispano-Suiza and many early Ford models.

Hours: Daily 9-8:30, June 15-Labor Day; daily 9-7:30, Apr. 1-June 14 and day after Labor Day-Oct. 31; Mon.-Fri. 9-5:30, Sat.-Sun. 9-6:30, rest of year. **Cost:** (includes Luray Caverns and Luray Valley Museum) $27; $23 (ages 62+); $14 (ages 6-12). **Phone:** (540) 743-6551.

The Garden Maze is at 970 US 211 at Luray Caverns. Visitors must navigate a half-mile path through 8-foot-high arborvitae trees by solving riddles along the way. The 1-acre ornamental garden features misting fog, fountains and a cave. **Time:** Allow 30 minutes minimum. **Hours:** Daily 9-7, June 15-Labor Day; otherwise varies rest of year. Phone ahead to confirm schedule. **Cost:** $9; $7 (ages 6-12). **Phone:** (540) 843-0769. [GT]

Luray Valley Museum, 970 US 211W at Luray Caverns, documents early Shenandoah Valley history and culture. Documents, period clothing and decorative items are displayed in a reconstructed log building; the highlight of the collection is a 1536 Swiss Bible in the German vernacular. Also on the grounds are a group of restored and reconstructed historical structures depicting a 19th-century farming community.

Time: Allow 1 hour minimum. **Hours:** Daily 10-8:30, June 15-Labor Day; daily 10-7:30, Apr. 1-June 14 and day after Labor Day-Oct. 31; Mon.-Fri. 10-5:30, Sat.-Sun. 10-6:30, rest of year. Closed major holidays. **Cost:** (includes Car and Carriage Caravan and Luray Caverns) $27; $23 (ages 62+); $14 (ages 6-12). **Phone:** (540) 743-6551. [A]

Singing Tower is 1 mi. w. on US 211 at the entrance to Luray Caverns. Situated in a parklike setting, the Belle Brown Northcott Memorial is built of sandstone from Massanutten Mountain. The 117-foot carillon, 25 feet square at the base, contains 47 bells; the largest weighs 7,640 pounds, the smallest 12.5 pounds. **Hours:** Recitals, which last about 45

▼ *See AAA listing p. 163* ▼

minutes, are given Tues., Thurs. and Sat.-Sun. at 8 p.m., June-Aug.; Sat.-Sun. at 3, Apr.-May and Sept.-Oct. **Cost:** Free. **Phone:** (540) 743-6551.

THE CABINS AT BROOKSIDE   540/743-5698
 Cabin. **Address:** 2978 US Hwy 211 E 22835

DAYS INN-LURAY   540/743-4521
Motel. **Address:** 138 Whispering Hill Rd 22835

THE MIMSLYN INN   540/743-5105

Hotel
Rates not provided
Address: 401 W Main St 22835 **Location:** 0.3 mi w on US 211 business route. **Facility:** 55 units, some houses and cottages. 3 stories, interior corridors. **Dining:** Circa '31 at The Mimslyn Inn, see separate listing. **Pool:** heated outdoor. **Activities:** hot tub, exercise room, massage.

QUALITY INN   (540)743-6511

Motel
$70-$85
Address: 410 W Main St 22835 **Location:** 0.3 mi w on US 211 business route. **Facility:** 40 units. 2 stories (no elevator), exterior corridors. **Terms:** 4 day cancellation notice-fee imposed. **Dining:** Alexander's, see separate listing. **Pool:** outdoor.

SHADOW MOUNTAIN ESCAPE   540/843-0584
 Cabin. **Address:** 1132 Jewell Hollow Rd 22835

WHERE TO EAT

ALEXANDER'S   540/743-6511
Breakfast
Casual Dining
$5-$19
AAA Inspector Notes: This family-oriented eatery has a wide-ranging menu. Don't miss the bread pudding. Southern hospitality is shown in abundance at this restaurant. **Address:** 410 W Main St 22835 **Location:** 0.3 mi w on US 211 business route; in Quality Inn.
Parking: on-site and street. B

BROOKSIDE RESTAURANT   540/743-5698
American
Casual Dining
$6-$21
AAA Inspector Notes: Diners in the mood for homemade soup, tasty, well-prepared salmon cakes or pot roast won't be disappointed. The basic eatery prepares a good variety of standard favorites and spreads out a tempting salad bar. Homespun decor and wonderful service are other strengths. Don't miss seeing the brook running beside the restaurant. **Features:** beer & wine. **Address:** 2978 US Hwy 211 E 22835 **Location:** 4.8 mi e; in The Cabins at Brookside. B L D

CIRCA '31 AT THE MIMSLYN INN   540/743-5105
 American. Fine Dining. **Address:** 401 W Main St 22835

THE PARKHURST RESTAURANT ON RAINBOW HILL
                                          540/743-6009
American. Casual Dining. **Address:** 2547 US 211 W 22835

RANCHO VIEJO MEXICAN GRILL & CANTINA   540/743-3775
Mexican. Casual Dining. **Address:** 709 E Main St 22835

LYNCHBURG (H-7) pop. 75,568, elev. 517'
• Hotels p. 166 • Restaurants p. 166

A ferry established by John Lynch in 1757 was the nucleus of the original settlement that became Lynchburg, laid out on 45 acres of Lynch's land. He built the region's first tobacco warehouse in 1785.

During the Civil War the city was a supply base for the Confederate Army. It was for the possession of these stores that the Battle of Lynchburg was fought June 18, 1864, when Union general David Hunter made an unsuccessful attempt to capture the city from Confederates commanded by Gen. Jubal A. Early. Throughout the Civil War Lynchburg served as a major hospital center.

Lynchburg has several 19th- and early 20th-century residential districts. Five hills in the "City of Seven Hills" are National Register Historic Districts. Court House Hill is home of Lynchburg Museum at the Old Courthouse (see attraction listing) and is named after the first courthouse built in 1813. Diamond and Garland hills represent the wealth of the tobacco era with magnificent residences of wealthy citizens. Federal Hill was Lynchburg's first suburb. On Daniel's Hill, Cabell Street is reminiscent of the Victorian elegance in the 1890s.

Lynchburg salutes the James River in mid-June with the James River Batteau Festival. It kicks off an 8-day trek in which flat-bottomed boats, once used to transport tobacco and other goods, pole their way from Lynchburg to Richmond.

Lynchburg Regional Convention and Visitors Bureau: 216 12th St., Lynchburg, VA 24504. **Phone:** (434) 485-7290 or (800) 732-5821.

Self-guiding tours: Brochures outlining walking and driving tours of Lynchburg's historic areas are available from the convention and visitors bureau.

AMAZEMENT SQUARE—THE RIGHTMIRE CHILDREN'S MUSEUM is at 27 Ninth St. This dynamic learning environment encourages children to play, learn and solve problems through four floors of hands-on exhibits. Visitors can explore global and regional topics, arts and humanities, science and health-related themes.

Note: Strollers are not permitted. Rental lockers are available. **Time:** Allow 1 hour minimum. **Hours:** Tues.-Sat. 10-5 (also second Sat. of the month 5-7), Sun. and Mon. holidays 1-5. Closed Jan. 1, Easter, Mother's Day, Father's Day, July 4, Thanksgiving and Christmas. **Cost:** $9; $6 (ages 60+); $3 (second Sat. of the month 4-7 p.m.); free (ages 0-1). **Phone:** (434) 845-1888.

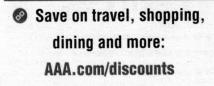

LYNCHBURG MUSEUM AT THE OLD COURTHOUSE

is at 901 Court St. Exhibits detail the history of Lynchburg and central Virginia. Built in 1855, the Greek Revival court building houses displays of Monacan Indian artifacts, Civil War memorabilia and historic photographs. Exhibits chronicle Lynchburg's transition from a tobacco trading center in the early 1800s to a modern industrial city. Displays also highlight railroad, architecture, firefighting and World War I history.

Time: Allow 30 minutes minimum. **Hours:** Mon.-Sat. 10-4, Sun. noon-4. Closed Jan. 1, Thanksgiving, Christmas Eve and Christmas. **Cost:** Free. **Phone:** (434) 455-6226.

MAIER MUSEUM OF ART is off Rivermont Ave. at 1 Quinlan St. on the campus of Randolph College. The museum's permanent collection focuses on American paintings of the 19th, 20th and 21st centuries. The galleries display works by such artists as Thomas Hart Benton, Mary Cassatt, Childe Hassam, Edward Hopper and Georgia O'Keeffe. Changing exhibits also are displayed. **Time:** Allow 30 minutes minimum. **Hours:** Tues.-Sun. 1-5, Sept.-Apr.; Wed.-Sun. 1-4, rest of year. Closed holidays and during Randolph College winter and spring breaks. Phone ahead to confirm schedule. **Cost:** Free. **Phone:** (434) 947-8136.

BAYMONT INN & SUITES LYNCHBURG   434/237-2986
WW Motel. **Address:** 2815 Candlers Mountain Rd 24502

COURTYARD BY MARRIOTT   (434)846-7900
WWW Hotel. **Address:** 4640 Murray Pl 24502
AAA Benefit: Members save 5% or more!

THE CRADDOCK TERRY HOTEL AND EVENT CENTER
(434)455-1500

Boutique Hotel
$149-$299

Address: 1312 Commerce St 24504 **Location:** US 29 business route exit 1A (Main St), just w. **Facility:** A turn-of-the-century shoe factory is now this chic boutique hotel that blends the urban architecture of two landmark brick warehouses with the fashionable styling of a modern hotel. 44 units. 4-5 stories, interior corridors. **Terms:** check-in 4 pm, cancellation fee imposed. **Amenities:** safes. **Dining:** Shoemakers American Grille, see separate listing. **Activities:** exercise room. **Guest Services:** valet laundry, area transportation.

ECONO LODGE   (434)847-1045
WW Motel. **Address:** 2400 Stadium Rd 24501

EXTENDED STAY AMERICA - LYNCHBURG - UNIVERSITY BLVD   (434)239-8863
WW Extended Stay Motel. **Address:** 1910 University Blvd 24502

FAIRFIELD INN & SUITES LYNCHBURG LIBERTY UNIVERSITY
(434)845-1700
WWWW Hotel. **Address:** 3777 Candlers Mountain Rd 24502
AAA Benefit: Members save 5% or more!

FEDERAL CREST INN B & B   (434)845-6155
WWW Historic Bed & Breakfast. **Address:** 1101 Federal St 24504

HOLIDAY INN DOWNTOWN LYNCHBURG   434/528-2500
WWW Hotel. **Address:** 601 Main St 24504

HOLIDAY INN EXPRESS   434/237-7771
WWW Hotel. **Address:** 5600 Seminole Ave 24502

KIRKLEY HOTEL & CONFERENCE CENTER   (434)237-6333
WWW Hotel. **Address:** 2900 Candlers Mountain Rd 24502

LA QUINTA INN & SUITES LYNCHBURG AT LIBERTY UNIVERSITY   (434)847-8655
WWW Hotel. **Address:** 3320 Candlers Mountain Rd 24502

MICROTEL & SUITES BY WYNDHAM LYNCHBURG
434/239-2300
WW Hotel. **Address:** 5704 Seminole Ave 24502

SLEEP INN LYNCHBURG   (434)846-6900

Hotel
$90-$169

Address: 3620 Candlers Mountain Rd 24502 **Location:** US 29 exit 8B. **Facility:** 75 units. 4 stories, interior corridors. **Activities:** exercise room. **Guest Services:** valet and coin laundry. **Featured Amenity: continental breakfast.**

SPRINGHILL SUITES BY MARRIOTT   (434)237-5848
WWW Hotel. **Address:** 15171 Wards Rd 24502
AAA Benefit: Members save 5% or more!

WHERE TO EAT

BULL'S STEAKHOUSE   434/385-7581
WW Tex-Mex. Casual Dining. **Address:** 1887 Graves Mill Rd 24551

CHARLEY'S   434/237-5988
WW American. Casual Dining. **Address:** 707 Graves Mill Rd 24502

THE DEPOT GRILLE   434/846-4464
WW American. Casual Dining. **Address:** 10 9th St 24504

DISH   434/528-0070
WWW American. Fine Dining. **Address:** 1120 Main St 24504

THE FARM BASKET   434/528-1107
W Deli. Quick Serve. **Address:** 2008 Langhorne Rd 24501

ISABELLA'S ITALIAN TRATTORIA   434/385-1660
WWW Northern Italian. Fine Dining. **Address:** 4925 Boonsboro Rd 24503

JIMMY'S ON THE JAMES   434/845-1116
WWW Southern American. Casual Dining. **Address:** 610 Commerce St 24504

MACADO'S   434/845-6464
♦♦ American. Casual Dining. **Address:** 3744 Candlers Mountain Rd 24502

MAGNOLIA FOODS   434/528-5442
♦ Specialty Sandwiches. Quick Serve. **Address:** 2476 Rivermont Ave 24503

MAIN ST EATERY   434/847-2526
♦♦♦ Continental. Fine Dining. **Address:** 907 Main St 24504

MARKET AT MAIN   434/847-9040
♦♦ American. Casual Dining. **Address:** 904 N Main St 24505

MILAN INDIAN CUISINE   434/237-7990
♦♦ Indian. Casual Dining. **Address:** 2124 Wards Rd 24502

MILANO'S ITALIAN RESTAURANT   434/384-3400
♦♦ Traditional Italian. Casual Dining. **Address:** 4327 Boonsboro Rd 24503

MONTE CARLO ITALIAN RESTAURANT   434/385-7711
♦♦ Italian. Casual Dining. **Address:** 3230 Old Forest Rd 24501

ROBIN ALEXANDER AN AMERICAN BISTRO   434/845-1601
♦♦ American. Casual Dining. **Address:** 1344 Main St 24504

SHOEMAKERS AMERICAN GRILLE   404/455-1510
♦♦♦ American. Fine Dining. **Address:** 1312 Commerce St 24504

WATERSTONE FIRE ROASTED PIZZA   434/455-1515
♦♦ Pizza. Casual Dining. **Address:** 1309 Jefferson St 24504

MACHIPONGO (A-5) elev. 40'

This barrier island on the Atlantic Ocean is part of Virginia's Eastern Shore, famed for its natural beauty, abundant wildlife, bountiful fishing and rural charm.

MADISON pop. 229

THE BAVARIAN CHEF   540/948-6505
♦♦♦ German. Casual Dining. **Address:** 5102 S Seminole Tr 22727

MANASSAS (B-11) pop. 37,821, elev. 312'
• Restaurants p. 168

The juncture of the Manassas Gap and the Orange & Alexandria railroads in the 1850s created the hamlet of Manassas (ma-NAS-sas). During the Civil War this tiny junction became a bloody pawn between two contending armies. Fought over and burned, Manassas was a key to the heart of Virginia and the site for hospitals, fortifications and supply depots for both North and South.

When the war ended, the railroad became the basis of the town's economy, which was further spurred in the last half of the 20th century by the growth of the Washington, D.C., metropolitan area.

Fall Jubilee, held on the first Saturday in October, draws crowds with live music, local celebrities, baking contests, arts and crafts, and children's activities. Also featured are the Chainsaw Chix, a group of women chainsaw artists whose creations are auctioned off at the end of the event.

Historic Manassas Visitor Center: 9431 West St., Manassas, VA 20110. **Phone:** (703) 361-6599.

Self-guiding tours: Brochures outlining driving and walking tours are available from the Historic Manassas Visitor Center and The Manassas Museum.

Shopping

Manassas Mall, 8300 Sudley Rd., has more than 80 stores, including Macy's and Sears.

BEST WESTERN BATTLEFIELD INN   (703)361-8000

Hotel
$125-$200

AAA Benefit: Members save 10% or more & earn 10% bonus points!

Address: 10820 Balls Ford Rd 20109 **Location:** I-66 exit 47A westbound; exit 47 eastbound, just s on SR 234 business route. Located in a commercial area. **Facility:** 123 units. 2 stories (no elevator), exterior corridors. **Terms:** cancellation fee imposed. **Amenities:** safes. **Pool:** outdoor. **Guest Services:** valet and coin laundry.

BEST WESTERN MANASSAS   (703)368-7070

Hotel
$99-$175

AAA Benefit: Members save 10% or more & earn 10% bonus points!

Address: 8640 Mathis Ave 20110 **Location:** I-66 exit 53 (SR 28 S), 5 mi s to Manassas Dr, just w, then just s. **Facility:** 59 units, some efficiencies. 2 stories (no elevator), interior corridors. **Terms:** 3 day cancellation notice-fee imposed. **Activities:** sauna, exercise room. **Guest Services:** coin laundry. **Featured Amenity:** breakfast buffet.

CANDLEWOOD SUITES MANASSAS   (703)530-0550
♦♦ Extended Stay Hotel. **Address:** 11220 Balls Ford Rd 20109

COMFORT SUITES MANASSAS   (703)686-1100
♦♦♦ Hotel. **Address:** 7350 Williamson Blvd 20109

COURTYARD BY MARRIOTT MANASSAS-BATTLEFIELD PARK
                                            (703)335-1300
♦♦♦ Hotel. **Address:** 10701 Battleview Pkwy 20109

AAA Benefit: Members save 5% or more!

HAMPTON INN BY HILTON MANASSAS   (703)369-1100
♦♦♦ Hotel. **Address:** 7295 Williamson Blvd 20109

AAA Benefit: Members save up to 10%!

HOLIDAY INN EXPRESS & SUITES MANASSAS
(703)393-9797

Hotel
$119-$129

Address: 10810 Battleview Pkwy 20109 **Location:** I-66 exit 47 eastbound; exit 47B westbound, just n on SR 234, then just e. **Facility:** 75 units. 3 stories, interior corridors. **Pool:** heated indoor. **Activities:** hot tub, exercise room. **Guest Services:** valet and coin laundry. **Featured Amenity: continental breakfast.**

HOLIDAY INN MANASSAS BATTLEFIELD   571/292-5400
♥♥♥ Hotel. **Address:** 10424 Balls Ford Rd 20109

LA QUINTA INN & SUITES MANASSAS   (703)393-9966
♥♥♥ Hotel. **Address:** 6950 Nova Way 20109

RED ROOF PLUS+ WASHINGTON DC-MANASSAS
(703)335-9333

♥♥
Motel
$69-$150

Address: 10610 Automotive Dr 20109 **Location:** I-66 exit 47A westbound; exit 47 eastbound, just s on SR 234 business route, then just e on Balls Ford Rd. **Facility:** 119 units. 3 stories, exterior corridors. **Amenities:** safes.

RESIDENCE INN BY MARRIOTT MANASSAS BATTLEFIELD PARK
(703)330-8808

Extended Stay Hotel
$89-$239

Residence Inn Marriott

AAA Benefit: Members save 5% or more!

Address: 7345 Williamson Blvd 20109 **Location:** I-66 exit 47A westbound; exit 47 eastbound, 0.5 mi s on SR 234 business route, then just e. **Facility:** 107 units, some two bedrooms, efficiencies and kitchens. 3 stories, interior corridors. **Terms:** cancellation fee imposed. **Pool:** heated indoor. **Activities:** exercise room. **Guest Services:** valet and coin laundry. **Featured Amenity:** breakfast buffet.

WHERE TO EAT

C.J. FINZ RAW BAR & GRILLE   571/292-1742
♥♥ Seafood. Casual Dining. **Address:** 9413 West St 20110

GLORY DAYS GRILL   703/361-9040
♥♥ American. Casual Dining. **Address:** 9516 Liberia Ave 20110

KATERINA'S GREEK CUISINE   703/361-4976
♥♥ Greek. Casual Dining. **Address:** 9112 Center St 20110

MARIACHIS TEQUILERIA & RESTAURANT   703/369-6022
♥♥ Mexican. Casual Dining. **Address:** 9428 Battle St 20110

OKRA'S CAJUN CREOLE   703/330-2729
♥♥ Regional American. Casual Dining. **Address:** 9110 Center St 20110

ZANDRA'S TAQUERIA   703/359-6767
♥♥ Mexican. Casual Dining. **Address:** 9114 Center St 20110

MANASSAS NATIONAL BATTLEFIELD PARK (B-11)

Manassas National Battlefield Park, on SR 234 between I-66 and US 29, marks the site north of the strategically important railroad junction at Manassas where two great battles of the Civil War—the First and Second Battles of Manassas, or Bull Run—were fought.

On July 21, 1861, picnickers and other sightseers observed a well-equipped but ill-trained Union Army under Gen. Irvin McDowell as it battled the Confederate Army under Gens. Pierre Beauregard and Joseph Johnston. After 10 hours of deadly fighting it became apparent that this conflict was not going to decide the war, as most had expected. The Union army, finally broken by Confederate forces, was forced to retreat toward Washington, D.C. It was at this battle that Gen. Thomas J. Jackson earned the nickname Stonewall.

When the armies returned to the plains of Manassas in August 1862, they were no longer young recruits in colorful new uniforms. A year of war had hardened both armies and brought the Confederacy to the peak of its power, soon to be realized with the outcome of this battle. The encounter also proved to be a bloody demonstration of Robert E. Lee's genius, as he defeated the larger army of Gen. John Pope in 3 days of fighting.

A walking trail on Henry Hill offers scenic views of the first battlefield. The focal point of the hill is an equestrian statue of Jackson. The Stone House, which served as a field hospital in both battles, is open seasonally. The Brawner Farm Interpretive Center offers various exhibits and multimedia programs.

The Henry Hill Visitor Center has a museum and theater that shows the 45-minute film "Manassas: End of Innocence"; a 3-D map illustrates the strategies of the first battle. Two 5-mile hikes around the battlefield are detailed in a pamphlet available at the visitor center. Various guided tours are offered throughout the year. A CD driving tour of the park also is available for purchase at the visitor center. The route encompasses the main points of the second battle as well as areas involved in both engagements.

Grounds open daily dawn-dusk. Visitor center open daily 8:30-5; closed Thanksgiving and Christmas. Stone House open daily 10-4:30, Memorial Day-Labor Day; Sat.-Sun. 10-4, early Apr.-day before Memorial Day and day after Labor Day-late Oct. (weather permitting). Brawner Farm Interpretive Center open daily 9-5, early Mar.-late Nov. (weather permitting). Phone ahead to confirm hours. Park admission is free. Phone (703) 361-1339 for the visitor center or (703) 754-1861 for the park headquarters.

MARION (H-4) pop. 5,968, elev. 2,172'

Marion was named for Gen. Francis Marion, known as the "Swamp Fox" during the Revolution because of the guerrilla warfare tactics he used against the British in South Carolina. A popular vacation base, Marion is surrounded by the George Washington and Jefferson National Forests *(see place listing p. 119).*

Chamber of Commerce of Smyth County: 214 W. Main St., P.O. Box 924, Marion, VA 24354. **Phone:** (276) 783-3161.

THE COLLINS HOUSE INN (276)781-0250
▼▼▼ Bed & Breakfast. **Address:** 204 W Main St 24354

GENERAL FRANCIS MARION HOTEL (276)783-4800

Hotel
$99-$300

Address: 107 E Main St 24354 **Location:** I-81 exit 45, 2.1 mi w on SR 16, then 0.4 mi s. **Facility:** 36 units. 5 stories, interior corridors. **Terms:** cancellation fee imposed. **Guest Services:** valet laundry. **Featured Amenity:** continental breakfast.

MARTINSVILLE (I-6) pop. 13,821, elev. 1,017'

VIRGINIA MUSEUM OF NATURAL HISTORY is at 21 Starling Ave. This state-of-the-art facility offers walk-through exhibits and hands-on experiences relating to the natural world and Virginia's ancient past. A collection of fossils includes a towering allosaurus skeleton and re-creations of important geologic sites. A behind-the-scenes look at research projects and objects in storage lets visitors see how a natural history museum works.

Time: Allow 2 hours minimum. **Hours:** Mon.-Sat. 9-5, Sun. 1-5, Memorial Day weekend-Labor Day weekend; Mon.-Sat. 9-5, rest of year. Last admission 30 minutes before closing. Closed Jan. 1, Thanksgiving and Christmas. **Cost:** $7; $5 (ages 3-18, ages 60+ and students and military with ID). **Phone:** (276) 634-4141.

BAYMONT INN & SUITES MARTINSVILLE 276/638-0478
▼▼ Hotel. **Address:** 378 Commonwealth Blvd W 24112

COMFORT INN MARTINSVILLE (276)666-6835
▼▼▼ Hotel. **Address:** 1895 Virginia Ave 24112

HAMPTON INN (276)647-4700
▼▼▼ Hotel. **Address:** 50 Hampton Dr 24112

AAA Benefit: Members save up to 10%!

WHERE TO EAT

CHECKERED PIG 276/632-1161
▼▼ Barbecue. Casual Dining. **Address:** 1014 Liberty St 24112

MI RANCHITO 276/632-6363
▼▼▼ Mexican. Casual Dining. **Address:** 1212 Memorial Blvd 24112

MAX MEADOWS pop. 562, elev. 2,028'

HAMPTON INN OF FT. CHISWELL (276)637-4027
▼▼▼ Hotel. **Address:** 199 Ft. Chiswell Rd 24360

AAA Benefit: Members save up to 10%!

SUPER 8 276/637-4141
▼▼ Motel. **Address:** 194 Ft. Chiswell Rd 24360

MCGAHEYSVILLE elev. 1,122'

HANK'S SMOKEHOUSE AND DELI 540/289-7667
▼▼ Barbecue. Casual Dining. **Address:** 49 Bloomer Springs Rd 22840

ROMANO'S ITALIAN BISTRO 540/289-5770
▼▼ Italian. Casual Dining. **Address:** 42 Island Ford Rd 22840

THUNDERBIRD CAFE 540/289-5094
▼ American. Casual Dining. **Address:** 42 Island Ford Rd 22840

MCLEAN (B-12) pop. 48,115, elev. 303'
- Hotels p. 170 • Restaurants p. 170
- Hotels & Restaurants map & index p. 38

SAVE **CLAUDE MOORE COLONIAL FARM** is 2.5 mi. e. on SR 193 from I-495 exit 44 to 6310 Georgetown Pike. This is a small-scale representation of a homestead during the late Colonial period, with costumed interpreters performing the farm tasks. In addition to field crops, heritage breeds of cattle, chickens, turkeys and hogs are on the farm. Re-enactments of Colonial market fairs are held the third full weekend in May, July and October.

Time: Allow 30 minutes minimum. **Hours:** Wed.-Sun. 10-4:30, early Apr. to mid-Dec. Closed July 4 and Thanksgiving. **Cost:** $5; $3 (ages 3-12 and 60+). During market fair days $8; $4 (ages 3-12 and 60+). An additional fee may be charged during events. **Phone:** (703) 442-7557.

GREAT FALLS PARK is at 9200 Old Dominion Dr. Here the Potomac River plunges a total of 77 feet in a series of picturesque falls and thundering rapids. One-mile-long Mather Gorge is walled by irregular palisades. Biking, hiking, cross-country skiing and kayaking are among the possible recreational activities.

Within the 800-acre park are remnants of a skirting canal constructed between 1785 and 1802 by the Patowmack Co., of which George Washington was founder and president. The canal had a series of locks that enabled boats to re-enter the river after having bypassed the falls. There is no direct access between the Virginia and Maryland sides. The Maryland side is part of Chesapeake and Ohio Canal National Historical Park.

Note: Extreme care must be taken when visiting this beautiful but hazardous natural area. Signs indicate treacherous spots. Stay on the trails and observe the signs. Alcoholic beverages are not

(See map & index p. 38.)

permitted. The park has a carry in, carry out policy in effect, and there are no trash cans on-site. **Hours:** Grounds daily 7 a.m.-dusk. Visitor center daily 10-5, early Mar.-early Nov.; 10-4, rest of year. Closed Christmas. **Cost:** (valid for 3 days) $10 (per private vehicle); $5 (per person arriving by other means). **Phone:** (703) 285-2965 or (703) 757-3101.

Visitor Center is at 9200 Old Dominion Dr. in Great Falls Park, within walking distance of the falls over-looks. The center has displays, a slide show about park history and changing exhibits. "The History of Great Falls," an 8-minute video presentation, is available by request. Games and puzzles in the Children's Room teach kids about the park's history. Ranger-led and historical programs vary with the seasons.

Hours: Daily 10-5, early Mar.-early Nov.; 10-4, rest of year. Closed Christmas. **Cost:** Included in Great Falls Park admission (valid for 3 days) of $5 (per private vehicle); $3 (per person arriving by other means). **Phone:** (703) 285-2965 or (703) 757-3101.

STAYBRIDGE SUITES TYSONS MCLEAN HOTEL (WASHINGTON, D.C. AREA) 703/448-5400 (32)

Extended Stay Hotel
Rates not provided

Address: 6845 Old Dominion Dr 22101 **Location:** I-495 exit 46B, 2 mi n on SR 123, then 0.3 mi e on SR 309. Located in a commercial area. **Facility:** 142 effi-ciencies, some two bedrooms. 5 stories, interior corridors. **Terms:** check-in 4 pm. **Amenities:** safes. **Pool:** outdoor. **Activities:** exercise room. **Guest Services:** complimentary and valet laundry, area transportation. **Featured Amenity: breakfast buffet.**

WHERE TO EAT

7SPICE FINE INDIAN CUISINE 703/827-0444 (29)
Indian. Casual Dining. **Address:** 1379 Beverly Rd 22101

CAFE OGGI 703/442-7360 (32)
Italian. Fine Dining. **Address:** 6671 Old Dominion Dr 22101

THE GREEK TAVERNA 703/556-0788 (30)
Greek. Casual Dining. **Address:** 6828-C Old Dominion Dr 22101

KAZAN RESTAURANT 703/734-1960 (31)
Turkish. Casual Dining. **Address:** 6813 Redmond Dr 22101

PULCINELLA THE ITALIAN HOST 703/893-7777 (28)
Southern Italian. Casual Dining. **Address:** 6852 Old Dominion Dr 22101

TACHIBANA 703/847-1771 (33)
Japanese Sushi. Casual Dining. **Address:** 6715 Lowell Ave 22101

MECHANICSVILLE pop. 36,348
• Hotels & Restaurants map & index p. 212
• Part of Richmond area — see map p. 193

HAMPTON INN (804)559-0559 (58)
Hotel. **Address:** 7433 Bell Creek Rd 23111

AAA Benefit: Members save up to 10%!

HOLIDAY INN EXPRESS-RICHMOND-MECHANICSVILLE 804/559-0022 (59)
Hotel. **Address:** 7441 Bell Creek Rd 23111

WHERE TO EAT

GINGER RED ASIAN BISTRO 804/427-7256 (66)
Asian Sushi. Casual Dining. **Address:** 7500 Jackson Arch Dr 23111

MEXICO RESTAURANT 804/559-8126 (67)
Mexican. Casual Dining. **Address:** 7162 Mechanicsville Tpke 23111

PEKING RESTAURANT 804/730-9898
Chinese. Casual Dining. **Address:** 7100 Mechanicsville Tpke 23111

MIDDLEBURG pop. 673, elev. 486'

SALAMANDER RESORT & SPA (540)326-4000

Resort Hotel
$295-$695

Address: 500 N Pendleton St 20117 **Location:** Off US 50, just n. **Facility:** This 340-acre resort is located in the heart of horse country. Features include a full-service spa, horse stables, fine and casual dining outlets, and luxurious public rooms, guest rooms and suites. 168 units. 5 stories, interior corridors. **Parking:** on-site and valet. **Terms:** check-in 4 pm, 7 day cancellation notice-fee imposed, resort fee. **Amenities:** safes. **Dining:** Harrimans, see separate listing. **Pool:** outdoor, heated indoor. **Activities:** sauna, tennis, recre-ation programs, bicycles, lawn sports, trails, exercise room, spa. **Guest Services:** valet laundry, area transportation.

WHERE TO EAT

HARRIMANS 540/326-4070
American. Fine Dining. **Address:** 500 N Pendleton St 20117

RED FOX INN 540/687-6301
American. Casual Dining. **Address:** 2 E Washington St 20117

MIDDLETOWN (E-8) pop. 1,265, elev. 660'

The Battle of Cedar Creek took place Oct. 19, 1864, when Confederate general Jubal Early ex-ecuted a surprise attack on Gen. Philip Sheridan's army encamped on Cedar Creek, south of Middle-town. Sheridan was at Winchester when the firing began, and he raced to the scene of the battle. Meeting the retreating soldiers about a mile north of Middletown, he not only halted the flight of his troops but also galvanized them to attack and defeat Early.

SAVE **BELLE GROVE PLANTATION** is 1 mi. s. on US 11, then .5 mi. w. on Belle Grove Rd. Maj. Isaac Hite Jr. acquired the 483-acre parcel in 1783, the same year he married Nelly Conway Madison, sister of the future president. During the Civil War, Union troops repeatedly occupied the estate, which was the focus of the Battle of Cedar Creek in October 1864. On the grounds of the 1797 limestone manor house are gardens, orchards, an overseer's house, a slave cemetery and original outbuildings.

Time: Allow 2 hours minimum. **Hours:** Mon.-Sat. 10:15-3:15, Sun. 1:15-4:15, late Mar.-late Oct.; schedule varies Nov.-Dec. **Cost:** $12; $11 (ages 60+ and military with ID); $6 (ages 6-16). **Phone:** (540) 869-2028. GT 🏃

NANA'S IRISH PUB   540/868-9877
🍷🍷 Irish. Casual Dining. **Address:** 7843 Main St 22645

MIDLOTHIAN (A-1) elev. 367'
• **Hotels & Restaurants map & index p. 212**
• **Part of Richmond area — see map p. 193**

CHILDREN'S MUSEUM OF RICHMOND-CHESTERFIELD, in the Winterpock Crossing Shopping Center at 6629 Lake Harbour Dr., features hands-on exhibits that focus on problem solving and creativity. Included among the fun interactive displays are an art studio, a theater/stage, a safari animal train, a climbing station, and sand and water play tables. There's also an enchanted forest area geared toward children ages 2 and under.

The centerpiece of the museum is Main Street, where kids learn real world concepts through role playing activities in a bank, a diner, a veterinary clinic, a bait and tackle shop, a grocery store and the Transportation Station, which features a restored fire truck and a city bus.

Time: Allow 1 hour, 30 minutes minimum. **Hours:** Daily 9:30-5. Closed Jan. 1, Easter, July 4, Thanksgiving and Christmas. **Cost:** $9; $8 (ages 60+ and military with ID); free (ages 0-11 months). **Phone:** (804) 474-7075.

HAMPTON INN-RICHMOND-SOUTHWEST-HULL STREET
                                (804)675-0000 **73**
🍷🍷🍷 Hotel. **Address:** 3620 Price Club Blvd 23112

AAA Benefit: Members save up to 10%!

HOLIDAY INN EXPRESS HOTEL & SUITES-BRANDERMILL
                                804/744-7303 **74**
🍷🍷🍷 Hotel. **Address:** 5030 W Village Green Dr 23112

LA QUINTA INN & SUITES-RICHMOND-MIDLOTHIAN
                                (804)794-4999 **72**
🍷🍷🍷 Hotel. **Address:** 1301 Huguenot Rd 23113

SLEEP INN & SUITES HARBOUR POINT   (804)639-3500 **75**
🍷🍷🍷 Hotel. **Address:** 6451 Bayside Ln 23112

🌐 **Get member rates and reservations at AAA.com/hertz**

BLUEFISH DELI   804/303-3561 **79**
🍷🍷 Asian Sushi Sandwiches. Casual Dining. **Address:** 4948 Millridge Pkwy 23112

THE BOATHOUSE AT SUNDAY PARK   804/744-2545 **80**
🍷🍷 American. Casual Dining. **Address:** 4602 Millridge Pkwy 23112

BONEFISH GRILL   804/639-2747 **81**
🍷🍷🍷 Seafood. Fine Dining. **Address:** 6081 Harbour Park Dr 23112

CAFE CATURRA   804/378-4955 **78**
🍷 American. Casual Dining. **Address:** 13830 Village Place Dr 23114

THE DESSERTERIE   804/639-9940 **82**
🍷🍷 Desserts Sandwiches. Casual Dining. **Address:** 6161 Harbourside Centre Loop 23112

GLORY DAYS GRILL   804/608-8350
🍷🍷 American. Casual Dining. **Address:** 6151 Harbourside Centre Loop 23112

THE HARD SHELL   804/464-1476 **77**
🍷🍷 Seafood. Casual Dining. **Address:** 11400 W Huguenot Rd 23113

PEKING RESTAURANT   804/794-1799
🍷🍷 Chinese. Casual Dining. **Address:** 13132 Midlothian Tpke 23113

RIVER CITY DINER   804/897-9518
🍷🍷 Breakfast Comfort Food. Casual Dining. **Address:** 11430 W Huguenot Rd 23113

RUTH'S CHRIS STEAK HOUSE   804/378-0600 **74**
🍷🍷🍷 Steak. Fine Dining. **Address:** 11500 W Huguenot Rd 23113

SUSHI-O   804/897-9878 **76**
🍷🍷🍷 Japanese Sushi. Casual Dining. **Address:** 1228 Alverser Dr 23113

TAZZA KITCHEN ALVERSER PLAZA   804/415-6224 **75**
🍷🍷🍷 American. Casual Dining. **Address:** 1244 Alverser Plaza 23113

MILLWOOD (E-8) elev. 520'

Millwood lies near the Shenandoah River. Descendants of Tidewater aristocrat Robert "King" Carter built several large estates in and around Millwood in the late 18th century. One of these wealthy settlers, Nathaniel Burwell, built Carter Hall 1790-98. Among Carter Hall's guests were Gen. Thomas J. "Stonewall" Jackson and Edmund Randolph.

MINERAL (G-9) pop. 467, elev. 463'

Originally known as Tolersville, the town of Mineral was renamed in 1890 after deposits of copper, gold, mica and sulfur were discovered in the area.

MINT SPRING

DAYS INN-STAUNTON   540/337-3031
🍷🍷 Motel. **Address:** 372 White Hill Rd 24401

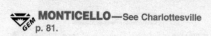

MONTICELLO—See Charlottesville p. 81.

MONTPELIER STATION (F-8) elev. 492'

JAMES MADISON'S MONTPELIER is at 11350 Constitution Hwy. (SR 20). The 2,650-acre property was the lifelong home of James Madison, fourth president of the United States, Father of the Constitution and architect of the Bill of Rights. Madison and his wife, Dolley—America's "first" first lady—are buried in the family cemetery.

The David M. Rubenstein Visitor Center houses the Potter Theater, which presents an orientation film, the Joe and Marge Grills Gallery and the William duPont Gallery. Also on the grounds is the Gilmore Cabin. The restored structure was built in the 1870s by George Gilmore, a freed Montpelier slave, and his wife Polly. The 1910 Train Depot houses a Jim Crow exhibit titled In the Time of Segregation.

Ongoing archeological excavations uncover details of plantation life, and curators continue to work to return the Madisons' furnishings and décor to the home. The cellar houses The Mere Distinction of Colour exhibit while the South Yard—the domestic slave quarters—features re-created slave dwellings, kitchens and a smokehouse. The grounds also include the Annie duPont Formal Garden, the Stable Quarter, the 200-acre James Madison Landmark Forest, an archeology lab, a Civil War encampment site, a slave cemetery and more than 8 miles of walking trails through old-growth forests and meadows.

Hours: Daily 9-5:30. Closed first 2 weeks in Jan., Thanksgiving and Christmas. Gilmore Cabin open Mon.-Fri. for self-guiding tours, Sat.-Sun. for guided tours, Apr.-Oct. Phone ahead to confirm schedule. **Cost:** Grounds, gardens, trails, lab and galleries free. Signature and specialty tours $22; $9 (ages 6-14). The Mere Distinction of Colour exhibit and Enslaved Community walking tour free with house ticket. Historic Landscape walking tour free first Sat. of the month, Apr.-Oct. **Phone:** (540) 672-2728. GT ⛔

MOSELEY (G-9) elev. 312'
• **Part of Richmond area — see map p. 193**

METRO RICHMOND ZOO is at 8300 Beaver Bridge Rd., just s. of jct. US 360 (Hull Street Rd.). The 40-acre zoo is home to more than 2,000 animals representing 180-plus species, including cheetahs, giraffes, tigers, rhinos, warthogs and penguins as well as some 200 monkeys. A petting area featuring barnyard animals also is on-site as is a jungle-themed carousel. The Safari Sky Ride takes visitors on a scenic 15-minute tour high above the park grounds. The Safari Train also offers views of the park's inhabitants. The Treetop Zoofari zipline zooms 3,000 feet through the forest, including a 600-foot zip over the zoo's lake.

Food is available seasonally. Picnic tables are available. **Time:** Allow 1 hour minimum. **Hours:** Mon.-Sat. 9:30-5 (weather permitting). Closed Jan. 1, Thanksgiving, Christmas Eve and Christmas. **Cost:** $17.25; $16.25 (ages 60+); $11.25 (ages 2-11). Carousel $2. Safari Sky Ride $3; free (ages 0-1). Safari Train $3; free (ages 0-1). Unlimited ride wristband (includes carousel, train and sky ride) $8. Treetop Zoofari $50 (ages 8+ or over 54 inches tall). **Phone:** (804) 739-5666. ⛔ ⛔

MOUNTAIN LAKE

MOUNTAIN LAKE LODGE   540/626-7121
▼▼▼ Resort Hotel. **Address:** 115 Hotel Cir 24136

MOUNT JACKSON pop. 1,994

THE WIDOW KIP'S   540/477-2400
▼▼▼ Historic Bed & Breakfast. **Address:** 355 Orchard Dr 22842

MOUNT ROGERS NATIONAL RECREATION AREA (I-4)

The visitor center for the Mount Rogers National Recreation Area, in the high country of southwestern Virginia, is at 3714 SR 16. The 200,000-acre recreation area is part of George Washington and Jefferson National Forests (see place listing p. 119). Mount Rogers is the highest point in the state at 5,729 feet; a trail to the top begins at Grindstone Campground and Grayson Highlands State Park (see Recreation Areas Chart).

Broad mountain meadows and forests of spruce, fir and northern hardwood provide settings for seven developed campgrounds, which are open April through October.

A network of trails includes a 60-mile segment of the Appalachian Trail and others suitable for cross-country skiing. Three primitive horse camps adjoin the Virginia Highlands Horse Trail. The 34-mile Virginia Creeper Trail is popular with bicyclists. Most prefer to take the shuttle to Whitetop Station, the mountain's highest point, and ride the 17 miles back down to Damascus. The area also offers good trout fishing and deer and turkey hunting.

The visitor center is open Mon.-Fri. 8-4:30, Sat.-Sun. 9-4, May 1-late Oct.; Mon.-Fri. 8-4:30, rest of year. Phone (276) 783-5196 or (800) 628-7202. See Recreation Areas Chart.

MOUNT VERNON (B-12) pop. 12,416, elev. 79'
• **Restaurants p. 174**

GEORGE WASHINGTON'S MOUNT VERNON is at the s. end of George Washington Memorial Pkwy., overlooking the Potomac River at 3200 Mount Vernon Memorial Hwy. George Washington's residence at Mount Vernon, from 1759 until his death in 1799, was interrupted by his tenure as president. George and Martha Washington rest in two marble sarcophagi within the family tomb vault.

John Washington, great-grandfather of George, was granted land on the upper Potomac between Little Hunting Creek and Dogue Run, which became the Mount Vernon homesite in 1674. Washington family members occupied Mount Vernon over the years, and in 1761, George acquired the plantation, enlarging and improving the mansion and estate.

The mansion has been restored to appear as it was during the last year of Washington's life and contains much of the original furniture. Displays include the bed in which Washington died and the key to the Bastille, presented to him by the Marquis de Lafayette. Visitors can tour Washington's tomb, gardens and 12 outbuildings. The Pioneer Farmer site offers hands-on activities and contains a reconstruction of Washington's round barn, where horses walk the second floor threshing wheat seasonally.

Various guided tours of the grounds are offered April through October. In mid-September, the ⇝Colonial Market and Fair at Mount Vernon features puppet and magic shows, sword-swallowers, fire-eaters and gypsies.

Note: Baby strollers and photography are not permitted inside the mansion. **Time:** Allow 3 hours minimum **Hours:** Daily 9-5, Apr.-Oct.; 9-4, rest of year. Grounds are cleared 30 minutes after closing. **Cost:** (includes Donald W. Reynolds Museum and Education Center, Ford Orientation Center, George Washington's Distillery & Gristmill, pioneer farm and outbuildings) $20; $19 (ages 62+); $10 (ages 6-11). Grounds audio tour $6. **Phone:** (703) 780-2000 or TTY (703) 799-8697. GT 🍴

⇝ **Donald W. Reynolds Museum and Education Center** is at George Washington's Mount Vernon, 3200 Mount Vernon Memorial Hwy. Visitors learn about George Washington in 23 galleries and theaters through interactive displays, short videos and a collection of some 700 items. Computers provide access to more than 20,000 letters penned by Washington.

Museum highlights include a bust of the first president sculpted by Jean-Antoine Houdon noted for its remarkable likeness; objects accumulated by Washington from Europe and other parts of the world; historic articles relating to Washington's military career and presidency; a gallery offering a behind-the-scenes glimpse into the daily lives of the Washington family; and a collection of books, manuscripts and maps.

Lives Bound Together: Slavery at George Washington's Mount Vernon provides insight into the daily lives of those who worked in the Washington household as well as George Washington's changing views on slavery through artwork, documents, furnishings, archaeological discoveries and interactive displays.

The education center features original videos produced by The History Channel offering viewers a state-of-the-art theater experience depicting Washington's life story. **Time:** Allow 1 hour minimum. **Hours:** Daily 9-5, Apr.-Oct.; 9-4, rest of year. Last admission 1 hour before closing. **Cost:** (includes George Washington's Mount Vernon, Ford Orientation Center, George Washington's Distillery & Gristmill, pioneer farm and outbuildings) $20; $19 (ages 62+); $10 (ages 6-11). **Phone:** (703) 780-2000 or TTY (703) 799-8697.

Ford Orientation Center is at George Washington's Mount Vernon, 3200 Mount Vernon Memorial Hwy. "We Fight to be Free," a 20-minute video, provides general information about Mount Vernon as well as insight into the challenges George Washington faced during his life. In addition visitors can explore a one-twelfth-scale replica of the Mount Vernon mansion, complete with operational windows, fireplaces and doorknobs.

Time: Allow 30 minutes minimum. **Hours:** Daily 9-5, Apr.-Oct.; 9-4, rest of year. Grounds are cleared 30 minutes after closing. **Cost:** (includes George Washington's Mount Vernon, Donald W. Reynolds Museum and Education Center, George Washington's Distillery & Gristmill, pioneer farm and outbuildings) $20; $19 (ages 62+); $10 (ages 6-11). **Phone:** (703) 780-2000 or TTY (703) 799-8697.

George Washington's Distillery & Gristmill is at 5514 Mount Vernon Memorial Hwy, in a small park 3.1 mi. w. of George Washington's Mount Vernon. Demonstrations by costumed distillers take visitors through the historic process of whiskey making in this reconstruction of what is reputedly the largest 18th-century distillery in America.

The distillery is adjacent to the reconstructed gristmill, a water-powered mill where guides in period garb grind corn into meal and wheat into flour just as it was done by millers more than 200 years ago. Together, these buildings showcase Washington's entrepreneurship and his vision for the nation's future.

Time: Allow 1 hour minimum. **Hours:** Daily 10-5, Apr.-Oct. **Cost:** (includes George Washington's Mount Vernon, Donald W. Reynolds Museum and Education Center, Ford Orientation Center, pioneer farm and outbuildings) $20; $19 (ages 62+); $10 (ages 6-11). **Phone:** (703) 780-2000 or TTY (703) 799-8697. GT 🎟

Mount Vernon Sightseeing Cruises on the Potomac River is at George Washington's Mount Vernon, 3200 Mount Vernon Memorial Hwy. Departing from Mount Vernon's wharf, the 45-minute cruise provides scenic views of the estate, with some narration provided. The boat travels just beyond Fort Washington then turns around.

Note: Guests should arrive 30 minutes before the scheduled tour time. **Time:** Allow 45 minutes minimum. **Hours:** Cruises depart Tues.-Sun., May-Aug.; Sat.-Sun. in Apr. and Sept. Departure times vary; phone ahead. **Cost:** $11; $7 (ages 6-11). **Phone:** (703) 780-2000 or TTY (703) 799-8697. GT

THE MOUNT VERNON INN   703/780-0011
▼▼ American. Fine Dining. **Address:** 3200 Mount Vernon Memorial Hwy 22121

NASSAWADOX pop. 499

THE GREAT MACHIPONGO CLAM SHACK   757/442-3800
▼▼ Seafood. Casual Dining. **Address:** 6468 Lankford Hwy 23413

LITTLE ITALY   757/442-7831
▼▼ Italian. Casual Dining. **Address:** 10227 Rogers Dr 23413

NATURAL BRIDGE (G-6) elev. 1,078'

Historic Natural Bridge, in the heart of the Blue Ridge Mountains, is home to the "rock bridge" (the county's namesake) and adjacent to George Washington and Jefferson National Forests *(see place listing p. 119)*. Natural Bridge became a retreat when Thomas Jefferson built a two-room log cabin for guests. By the 19th century, the railway dropped off thousands of people at Natural Bridge station for a mountain respite, during which they would view the renowned rock bridge that Jefferson called "the most sublime of nature's works." The site is now known as Natural Bridge State Park *(see attraction listing this page)*.

NATURAL BRIDGE STATE PARK is off I-81 exit 175 or 180 on US 11 or off the Blue Ridge Pkwy. Mileposts 61.6 and 63.7. The 215-foot tall limestone arch spanning Cedar Creek, known by the Monacan Indians as the "Bridge of God," is an ancient natural wonder, a Virginia Civil War Trails site and a Virginia Birding and Wildlife Trail site. It was purchased in 1774 by Thomas Jefferson, and surveyed by George Washington.

In early American history the Natural Bridge ranked with Niagara Falls in the top tier of the country's natural wonders and continues to inspire awe today. Those exploring the serene Cedar Creek Trail view tall rock walls, lush vegetation and a beautiful creek. A re-created Monacan Indian village allows visitors to delve into the history of Virginia's native peoples. When darkness falls, the Natural Bridge comes alive with choreographed lighting, words and music during "The Drama of Creation," a bridge tradition since 1927.

Hours: Grounds daily 8 a.m.-dusk. "The Drama of Creation" is presented daily at dusk, Mar.-Oct. Phone ahead to confirm schedule. **Cost:** $8; $6 (ages 6-12). **Phone:** (540) 291-1326. ⒶT

Natural Bridge Monacan Indian Village is along Cedar Creek Trail at Natural Bridge State Park on US 11. Visitors travel back in time 3 centuries at this re-created 17th-century village, which features interpreters in period costume. Enhancing the educational experience are demonstrations of rope making, weaving, weapon production, meal preparation, wigwam building, hide tanning and other activities typical of the Monacan lifestyle. **Time:** Allow 1 hour minimum. **Hours:** Daily 10-5, Apr.-Oct.; daily 10-4, mid-Mar. through Mar. 31 and in Nov. Outdoor exhibits closed Dec. to mid-Mar. **Cost:** Natural Bridge State Park admission $8; $6 (ages 6-12). **Phone:** (540) 291-1324. GT

VIRGINIA SAFARI PARK is at 229 Safari Ln. This 180-acre, drive-through zoo permits close contact with free-roaming buffalo, elk, zebras and other large herd animals. Buckets of feed are available for purchase. Safari wagon rides also are available.

Time: Allow 1 hour minimum. **Hours:** Daily 9-6:30, Memorial Day-Labor Day; 9-5:30, mid-Mar. through day before Memorial Day and day after Labor Day-late Nov. Safari wagon rides are given daily at 11:30, 1 and 3, mid-June through Labor Day; Sat.-Sun. at 11:30, 1 and 3, mid-Mar. to mid-June and day after Labor Day-late Nov. Last admission 90 minutes before closing. Closed Thanksgiving. **Cost:** $19.95; $18.95 (ages 65+); $12.95 (ages 2-12). Safari wagon ride $6.50. **Phone:** (540) 291-3205.

PINK CADILLAC DINER   540/291-2378
▼▼ American. Casual Dining. **Address:** 4347 S Lee Hwy 24578

RED FOX RESTAURANT   540/291-2121
▼▼▼ American. Fine Dining. **Address:** 15 Appledore Ln 24578

NEW CHURCH pop. 205

GARDEN AND SEA INN   (757)824-4123
▼▼▼ Historic Bed & Breakfast. **Address:** 4188 Nelson Rd 23415

NEW KENT (A-2) pop. 239, elev. 135'
• Part of Richmond area — see map p. 193

WINERIES
• **New Kent Winery** is at 8400 Old Church Rd. **Hours:** Daily 10-6. Closed major holidays. **Phone:** (804) 932-8240. GT

NEW MARKET (F-8) pop. 2,146, elev. 1,060'

One of the more spectacular events of the Civil War occurred during the Battle of New Market on May 15, 1864. Compelled by necessity, Gen. John Breckinridge ordered 257 cadets from Virginia Military Institute to confront the Union forces under Gen. Franz Sigel. The boys were to be kept in reserve until needed to fill a gap in the advancing line, but in the confusion of battle, they were accidentally put on the front line. Ten were killed and 45 wounded. The cadets' heroism in holding the line helped to defeat Sigel's seasoned troops, who then retreated north.

ENDLESS CAVERNS is off I-81 exit 264; take US 211 .2 mi. e., US 11 3.1 mi. s.w., then Endless Caverns Rd. 1.8 mi. s.e. No end has been discovered to these caverns, which include an impressive array of stalactites, stalagmites, giant columns, flowstone and limestone pendants, and such chambers as Snowdrift, Fairyland and Grand Canyon. **Time:** Allow 1 hour, 15 minutes minimum. **Hours:** Guided tours daily on the hour 10-4, Memorial Day-Labor Day; every 2 hours 10-4, Apr. 1-day before Memorial Day and day after Labor Day-Nov. 15. **Cost:** $20; $9 (ages 4-12). **Phone:** (540) 896-2283, ext. 3, or (800) 544-2283.

SHENANDOAH CAVERNS—see Shenandoah Caverns p. 240.

VIRGINIA MUSEUM OF THE CIVIL WAR is off I-81 exit 264 at 8895 George R. Collins Pkwy. On display are exhibits, dioramas and artifacts documenting the Civil War. Special emphasis is paid to the 1864 Battle of New Market, when 257 cadets from the Virginia Military Institute aided veteran Confederate troops in victory over Union forces. The Emmy-winning film "Field of Lost Shoes" is shown in the museum theater hourly. Of interest is the Kaminsky Gallery of Civil War Firearms.

Administered by the Virginia Military Institute, the 300-acre site includes New Market Battlefield State Historical Park and is accessible by foot or car. Two 1-mile walking trails cross the property and terminate atop Bushong's Hill, where scenic overlooks offer views of the Shenandoah River 100 feet below. Also on the park grounds is the historic Bushong Farm; dating from the early 1800s, it features seven buildings, such as the 1825 House, a barn and the Wheelwright Shop.

Time: Allow 2 hours minimum. **Hours:** Daily 9-5. Closed Jan. 1, Thanksgiving, Christmas Eve and Christmas. **Cost:** (includes museum, farm complex and battlefield walking tour) $10; $9 (ages 65+ and military with ID); $6 (ages 6-12). **Phone:** (866) 515-1864.

SOUTHERN KITCHEN   540/740-3514
American. Casual Dining. **Address:** 9576 S Congress St 22844

NEWPORT NEWS (H-10) pop. 180,719, elev. 20'
• Hotels p. 177 • Restaurants p. 177
• Hotels & Restaurants map & index p. 128
• Part of Hampton Roads Area — see map p. 124

It is said this city gained its name from Capt. Christopher Newport, commander of a three-ship English fleet that landed at Jamestown Island in 1607. The captain played a key role in the permanent settlement of Virginia, making five transatlantic voyages between 1607 and 1619. "News" may refer to the supplies and reinforcements his ships carried over from England, hence "Newport's good news."

Offering holiday festivities in several towns, 100 Miles of Lights kicks off Newport News in late November with Celebration in Lights, a 2-mile-long, drive-through light display at Newport News Park.

Newport News Visitor Center: 13560 Jefferson Ave., Newport News, VA 23603. **Phone:** (757) 886-7777, (757) 886-7920 or (888) 493-7386. *(See ad p. 286.)*

HUNTINGTON PARK is at Riverpark Dr. and Mercury Blvd. Overlooking the James River, the site is home to the Virginia War Museum *(see attraction listing)*; a rose garden with more than 70 varieties of roses; and Vietnam War and Holocaust memorials. The grounds also feature tennis courts, two fishing piers, a boat ramp, a beach with a swimming area and athletic fields. Fort Fun is a 14,000-square-foot children's playground on the waterfront. *See Recreation Areas Chart.*

Food is available Memorial Day weekend-Labor Day. **Hours:** Park open daily dawn-dusk. Beach area open (and staffed with lifeguards) Memorial Day weekend-Labor Day. **Cost:** Free. **Phone:** (757) 886-7912 or (757) 888-3333.

Virginia War Museum is at 9285 Warwick Blvd. in Huntington Park. More than 60,000 artifacts document U.S. military history from 1775 to the present. Exhibits include propaganda posters, uniforms, vehicles, weapons and accouterments. The museum also has educational programs, a military history film collection and a research library.

Time: Allow 1 hour minimum. **Hours:** Museum open Mon.-Sat. 9-5, Sun. noon-5. Last admission 30 minutes before closing. Library open by appointment. Closed Jan. 1, Easter, Thanksgiving, Christmas Eve and Christmas. **Cost:** $8; $7 (ages 62+ and active military with ID); $6 (ages 7-18). Combination ticket with Endview Plantation and Lee Hall Mansion $21; $18 (ages 62+); $15 (ages 7-18). **Phone:** (757) 247-8523.

THE MARINERS' MUSEUM AND PARK is off I-64 exit 258A, following US 17S to 100 Museum Dr. Dedicated to preserving and interpreting the heritage of the sea, the museum features one of the world's most comprehensive maritime collections. The rambling, one-story building contains some 35,000 artifacts, including figureheads, scrimshaw, ship models, decorative arts, rare books, maps and navigational instruments as well as the USS *Monitor* Center *(see attraction listing)*.

The 15th through 18th centuries are the focus of the Age of Exploration gallery, where visitors learn about the intrepid explorers who ventured across seas to new lands.

(See map & index p. 128.)

The Defending the Seas gallery explores the history of the U.S. Navy using re-created sections of military ships, including the ready room of an aircraft carrier and the helm section of a submarine.

Detailed handcrafted models of the commercial steamships that once sailed the world's oceans form the core of the Ship Model gallery. The ORACLE Team USA's 72-foot-long racing yacht that won the 2013 America's Cup is featured in the Speed and Innovation in the America's Cup gallery.

A highlight of the museum is the gallery devoted to the intricately carved works of art created by August and Winifred Crabtree. The Crabtree Miniature Ships collection features 16 of these models, crafted in amazingly exquisite detail.

The International Small Craft Center houses close to 75 watercraft ranging from dugout canoes, fishing boats, a boat used by Cuban refugees and surfboards. The museum is set in a 550-acre park, which boasts Lake Maury, rimmed by the 5-mile Noland Trail, and the Lion's Bridge, the dam forming the lake.

Time: Allow 2 hours minimum. **Hours:** Museum Mon.-Sat. 9-5, Sun. 11-5. Noland Trail daily 6:30 a.m.-dusk. Closed Thanksgiving and Christmas. **Cost:** (includes all The Mariners' Museum facilities) $13.95; $12.95 (ages 65+ and military with ID); $8.95 (ages 4-12). **Phone:** (757) 596-2222 or (800) 581-7245. 🍴 🎦

USS *Monitor* **Center** is at The Mariners' Museum at 100 Museum Dr. The facility houses such artifacts as the gun turret and the steam engine from the USS *Monitor,* an ironclad warship that came head to head with the CSS *Virginia* during the Battle of Hampton Roads. Videos depict the personal experiences of crew members, while interactive exhibits allow visitors to build their own ironclad warship, maneuver a sailing frigate in battle, walk through re-creations of the *Monitor's* living quarters and feel the action of the Civil War skirmish in the Battle Theater.

Time: Allow 1 hour minimum. **Hours:** Mon.-Sat. 9-5, Sun. 11-5. **Cost:** (includes all The Mariners' Museum facilities) $13.95; $12.95 (ages 65+ and military with ID); $8.95 (ages 4-12). **Phone:** (757) 596-2222 or (800) 581-7245.

U.S. ARMY TRANSPORTATION MUSEUM is s.w. of I-64 exit 250A at 300 Washington Blvd. During World War I Fort Eustis was established at Newport News as a U.S. Coast Artillery training center. Today the fort is the home of the U.S. Army Transportation Corps.

The museum displays uniforms, equipment, models and dioramas as well as full-size vehicles, helicopters, airplanes, trains and marine vessels. Exhibits cover Army transportation history from the Revolutionary War through current operations in Iraq and Afghanistan. Included are an L-19 airplane, a Huey helicopter, a gun truck used during the

Vietnam War, the third CH47 Chinook helicopter ever built, a M1070 heavy equipment transporter from Iraq, a M1114 vehicle from Afghanistan and a VH60 helicopter used to transport high-ranking military and political figures. **Hours:** Tues.-Sat. 9-4:30. Closed major holidays. **Cost:** Free. **Phone:** (757) 878-1115.

VIRGINIA LIVING MUSEUM is at 524 J. Clyde Morris Blvd., off I-64 exit 258A between SR 143 and US 60. Virginia's natural heritage is explored through indoor and outdoor exhibits that highlight regional geography, geology, ecosystems, plants and animals. Although modern, the museum's exterior blends well with its wooded surroundings.

Six indoor galleries on two levels present habitats found in Virginia and introduce visitors to the state's diverse regions. Interactive discovery centers and touch tanks invite visitors to handle natural science specimens and live animals.

In the aquariums of the Coastal Plain Gallery you can see marine life from the Chesapeake Bay estuary, including large turtles. Gators, ducks, longnose gar and catfish inhabit the wetland habitat of the Cypress Swamp.

The cool environment of the Appalachian Mountain Cove exhibit is where you'll find a waterfall, a mountain stream and a lake. Creatures you'll likely see there include native songbirds, trout and the endangered Roanoke Logperch. The James River ecosystem is depicted in the Piedmont and Mountains Gallery where smallmouth bass, perch, catfish and wood turtles are joined by pine snakes and chipmunks.

Jellyfish, owls, sharks, flying squirrels, bats, tree frogs and other live nocturnal animals dwell within the Virginia's World of Darkness Gallery, and gems, fossils and cave-dwelling creatures are found in the Virginia Underground Gallery.

Outdoor exhibits can be seen from a looping .75-mile elevated lakeside boardwalk that winds through a 10-acre nature area. As they walk along the boardwalk, visitors are offered views of animals native to Virginia such as foxes, wild turkeys, beavers, otters, raccoons, red wolves (an endangered species), bobcats, eagles, deer and coyotes. A children's nature playground and a learning center are available.

An interesting feature along the boardwalk is the Coastal Plain Aviary. Visitors can walk through the structure and admire more than 16 species, including egrets, pelicans and herons. The Living Green House is an environmental education center with the latest in what it takes to make a home "green."

Time: Allow 2 hours minimum. **Hours:** Museum daily 9-5 (also Thurs. 5-8, June-Aug.). Planetarium schedule varies; phone ahead. Closed Jan. 1, Thanksgiving, Christmas Eve and Christmas. **Cost:** Museum $20; $15 (ages 3-12). Daytime planetarium show $4; evening show $6. Double feature with

(See map & index p. 128.)

planetarium show and laser show $10. Combination tickets are available. **Phone:** (757) 595-1900. GT

BEST WESTERN PLUS NEWPORT NEWS INN & SUITES
(757)952-1182   **7**

Hotel
$79-$199

AAA Benefit: Members save 10% or more & earn 10% bonus points!

Address: 500 Operations Dr 23602 **Location:** I-64 exit 255A, just s on Jefferson Ave. **Facility:** 65 units. 3 stories, interior corridors. **Terms:** cancellation fee imposed. **Pool:** outdoor. **Activities:** hot tub, exercise room. **Guest Services:** coin laundry. **Featured Amenity:** full hot breakfast.

SAVE 🍴⁺ 🏊 ♿ BIZ HS 🛜
🖨 📷 💻

COMFORT INN NEWPORT NEWS-FT EUSTIS   757/887-3300
♦♦♦ Hotel. **Address:** 14900 Warwick Blvd 23603

COMFORT SUITES AIRPORT   (757)947-1333   **1**
♦♦♦ Hotel. **Address:** 12570 Jefferson Ave 23602

COURTYARD BY MARRIOTT NEWPORT NEWS AIRPORT
(757)842-6212   **5**
♦♦♦ Hotel. **Address:** 530 St. Johns Rd 23602

AAA Benefit: Members save 5% or more!

HAMPTON INN   (757)989-8977   **2**
♦♦♦ Hotel. **Address:** 151 Ottis St 23602

AAA Benefit: Members save up to 10%!

HAMPTON INN & SUITES   (757)249-0001   **6**
♦♦♦ Hotel. **Address:** 12251 Jefferson Ave 23602

AAA Benefit: Members save up to 10%!

HILTON GARDEN INN   (757)947-1080   **3**
♦♦♦ Hotel. **Address:** 180 Regal Way 23602

AAA Benefit: Members save up to 10%!

HOLIDAY INN EXPRESS & SUITES   757/596-6417   **8**
♦♦♦ Hotel. **Address:** 943 J Clyde Morris Blvd 23601

NEWPORT NEWS MARRIOTT AT CITY CENTER
(757)873-9299   **9**

Hotel
$79-$340

AAA Benefit: Members save 5% or more!

Address: 740 Town Center Dr 23606 **Location:** I-64 exit 255A, 2.5 mi s on Jefferson Ave, then just e on Thimble Shoals Dr. Located in City Center of Oyster Point. **Facility:** 256 units. 11 stories, interior corridors. **Parking:** on-site (fee) and valet. **Terms:** check-in 4 pm, cancellation fee imposed. **Amenities:** safes. **Pool:** heated indoor. **Activities:** exercise room. **Guest Services:** valet and coin laundry, boarding pass kiosk.

SAVE ECO 🍴 🎯 🍷 CALL ♿ 🏊 ♿ BIZ HS
🛜 ✉ 🖨 💻

RESIDENCE INN BY MARRIOTT NEWPORT NEWS AIRPORT
(757)842-6214   **4**
♦♦♦ Extended Stay Hotel. **Address:** 531 St. Johns Rd 23602

AAA Benefit: Members save 5% or more!

SUPER 8 MOTEL NEWPORT NEWS   757/825-1422   **10**
♦ Hotel. **Address:** 6105 Jefferson Ave 23605

WHERE TO EAT

2ND STREET AMERICAN BISTRO   757/234-4448   **3**
♦♦ American. Casual Dining. **Address:** 115 Arthur Way 23601

AL FRESCO RISTORANTE   757/873-0644   **14**
♦♦ Italian. Casual Dining. **Address:** 11710 Jefferson Ave 23606

AROMAS   757/240-4650   **9**
♦ Coffee/Tea Sandwiches. Casual Dining. **Address:** 706 Town Center Dr, Suite 104 23606

BALKAN CUISINE   757/874-0100   **5**
♦♦ European. Casual Dining. **Address:** 13678 Warwick Blvd 23602

CHIC N FISH   757/223-6517   **6**
♦♦ Korean Chicken. Casual Dining. **Address:** 954 J Clyde Morris Blvd 23601

CRAB SHACK ON THE JAMES   757/245-2722   **18**
♦♦ Seafood. Casual Dining. **Address:** 7601 River Rd 23607

FIN   757/599-5800   **11**

Seafood
Fine Dining
$14-$55

AAA Inspector Notes: The chef-owner at this chic spot overlooking the square has built his menu around some of the freshest and best products he can find. His father is a fisherman, which means you can be assured the seafood is the best available as are the organic produce from local farms, specialty meats and artisan cheeses. Grab a seat indoors to watch the chef in action or on the pleasant sidewalk patio. Specialties include sweet corn and crab soup with truffle oil, soft-shell crab and lobster mashed potatoes. **Features:** full bar, patio dining, Sunday brunch, happy hour. **Reservations:** suggested. **Address:** 3150 William Styron Square 23606 **Location:** I-64 exit 225A, 2.4 mi s on Jefferson Ave to Port Warwick. **Parking:** street only.
L D CALL ♿ 🎯

HARPOON LARRY'S FISH HOUSE & OYSTER BAR
757/827-0600   **15**
♦♦ Seafood. Casual Dining. **Address:** 621 J Clyde Morris Blvd 23601

(See map & index p. 128.)

HAYASHI SUSHI & GRILL 757/223-5783 (10)
♦♦ Japanese. Casual Dining. **Address:** 11820 Merchants Walk 23606

KYUNG SUNG KOREAN RESTAURANT 757/877-2797 (4)
♦♦ Korean. Casual Dining. **Address:** 13748 Warwick Blvd 23602

LA PENA HOREB 757/969-1444 (2)
♦ Puerto Rican. Casual Dining. **Address:** 14349 Warwick Blvd 23602

THE LUNCH BELL 757/873-1839 (8)
♦♦ American. Casual Dining. **Address:** 694 Town Center Dr 23606

MIDTOWN EATS 757/223-5025 (7)
♦♦ American. Casual Dining. **Address:** 88 J. Clyde Morris Blvd 23601

NAWAB INDIAN CUISINE 757/591-9200
♦♦ Indian. Casual Dining. **Address:** 11712-K Jefferson Ave 23606

PHO 79 757/877-1213 (1)
♦♦ Vietnamese. Casual Dining. **Address:** 12551 Jefferson Ave, Suite 213 23602

PLAZA AZTECA MEXICAN RESTAURANT 757/833-0271
♦♦ Mexican. Casual Dining. **Address:** 12835 Jefferson Ave 23608

ROCKY MOUNT BBQ 757/596-0243 (17)
♦♦ Southern American. Casual Dining. **Address:** 10113 Jefferson Ave 23605

SAGE KITCHEN AT ANDERSON'S SHOWPLACE
757/599-3510 (16)
♦♦ American. Casual Dining. **Address:** 11250 Jefferson Ave 23601

SAISAKI ASIAN BISTRO & SUSHI BAR 757/886-1988 (19)
♦♦ Japanese Sushi. Casual Dining. **Address:** 101 Regal Way 23602

SCHLESINGER'S CHOPHOUSE 757/599-4700 (12)
♦♦♦ Steak. Fine Dining. **Address:** 1106 William Styron Square 23606

TASTE UNLIMITED 757/596-8651
♦ Specialty Sandwiches. Quick Serve. **Address:** 702 Mariners Row, Suite 104 23606

THAIJINDESU THAI & SUSHI BAR 757/595-8410 (13)
♦♦ Thai. Casual Dining. **Address:** 2180 William Styron Square S 23606

NORFOLK (H-11) pop. 242,803, elev. 10'
- **Hotels p. 181 • Restaurants p. 182**
- **Hotels & Restaurants map & index p. 131, 134**
- **Part of Hampton Roads Area — see map p. 124**

Where important military battles once raged, maritime attractions and cultural sites now stand. Inscriptions from letters written by U.S. service people who lost their lives in war are cast on 20 thin bronze sheets scattered about the Armed Forces Memorial. The touching tribute overlooks the Elizabeth River and is connected to Town Point Park by two bridges.

Seven-acre Town Point Park hosts numerous outdoor concerts and festivals throughout the year, including the ♦ Norfolk Harborfest and the Bayou Boogaloo and Cajun Food Festival in June, the Norfolk Waterfront Jazz Festival in mid-July and mid-October's Spring Town Point Virginia Wine Festival.

Norfolk's PrideFest, held near the waterfront in summer, attracts thousands of people for a weekend of games, live music, a family fun park, a block party and a boat parade.

Choral groups, Celtic dancers, color guards, marching bands and military drill teams embody the ♦ Virginia International Tattoo, which takes place in late April. Celebrating Thanksgiving, Hanukkah, Christmas, Kwanzaa and New Year's Eve, ♦ Holidays in the City begins in mid-November and features 6 weeks of festivities.

The creations of local artisans can be found on several downtown streets. The Mermaid Heart and Art Walking Trail features mermaid sculptures depicting the city's culture and heritage.

From April through September catch a baseball game at Harbor Park. The home park of the Norfolk Tides, the Baltimore Orioles AAA affiliate, is located downtown on the Elizabeth River.

A convenient way to get around Norfolk is The Tide, Virginia's first light rail system. The 7.4-mile route stretches between the Eastern Virginia Medical Center complex in the west to Newtown Road in the east. One-way fare is $1.75; 75c (senior citizens); free (ages 0-17 with adult). A 1-day Go-Pass is $4. Phone Hampton Roads Transit at (757) 222-6100 for more information.

VisitNorfolk: 232 E. Main St., Norfolk, VA 23510. **Phone:** (757) 664-6620 or (800) 368-3097.

Self-guiding tours: A brochure detailing Norfolk's Civil War heritage is available from VisitNorfolk. The self-guiding tour covers such sites as Fort Norfolk, occupied by Confederate troops 1861-62, and the Freemason Historic District. Visitors also can pick up maps and information about other self-guiding tours such as Waterways to Freedom and Cannonball Trail.

Shopping: Norfolk's pre-eminent shopping mecca, the MacArthur Center (300 Monticello Ave.), is in the heart of downtown. The huge, three-level mall has Dillard's and Nordstrom as its anchors. With 1 million square feet of shops, there are plenty of choices for even the pickiest of buyers. Chico's, Coach, Eddie Bauer, H&M, J. Crew, Johnston & Murphy, Pottery Barn and Williams-Sonoma are among the 140 retail offerings.

The Historic Ghent district along Colley Avenue and Granby and 21st streets is a shopper's delight. The historic character of stately turn-of-the-20th-century homes and tree-lined streets blends well with comfortable bungalows, apartment buildings and newly converted condominiums. Add to this mix an assortment of antiques dealers (centered around Granby and 21st streets), chic boutiques, cafes and restaurants and it's easy to understand why this diverse neighborhood is one of Norfolk's most popular areas. If all that shopping makes you hungry, head to one of Ghent's favorite eateries, Doumar's Cones & Barbecue (1919 Monticello Ave.). Abe Doumar,

(See maps & indexes p. 131, 134.)

the drive-in's original owner, was among several entrepreneurs who claimed to have invented the ice cream cone at the 1904 St. Louis World's Fair; Doumar's family still uses a machine from 1905 to hand-roll cones.

If you're in the market for a piece of original art, head to the NEON District, a hot spot for artistic types. That's the location of the d'ART Center (740 Duke St.), where resident artists create paintings, glassworks, jewelry and ceramics; phone (757) 625-4211.

Nightlife: Downtown Norfolk, and Granby Street, also known as "restaurant row," is where you'll find a concentration of Norfolk's nightlife scene. Monticello Street also has its share of nightspots. Have a nice meal (there's an abundance of restaurants to choose from as well), then take a stroll down the street and see what looks appealing. There are plenty of places to dance 'til you drop or just stop in for a drink or two.

Despite its sketchy-sounding name, Hell's Kitchen (124 Granby St.) is a great place to go for some local flavor and alternative and rock music. It's not as fancy as many of the other Granby Street nightspots, and its black floors and brick accent walls contribute to its edgy vibe; phone (757) 624-1906.

At The NorVa (317 Monticello Ave.), you can catch some of the best concerts in Norfolk; there's something going on almost every night. The venue, built as a theater in the 1920s (notice the old marquee out front), now hosts local and national music acts representing all genres. Phone (757) 627-4547.

If your drink of choice is wine, stop by Mermaid Winery (330 W. 22nd St.) in Norfolk's trendy Ghent section. Beer lovers will like The Birch (1231 W. Olney Rd.), O'Connor Brewing Co. (211 W. 24th St.) and Smartmouth Brewing Co. (1309 Raleigh Ave.), all located in historic Ghent. These breweries serve fresh, handcrafted beer which can be found on tap at many restaurants throughout the Coastal Virginia region. Phone (757) 962-5400 for The Birch, (757) 623-2337 for O'Connor Brewing Co. or (757) 624-3939 for Smartmouth Brewing Co.

CHRYSLER MUSEUM OF ART is at Olney Rd. and W. Virginia Beach Blvd. at 1 Memorial Pl. Originally known as the Norfolk Museum of Arts and Sciences, the museum was renamed in 1971 when Walter P. Chrysler Jr., the son of the founder of the Chrysler Corporation and an avid lifelong art collector, donated his vast collection to the city of Norfolk. Chrysler's wife Jean was a Norfolk native. The imposing Italianate-style building on the city's Hague Inlet of the Elizabeth River is a fitting repository for the museum's collection of objects that encompass a 5,000-year span.

Comprising approximately 30,000 pieces, the museum's diverse holdings include art treasures from Egypt, ancient Greece, Rome, Asia and Mesoamerica; European and American paintings and sculpture; decorative arts from the 12th century to the present; and modern and contemporary art. It also boasts an extensive photography collection that includes early daguerreotypes, Civil War battlefield albumen prints, 20th-century documentary photographs and portraits, and contemporary explorations using digital media.

Among artists represented in the museum's collection are Mary Cassatt, Nick Cave, Winslow Homer, Henri Matisse, Pablo Picasso, Jackson Pollock, Auguste Rodin, Mark Rothko, Andy Warhol and Kehinde Wiley.

The museum's collection of American painting and sculpture goes as far back as Colonial portraits and folk art. More recent examples include works by American Impressionists and a highly regarded group of 19th-century marble sculpture.

Representing Europe are strong collections of works by masters from the Italian Renaissance and the Baroque period such as Gianlorenzo Bernini and paintings by Dutch and Flemish artists, including examples by Peter Paul Rubens and Anthony van Dyck. England and Spain are represented by Thomas Gainsborough and Diego Velazquez, and paintings by Edgar Degas, Paul Gauguin and Pierre Auguste Renoir constitute a portion of the museum's 19th-century French works.

One of the country's most comprehensive glass collections includes more than 10,000 pieces of carved and blown sculptural works. Major pieces by Emile Gallé, Rene Lalique and Louis Comfort Tiffany also are on display. The Tiffany collection contains magnificent grand windows and lamps in addition to blown glass pieces.

Time: Allow 1 hour minimum. **Hours:** Tues.-Sat. 10-5 (also third Thurs. 5-10 p.m.), Sun. noon-5. Hours may vary. Closed select holidays. Phone ahead to confirm schedule. **Cost:** Free. A fee may be charged for special exhibits and events. **Phone:** (757) 664-6200. [📷]

Chrysler Museum Perry Glass Studio is adjacent to the Chrysler Museum of Art at 745 Duke St. near W. Olney Rd. and W. Virginia Beach Blvd. At this state-of-the-art working glass studio, visitors can watch artists collaborating on glass pieces during free demonstrations. While the pride and joy of this 7,000-square foot facility is a furnace capable of melting up to 560 pounds of glass, the skilled artisans on-site also utilize such handheld tools as blowpipes, torches, jacks and shears. Most glassmaking demonstrations last about an hour. The Studio also has flame-working, kiln-working and cold-working areas. Classes, workshops and other educational programs are offered; advance reservations are required.

Time: Allow 1 hour minimum. **Hours:** Tues.-Sat. 10-5 (also third Thurs. 7-10 p.m.), Sun. noon-5. Glassmaking demonstrations take place Tues.-Sun. at noon. Closed select holidays. Phone ahead to

(See maps & indexes p. 131, 134.)

confirm schedule. **Cost:** Free. Evening and performing arts events may have admission fees. **Phone:** (757) 664-6200.

MACARTHUR MEMORIAL is on City Hall Ave. Nine galleries in the former 1847 city hall portray Gen. Douglas MacArthur's life and military career through displays of gifts, art objects, maps, murals, pictures, models and mementos. MacArthur's trademark military cap, corncob pipe and sunglasses and his 1950 Chrysler Imperial limousine are among the relics. The general's books and an extensive collection of correspondence, photographs, scrapbooks and newspapers are housed in a library and archives.

In the main rotunda, the tomb containing MacArthur and his wife is surrounded by inscriptions and flags from the general's military career. A documentary is shown every 30 minutes. **Hours:** Tues.-Sat. 10-5, Sun. 11-5. Last movie begins at 4. Closed Jan. 1, Thanksgiving and Christmas. **Cost:** Donations. **Phone:** (757) 441-2965.

NAUTICUS is at One Waterside Dr., downtown on the Elizabeth River. The Norfolk waterfront maritime science museum features hands-on exhibits that explore the naval, economic and natural power of the sea. Visitors can observe weather patterns on a 6-foot globe, touch horseshoe crabs, see live science demonstrations, construct an ROV (remotely operated vehicle), watch 3-D movies and learn about sharks.

The museum manages the day-to-day operations of The Battleship *Wisconsin,* berthed adjacent to Nauticus. Visitors can "walk the decks of history" and explore many areas of the vessel. A chronology of the battleship's history is presented in Wisky Walk: 50 Years of Service.

Time: Allow 2 hours minimum. **Hours:** Daily 10-5, Memorial Day-Labor Day; Tues.-Sat. 10-5, Sun. noon-5, rest of year. Closed Jan. 1, Thanksgiving, Christmas Eve and Christmas. **Cost:** Gold Ticket (includes all Nauticus facilities and guided and self-guiding tours of The Battleship *Wisconsin*) $35.95; $32.95 (active military with ID); $31.50 (ages 4-12). White Ticket (includes all Nauticus facilities and self-guiding tour of The Battleship *Wisconsin*) $15.95; $14.95 (ages 55+); $12.95 (active military with ID); $11.50 (ages 4-12). **Parking:** Pay garages are available nearby, including off Plume and Main streets. **Phone:** (757) 664-1000 or (800) 664-1080. ⑪

The Battleship *Wisconsin* is berthed next to Nauticus at One Waterside Dr. One of the last and largest battleships built by the U.S. Navy, this vessel was used in World War II, the Korean War and Operation Desert Storm. A self-guiding tour of the main deck includes interactive exhibits depicting the history of the ship and life on board.

Time: Allow 1 hour minimum. **Hours:** Daily 10-5, Memorial Day-Labor Day; Tues.-Sat. 10-5, Sun. noon-5, rest of year. Closed Jan. 1, Thanksgiving,

Christmas Eve and Christmas. **Cost:** (includes all Nauticus facilities) $15.95; $14.95 (ages 55+); $12.95 (active military with ID); $11.50 (ages 4-12). **Parking:** Pay garages are available nearby, including off Plume and Main streets. **Phone:** (757) 664-1000 or (800) 664-1080. ⑰

NORFOLK BOTANICAL GARDEN is next to Norfolk International Airport at 6700 Azalea Garden Rd. The 175-acre garden includes one of the largest collections of azaleas, camellias, rhododendrons and roses on the East Coast and features 53 themed gardens and natural areas. The climate-controlled Tropical Pavilion houses over 100 varieties of plants from tropical regions around the world. Visitors may tour the gardens by foot on more than 12 miles of pathways; guided tours are offered aboard trams. A 45-minute narrated boat tour and a 3-acre interactive children's garden with water features also are available.

Hours: Grounds daily 9-7, Apr. 1-Oct. 15; 9-5, rest of year. Children's garden daily 9:30-6:30, Apr. 1-Oct. 15; 9:30-4:30, rest of year. Tram tours are offered Mon.-Fri. every hour 10-4, Sat.-Sun. every half-hour 10-4:30, Apr. 1-Oct. 15; otherwise varies. Boat tours are given daily at noon, 2, 4 and 5, May-Oct. Closed Jan. 1, Thanksgiving and Christmas. Phone ahead to confirm schedule. **Cost:** (includes tram tour) $12; $10 (ages 3-18, ages 62+ and military with ID). Boat tour $8; $5 (ages 3-17). **Phone:** (757) 441-5830. ⑰ ⑪

***VICTORY ROVER* NAVAL BASE CRUISES** departs from the downtown waterfront; tickets are available at the Nauticus museum at One Waterside Dr. Passengers aboard the Navy-themed *Victory River* enjoy a 2-hour narrated nautical sightseeing tour. Both enclosed and open-air decks on the vessel afford views of Naval Station Norfolk and its aircraft carriers, nuclear submarines and guided missile cruisers.

Time: Allow 2 hours minimum. **Hours:** Cruises depart daily at 11, 2 and 5:30, Memorial Day weekend-Labor Day; daily at 11 and 2, Apr. 1-day before Memorial Day weekend and day after Labor Day-Oct. 31; Tues.-Sun. at 2 in Mar. and Nov.-Dec. Phone ahead to confirm schedule. **Cost:** $24; $14 (ages 4-12). Reservations are recommended. **Phone:** (757) 627-7406. ⑰ ⑪

(See maps & indexes p. 131, 134.)

BEST WESTERN PLUS HOLIDAY SANDS INN & SUITES   (757)583-2621   **1**

◆◆◆
Hotel
$79-$259

AAA Benefit:
Members save 10% or more & earn 10% bonus points!

Address: 1330 E Ocean View Ave 23503 **Location:** Oceanfront. US 60, 4 mi e of Hampton Roads Bridge Tunnel. **Facility:** 89 units, some two bedrooms and kitchens. 2-5 stories, exterior corridors. **Terms:** check-in 4 pm, 3 day cancellation notice-fee imposed. **Amenities:** safes. **Pool:** outdoor. **Activities:** exercise room. **Guest Services:** coin laundry.

[SAVE] [ECO] 🛏 🖐 [BIZ] [HS] 📶 ✕ ▤ 📠
▭ / SOME UNITS 🐾

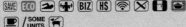

BW Best Western PLUS.
Located directly on Chesapeake Bay. Spacious 2 room suites with full kitchens. Bayfront balconies

---

CANDLEWOOD SUITES NORFOLK AIRPORT
757/605-4001   **9**
◆◆◆ Extended Stay Hotel. **Address:** 5600 Lowery Rd 23502

COURTYARD BY MARRIOTT   (757)963-6000   **6**
◆◆◆ Hotel. **Address:** 520 Plume St 23510

AAA Benefit: Members save 5% or more!

DOUBLETREE HOTEL NORFOLK AIRPORT
(757)466-8000   **5**
◆◆◆ Hotel. **Address:** 1500 N Military Hwy 23502

AAA Benefit: Members save 5% or more!

FREEMASON INN BED AND BREAKFAST   757/963-7000   **5**
◆◆◆ Historic Bed & Breakfast. **Address:** 411 W York St 23510

HAMPTON INN & SUITES NORFOLK AIRPORT
(757)605-9999   **6**
◆◆◆ Hotel. **Address:** 1511 USAA Dr 23502

AAA Benefit: Members save up to 10%!

HAMPTON INN NORFOLK NAVAL BASE   (757)489-1000   **2**
◆◆◆ Hotel. **Address:** 8501 Hampton Blvd 23505

AAA Benefit: Members save up to 10%!

HOLIDAY INN EXPRESS HOTEL & SUITES-NORFOLK AIRPORT
757/455-5055   **8**

◆◆◆
Hotel
Rates not provided

Address: 1157 N Military Hwy 23502 **Location:** I-264 exit 13B (US 13/Military Hwy), 1.3 mi n, then just w. **Facility:** 104 units. 5 stories, interior corridors. **Terms:** check-in 4 pm. **Amenities:** safes. **Pool:** heated indoor. **Activities:** hot tub, exercise room. **Guest Services:** valet and coin laundry. **Featured Amenity:** breakfast buffet.

[SAVE] [ECO] 🔌 🍽 CALL 🛗 🛏
🖐 [BIZ] [HS] 📶 ✕ ▤ 📠
▭

HOLIDAY INN NORFOLK AIRPORT   757/213-2231   **4**
◆◆◆ Hotel. **Address:** 1570 N Military Hwy 23502

LA QUINTA INN & SUITES NORFOLK AIRPORT
(757)466-7001   **7**
◆◆◆ Hotel. **Address:** 1387 N Military Hwy 23502

NORFOLK WATERSIDE MARRIOTT   (757)627-4200   **7**

◆◆◆
Hotel
$93-$305

Ⓜ MARRIOTT

AAA Benefit: Members save 5% or more!

Address: 235 E Main St 23510 **Location:** Corner of Main and Atlantic sts; center of downtown. **Facility:** 405 units. 24 stories, interior corridors. **Parking:** on-site (fee) and valet. **Terms:** check-in 4 pm, cancellation fee imposed. **Dining:** Shula's 347, see separate listing. **Pool:** heated indoor. **Activities:** hot tub, exercise room. **Guest Services:** valet and coin laundry.

[SAVE] [ECO] 🍽 🖐 🍷 CALL 🛗 🛏 🖐 [BIZ] 📶
✕ ▭ / SOME UNITS [HS] 📠 📠

PAGE HOUSE INN BED & BREAKFAST   757/625-5033   **3**
◆◆◆ Historic Bed & Breakfast. **Address:** 323 Fairfax Ave 23507

RESIDENCE INN BY MARRIOTT DOWNTOWN
(757)842-6216   **4**
◆◆◆ Extended Stay Hotel. **Address:** 227 W Brambleton Ave 23510

AAA Benefit: Members save 5% or more!

RESIDENCE INN BY MARRIOTT NORFOLK AIRPORT
(757)333-3000   **3**
◆◆◆ Extended Stay Hotel. **Address:** 1590 N Military Hwy 23502

AAA Benefit: Members save 5% or more!

SHERATON NORFOLK WATERSIDE HOTEL
(757)622-6664   **8**

◆◆◆
Hotel
$89-$289

Ⓢ Sheraton

AAA Benefit: Members save 5% or more!

Address: 777 Waterside Dr 23510 **Location:** Waterfront. I-264 exit 9 (Waterside Dr); downtown. Adjacent to Waterside District. **Facility:** 468 units. 10 stories, interior corridors. **Parking:** on-site (fee) and valet. **Terms:** 2 night minimum stay - seasonal and/or weekends, cancellation fee imposed. **Amenities:** Some: safes. **Pool:** outdoor. **Activities:** exercise room. **Guest Services:** valet and coin laundry, area transportation.

[SAVE] [ECO] 🍽 🖐 🍷 CALL 🛗 🛏 🖐 [BIZ] 📶
✕ 📷 📠 📠 ▭ / SOME UNITS 🐾

(See maps & indexes p. 131, 134.)

SPRINGHILL SUITES BY MARRIOTT NORFOLK/VA BEACH
(757)333-3100 **10**
♦♦♦♦ Hotel. **Address:** 6350 Newtown Rd 23502

AAA Benefit:
Members save 5%
or more!

SPRINGHILL SUITES BY MARRIOTT-ODU
(757)423-4100 **1**
♦♦♦♦ Hotel. **Address:** 4500 Hampton Blvd 23508

AAA Benefit:
Members save 5%
or more!

WYNDHAM GARDEN NORFOLK DOWNTOWN
757/627-5555 **2**

Hotel
Rates not provided

Address: 700 Monticello Ave 23510 **Location:** Jct Brambleton Ave and St Pauls Blvd; downtown. Across from Scope Arena. **Facility:** 204 units. 12 stories, interior corridors. **Parking:** on-site (fee). **Terms:** check-in 4 pm. **Pool:** outdoor. **Activities:** exercise room, massage. **Guest Services:** valet and coin laundry.

[SAVE] [⊞] [♨] [Y] CALL [&] [≋]
[▦] [BIZ] [📶] [✉] [🔋] [📷] [▤]
/ SOME UNITS [🐾]

WHERE TO EAT

219 AMERICAN BISTRO
757/416-6219 **50**
♦♦♦ New American. Casual Dining. **Address:** 219 Granby St 23510

3 WAY CAFE
757/625-3929 **52**
♦ Sandwiches. Quick Serve. **Address:** 216 E Plume St 23520

456 FISH
757/625-4444 **35**
♦♦♦ Seafood. Fine Dining. **Address:** 456 Granby St 23510

80/20 BURGER BAR
757/233-7900 **21**
♦♦ Burgers. Casual Dining. **Address:** 123 W 21st St 23517

A.W. SHUCKS RAW BAR & GRILL
757/664-9117 **12**
♦♦ Seafood. Casual Dining. **Address:** 2200 Colonial Ave, Suite 14 23517

THE AZALEA INN
757/587-4649 **7**
♦♦ Greek Pizza. Casual Dining. **Address:** 2344 E Little Creek Rd 23518

THE BAKEHOUSE AT CHELSEA
757/644-6939 **18**
♦ Breads/Pastries Pizza. Quick Serve. **Address:** 1233 W Olney Rd 23507

BAKER'S CRUST
757/625-3600
♦♦ American. Casual Dining. **Address:** 330 W 21st St 23517

BANGKOK GARDEN
757/622-5047
♦♦ Thai. Casual Dining. **Address:** 417 W 21st St 23517

BARDO EDIBLES & ELIXIRS
757/622-7362 **17**
♦♦ Asian Small Plates. Casual Dining. **Address:** 430 W 21st St 23517

BAXTER'S SPORTS LOUNGE
757/622-9837 **34**
♦♦ American. Casual Dining. **Address:** 500 Granby St 23510

BITE RESTAURANT & CATERING
757/486-0035 **39**
♦♦ American. Casual Dining. **Address:** 440 Monticello Ave 23510

BODEGA
757/622-8527 **37**
♦♦ Spanish. Casual Dining. **Address:** 442 Granby St 23510

BYRD & BALDWIN BROTHERS STEAKHOUSE
757/222-9191 **48**
♦♦♦ Steak. Fine Dining. **Address:** 116 Brooke Ave 23510

CAFE STELLA
757/625-0461 **25**
♦♦ Coffee/Tea Natural/Organic. Quick Serve. **Address:** 1907 Colonial Ave 23517

CAPT. GROOVY'S GRILL & RAW BAR
757/965-4667 **6**
♦♦ Seafood. Casual Dining. **Address:** 8101 Shore Dr 23518

CHARTREUSE BISTRO
757/965-2137 **51**
♦♦♦ American. Fine Dining. **Address:** 205 E City Hall Ave 23510

CHOW RESTAURANT & BAR
757/321-2923 **10**
♦♦ Southern American. Casual Dining. **Address:** 5103 Colley Ave 23508

CILANTRO BANGLADESHI BISTRO
757/962-1004 **14**
♦♦ Asian. Casual Dining. **Address:** 1011 Kempsville Rd 23502

COGAN'S PIZZA
757/627-6428 **26**
♦♦ Pizza. Casual Dining. **Address:** 1901 Colonial Ave 23517

COGAN'S PIZZA NORTH
757/627-6428 **2**
♦♦ Pizza. Casual Dining. **Address:** 4311 Colley Ave 23517

COLLEY CANTINA
757/622-0033 **30**
♦♦ Mexican. Casual Dining. **Address:** 1316 Colley Ave 23517

CRACKERS LITTLE BAR BISTRO
757/640-0200 **11**
♦♦♦ New Small Plates. Casual Dining. **Address:** 4226 Granby St 23505

CURE COFFEEHOUSE & BRASSERIE
757/321-0044 **41**
♦♦ Coffee/Tea Natural/Organic. Quick Serve. **Address:** 503 Botetourt St 23510

D'EGG DINER
757/626-3447 **55**
♦ Breakfast Comfort Food. Casual Dining. **Address:** 204 E Main St 23510

DOG-N-BURGER GRILLE
757/623-1667 **20**
♦ Burgers Hot Dogs. Quick Serve. **Address:** 2001 Manteo St 23517

DOUMAR'S CONES & BARBECUE
757/627-4163 **28**
♦ Barbecue Burgers. Quick Serve. **Address:** 1919 Monticello Ave 23517

EL AZTECA RESTAURANTE MEXICANO
757/587-6016 **8**
♦♦ Mexican. Casual Dining. **Address:** 1522 E Little Creek Rd 23518

FELLINI'S
757/625-3000 **4**
♦♦ Pizza. Casual Dining. **Address:** 3910 Colley Ave 23508

FIELD GUIDE
40
♦♦ American. Gastropub. **Address:** 429 Granby St 23510

FRANCO'S BY THE BAY
757/531-8100 **2**
♦♦ Italian. Casual Dining. **Address:** 169 W Ocean View Ave 23503

FRANCO'S ITALIAN RESTAURANT
757/853-0177 **9**
♦♦♦ Italian. Casual Dining. **Address:** 6200 N Military Hwy, Suite A 23518

FREEMASON ABBEY
757/622-3966 **43**
♦♦ American. Casual Dining. **Address:** 209 W Freemason St 23510

THE GOURMET GANG
757/557-0294 **16**
♦ Specialty Sandwiches. Quick Serve. **Address:** 715 Newtown Rd 23502

(See maps & indexes p. 131, 134.)

THE GOURMET GANG   757/640-1065 **54**
🍴 Sandwiches. Quick Serve. **Address:** 482 E Main St 23510

GRANBY BISTRO & DELI   757/622-7003 **49**
🍴🍴 Mediterranean. Casual Dining. **Address:** 225 Granby St 23510

GRANBY STREET PIZZA   757/622-5084 **47**
🍴 Italian Pizza. Quick Serve. **Address:** 235 Granby St 23510

THE GREEN ONION   757/963-1200 **24**
🍴🍴🍴 American. Casual Dining. **Address:** 1603 Colley Ave 23517

THE GRILLED CHEESE BISTRO   757/233-2512 **44**
🍴🍴 Sandwiches. Casual Dining. **Address:** 345 Granby St 23510

GUY FIERI'S SMOKEHOUSE   757/426-7433 **59**
🍴 Barbecue. Casual Dining. **Address:** 333 Waterside Dr 23510

HANDSOME BISCUIT   **5**
🍴 Specialty. Quick Serve. **Address:** 2511 Colonial Ave 23517

ICHRAN JAPANESE RAMEN   757/461-8630 **17**
🍴🍴 Japanese Soup. Casual Dining. **Address:** 5720 Hoggard Rd 23502

JESSY'S TACO BISTRO   757/216-9922 **23**
🍴🍴 Mexican. Casual Dining. **Address:** 328 W 20th St 23517

KAPPO NARA RAMEN   757/622-2045 **22**
🍴🍴 Asian Soup. Casual Dining. **Address:** 2000 Colonial Ave 23517

KATANA JAPANESE STEAK HOUSE & SUSHI
  757/640-8898 **16**
🍴🍴 Japanese Steak Sushi. Casual Dining. **Address:** 520 W 21st St, Unit E 23517

KELLY'S TAVERN   757/623-3216
🍴🍴 American. Casual Dining. **Address:** 1408 Colley Ave 23507

KOTOBUKI   757/628-1025 **14**
🍴🍴 Japanese. Casual Dining. **Address:** 721 W 21st St 23517

LA BELLA IN GHENT   757/622-6172 **7**
🍴🍴🍴 Italian. Casual Dining. **Address:** 738 W 22nd St 23517

LEGRAND KITCHEN   **13**
🍴🍴 New American. Casual Dining. **Address:** 4515 Colley Ave 23508

LEONE'S   757/624-1455 **36**
🍴🍴🍴 Italian. Fine Dining. **Address:** 455 Granby St 23510

THE LIZARD CAFE AT PRINCE BOOKS   757/622-5973 **56**
🍴🍴 Deli. Casual Dining. **Address:** 109 E Main St 23510

LUCE   757/502-7260 **46**
🍴🍴🍴 Italian. Fine Dining. **Address:** 245 Granby St 23510

LUNA MAYA CANTINA   757/622-6986 **15**
🍴🍴 Latin American. Casual Dining. **Address:** 2010 Colley Ave 23517

MERMAID WINERY   757/233-4155 **10**
🍴🍴 American. Casual Dining. **Address:** 330 W 22nd St, #106 23517

MI HOGAR MEXICAN RESTAURANT   757/640-7705 **12**
🍴🍴 Mexican. Casual Dining. **Address:** 4201 Granby St 23504

NAWAB INDIAN CUISINE   757/455-8080
🍴🍴 Indian. Casual Dining. **Address:** 888 N Military Hwy 23502

NO FRILL BAR & GRILL   757/627-4262
🍴🍴 American. Casual Dining. **Address:** 806 Spotswood Ave 23517

NOUVELLE   757/248-3712 **33**
🍴🍴🍴 New French. Casual Dining. **Address:** 217 Grace St 23510

OCEAN VIEW FISHING PIER RESTAURANT
  757/583-6000 **1**
🍴 Seafood. Casual Dining. **Address:** 400 W Ocean View Ave 23503

OMAR'S CARRIAGE HOUSE   757/622-4990 **42**
🍴🍴🍴 International. Fine Dining. **Address:** 313 W Bute St 23510

PELON'S BAJA GRILL   757/961-4673 **8**
🍴 Mexican. Quick Serve. **Address:** 738 W 22nd St, Suite 15 23517

PHO 79   757/333-4266 **13**
🍴🍴 Vietnamese. Casual Dining. **Address:** 723 W 21st St 23517

PIZZA CHEF   757/588-7600 **5**
🍴 Pizza. Casual Dining. **Address:** 1007 E Bayview Blvd 23503

PRESS 626   757/202-0204 **31**
🍴🍴🍴 American. Fine Dining. **Address:** 626 W Olney Rd 23507

RAJPUT INDIAN CUISINE   757/625-4634 **11**
🍴🍴 Indian. Casual Dining. **Address:** 742 W 21st St 23517

RAZZO   757/962-3630 **3**
🍴🍴 Italian. Casual Dining. **Address:** 3248 E Ocean View Ave 23518

RECOVERY SPORTS GRILL   757/423-4100 **3**
🍴🍴 American. Casual Dining. **Address:** 4500 Hampton Blvd 23508

SAINT GERMAIN   757/321-9445 **45**
🍴🍴🍴 New American. Fine Dining. **Address:** 255 Granby St 23510

SANDFIDDLER CAFE   757/227-3484 **4**
🍴🍴 Breakfast Comfort Food. Casual Dining. **Address:** 0561 Shore Dr 23518

SHIPTOWN   **1**
🍴🍴 Seafood. Casual Dining. **Address:** 4314 Colley Ave 23508

SHULA'S 347   757/282-6347 **57**

🍴🍴🍴🍴
Steak
Casual Dining
$11-$39

AAA Inspector Notes: Guaranteed to be the smoothest sports bar you've entered, this place offers Prime Black Angus steaks, fresh seafood, a rich crab soup with lots of meat on Fridays, and a great burger with thin, crispy fries. Enjoy all this fine fare while watching a bevy of sports on the restaurant's numerous flat-screen TVs; you'll even find them in the restrooms. **Features:** full bar. **Reservations:** suggested. **Address:** 235 E Main St 23510 **Location:** Corner of Main and Atlantic sts; center of downtown; in Norfolk Waterside Marriott. **Parking:** street only. L D LATE CALL ♿

STREATS   757/233-8933 **9**
🍴🍴 Small Plates. Casual Dining. **Address:** 915 W 21st St 23517

SUPPER SOUTHERN MORSELS   757/383-6800 **19**
🍴🍴🍴 Southern American. Casual Dining. **Address:** 319 W 21st St 23517

SURF RIDER RESTAURANT   757/480-5000
🍴🍴 Seafood. Casual Dining. **Address:** 8180 Shore Dr 23518

(See maps & indexes p. 131, 134.)

SURF RIDER WEST   757/461-6488 (15)
Seafood. Casual Dining. **Address:** 723 Newtown Rd 23502

TASTE UNLIMITED   757/623-7770
Specialty Sandwiches. Quick Serve. **Address:** 6464 Hampton Blvd 23508

THE TEN TOP   757/622-5422 (29)
American. Quick Serve. **Address:** 748 Shirley Ave 23517

TOAST   (6)
Breads/Pastries. Casual Dining. **Address:** 2406 Colonial Ave 23517

TODD JURICH'S BISTRO   757/622-3210 (53)

New American Fine Dining $9-$42

AAA Inspector Notes: This longtime downtown staple is famed for bringing urban elegance to this once humble area. The setting is cool and modern with a lively scene in the bar on most nights. The menu changes seasonally, but perennial favorites include house-made truffle ravioli, mozzarella-and-tomato short stack, local soft-shell crabs in season and crabcakes. Upscale sandwiches and burgers round out the lunch menu. Valet parking is available in the evening. Lunch is not served on Saturday. **Features:** full bar, patio dining, happy hour. **Reservations:** suggested. **Address:** 150 W Main St, Suite 100 23510 **Location:** Downtown; entrance on Boush St; across from Nauticus. **Parking:** on-site (fee) and valet.

L   D   CALL 🔊 ♿ 🐾

TORTILLA WEST   757/440-3777 (19)
Mexican. Casual Dining. **Address:** 508 Orapax St 23507

VINTAGE KITCHEN   757/625-3370 (58)
Regional American. Fine Dining. **Address:** 999 Waterside Dr 23510

VOILA CUISINE INTERNATIONAL   757/640-0343 (38)
Continental. Fine Dining. **Address:** 509 Botetourt St 23510

VOLCANO SUSHI AND CHINA BISTRO   757/683-2688 (18)
Asian Sushi. Casual Dining. **Address:** 339 W 21st St 23517

YNOT PIZZA & ITALIAN CUISINE   757/624-9111 (27)
Italian Pizza. Casual Dining. **Address:** 1517 Colley Ave 23517

ZEKE'S BEANS & BOWLS   757/963-5220 (32)
Natural/Organic Coffee/Tea. Quick Serve. **Address:** 800 Granby St 23510

NORTON pop. 3,958

DAYS INN   276/679-5340
Motel. **Address:** 375 Wharton Ln 24273

SUPER 8-NORTON   276/679-0893
Motel. **Address:** 425 Wharton Ln 24273

OCCOQUAN (B-12) pop. 934, elev. 80'

The historic town of Occoquan, its name taken from a Dogue Indian word meaning "at the end of the water," was a recognized community in 1734. By the late 18th century the area was a thriving port and milling town dependent on the waterpower of the Occoquan River. During the Civil War Gen. Wade Hampton made his headquarters in the Hammill Hotel, today a collection of shops and offices.

One of Virginia's first cotton mills, built in 1828, hummed with 1,000 spindles before it was silenced by fire during the Civil War. The village flourished until deepening silt in the Occoquan River prevented vessels from reaching the mills.

Prince William County Visitor Information Center: 200 Mill St., Occoquan, VA 22125. **Phone:** (703) 491-4045.

Self-guiding tours: A brochure offering a walking tour of the historic district and a list of local artists and galleries is available at the visitor information center.

Shopping: There are more than 80 specialty shops in the compact historic district. Many are housed in original historic buildings and offer antiques and crafts.

MADIGAN'S WATERFRONT   703/494-6373
American. Casual Dining. **Address:** 201 Mill St 22125

ONANCOCK (G-11) pop. 1,263, elev. 20'

This waterfront village was established in 1680 on the Chesapeake Bay's eastern shore. The name is said to come from a Native American word meaning "a foggy place." Onancock-Tangier Island passenger ferries operate May through September. Reservations are recommended; phone (757) 891-2505.

1890 SPINNING WHEEL BED & BREAKFAST   757/787-7311
Historic Bed & Breakfast. **Address:** 31 North St 23417

CHARLOTTE HOTEL   (757)787-7400
Boutique Country Inn. **Address:** 7 North St 23417

THE INN & GARDEN CAFE   757/787-8850
Country Inn. **Address:** 145 Market St 23417

WHERE TO EAT

BIZZOTTO'S GALLERY-CAFFE   757/787-3103
Continental. Casual Dining. **Address:** 41 Market St 23417

CHARLOTTE RESTAURANT   757/787-7400
American. Fine Dining. **Address:** 7 North St 23417

THE INN & GARDEN CAFE   757/787-8850
American. Casual Dining. **Address:** 145 Market St 23417

JANET'S ONANCOCK GENERAL STORE CAFE   757/787-9495
American. Casual Dining. **Address:** 49 King St 23417

MALLARD'S AT THE WHARF   757/787-8558
Seafood. Casual Dining. **Address:** 2 Market St 23417

ONLEY pop. 516

SAGE DINER   757/787-9341
American. Casual Dining. **Address:** 25558 Lankford Hwy 23418

ORANGE (F-8) pop. 4,721, elev. 522'

This small rural town in the state's north-central region was named after Prince William of Orange, who married King George II's oldest daughter in 1734, the year Orange County was founded. The town was home to Col. James Taylor II, great-grandfather to two American presidents, James Madison and Zachary Taylor.

During the Civil War Orange County was Confederate stomping ground. Robert E. Lee's army camped there in the winter of 1863-64 and on the eve of the May 1864 Battle of the Wilderness, the opening conflict in Ulysses S. Grant's bloody Overland Campaign. Lee regularly worshipped at St. Thomas's Episcopal Church on Caroline Street; the locust tree to which he tied his horse, Traveller, is labeled.

As you're exploring Orange, keep your eyes peeled for a series of markers that highlight other historically significant sites. Among these points of interest is the 1909-10 Colonial Revival-style Orange Train Station, 122 E. Main St. The original building and several nearby structures burned down in a 1908 fire that swept through the eastern part of town. The station ceased its passenger train operations along the Orange & Alexandria Railroad in the early 1970s; today it houses the Orange County Visitors Center.

Architecture and history buffs won't want to miss the Orange County Courthouse at Main Street and Madison Road. Constructed 1858-59, the Italianate building exemplifies Virginia's bold departure from the conventional Classical style of architecture. The Confederate 7th Virginia Cavalry and three Union cavalries clashed at the site in August 1862.

If history isn't your cup of tea (or glass of Chardonnay), visit a local winery—be sure to drink in the sensational views of rolling hills, spacious farmland and the Blue Ridge Mountains en route. For a shopping experience that won't leave you empty-handed, check out the antiques shops and art galleries on Main Street.

If you're in the mood for some outdoor R & R, cast a line, munch on a picnic lunch or immerse yourself in a book at scenic Lake Orange, off SR 739. If an adrenaline-filled adventure is what you crave, try free-falling from a whopping 13,000 feet at Skydive Orange, 11339 Bloomsbury Rd.; phone (703) 759-3483. (Now *that's* a view you won't soon forget.)

Orange County Visitors Center: 122 E. Main St., Orange, VA 22960. **Phone:** (540) 672-1653 or (877) 222-8072.

 JAMES MADISON'S MONTPELIER—see Montpelier Station p. 172.

COMFORT INN & SUITES   (540)672-3121
Hotel. **Address:** 334 Caroline St 22960

ROUND HILL INN   540/672-6691

Hotel
Rates not provided

Address: 750 Round Hill Dr 22960 **Location:** US 15, 2.1 mi n of jct SR 20. **Facility:** 65 units. 2 stories, interior corridors. **Pool:** outdoor. **Activities:** exercise room. **Guest Services:** coin laundry. **Featured Amenity:** breakfast buffet.

WHERE TO EAT

ELMWOOD AT SPARKS   540/672-0060
American. Fine Dining. **Address:** 124 W Main St 22960

REAL FOOD   540/661-7261
American. Casual Dining. **Address:** 12267 Old Gordonsville Rd 22960

SILK MILL GRILLE   540/672-4010
American. Casual Dining **Address:** 101-A Woodmark St 22960

PARKSLEY (G-11) pop. 842, elev. 43'

Henry R. Bennett, a traveling salesman, laid out the town of Parksley in 1884 during construction of the Eastern Shore Railway. In the 160-acre planned community, selling liquor meant the immediate loss of one's property. Benjamin Parks, upon whose farm Parksley was built, soon fled the constraints of town life for a new seaside home.

PENN LAIRD

VITO'S PIZZA PIE   540/433-8486
Pizza. Casual Dining. **Address:** 4741 Spotswood Tr 22846

PETERSBURG (B-1) pop. 32,420, elev. 100'
• Hotels p. 186 • Restaurants p. 187
• Hotels & Restaurants map & index p. 219

Petersburg began in 1645 as Fort Henry, a frontier fort and trading post. In 1781 a British force under generals William Phillips and Benedict Arnold marched on the town, which was inadequately garrisoned by 1,000 men under Maj. Gen. Friedrich von Steuben. After a short skirmish to cover his retreat, von Steuben withdrew across Pocahontas Bridge, burning it behind him. Later the Marquis de Lafayette bombarded the city. It was in Petersburg that Gen. Charles Cornwallis gathered British troops for the Yorktown campaign.

By the time it was incorporated as a city in 1850, Petersburg had become a thriving industrial and commercial center, with tobacco warehouses, cotton and flour mills and iron foundries. Economic success was followed by a cultural blossoming; schools, colleges, churches and theaters flourished.

Unfortunately, Petersburg's importance as an industrial and transportation center of the Confederacy made it a prime target for Gen. Ulysses S. Grant's armies. In the summer of 1864 the surrounding countryside turned into a battlefield. Stray

(See map & index p. 219.)

shells struck 800 homes. For 10 months the city suffered hunger and cannon bombardment before it fell to the Union near the close of the Civil War *(see Petersburg National Battlefield p. 187).*

Not long after the war's end, Mary Logan, wife of Union commander Gen. John A. Logan, witnessed a group of schoolgirls placing flowers on the graves of Petersburg defenders at the Old Blandford Church. Deeply moved when she saw the ritual repeated the next year, she related the story to her husband, who took steps that ultimately led to the observance of Memorial Day as a national holiday.

Petersburg Area Regional Tourism: 1964 Wakefield Ave., P.O. Box 1808, Petersburg, VA 23805. **Phone:** (804) 861-1666 or (877) 730-7278.

Self-guiding tours: The visitor center offers a variety of maps outlining tours of Petersburg and its Old Towne historic district as well as Lee's Retreat. This 26-stop driving tour through seven counties connecting Petersburg to Appomattox follows the route of Gen. Robert E. Lee at the end of the Civil War.

Petersburg's African-American heritage is one of the oldest in the country. By the mid-19th century, the area had one of the largest free black populations in the state. A brochure outlining a self-guiding tour of Petersburg's African-American historic sites is available at the visitor center and at Petersburg museums.

BLANDFORD CHURCH AND RECEPTION CENTER is at 319 S. Crater Rd. in Blandford Cemetery. Known in Colonial times as the Brick Church on Well's Hill, the church was built 1735-37. Its 15 stained glass windows by Tiffany Studios are memorials donated by the Confederate States. The 189-acre Blandford Cemetery contains the graves of 30,000 Confederate soldiers and the unmarked grave of British general William Phillips.

Guided tours leave from the reception center at 111 Rochelle Ln. inside the cemetery. **Hours:** Mon.-Sat. 10-5, Sun. 1-5, Apr.-Sept. Closed Jan. 1, Thanksgiving, Christmas Eve and Christmas. Phone ahead to confirm schedule. **Cost:** $5; $4 (ages 7-12 and 60+). Combination ticket with Centre Hill Mansion $9; $7 (ages 7-12 and 60+). **Phone:** (804) 733-2396. GT

CENTRE HILL MANSION is at 1 Centre Hill Ave. off Franklin St. Extensive renovations to this 1823 Federal-style mansion took place in the 1840s and again in 1901, thereby depicting the architectural evolution that paralleled the Victorian era. Period antiques include a rare 1886 Knabe Art grand piano that is 9 feet long.

Hours: Thurs.-Sat. 10-4, Sun. 1-4. Closed Jan. 1, Thanksgiving, Christmas Eve and Christmas. Phone ahead to confirm schedule. **Cost:** $5; $4 (ages 7-12 and 60+). Combination ticket with Blandford Church

and Reception Center $9; $7 (ages 7-12 and 60+). **Phone:** (804) 733-2401.

PAMPLIN HISTORICAL PARK AND THE NATIONAL MUSEUM OF THE CIVIL WAR SOLDIER is off I-85 exit 63A at 6125 Boydton Plank Rd. A premier Civil War history destination, this 424-acre park features four antebellum homes, four museums and daily living-history demonstrations. The park also is the site of the Breakthrough Battle of April 2, 1865, a decisive point in the Petersburg Campaign that led to Gen. Robert E. Lee's retreat from Richmond.

Appealing to casual visitors, serious students of Civil War history and families, the park explores the experiences of common soldiers and life in the antebellum South. The National Museum of the Civil War Soldier displays more than 3,000 artifacts, supplying visitors with personal audio players to follow the true-life stories of individuals who fought in the conflict.

The site includes a military encampment, slave quarters, fortifications and nearly a mile of original earthworks.

Time: Allow 3 hours minimum. **Hours:** Daily 9-5, Mar.-Nov.; Sat.-Sun. 9-5, rest of year. Phone ahead to confirm schedule. **Cost:** $13; $12 (ages 62+ and military with ID); $8 (ages 6-12). **Phone:** (804) 861-2408 or (877) 726-7546. 🎟

SIEGE MUSEUM is at 15 W. Bank St. The human side of the Civil War is presented through exhibits depicting the lives of the citizens of Petersburg while under siege. A 20-minute film shows the contrast between the city before the war and as it was during the 10 months preceding Gen. Robert E. Lee's surrender.

Note: The museum is undergoing renovations and is closed to the public; phone ahead for updates. **Hours:** Mon.-Sat. 10-5, Sun. noon-5. Closed Jan. 1, Thanksgiving, Christmas Eve and Christmas. Phone ahead to confirm schedule. **Cost:** $5; $4 (ages 7-12 and 60+). Combination ticket with Blandford Church and Reception Center and Centre Hill Mansion $11; $9 (ages 7-12 and 60+). **Phone:** (804) 733-2402.

COMFORT INN-PETERSBURG SOUTH   (804)732-2000 **4**
▼▼ Hotel. **Address:** 12001 S Crater Rd 23805

COUNTRY INN & SUITES BY CARLSON
                                (804)861-4355 **1**

Hotel
$110-$150

Address: 130 Wagner Rd 23805 **Location:** I-95 exit 48B, just w. **Facility:** 70 units. 3 stories, interior corridors. **Pool:** heated indoor. **Activities:** hot tub, exercise room. **Guest Services:** valet and coin laundry. **Featured Amenity:** continental breakfast.

SAVE CALL 🔧 🛏 🛗 BIZ HS
📶 🚫 🔌 🖥 📺

(See map & index p. 219.)

HAMPTON INN | (804)732-1400
▼▼▼ Hotel. **Address:** 11909 S Crater Rd 23805 | **AAA Benefit:** Members save up to 10%!

HOLIDAY INN EXPRESS HOTEL & SUITES
804/518-1800 **3**
▼▼▼▼ Hotel. **Address:** 11979 S Crater Rd 23805

HOLIDAY INN EXPRESS HOTEL & SUITES PETERSBURG/DINWIDDIE   804/518-1515 **7**

▼▼▼▼ **Hotel**
Rates not provided

Address: 5679 Boydton Plank Rd 23803 **Location:** I-85 exit 63A, just s on US 1. **Facility:** 67 units. 3 stories, interior corridors. **Pool:** outdoor. **Activities:** exercise room. **Guest Services:** valet laundry. **Featured Amenity:** full hot breakfast.

SAVE 🍴 CALL ♿ 🛎 📶 BIZ
📶 ✕ 🍴 📺 📋

WHERE TO EAT

ALEXANDER'S FINE FOOD   804/733-7134 **7**
▼▼ Greek. Casual Dining. **Address:** 101 W Bank St 23803

THE BRICKHOUSE RUN   804/862-1815 **3**
▼▼ British. Gastropub. **Address:** 407-409 Cockade Alley 23803

DEMOLITION COFFEE   804/732-2991 **5**
▼ Coffee/Tea. Quick Serve. **Address:** 215 E Bank St 23803

DIXIE RESTAURANT   804/732-7425 **8**
▼ Southern Breakfast Comfort Food. Casual Dining. **Address:** 250 N Sycamore St 23803

KING'S BARBECUE   804/732-0975 **10**
▼ Barbecue Comfort Food. Casual Dining. **Address:** 2910 S Crater Rd 23805

LONGSTREET'S DELICATESSEN   804/722-4372 **6**
▼▼ Deli. Casual Dining. **Address:** 302 N Sycamore St 23803

MARIA'S OLD TOWN 21 RISTORANTE ITALIANO
804/862-3100 **2**
▼▼ Italian. Casual Dining. **Address:** 21 W Old St 23803

NANNY'S FAMILY RESTAURANT   804/733-6619 **11**
▼ Southern. Casual Dining. **Address:** 11900 S Crater Rd 23805

SAUCY'S SIT DOWN BBQ   804/504-3075 **1**
▼ Barbecue. Casual Dining. **Address:** 5th & Bollingbrook Sts 23803

WABI-SABI SUSHI & TAPAS   804/862-1365 **4**
▼▼ Japanese Sushi Small Plates. Casual Dining. **Address:** 29 Bollingbrook St 23803

YANKEE COFFEE SHOPPE   804/861-4990 **9**
▼ Breakfast Comfort Food. Casual Dining. **Address:** 2557-B S Crater Rd 23805

PETERSBURG NATIONAL BATTLEFIELD (B-1)

The 2,659-acre Petersburg National Battlefield, 2 miles east of Petersburg via Washington/Oaklawn St. (SR 36), was established to preserve and interpret the battlefields where 10 months of grim trench warfare sapped the strength of Gen. Robert E. Lee's Confederate army and led to the fall of Richmond.

Petersburg was an important point through which supplies moved to Richmond, as five railroads converged at Petersburg with only one line leading to the capital city.

Despite disastrous losses at Wilderness, Spotsylvania Court House and Cold Harbor, Gen. Ulysses S. Grant moved on from Richmond, intending to cut off its line of communication with the South at Petersburg and compel the evacuation of the Confederate capital. Four days of furious fighting—June 15-18, 1864—forced the Confederate line back about a mile, where the armies entrenched and Grant began his siege.

Between June 25 and July 23, Union volunteers, including many Pennsylvania coal miners, dug a 511-foot-long mine shaft that ended beneath the Confederate line. Quietly carrying out tons of soil in cracker boxes, the Union men packed the shaft with 4 tons of black powder which, when ignited, created a 170-by-60-foot crater 30 feet deep. The blast produced 278 casualties. Only faulty Union plans in the following battle and the prompt action of Confederate troops saved the city. The deep depression created by the explosion is called The Crater.

Confederate lines stretched farther south and west as the soldiers were forced to defend both the eastern and western sectors against the Union's attempt to take the city. On April 3, 1865, Lee evacuated Petersburg and Richmond, an action that culminated 1 week later in his surrender at Appomattox Court House. About 42,000 Union and 28,000 Confederate soldiers were casualties in the Petersburg Campaign.

The park includes miles of original earthworks. Outstanding features are The Crater; Battery Five, where Grant's army first struck and from which he later shelled Petersburg with a 17,000-pound seacoast mortar known as "The Dictator"; Fort Stedman, where Lee's last grand offensive failed; the site of Fort Morton, near which the concentration of Union artillery used at the Battle of The Crater was stored; City Point, the Union supply center and logistics base where Grant and President Lincoln conferred for 2 weeks near the end of the siege; Five Forks Battlefield, about 17 miles southwest of Petersburg, site of the last major battle for the South Side Railroad on April 1, 1865; and Poplar Grove National Cemetery, where 6,000 Union soldiers are buried.

The 4-mile self-guiding Battlefield Tour begins at the Eastern Front Visitor Center; part of the tour road is reserved for hikers and cyclists. From four points on the tour road, walks lead to major battle sites. The 16-mile Siege Line Tour picks up where the Battlefield Tour ends and leads to park areas south and west of Petersburg. The park is open daily 8-dusk. Closed Jan. 1, Thanksgiving and Christmas. Admission is free. Phone (804) 732-3531.

EASTERN FRONT VISITOR CENTER is at the entrance to Petersburg National Battlefield off Washington Ave. (SR 36). The Petersburg campaign is depicted through exhibits, battlefield relics, maps and models. Self-guiding tour maps and a recorded narration of the 37-mile driving tour of the battlefield are available. **Hours:** Grounds daily 9-8, Apr.-Oct.; 9-5, rest of year. Visitor center daily 9-5. Closed Jan. 1, Thanksgiving and Christmas. **Cost:** Free. **Phone:** (804) 732-3531, ext. 200.

POCAHONTAS (H-4) pop. 389, elev. 2,300'

In 1873 Maj. Jed Hotchkiss hired a surveyor to explore a 500,000-acre tract along the Bluestone River. The report noted a coal bed used for fuel by a local blacksmith, and Hotchkiss brought the discovery to the attention of investors. A railroad was built to the site, and the first shipment of "smokeless" Pocahontas coal was delivered to Norfolk in 1883. When the original shaft was depleted decades later, the company town turned it into a show mine.

PORT ROYAL

| RIVER HAVEN RESTAURANT | 804/742-5113 |

American Casual Dining

$7-$29

AAA Inspector Notes: This casual restaurant occupies a beautiful spot overlooking "the rivah" and includes a small fishing pier and boat dock. Grab a spot by the windows and enjoy fresh local seafood such as jumbo lump crab cakes, fried catfish, fried oysters and Maryland-style crab soup. Other specialties include great burgers, hand-cut fries cooked in peanut oil, chili and meatloaf. The Sunday breakfast buffet starts at 10 a.m. **Features:** full bar, patio dining. **Address:** 136 Main St 22535 **Location:** On US 301, just n of jct US 17; on Rappahannock River.

PORTSMOUTH (H-10) pop. 95,535, elev. 11'

• Hotels & Restaurants map & index p. 134
• Part of Hampton Roads Area — see map p. 124

Because of the location's accessibility to water and a ready supply of timber for shipbuilding, Portsmouth earned a king's grant for settlement in 1620. Ownership alternated between the crown and mariners until it was re-patented in 1716 by Col. William Crawford, presiding justice of Norfolk County. Crawford donated the four corners of High and Court streets for a market, a jail, a courthouse and a church. The restored 1762 Trinity Episcopal Church is the town's oldest building.

Portsmouth was a strategic military objective in early U.S. conflicts. During the Revolution, after seven British vessels had bombarded and set fire to Portsmouth and the surrounding Tidewater areas, Benedict Arnold set up headquarters and the British line of defense on Hospital Point, then called Fort Nelson.

During the early months of the Civil War the Virginia Militia wrested control of the naval shipyard from the Union. After the Federal troops burned and abandoned Portsmouth, the Confederates raised the frigate *Merrimac* and turned it into the world's first ironclad battleship, the CSS *Virginia.*

Beginning as a marine yard in 1767, the Norfolk Naval Shipyard is the largest in the world. Besides the CSS *Virginia,* the shipyard produced the *Chesapeake,* the sister of the *Constitution* and one of the Navy's first warships.

The Olde Towne Historic District is distinguished by a fine collection of period homes with a rich diversity of architectural styles. The Art Deco marquee of the Commodore Theatre at 421 High St. is a local landmark. The theater, which was built in 1945, features first-run films and dining; phone (757) 393-6962.

(See map & index p. 134.)

Ferry service between Norfolk and Portsmouth resumed on the Elizabeth River in the early 1980s; the river was first crossed in 1636 by North America's first pedestrian ferry. The ferry is operated by Hampton Roads Transit; an information station is at North Landing, 6 Crawford Pkwy.

Portsmouth Visitor Information Center: 6 Crawford Pkwy., Portsmouth, VA 23704. **Phone:** (757) 393-5111.

Self-guiding tours: A brochure describing a walking tour of the Olde Towne Historic District is available from the visitor information center.

Shopping: Centered on High Street, the Olde Towne Historic District offers various small specialty shops, including antiques stores and art galleries.

CHILDREN'S MUSEUM OF VIRGINIA is at 221 High St. More than 90 hands-on displays challenge the imagination of both children and adults. Changing exhibits focus on science, art, music, communications, cultural diversity and technology. Immersive planetarium shows inspire young ones with the wonders and mysteries of the universe.

Time: Allow 2 hours minimum. **Hours:** Mon.-Sat. 9-5, Sun. 11-5, Memorial Day-Labor Day; Tues.-Sat. and Mon. holidays 9-5, Sun. 11-5, rest of year. Closed Jan. 1, Thanksgiving and Christmas. **Cost:** $11; $10 (ages 2-17, military with ID and senior citizens); $9 (military dependents ages 2-17). **Phone:** (757) 393-5258.

RENAISSANCE PORTSMOUTH-NORFOLK WATERFRONT (757)673-3000 [13]

Hotel
$101-$252

R RENAISSANCE HOTELS

AAA Benefit: Members save 5% or more!

Address: 425 Water St 23704 **Location:** Waterfront. Jct Crawford St, just n; downtown. **Facility:** 249 units. 13 stories, interior corridors. **Parking:** on-site (fee) and valet. **Terms:** check-in 4 pm, cancellation fee imposed. **Pool:** heated indoor. **Activities:** hot tub, exercise room. **Guest Services:** valet and coin laundry.

WHERE TO EAT

BANGKOK GARDEN 757/483-0799
Thai. Casual Dining. **Address:** 5774 Churchland Blvd 23703

THE BIER GARDEN 757/393-6022 [30]
German. Casual Dining. **Address:** 438 High St 23704

CAFE EUROPA 757/399-6652 [28]
Continental. Fine Dining. **Address:** 319 High St 23704

COMMODORE THEATRE 757/393-6962 [29]

American Dinner Theatre
$5-$12

AAA Inspector Notes: *Historic.* This classic 1940s-era Art Deco cinema is a fantastic place to relax and enjoy a movie. Cozy armchairs on wheels provide ample space and ordering your meal via the tabletop telephone is quaint. The short menu lists deli sandwiches, nachos, pizzas, deep-fried favorites and great cinnamon loaves. Of course there's popcorn topped with real butter—no fake stuff here. Be sure to check out the original murals on the wall before the theater lights dim. **Features:** beer & wine. **Address:** 421 High St 23704 **Location:** Jct Dinwiddie St; in Olde Towne. **Parking:** street only.

HOME GROWN 757/399-1490 [26]
Pizza. Casual Dining. **Address:** 455 Court St 23704

JOJACK'S ESPRESSO BAR & CAFE 757/483-1483 [22]
Coffee/Tea Sandwiches. Quick Serve. **Address:** 5700 Churchland Blvd, Suite 39 23703

MANNINO'S ITALIAN BISTRO 757/966-7522 [31]
Italian. Fine Dining. **Address:** 600 High St 23704

ONO HAWAII BBQ 757/686-2219 [23]
Hawaiian Barbecue. Casual Dining. **Address:** 6071 W High St 23703

ROGER BROWN'S RESTAURANT & SPORTS BAR 757/399-5377 [27]
American. Casual Dining. **Address:** 316 High St 23704

STILL WORLDLY ECLECTIC TAPAS 757/000-7222 [25]
Small Plates. Gastropub. **Address:** 450 Court St 23704

STOVE 757/397-0900 [24]
American. Fine Dining. **Address:** 2622 Detroit St 23707

POUNDING MILL

CLAYPOOL HILL HOLIDAY INN EXPRESS HOTEL & SUITES 276/596-9880
Hotel. **Address:** 180 Clay Dr 24637

CLAYPOOL HILL SUPER 8 276/964-9888
Motel. **Address:** 12367 Governor GC Peery Hwy 24637

PRINCE GEORGE pop. 2,066
• Hotels & Restaurants map & index p. 219

BAYMONT INN & SUITES PRINCE GEORGE 804/452-0022 [25]

fyi
Hotel
Rates not provided

Under major renovation, scheduled to be completed December 2017. **Last Rated:** **Address:** 5380 Oaklawn Blvd 23875 **Location:** I-295 exit 9B (SR 36), just w. **Facility:** 144 units, some efficiencies and kitchens. 2-4 stories, interior corridors. **Amenities:** safes. **Pool:** outdoor. **Activities:** sauna, exercise room. **Guest Services:** complimentary and valet laundry. **Featured Amenity:** full hot breakfast.

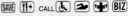

(See map & index p. 219.)

SLEEP INN & SUITES AT FT LEE   (804)732-3737

Hotel
$90-$200

Address: 2200 Waterside Rd 23875 **Location:** I-95 exit 54, 2 mi e on SR 144 (Temple Ave), then just s on Puddledock Rd; in Waterside Commons. **Facility:** 60 units, some efficiencies. 3 stories, interior corridors. **Amenities:** safes. **Pool:** heated indoor. **Activities:** hot tub, exercise room. **Guest Services:** valet and coin laundry. **Featured Amenity:** continental breakfast.

PURCELLVILLE

GRANDALE RESTAURANT   540/668-6000

American. Fine Dining. **Address:** 14001 Harpers Ferry Rd 20132

QUANTICO (C-12) pop. 480, elev. 35'

Quantico is one of the nation's largest Marine Corps installations and the site of the Marine Corps Combat Development Command. At the entrance is a replica of the Marine Corps War Memorial, a statue depicting the flag raising on Mount Suribachi during the World War II battle for Iwo Jima. The original stands at the north end of Arlington National Cemetery *(see place listing p. 66).*

Quantico National Cemetery is off I-95 on CR 619W. Ceremonies on Memorial Day and Veterans Day feature color guards from area veterans' organizations.

NATIONAL MUSEUM OF THE MARINE CORPS is adjacent to the Quantico Marine Corps Base in Triangle, just off I-95. The building's stunning design captivates visitors as they enter by way of the Leatherneck Gallery, where aircraft—including a restored SBD Dauntless dive bomber from World War II and a Vietnam-era Sikorsky UH-34D helicopter—hang from the ceiling. Adjacent to the gallery, the Legacy Walk contains a timeline and leads to areas depicting various actions in which the Marines have been involved.

Visitors learn about Marines in boot camp, World War II, and the Korean and Vietnam wars. Also discussed is the role of the Marines in the global war on terrorism. **Time:** Allow 4 hours minimum. **Hours:** Daily 9-5. Guided tours depart daily at 10 and 2 (based on staff availability). Closed Christmas. **Cost:** Free. **Phone:** (877) 635-1775.

RADFORD pop. 16,408

BEST WESTERN RADFORD INN   (540)639-3000

Hotel
$69-$249

 Best Western.

AAA Benefit: Members save 10% or more & earn 10% bonus points!

Address: 1501 Tyler Ave 24141 **Location:** I-81 exit 109, 2.7 mi nw on SR 177. **Facility:** 72 units. 2 stories, interior corridors. **Terms:** cancellation fee imposed. **Pool:** heated indoor. **Activities:** sauna, hot tub, exercise room. **Guest Services:** valet and coin laundry. **Featured Amenity:** full hot breakfast.

COMFORT INN & SUITES   (540)639-3333

Hotel
$80-$299

Address: 2331 Tyler Ave 24073 **Location:** I-81 exit 109, just w. **Facility:** 72 units. 3 stories, interior corridors. **Amenities:** safes. **Pool:** heated indoor. **Activities:** hot tub, exercise room. **Guest Services:** coin laundry. **Featured Amenity:** breakfast buffet.

LA QUINTA INN RADFORD   (540)633-6800

Motel
$64-$144

Address: 1450 Tyler Ave 24141 **Location:** I-81 exit 109, 2.6 mi w on SR 177. **Facility:** 51 units. 2 stories (no elevator), interior corridors. **Activities:** exercise room. **Guest Services:** valet laundry. **Featured Amenity:** breakfast buffet.

SUPER 8-RADFORD   540/731-9355

Motel. **Address:** 1600 Tyler Ave 24141

WHERE TO EAT

SAL'S RISTORANTE ITALIANO   540/639-9669

Italian. Casual Dining. **Address:** 709 W Main St 24141

RAPHINE

COMFORT INN & SUITES   540/377-2604

Motel
Rates not provided

Address: 584 Oakland Cir 24472 **Location:** I-81 exit 205, just sw. Located in a commercial area. **Facility:** 86 units. 3 stories, interior corridors. **Pool:** outdoor. **Activities:** exercise room. **Guest Services:** coin laundry. **Featured Amenity:** full hot breakfast.

REEDVILLE (G-11) elev. 10'

Reedville's history is intertwined with that of the Potomac River and Chesapeake Bay. On Virginia's Northern Neck, the city was the home of wealthy fishermen and factory owners whose fortunes were made from the menhaden that populated those waters. Their Victorian mansions can be seen along Main Street. Reedville retains its ties to the water, as fishing charters and cruises to nearby Smith and Tangier islands are popular with visitors.

RESTON pop. 58,404
• Hotels & Restaurants map & index p. 38

EXTENDED STAY AMERICA WASHINGTON DC-RESTON
(703)707-9700　27

Extended Stay Motel. **Address:** 12190 Sunset Hills Rd 20190

HYATT REGENCY RESTON　(703)709-1234　26

Hotel
$109-$389

HYATT REGENCY

AAA Benefit: Members save 10%!

Address: 1800 Presidents St 20190 **Location:** SR 267 (Dulles Toll Rd) exit 12 (Reston Pkwy); center. **Facility:** This hotel is part of a Town Center that incorporates numerous shops, restaurants and movie theaters. The guest rooms have upgraded bedding, flat-panel TVs and good work space. 518 units. 15 stories, interior corridors. **Parking:** on-site (fee) and valet. **Terms:** cancellation fee imposed. **Amenities:** safes. **Pool:** heated indoor. **Activities:** health club. **Guest Services:** valet laundry, boarding pass kiosk.

SHERATON RESTON HOTEL　703/620-9000　29

Hotel. **Address:** 11810 Sunrise Valley Dr 20191

AAA Benefit: Members save 5% or more!

THE WESTIN RESTON HEIGHTS　703/391-9000　28

Hotel. **Address:** 11750 Sunrise Valley Dr 20191

AAA Benefit: Members save 5% or more!

WHERE TO EAT

BUSARA　703/435-4188　20

Thai. Casual Dining. **Address:** 11964 Market St 20190

CLYDE'S OF RESTON　703/787-6601

American. Casual Dining. **Address:** 11905 Market St 20190

JACKSON'S MIGHTY FINE FOOD & LUCKY LOUNGE
703/437-0800　24

American. Casual Dining. **Address:** 11927 Democracy Dr 20190

M & S GRILL　703/787-7766　21

Steak Seafood. Casual Dining. **Address:** 11901 Democracy Dr 20190

MCCORMICK & SCHMICK'S　703/481-6600　22

Seafood. Fine Dining. **Address:** 11920 Democracy Dr 20190

MON AMI GABI　703/707-0233　23

French Steak. Casual Dining. **Address:** 11950 Democracy Dr 20190

MORTON'S THE STEAKHOUSE　703/796-0128　19

Steak. Fine Dining. **Address:** 11956 Market St 20190

NEYLA MEDITERRANEAN BISTRO　703/318-8920　18

Mediterranean. Casual Dining. **Address:** 11898 Market St 20190

PASSIONFISH　703/230-3474　25

Seafood. Fine Dining. **Address:** 11960 Democracy Dr 20190

SILVER DINER　703/742-0801

American. Casual Dining. **Address:** 11951 Killingsworth Ave 20194

Richmond

Then & Now

Not many state capitals can claim to have also been the capital of a nation. As capital of the Confederacy during the Civil War, Richmond can, which is why many folks associate the city with that battle between North and South. What they might not know, however, is the role the city played in an earlier struggle, the war for American independence.

The rallying cry of the Revolution, Patrick Henry's stirring "Give me liberty or give me death" speech was delivered in 1775 at stately St. John's Church. In attendance were such patriots as George Washington, Thomas Jefferson and Richard Henry Lee. Henry's impassioned plea moved the Colonies closer to their inevitable split with England.

Many of the Revolution's respected names were also members of Virginia's senate and house of delegates that met in the state Capitol. Designed by Thomas Jefferson and in continuous use since 1788, "Mr. Jefferson's temple" sits majestically on a hill above the James River, its six columns reminiscent of traditional Roman design. In its elegant rotunda stands Houdon's life-size statue of George Washington. Another period icon, John Marshall, the fourth chief justice of the U.S. Supreme Court, built his home in Court End in 1790.

Richmond's compact downtown is very walkable. Historic 18th-century buildings coexist seamlessly with those from a more turbulent part of American history, the War Between the States. The White House of the Confederacy served as the executive mansion of Jefferson Davis. The Davis family as well as Gen. Robert E. Lee and his wife worshiped at nearby St. Paul's Episcopal Church. The 1845 Greek Revival church is a perfect architectural complement to the Classical Virginia State Capitol across the street.

Richmond's early years were, indeed, a who's who of early American history. On the James River just outside downtown's historic district is Hollywood Cemetery, the city skyline intruding as a modern backdrop. Named for its profusion of holly trees, the tranquil, beautiful burial ground is the final resting place of two U.S. presidents, James Monroe and John Tyler; Jefferson Davis; six Virginia governors; Confederate generals J.E.B. Stuart and George Pickett; and more than 18,000 Confederate soldiers.

The War Between the States greatly impacted Richmond. A succession of Union generals tried but failed to capture the Southern capital, but it wasn't until Gen. Ulysses S. Grant's victory at Petersburg (a week before the South's

AAA.com/travelguides—
more ways to look, book and save

James River

(Continued on p. 194.)

Destination Richmond

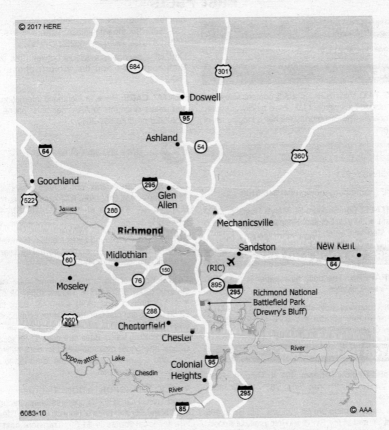

This map shows cities in the Richmond vicinity where you will find attractions, hotels and restaurants. Cities are listed alphabetically in this book on the following pages.

Fast Facts

ABOUT THE CITY

POP: 204,214 ▪ **ELEV:** 15 ft.

MONEY

SALES TAX: Virginia levies a 5.3 percent sales tax, which includes a 1 percent tax levied by city or county governments. The Richmond area has a lodging tax of 8 percent.

WHOM TO CALL

EMERGENCY: 911

POLICE (non-emergency): (804) 646-5100

HOSPITALS: Bon Secours-St. Mary's Hospital, (804) 285-2011 ▪ Henrico Doctors' Hospital, (804) 289-4500 ▪ VCU Medical Center, (804) 828-9000.

WHERE TO LOOK AND LISTEN

NEWSPAPERS: The daily newspaper is the *Richmond Times-Dispatch*.

RADIO: Richmond radio station WRVA (1140 AM) is an all news/talk station ▪ WCVE (88.9 FM) is a member of National Public Radio.

VISITOR INFORMATION

Richmond Region Tourism: 401 N. Third St., Richmond, VA 23219. **Phone:** (804) 783-7450 or (800) 370-9004.

Walk-in visitor centers are off I-95 exit Fifth St. at 405 N. Third St. and at the Richmond International Airport.

TRANSPORTATION

AIR TRAVEL: Richmond International Airport (RIC), off I-64 exit 197A, is served by Air Canada, (888) 247-2262; AirTran, (800) 247-8726; Allegiant, (702) 505-8888; American Airlines, (800) 433-7300; Delta Airlines, (800) 221-1212; JetBlue Airways, (800) 538-2583; Southwest Airlines, (800) 435-9792; and United Airlines, (800) 241-6522.

Limousine service is available between the greater Richmond area and the airport; phone (804) 360-2122.

RENTAL CARS: Hertz, at Richmond International Airport, offers discounts to AAA members; phone (804) 222-7228 or (800) 654-3080.

 Book and save at AAA.com/hertz

RAIL SERVICE: Amtrak train service is available at 7519 Staples Mill Rd., (800) 872-7245, and at historic Main Street Station at 500 E. Main St., (804) 646-2041.

BUSES: The Greyhound Lines Inc. bus terminal is at 2910 N. Boulevard St. across from The Diamond baseball field; phone (804) 254-5910.

TAXIS: Some of the larger cab companies include Galaxy, (804) 560-4408 ▪ Yellow, (804) 222-7300 ▪ and Richmond Taxi, (804) 439-0009. Base fare is $2.50 for the first one-fifth mile, 50c for each additional one-fifth mile and 50c for each 80-second period of delay, including traffic. Base fare rises $1 for each additional passenger over age 6 and for rides between 9 p.m. and 6 a.m. A $2 access fee is added to fares originating at the airport.

PUBLIC TRANSPORTATION: The Greater Richmond Transit Co. (GRTC) operates buses throughout most of the city and parts of Henrico County. The base fare for local routes is $1.50. Transfers cost 25c. Transfers must be purchased at the time your initial fare is paid. Reduced rates are available for senior citizens and the physically impaired. Go Cards, used in lieu of cash by customers boarding GRTC vehicles, are available for advance purchase at retail locations throughout the Richmond area for $10. Phone (804) 358-4782.

(Continued from p. 192.)

surrender at Appomattox) that the city was evacuated.

Civil War heroes are honored along Monument Avenue, a historic landmark that also is considered one of the country's most beautiful streets. The tree-lined avenue, graced by restored historic gems, is known for the statues of Confederate champions Jefferson Davis, Thomas J. "Stonewall" Jackson, Robert E. Lee and J.E.B. Stuart. A more recent addition is the statue of tennis legend and humanitarian Arthur Ashe, a Richmond native and the first black man to win Wimbledon.

Though the Revolutionary and Civil wars certainly helped mold Richmond, the city has built on its past to become a modern, progressive destination. The downtown area, in particular, has undergone a revival. Shockoe Slip, once a warehouse district, is now the center of Richmond's nightlife scene. Nearby Shockoe Bottom also boasts nightclubs as well as trendy warehouse apartments. Jackson Ward, a historically African-American neighborhood, was home to Maggie Walker, the first woman to found a U.S. bank, and celebrated tap dancer Bill "Bojangles" Robinson.

Just west is the Fan District, so-called because its streets "fan out" from the downtown core. The genteel residential area, a mix of affluent Richmonders and Virginia Commonwealth University students, is known for its Victorian homes and shady lanes.

Must Do: AAA Editor's Picks

- Explore 🐝 **Maymont** (2201 Shields Lake Dr.), a dairy farm-turned-Gilded Age showstopper that has been enjoyed as a public park and museum since 1925. The 100-acre site on the James River, once the home of business leader James H. Dooley and his wife, has got it all: a luxurious 33-room mansion, zoological exhibits, historical carriages, meticulously groomed gardens and more than a few captivated guests.

- Lose count at 🐝 **The Museum of the Confederacy** (1201 E. Clay St.), whose imposing collection of relics, manuscripts and photographs includes 1,500 decorative objects, 550 flags, 177 firearms and 150 paintings. After viewing the displays, tour the adjacent 🐝 **The White House of the Confederacy.** During 40-minute guided tours, docents lead visitors through this gray-stuccoed Court End mansion, which Confederate President Jefferson Davis and his family inhabited 1861-65.

- Take in Grace Arents' gift to the city, the 🐝 **Lewis Ginter Botanical Garden** (1800 Lakeside Ave.). In her will, the green-thumbed philanthropist stipulated that a botanical garden be established on the property in honor of her uncle Lewis Ginter, a local businessman who bought the site in 1884. Today, the year-round site attracts both locals and out-of-towners with more than a dozen themed gardens and a striking conservatory crowned by a 63-foot-tall dome.

- Catch a second-run flick for $1.99 at **The Byrd Theatre** (2908 W. Cary St.), a restored 1920s movie palace in the funky Carytown shopping district. Go on a Saturday, when an organist named Bob puts on a rocking pre-show recital on a "Mighty Wurlitzer," a pipe organ originally designed to accompany silent films.

- Conserve your souvenir shopping fund at the 🐝 **Virginia Museum of Fine Arts** (200 N. Boulevard), where admission to the permanent collection of more than 23,000 works—from French Impressionist paintings to glittering Fabergé eggs—is always free.

- Revel in all things touristy in **Capitol Square,** between 9th, Governor, Broad and Bank streets. Ask a passerby to snap a pic of you with the Washington Monument as your backdrop. Pick up brochures at the state visitor center in the 1825 Bell Tower. Take a guided tour of the neoclassical 🐝 **Virginia State Capitol** (1000 Bank St.), then hit up the gift shop for "Virginia is for Lovers" shot glasses, paperweights etched with the state seal and a wide selection of presidential bobbleheads.

- Enjoy a hair-raising day o' fun at 🐝 **Kings Dominion** (16000 Theme Park Dr. in Doswell), where coasters with names like Dominator and Intimidator 305 attract would-be daredevils.

- Walk along tree-shaded **Monument Avenue.** Located in the heart of the historic Fan District, the architecturally noteworthy residential street boasts statues of Confederate heroes, including generals Robert E. Lee and Thomas J. "Stonewall" Jackson; the "Pathfinder of the Seas," Matthew Fontaine Maury; and Richmond-born tennis champ Arthur Ashe.

- Riddle me this: What do a pair of 19th-century boot hooks, a lock of hair glued to the back of an envelope, and a stuffed raven (come on, this one's a dead giveaway) have in common? All are exhibits at the **Poe Museum** (1914 E. Main St.), which relates the life of onetime Richmond resident Edgar Allan Poe.

- Tour **Richmond National Battlefield Park.** Headquartered in Richmond, the park encompasses Civil War battlefields in Hanover, Henrico and Chesterfield counties. Get out and stretch your legs during the 60-mile drive at the **Fort Harrison Visitor Center** (8621 Battlefield Park Rd.), the **Civil War Visitor Center at Tredegar Iron Works** (470 Tredegar St.), the **Chimborazo Medical Museum** (3215 E. Broad St.) and **The American Civil War Museum at Historic Tredegar** (500 Tredegar St.).

Virginia Museum of Fine Arts

Richmond 1-day Itinerary

AAA editors suggest these activities for a great short vacation experience.

Morning

- It's tough choosing between the seasonally changing French toast recipe and the crawfish hollandaise sauce-smothered egg and fried catfish platter at **The Black Sheep** (901 W. Marshall St.). Plus, a few hard-to-resist lunch items are thrown into the mix beginning at 11 a.m., with most patrons targeting the sub-style "battleships" served on supersize French baguettes.

- From The Black Sheep it's less than 2 miles south to **Hollywood Cemetery** (412 S. Cherry St.), the final resting place of two U.S. presidents (James Monroe and John Tyler) as well as Confederate President Jefferson Davis. In addition to elaborate mausoleums and tombstones, the graveyard safeguards a 90-foot-high pyramid honoring 18,000 fallen Confederate soldiers, some of whom are said to haunt the grounds.

- Spend the rest of your morning (and, if you're really interested in the subject, your afternoon) learning about Richmond's past life as the capital of the Confederate States of America. Just a short jaunt east of Hollywood Cemetery are the **Civil War Visitor Center at Tredegar Iron Works** (470 Tredegar St.), the main visitor center for **Richmond National Battlefield Park**, and **The American Civil War Museum at Historic Tredegar** (500 Tredegar St.), which offers Confederate, Union and African-American perspectives on the 4-year conflict.

Afternoon

- Civil War buffs should certainly check out the impressive 15,000-piece collection of ⚑ **The Museum of the Confederacy** (1201 E. Clay St.), along with ⚑ **The White House of the Confederacy.** Both the museum and the South's former executive mansion are within walking distance to several other historic sites and attractions, including the ⚑ **Virginia State Capitol** (1000 Bank St.) and ⚑ **The Valentine** (1015 E. Clay St.).

- When hunger strikes, **Millie's Diner** (2603 E. Main St.), flaunting a righteous compilation of 45s and old-timey Wall-O-Matic jukebox selectors, is a good bet. FYI: Seats at this tiny joint go quick, especially during brunch hours.

- As an alternative to the game plan above, make your way to the Fan District. Despite the parking headaches of the Fan, the grandma-approved boxed lunches from **Sally Bell's Kitchen** (2337 W. Broad St.) are worth the stop. On weekdays, polite Virginians form ranks outside this tiny Richmond institution founded in the 1920s. Half the fun is in scooting off the butcher's string and peeling back the wax paper to reveal a sandwich, a deviled egg, potato or macaroni salad, a cheese wafer and an upside-down

The Jefferson Hotel

cupcake.

- After refueling, while away your remaining daylight hours at ⚑ **Maymont** (2201 Shields Lake Dr.), whose manicured gardens and 12,000-square-foot mansion will have you daydreaming about winning the Virginia Lottery. The ethereal Gilded Age estate is on the banks of the James River.

Evening

- Change into your stepping out clothes and spend the evening in Shockoe Slip. Once the city's mercantile hub, the historic district flaunting Italianate-style brick and iron front buildings is now the epicenter of Richmond nightlife.

- A funkier bar scene continues down the hill into Shockoe Bottom, where refurbished warehouses now accommodate hip cafés, taverns and other businesses. Chill out at a manly wood-paneled watering hole or see a band play at a divey live music venue. If your dining tastes swing toward the casual end of the spectrum, duck into **Bottoms Up Pizza** (1700 Dock St.), a local hangout celebrated for tasty pies and, thanks to its location beneath the railroad tracks, raucous urban atmosphere.

- For a more upscale meal, reserve a candlelit table at **Julep's, New Southern Cuisine** (420 E. Grace St.), housed in a former lumber storehouse. Or, rub shoulders with Richmond VIPs at **Lemaire;** heralded for its farm-to-table approach, this special occasions spot is in downtown Richmond's lavish 19th-century masterpiece **The Jefferson Hotel** (101 W. Franklin St.).

Arriving
By Car

Richmond is served by numerous highways, including two major interstates. To the southwest, I-295 misses Richmond by sprouting off I-95 in Petersburg and catches up with I-95 north of Richmond in northern Henrico County; I-295 continues westward until it dead-ends into I-64 near Short Pump. The 3rd Street approach offers access to downtown on I-95 (Richmond-Petersburg Turnpike) from the north; take Broad Street if entering from the south.

East-west I-64 from Williamsburg enters the city from the southeast, joins up with I-95 downtown and then re-emerges south of Dumbarton near Joseph Bryan Park to continue its trek northwest toward Charlottesville. The 3rd Street exit off I-64 provides access to downtown if coming from the west; the 5th Street exit off I-64 takes you downtown from the east.

SR 150 semicircles the western side of the city, coming in from the south as the Chippenham Parkway on the James River in eastern Chesterfield County, crossing the James River to the west of Richmond as Parham Road, crossing I-64 northwest of the city and joining US 301/Chamberlayne Road north of Richmond near I-295.

US 1/301 enters the city from the south as Jefferson Davis Highway, crosses the James River over the Robert E. Lee Bridge, becomes Belvidere Street as it runs through downtown, and splits just north of I-95 (Richmond-Petersburg Parkway) with US 1 heading north as Brook Road and US 301 heading northeast as Chamberlayne Road.

Getting Around
Street System

Downtown Richmond is bounded by the James River to the south and I-95 to the north and east. Belvidere Street (US 1/301) is roughly the eastern edge of downtown. Broad Street (US 250) bisects the area.

Richmond resembles a grid pattern. Numbered streets 1st through 40th fall either in the East End (in the Church Hill and Shockoe Bottom area) or on the South Side (in the Forest Hill and Bainbridge area). Some streets change names, including Monument Avenue, which becomes W. Franklin Street at Stuart Circle; Malvern becomes Westwood as it crosses Broad Street; and The Boulevard flows into Hermitage Road northbound and Westover Hill Boulevard southbound as it traverses the river (it changes again to Belt Boulevard as it crosses Midlothian Turnpike).

Six bridges cross the James River east to west: I-95/Richmond-Petersburg Turnpike, Mayo's Bridge (US 360), Manchester Bridge (US 60), Robert E. Lee Bridge (US 1/301/Belvidere Street), Boulevard Bridge (SR 161) and Powhite Parkway (SR 76).

Many of the roads throughout Richmond are toll roads, including the Boulevard Bridge (SR 161) over the James River; SR 195/Downtown Expressway from Powhite Parkway to I-95; and the Powhite Parkway Bridge over the James River.

The city speed limit is 30 mph, or as posted. Rush hours are usually 7:30-9 a.m. and 4-6 p.m. Unless otherwise posted, a right turn on red is permitted.

Parking

Like any big city, Richmond has some downtown street parking; metered parking is limited and strictly monitored. If your car is towed from a downtown street, phone police information at (804) 646-5100 or Seibert's Towing at (804) 233-5757. Numerous parking lots and garages are available throughout the city. Hourly rates vary from $3-$5.

Shopping

There's lots more to shopping in Richmond than just malls.

Let's start with downtown. **Shockoe Slip,** originally a 1600s trading post near the James River, has been transformed into a trendy shopping area. The renovated 19th-century brick warehouses that line several blocks of cobblestoned E. Cary Street now house fashionable gift shops, boutiques, galleries, antique shops, restaurants and clubs.

Nearby **Shockoe Bottom,** just down the hill from Shockoe Slip, is a little less polished though still an interesting place to shop; expect shops similar to those in Shockoe Slip. A fixture in Shockoe Bottom is the **17th Street Farmers' Market**, at 17th and Main streets, one of the country's oldest public markets. You'll find homegrown fresh produce, meats, cheeses, baked items and crafts at the market, which is open Saturday and Sunday from early May to early December.

Carytown, on W. Cary Street between Boulevard and Thompson Street, is an eclectic area of small,

Farmers' market

Maymont estate

locally owned shops ranging from casual to funky to chic, all with a distinctly bohemian vibe. Numerous restaurants and sidewalk cafes are perfect spots for relaxing and people watching.

For a more upscale experience, head to **Libbie, Grove and Patterson,** a decidedly stylish area in the city's fashionable West End. The shops and restaurants locals refer to as "on the Avenues" are known for their service and attention to detail. Clothing boutiques, home goods stores and jewelers are among the avenues' specialty shops.

If you have an interest in collectibles, check out the **West End Antiques Mall** at 2004 Staples Mill Rd., in the **Crossroads Shopping Center** near W. Broad Street. You'll find an amazing assortment of treasures, including furniture, glassware, pottery, silver and jewelry in the mall's more than 250 booths. At the adjoining **Crossroads Art Center,** you can peruse the vibrant works of painters, sculptors and other creative types.

When you *are* looking for a classic mall experience, it's a short ride to **Chesterfield Towne Center,** built in 1975. Home to such national retailers as JCPenney, Macy's and Sears, the mall is about 12 miles southwest of downtown Richmond at US 60 (Midlothian Turnpike) and SR 147 (Huguenot Road). Another venue for browsing is **Short Pump Town Center,** about 16 miles northwest of downtown Richmond via I-95 N/I-64 W. The two-level, open-air mall draws savvy shoppers with names like Apple, Hollister and Urban Outfitters. Dick's Sporting Goods and Dillard's locations are anchors of both Short Pump Town Center and its rival, **Stony Point Fashion Park,** a fashion-forward outdoor shopping center about 12 miles west of downtown Richmond at 9200 Stony Point Pkwy. Stony Point also features a Saks Fifth Avenue as well as smaller upmarket chains like Anthropologie and Restoration Hardware.

Nightlife

If you're in Richmond and looking for nightlife, the place to be is **Shockoe Slip.** Founded as a trading post in the 1600s, the Slip grew to become Richmond's commercial center, aided by its proximity to the James River. This historic district, which roughly runs from 12th to 15th streets and from Main to Dock streets, maintains a late 19th-century feel. Restored brick warehouses along cobblestone streets are repurposed as hip restaurants and shops, taverns, offices and residences. Just down the hill is **Shockoe Bottom,** equally lively as a nightspot, but not as renovated and somewhat less chic than the Slip.

South of Shockoe Bottom in the Rocketts Landing neighborhood is **The Boathouse at Rocketts Landing** (4708 E. Old Main St.), which looks like a crystal structure rising out of the James River. This contemporary glass-enclosed spot with views of the river on all sides is a perfect place at sunset to have a drink on the open-air deck and admire the Richmond skyline. Phone (804) 622-2628.

The place to go for concerts in Richmond is **The National** (708 E. Broad St.). Both local and nationally known performers play dates at this beautifully restored three-tiered venue. Phone (804) 612-1900.

Big Events

February is a busy month in the capital, with the **Richmond Camping RV Expo** early in the month and the **Richmond Boat Show** mid-month; both are held at the **Richmond Raceway Complex.**

In April, **Dominion Family Easter** draws families with young kids to the **Maymont** estate with Easter egg hunts, puppet and magic shows and hands-on activities. Occurring along four blocks of Monument Avenue every Easter Sunday, the **Easter on Parade** event includes arts and crafts vendors, music and a petting zoo.

Historic Garden Week takes place throughout the state at various times in late April. During this special event, private homes and gardens, and historic venues are opened up to the public for viewing. In early May **Byrd Park** is home to **Arts in the Park,** one of the largest outdoor craft shows on the East Coast.

In November the **Science Museum of Virginia** presents the **Craft and Design Show,** during which more than 50 craftspeople display their wares. Also in November is the **Capital of The Confederacy Civil War Show,** with exhibitors and vendors setting up shop at the Richmond Raceway Complex. Running from late November to mid-January at the **Lewis Ginter Botanical Garden, Dominion GardenFest of Lights** features holiday lights and decorations, along with plenty of fun family-friendly activities.

Sports & Rec

Centrally located, Richmond offers a wealth of recreational opportunities. To the west are the **Blue**

Ridge and Shenandoah mountains and the chance for such winter sports as skiing and sledding. To the east are Chesapeake Bay and the Atlantic Ocean where anglers and water sports enthusiasts alike can revel in the miles of shoreline.

The James River is a great place to lure in smallmouth bass; catfish, bream, largemouth bass and muskie also can be caught. Saltwater fishing can be found nearby in the Hampton Roads area and in Chesapeake Bay. For information about fishing licenses contact the Virginia Department of Game and Inland Fisheries; phone (804) 367-1000.

Richmond boasts the only urban class IV rapids in the country. Rafting and tubing trips on the James River are available through River City Adventures; phone (804) 233-4000. Riverside Outfitters, (804) 560-0068, also offers rafting trips as well as tube, canoe and kayak rentals.

Some 60 parks can be found throughout the greater Richmond area. Some of the activities available at the parks include tennis, bicycling, hiking, picnicking, swimming, boating and horseback riding. For information contact the Department of Parks and Recreation; phone (804) 646-5733 in Richmond, (804) 748-1623 in Chesterfield County, (804) 501-7275 in Henrico County or (804) 365-4695 in Hanover County.

James River Park, at 22nd Street and Riverside Drive, is a good place to fish or hike. As part of the park, Belle Isle is reached via a footbridge on Tredegar Street or from the parking lot on 22nd Street. The island has walking trails with interpretive signs, a floating fishing pier and the opportunity for kayaking, canoeing, bicycling and rock climbing.

Pocahontas State Park (see Recreation Areas Chart), in nearby Chesterfield, offers 7,920 acres of outdoor opportunities for camping, swimming, hiking, boating and fishing.

More than 20 public and private golf courses can be found within the Richmond area. Some of the public and semi-private courses are Birkdale, (804) 739-8800, 8511 Royal Birkdale Dr. in Chesterfield; The Crossings, (804) 261-0000, 800 Virginia Center Pkwy. in Glen Allen; Glenwood, (804) 226-1793, 3100 Creighton Rd.; The Hollows, (804) 883-5381, 14501 Greenwood Church Rd. in Montpelier; and Sycamore Creek, (804) 784-3544, 1991 Manakin Rd. in Manakin-Sabot.

The Richmond Kickers play soccer in the United Soccer League's Professional Division at Richmond City Stadium, 3201 Maplewood Ave.; phone (804) 644-5425 for schedule and tickets.

With four major colleges and universities in the area, Richmond is home to many rivalrous collegiate games. Basketball and football are popular at the University of Richmond where the Spiders play ball in Robins Center and Robins Stadium, respectively; phone (804) 289-8388. The Virginia Commonwealth University Rams play basketball at the Stuart C. Siegel Center; phone (804) 828-7267. The Panthers at Virginia Union University play football on campus at Hovey Field and basketball at the

Barco-Stevens Hall; phone (804) 342-1484. A variety of sports is offered at Randolph-Macon College in Ashland, including baseball, football and both men's and women's soccer, basketball, tennis, lacrosse and field hockey; phone (804) 752-7223.

Richmond is home to the Richmond International Raceway, which hosts several NASCAR automobile racing events throughout the year. Located at the Richmond Raceway Complex, the raceway houses some 105,000 reserved seats; phone (866) 455-7223 for tickets and information.

Performing Arts

Built upon a rich history, Richmond's cultural scene began in 1786 with the opening of the city's first theater. The Altria Theater, 6 N. Laurel St., was formerly known as the Mosque because of its resemblance to a Moslem Temple. Built in 1926 by the Shriners, the 3,500-seat theater today offers performances by national touring companies; phone (804) 646-0546. On the corner of 6th and Grace streets, Dominion Arts Center is home to three performance venues: Carpenter Theatre, Libby S. Gottwald Playhouse and Rhythm Hall. Phone (804) 592-3330 for ticket and event information.

The Byrd Theatre, 2908 W. Cary St., was built in 1928 and shows second-run movies as well as classic films; phone (804) 353-9911. The Sara Belle and Neil November Theatre, 114 W. Broad St., originally was founded in 1911 as the Empire Theatre and underwent

James River rafting

restoration in the early 1990s. It is now home to the **Virginia Repertory Theatre** company, which also stages productions at **The Children's Theatre at Willow Lawn,** in The Shops at Willow Lawn at 1601 Willow Lawn Dr., and at **November Theatre,** 114 W. Broad St. For more information, phone the Virginia Rep box office at (804) 282-2620.

Offering five major concerts and several smaller venues, the **Richmond Symphony** is for classical music lovers; phone (804) 788-1212. The **Richmond Philharmonic** also presents five concerts a year throughout town; phone (804) 673-7400 for information. Concerts by top-name performers regularly take place at the **Richmond Coliseum,** 601 E. Leigh St.; phone (804) 780-4970 for the box office.

The **Richmond Ballet,** the commonwealth's only professional troupe, performs year-round and travels throughout Virginia presenting its repertoire of both classical and contemporary works; phone (804) 344-0906.

ATTRACTIONS

 For a complete list of attractions, visit AAA.com/travelguides/attractions

AGECROFT HALL is at 4305 Sulgrave Rd. in Windsor Farms. Built in the late 15th century in Lancashire, England, this Tudor manor house was dismantled in the late 1920s and shipped to its present location overlooking the James River. Outstanding features include the original hand-carved oak paneling, leaded-glass windows and furnishings from the Tudor and early Stuart periods (1580-1640). The house is surrounded by 23 acres of lawns, woodlands and several Elizabethan gardens.

Tours begin with a 12-minute film. **Hours:** Tues.-Sat. 10-4, Sun. 12:30-5. Closed major holidays. **Cost:** $8; $7 (ages 65+); $5 (students with ID); free (ages 0-5 and active military with ID). **Phone:** (804) 353-4241. GT

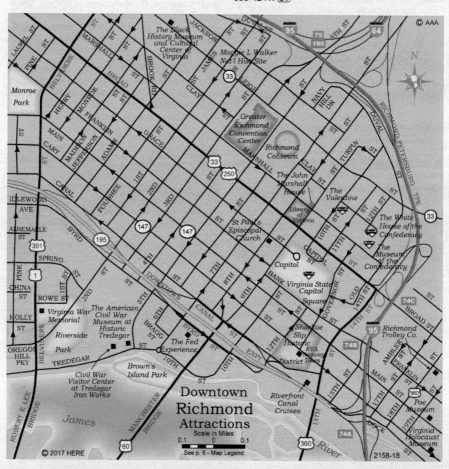

Downtown Richmond Attractions

Scale in Miles
0.1   0   0.1

See p. 6 - Map Legend

© 2017 HERE

© AAA

2158-18

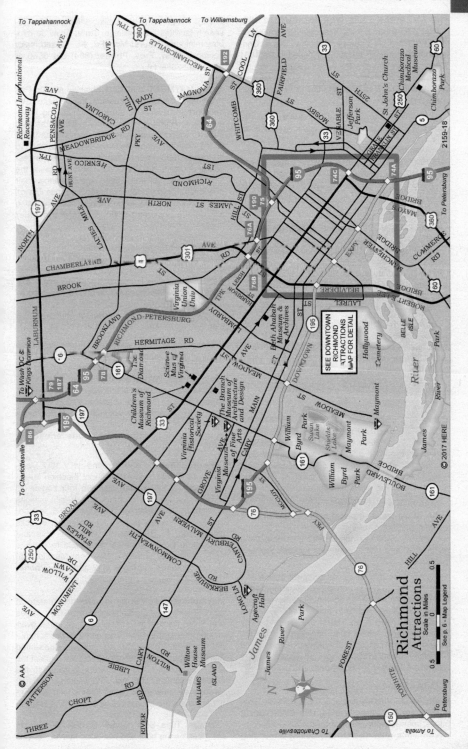

Richmond
Attractions

Scale in Miles

See p. 6 - Map Legend

© 2017 HERE

© AAA

THE AMERICAN CIVIL WAR MUSEUM AT HIS-TORIC TREDEGAR, 500 Tredegar St., interprets the Civil War from three perspectives: Union, Confederate and African-American. Housed in the 1861 Tredegar Gun Foundry, the center's flagship exhibit, In the Cause of Liberty, discusses the war's causes, course and legacies through films, interactive displays and artifacts.

The center affords picturesque views of the James River and is a national historic landmark located near the joint visitor center for the American Civil War Museum and Richmond National Battlefield Park *(see place listing p. 229).* **Time:** Allow 1 hour minimum. **Hours:** Daily 9-5. Closed Jan. 1, Thanksgiving, Christmas and Dec. 31. **Cost:** $10; $8.50 (ages 62+); $5 (ages 6-17). **Phone:** (804) 649-1861.

CHILDREN'S MUSEUM OF RICHMOND-SHORT PUMP, 11800 W. Broad St. at Short Pump Town Center, features 13 "learning through play" activity zones, including an art studio and a puppet theater. Geared toward children under age 6, the hands-on museum also features a miniature grocery store, diner and farm. Also popular among pint-size visitors is the Dino Dig Pit.

Time: Allow 2 hours minimum. **Hours:** Daily 9:30-5. Closed Jan. 1, Easter, July 4, Thanksgiving and Christmas. **Cost:** $9; $8 (ages 60+ and military with ID); free (ages 0-11 months). **Phone:** (804) 474-7070.

KINGS DOMINION—see Doswell p. 101.

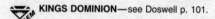 **LEWIS GINTER BOTANICAL GARDEN** is 1.5 mi. n. of I-95 exit 80 (Lakeside Ave./Hilliard Rd.) at 1800 Lakeside Ave. This popular garden offers year-round beauty on a historic property of more than 50 landscaped acres. A classical domed conservatory contains changing displays, including more than 200 orchids in bloom.

More than a dozen themed gardens include the Asian Valley, featuring plants native to East Asia; a fountain garden; a rose garden with 1,800 fragrant species; a Victorian garden; a healing garden; and a wetland environment explored via bridges and boardwalks.

Also on-site is a seasonal butterfly house and children's garden, which offers a wheelchair-accessible tree house, an adventure pathway, an international village and sand and water play areas. **Hours:** Daily 9-5 (also Thurs. 5-9, June 1-early Sept.). Butterfly house open mid-Apr. to mid-Oct. Closed Thanksgiving, Christmas Eve and Christmas. **Cost:** $13; $11 (ages 55+); $10 (military with ID); $8 (ages 3-12). **Phone:** (804) 262-9887.

LIBRARY OF VIRGINIA is at 800 E. Broad St. Treasures from the library's extensive collection of books, manuscripts, maps and artwork—the commonwealth's records from the colony's founding through the present—are available to the public. Research facilities are available. **Time:** Allow 30 minutes minimum. **Hours:** Mon.-Fri. 9-5. Closed major holidays. **Cost:** Free. **Phone:** (804) 692-3500 or (804) 692-3588.

MAYMONT is at 2201 Shields Lake Dr. Part public park, part museum, this beautiful 100-acre property is a treasured gem among Richmonders. Popular with picnicking couples and parents toting young kids, the lush site boasting rolling hills and sunny meadows was bequeathed to the city in 1925. Prior to that, it was the country estate of James and Sallie Dooley, who purchased the land in 1886; typifying Gilded Age opulence, their residence, Maymont Mansion *(see attraction listing),* was finished in 1893. Other historical buildings also are on-site, including a stone barn and a water tower.

The elegant, manicured grounds feature such specialty gardens as Marie's Butterfly Trail, Jack's Vegetable Garden and a herb garden. The Italian Garden showcases fountains, sculptures and a long pergola, while the Japanese Garden is accented by a 40-foot waterfall, stone lanterns, paths and bridges. In addition, an arboretum shelters more than 200 exotic species of trees and plants.

Maymont also includes the Robins Nature & Visitor Center *(see attraction listing)* and a farm, home to chickens, cows, goats, sheep, rabbits and other animals. Wildlife exhibits featuring native Virginia fauna, including black bears, a bobcat and various birds of prey, are scattered throughout a 40-acre valley. A carriage house built in 1904 displays a collection of period vehicles. Carriage rides are available by appointment; phone ahead for information.

Hours: Grounds and gardens daily 10-7, Apr.-Sept.; 10-5, rest of year. Maymont Mansion Tues.-Sun. noon-5; last guided mansion tour begins 30 minutes before closing. Farm and wildlife exhibits daily 10-5. Nature center Tues.-Sun. 10-5; last admission 15 minutes before closing. Indoor exhibits closed Jan. 1, Thanksgiving, Christmas Eve and Christmas. **Cost:** Grounds, farm, wildlife exhibits and gardens by donation. Maymont Mansion $5. Nature center $4; $3 (ages 4-12 and 60+). **Phone:** (804) 358-7166.

Maymont Mansion is on the Maymont estate at 2201 Shields Lake Dr. Completed in 1893 by James and Sallie Dooley, the stately 33-room home overlooking the James River was gifted to the community in 1925. Today, the art- and antiques-filled manor is open to the public, with guided tours of the luxurious upstairs rooms offered. In contrast, the Dooleys' domestic staff lived and worked in the austere belowstairs; eight period rooms with informational panels are accessible by self-guiding tour.

Hours: Tues.-Sun. noon-5. Guided house tours are given on the hour and half-hour; last tour begins

30 minutes before closing. Closed Jan. 1, Thanksgiving, Christmas Eve and Christmas. **Cost:** $5. **Phone:** (804) 358-7166. GT

Robins Nature & Visitor Center is at Maymont, 2201 Shields Lake Dr. Dedicated to native Virginia wildlife, the center offers a glimpse into life on the James River. Thirteen giant, linked aquariums are filled with turtles, fish and river otters. Reptiles take center stage in two galleries, the American Alligators Exhibit and the Venomous Snakes Exhibit. Interactive displays also help educate visitors about the local ecosystem. **Hours:** Tues.-Sun. 10-5; last admission 15 minutes before closing. Closed Jan. 1, Thanksgiving, Christmas Eve and Christmas. **Cost:** $4; $3 (ages 4-12 and 60+). **Phone:** (804) 358-7166. GT ⓘ 🏧

THE MUSEUM OF THE CONFEDERACY is 2 blks. n. of Broad St. at 1201 E. Clay St. Founded in 1890, the museum interprets the Civil War through one of the largest collections of Confederate artifacts, paintings and documents.

Some 20,000 artifacts include military equipment and clothing that belonged to Confederate leaders, among them Jefferson Davis, Robert E. Lee, J.E.B. Stuart and Thomas J. "Stonewall" Jackson; artifacts documenting the lives of free and enslaved African-Americans; art illustrating the Confederate experience; and flags relating to the Confederate armed forces and government. On display is the 1869 painting "The Last Meeting of Lee and Jackson," a 15-foot painting depicting the moment Jackson went off to Chancellorsville, where he was mortally wounded.

Free parking is available at the Virginia Commonwealth University Medical Center visitor/patient parking deck on 12th Street (museum will validate parking slip). **Time:** Allow 1 hour minimum. **Hours:** Daily 10-5. Closed Jan. 1, Thanksgiving, Christmas and Dec. 31. **Cost:** $10; $8.50 (ages 62+); $5 (ages 6-17). Combination ticket with The White House of the Confederacy $18; $16 (ages 62+); $9 (ages 6-17). **Phone:** (804) 649-1861.

The White House of the Confederacy is next to The Museum of the Confederacy at 1201 E. Clay St. This was the executive mansion of President Jefferson Davis and his family during the Civil War. The house was built in Richmond's fashionable Court End neighborhood in 1818. The neoclassical structure was expanded over the years; in the process a third story was added as were a carriage house and stable. Wallpaper, gasoliers, carpet and draperies were among the decorative enhancements.

When the capitol of the Confederacy moved to Richmond, the city purchased the home and leased it to the Confederate States of America. And, although the building came to be known as The White House of the Confederacy, it is actually not white at all, but a light gray color.

The mansion became the hub of Richmond's social and political scene, and visitors were welcome at public receptions. Because of health issues, Davis used his home office to conduct state and military business, and cabinet members and military advisors were frequent guests.

A 45-minute guided tour, which departs from The Museum of the Confederacy lobby, starts in the mansion's basement and explores the first and second floors. Visitors see the first-floor entrance hall, parlor, library and elegant dining room, where formal dinners and cabinet meetings were held. Davis' office, his secretary's office, and the family's private quarters, including a large nursery, are on the second floor.

As the city has grown over the years, the house is now virtually surrounded by the VCU Medical Center and other office buildings. **Time:** Allow 1 hour minimum. **Hours:** Guided tours are given daily; phone ahead for departure times. Closed Jan. 1, Thanksgiving, Christmas and Dec. 31. **Cost:** $10; $8 (ages 62+); $6 (ages 7-13). Combination ticket with The Museum of the Confederacy $18; $16 (ages 62+); $9 (ages 6-17). **Phone:** (804) 649-1861. GT

POE MUSEUM is at 1914 E. Main St. Although Edgar Allan Poe never resided in the 1737 Old Stone House—Richmond's oldest residence—he lived and worked in the area for much of his life. The museum features a complex of four buildings that house Poe's manuscripts, clothing, childhood bed and rare first editions, along with a large-scale model of early 19th-century Richmond focusing on Poe's life in the city. **Hours:** Tues.-Sat. 10-5, Sun. 11-5. Closed major holidays. **Cost:** $6; $5 (ages 60+ and students and military with ID). **Phone:** (804) 648-5523. GT

SCIENCE MUSEUM OF VIRGINIA is off US 95 and US 64, at 2500 W. Broad St. The museum, housed in a former train station built in 1919, offers more than 250 hands-on exhibits as well as demonstrations, displays and touring exhibitions. An IMAX theater features large-format films and multimedia shows.

Hours: Mon.-Sat. 9:30-5, Sun. 11:30-5, Memorial Day-Labor Day; Tues.-Sat. 9:30-5, Sun. 11:30-5, rest of year. IMAX schedule varies; phone ahead. Closed Thanksgiving, Christmas Eve and Christmas. **Cost:** Museum $14.50; $13.50 (ages 4-12 and 60+); free (ages 0-3 with adult and active military with ID). IMAX film $9; free (ages 0-3 with adult). Combination ticket $18.50; $17.50 (ages 4-12 and 60+). **Phone:** (804) 864-1400. ⊟ ⓘ

THE VALENTINE is at 1015 E. Clay St. in the Court End district. The museum's founder, Mann S. Valentine Jr., bequeathed his personal collection of art and artifacts to the city in 1892, along with ownership of the 1812 John Wickham House. With its focus on the history of

Richmond and the people who shaped it, the history center offers changing exhibits, tours and a research library.

Displays include decorative and industrial arts, paintings, prints, manuscripts and books. Complementing these artifacts are more than half a million photographs of the city and the surrounding area. The museum also features a dynamic new permanent exhibition documenting the city's history entitled This is Richmond, Virginia.

The Wickham House was built by John and Elizabeth Wickham, one of Richmond's wealthiest couples, in 1812. Guided tours of the house address the lives of numerous residents, black and white, including the Wickhams' many children and enslaved servants. The elegant house, with its magnificent freestanding stairway, rare neoclassical wall paintings and carved ornamentation, typifies late Federal architecture.

Hours: Tues.-Sun. and Mon. holidays 10-5. Closed Jan. 1, Thanksgiving, Christmas Eve and Christmas. **Cost:** (includes museum galleries, 1812 John Wickham House and Edward V. Valentine Sculpture Studio) $10; $8 (ages 55+ and students with ID); free (ages 0-18 and active military with ID). **Phone:** (804) 649-0711. ⒼⓉ

VIRGINIA HISTORICAL SOCIETY is at 428 N. Boulevard. The museum's impressive neoclassical building was built in 1913. Known locally as Battle Abbey, its original function was to serve as a memorial to the state's Confederate soldiers and to store Confederate records. Several enlargements later, it is now a repository of 4 centuries worth of Virginia's historical treasures. Included are 13 gallery spaces, a 5,200-square-foot reading room and seven permanent exhibitions providing insights into the state's past.

The Story of Virginia, an American Experience, explores the development of Virginia from prehistoric times to the present. The 10,500-square-foot exhibit space features more than 1,000 objects, films and oral history interviews, and interactive displays that touch on such themes as electrification, urbanization, the Civil War, World War II and the civil rights movement. Four Seasons of the Confederacy: Murals by Charles Hoffbauer showcases memorial military murals painted in the early 20th-century by Hoffbauer, a Paris-born artist who immigrated to America in 1909. The works illustrate such dramatic Civil War-era scenes as J.E.B. Stuart leading his cavalrymen through Virginia woods and an artillery battery retreating in the snow.

The museum's vast collection also includes nearly 300,000 prints and photographs; more than 1,500 paintings; and textiles, silver, furniture and weaponry.

Time: Allow 2 hours minimum. **Hours:** Museum galleries daily 10-5; closed Jan. 1, Easter, July 4, Thanksgiving and Christmas. Library Mon.-Sat. 10-5; closed major holidays. **Cost:** Free. Admission

may be charged during special events. **Phone:** (804) 358-4901. Ⓐ

VIRGINIA HOLOCAUST MUSEUM is in Shockoe Bottom at 2000 E. Cary St. The museum contains memorabilia, archives, audiovisual presentations and re-creations of scenes related to the Holocaust. Also on-site are a replicated Nuremberg courtroom (the original was the setting of the Nazi International War Crimes Trials of 1945-46) and a re-created, full-size Chor Schul (synagogue) from Kovno, Lithuania. A special exhibit is dedicated to the Ipson family, who fled from the Kovno Ghetto and survived in an underground bunker for 6 months. Visitors can climb into a model of the 9-by-12-foot hiding place, which sheltered 13 people. The Modern Genocide Gallery is open to visitors, though construction is ongoing.

Time: Allow 1 hour minimum. **Hours:** Mon.-Fri. 10-5, Sat.-Sun. 11-5. Closed Jan. 1, Easter, first day of Rosh Hashanah, Yom Kippur, Thanksgiving, Christmas Eve, Christmas and Dec. 31. **Cost:** Donations. Not recommended for children ages 0-10. **Phone:** (804) 257-5400.

VIRGINIA MUSEUM OF FINE ARTS is at 200 N. Boulevard. Ancient to contemporary art is represented at this museum, with more than 35,000 works of art spanning 5,000 years of world history. The collection includes Art Nouveau, Art Deco, Fabergé, Impressionist, Post-Impressionist, American, British, Modern and Contemporary paintings, prints, jewelry, decorative arts and sculpture.

Among the highlights are the Mellon Collection of French Art; the Lewis Collection of Late 19th- and Early 20th-Century Decorative Arts; European and American masterpieces, including works by Goya, Sargent and Monet; ancient Egyptian, Greek and Roman art, including a life-size marble statue of the emperor Caligula; one of the world's leading collections of the art of South Asia; African art; and an extensive array of English silver.

In addition the museum features a sculpture garden as well as special exhibitions, educational activities, studio classes and concerts. **Time:** Allow 2 hours minimum. **Hours:** Daily 10-5 (also Thurs.-Fri. 5-9). **Cost:** Free. A fee is charged for special exhibitions, lectures and concerts. **Phone:** (804) 340-1400. ⒾⒾ

VIRGINIA STATE CAPITOL is on Capitol Square at 1000 Bank St. Designed by Thomas Jefferson, this "Temple on the Hill" was first occupied in 1788 and is still home to America's oldest elected legislature.

The U.S. Bill of Rights was ratified here in 1791. Among other significant American events, former Vice President Aaron Burr was tried for treason at the Capitol in 1807, and Robert E. Lee received his commission as commander of the Virginia forces in 1861. Winston Churchill addressed the Virginia Assembly in 1946, and L. Douglas Wilder was sworn in as the country's first elected African-American governor in 1990.

Visitors will find important historical statuary and paintings, rare exhibit objects and beautifully restored old and new legislative chambers. A magnificent statue of George Washington stands under the interior dome of the two-story rotunda, surrounded by marble busts of seven other Virginia-born presidents.

Metered street parking and parking garages are nearby. **Hours:** Mon.-Sat. 9-5, Sun. 1-5. Guided tours are offered daily. Last tour begins 1 hour before closing. Closed Jan. 1, Thanksgiving and Christmas. **Cost:** Free. **Phone:** (804) 698-1788. (GT) (Y)

VIRGINIA WAR MEMORIAL is at the n. end of Robert E. Lee Bridge at 621 S. Belvidere St. (US 1). Overlooking the Richmond skyline and the James River, the memorial honors nearly 12,000 Virginians killed in World War II, Korea, Vietnam, the Persian Gulf and the Global War on Terrorism. The memorial includes the inspiring glass and marble Shrine of Memory.

Military artifacts, including uniforms, weapons and medals, are displayed in the Paul and Phyllis Galanti Education Center, which also features an auditorium, a lecture hall and an outdoor amphitheater. A theater features the film "Into Battle" and the video series "Virginians at War." **Time:** Allow 1 hour minimum. **Hours:** Site daily 5 a.m.-midnight. Visitor center Mon.-Sat. 9-4, Sun. noon-4. Closed Jan. 1, Easter, Thanksgiving and Christmas. **Cost:** Donations. **Phone:** (804) 786-2060.

Sightseeing
Boat Tours

RIVERFRONT CANAL CRUISES is at 139 Virginia St. (on the Canal Walk at 14th and Dock sts.). These narrated cruises of the James River and Kanawha Canal highlight Richmond's canal system, which dates to 1789, and the development of Richmond's waterfront. Many historic sites can be seen during the 40-minute narrated sightseeing excursion, which also offers glimpses of the city skyline; the floodwall and lock systems; and local wildlife, including egrets, great blue herons and turtles.

Time: Allow 1 hour minimum. **Hours:** Cruises depart on the hour Mon.-Fri. noon-7, Sat. 11-8, Sun. 11-7, May-Sept.; Thurs.-Sat. noon-7, Sun. noon-5, in Oct.; Fri.-Sat. noon-7, Sun. noon-5, in Apr.; Fri.-Sun. noon-5, Nov. 1 to mid-Nov. (weather permitting). Phone ahead to confirm schedule. **Cost:** $8; $6 (ages 5-12 and 65+). **Phone:** (804) 649-2800 or (804) 788-6466. (GT)

Segway Tours

RVA SEGWAY TOURS departs from 1301 E. Cary St. Guided 1- or 2-hour Segway tours describe Richmond's architectural standouts, including such local landmarks as St. Paul's Episcopal Church, the Federal Reserve building and the Virginia State Capitol.

Virginia State Capitol

Along the way, guides impart their knowledge of local history as well as fun tidbits, facts and stories about the area. Among the wide variety of special-interest tours are the Public Art Tour, the Lincoln's Walk Tour, the Hollywood Cemetery Tour and the Black History Tour.

Guests must arrive 30 minutes before the scheduled tour time for a safety lesson. Comfortable, flat-bottom, closed-toed shoes are recommended. Tours are not recommended for pregnant women. **Time:** Allow 2 hours, 30 minutes minimum. **Hours:** Two-hour tours depart daily at 10 and 2. One-hour tours depart daily at 12:30 and 5. Phone ahead to confirm schedule. **Cost:** $50-$68. Ages 0-13 are not permitted on the tour. Reservations are recommended. **Phone:** (804) 343-1850. (GT)

Walking Tours

Richmond History Tours, a service of The Valentine *(see attraction listing p. 203)*, offers 380 guided walking tours of downtown and surrounding areas April through October. The tours cover such historic sites as the Byrd Theatre, Carytown, Riverfront, Hollywood Cemetery, Shockoe Bottom, Church Hill, the Court End, Jackson Ward and Richmond's Wall Street. Year-round specialty bus tours also are offered; phone (804) 649-0711.

More than 30 markers and exhibits along Canal Walk, a 1.25-mile interpretive path, convey tidbits about Richmond's heritage. Stretching between 5th and 17th streets, the pathway is adjacent to the north bank of the James River. Visitors can view remnants of the James River and Kanawha Canal that once flowed westward 197 miles to the Allegheny Mountains. Highlights include views of Belle

Isle, Brown's Island, Tredegar Iron Works, and the James River and Kanawha Tidewater Connection Locks.

Belle Isle, once home to a Civil War prison camp, can be reached by the pedestrian bridge under the Lee Bridge at 7th and Tredegar streets. A 1-mile walking trail allows visitors to walk along the falls and view the historic earthworks. Brown's Island is the former site of the Confederate Laboratory that exploded in 1863, killing some 50 workers.

Visitors can view remnants of the buildings of Tredegar Iron Works, the most important iron works in the South during the Civil War. The armor used for the CSS *Virginia*, formerly the USS *Merrimac*, was manufactured at this plant.

Running along the James River, the Richmond Floodwall is a 1-mile-long concrete levee that varies in height from 7 feet to 30 feet. Highlights of the walk atop the levee include views of the river where walkers can spot various wildlife, including blue herons, Canada geese and turtles.

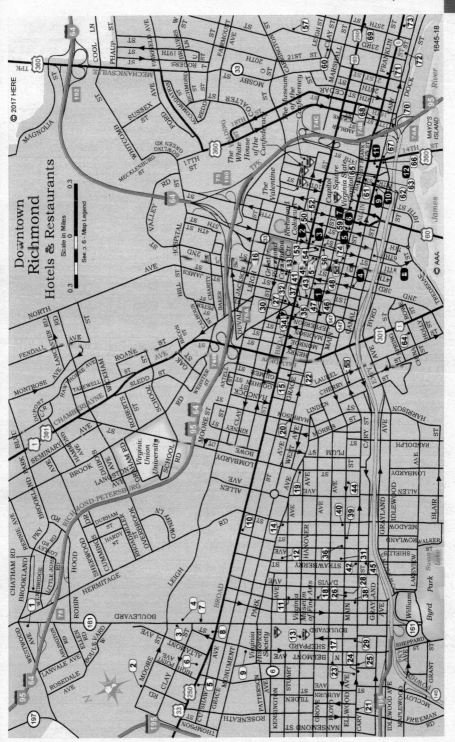

Downtown
Richmond
Hotels & Restaurants

Scale in Miles

See ▷ 6 - Map Legend

© 2017 HERE

1645-18

Downtown Richmond

This index helps you "spot" where approved hotels and restaurants are located on the corresponding detailed maps. Hotel daily rate range is for comparison only. Restaurant price range is a combination of lunch and/or dinner. Turn to the listing page for more information and consult display ads for special promotions.

 For more details, rates and reservations: **AAA.com/travelguides/hotels**

DOWNTOWN RICHMOND

Map Page	Hotels	Diamond Rated	Rate Range	Page
1 p. 207	**The Jefferson Hotel** *(See ad p. 222.)*	♦♦♦♦♦	$275-$455 SAVE	222
2 p. 207	**Richmond Marriott Downtown**	♦♦♦	$97-$320 SAVE	223
3 p. 207	**Hilton Richmond Downtown**	♦♦♦	$179-$299 SAVE	221
4 p. 207	Holiday Inn Express Downtown	♦♦	Rates not provided	221
5 p. 207	Hampton Inn & Suites by Hilton Richmond-Downtown	♦♦♦	Rates not provided	221
6 p. 207	Homewood Suites by Hilton Richmond-Downtown	♦♦♦	Rates not provided	221
7 p. 207	The Commonwealth	fyi	$199-$269	221
8 p. 207	**Delta Marriott Richmond Downtown**	♦♦♦	$159-$209 SAVE	221
9 p. 207	Omni Richmond Hotel	♦♦♦	Rates not provided	222
10 p. 207	**The Berkeley Hotel**	♦♦♦	$149-$269 SAVE	221
11 p. 207	**Residence Inn by Marriott Richmond Downtown**	♦♦♦	$71-$346 SAVE	222
12 p. 207	**Courtyard by Marriott Richmond Downtown**	♦♦♦	$108-$348 SAVE	221

Map Page	Restaurants	Diamond Rated	Cuisine	Price Range	Page
1 p. 207	Kitchen 64	♦♦	American	$8-$23	224
2 p. 207	The Dairy Bar	♦♦	American	$6-$10	223
3 p. 207	Fat Dragon	♦♦	Chinese	$10-$21	223
4 p. 207	**Buz and Neds Real Barbecue**	♦	Barbecue	$6-$16	223
5 p. 207	Lemon Cuisine of India	♦♦	Indian	$12-$16	224
6 p. 207	Lunch	♦♦	American	$8-$15	224
7 p. 207	En Su Boca	♦♦	Tex-Mex	$8-$11	223
8 p. 207	Peter Chang China Cafe	♦♦	Szechuan	$10-$22	224
9 p. 207	Akida	♦♦	Japanese Sushi	$7-$20	223
10 p. 207	The Savory Grain	♦♦	American	$7-$16	224
11 p. 207	Secco Wine Bar	♦♦♦	European	$11-$24	224
12 p. 207	Strawberry Street Cafe	♦♦	American	$6-$18	224
13 p. 207	Amuse	♦♦♦	New American	$16-$32	223
14 p. 207	Garnett's Cafe	♦♦	Sandwiches	$10	224
15 p. 207	The Black Sheep	♦♦	American	$8-$16	223
16 p. 207	The Rogue Gentlemen	♦♦♦	New American	$24-$30	224
17 p. 207	Belmont Food Shop	♦♦♦	Steak	$35	223
18 p. 207	Early Bird Biscuit Company	♦	Breads/Pastries Breakfast	$3-$8	223
19 p. 207	Kuba Kuba	♦♦	Cuban	$6-$20	224
20 p. 207	Edo's Squid	♦♦	Italian	$8-$35	223
21 p. 207	Amici Ristorante	♦♦♦	Northern Italian	$8-$28	223

Map Page	Restaurants (cont'd)	Diamond Rated	Cuisine	Price Range	Page
22 p. 207	Sally Bell's Kitchen	◆	Seafood Desserts	$6-$7	224
23 p. 207	Can Can Brasserie	◆◆◆	French	$11-$26	223
24 p. 207	Galaxy Diner	◆◆	American	$7-$10	224
25 p. 207	Farouk's House of India	◆◆	Indian	$7-$14	223
26 p. 207	Helen's	◆◆◆	American	$13-$26	224
27 p. 207	Saison	◆◆◆	American	$13-$23	224
28 p. 207	3 Monkeys Bar & Grill	◆◆	American	$9-$24	223
29 p. 207	Coppola's Deli	◆	Italian Deli	$8-$13	223
30 p. 207	Comfort	◆◆	Regional American	$10-$20	223
31 p. 207	Sticky Rice	◆◆	Japanese Sushi	$5-$10	224
32 p. 207	Max's on Broad	◆◆	American	$15-$36	224
33 p. 207	Lucy's	◆◆◆	American	$8-$23	224
34 p. 207	Maple & Pine	◆◆◆	American	$9-$33	224
35 p. 207	Graffiato	◆◆◆	Italian	$9-$16	224
36 p. 207	Rowland	◆◆◆	American	$16-$27	224
37 p. 207	Bistro 27	◆◆◆	European	$15-$26	223
38 p. 207	Acacia Mid-Town	◆◆◆	American	$18-$30	223
39 p. 207	Sidewalk Cafe	◆	American	$8-$16	224
40 p. 207	Bacchus	◆◆◆	Continental	$8-$25	223
41 p. 207	Tarrant's Cafe	◆◆	American	$9-$25	225
42 p. 207	Fresca...on Addison	◆	Vegetarian Vegan	$8-$12	224
43 p. 207	Chez Foushee	◆◆◆	American	$12-$32	223
44 p. 207	Heritage	◆◆◆	American	$13-$22	224
45 p. 207	Lamplighter Roasting Company	◆	Coffee/Tea Vegetarian	$5-$9	224
46 p. 207	T. J.'s Restaurant and Lounge	◆◆◆	American	$7-$25	225
47 p. 207	Lemaire	◆◆◆◆	New American	$18-$30	224
48 p. 207	Perly's	◆◆	Kosher Deli	$7-$18	224
49 p. 207	Rapp Session	◆◆	Seafood Small Plates	$8-$15	224
50 p. 207	La Grotta Ristorante	◆◆◆	Italian	$8-$28	224
51 p. 207	Rappahannock Restaurant	◆◆◆	Seafood	$24-$32	224
52 p. 207	Vagabond	◆◆◆	American	$12-$24	225
53 p. 207	Julep's, New Southern Cuisine	◆◆◆	Southern American	$25-$34	224
54 p. 207	Pasture	◆◆	Southern American	$10-$22	224
55 p. 207	Dinamo	◆◆	Italian	$10-$24	223
56 p. 207	Pop's Market on Grace	◆	Sandwiches	$9-$16	224
57 p. 207	Metzger Bar and Butchery	◆◆◆	German	$15-$24	224
58 p. 207	Cafe Rustica	◆◆	Mediterranean	$14-$34	223
59 p. 207	Belle & James	◆◆◆	American	$14-$28	223
60 p. 207	Alamo BBQ	◆	Barbecue	$6-$14	223

Map Page	Restaurants (cont'd)	Diamond Rated	Cuisine	Price Range	Page
61 p. 207	Citizen	◆◆	American	$9-$21	223
62 p. 207	The Dining Room at The Berkeley Hotel	◆◆◆	Southern American	$9-$30	223
63 p. 207	Bistro Bobette	◆◆◆	French	$8-$32	223
64 p. 207	L'Opossum	◆◆◆	American	$7-$29	224
65 p. 207	Urban Farmhouse Market & Cafe	◆	Natural/Organic Sandwiches	$7-$14	225
66 p. 207	Kitchen on Cary	◆◆◆	American	$12-$26	224
67 p. 207	The Hard Shell	◆◆◆	Seafood	$12-$60	224
68 p. 207	Addis Ethiopian Restaurant	◆◆	Ethiopian	$13-$20	223
69 p. 207	Proper Pie Co.	◆	Specialty	$4-$6	224
70 p. 207	Bottoms Up Pizza	◆◆	Pizza	$8-$15	223
71 p. 207	Nota Bene Restaurant & Bar	◆◆◆	Italian	$15-$24	224
72 p. 207	Old Original Bookbinder's	◆◆◆	Seafood Steak	$22-$96	224
73 p. 207	Millie's Diner	◆◆	American	$7-$27	224
74 p. 207	Secret Sandwich Society	◆◆	Sandwiches	$10-$12	224

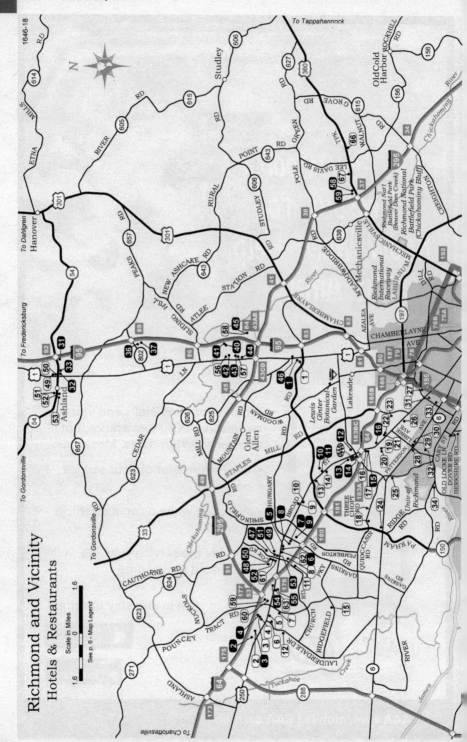

Richmond and Vicinity
Hotels & Restaurants

See p. 6 - Map Legend

Scale in Miles

1.6 0 1.6

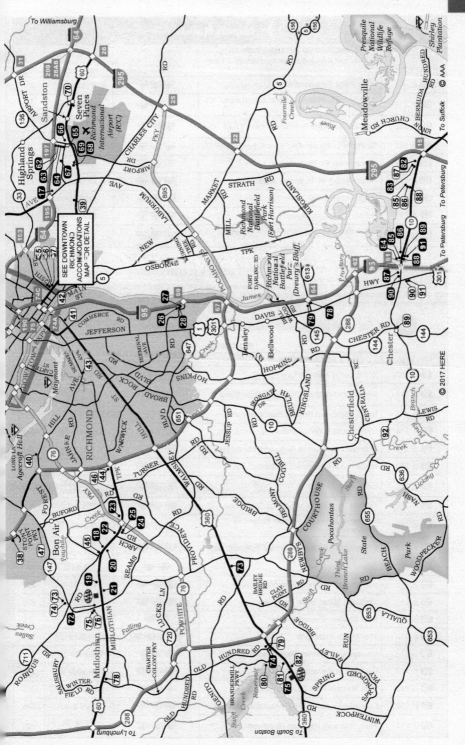

✈ Airport Hotels

Map Page	RICHMOND INTERNATIONAL (Maximum driving distance from airport: 3.1 mi)	Diamond Rated	Rate Range	Page
17 p. 212	**Hyatt Place Richmond Airport, 3.1 mi**	♦♦♦	$104-$299 SAVE	227
68 p. 212	**Best Western Plus Richmond Airport Hotel, 1.6 mi**	♦♦♦	$89-$250 SAVE	239
67 p. 212	Candlewood Suites Richmond Airport, 2.0 mi	♦♦♦	Rates not provided	239
69 p. 212	Courtyard by Marriott-Richmond Airport, 1.9 mi	♦♦♦	$88-$218	239
62 p. 212	Hampton Inn Richmond Airport, 1.8 mi	♦♦♦	$99-$169	239
63 p. 212	Hilton Garden Inn Richmond Airport, 1.8 mi	♦♦♦	$139-$229	239
65 p. 212	Holiday Inn Express, 1.6 mi	♦♦♦	$124-$127	239
64 p. 212	Holiday Inn Richmond Airport, 1.8 mi	♦♦♦	$119-$179	239
66 p. 212	Homewood Suites by Hilton Richmond Airport, 1.5 mi	♦♦♦	$99-$169	239

Richmond and Vicinity

This index helps you "spot" where approved hotels and restaurants are located on the corresponding detailed maps. Hotel daily rate range is for comparison only. Restaurant price range is a combination of lunch and/or dinner. Turn to the listing page for more information and consult display ads for special promotions.

 For more details, rates and reservations: AAA.com/travelguides/hotels

RICHMOND

Map Page	Hotels	Diamond Rated	Rate Range	Page
1 p. 212	Econo Lodge North-Parham Rd	♦♦	$55-$100	225
2 p. 212	Wingate by Wyndham-Richmond, Short Pump	♦♦♦	Rates not provided	228
3 p. 212	**Hilton Richmond Hotel & Spa/Short Pump**	♦♦♦♦	$139-$279 SAVE	226
4 p. 212	**Hyatt House Richmond-West** (See ad p. 226.)	♦♦♦	$99-$219 SAVE	227
5 p. 212	**Courtyard by Marriott Richmond Northwest**	♦♦♦	$79-$225 SAVE	225
6 p. 212	Residence Inn by Marriott Northwest	♦♦♦	$84-$206	228
7 p. 212	Holiday Inn Express	♦♦♦	Rates not provided	226
8 p. 212	Fairfield Inn & Suites by Marriott Short Pump	♦♦♦	$68-$171	226
9 p. 212	**SpringHill Suites by Marriott Richmond Northwest**	♦♦♦	$72-$183 SAVE	228
10 p. 212	Country Inn & Suites By Carlson, Richmond West	♦♦♦	Rates not provided	225
11 p. 212	Quality Inn West End	♦♦	$71-$142	227
12 p. 212	Hampton Inn & Suites-Richmond/Glenside	♦♦♦	$129-$229	226
13 p. 212	**Embassy Suites Hotel by Hilton**	♦♦♦	$159-$329 SAVE	225
14 p. 212	**Best Western Executive Hotel**	♦♦	$89-$209 SAVE	225
15 p. 212	**The Westin Richmond**	♦♦♦♦	$149-$299 SAVE	228
16 p. 212	**Courtyard by Marriott Richmond-West**	♦♦♦	$90-$199 SAVE	225
17 p. 212	**Hyatt Place Richmond Airport**	♦♦♦	$104-$299 SAVE	227
18 p. 212	**Best Western Plus Governor's Inn**	♦♦♦	$89-$159 SAVE	225
19 p. 212	DoubleTree Hotel Richmond-Midlothian	♦♦♦	$109-$149	225
20 p. 212	**Four Points by Sheraton Richmond**	♦♦♦	Rates not provided SAVE	226

RICHMOND (cont'd)

Map Page	Hotels (cont'd)	Diamond Rated	Rate Range	Page
21 p. 212	Hampton Inn-Midlothian Turnpike	◈◈◈	$119-$209	226
22 p. 212	Fairfield Inn & Suites by Marriott Richmond-Midlothian	◈◈◈	$89-$218	226
23 p. 212	Holiday Inn Express Midlothian Turnpike	◈◈◈	Rates not provided	227
24 p. 212	**Hyatt Place Richmond/Arboretum** *(See ad p. 227.)*	◈◈◈	$59-$169 SAVE	227
25 p. 212	Extended Stay America North Chesterfield Arboretum	◈◈	$55-$75	226
26 p. 212	Candlewood Suites	◈◈◈	$89-$159	225
27 p. 212	Hampton Inn I-95 South Bells Rd	◈◈◈	$139-$159	226
28 p. 212	Holiday Inn South - Bells Road	◈◈◈	$119-$129	227

Map Page	Restaurants	Diamond Rated	Cuisine	Price Range	Page
1 p. 212	Bella Luna Ristorante Italiano	◈◈	Italian	$6-$18	228
2 p. 212	Shula's America's Steak House	◈◈◈	Steak	$10-$50	229
3 p. 212	Lehja	◈◈◈	Indian	$11-$25	229
4 p. 212	Firebirds Wood Fired Grill	◈◈◈	American	$11-$50	228
5 p. 212	Umi Sushi Bistro	◈◈◈	Japanese Sushi	$9-$30	229
6 p. 212	Anokha-Unique Cuisine of India	◈◈◈	Indian	$10-$22	228
7 p. 212	Tazza Kitchen	◈◈◈	American	$10-$19	229
8 p. 212	Cupertino's New York Bagels and Deli	◈	American	$5-$9	228
9 p. 212	Zorba's	◈◈	Greek	$6-$16	229
10 p. 212	Vietnam Garden	◈◈	Vietnamese	$9-$23	229
11 p. 212	The Grapevine II	◈◈	Greek	$7-$22	228
12 p. 212	Malabar Indian Cuisine	◈◈	Indian	$7-$17	229
13 p. 212	Buz and Ned's Real Barbecue	◈	Barbecue	$6-$15	228
14 p. 212	Chicken Fiesta	◈	Tex-Mex Chicken	$8-$15	228
15 p. 212	Ichiban Japanese Cuisine	◈◈	Japanese	$9-$26	228
16 p. 212	Plaza Azteca Mexican Restaurant	◈◈	Mexican	$6-$20	229
17 p. 212	Crossings Restaurant & Lounge	◈◈◈	American	$8-$29	228
18 p. 212	Melito's	◈◈	American	$6-$11	229
19 p. 212	Full Kee Chinese Restaurant	◈◈	Chinese	$6-$15	228
20 p. 212	Original Mexican Restaurant	◈◈	Mexican	$4-$13	229
21 p. 212	Mekong Restaurant	◈◈	Vietnamese	$7-$20	229
22 p. 212	The Answer Brewpub	◈◈	Vietnamese	$8-$13	228
23 p. 212	Shagbark	◈◈◈◈	Southern American	$17-$29	229
24 p. 212	Buckhead's	◈◈◈	Steak	$29-$52	228
25 p. 212	Toast	◈◈	American	$10-$21	229
26 p. 212	Sticks Kebab Shop	◈	Middle Eastern	$5-$11	229
27 p. 212	Greek Grill Cafe	◈◈	Greek	$8-$20	228
28 p. 212	Barrel Thief Wine Shop & Cafe	◈◈◈	Small Plates	$8-$16	228
29 p. 212	Superstars Pizza	◈	Pizza Sandwiches	$5-$17	229

Map Page	Restaurants (cont'd)	Diamond Rated	Cuisine	Price Range	Page
㉚ p. 212	Yum Yum Good	◆◆	Chinese	$5-$15	229
㉛ p. 212	Su Casa Mexican Restaurant	◆◆	Mexican	$5-$14	229
㉜ p. 212	The Continental Westhampton	◆◆	American	$8-$24	228
㉝ p. 212	Stella's	◆◆◆	Greek	$9-$24	229
㉞ p. 212	Azzurro	◆◆◆	Italian	$9-$32	228
㉟ p. 212	The Roosevelt	◆◆◆	New American	$10-$30	229
㊱ p. 212	Dutch & Company	◆◆◆	American	$24-$27	228
㊲ p. 212	The Hill Cafe	◆◆	American	$8-$22	228
㊳ p. 212	Brio Tuscan Grille	◆◆◆	Italian	$12-$32	228
㊴ p. 212	Carini Italian Restaurant	◆◆	Italian	$8-$16	228
㊵ p. 212	Max's Positive Vibe Cafe	◆◆	American	$8-$19	229
㊶ p. 212	Plant Zero Cafe	◆	Sandwiches	$5-$9	229
㊷ p. 212	The Boathouse at Rocketts Landing	◆◆◆	Seafood	$8-$25	228
㊸ p. 212	Laura Lee's	◆◆	American	$12-$22	229
㊹ p. 212	Carena's Jamaican Grille	◆◆	Jamaican	$10-$17	228
㊺ p. 212	Hiro Sushi	◆◆	Japanese Sushi	$7-$17	228
㊻ p. 212	Chicken Fiesta	◆	Tex-Mex Chicken	$8-$14	228
㊼ p. 212	Southbound	◆◆◆	Southern American	$14-$25	229

ASHLAND

Map Page	Hotels	Diamond Rated	Rate Range	Page
㉛ p. 212	Holiday Inn Express Hotel & Suites	◆◆◆	Rates not provided	68
㉜ p. 212	Hampton Inn by Hilton	◆◆◆	$99-$209	68
㉝ p. 212	Sleep Inn & Suites	◆◆◆	$79-$214	68
㊱ p. 212	Fairfield Inn & Suites by Marriott Richmond Ashland	◆◆◆	$120-$191	68
㊲ p. 212	Country Inn & Suites By Carlson, Ashland-Hanover	◆◆◆	Rates not provided	68

Map Page	Restaurants	Diamond Rated	Cuisine	Price Range	Page
㊾ p. 212	Yokozuna Sushi	◆◆	Japanese Sushi	$6-$15	68
㊿ p. 212	El Azteca	◆◆	Mexican	$6-$15	68
(51) p. 212	Homemades by Suzanne	◆	Regional American	$10	68
(52) p. 212	Iron Horse Restaurant	◆◆◆	Regional American	$8-$28	68
(53) p. 212	The Caboose Market & Cafe	◆◆	Small Plates	$8-$12	68

GLEN ALLEN

Map Page	Hotels	Diamond Rated	Rate Range	Page
㊵ p. 212	Candlewood Suites Virginia Center Commons	◆◆◆	Rates not provided	121
㊶ p. 212	Comfort Suites Virginia Center Commons	◆◆◆	$94-$439	121
㊷ p. 212	Courtyard by Marriott Richmond North/Glen Allen	◆◆◆	$103-$179	121
㊸ p. 212	Hampton Inn & Suites Richmond Virginia Center	◆◆◆	$104-$139	121
㊹ p. 212	SpringHill Suites by Marriott	◆◆◆	$72-$171	121
㊺ p. 212	**Virginia Crossings Hotel & Conference Center**	◆◆◆◆	$99-$259 SAVE	122

GLEN ALLEN (cont'd)

Map Page	Hotels (cont'd)	Diamond Rated	Rate Range	Page
46 p. 212	**Best Western Plus Glen Allen Inn**	◆◆◆	$78-$129 (SAVE)	121
47 p. 212	**TownePlace Suites by Marriott**	◆◆	$67-$207 (SAVE)	121
48 p. 212	**Richmond Marriott Short Pump**	◆◆◆	$81-$332 (SAVE)	121
49 p. 212	Homewood Suites by Hilton Richmond West End-Innsbrook	◆◆◆	$109-$239	121
50 p. 212	**Hyatt Place Richmond/Innsbrook**	◆◆◆	$79-$179 (SAVE)	121
51 p. 212	Comfort Suites-Innsbrook	◆◆◆	$99-$189	121
52 p. 212	Hilton Garden Inn Richmond Innsbrook	◆◆◆	$109-$219	121
53 p. 212	Hampton Inn-Richmond West	◆◆◆	$99-$149	121
54 p. 212	Candlewood Suites Richmond-West	◆◆	Rates not provided	121
55 p. 212	**Aloft Richmond West**	◆◆◆	$119-$289 (SAVE)	120

Map Page	Restaurants	Diamond Rated	Cuisine	Price Range	Page
56 p. 212	Plaza Azteca Mexican Restaurant	◆◆	Mexican	$8-$16	122
57 p. 212	True Taste Chinese Restaurant	◆◆	Chinese	$6-$15	122
58 p. 212	The Glen Restaurant and The Tavern	◆◆◆	American	$13-$33	122
59 p. 212	Noodles & Dumplings by Peter Chang	◆	Chinese Noodles Dim Sum	$4-$10	122
60 p. 212	Peter Chang China Cafe	◆◆	Chinese	$8-$20	122
61 p. 212	Mama Cucina	◆◆	Italian	$8-$20	122
62 p. 212	burgerworks	◆	Burgers	$6-$10	122
63 p. 212	The Wine Loft	◆◆	American	$10-$15	122

MECHANICSVILLE

Map Page	Hotels	Diamond Rated	Rate Range	Page
58 p. 212	Hampton Inn	◆◆◆	$138-$157	170
59 p. 212	Holiday Inn Express-Richmond-Mechanicsville	◆◆◆	Rates not provided	170

Map Page	Restaurants	Diamond Rated	Cuisine	Price Range	Page
66 p. 212	Ginger Red Asian Bistro	◆◆	Asian Sushi	$8-$20	170
67 p. 212	Mexico Restaurant	◆◆	Mexican	$5-$16	170

SANDSTON

Map Page	Hotels	Diamond Rated	Rate Range	Page
02 p. 212	Hampton Inn Richmond Airport	◆◆◆	$99-$169	239
63 p. 212	Hilton Garden Inn Richmond Airport	◆◆◆	$139-$229	239
64 p. 212	Holiday Inn Richmond Airport	◆◆◆	$119-$179	239
65 p. 212	Holiday Inn Express	◆◆◆	$124-$127	239
66 p. 212	Homewood Suites by Hilton Richmond Airport	◆◆◆	$99-$169	239
67 p. 212	Candlewood Suites Richmond Airport	◆◆◆	Rates not provided	239
68 p. 212	**Best Western Plus Richmond Airport Hotel**	◆◆◆	$89-$250 (SAVE)	239
69 p. 212	Courtyard by Marriott-Richmond Airport	◆◆◆	$88-$218	239

Map Page	Restaurant	Diamond Rated	Cuisine	Price Range	Page
70 p. 212	Hillbilly Red's Barbeque	◆	Barbecue	$10-$26	239

MIDLOTHIAN

Map Page	Hotels	Diamond Rated	Rate Range	Page
72 p. 212	La Quinta Inn & Suites-Richmond-Midlothian	◆◆◆	$79-$139	171
73 p. 212	Hampton Inn-Richmond-Southwest-Hull Street	◆◆◆	$132-$162	171
74 p. 212	Holiday Inn Express Hotel & Suites-Brandermill	◆◆◆	Rates not provided	171
75 p. 212	Sleep Inn & Suites Harbour Point	◆◆◆	$125-$229	171

Map Page	Restaurants	Diamond Rated	Cuisine	Price Range	Page
73 p. 212	The Hard Shell	◆◆	Seafood	$17-$26	171
74 p. 212	Ruth's Chris Steak House	◆◆◆	Steak	$33-$80	171
75 p. 212	Tazza Kitchen Alverser Plaza	◆◆◆	American	$9-$20	171
76 p. 212	Sushi-O	◆◆◆	Japanese Sushi	$9-$22	171
78 p. 212	Cafe Caturra	◆	American	$8-$20	171
79 p. 212	Bluefish Deli	◆◆	Asian Sushi Sandwiches	$8-$11	171
80 p. 212	The Boathouse at Sunday Park	◆◆◆	American	$15-$30	171
81 p. 212	Bonefish Grill	◆◆◆	Seafood	$15-$30	171
82 p. 212	The Desserterie	◆◆	Desserts Sandwiches	$8-$16	171

CHESTERFIELD

Map Page	Hotels	Diamond Rated	Rate Range	Page
78 p. 212	Sleep Inn Richmond	◆◆	$72-$104	93
79 p. 212	La Quinta Inn Richmond South	◆◆	$75-$164	93

CHESTER

Map Page	Hotels	Diamond Rated	Rate Range	Page
82 p. 212	Residence Inn by Marriott	◆◆◆	$118-$252	92
83 p. 212	**Hyatt Place Richmond/Chester**	◆◆◆	$89-$199 SAVE	92
84 p. 212	Hampton Inn	◆◆◆	$129-$209	92
85 p. 212	Comfort Inn-Richmond/Chester	◆◆	$79-$215	92
86 p. 212	Quality Inn & Suites	◆◆	$80-$150	92
87 p. 212	**Fairfield Inn by Marriott**	◆◆◆	$77-$163 SAVE	92
88 p. 212	Courtyard by Marriott Richmond/Chester	◆◆◆	$88-$189	92
89 p. 212	Holiday Inn Express	◆◆◆	Rates not provided	92
90 p. 212	Country Inn & Suites By Carlson	◆◆◆	Rates not provided	92
91 p. 212	Homewood Suites by Hilton Richmond/Chester	◆◆◆	$139-$189	92

Map Page	Restaurants	Diamond Rated	Cuisine	Price Range	Page
85 p. 212	Divine	◆◆	American	$12-$28	92
86 p. 212	Narita Japanese Restaurant	◆◆	Japanese Sushi	$6-$24	92
87 p. 212	Jalapenos	◆◆	Mexican	$5-$18	92
88 p. 212	Antonio's Ristorante, Pizzeria & Wine Bar	◆◆	Italian	$6-$21	92
89 p. 212	Sibley's Bar-B-Q	fyi	Southern Barbecue	$5-$12	92
90 p. 212	Central Park Deli	◆	Deli	$7-$19	92
91 p. 212	Don Papa Grande Mexican Restaurant	◆◆	Mexican	$5-$17	92
92 p. 212	Brock's Bar-B-Que	◆◆	Barbecue	$5-$17	92

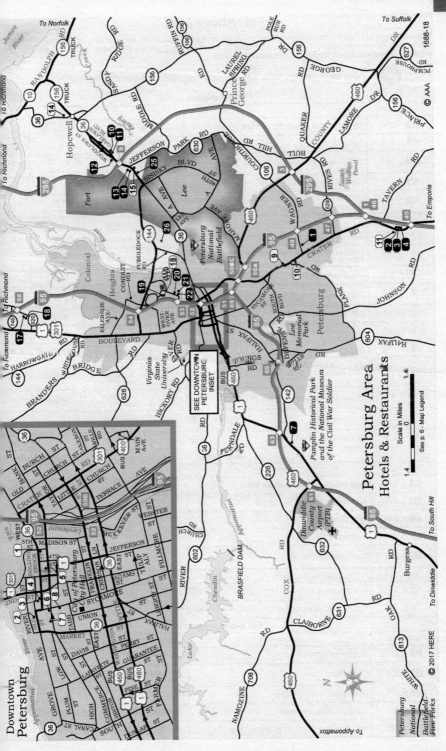

Petersburg Area
Hotels & Restaurants

Downtown
Petersburg

Petersburg Area

This index helps you "spot" where approved hotels and restaurants are located on the corresponding detailed maps. Hotel dail rate range is for comparison only. Restaurant price range is a combination of lunch and/or dinner. Turn to the listing page fc more information and consult display ads for special promotions.

 For more details, rates and reservations: AAA.com/travelguides/hotels

PETERSBURG

Map Page	Hotels	Diamond Rated	Rate Range	Page
1 p. 219	**Country Inn & Suites By Carlson**	◆◆◆	$110-$150 SAVE	186
2 p. 219	Hampton Inn	◆◆◆	$109-$149	187
3 p. 219	Holiday Inn Express Hotel & Suites	◆◆◆	Rates not provided	187
4 p. 219	Comfort Inn-Petersburg South	◆◆	$75-$130	186
7 p. 219	**Holiday Inn Express Hotel & Suites Petersburg/ Dinwiddie**	◆◆◆	Rates not provided SAVE	187

Map Page	Restaurants	Diamond Rated	Cuisine	Price Range	Page
① p. 219	Saucy's Sit Down BBQ	◆	Barbecue	$5-$11	187
② p. 219	Maria's Old Town 21 Ristorante Italiano	◆◆	Italian	$7-$18	187
③ p. 219	The Brickhouse Run	◆◆	British	$9-$21	187
④ p. 219	Wabi-Sabi Sushi & Tapas	◆◆	Japanese Sushi Small Plates	$7-$25	187
⑤ p. 219	Demolition Coffee	◆	Coffee/Tea	$7-$9	187
⑥ p. 219	Longstreet's Delicatessen	◆◆	Deli	$6-$15	187
⑦ p. 219	Alexander's Fine Food	◆◆	Greek	$5-$19	187
⑧ p. 219	Dixie Restaurant	◆	Southern Breakfast Comfort Food	$5-$10	187
⑨ p. 219	Yankee Coffee Shoppe	◆	Breakfast Comfort Food	$4-$11	187
⑩ p. 219	King's Barbecue	◆	Barbecue Comfort Food	$6-$16	187
⑪ p. 219	Nanny's Family Restaurant	◆	Southern	$3-$34	187

HOPEWELL

Map Page	Hotels	Diamond Rated	Rate Range	Page
10 p. 219	**Best Western Plus Hopewell Inn**	◆◆◆	$89-$125 SAVE	155
11 p. 219	Fairfield Inn & Suites by Marriott	◆◆◆	$63-$133	155
12 p. 219	Stay Over Suites	◆◆◆	$87-$129	155
13 p. 219	Hampton Inn-Ft Lee	◆◆◆	$139-$179	155
14 p. 219	Candlewood Suites	◆◆	Rates not provided	155

Map Page	Restaurants	Diamond Rated	Cuisine	Price Range	Page
⑭ p. 219	K&L Barbecue	◆	Barbecue	$6-$14	155
⑮ p. 219	Katcha Thai Restaurant	◆◆	Thai	$8-$14	155

COLONIAL HEIGHTS

Map Page	Hotels	Diamond Rated	Rate Range	Page
17 p. 219	Comfort Inn Colonial Heights	◆◆◆	$85-$155	96
18 p. 219	Candlewood Suites	◆◆◆	Rates not provided	96
19 p. 219	Hilton Garden Inn-Southpark	◆◆◆	$139-$189	96
20 p. 219	Comfort Suites Southpark	◆◆◆	$90-$210	96
21 p. 219	Hampton Inn Petersburg-Southpark Mall	◆◆◆	$149-$209	96

COLONIAL HEIGHTS (cont'd)

Map Page	Hotels (cont'd)	Diamond Rated	Rate Range	Page
🞂 p. 219	Holiday Inn Petersburg North-Ft Lee	◆◆◆	Rates not provided	96

Map Page	Restaurant	Diamond Rated	Cuisine	Price Range	Page
18 p. 219	Koreana Oriental Restaurant	◆◆	Korean	$8-$19	97

PRINCE GEORGE

Map Page	Hotels	Diamond Rated	Rate Range	Page
25 p. 219	Baymont Inn & Suites Prince George	fyi	Rates not provided SAVE	189
26 p. 219	Sleep Inn & Suites at Ft Lee	◆◆◆	$90-$200 SAVE	190

DOWNTOWN RICHMOND
- Restaurants p. 223
- Hotels & Restaurants map & index p. 207

THE BERKELEY HOTEL   (804)780-1300 10
◆◆◆
Boutique Hotel
$149-$209

Address: 1200 E Cary St 23219 Location: Just s of state Capitol; jct 12th St. Located in Historic Shockoe Slip District. Facility: This petite hotel offers suites and some rooms with balconies just steps from the cobblestone streets of the Historic Shockoe Slip District. Privileges are available at the neighboring YMCA. 55 units. 6 stories, interior corridors. Parking: valet only. Terms: check-in 4 pm, cancellation fee imposed. Amenities: safes. Dining: The Dining Room at The Berkeley Hotel, see separate listing. Guest Services: valet laundry, area transportation. Featured Amenity: full hot breakfast.

THE COMMONWEALTH   (804)343-7300 7
fyi Historic Boutique Hotel. Under major renovation, scheduled to be completed December 2017. Last Rated: ◆◆ Address: 901 Bank St 23219

COURTYARD BY MARRIOTT RICHMOND DOWNTOWN   (804)754-0007 12
◆◆◆
Hotel
$108-$348
COURTYARD Marriott
AAA Benefit: Members save 5% or more!

Address: 1320 E Cary St 23219 Location: Jct S 14th St; in Historic Shockoe Slip District. Facility: 135 units. 6 stories, interior corridors. Parking: on-site (fee) and street. Terms: cancellation fee imposed. Activities: exercise room. Guest Services: valet and coin laundry, boarding pass kiosk.

DELTA MARRIOTT RICHMOND DOWNTOWN   (804)788-0900 8
◆◆◆
Hotel
$159-$209
DELTA HOTELS
AAA Benefit: Members save 5% or more!

Address: 555 E Canal St 23219 Location: I-95 exit 74A (I-195) exit Canal St. Facility: 298 units. 16 stories, interior corridors. Parking: on site (fee) and valet. Terms: 3 day cancellation notice-fee imposed. Pool: heated indoor. Activities: hot tub, exercise room. Guest Services: complimentary and valet laundry, area transportation. Featured Amenity: full hot breakfast.

HAMPTON INN & SUITES BY HILTON RICHMOND-DOWNTOWN   804/643-5400 5
◆◆◆ Hotel. Address: 700 E Main St, Suite A 23219
AAA Benefit: Members save up to 10%!

HILTON RICHMOND DOWNTOWN   (804)344-4300 3
◆◆◆
Hotel
$179-$299
Hilton HOTELS & RESORTS
AAA Benefit: Members save 5% or more!

Address: 501 E Broad St 23219 Location: At 5th and E Broad sts. Facility: 250 units. 7 stories, interior corridors. Parking: on-site (fee) and valet. Terms: check-in 4 pm, 1-7 night minimum stay, cancellation fee imposed. Amenities: safes. Dining: 2 restaurants, also, La Grotta Ristorante, see separate listing. Pool: heated indoor. Activities: hot tub, exercise room. Guest Services: valet and coin laundry, area transportation.

HOLIDAY INN EXPRESS DOWNTOWN   804/788-1600 4
◆◆ Hotel. Address: 201 E Cary St 23219

HOMEWOOD SUITES BY HILTON RICHMOND-DOWNTOWN   804/643-2900 6
◆◆◆ Extended Stay Hotel. Address: 700 E Main St 23219
AAA Benefit: Members save up to 10%!

🔗 For exclusive AAA member savings and benefits: AAA.com/hertz

(See map & index p. 207.)

THE JEFFERSON HOTEL (804)788-8000

Classic Historic Hotel
$275-$455

Address: 101 W Franklin St 23220 **Location:** Jct Franklin and Adams sts; center. **Facility:** This ornate 1895 Beaux-Arts hotel is a historic landmark with striking architectural details, including a Tiffany stained-glass rotunda, a marble statue of Thomas Jefferson and a grand staircase. 181 units. 6 stories, interior corridors. **Parking:** on-site (fee) and valet. **Terms:** check-in 4 pm, cancellation fee imposed. **Amenities:** safes. **Dining:** 2 restaurants, also, Lemaire, T. J.'s Restaurant and Lounge, see separate listings. **Pool:** heated indoor. **Activities:** bicycles, exercise room, massage. **Guest Services:** valet laundry, area transportation. Affiliated with Preferred Hotels & Resorts. *(See ad this page.)*

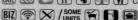

OMNI RICHMOND HOTEL   804/344-7000
Hotel. **Address:** 100 S 12th St 23219

RESIDENCE INN BY MARRIOTT RICHMOND DOWNTOWN (804)225-5550

Extended Stay Hotel
$71-$346

Residence Inn Marriott
AAA Benefit: Members save 5% or more!

Address: 14 S 14th St 23219 **Location:** Jct E Cary St; in Historic Shockoe Slip District. **Facility:** 75 efficiencies. 6 stories, interior corridors. **Parking:** on-site (fee) and valet. **Terms:** cancellation fee imposed. **Activities:** exercise room. **Guest Services:** valet and coin laundry. **Featured Amenity:** breakfast buffet.

▼ *See AAA listing this page* ▼

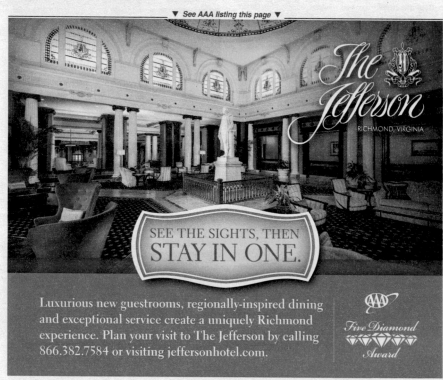

SEE THE SIGHTS, THEN
STAY IN ONE.

The Jefferson
RICHMOND, VIRGINIA

Luxurious new guestrooms, regionally-inspired dining and exceptional service create a uniquely Richmond experience. Plan your visit to The Jefferson by calling 866.382.7584 or visiting jeffersonhotel.com.

Five Diamond Award

Make the Connection

Find this symbol for places to look, book and save on AAA.com.

(See map & index p. 207.)

RICHMOND MARRIOTT DOWNTOWN

(804)643-3400

Hotel
$97-$320

AAA Benefit: Members save 5% or more!

MARRIOTT

Address: 500 E Broad St 23219 **Location:** I-95 exit 74C; jct 5th and E Broad sts. **Facility:** 410 units, 18 stories, interior corridors. **Parking:** on-site (fee) and valet. **Terms:** check-in 4 pm, cancellation fee imposed. **Dining:** 2 restaurants. **Pool:** heated indoor. **Activities:** exercise room. **Guest Services:** valet and coin laundry, boarding pass kiosk, area transportation.

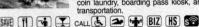

WHERE TO EAT

3 MONKEYS BAR & GRILL 804/204-2525 (28)
American. Casual Dining. **Address:** 2525 W Main St 23221

ACACIA MID-TOWN 804/562-0138 (38)
American. Fine Dining. **Address:** 2601 W Cary St 23220

ADDIS ETHIOPIAN RESTAURANT 804/308-3649 (68)
Ethiopian. Casual Dining. **Address:** 0 N 17th St 23219

AKIDA 804/359-8036 (9)
Japanese Sushi. Casual Dining. **Address:** 606 N Sheppard St 23221

ALAMO BBQ 804/592-3138 (60)
Barbecue. Quick Serve. **Address:** 2202 Jefferson Ave 23223

AMICI RISTORANTE 804/353-4700 (21)
Northern Italian. Fine Dining. **Address:** 3343 W Cary St 23221

AMUSE 804/340-1580 (13)
New American. Fine Dining. **Address:** 200 N Boulevard 23220

BACCHUS 804/355-9919 (40)
Continental. Fine Dining. **Address:** 2 N Meadow St 23220

BELLE & JAMES 804/643-0366 (59)
American. Fine Dining. **Address:** 700 E Main St 23219

BELMONT FOOD SHOP 804/358-7467 (17)
Steak. Fine Dining. **Address:** 27 N Belmont Ave 23221

BISTRO 27 804/780-0086 (37)
European. Fine Dining. **Address:** 27 W Broad St 23219

BISTRO BOBETTE 804/225-9116 (63)
French. Fine Dining. **Address:** 1209 E Cary St 23219

THE BLACK SHEEP 804/648-1300 (15)
American. Casual Dining. **Address:** 901 W Marshall St 23220

BOTTOMS UP PIZZA 804/644-4400 (70)
Pizza. Casual Dining. **Address:** 1700 Dock St 23223

BUZ AND NEDS REAL BARBECUE 804/355-6055 (4)

Barbecue
Casual Dining
$6-$16

AAA Inspector Notes: After traveling the country researching the world of barbecue, Buz perfected his spicy-sweet version and proved his dominance by beating one of TV's famed chefs. Guests can sample brisket, pork, chicken and ribs with such traditional Southern sides as baked beans, macaroni and cheese, and sweet potato fries. **Features:** beer & wine, patio dining. **Address:** 1119 N Boulevard 23230 **Location:** Just n of W Broad St. **Parking:** no self-parking.

CAFE RUSTICA 804/225-8811 (58)
Mediterranean. Casual Dining. **Address:** 414 E Main St 23219

CAN CAN BRASSERIE 804/358-7274 (23)
French. Casual Dining. **Address:** 3120 W Cary St 23221

CAPITAL ALE HOUSE 804/780-2537
American. Casual Dining. **Address:** 623 E Main St 23219

CHEZ FOUCHEE 804/648-3225 (43)
American. Fine Dining. **Address:** 203 N Foushee St 23220

CITIZEN 804/780-9038 (61)
American. Casual Dining. **Address:** 1203 E Main St 23219

COMFORT 804/780-0004 (30)
Regional American. Casual Dining. **Address:** 200 W Broad St 23220

COPPOLA'S DELI 804/359-6969 (29)
Italian Deli. Quick Serve. **Address:** 2900 W Cary St 23221

THE DAIRY BAR 804/355-1937 (2)
American. Casual Dining. **Address:** 1602 Roseneath Rd 23230

DINAMO 804/678-9706 (55)
Italian. Casual Dining. **Address:** 821 W Cary St 23220

THE DINING ROOM AT THE BERKELEY HOTEL

804/225-5105 (62)

Southern
American
Fine Dining
$9-$30

AAA Inspector Notes: Slide into a seat along the window with views of the street, just where the pavement meets the cobblestone in Shockoe Slip, for a meal filled with prime people watching. The menu presents classic Southern favorites such as crab bisque, fried green tomatoes, shrimp and grits and fried oysters. **Features:** full bar, Sunday brunch. **Reservations:** suggested. **Address:** 1200 E Cary St 23219 **Location:** Just s of state Capitol; jct 12th St; in The Berkeley Hotel. **Parking:** valet and street only.

EARLY BIRD BISCUIT COMPANY 804/335-4570 (18)
Breads/Pastries Breakfast. Quick Serve. **Address:** 119 N Robinson St 23228

EDO'S SQUID 804/864-5488 (20)
Italian. Casual Dining. **Address:** 411 N Harrison St 23220

EN SU BOCA 804/359-0768 (7)
Tex-Mex. Casual Dining. **Address:** 1001 N Boulevard 23230

FAROUK'S HOUSE OF INDIA 804/355-0378 (25)
Indian. Casual Dining. **Address:** 3033 W Cary St 23221

FAT DRAGON 804/359-0202 (3)
Chinese. Casual Dining. **Address:** 1200 N Boulevard 23230

(See map & index p. 207.)

FRESCA...ON ADDISON   804/359-8638   (42)
💎 Vegetarian Vegan. Quick Serve. **Address:** 22 S Addison St 23220

GALAXY DINER   804/213-0510   (24)
💎💎 American. Casual Dining. **Address:** 3109 W Cary St 23221

GARNETT'S CAFE   804/367-7909   (14)
💎💎 Sandwiches. Casual Dining. **Address:** 2001 Park Ave 23220

GRAFFIATO   804/918-9454   (35)
💎💎💎 Italian. Casual Dining. **Address:** 123 W Broad St 23220

THE HARD SHELL   804/643-2333   (67)
💎💎💎 Seafood. Casual Dining. **Address:** 1411 E Cary St 23219

HELEN'S   804/358-4370   (26)
💎💎💎 American. Fine Dining. **Address:** 2527 W Main St 23220

HERITAGE   804/353-4060   (44)
💎💎💎 American. Gastropub. **Address:** 1627 W Main St 23220

JULEP'S, NEW SOUTHERN CUISINE   804/377-3968   (53)
💎💎💎 Southern American. Fine Dining. **Address:** 420 E Grace St 23219

KITCHEN 64   804/358-0064   (1)
💎💎 American. Casual Dining. **Address:** 3336 N Boulevard 23227

KITCHEN ON CARY   804/643-1315   (66)
💎💎💎 American. Fine Dining. **Address:** 1331 E Cary St 23219

KUBA KUBA   804/355-8817   (19)
💎💎 Cuban. Casual Dining. **Address:** 1601 Park Ave 23220

LA GROTTA RISTORANTE   804/644-2466   (50)
💎💎💎 Italian. Fine Dining. **Address:** 529 E Broad St 23219

LAMPLIGHTER ROASTING COMPANY   804/728-2292   (45)
💎 Coffee/Tea Vegetarian. Quick Serve. **Address:** 116 Addison St 23220

LEMAIRE   804/649-4644   (47)
💎💎💎💎 New American. Fine Dining. **Address:** 101 W Franklin St 23220

LEMON CUISINE OF INDIA   804/204-1800   (5)
💎💎 Indian. Casual Dining. **Address:** 3215 W Broad St 23230

L'OPOSSUM   804/918-6028   (64)
💎💎💎 American. Fine Dining. **Address:** 626 China St 23220

LUCY'S   804/562-1444   (33)
💎💎💎 American. Casual Dining. **Address:** 404 N 2nd St 23219

LUNCH   804/353-0111   (6)
💎💎 American. Casual Dining. **Address:** 1213 Summit Ave 23230

MAPLE & PINE   804/340-6050   (34)
💎💎💎 American. Fine Dining. **Address:** 201 W Broad St 23220

MAX'S ON BROAD   804/225-0400   (32)
💎💎 American. Casual Dining. **Address:** 305 Brook Rd 23220

METZGER BAR AND BUTCHERY   804/325-3147   (57)
💎💎💎 German. Fine Dining. **Address:** 801 N 23rd St 23223

MILLIE'S DINER   804/643-5512   (73)
💎💎 American. Casual Dining. **Address:** 2603 E Main St 23223

NOTA BENE RESTAURANT & BAR   804/477-3355   (71)
💎💎💎 Italian. Casual Dining. **Address:** 2110 E Main St 23223

OLD ORIGINAL BOOKBINDER'S   804/643-6900   (72)
💎💎💎 Seafood Steak. Fine Dining. **Address:** 2306 E Cary St 23223

PASTURE   804/780-0416   (54)
💎💎 Southern American. Casual Dining. **Address:** 416 E Grace St 23219

PEKING RESTAURANT   804/649-8888
💎💎 Chinese. Casual Dining. **Address:** 1302 E Cary St 23219

PERLY'S   804/649-2779   (48)
💎💎 Kosher Deli. Casual Dining. **Address:** 111 E Grace St 23219

PETER CHANG CHINA CAFE   804/728-1820   (8)
💎💎 Szechuan. Casual Dining. **Address:** 2816 W Broad St 23230

POP'S MARKET ON GRACE   804/644-7677   (56)
💎 Sandwiches. Quick Serve. **Address:** 415 E Grace St 23219

PROPER PIE CO.   804/343-7437   (69)
💎 Specialty. Quick Serve. **Address:** 2505 E Broad St 23223

RAPPAHANNOCK RESTAURANT   804/545-0565   (51)
💎💎 Seafood. Casual Dining. **Address:** 320 E Grace St 23219

RAPP SESSION   804/545-0565   (49)
💎💎 Seafood Small Plates. Gastropub. **Address:** 318 E Grace St 23219

THE ROGUE GENTLEMEN   804/477-3456   (16)
💎💎💎 New American. Fine Dining. **Address:** 618 N 1st St 23219

ROWLAND   804/257-9885   (36)
💎💎💎 American. Fine Dining. **Address:** 2132 W Main St 23220

SAISON   804/269-3689   (27)
💎💎💎 American. Gastropub. **Address:** 23 W Marshall St 23220

SALLY BELL'S KITCHEN   804/644-2838   (22)
💎 Seafood Desserts. Quick Serve. **Address:** 2337 W Broad St 23220

THE SAVORY GRAIN   804/592-4000   (10)
💎💎 American. Casual Dining. **Address:** 2043 W Broad St 23220

SECCO WINE BAR   804/353-0670   (11)
💎💎💎 European. Fine Dining. **Address:** 325 N Robinson St 23220

SECRET SANDWICH SOCIETY   804/644-4777   (74)
💎💎 Sandwiches. Casual Dining. **Address:** 501 E Grace St 23219

SIDEWALK CAFE   804/358-0645   (39)
💎 American. Casual Dining. **Address:** 2101 W Main St 23220

STICKY RICE   804/358-7870   (31)
💎💎 Japanese Sushi. Casual Dining. **Address:** 2232 W Main St 23220

STRAWBERRY STREET CAFE   804/353-6860   (12)
💎💎 American. Casual Dining. **Address:** 421 N Strawberry St 23220

(See map & index p. 207.)

TARRANT'S CAFE   804/225-0035   41
♦♦♦ American. Casual Dining. **Address:** 1 W Broad St 23220

T. J.'S RESTAURANT AND LOUNGE   804/649-4672   46
♦♦♦ American. Casual Dining. **Address:** 101 W Franklin St 23220

URBAN FARMHOUSE MARKET & CAFE   804/325-3988   65
♦ Natural/Organic Sandwiches. Quick Serve. **Address:** 1217 E Cary St 23219

VAGABOND   804/643-2632   52
♦♦♦ American. Fine Dining. **Address:** 700 E Broad St 23219

RICHMOND elev. 15'

BEST WESTERN EXECUTIVE HOTEL
(804)672-7007   14

♦♦♦ Hotel $89-$209 | Best Western. | **AAA Benefit.** Members save 10% or more & earn 10% bonus points!

Address: 7007 W Broad St 23294 **Location:** I-64 exit 183C (W Broad St); jct Glenside Dr. **Facility:** 114 units. 4 stories, interior corridors. **Terms:** cancellation fee imposed. **Pool:** outdoor. **Activities:** exercise room. **Guest Services:** coin laundry. **Featured Amenity:** full hot breakfast.

BEST WESTERN PLUS GOVERNOR'S INN
(804)323-0007   18

♦♦♦ Hotel $89-$159 | Best Western PLUS. | **AAA Benefit:** Members save 10% or more & earn 10% bonus points!

Address: 9826 Midlothian Tpke 23235 **Location:** 1.5 mi w of jct Powhite Pkwy (SR 76). **Facility:** 80 units. 3 stories, interior corridors. **Terms:** 3 day cancellation notice-fee imposed. **Amenities:** safes. **Pool:** outdoor. **Activities:** exercise room. **Featured Amenity:** continental breakfast.

CANDLEWOOD SUITES   (804)271-0016   26
♦♦♦ Extended Stay Hotel. **Address:** 4301 Commerce Rd 23234

COUNTRY INN & SUITES BY CARLSON, RICHMOND WEST
804/755-6605   10
♦♦♦ Hotel. **Address:** 8010 W Broad St 23294

COURTYARD BY MARRIOTT RICHMOND NORTHWEST
(804)346-5427   5

♦♦♦ Hotel $79-$225 | 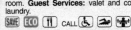 COURTYARD Marriott | **AAA Benefit:** Members save 5% or more!

Address: 3950 Westerre Pkwy 23233 **Location:** I-64 exit 178B, 0.5 mi e; jct W Broad St and Westerre Pkwy. **Facility:** 154 units. 4 stories, interior corridors. **Terms:** cancellation fee imposed. **Pool:** heated indoor. **Activities:** exercise room. **Guest Services:** valet and coin laundry.

COURTYARD BY MARRIOTT RICHMOND-WEST
(804)282-1881   16

♦♦♦ Hotel $90-$199 | COURTYARD Marriott | **AAA Benefit:** Members save 5% or more!

Address: 6400 W Broad St 23230 **Location:** I-64 exit 183B westbound; exit 183 eastbound; jct US 250, 0.5 mi e. **Facility:** 145 units. 2-3 stories, interior corridors. **Terms:** cancellation fee imposed. **Pool:** outdoor. **Activities:** exercise room. **Guest Services:** valet and coin laundry, boarding pass kiosk.

DOUBLETREE HOTEL RICHMOND-MIDLOTHIAN
(804)379-3800   19
♦♦♦ Hotel. **Address:** 1021 Koger Center Blvd 23235   **AAA Benefit:** Members save 5% or more!

ECONO LODGE NORTH-PARHAM RD
(804)262-7070   1
♦♦ Motel. **Address:** 8350 Brook Rd 23227

EMBASSY SUITES HOTEL BY HILTON
(804)672-8585   13

♦♦♦ Hotel $159-$329 | EMBASSY SUITES by HILTON | **AAA Benefit:** Members save 5% or more!

Address: 2925 Emerywood Pkwy 23294 **Location:** I-64 exit 183C (W Broad St) eastbound, just s; exit 183 westbound, just n on Glenside Dr, then just w on W Broad St. **Facility:** 224 units. 8 stories, interior corridors. **Terms:** 1-7 night minimum stay, cancellation fee imposed. **Pool:** heated indoor. **Activities:** sauna, hot tub, exercise room. **Guest Services:** valet and coin laundry, area transportation. **Featured Amenity:** full hot breakfast.

(See map & index p. 212.)

EXTENDED STAY AMERICA NORTH CHESTERFIELD ARBORETUM (804)272-1800 **25**
◈◈ Extended Stay Hotel. **Address:** 241 Arboretum Pl 23236

FAIRFIELD INN & SUITES BY MARRIOTT RICHMOND-MIDLOTHIAN (804)447-8326 **22**
◈◈◈ Hotel. **Address:** 150 N Pinetta Dr 23235

AAA Benefit: Members save 5% or more!

FAIRFIELD INN & SUITES BY MARRIOTT SHORT PUMP (804)545-4200 **8**
◈◈◈ Hotel. **Address:** 9937 Mayland Dr 23233

AAA Benefit: Members save 5% or more!

FOUR POINTS BY SHERATON RICHMOND
804-323-1144 **20**

◈◈◈
Hotel
Rates not provided

FOUR POINTS BY SHERATON

AAA Benefit: Members save 5% or more!

Address: 9901 Midlothian Tpke 23235 **Location:** 1 mi w of Powhite Pkwy (SR 76). **Facility:** 194 units. 7 stories, interior corridors. **Amenities:** safes. **Pool:** heated outdoor, heated indoor. **Activities:** exercise room. **Guest Services:** valet laundry, area transportation.

[SAVE] [ECO] [🍴] [♿] [▼] CALL [♿]
[🛏] [👥] [BIZ] [📶] [✕] [📺] [🛎]
[🍽] [💻] / SOME UNITS [🐾]

HAMPTON INN & SUITES-RICHMOND/GLENSIDE
(804)756-1777 **12**
◈◈◈ Hotel. **Address:** 5406 Glenside Dr 23228

AAA Benefit: Members save up to 10%!

HAMPTON INN I-95 SOUTH BELLS RD (804)743-3550 **27**
◈◈ Hotel. **Address:** 4300 Commerce Rd 23234

AAA Benefit: Members save up to 10%!

HAMPTON INN-MIDLOTHIAN TURNPIKE (804)897-2800 **21**
◈◈◈ Hotel. **Address:** 800 Research Rd 23236

AAA Benefit: Members save up to 10%!

HILTON RICHMOND HOTEL & SPA/SHORT PUMP (804)364-3600 **3**

◈◈◈◈
Hotel
$139-$279

Hilton
HOTELS & RESORTS

AAA Benefit: Members save 5% or more!

Address: 12042 W Broad St 23233 **Location:** I-64 exit 178, 2 mi w. **Facility:** Adjacent to Short Pump Town Center, this elegant hotel offers modern style and a luxurious spa. 254 units. 8 stories, interior corridors. **Parking:** on-site and valet. **Terms:** 1-7 night minimum stay, cancellation fee imposed. **Amenities:** safes. **Dining:** Shula's America's Steak House, see separate listing. **Pool:** heated indoor. **Activities:** hot tub, exercise room, spa. **Guest Services:** valet laundry, area transportation.

[SAVE] [ECO] [🍴] [♿] CALL [♿] [🛏] [👥] [BIZ] [HS] [📶]
[✕] [🛎] [💻]

HOLIDAY INN EXPRESS 804/934-9300 **7**
◈◈◈ Hotel. **Address:** 9933 Mayland Dr 23233

🔗 **Get the scoop**

from AAA inspectors:

AAA.com/travelguides/restaurants

▼ See AAA listing p. 227 ▼

(See map & index p. 212.)

HOLIDAY INN EXPRESS MIDLOTHIAN TURNPIKE
804/320-8900 **23**
WWW Hotel. **Address:** 8710 Midlothian Tpke 23235

HOLIDAY INN SOUTH - BELLS ROAD (804)592-2900 **28**
WWW Hotel. **Address:** 4303 Commerce Rd 23234

HYATT HOUSE RICHMOND-WEST
(804)360-7021 **4**

WWW
Extended Stay
Contemporary
Hotel
$99-$219

H HYATT house™

AAA Benefit: Members save 10%!

Address: 11800 W Broad St, Suite 1098 23233 **Location:** I-64 exit 178, 1.3 mi w; in Short Pump Town Center. **Facility:** 134 units, some efficiencies. 6 stories, interior corridors. **Terms:** check-in 4 pm, cancellation fee imposed. **Pool:** heated outdoor. **Activities:** hot tub, exercise room. **Guest Services:** valet and coin laundry. **Featured Amenity:** full hot breakfast. *(See ad p. 226.)*

SAVE ⊞ Y CALL ♿ ⛟ ⊞ BIZ HS 📶 ✕
⊟ 🖥 ⊡

🌐 **For complete hotel,**

dining and attraction listings:

AAA.com/travelguides

HYATT PLACE RICHMOND AIRPORT
(804)549-4865 **17**

WWW
Hotel
$104-$299

⭐HYATT PLACE®

AAA Benefit: Members save 10%!

Address: 4401 S Laburnum Ave 23231 **Location:** I-64 exit 195, just s; in White Oak Village. **Facility:** 151 units. 7 stories, interior corridors. **Terms:** cancellation fee imposed. **Pool:** heated indoor. **Activities:** exercise room. **Guest Services:** valet laundry, area transportation. **Featured Amenity:** full hot breakfast.

SAVE ⊞ ⊞ CALL ♿ ⛟ ⊞
BIZ HS 📶 ✕ ⊟ ⊡

 / SOME UNITS 🐾

HYATT PLACE RICHMOND/ARBORETUM
(804)560-1566 **24**

WWW
Hotel
$59-$169

⭐HYATT PLACE®

AAA Benefit: Members save 10%!

Address: 201 Arboretum Pl 23236 **Location:** Jct Powhite Pkwy (SR 76) and Midlothian Tpke (US 60), just w. **Facility:** 127 units. 6 stories, interior corridors. **Terms:** cancellation fee imposed. **Amenities:** *Some:* safes. **Pool:** heated outdoor. **Activities:** exercise room. **Guest Services:** valet laundry. **Featured Amenity:** full hot breakfast. *(See ad this page.)*

SAVE Y CALL ♿ ⛟ ⊞ BIZ 📶 ✕ 📹 ⊟

🖥 / SOME UNITS 🐾

QUALITY INN WEST END (804)346-0000 **11**
WW Hotel. **Address:** 0008 W Broad St 23294

▼ *See AAA listing this page* ▼

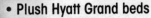

(See map & index p. 212.)

RESIDENCE INN BY MARRIOTT NORTHWEST
(804)762-9852

Extended Stay Hotel. Address: 3940 Westerre Pkwy 23233

AAA Benefit: Members save 5% or more!

SPRINGHILL SUITES BY MARRIOTT RICHMOND NORTHWEST
(804)217-7075

Hotel
$72-$183

SPRINGHILL SUITES MARRIOTT
AAA Benefit: Members save 5% or more!

Address: 9960 Independence Park Dr 23233 **Location:** I-64 exit 180B, just n to Mayland Dr, then just e on Mayland Ct. **Facility:** 103 units. 4 stories, interior corridors. **Terms:** cancellation fee imposed. **Pool:** heated indoor. **Activities:** hot tub, exercise room, and coin laundry. **Guest Services:** valet **Featured Amenity: full hot breakfast.**

THE WESTIN RICHMOND
(804)282-8444

Contemporary Hotel
$149-$299

WESTIN HOTELS & RESORTS
AAA Benefit: Members save 5% or more!

Address: 6631 W Broad St 23230 **Location:** I-64 exit 183 eastbound; exit 183B westbound; in Reynolds Crossing. **Facility:** Offering crisp, contemporary décor with clean lines and soothing shades of gray, the atmosphere here is designed to relax and renew. Spaces are infused with the scent of white tea. 250 units. 7 stories, interior corridors. **Parking:** on-site and valet. **Terms:** cancellation fee imposed. **Amenities:** safes. **Dining:** Crossings Restaurant & Lounge, see separate listing. **Pool:** heated indoor. **Activities:** hot tub, exercise room, massage. **Guest Services:** valet laundry, area transportation.

WINGATE BY WYNDHAM-RICHMOND, SHORT PUMP
804/421-1600

Hotel. Address: 13991 N Gayton Rd 23233

WHERE TO EAT

ANOKHA-UNIQUE CUISINE OF INDIA 804/360-8686 ⑥
Indian. Fine Dining. **Address:** 4015 Lauderdale Dr 23233

THE ANSWER BREWPUB 804/282-1248 ㉒
Vietnamese. Brewpub. **Address:** 6008 W Broad St 23230

AZZURRO 804/282-1509 ㉞
Italian. Casual Dining. **Address:** 6221 River Rd 23229

BAKER'S CRUST
American. Casual Dining.
LOCATIONS:
Address: 3553 W Cary St 23221 **Phone:** 804/213-0800
Address: 11800 W Broad St, Suite 1102 23233
Phone: 804/377-9060

BARREL THIEF WINE SHOP & CAFE 804/612-9232 ㉘
Small Plates. Casual Dining. **Address:** 5805 Patterson Ave 23226

BELLA LUNA RISTORANTE ITALIANO 804/497-4681 ①
Italian. Casual Dining. **Address:** 1212 Concord Ave 23228

THE BOATHOUSE AT ROCKETTS LANDING 804/622-2628 ㊷
Seafood. Fine Dining. **Address:** 4708 E Old Main St 23231

BRIO TUSCAN GRILLE 804/272-2255 ㊳
Italian. Fine Dining. **Address:** 9210 Stony Point Pkwy 23235

BUCKHEAD'S 804/750-2000 ㉔
Steak. Fine Dining. **Address:** 8510 Patterson Ave 23229

BUZ AND NED'S REAL BARBECUE 804/346-4227 ⑬
Barbecue. Quick Serve. **Address:** 8205 W Broad St 23294

CARENA'S JAMAICAN GRILLE 804/422-5375 ㊹
Jamaican. Casual Dining. **Address:** 7102 Midlothian Tpke 23225

CARINI ITALIAN RESTAURANT 804/222-0715 ㊴
Italian. Casual Dining. **Address:** 3718 W Williamsburg Rd 23231

CHICKEN FIESTA 804/320-1112 ㊻
Tex-Mex Chicken. Quick Serve. **Address:** 7748 Midlothian Tpke 23235

CHICKEN FIESTA 804/527-0009 ⑭
Tex-Mex Chicken. Quick Serve. **Address:** 7925 W Broad St 23294

THE CONTINENTAL WESTHAMPTON 804/285-0911 ㉜
American. Casual Dining. **Address:** 5704 Grove Ave 23226

CROSSINGS RESTAURANT & LOUNGE 804/282-8444 ⑰
American. Casual Dining. **Address:** 6631 W Broad St 23230

CUPERTINO'S NEW YORK BAGELS AND DELI 804/747-4005 ⑧
American. Quick Serve. **Address:** 3621A Cox Rd 23233

DUTCH & COMPANY 804/643-8824 ㊱
American. Fine Dining. **Address:** 400 N 27th St 23223

FIREBIRDS WOOD FIRED GRILL 804/364-9744 ④
American. Casual Dining. **Address:** 11800 W Broad St, Suite 1068 23233

FULL KEE CHINESE RESTAURANT 804/673-2233 ⑲
Chinese. Casual Dining. **Address:** 6400 Horsepen Rd 23226

GLORY DAYS GRILL 804/754-3710
American. Casual Dining. **Address:** 10466 Ridgefield Pkwy 23233

THE GRAPEVINE II 804/440-9100 ⑪
Greek. Casual Dining. **Address:** 11055 Three Chopt Rd 23233

GREEK GRILL CAFE 804/355-4001 ㉗
Greek. Casual Dining. **Address:** 2313 Westwood Ave 23230

THE HILL CAFE 804/648-0360 ㊲
American. Casual Dining. **Address:** 2800 E Broad St 23223

HIRO SUSHI 804/323-8108 ㊺
Japanese Sushi. Casual Dining. **Address:** 9958 Midlothian Tpke 23235

ICHIBAN JAPANESE CUISINE 804/750-2380 ⑮
Japanese. Casual Dining. **Address:** 10490 Ridgefield Pkwy 23233

(See map & index p. 212.)

LAURA LEE'S   804/233-9672 43
♥♥ American. Casual Dining. Address: 3410 Semmes Ave
23225

LEHJA   804/364-1111 3
♥♥♥ Indian. Fine Dining. Address: 11800 W Broad St, Suite
910 23233

MALABAR INDIAN CUISINE   804/364-7077 12
♥♥ Indian. Casual Dining. Address: 3456 Lauderdale Dr
23233

MAX'S POSITIVE VIBE CAFE   804/560-9622 40
♥♥ American. Casual Dining. Address: 2825 Hathaway Rd
23225

MEKONG RESTAURANT   804/288-8929 21
♥♥ Vietnamese. Casual Dining. Address: 6004 W Broad St
23230

MELITO'S   804/285-1899 18
♥♥ American. Casual Dining. Address: 8815 Three Chopt Rd
23229

ORIGINAL MEXICAN RESTAURANT   804/202-7357 20
♥♥ Mexican. Casual Dining. Address: 6406 Horsepen Rd
23226

PEKING RESTAURANT   804/270-9898
♥♥ Chinese. Casual Dining. Address: 8904-F W Broad St
23294

PLANT ZERO CAFE   804/231-6500 41
♥ Sandwiches. Casual Dining. Address: 3 E 3rd St 23224

PLAZA AZTECA MEXICAN RESTAURANT   804/888-9984 16
♥♥ Mexican. Casual Dining. Address: 6623 W Broad St
23230

RIVER CITY DINER   804/266-1500
♥♥ American. Casual Dining. Address: 803 E Parham Rd
23227

THE ROOSEVELT   804/658-1935 35
♥♥♥ New American. Gastropub. Address: 623 N 25th St
23223

SHAGBARK   804/358-7424 23
♥♥♥♥ Southern American. Fine Dining. Address: 4901
Libbie Mill Blvd E, Suite 175 23230

SHULA'S AMERICA'S STEAK HOUSE   804/565-7000 2
♥♥♥♥ Steak. Fine Dining. Address: 12042 W Broad St 23233

SOUTHBOUND   804/918-5431 47
♥♥♥♥ Southern American. Casual Dining. Address: 3036
Stony Point Rd 23235

STELLA'S   804/358-2011 33
♥♥♥ Greek. Casual Dining. Address: 1012 Lafayette St
23221

STICKS KEBAB SHOP   804/282-7010 26
♥ Middle Eastern. Quick Serve. Address: 1700 Willow Lawn Dr
23221

SU CASA MEXICAN RESTAURANT   804/355-6805 31
♥♥ Mexican. Casual Dining. Address: 4013 W Broad St
23230

SUPERSTARS PIZZA   804/673-3663 29
♥ Pizza Sandwiches. Quick Serve. Address: 5700 Patterson
Ave 23226

TAZZA KITCHEN   804/716-6448 7
♥♥♥ American. Casual Dining. Address: 3332 Pump Rd
23233

TOAST   804/525-4525 25
♥♥ American. Gastropub. Address: 7007 Three Chopt Rd
23226

UMI SUSHI BISTRO   804/360-2077 5
♥♥♥ Japanese Sushi. Fine Dining. Address: 11645 W
Broad St 23233

VIETNAM GARDEN   804/262-6114 10
♥♥ Vietnamese. Casual Dining. Address: 9031 W Broad St
23294

YUM YUM GOOD   804/673-9226 30
♥♥ Chinese. Casual Dining. Address: 5612 Patterson Ave
23226

ZORBA'S   804/270-6026 9
♥♥ Greek. Casual Dining. Address: 9068 W Broad St 23294

RICHMOND NATIONAL BATTLEFIELD PARK (A-2)

• Part of Richmond area — see map p. 193

Headquartered in Richmond with battlefields in Hanover, Henrico and Chesterfield counties, the park commemorates the struggle for possession of the Confederate capital. Seven Federal attacks on Richmond took place during the Civil War. The park, consisting of 13 units, preserves the sites of the two efforts that came close to success—Gen. George McClellan's Peninsula Campaign of 1862 and Gen. Ulysses S. Grant's Overland Campaign in 1864. Completely touring the park involves a 60-mile drive.

Of McClellan's campaign, the park includes the sites of the important Seven Days' Battles at Beaver Dam Creek, Gaines' Mill Glendale and Malvern Hill. Grant's campaign is represented by the battlefields at Totopotomoy Creek and Cold Harbor, where on June 3, 1864, Grant hurled his army at strongly fortified Confederate positions, resulting in nearly 5,000 casualties. That September, Grant also made several more attacks across the James River on Confederates at Fort Harrison and New Market Heights.

Several Confederate strongholds, including Fort Harrison and Drewry's Bluff (Fort Darling), and Union-built Fort Brady are in the park. Living-history programs are presented in summer. The park's units are open daily dawn-dusk. Visitor center hours vary by location. Closed Jan. 1, Thanksgiving and Christmas. Free. Phone (804) 226-1981.

CHIMBORAZO MEDICAL MUSEUM is at 3215 E. Broad St. in Richmond National Battlefield Park. The massive Chimborazo Hospital, built in 1861, treated more than 76,000 Confederate patients during the Civil War. The 40-acre hilltop site was said to be named by a Richmond traveler for a volcano in Ecuador. Exhibits and a film tell the story of hospital life and the Confederate Medical Service. Hours: Daily 9-4:30. Closed Jan. 1, Thanksgiving and Christmas. Cost: Free. Phone: (804) 226-1981.

CIVIL WAR VISITOR CENTER AT TREDEGAR IRON WORKS is at 470 Tredegar St. The main visitor center to Richmond National Battlefield Park contains three floors of audiovisual presentations and exhibits about Richmond's role in the Civil War.

Park maps are offered at the center, which is the beginning point for a self-guiding driving tour of the 1862 Seven Days' Battles and 1864 Overland Campaign sites. **Hours:** Daily 9-5. Closed Jan. 1, Thanksgiving and Christmas. **Cost:** Free. **Phone:** (804) 771-2145.

COLD HARBOR BATTLEFIELD VISITOR CENTER is 5 mi. s.e. of Mechanicsville on SR 156. This facility serves as the starting point for tours of the Cold Harbor and Gaines' Mill battlefields within Richmond National Battlefield Park. The center contains exhibits and an electronic battle map for both engagements. **Hours:** Daily 9-4:40. Closed Jan. 1, Thanksgiving and Christmas. **Cost:** Free. **Phone:** (804) 730-5025 or (804) 226-5023.

FORT HARRISON VISITOR CENTER is off SR 5 at 8621 Battlefield Park Rd. This summer facility for Richmond National Battlefield Park offers brochures and exhibits. A walking trail leads through the remains of the fort, which was captured by 2,500 union soldiers on Sept. 29, 1864. **Hours:** Walking trail daily dawn-dusk. Visitor center daily 9-5, June-Aug. Phone ahead to confirm schedule. **Cost:** Free. **Phone:** (804) 226-1981 or (804) 795-2217.

GLENDALE/MALVERN HILL BATTLEFIELDS VISITOR CENTER is at 8301 Willis Church Rd. Part of Richmond National Battlefield Park, this center features exhibits and an electronic battle map about the Glendale and Malvern Hill battles of the 1862 Seven Days Campaign. **Hours:** Daily 9-5, June-Aug. Phone ahead to confirm schedule. **Cost:** Free. **Phone:** (804) 226-1981.

ROANOKE (H-6) pop. 97,032, elev. 940'
• Hotels p. 235 • Restaurants p. 237
• Hotels & Restaurants map & index p. 232

Roanoke, the commercial and medical center of western Virginia, is rich in history and Virginia tradition. Diverse products manufactured include railroad cars, fabricated steel, electronic components, furniture, plastics, textiles and clothing.

Surrounding lakes, state parks and national forests offer recreational opportunities, including hiking, picnicking and camping along the Appalachian Trail and the Blue Ridge Parkway *(see place listing p. 71)*. Fishing and boating are popular activities at nearby Smith Mountain Lake State Park *(see Recreation Areas Chart)*.

Downtown Roanoke boasts many historic landmarks, including a 1907 fire station, a historic farmers market and the Tudor-style Hotel Roanoke. The city's farmers market was first opened in 1882; it still operates daily on the same site, downtown on Market Square. The 3-day ☙ Roanoke Festival in the Park, a local tradition since 1968, takes place Memorial Day weekend in Elmwood Park at Elm Avenue (SR 24) and Williamson Road (SR 116). A city landmark, the 100-foot-tall Roanoke Star was erected on top of Mill Mountain in 1949; the star is illuminated each night, and the site offers a scenic overlook of the Roanoke Valley.

Visit Virginia's Blue Ridge: 101 Shenandoah Ave. N.E., Roanoke, VA 24016. **Phone:** (540) 342-6025 or (800) 635-5535.

Self-guiding tours: The visitor information center offers a map detailing a walking tour of downtown Roanoke.

Shopping: Off I-581 exit 3E, Valley View Mall (4802 Valley View Blvd. N.W.) offers more than 100 stores, including Belk, JCPenney, Macy's and Sears. Tanglewood Mall (4420-A Electric Rd.) features Barnes & Noble, Belk and T.J.Maxx.

CENTER IN THE SQUARE is off I-581 downtown at 1 Market Sq. S.E. This restored 1914 warehouse is adjacent to Roanoke's historic farmers market. The atrium features a 6,000-gallon living coral reef aquarium, two jellyfish aquaria joined by a seahorse estuary and a butterfly garden on the fifth floor. Several independent cultural organizations are housed here and include the Mill Mountain Theatre, Harrison Museum of African American Culture, History Museum of Western Virginia and Science Museum of Western Virginia. **Phone:** (540) 342-5700.

Harrison Museum of African American Culture is off I-581 downtown at 1 Market Sq. S.E. in Center in the Square. With a focus on African-American culture and history, the museum details the emergence of Roanoke as well as the growth of Virginia. Permanent and temporary exhibitions range from contemporary art installations to oral histories. **Time:** Allow 1 hour minimum. **Hours:** Mon.-Sat.-10-5, Sun. 1-5. Closed Jan. 1, Easter and Christmas. **Cost:** $7; $4.75 (ages 5-17). **Phone:** (540) 857-4395.

History Museum of Western Virginia is at 101 Shenandoah Ave. in the historic Passenger Station. Historical collections pertain to the history of western Virginia. Hands-on exhibits help guests learn about Virginia's past while rotating exhibits focus on local history.

Hours: Museum Tues.-Sat. 10-5, Sun. 1-5. Closed major holidays. **Cost:** $6; $5.50 (ages 60+ and students and military with ID); $5 (ages 3-12). **Phone:** (540) 982-5465.

Science Museum of Western Virginia is off I-581 downtown at 1 Market Sq. S.E. in Center in the Square. Interactive galleries, such as Healthy Bodies, Healthy Earth and How it Works, explore the wonders of science. Live animal exhibits include Butterfly Garden & Bug Zoo and the Living River & Touch Tank. The Bubble is a multisensory play area for preschoolers. Traveling exhibits also are offered.

Hours: Mon.-Sat. 10-5, Sun. 1-5, Memorial Day-Labor Day; Tues.-Sat. 10-5, Sun. 1-5, rest of year. Closed major holidays. **Cost:** Museum $15; $13.50 (ages 6-17, ages 60+ and students and military with ID); $7.50 (ages 3-5). Butterfly Garden & Bug Zoo only $7.60; free (ages 0-2). Prices may vary; phone ahead. **Phone:** (540) 342-5710.

(See map & index p. 232.)

O. WINSTON LINK MUSEUM is at 101 Shenandoah Ave. The museum is dedicated to O. Winston Link, whose black-and-white photographs documented the final days of railroad steam engines. Many works captured Norfolk & Western Railway trains as they passed through Virginia, Maryland and North Carolina 1955-60. Displays of photographic equipment and railway artifacts also are presented.

Time: Allow 1 hour minimum. **Hours:** Tues.-Sat. 10-5. Closed Jan. 1, Easter, Thanksgiving and Christmas. **Cost:** $6; $5.50 (ages 60+); $5 (ages 3-11). Combination ticket with Virginia Museum of Transportation $13; $11 (ages 60+); $9 (ages 3-11). **Phone:** (540) 982-5465.

TAUBMAN MUSEUM OF ART is off I-581 at 110 Salem Ave. S.E. Housed in a striking glass-and-steel structure, the museum features a permanent collection of American art and decorative arts from the 19th and 20th centuries. Modern, contemporary and changing exhibitions also are featured. Art Venture, an interactive gallery and art center, offers children a hands-on experience and includes a lab, stage area and printing station.

Time: Allow 1 hour minimum. **Hours:** Wed.-Sat. 10-5 (also third Thurs. and first Fri. of the month 5-9), Sun. noon-5. Closed Jan. 1, Memorial Day, Labor Day, Thanksgiving and Christmas. Phone

ahead to confirm schedule. **Cost:** Museum free. Art Venture $5; free (ages 0-23 months). Some exhibitions require an admission fee. **Phone:** (540) 342-5760.

VIRGINIA MUSEUM OF TRANSPORTATION is at 303 Norfolk Ave. S.W. A historic freight station houses steam, electric and diesel locomotives, railcars and cabooses; a large two-tier, O-gauge model train layout; a model circus; antique carriages, automobiles and trucks; and aviation equipment. The museum collection includes more than 50 pieces of rolling stock, including the Norfolk & Western Class A #1218, one of the world's most technologically advanced steam locomotives. A 48-seat theater in a railcar offers films about rail history.

Also at the museum is the N & O Class J611 steam passenger locomotive known as the "Spirit of Roanoke." One of only 14 of its kind ever built, it is the only one still in existence. It takes passengers out on special excursions several times a year. Reservations are required and an additional fee is charged; phone ahead for more information.

Hours: Museum Mon.-Sat. 10-5, Sun. 1-5. Phone ahead to confirm holiday schedule. Closed Jan. 1, Easter, Thanksgiving and Christmas. **Cost:** Museum $10; $8 (ages 13-18, ages 60+ and students ages 19-25 with ID); $6 (ages 3-12). Combination ticket with O. Winston Link Museum $13; $11 (ages 60+); $9 (ages 3-11). **Phone:** (540) 342-5670.

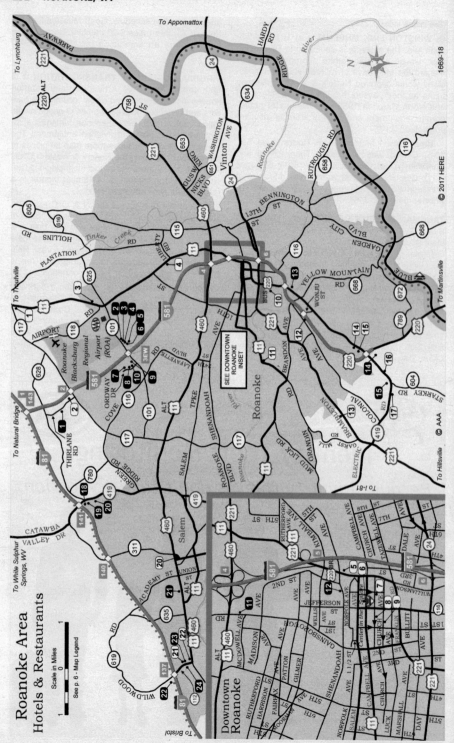

Roanoke Area
Hotels & Restaurants

Scale in Miles

See p. 6 - Map Legend

© 2017 HERE

© AAA

1669-18

Downtown Roanoke

✈ Airport Hotels

Map Page	ROANOKE REGIONAL-WOODRUM FIELD (Maximum driving distance from airport: 3.5 mi)	Diamond Rated	Rate Range	Page
4 p. 232	Best Western Plus Inn at Valley View, 1.9 mi	◈◈◈	$85-$199 [SAVE]	235
3 p. 232	Comfort Inn Airport, 1.8 mi	◈◈◈	$99-$175	235
10 p. 232	Courtyard by Marriott Roanoke Airport, 1.6 mi	◈◈◈	$84-$206	235
5 p. 232	Hampton Inn & Suites Roanoke Airport/Valley View Mall, 1.7 mi	◈◈◈	Rates not provided	235
7 p. 232	Holiday Inn Roanoke Valley View, 1.7 mi	◈◈◈	$129-$239	236
6 p. 232	Hyatt Place Roanoke Airport/Valley View Mall, 2.0 mi	◈◈◈	$99-$249 [SAVE]	237
2 p. 232	MainStay Suites Roanoke Airport, 1.9 mi	◈◈◈	$89-$219	237
8 p. 232	Residence Inn by Marriott Roanoke Airport, 1.6 mi	◈◈◈	$78-$211	237
9 p. 232	Sheraton Roanoke Hotel & Conference Center, 1.6 mi	◈◈◈	$79-$229 [SAVE]	237
1 p. 232	Super 8, 3.5 mi	◈	Rates not provided [SAVE]	237

Roanoke Area

This index helps you "spot" where approved hotels and restaurants are located on the corresponding detailed maps. Hotel daily rate range is for comparison only. Restaurant price range is a combination of lunch and/or dinner. Turn to the listing page for more information and consult display ads for special promotions.

 For more details, rates and reservations: AAA.com/travelguides/hotels

ROANOKE

Map Page	Hotels	Diamond Rated	Rate Range	Page
1 p. 232	Super 8	◈	Rates not provided [SAVE]	237
2 p. 232	MainStay Suites Roanoke Airport	◈◈◈	$89-$219	237
3 p. 232	Comfort Inn Airport	◈◈◈	$99-$175	235
4 p. 232	Best Western Plus Inn at Valley View	◈◈◈	$85-$199 [SAVE]	235
5 p. 232	Hampton Inn & Suites Roanoke Airport/Valley View Mall	◈◈◈	Rates not provided	235
6 p. 232	Hyatt Place Roanoke Airport/Valley View Mall	◈◈◈	$99-$249 [SAVE]	237
7 p. 232	Holiday Inn Roanoke Valley View	◈◈◈	$129-$239	236
8 p. 232	Residence Inn by Marriott Roanoke Airport	◈◈◈	$78-$211	237
9 p. 232	Sheraton Roanoke Hotel & Conference Center	◈◈◈	$79-$229 [SAVE]	237
10 p. 232	Courtyard by Marriott Roanoke Airport	◈◈◈	$84-$206	235
11 p. 232	Holiday Inn Express	◈◈◈	$109-$229	236
12 p. 232	The Hotel Roanoke & Conference Center, Curio - A Collection by Hilton (See ad p. 236.)	◈◈◈	$109-$289 [SAVE]	236
13 p. 232	Cambria Hotel & Suites Roanoke (See ad p. 235.)	◈◈◈	$119-$289 [SAVE]	235
14 p. 232	Hilton Garden Inn Roanoke	◈◈◈	Rates not provided	235
15 p. 232	Holiday Inn Tanglewood/Roanoke	◈◈◈	$99-$149 [SAVE]	236

Map Page	Restaurants	Diamond Rated	Cuisine	Price Range	Page
1 p. 232	Alejandro's Mexican Grill	◈◈	Mexican	$7-$18	237
2 p. 232	El Toreo	◈◈	Mexican	$6-$17	237
3 p. 232	Coach and Four	◈◈	Steak Seafood	$10-$35	237

Map Page	Restaurants (cont'd)	Diamond Rated	Cuisine	Price Range	Page
④ p. 232	New Yorker Delicatessen and Restaurant	◆	American	$4-$12	237
⑤ p. 232	The Regency Room	◆◆◆	American	$11-$42	237
⑥ p. 232	Metro!	◆◆◆	American	$12-$32	237
⑦ p. 232	On the Rise Bread Company	◆	Breads/Pastries Sandwiches	$4-$14	237
⑧ p. 232	Lucky	◆◆◆	French Comfort Food	$15-$39	237
⑨ p. 232	Bread Craft, an Artisan Bakery	◆	Breads/Pastries Sandwiches	$6-$11	237
⑩ p. 232	Wildflour Market and Bakery	◆◆	American	$7-$20	238
⑪ p. 232	Local Roots	◆◆◆	Natural/Organic	$20-$34	237
⑫ p. 232	**The Roanoker Restaurant**	◆◆	Southern American	$7-$22	237
⑬ p. 232	Luigi's	◆◆◆	Italian	$15-$40	237
⑭ p. 232	Taste of Asia	◆◆	Thai	$9-$29	238
⑮ p. 232	Montano's International Gourmet	◆◆	Continental	$9-$27	237
⑯ p. 232	Carlos Brazilian International Cuisine	◆◆◆	Brazilian	$10-$34	237
⑰ p. 232	419 West	◆◆◆	American	$11-$29	237

SALEM

Map Page	Hotels	Diamond Rated	Rate Range	Page
⑱ p. 232	**Baymont Inn & Suites Salem Roanoke Area**	◆◆	Rates not provided [SAVE]	238
⑲ p. 232	La Quinta Inn Roanoke Salem	◆◆	$75-$144	238
⑳ p. 232	**Holiday Inn Express & Suites Salem Civic Center**	◆◆◆	$100-$139 [SAVE]	238
㉑ p. 232	Inn at Burwell Place	◆◆◆	Rates not provided	238
㉒ p. 232	Hampton Inn Salem I-81	◆◆◆	Rates not provided	238
㉓ p. 232	Comfort Suites Salem	◆◆◆	$90-$180	238
㉔ p. 232	Quality Inn	◆◆	$64-$180	238

Map Page	Restaurants	Diamond Rated	Cuisine	Price Range	Page
⑳ p. 232	Mac and Bob's Restaurant	◆◆	American	$8-$27	238
㉑ p. 232	El Rodeo	◆	Mexican	$7-$18	238
㉒ p. 232	**Mamma Maria's Italian Restaurant**	◆◆	Italian	$8-$23	238

(See map & index p. 232.)

BEST WESTERN PLUS INN AT VALLEY VIEW
(540)362-2400 **4**

Hotel
$85-$199

 Best Western PLUS. **AAA Benefit:** Members save 10% or more & earn 10% bonus points!

Address: 5050 Valley View Blvd 24012 **Location:** I-581 exit 3E, just e, then just s via shopping center exit. **Facility:** 84 units. 3 stories, interior corridors. **Terms:** 3 day cancellation notice-fee imposed. **Amenities:** safes. **Pool:** heated indoor. **Activities:** exercise room. **Guest Services:** coin laundry. **Featured Amenity:** breakfast buffet.

CAMBRIA HOTEL & SUITES ROANOKE
(540)400-6226 **13**

Hotel
$119-$289

Address: 301 Reserve Ave 24016 **Location:** Just e of jct US 220 business route (Franklin Rd SW). Near Carilion Roanoke Memorial Hospital. **Facility:** 127 units. 5 stories, interior corridors. **Pool:** heated indoor. **Activities:** hot tub, bicycles, exercise room. **Guest Services:** valet and coin laundry. (See ad this page.)

COMFORT INN AIRPORT
(540)527-2020 **3**
Hotel. **Address:** 5070 Valley View Blvd 24012

COUNTRY INN & SUITES BY CARLSON
(540)366-5678
Hotel. **Address:** 7860 Plantation Rd 24019

COURTYARD BY MARRIOTT ROANOKE AIRPORT
(540)563-5002 **10**
Hotel. **Address:** 3301 Ordway Dr 24017

AAA Benefit: Members save 5% or more!

DAYS INN
540/366-0341

Motel
Rates not provided

Address: 8118 Plantation Rd 24019 **Location:** I-81 exit 146, just e on SR 115. **Facility:** 115 units. 2 stories (no elevator), interior/exterior corridors. **Pool:** outdoor. **Activities:** exercise room. **Guest Services:** coin laundry. **Featured Amenity:** continental breakfast.

FAIRFIELD INN & SUITES BY MARRIOTT ROANOKE NORTH
(540)362-4200
Hotel. **Address:** 7944 Plantation Rd 24019

AAA Benefit: Members save 5% or more!

HAMPTON INN & SUITES ROANOKE AIRPORT/VALLEY VIEW MALL
540/336-6300 **5**
Hotel. **Address:** 5033 Valley View Blvd N 24012

AAA Benefit: Members save up to 10%!

HAMPTON INN ROANOKE/HOLLINS
(540)563-5656
Hotel. **Address:** 7922 Plantation Rd 24019

AAA Benefit: Members save up to 10%!

HILTON GARDEN INN ROANOKE
540/776-3400 **14**
Hotel. **Address:** 4500 S Peak Blvd 24018

AAA Benefit: Members save up to 10%!

▼ See AAA listing this page ▼

(See map & index p. 232.)

HOLIDAY INN EXPRESS   (540)982-0100 **11**
Hotel. **Address:** 815 Gainsboro Rd 24016

HOLIDAY INN ROANOKE VALLEY VIEW   (540)362-4500 **7**
Hotel. **Address:** 3315 Ordway Dr 24017

HOLIDAY INN TANGLEWOOD/ROANOKE
                               (540)774-4400 **15**

Hotel
$99-$149

Address: 4468 Starkey Rd 24018 **Location:** I-581 exit US 220 (Franklin Rd/Salem), 0.8 mi s on SR 419 (Electric Rd). **Facility:** 196 units. 5 stories, interior corridors. **Terms:** 15 day cancellation notice. **Pool:** heated outdoor. **Activities:** exercise room. **Guest Services:** valet and coin laundry, area transportation.

/ SOME UNITS

THE HOTEL ROANOKE & CONFERENCE CENTER, CURIO - A COLLECTION BY HILTON
                    (540)985-5900 **12**

Classic Historic Hotel
$109-$289

AAA Benefit:
Members save 5% or more!

Address: 110 Shenandoah Ave 24016 **Location:** I-581 exit 5 southbound; exit 4E northbound, 0.5 mi s on US 11/221/SR 16, then just w on Wells Ave. **Facility:** The grand historic hotel was built in 1882 and features Tudor-style elegance on the hillside grounds and the grand lobby. Guest rooms feature modern fittings that borrow styling from the historic era. 331 units. 7 stories, interior corridors. **Parking:** on-site (fee) and valet. **Terms:** check-in 4 pm, 1-7 night minimum stay, cancellation fee imposed. **Amenities:** video games. **Dining:** The Regency Room, see separate listing, entertainment. **Pool:** outdoor. **Activities:** hot tub, exercise room, massage. **Guest Services:** valet laundry, area transportation. *(See ad this page.)*

/ SOME UNITS

Located in the heart of the Blue Ridge Mountains in beautiful downtown Roanoke.

▼ *See AAA listing this page* ▼

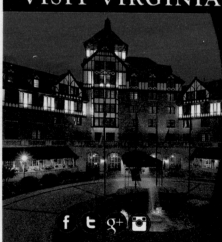

(See map & index p. 232.)

HYATT PLACE ROANOKE AIRPORT/VALLEY VIEW MALL
(540)366-4700   **6**

Hotel
$99-$249

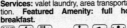
HYATT PLACE
AAA Benefit: Members save 10%!

Address: 5040 Valley View Blvd 24012 **Location:** I-581 exit 3E, just e, then just s via shopping center exit. **Facility:** 126 units. 6 stories, interior corridors. **Terms:** cancellation fee imposed. **Pool:** heated indoor. **Activities:** exercise room. **Guest Services:** valet laundry, area transportation. **Featured Amenity: full hot breakfast.**

MAINSTAY SUITES ROANOKE AIRPORT   (540)527-3030   **2**

Extended Stay Hotel. **Address:** 5080 Valley View Blvd 24012

RESIDENCE INN BY MARRIOTT ROANOKE AIRPORT
(540)265-1119   **8**

Extended Stay Hotel. **Address:** 3305 Ordway Dr NW 24017

AAA Benefit: Members save 5% or more!

SHERATON ROANOKE HOTEL & CONFERENCE CENTER
(540)563-9300   **9**

Hotel
$79-$229

Sheraton
AAA Benefit: Members save 5% or more!

Address: 2801 Hershberger Rd 24017 **Location:** I-581 exit 3W, just w to Ordway Dr, then just n via service road. **Facility:** 320 units. 7-8 stories, interior corridors. **Terms:** cancellation fee imposed. **Dining:** ? restaurants. **Pool:** outdoor, heated indoor. **Activities:** sauna, hot tub, exercise room. **Guest Services:** valet laundry.

SUPER 8
540/563-8888   **1**

Motel
Rates not provided

Address: 6616 Thirlane Rd 24019 **Location:** I-581 exit 25, s on SR 117 (Peters Creek Rd), then just w. **Facility:** 59 units. 2-3 stories (no elevator), interior corridors. **Amenities:** safes. **Featured Amenity: continental breakfast.**

WHERE TO EAT

419 WEST   540/776-0419   **17**
American. Casual Dining. **Address:** 3865 Electric Rd 24014

ALEJANDRO'S MEXICAN GRILL   540/904-5825   **1**
Mexican. Casual Dining. **Address:** 7212 Williamson Rd 24019

BREAD CRAFT, AN ARTISAN BAKERY   540/562-4112   **9**
Breads/Pastries Sandwiches. Quick Serve. **Address:** 24 Church St 24011

CARLOS BRAZILIAN INTERNATIONAL CUISINE
540/776-1117   **16**
Brazilian. Casual Dining. **Address:** 4167 Electric Rd 24018

COACH AND FOUR   540/362-4220   **3**
Steak Seafood. Casual Dining. **Address:** 5206 Williamson Rd 24012

EL TOREO   540/265-9116   **2**
Mexican. Casual Dining. **Address:** 6617 Thirlane Rd 24019

HARBOR INN SEAFOOD RESTAURANT   540/563-0001
Seafood. Casual Dining. **Address:** 7416 Williamson Rd NE 24019

HOLLYWOOD'S RESTAURANT & BAKERY   540/362-1812
American. Casual Dining. **Address:** 7770 Williamson Rd 24019

LOCAL ROOTS   540/206-2610   **11**
Natural/Organic. Fine Dining. **Address:** 1314 Grandin Rd SW 24015

LUCKY   540/982-1249   **8**
French Comfort Food. Gastropub. **Address:** 18 Kirk Ave SW 24011

LUIGI'S   540/989-6277   **13**
Italian. Fine Dining. **Address:** 3301 Brambleton Ave SW 24018

MACADO'O   540/776-9884
American. Casual Dining. **Address:** 4927 Electric Rd 24014

METRO!   540/345-6645   **6**
American. Fine Dining. **Address:** 14 Campbell Ave SW 24011

MONTANO'S INTERNATIONAL GOURMET   540/344-8960   **15**
Continental. Casual Dining. **Address:** 3733 Franklin Rd SW 24014

NAWAB INDIAN CUISINE   540/345-5150
Indian. Casual Dining. **Address:** 118-A Campbell Ave SE 24011

NEW YORKER DELICATESSEN AND RESTAURANT
540/366-0935   **4**
American. Casual Dining. **Address:** 2802 Williamson Rd 24012

ON THE RISE BREAD COMPANY   540/344-7715   **7**
Breads/Pastries Sandwiches. Quick Serve. **Address:** 303 Market St 24011

THE REGENCY ROOM   540/853-8280   **5**
American. Fine Dining. **Address:** 110 Shenandoah Ave 24016

THE ROANOKER RESTAURANT   540/344-7746   **12**

Southern American Casual Dining
$7-$22

AAA Inspector Notes: *Classic.* This family-run mainstay has been a local favorite since 1941, when it started as a downtown lunch counter. It's known for comfort food, great breakfasts and specialties such as great homemade breads: biscuits, rolls and sweet corn sticks; fried and broiled Atlantic seafood, spaghetti casserole, grilled pork tenderloin and apples; a stuffed grilled cheese sandwich and more choices like great country-style vegetables. **Features:** full bar. **Address:** 2522 Colonial Ave SW 24015 **Location:** I-581 exit Colonial Ave, just sw.

B **L** **D**

(See map & index p. 232.)

TASTE OF ASIA   540/342-1001 [14]
♥♥ Thai. Casual Dining. **Address:** 3603 Franklin Rd SW 24014

WILDFLOUR MARKET AND BAKERY   540/343-4543 [10]
♥♥ American. Casual Dining. **Address:** 1212 4th St SW 24016

ROCKY MOUNT pop. 4,799

COMFORT INN-ROCKY MOUNT   (540)489-4000
♥♥ Hotel. **Address:** 1730 N Main St 24151
HOLIDAY INN EXPRESS HOTEL & SUITES   540/489-5001
♥♥♥ Hotel. **Address:** 395 Old Franklin Tpke 24151

WHERE TO EAT

IPPY'S RESTAURANT & BAR   540/489-5600
♥♥ American. Casual Dining. **Address:** 1760 N Main St 24151

RUCKERSVILLE pop. 1,141

HOLIDAY INN EXPRESS & SUITES CHARLOTTESVILLE RUCKERSVILLE   434/985-1855
♥♥♥ Hotel. **Address:** 5920 Seminole Tr 22968

WHERE TO EAT

BLUE RIDGE CAFE   434/985-3633
♥ American. Casual Dining. **Address:** 8315 Seminole Tr 22968

SALEM (H-6) pop. 24,802, elev. 1,066'
• Restaurants p. 238
• Hotels & Restaurants map & index p. 232

Fort Lewis was built near present-day Salem in 1752 to protect area settlers. The town was chartered in 1802 upon land previously owned by the son of Gen. Andrew Lewis, the fort's namesake. Roanoke College, then a Lutheran men's school, moved to Salem in 1847. After the Civil War, the growing town marketed itself as the "Switzerland of the South." A major blizzard devastated the local economy in 1890.

City of Salem Visitor's Center: 1001 Roanoke Blvd., Salem, VA 24153. **Phone:** (540) 375-4044 or (888) 827-2536.

BAYMONT INN & SUITES SALEM ROANOKE AREA
540/562-1912 [18]

♥♥ Hotel
Rates not provided
Address: 179 Sheraton Dr 24153 **Location:** I-81 exit 141, 0.4 mi e on SR 419. **Facility:** 115 units. 2 stories (no elevator), interior corridors. **Pool:** outdoor. **Activities:** exercise room. **Guest Services:** coin laundry. **Featured Amenity:** full hot breakfast.

COMFORT SUITES INN AT RIDGEWOOD FARM
(540)375-4800
♥♥♥ Hotel. **Address:** 2898 Keagy Rd 24153

COMFORT SUITES SALEM   (540)389-7171 [23]
♥♥♥ Hotel. **Address:** 100 Wildwood Rd 24153

HAMPTON INN SALEM   (540)776-6500
♥♥♥ Hotel. **Address:** 1886 Electric Rd 24153
AAA Benefit: Members save up to 10%!

HAMPTON INN SALEM I-81   540/389-2424 [22]
♥♥♥ Hotel. **Address:** 450 Litchell Rd 24153
AAA Benefit: Members save up to 10%!

HOLIDAY INN EXPRESS & SUITES SALEM CIVIC CENTER   (540)562-3229 [20]

♥♥♥ Hotel
$100-$139
Address: 991 Russell Dr 24153 **Location:** I-81 exit 141, just e. **Facility:** 75 units. 3 stories, interior corridors. **Pool:** outdoor. **Activities:** hot tub, exercise room. **Guest Services:** coin laundry. **Featured Amenity:** breakfast buffet.

INN AT BURWELL PLACE   540/387-0250 [21]
♥♥♥ Bed & Breakfast. **Address:** 601 W Main St 24153
LA QUINTA INN ROANOKE SALEM   (540)562-2717 [19]
♥♥ Hotel. **Address:** 140 Sheraton Dr 24153
QUALITY INN   (540)387-1600 [24]
♥♥ Motel. **Address:** 151 Wildwood Rd 24153

WHERE TO EAT

CHIP & JO'S RESTAURANT   540/387-9585
♥ American. Casual Dining. **Address:** 315 8th St 24153
EL RODEO   540/387-4045 [21]
♥ Mexican. Casual Dining. **Address:** 260 Wildwood Rd 24153
MAC AND BOB'S RESTAURANT   540/389-5999 [20]
♥♥ American. Casual Dining. **Address:** 316 E Main St 24153
MAMMA MARIA'S ITALIAN RESTAURANT
540/389-2848 [22]
♥♥ Italian
Casual Dining
$8-$23
AAA Inspector Notes: A Southern Virginia favorite, the restaurant prepares a wide variety of pizza and pasta dishes. Service is upbeat and friendly. The buffet at lunchtime is very popular. **Features:** full bar. **Address:** 2025 W Main St 24153 **Location:** I-81 exit 137, just e.
[L] [D]

SANDSTON (A-1) pop. 7,571, elev. 167'
• Hotels & Restaurants map & index p. 212
• Part of Richmond area — see map p. 193

Sandston is a census-designated place in Henrico County, just east of Richmond and adjacent to the Richmond International Airport. The Richmond Dragway, at 1955 Portugee Rd. in Sandston, is an International Hot Rod Association-sanctioned facility that hosts more than 60 racing events a year from March through November. Phone (804) 737-1193.

(See map & index p. 212.)

BEST WESTERN PLUS RICHMOND AIRPORT HOTEL
(804)222-8200   **68**

Hotel
$89-$250

Best Western PLUS

AAA Benefit: Members save 10% or more & earn 10% bonus points!

Address: 5300 Airport Square Ln 23150 **Location:** I-64 exit 197A (Sandston-RIC Airport), just s to Williamsburg Rd, then 1 mi w. **Facility:** 119 units. 4 stories, interior corridors. **Terms:** cancellation fee imposed. **Pool:** outdoor. **Activities:** exercise room. **Guest Services:** valet and coin laundry, area transportation.

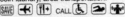

/ SOME UNITS

CANDLEWOOD SUITES RICHMOND AIRPORT
804/652-1888   **67**
Extended Stay Hotel. **Address:** 6400 Audubon Dr 23231

COURTYARD BY MARRIOTT-RICHMOND AIRPORT
(804)652-0500   **69**
Hotel. **Address:** 5400 Williamsburg Rd 23150

AAA Benefit: Members save 5% or more!

HAMPTON INN RICHMOND AIRPORT
(804)226-1888   **62**
Hotel. **Address:** 421 International Center Dr 23150

AAA Benefit: Members save up to 10%!

HILTON GARDEN INN RICHMOND AIRPORT
(804)222-3338   **63**
Hotel. **Address:** 441 International Center Dr 23150

AAA Benefit: Members save up to 10%!

HOLIDAY INN EXPRESS
(804)222-1499   **65**
Hotel. **Address:** 491 International Center Dr 23150

HOLIDAY INN RICHMOND AIRPORT
(804)236-1111   **64**
Hotel. **Address:** 445 International Center Dr 23150

HOMEWOOD SUITES BY HILTON RICHMOND AIRPORT
(804)737-1600   **66**
Extended Stay Hotel. **Address:** 5996 Audubon Dr 23150

AAA Benefit: Members save up to 10%!

WHERE TO EAT

HILLBILLY RED'S BARBEQUE
804/737-2007   **70**
Barbecue. Quick Serve. **Address:** 353 E Williamsburg Rd 23150

MEXICO RESTAURANT
804/226-2388
Mexican. Casual Dining. **Address:** 5213 Williamsburg Rd 23150

SCHUYLER (G-8) pop. 298, elev. 400'

It was in Schuyler, in the foothills of the Blue Ridge Mountains, that author Earl Hamner Jr. grew up and recorded his childhood memories in journals that were to be the basis for the popular television show "The Waltons."

SCOTTSVILLE pop. 566, elev. 279'

TAVERN ON THE JAMES   434/286-3500
American Casual Dining $9-$27

AAA Inspector Notes: Located close to the James River, this restaurant offers a wide variety of classic menu options, including steak and chicken. **Features:** full bar, patio dining, senior menu, happy hour. **Address:** 280 Valley St 24590 **Location:** 1.1 mi s on SR 20.

B L D

SHENANDOAH
- Part of Shenandoah National Park area — see map p. 241

MAMMA MIA ITALIAN RESTAURANT   540/652-6062
◈◈ Italian. Casual Dining. **Address:** 701 S Third St 22849

SHENANDOAH CAVERNS (E-7) elev. 945'

◈ GEM SAVE **SHENANDOAH CAVERNS** is 1 mi. w. of I-81 exit 269 at 261 Caverns Rd. Local legend says that two boys descended into these caverns after railroad workers broke through the limestone ceiling. The cave opened to the public in 1922, providing natural air-conditioning to a hotel that was formerly located at the entrance.

A guided 1-hour tour begins with an elevator descent to the cave's subterranean entrance hall. Colorful and pure-white formations are visible in 17 rooms, which are connected by a mile of gravel pathways. Fault lines are visible in the ceilings of many of the rooms since the caverns were largely formed by earthquake movement. Gemstone panning and an extended 2-hour tour also are available.

Among the highlights are the crystal-laden Diamond Cascade, the Bacon Formations, the Grotto of the Gods and the Oriental Garden. The temperature in the caverns remains a constant 56 F.

Food is available June-Aug. A jacket and comfortable walking shoes are recommended. **Hours:** Guided cave tours daily 9-6, mid-June through Labor Day; 9-5, mid-Mar. to mid-June and day after Labor Day-Oct. 31; 9-4, rest of year. Closed Christmas. **Cost:** (includes all Shenandoah Caverns attractions) $24; $21 (ages 62+); $12 (ages 6-12). **Phone:** (540) 477-3115. *(See ad this page.)* GT ⑪ ⑯

American Celebration on Parade is at 397 Caverns Rd. at Shenandoah Caverns. A 40,000-square-foot exhibit hall contains a collection of parade floats, props and stage settings from America's entertainment and political history, including the Rose Parade, presidential inaugurations, the Miss America pageant, Thanksgiving parades and world summit meetings.

Food is available June-Aug. **Hours:** Daily 10-6, mid-June through Labor Day; Sat.-Sun. 10-6, Easter to mid-June and day after Labor Day-Oct. 31; Sat.-Sun. 10-5, Nov. 1-Thanksgiving. Closed Christmas. **Cost:** (includes all Shenandoah Caverns attractions) $24; $21 (ages 62+); $12 (ages 6-12). **Phone:** (540) 477-3115. ⑪ ⑯

Main Street of Yesteryear is at 261 Caverns Rd. at Shenandoah Caverns. Antique, animated window displays that appeared in famous department stores include Cinderella at the ball, a 100-figure circus parade, toy soldiers and a miniature presidential inaugural parade.

Food is available June-Aug. **Hours:** Daily 9-6, mid-June through Labor Day; 9-5, mid-Mar. to mid-June and day after Labor Day-Oct. 31; 9-4, rest of year. Closed Christmas. **Cost:** (includes all Shenandoah Caverns attractions) $24; $21 (ages 62+); $12 (ages 6-12). **Phone:** (540) 477-3115. *(See ad this page.)* ⑪ ⑯

The Yellow Barn at Shenandoah Caverns, 261 Caverns Rd. at Shenandoah Caverns, relates the area's agricultural and rural heritage. Exhibits include antiques, model trains, restored farm vehicles and an indoor beehive. Food is available June-Aug. **Hours:** Daily 10-6, mid-June through Labor Day; 9-5, rest of year. Hours may vary due to private events; phone ahead. Closed Christmas. **Cost:** (includes all Shenandoah Caverns attractions) $24; $21 (ages 62+); $12 (ages 6-12). **Phone:** (540) 477-2432. *(See ad this page.)* ⑪ ⑯

SHENANDOAH NATIONAL PARK (F-8)

Elevations in the park range from 600 ft. at the north entrance to 4,050 ft. at the summit of Hawksbill Peak. Refer to AAA maps for additional elevation information.

Established in December 1935, the park extends approximately 70 miles along the crest of the Blue Ridge Mountains, between Front Royal on the north and Waynesboro on the south. In one of the most beautiful and historic regions of the East, Shenandoah National Park embraces one of the highest and most scenic portions of the Blue Ridge. Shenandoah, a Native American name, is thought to mean "Daughter of the Stars."

Spur ridges from the mountain crest blend into the rolling land of the Shenandoah Valley on the west and the wooded hills, orchards and fields of the Piedmont on the east. Between these ridges are deep, timbered hollows and cascading streams.

The 4,050-foot Hawksbill Peak and the 4,010-foot Stony Man are among the highest points in northern Virginia. Notable among the passes through the Blue Ridge are Thornton, Swift Run and Rockfish gaps, which form three of the four primary entrances into the park.

The park's 197,439 acres contain hundreds of miles of hiking trails and scenic viewpoints and are home to many species of plant and animal life. The park is a wildlife sanctuary harboring about 50 varieties of mammals, from chipmunks and groundhogs to deer and bears. Some 200 kinds of birds and a number of reptiles have been observed. The only poisonous snakes are rattlesnakes and copperheads, neither of which is encountered often. It is illegal to feed or harm wild animals.

There are nearly 100 species of trees. Most common are the hardwoods, which produce the annual blaze of autumn color; their height of brilliance usually occurs from mid- to late October. About

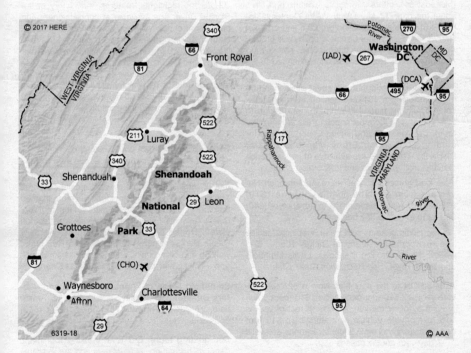

This map shows cities in Shenandoah National Park where you will find attractions, hotels and restaurants. Cities are listed alphabetically in this book on the following pages.

1,100 species of flowering plants have been identified. Wildflowers typically bloom from May through late fall. Azaleas and mountain laurel are strikingly beautiful in late spring; redbud and dogwood trees also flower at lower elevations in early spring.

General Information and Activities

Shenandoah National Park is open all year, although facilities close in winter. Permits for backcountry camping are required and are available free of charge at the park headquarters, entrance stations and visitor centers.

Free guided hikes and walks, slide shows and campfire programs are available; schedules are posted on park bulletin boards and published in *Explore Shenandoah,* a park guide.

Information is available on weekdays at park headquarters, approximately 4 miles west of Thornton Gap on US 211.

Harry F. Byrd Sr. Visitor Center, at Big Meadows (Milepost 51), offers interactive exhibits and films about the park. Dickey Ridge Visitor Center (Milepost 4.6) offers an orientation program and exhibits. Harry F. Byrd Sr. Visitor Center is open daily 8:30-5, Apr.-Nov. Dickey Ridge is open 8:30-5, early spring through late fall. Both centers offer extended hours in summer.

Hiking trails within the park cover more than 500 miles, including a 101-mile section of the Appalachian Trail, the mountain footpath from Maine to Georgia. Among the most popular trails are the Whiteoak Canyon Trail and several shorter trails, including Limberlost, Stony Man and Frazier Discovery. Trail maps are available at park entrance stations, visitor centers and concession units.

Guided horseback rides leave April through November from Skyland Stables; phone (540) 999-2212 to make reservations in advance or (540) 999-2210 for same-day bookings.

Free picnic grounds with water, fireplaces, tables and restrooms are found at Dickey Ridge, Elkwallow, Pinnacles, Big Meadows, Lewis Mountain and South River. *See Recreation Areas Chart.*

ADMISSION to the park Mar.-Nov. is $25 (per private vehicle); $20 (per motorcycle); $10 (per person arriving by other means). Admission rest of year is $15 (per private vehicle or motorcycle); $10 (per person arriving by other means). Permits are valid for 7 days. An annual pass is $50.

PETS are permitted in the park only if they are leashed, crated or otherwise restricted at all times. Some trails are closed to pets.

ADDRESS inquiries to the Superintendent, Shenandoah National Park, 3655 US 211E, Luray, VA 22835; phone (540) 999-3500.

SKYLINE DRIVE runs along the ridge crest the entire length of the park and can be entered at four points: near Front Royal on US 340; at Thornton Gap between Luray and Sperryville on US

211; at Swift Run Gap between Stanardsville and Elkton on US 33; and at Rockfish Gap between Charlottesville and Waynesboro on US 250/I-64. The speed limit is 35 mph.

The 105-mile drive is one of the most spectacular scenic highways in the East. Parking overlooks offer views of the Piedmont to the east and the Shenandoah Valley to the west. Across the Shenandoah Valley rise Massanutten Mountain and, farther away, the Allegheny Mountains.

Not far from Thornton Gap is a 610-foot tunnel through the solid granodiorite of Marys Rock. The highest point on the road is at the north entrance to Skyland, where the elevation is 3,680 feet. Blue Ridge Parkway *(see place listing p. 71)* extends 469 miles from the southern end of Skyline Drive to Great Smoky Mountains National Park in North Carolina and Tennessee.

An audio tour running from north to south describes the highlights, features and history of the Skyline Drive; it is available at concessioners and park visitor centers. **Time:** Allow 3 hours minimum. **Hours:** Skyline Drive is closed 5 p.m.-8 a.m., mid-Nov. to early Jan. and during inclement weather. **Cost:** (valid for 7 consecutive days) $25 (per private vehicle); $20 (per motorcycle); $10 (per person arriving on foot or by bicycle). Audio tour $10 (CD). **Phone:** (540) 999-3582 to order audio tour, or (540) 999-3500 for recorded information.

SMITHFIELD (C-3) pop. 8,089, elev. 33'
• Part of Hampton Roads Area — see map p. 124

Known internationally for its hams, Smithfield is one of Virginia's best preserved Colonial seaports. The downtown historic district features more than 60 buildings, including the 1752 Smithfield Inn, that represent Colonial, Federal and Victorian architectural styles. Dotted by historical structures, Windsor Castle Park, downtown at 301 Jericho Rd., offers walking and biking trails, a canoe and kayak launch and a fishing pier *(see Recreation Areas Chart).*

Smithfield & Isle of Wight Convention and Visitors Bureau: 319 B Main St., P.O. Box 37, Smithfield, VA 23431. **Phone:** (757) 357-5182 or (800) 365-9339.

Self-guiding tours: Old Town Walking Tour maps detail 65 historic points of interest and are available at the convention and visitors bureau.

Shopping: Centered on Main and Church streets, the Smithfield Historic District offers antique shops, art galleries and specialty stores.

FORT HUGER, 15080 Talcott Terr., was known as the "Gateway to the Confederate Capital" and was the site of the Battle of Suffolk at Hill's Point in 1863. Various interpretive walking trails highlight the historic fort's Civil War history. **Time:** Allow 30 minutes minimum. **Hours:** Daily dawn-dusk. Guided tours depart the first Sat. of the month at 10, Mar.-Oct.; phone ahead to confirm schedule. **Cost:** Free. Reservations are required for guided tours. **Phone:** (757) 357-0115, or (757) 356-1223 for tour information. GT

HAMPTON INN & SUITES   (757)365-4760
WWW Hotel. **Address:** 200 Vincents Crossing 23430

AAA Benefit: Members save up to 10%!

WHERE TO EAT

SMITHFIELD GOURMET BAKERY AND CAFE   757/357-0045
WW Breads/Pastries. Casual Dining. **Address:** 218 Main St 23430

SMITHFIELD STATION RESTAURANT   757/357-7700
WW Regional Seafood. Casual Dining. **Address:** 415 S Church St 23430

SOUTH BOSTON pop. 8,142

THE BERRY HILL RESORT AND CONFERENCE CENTER
                                                          (434)517-7000
WWW Historic Hotel. **Address:** 3105 River Rd S 24592

DAYS INN & SUITES SOUTH BOSTON   434/575-4000
WWW Hotel. **Address:** 1074 Bill Tuck Hwy 24592

FAIRFIELD INN & SUITES BY MARRIOTT SOUTH BOSTON
                                                          (434)575-6000
WWW Hotel. **Address:** 1120 Bill Tuck Hwy 24592

AAA Benefit: Members save 5% or more!

SUPER 8   434/572-8868
WW Motel. **Address:** 1040 Bill Tuck Hwy 24592

WHERE TO EAT

BISTRO 1888   434/572-1888
WWW New American. Fine Dining. **Address:** 221 Main St 24592

CAFFE PERONI   434/575-5645
WW Italian Sandwiches Coffee/Tea. Casual Dining. **Address:** 303 Main St 24592

ERNIE'S RESTAURANT INC   434/572-3423
WW Southern. Casual Dining. **Address:** 1010 John Randolph Blvd 24592

MEXICO VIEJO MEXICAN GRILL   434/575-1775
WW Mexican. Casual Dining. **Address:** 1020 Bill Tuck Hwy, Suite 800 24592

SOUTHERN PLENTY CAFE   434/575-7675
WW American. Casual Dining. **Address:** 206 Main St 24592

🍽 **Booth or table?**

AAA.com/travelguides/restaurants

WINDMILL FARM BAKE SHOP   434/572-4444
W Breads/Pastries Sandwiches. Quick Serve. **Address:** 2221 Wilborn Ave 24592

SOUTH HILL pop. 4,650

BEST WESTERN PLUS SOUTH HILL INN   (434)955-2777

Hotel
$95-$300

AAA Benefit: Members save 10% or more & earn 10% bonus points!

Address: 101 Thompson St 23970 **Location:** I-85 exit 12A, just e on US 58. **Facility:** 57 units, some efficiencies. 2 stories, interior corridors. **Parking:** winter plug-ins. **Terms:** cancellation fee imposed. **Pool:** outdoor. **Activities:** exercise room. **Guest Services:** coin laundry.

SAVE CALL 🏊 📶 BIZ HS 📡 🔌 🛎 🖥

COMFORT INN & SUITES   (434)447-2200

Hotel
$84-$178

Address: 250 Thompson St 23970 **Location:** I-85 exit 12A, just n. **Facility:** 52 units. 3 stories, interior corridors. **Parking:** winter plug-ins. **Amenities:** safes. **Activities:** exercise room. **Guest Services:** coin laundry. **Featured Amenity:** continental breakfast.

SAVE 🍴 CALL 🏊 📶 BIZ 📡 ✕ 🔌 🛎 🖥 /SOME UNITS 🦮

FAIRFIELD INN & SUITES BY MARRIOTT SOUTH HILL I-85
                                                   (434)447-6800
WWW Hotel. **Address:** 150 Arnold Dr 23970

AAA Benefit: Members save 5% or more!

HAMPTON INN   (434)447-4600

Hotel
$99-$159

AAA Benefit: Members save up to 10%!

Address: 200 Thompson St 23970 **Location:** I-85 exit 12A, just e on US 58. **Facility:** 54 units. 3 stories, interior corridors. **Parking:** winter plug-ins. **Terms:** check-in 4 pm, 1-7 night minimum stay, cancellation fee imposed. **Pool:** outdoor. **Activities:** exercise room. **Guest Services:** coin laundry.

SAVE 🍴 CALL 🏊 📶 BIZ HS 📡 ✕ 🔌 🛎 🖥

WHERE TO EAT

THE HORSESHOE RESTAURANT   434/447-7781
WW Southern American. Casual Dining. **Address:** 311 W Danville St 23970

KAHILL'S   434/447-6941
WW American. Casual Dining. **Address:** 1791 N Mecklenburg Ave 23950

LUCA'S ITALIAN RESTAURANT   434/447-3211
WW Italian. Casual Dining. **Address:** 932 Cycle Ln 23970

SPERRYVILLE pop. 342

THORNTON RIVER GRILLE   540/987-8790
WWW American. Casual Dining. **Address:** 3710 Sperryville Pike 22740

SPOTSYLVANIA (D-11) elev. 308'

The Battle of Spotsylvania Court House was fought May 8-21, 1864. The site is preserved as part of Fredericksburg and Spotsylvania National Military Park *(see place listing p. 117).*

In spite of losing about 17,000 men in the Battle of the Wilderness, Gen. Ulysses S. Grant pressed on toward Richmond. On May 8, north of Spotsylvania, the Union Army of the Potomac met Gen. Robert E. Lee's Confederate Army of Northern Virginia. Fighting continued for 2 weeks, resulting in approximately 30,000 casualties; among them was Union general John Sedgwick, who was killed by a sharpshooter.

The fighting reached its zenith May 12 when Union and Confederate armies struggled for 20 hours over a turn in the Confederate logworks known as the Bloody Angle. Though neither side could claim victory, Grant continued toward Richmond.

Spotsylvania County Visitor Center: 4704 Southpoint Pkwy., Fredericksburg, VA 22407. **Phone:** (540) 507-7090 or (877) 515-6197.

SPRINGFIELD (B-12) pop. 30,484, elev. 246'
• Hotels & Restaurants map & index p. 38

Just over 30,000 people live in Springfield, a census-designated place in Fairfax County. At the center of the community is the Springfield Interchange, where I-95, I-395 and I-495 intersect. An average of about 430,000 vehicles pass through interchange daily, making the highway junction one of the country's busiest.

Shopping: Springfield Town Center (6500 Springfield Mall) is anchored by JCPenney and Macy's. It also features an outdoor farmers market on Saturdays from early May through October.

BEST WESTERN SPRINGFIELD   (703)922-6100 **136**

Hotel
$99-$299

AAA Benefit: Members save 10% or more & earn 10% bonus points!

Address: 6721 Commerce St 22150 **Location:** I-95 exit 169A, just e on SR 644 E, then n; jct I-395 and 495, 0.8 mi s. Located in a commercial area. **Facility:** 177 units. 6 stories, interior corridors. **Terms:** cancellation fee imposed. **Amenities:** safes. **Pool:** outdoor. **Activities:** exercise room. **Guest Services:** valet laundry, area transportation.

COURTYARD BY MARRIOTT-SPRINGFIELD
(703)924-7200 **135**
Hotel. **Address:** 6710 Commerce St 22150

AAA Benefit: Members save 5% or more!

EMBASSY SUITES BY HILTON SPRINGFIELD
(571)339-2000 **143**
Hotel. **Address:** 8100 Loisdale Rd 22150

AAA Benefit: Members save 5% or more!

HILTON SPRINGFIELD   (703)971-8900 **142**

Hotel
$119-$199

AAA Benefit: Members save 5% or more!

Address: 6550 Loisdale Rd 22150 **Location:** I-95 exit 169A, just e on SR 644 E; jct I-395 and 495, 0.7 mi s. Located near Springfield Town Center. Franconia-Springfield, 93. **Facility:** 244 units. 12 stories, interior corridors. **Terms:** 1-7 night minimum stay, cancellation fee imposed. **Amenities:** safes. **Pool:** heated indoor. **Activities:** exercise room. **Guest Services:** valet and coin laundry, area transportation.

HOLIDAY INN EXPRESS SPRINGFIELD   703/644-5555 **137**
Hotel. **Address:** 6401 Brandon Ave 22150

HOMEWOOD SUITES BY HILTON SPRINGFIELD
(703)866-6045 **139**

Extended Stay Hotel
$149-$500

HOMEWOOD SUITES BY HILTON
AAA Benefit: Members save up to 10%!

Address: 7010 Old Keene Mill Rd 22150 **Location:** I-95 exit 169A, just nw of SR 644; jct I-395 and 495, 0.8 mi s. Located in a commercial area. **Facility:** 165 efficiencies. 6 stories, interior corridors. **Terms:** 1-7 night minimum stay, cancellation fee imposed. **Amenities:** safes. **Pool:** heated indoor. **Activities:** exercise room. **Guest Services:** valet and coin laundry, area transportation.
Featured Amenity: breakfast buffet.

RESIDENCE INN BY MARRIOTT SPRINGFIELD OLD KEENE MILL   (703)644-0020 **138**
Extended Stay Hotel. **Address:** 6412 Backlick Rd 22150

AAA Benefit: Members save 5% or more!

(See map & index p. 38.)

TOWNEPLACE SUITES BY MARRIOTT SPRINGFIELD
(703)569-8060   **134**

Extended Stay Hotel
$89-$263

| TOWNEPLACE SUITES MARRIOTT | **AAA Benefit:** Members save 5% or more! |

Address: 6245 Brandon Ave 22150 **Location:** I-95 exit 169B, just nw of SR 644; jct I-395 and 495, 0.8 mi s. Located near shopping and businesses. **Facility:** 148 units, some two bedrooms, efficiencies and kitchens. 4 stories, interior corridors. **Terms:** cancellation fee imposed. **Amenities:** Some: safes. **Pool:** heated outdoor. **Activities:** exercise room. **Guest Services:** valet and coin laundry, area transportation. **Featured Amenity: breakfast buffet.**

WINGATE BY WYNDHAM SPRINGFIELD   703/924-9444   **140**
Hotel. **Address:** 6550 Loisdale Ct 22150

WHERE TO EAT

AUSTIN GRILL   703/644-3111
Tex-Mex. Casual Dining. **Address:** 8430-A Old Keene Mill Rd 22152

BGR-THE BURGER JOINT   703/451-4651   **154**
Burgers. Quick Serve. **Address:** 8420 Old Keene Mill Rd 22152

ELENI'S GREEK TAVERNA   703/912-1400   **150**
Greek. Casual Dining. **Address:** 6131 Backlick Rd 22150

MAGGIANO'S LITTLE ITALY   703/923-9309   **153**
Italian. Casual Dining. **Address:** 6805 Springfield Mall 22150

MIKE'S AMERICAN GRILL   703/644-7100   **151**
American. Casual Dining. **Address:** 6210 Backlick Rd 22150

MONTY'S STEAKHOUSE   703/942-8676   **155**
Steak Seafood. Fine Dining. **Address:** 8426 Old Keene Mill Rd 22152

SANDWICH REPUBLIC   703/451-1655   **152**
Sandwiches. Quick Serve. **Address:** 7320 Old Keene Mill Rd 22150

SILVER DINER   703/924-1701
American. Casual Dining. **Address:** 6592 Springfield Mall 22150

STAFFORD (C-11) elev. 184'
• Restaurants p. 246

For those traveling along I-95 or Jefferson Davis Highway (US 1), Stafford is an inviting stopover offering a good selection of restaurants and hotels. This census-designated place just north of Fredericksburg also features Colonial buildings, including the Aquia Episcopal Church, 2938 Jefferson Davis Hwy., and such historic sites as 17-acre Government Island, 191 Coal Landing Rd. Stafford Civil War Park, 400 Mount Hope Church Rd., preserves earthen artillery fortifications and other remnants from the Army of the Potomac's winter encampment here 1862-63. Phone (540) 659-4007 for Aquia Episcopal Church, or (540) 658-4871 for information about Government Island or Stafford Civil War Park.

BEST WESTERN AQUIA/QUANTICO INN   (540)659-0022

Hotel
$79-$139

| Best Western. | **AAA Benefit:** Members save 10% or more & earn 10% bonus points! |

Address: 2868 Jefferson Davis Hwy 22554 **Location:** I-95 exit 143A; jct US 1 and SR 610. **Facility:** 118 units. 2 stories (no elevator), exterior corridors. **Terms:** cancellation fee imposed. **Pool:** outdoor. **Activities:** exercise room. **Guest Services:** coin laundry.

COMFORT INN STAFFORD/QUANTICO   (540)659-8999
Hotel. **Address:** 20 Salisbury Dr 22554

COURTYARD BY MARRIOTT STAFFORD QUANTICO
(703)221-6293
Hotel. **Address:** 375 Corporate Dr 22554

| | **AAA Benefit:** Members save 5% or more! |

HAMPTON INN BY HILTON AQUIA/STAFFORD/QUANTICO
(540)657-0999
Hotel. **Address:** 2925 Jefferson Davis Hwy 22554

| | **AAA Benefit:** Members save up to 10%! |

HOLIDAY INN EXPRESS & SUITES QUANTICO-STAFFORD
540/659-3600
Hotel. **Address:** 15 Salisbury Dr 22554

HOME2 SUITES BY HILTON STAFFORD/QUANTICO
540/657-8001
Extended Stay Hotel. **Address:** 3051 Jefferson Davis Hwy 22554

| | **AAA Benefit:** Members save up to 10%! |

QUALITY INN & SUITES   (540)657-5566
Hotel. **Address:** 28 Greenspring Dr 22554

RED ROOF INN & SUITES STAFFORD   (540)659-4330
Hotel. **Address:** 153 Garrisonville Rd 22554

STAYBRIDGE SUITES STAFFORD/QUANTICO   540/720-2111
Extended Stay Hotel. **Address:** 2996 Jefferson Davis Hwy 22554

SUBURBAN EXTENDED STAY HOTEL-QUANTICO
(540)288-9051
Extended Stay Hotel. **Address:** 3097 Jefferson Davis Hwy 22554

For highways, byways and more: AAA.com/maps

TOWNEPLACE SUITES BY MARRIOTT
QUANTICO-STAFFORD
(540)657-1990

Extended Stay Hotel
$82-$217

TOWNEPLACE SUITES MARRIOTT

AAA Benefit: Members save 5% or more!

Address: 2772 Jefferson Davis Hwy 22554 **Location:** I-95 exit 143A, just s on US 1. **Facility:** 93 units, some two bedrooms, efficiencies and kitchens. 3 stories, interior corridors. **Terms:** cancellation fee imposed. **Pool:** heated outdoor. **Activities:** exercise room. **Guest Services:** valet and coin laundry. **Featured Amenity:** full hot breakfast.

WHERE TO EAT

THE LOG CABIN 540/659-5067
Seafood Steak. Casual Dining. **Address:** 1749 Jefferson Davis Hwy 22554

PANCHO VILLA MEXICAN RESTAURANT 540/658-0895
Mexican. Casual Dining. **Address:** 155 Garrisonville Rd 22554

VINNY'S ITALIAN GRILL & PIZZERIA 540/657-8400
Italian Pizza. Casual Dining. **Address:** 397 Garrisonville Rd 22554

ZIBIBBO 73 TRATTORIA & BAR 540/288-3349
Italian. Casual Dining. **Address:** 2757 Jefferson Davis Hwy 22554

ZUM RHEINGARTEN RESTAURANT 703/221-4635
German. Casual Dining. **Address:** 3998 Jefferson Davis Hwy 22554

STANARDSVILLE pop. 367

THE LAFAYETTE INN 434/985-6345
American. Fine Dining. **Address:** 146 Main St 22973

STANLEY pop. 1,689

HAWKSBILL DINER 540/778-2006
American. Casual Dining. **Address:** 1388 Main St 22851

STAUNTON (F-7) pop. 23,746, elev. 1,382'

One of the oldest cities west of the Blue Ridge Mountains, Staunton (STAN-tun) was settled by John Lewis in 1732. It was named for Lady Rebecca Staunton, the wife of Gov. William Gooch. The town was laid out in 1747, and by 1800 its population had reached 1,000. Staunton's growth was aided by the opening of rail service in 1854 and its proximity to extensive mining operations.

Because it remained largely unscathed during the Civil War, Staunton has one of Virginia's finest collections of 19th-century architecture. Trinity Episcopal Church on Beverley Street was built in 1855 on the site of the building in which the Virginia Assembly took refuge in 1781, after escaping the British. Visitors can view 12 Tiffany stained glass windows in the church; phone (540) 886-9132.

Staunton also is noted as the early home of Woodrow Wilson, the most recent of the eight Virginia-born presidents. Departing from the Woodrow Wilson Presidential Library and Museum *(see attraction listing)* are free 2-hour guided walking tours of the city. Offered by the Historic Staunton Foundation, the tours are given Saturday at 10, May through October; phone (540) 885-7676.

Staunton Visitor Center: 35 S. New St., Staunton, VA 24401. **Phone:** (540) 332-3971.

Self-guiding tours: The visitor center has maps detailing a walking tour of Staunton, which features six National Historic Districts: Beverley, Gospel Hill, Newtown, Stuart Addition, The Villages and The Wharf.

AMERICAN SHAKESPEARE CENTER— BLACKFRIARS PLAYHOUSE is at 10 S. Market St. The company presents Elizabethan plays and other works at the Blackfriars Playhouse, modeled after Shakespeare's original indoor theater. In 17th-century tradition the audience closely surrounds the stage and often interacts with the performers. Pre-show lectures and educational programs also are offered.

Allow 1 hour minimum for guided tours. **Hours:** Guided backstage tours are given Mon.-Fri. at 11 and 2, Sat. at 11, Apr.-Oct.; Mon.-Fri. at 2, Sat. at 11, rest of year. Schedule varies on Thurs.; phone ahead. Evening and matinee performances are presented Wed.-Sun. and on select Mon. and Tues.; showtimes vary. **Cost:** Guided tour $7. Performance tickets $26-$60. Prices may vary for performances. Ages 0-6 are not permitted to most performances. **Phone:** (540) 851-1733 or (877) 682-4236. [GT]

FRONTIER CULTURE MUSEUM is off I-81 exit 222, then .3 mi. w. on US 250. The outdoor living-history facility features reconstructed working farms of the 17th, 18th and 19th centuries. Costumed interpreters depict life in West Africa, Germany, Northern Ireland, England and the Americas. Living-history demonstrations show a rich European influence on Appalachian cultural traditions.

Typical farms from Germany, England, Ireland and the Shenandoah Valley have been moved and re-assembled at the museum. Many of Virginia's early colonists were representative of the farmers who occupied these historic homes. A short film about the development of the museum project is available. Changing exhibits focus on European and American culture. The self-guiding tour covers 1.5 miles.

Time: Allow 2 hours minimum. **Hours:** Daily 9-5, mid-Mar. through Nov. 30; 10-4, rest of year. Closed Jan. 1, Thanksgiving and Christmas. **Cost:** $12; $11.50 (ages 61+); $11 (ages 13+ and college students with ID); $7 (ages 6-12). **Phone:** (540) 332-7850.

SUNSPOTS STUDIOS is at 202 S. Lewis St. Working artisans at this gallery and studio demonstrate the techniques they use to blow molten glass into handcrafted decorative objects. With the help of an expert glassblower, visitors can make their own ornament. **Time:** Allow 1 hour minimum. **Hours:** Mon.-Sat. 10-6, Sun. 11:30-5. Extended hours are offered in summer and in Nov. and Dec. Glassblowing demonstrations are offered most days until 4. Closed Jan. 1, Easter, Thanksgiving and Christmas. Phone ahead to confirm schedule. **Cost:** Free. **Phone:** (540) 885-0678.

WOODROW WILSON PRESIDENTIAL LIBRARY AND MUSEUM, 20 N. Coalter St. at jct. E. Frederick St., is dedicated to the life and legacy of the 28th president of the United States. Multiple galleries interpret Wilson's other roles: scholar, university president and New Jersey governor. Exhibits include presidential campaign memorabilia, historical documents and Wilson's Pierce Arrow limousine. A World War I trench experience with lights and sounds brings visitors to the battlefront.

Also offered are guided tours of his birthplace, the Presbyterian Manse, an elegant Greek Revival house adjacent to the museum. The home has been restored to depict the Wilsons' family life in the Shenandoah Valley before the Civil War. A Victorian garden, one of 13 historic gardens in Virginia, is on the grounds.

Time: Allow 1 hour minimum. **Hours:** Mon.-Sat. 9-5, Sun. noon-5, Mar.-Dec.; Thurs.-Mon. 9-5, rest of year. Last birthplace tour begins 1 hour before closing. Research library open by appointment. Closed Jan. 1, Easter, Thanksgiving, Christmas Eve and Christmas. Phone ahead to confirm schedule. **Cost:** $14; $12 (ages 60+ and active military with ID); $7 (students with ID); $5 (ages 6-12). **Phone:** (540) 885-0897 or (888) 496-6376. GT

BEST WESTERN STAUNTON INN (540)885-1112

Hotel
$99-$189

 Best Western. **AAA Benefit:** Members save 10% or more & earn 10% bonus points!

Address: 92 Rowe Rd 24401 **Location:** I-81 exit 222, just e on US 250. **Facility:** 80 units. 4 stories, interior corridors. **Terms:** cancellation fee imposed. **Pool:** heated indoor.

COMFORT INN (540)886-5000
Hotel. **Address:** 1302 Richmond Ave 24401

🔗 **Get an expert view from AAA inspectors:**
AAA.com/travelguides/hotels

ECONO LODGE STAUNTON (540)885-5158

Motel
$64-$109

Address: 1031 Richmond Ave 24401 **Location:** I-81 exit 222, 0.7 mi w on US 250. **Facility:** 88 units. 2 stories (no elevator), interior/exterior corridors. **Guest Services:** coin laundry. **Featured Amenity: continental breakfast.**

FREDERICK HOUSE 540/885-4220
Historic Hotel. **Address:** 28 N New St 24401

HAMPTON INN (540)886-7000
Hotel. **Address:** 40 Payne Ln 24401

AAA Benefit: Members save up to 10%!

HOLIDAY INN STAUNTON CONFERENCE CENTER (540)248-6020

Hotel
$99-$289

Address: 152 Fairway Ln 24401 **Location:** I-81 exit 225, 0.3 mi w on SR 262. **Facility:** 117 units. 6 stories, interior corridors. **Terms:** cancellation fee imposed. **Pool:** outdoor, heated indoor. **Activities:** health club. **Guest Services:** valet laundry.

QUALITY INN & SUITES (540)887-0200
Motel. **Address:** 200 Frontier Dr 24401

RED ROOF INN-STAUNTON (540)885-3117
Motel. **Address:** 42 Sangers Ln 24401

SLEEP INN (540)887-6500
Hotel. **Address:** 222 Jefferson Hwy 24401

STONEWALL JACKSON HOTEL & CONFERENCE CENTER 540/885-4848

Hotel
Rates not provided

Address: 24 S Market St 24401 **Location:** Between Beverley and Johnson sts; downtown. **Facility:** 124 units. 5 stories, interior corridors. **Terms:** check-in 4 pm. **Pool:** heated indoor. **Activities:** hot tub, exercise room, massage. **Guest Services:** valet and coin laundry.

WHERE TO EAT

AIOLI 540/885-1414
Mediterranean Small Plates. Fine Dining. **Address:** 29 N Augusta St 24401

BYERS STREET BISTRO 540/887-6100
Southern American. Casual Dining. **Address:** 18 Byers St 24401

CLOCKTOWER RESTAURANT & BAR 540/213-0665
American. Casual Dining. **Address:** 27 W Beverley St 24401

THE DEPOT GRILLE   540/885-7332

▼▼▼ American. Casual Dining. **Address:** 42 Middlebrook Ave 24401

EL PUERTO MEXICAN RESTAURANT   540/886-3578

▼▼ Mexican. Casual Dining. **Address:** 830 Greenville Ave 24401

EMILIO'S ITALIAN RESTAURANT   540/885-0102

▼▼ Italian. Casual Dining. **Address:** 23 E Beverley St 24401

HOMETOWN GRILL OF STAUNTON   540/885-2200

▼ American. Casual Dining. **Address:** 30 Sangers Ln 24401

KATHY'S   540/885-4331

▼▼ American. Casual Dining. **Address:** 705 Greenville Ave 24401

MILL STREET GRILL   540/886-0656

▼▼▼▼
**American
Casual Dining
$10-$32**

AAA Inspector Notes: The restaurant boasts a lively, contemporary atmosphere, brick facades, local artwork and a stylish bar. Guests soon realize why it is known for prime rib and American favorites like chicken and pasta. Don't miss the popular and locally made cheesecake. **Features:** full bar. **Reservations:** suggested, weekends. **Address:** 1 Mill St 24401 **Location:** I-81 exit 222, just w.

L   D

MRS ROWE'S FAMILY RESTAURANT & BAKERY
                                              540/886-1833

▼▼ American. Casual Dining. **Address:** Rowe Rd 24401

SHENANDOAH PIZZA AND TAP HOUSE   540/213-0008

▼ Pizza. Casual Dining. **Address:** 19 E Beverley St 24401

WRIGHT'S DAIRY-RITE FAMILY RESTAURANT   540/886-0435

▼ American. Casual Dining. **Address:** 346 Greenville Ave 24401

ZYNODOA RESTAURANT   540/885-7775

▼▼▼ Southern American. Casual Dining. **Address:** 115 E Beverley St 24401

STEELES TAVERN (G-7) elev. 1,680'

David Steele settled here in 1781, offering lodging to travelers on the road between Staunton and Lexington. The village that grew up around the tavern would be the birthplace of two revolutionary labor-saving devices, the Gibbs sewing machine and the McCormick reaper.

STEPHENS CITY pop. 1,829

COMFORT INN-STEPHENS CITY   (540)869-6500

▼▼▼
**Hotel
$85-$120**

Address: 167 Town Run Ln 22655 **Location:** I-81 exit 307, just se. **Facility:** 59 units. 2 stories (no elevator), interior corridors. **Pool:** outdoor. **Activities:** exercise room. **Guest Services:** coin laundry.

SAVE ▐▌↑ ⚓ ▐▌ BIZ HS 🛜
✕ 🛏 🖨 💻 / SOME UNITS 🐾

HOLIDAY INN EXPRESS   540/869-0909

▼▼▼ Hotel. **Address:** 165 Town Run Ln 22655

WHERE TO EAT

DEL RIO MEXICAN RESTAURANT   540/868-0111

▼▼ Mexican. Casual Dining. **Address:** 356 Fairfax Pike 22655

STERLING (A-11) pop. 27,822, elev. 300'

- **Restaurants p. 250**
- **Hotels & Restaurants map & index p. 38**

LOUDOUN HERITAGE FARM MUSEUM is 2 mi. n. on SR 28, 1 mi. e. on Church Rd., then .4 mi. n. on Cascades Pkwy. to the Claude Moore Park entrance. Some 300 years of agricultural history unfold at this facility tracing the ventures of 10 generations of Loudoun County residents. Much of the original Waxpool General Store, in operation 1890-1946, has been reconstructed inside the interactive museum. Of interest is the farm kitchen and schoolhouse exhibits.

Time: Allow 1 hour minimum. **Hours:** Tues.-Sat. 9:30-4:30, Sun. 11:30-4:30. Closed Jan. 1, Easter, July 4, Thanksgiving, Christmas Eve, Christmas and Dec. 31. **Cost:** $5; $4 (ages 55+ and military with ID); $3 (ages 2-12). **Phone:** (571) 258-3800.

BEST WESTERN DULLES AIRPORT INN
                                    (703)471-8300   **20**

▼▼▼
**Motel
$79-$189**

BW **Best Western.** **AAA Benefit:** Members save 10% or more & earn 10% bonus points!

Address: 45440 Holiday Dr 20166 **Location:** 1.7 mi n on SR 28 from jct SR 267 (Dulles Toll Rd), just e on SR 846, just s on Shaw Rd. **Facility:** 122 units. 2 stories (no elevator), exterior corridors. **Terms:** cancellation fee imposed. **Activities:** exercise room. **Guest Services:** valet and coin laundry.

SAVE ECO ✈ ▐▌ BIZ HS 🛜
✕ 🛏 🖨 💻 / SOME UNITS 🐾

CANDLEWOOD SUITES WASHINGTON DULLES/STERLING
                                              703/674-2288

▼▼▼ Extended Stay Hotel. **Address:** 45520 Severn Way 20166

COUNTRY INN & SUITES BY CARLSON, WASHINGTON DULLES INTERNATIONAL AIRPORT   703/435-2700   **21**

▼▼▼ Hotel. **Address:** 45620 Falke Plaza 20166

COURTYARD BY MARRIOTT DULLES TOWN CENTER
                                    (571)434-6400

▼▼▼
**Hotel
$59-$258**

COURTYARD Marriott **AAA Benefit:** Members save 5% or more!

Address: 45500 Majestic Dr 20166 **Location:** 0.4 mi e on SR 7 from jct SR 28, just s on CR 1582 (Algonkian Pkwy). Adjacent to Dulles Town Center Mall. **Facility:** 157 units. 4 stories, interior corridors. **Terms:** cancellation fee imposed. **Amenities:** safes. **Pool:** heated indoor. **Activities:** hot tub, exercise room. **Guest Services:** valet and coin laundry, boarding pass kiosk, area transportation. **Featured Amenity:** full hot breakfast.

SAVE ECO ✈ ▐▌↑ 🍽 CALL 🖥 ⚓ ▐▌ BIZ 🛜
✕ 🛏 💻 / SOME UNITS 🖥

(See map & index p. 38.)

DOUBLETREE BY HILTON HOTEL STERLING - DULLES AIRPORT (703)230-0077 **14**
🔷🔷🔷 Hotel. **Address:** 21611 Atlantic Blvd 20166

AAA Benefit: Members save 5% or more!

FAIRFIELD INN & SUITES BY MARRIOTT DULLES AIRPORT (703)435-5300 **22**
🔷🔷🔷 Hotel. **Address:** 23000 Indian Creek Dr 20166

AAA Benefit: Members save 5% or more!

HAMPTON INN & SUITES BY HILTON DULLES AIRPORT (703)537-7800 **17**
🔷🔷🔷 Hotel. **Address:** 22700 Holiday Park Dr 20166

AAA Benefit: Members save up to 10%!

HAMPTON INN BY HILTON-DULLES/CASCADES (703)450-9595
🔷🔷🔷 Hotel. **Address:** 46331 McClellan Way 20165

AAA Benefit: Members save up to 10%!

HAWTHORN SUITES BY WYNDHAM DULLES STERLING 703/444-2111
🔷🔷 Extended Stay Hotel. **Address:** 21123 Whitfield Pl 20165

HOLIDAY INN WASHINGTON DULLES INTERNATIONAL AIRPORT (703)471-7411 **19**
🔷🔷🔷 Hotel. **Address:** 45425 Holiday Dr 20166

HYATT HOUSE STERLING/DULLES AIRPORT NORTH (703)435-9002 **23**

🔷🔷🔷 Extended Stay Hotel $74-$199

HYATT house
AAA Benefit: Members save 10%!

Address: 45520 Dulles Plaza 20166 **Location:** 1 mi n on SR 28 from jct SR 267 (Dulles Toll Rd), just e on CR 606. **Facility:** 162 units, some efficiencies. 6 stories, interior corridors. **Terms:** cancellation fee imposed. **Pool:** heated outdoor. **Activities:** hot tub, exercise room. **Guest Services:** valet and coin laundry, area transportation. **Featured Amenity: full hot breakfast.** *(See ad this page.)*

SAVE 🔌 🍽 CALL 🚰 ✈ 👨 BIZ HS 📶 ✕ 🔲 🔲 🔲 / SOME UNITS 🐾

HYATT PLACE STERLING/DULLES AIRPORT-NORTH (703)444-3909

🔷🔷🔷 Hotel $69-$199

HYATT PLACE
AAA Benefit: Members save 10%!

Address: 21481 Ridgetop Cir 20166 **Location:** 1.3 mi e on SR 7 from jct SR 28. Located in a shopping and business area. **Facility:** 134 units. 6 stories, interior corridors. **Terms:** cancellation fee imposed. **Pool:** outdoor. **Activities:** exercise room. **Guest Services:** valet laundry, area transportation. **Featured Amenity: full hot breakfast.**

SAVE 🔌 🍽 🍽 CALL 🚰 ✈

👨 BIZ 📶 ✕ 🎬 🔲 🔲 / SOME UNITS 🐾

(See map & index p. 38.)

RESIDENCE INN BY MARRIOTT DULLES AIRPORT @ DULLES 28 CENTRE   (703)421-2000 **15**

Extended Stay Hotel
$92-$260

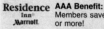

Residence Inn® Marriott

AAA Benefit: Members save 5% or more!

Address: 45250 Monterey Pl 20166 **Location:** SR 28 exit CR 625 (Waxpool Rd), just w, just n on Pacific Blvd, then just e on Commercial Dr. Located in a commercial area. **Facility:** 151 units, some two bedrooms, efficiencies and kitchens. 4 stories, interior corridors. **Terms:** cancellation fee imposed. **Amenities:** safes. **Pool:** heated indoor. **Activities:** hot tub, exercise room. **Guest Services:** valet and coin laundry, area transportation. **Featured Amenity:** breakfast buffet.

SPRINGHILL SUITES BY MARRIOTT WASHINGTON DULLES AIRPORT   (703)444-3944 **16**
Hotel. **Address:** 22595 Shaw Rd 20166

AAA Benefit: Members save 5% or more!

SUBURBAN EXTENDED STAY HOTEL WASHINGTON-DULLES/STERLING   (703)674-2299
Extended Stay Hotel. **Address:** 45510 E Severn Way 20166

TOWNEPLACE SUITES BY MARRIOTT AT DULLES AIRPORT   (703)707-2017 **18**
Extended Stay Hotel. **Address:** 22744 Holiday Park Dr 20166

AAA Benefit: Members save 5% or more!

WHERE TO EAT

A TASTE OF BURMA   703/444-8510
Burmese. Casual Dining. **Address:** 126 Edds Ln 20165

O'FAOLAIN'S   703/444-9796
Irish. Casual Dining. **Address:** 20921 Davenport Dr 20165

SORTREL THAI RESTAURANT & BAR   703/433-9720
Thai. Casual Dining. **Address:** 46 Pidgeon Hill Dr 20165

SWEETWATER TAVERN   571/434-6500
American. Gastropub. **Address:** 45980 Waterview Plaza 20166

STONY CREEK pop. 198

HAMPTON INN-STONY CREEK   (434)246-5500
Hotel. **Address:** 10476 Blue Star Hwy 23882

AAA Benefit: Members save up to 10%!

SLEEP INN & SUITES   (434)246-5100
Hotel. **Address:** 11019 Blue Star Hwy 23882

STRASBURG (E-8) pop. 6,398, elev. 637'

German settlers were drawn to the Bavarian-like countryside around Strasburg in the late 1700s. Beginning in the 19th century, pottery-making rose to such prominence that the community was dubbed "Pot Town." By 1908, however, its six potteries had closed. Strasburg's economy is based primarily on printing and the manufacture of automotive parts. The city also is a favorite stop for antique hunters.

Strasburg Chamber of Commerce: 132 W. King St., P.O. Box 42, Strasburg, VA 22657. **Phone:** (540) 465-3187.

Self-guiding tours: A self-guiding walking tour brochure is available from the chamber of commerce.

Shopping: Strasburg Antique Emporium (160 N. Massanutten St.) features a multitude of vendors specializing in Civil War memorabilia, furniture, vintage clothing, reproductions and art. Shops, galleries and other members of the O Shenandoah County Artisan Trail, which runs from Strasburg to New Market, specialize in local artisan-made products.

STRASBURG MUSEUM is at 440 E. King St. The town's old railroad station houses a pottery collection, toys, apparel, home implements, farm tools and shop machines that date from the mid-1800s. Settings include Colonial and Victorian rooms and cooper's, potter's and blacksmith's shops. Civil War exhibits also are on display, as are a red caboose and a model railroad depicting Strasburg and the Southern Railway in the 1930s. **Hours:** Daily 10-4, May-Oct. **Cost:** $3; $1 (ages 13-18); 50c (ages 0-12). Cash only. **Phone:** (540) 465-3175.

FAIRFIELD INN & SUITES BY MARRIOTT STRASBURG SHENANDOAH VALLEY   (540)465-1600
Hotel. **Address:** 33760 Old Valley Pike 22657

AAA Benefit: Members save 5% or more!

HOTEL STRASBURG   540/465-9191
Historic Country Inn. **Address:** 213 S Holliday St 22657

THE RAMADA STRASBURG   540/465-2444
Hotel. **Address:** 21 Signal Knob Dr 22657

WHERE TO EAT

HOTEL STRASBURG RESTAURANT   540/465-9191
Regional American. Fine Dining. **Address:** 213 Holliday St 22657

JALISCO MEXICAN RESTAURANT   540/465-5300
Mexican. Casual Dining. **Address:** 348 E King St 22657

STRATFORD (F-10) elev. 148'

The land for Stratford Hall was purchased in 1717 by Thomas Lee, president of the Council of Virginia and acting governor 1749-50. The manor he built overlooking the Potomac River would be home to four generations of the Lee family, including Gen. Robert E. Lee, who was born there in 1807. Thomas' sons, Richard Henry and Francis Lightfoot, were the only brothers to sign the Declaration of Independence. Henry "Light Horse Harry" Lee,

Robert E. Lee's father, was a Revolutionary War general.

 STRATFORD HALL is off SR 3 to SR 214, then 1 mi. following signs. The house, the birthplace of Robert E. Lee, was built circa 1738 in the shape of an H and is among the finest examples of Colonial architecture in the United States. Owned by the Lee family 1717-1822, the plantation still is operated in the manner of that era. Visitors can wander more than 1,900 acres of woods, meadows, gardens and cultivated fields.

The visitor center offers several galleries featuring interpretive displays, artifacts and temporary exhibitions. Auxiliary buildings include an 18th-century kitchen and a coach house. A reconstructed mill grinds corn, wheat, oats and barley (weather permitting) on the second Saturday of each month April through October. More than 2 miles of nature trails crisscross the plantation.

Food is available daily 11-3, early Mar.-late Dec. Pets are not permitted inside buildings. **Hours:** Grounds daily 9:30-4. House tours are given daily on the hour 10-4, early Mar.-late Dec; Sat.-Sun. and Mon. holidays on the hour 10-4, rest of year. Closed Jan. 1, Christmas, Christmas Eve and Dec. 31. Phone ahead to confirm schedule. **Cost:** House tour $12; $11 (ages 60+ and active military with ID); $7 (ages 6-11). Grounds only $7; $5 (ages 6-11). **Phone:** (804) 493-8038. GT ⑪ 🛪

STUARTS DRAFT pop. 9,235

SANZONE'S ITALIAN RESTAURANT   540/337-3373
♥♥ Italian. Casual Dining. **Address:** 2897 Stuarts Draft Hwy 24477

SUFFOLK pop. 84,585, elev. 49'
• Hotels & Restaurants map & index p. 134
• Part of Hampton Roads Area — see map p. 124

COMFORT SUITES SUFFOLK/CHESAPEAKE
(757)215-0700 ㊺

♥♥♥♥
Hotel
$84-$179

Address: 5409 Plummer Blvd 23435 **Location:** I-664 exit 9A, just n on US 17. **Facility:** 116 units. 5 stories, interior corridors. **Amenities:** safes. **Pool:** heated indoor. **Activities:** hot tub, exercise room. **Guest Services:** valet and coin laundry. **Featured Amenity:** breakfast buffet.

🅰 **Book and save at AAA.com/hertz**

COURTYARD BY MARRIOTT   (757)483-5777 ㊸
 Hotel. **Address:** 8060 Harbour View Blvd 23435

AAA Benefit: Members save 5% or more!

HAMPTON INN SUFFOLK   757/935-5880

Hotel
Rates not provided

AAA Benefit: Members save up to 10%!

Address: 1017 Centerbrooke Ln 23434 **Location:** From US 58/460, just n on Godwin Blvd (SR 10/32). **Facility:** 94 units. 5 stories, interior corridors. **Pool:** heated indoor. **Activities:** exercise room. **Guest Services:** valet and coin laundry.

SAVE CALL 🦽 ➦ 🛏 BIZ HS 🛜 ✉ 🚪 🖥 📺

HILTON GARDEN INN & SUFFOLK CONFERENCE CENTER
(757)925-1300
♥♥♥♥ Hotel. **Address:** 100 E Constance Rd 23434

AAA Benefit: Members save up to 10%!

HILTON GARDEN INN CHESAPEAKE/SUFFOLK
(757)484-9001 ㊹
♥♥♥♥ Hotel. **Address:** 5921 Harbour View Blvd 23435

AAA Benefit: Members save up to 10%!

TOWNEPLACE SUITES BY MARRIOTT   (757)483-5177 ㊻
♥♥♥♥ Extended Stay Hotel. **Address:** 8050 Harbour View Blvd 23435

AAA Benefit: Members save 5% or more!

WHERE TO EAT

BELLA NAPOLI ITALIAN RESTAURANT   757/483-0720 ㉒
♥♥ Italian Pizza. Casual Dining. **Address:** 6550 Hampton Roads Pkwy 23435

THE EGG BISTRO   757/967-0103 ㉓
♥♥ Breakfast. Casual Dining. **Address:** 5860 Harbour View Blvd 23435

NANA SUSHI   757/686-1560 ㉐
♥♥ Japanese Sushi. Casual Dining. **Address:** 6255 College Dr 23435

THE PLAID TURNIP   757/923-9740
♥♥ American. Casual Dining. **Address:** 115 N Main St 23434

RIVER STONE CHOPHOUSE   757/638-7990 ㉙
♥♥♥ Steak Seafood. Fine Dining. **Address:** 8032 Harbour View Blvd 23435

TASTE UNLIMITED   757/967-0895
♥ Sandwiches. Quick Serve. **Address:** 5911 Harbour View Blvd, Suite 100 23435

TOTOY'S FILIPINO STORE   757/483-1971 ㉑
♥ Philippine. Quick Serve. **Address:** 6550 Hampton Roads Pkwy, Suite 107 23435

VINTAGE TAVERN   757/238-8808
♥♥♥ Southern American. Fine Dining. **Address:** 1900 Governor's Pointe Dr 23436

SURRY (B-3) pop. 244, elev. 121'
• Part of Hampton Roads Area — see map p. 124

Surry County, on the southern banks of the James River, harbors several historic sites—from a rare castle to church ruins reputed to be haunted (Second Southwark Church off SR 10). Until 1652 these lands were part of the James City Shire, which also encompassed Jamestown *(see place listing p. 156)*, the first permanent English settlement in North America.

At the core of Surry County is the town of Surry, a small country village exuding old-world sensibility. To fully appreciate Surry's charm, take a walk past some of its long-standing structures. Jacobean Bacon's Castle, with its three chimneys and cruciform shape, is one of Surry's most distinctive landmarks. Stroll along the sand walkways of its garden for closer inspection of the colorful hollyhocks, snapdragons and columbine.

The 1854 mansion at Chippokes Plantation State Park also is surrounded by formal gardens comprising azaleas, crape myrtles and boxwoods. (If you're visiting the state park in July, the crape myrtles will be in full bloom, plus the Pork, Peanut and Pine Festival takes place the third weekend of the month. You'll sway to country, bluegrass and gospel music during this event highlighting the county's three main industries.) And though its brick exterior is lovely, the house at Smith's Fort Plantation shelters such delightful architectural elements as fluted pilasters, a cornice, arched cupboards and pine wood paneling.

If you're an adventure seeker, explore the 3.5 miles of hiking and bicycling trails at Chippokes Plantation State Park or visit the Hog Island Wildlife Management Area, which covers 3,908 acres of land in Surry and Isle of Wight counties. Hog Island is ideal for fishing, with carp, blue catfish and striped bass often found near the entrance to the Hog Island tract (located on a peninsula just north of the junction of SRs 10 and 617). In this section of the wildlife management area, you can access two observation platforms off Hog Island Road. The tidal marshes, ponds and pine forests found here attract a variety of fauna, including eagles and assorted shorebirds.

From late April to early May you can pick your own strawberries at College Run Farms at 2051 Alliance Rd. Other fresh produce items are available in summer and fall; phone (757) 294-3970.

SURRY NUCLEAR INFORMATION CENTER is 10 mi. e. on SR 10 to SR 650, then 5 mi. n. to 5570 Hog Island Rd. Innovative displays and interactive exhibits illuminate the science behind nuclear-generated electricity. Using muscle power, visitors produce electricity with a bicycle generator or control the power level in a model reactor core. They also can measure radioactivity with a Geiger counter, learn about nuclear power from uranium mining to electricity generation, and take the carbon footprint challenge to see what impact their lifestyle has on the Earth.

Film topics include electrical safety and managing used nuclear fuel. **Hours:** Mon.-Fri. 9-4 (based on staff availability). Closed major holidays. Phone ahead to confirm schedule. **Cost:** Free. **Phone:** (757) 357-5410.

TANGIER (G-11) pop. 727, elev. 0'

Discovered and named in 1608 by Capt. John Smith, Tangier Island was settled in 1686 by John Crockett and his sons' families. In 1814 it was headquarters of a British fleet that ravaged the Chesapeake Bay. Many customs and much of the appearance of an earlier era remain. Natives of the island still speak with a trace of an Elizabethan accent.

Since the 1800s Tangier's fishermen have supplied the Eastern Shore of Maryland with crabs and oysters. Crab farms lie along the island's shore and in open tanks perched on pilings in the harbor, which is crowded with fishing craft and sailboats. Duck hunting, fishing and swimming are permitted.

There are only a few cars and trucks on the island; bicycles and motor scooters are popular means of transportation. The island's two streets are only 8 to 10 feet wide.

Boat trips to the island depart from Onancock *(see place listing p. 184)* and Reedville *(see place listing p. 191)* as well as from Crisfield, Md. Reservations are required.

TAPPAHANNOCK (G-10) pop. 2,375, elev. 23'

In 1680 the General Assembly passed an act for "cohabitation," creating Tappahannock and 15 other towns. The act was vetoed by King Charles II, but later revived under William and Mary. Despite these delays in sanctioning its existence, Tappahannock grew into a prosperous Colonial port and county seat.

Tappahannock-Essex County Chamber of Commerce: 205 Cross St., P.O. Box 481, Tappahannock, VA 22560. **Phone:** (804) 443-5241.

THE ESSEX INN   (804)443-9900
Historic Bed & Breakfast. **Address:** 203 Duke St 22560

HOLIDAY INN EXPRESS HOTEL & SUITES   (804)445-1200
Hotel. **Address:** 1648 Tappahannock Blvd 22560

SUPER 8   804/443-3888
Motel. **Address:** 1800 Tappahannock Blvd 22560

WHERE TO EAT

LOWERY'S SEAFOOD RESTAURANT   804/443-2800
Regional Seafood. Casual Dining. **Address:** 528 Church Ln 22560

NORTHERN NECK BURGER   804/925-6100
Burgers. Quick Serve. **Address:** 303 Queen St 22560

TO DO CAFE   804/443-2002
Seafood. Casual Dining. **Address:** 1008 S Church Ln 22560

THORNBURG

BEST WESTERN PLUS THORNBURG INN & SUITES
(540)805-5023

Hotel
$139-$200

Best Western PLUS

AAA Benefit: Members save 10% or more & earn 10% bonus points!

Address: 5217 Mudd Tavern Rd 22580 **Location:** I-95 exit 118, just w. **Facility:** 82 units, some efficiencies. 8 stories, interior corridors. **Terms:** cancellation fee imposed. **Pool:** heated indoor. **Activities:** exercise room. **Guest Services:** complimentary laundry.

SAVE CALL ♿ 🏊 🛗 BIZ 📶
✕ 🛏 🍳 🖥

HOLIDAY INN EXPRESS & SUITES   (540)604-9690
♥♥♥ Hotel. **Address:** 6415 Dan Bell Ln 22565

TOPPING

MERROIR   804/758-2871
♥♥ Seafood. Casual Dining. **Address:** 784 Locklies Creek Rd 23169

TRIANGLE (C-12) pop. 8,188, elev. 161'

PRINCE WILLIAM FOREST PARK is accessed by taking I-95 s. to exit 150B, then .2 mi. w. to Joplin Rd. (SR 010). Covering more than 15,000 acres, the park offers hikers more than 37 miles of hiking trails and 21 miles of biking trails. During summer months, park rangers offer interpretive programs. Historic and nature exhibits are displayed at the Visitor Center.

Only campers and cabin occupants are admitted after dark, except when there are evening programs. **Hours:** Park open daily dawn-dusk. Visitor center open daily 9-5, Mar.-Oct.; 8-4, rest of year. Visitor center closed Jan. 1, Thanksgiving and Christmas. **Cost:** (valid for 7 days) $7 (per private vehicle); $5 (per person arriving by other means). **Phone:** (703) 221-7181. 🏔 ✕ 🎣 🏕

TROUTVILLE pop. 431

COMFORT INN   (540)992-5600
♥♥ Hotel. **Address:** 2545 Lee Hwy S 24175
HOLIDAY INN EXPRESS ROANOKE/TROUTVILLE
(540)966-4444
♥♥♥ Hotel. **Address:** 3200 Lee Hwy S 24175
QUALITY INN   (540)992-5335
♥♥♥ Hotel. **Address:** 3139 Lee Hwy S 24175

WHERE TO EAT

THE GREENWOOD RESTAURANT   540/992-3550
♥ American. Casual Dining. **Address:** 8176 Lee Hwy 24175

TYSONS CORNER (B-12) pop. 19,627, elev. 479'
• **Restaurants p. 254**
• **Hotels & Restaurants map & index p. 38**

Capital One, Hilton and many other companies have their corporate headquarters in Tysons Corner,

Fairfax County's central business district. Located between McLean and Vienna *(see place listings p. 169 and p. 255)* along the Capital Beltway (I-495), the census-designated place also boasts the state's largest shopping mall, Tysons Corner Center.

Fairfax County/Capital Region Visitors Center-Tysons Corner Center: 1961 Chain Bridge Rd., McLean, VA 22102. **Phone:** (703) 752-9500 or (800) 732-4732.

Shopping: Tysons Galleria, SR 123 and International Drive, includes Macy's, Neiman Marcus and Saks Fifth Avenue as well as some 100 specialty shops. Bloomingdale's, Lord & Taylor, Macy's and Nordstrom, plus more than 200 other stores, can be found at Tysons Corner Center, off SRs 7 and 123.

COURTYARD BY MARRIOTT, TYSONS CORNER
(703)790-0207   **61**

Hotel
$63-$528

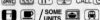
COURTYARD Marriott

AAA Benefit: Members save 5% or more!

Address: 1960A Chain Bridge Rd 22102 **Location:** I-495 exit 46A, 0.5 mi s on SR 123, just nw on International Dr, then just se on Greensboro Dr. Located near shopping malls, business offices and Tysons Corner Metro. 🚇 Tysons Corner, 101. **Facility:** 229 units. 11 stories, interior corridors. **Parking:** on-site (fee). **Terms:** 3 day cancellation notice fee imposed. **Activities:** exercise room. **Guest Services:** valet and coin laundry, boarding pass kiosk, area transportation.

SAVE ECO 🍴 ▼ CALL ♿ 🛗 BIZ HS 📶 ✕
🛏 🖥 /SOME UNITS 🍳 🚌

DOUBLETREE BY HILTON MCLEAN TYSONS
703/893-2100   **60**

Hotel
Rates not provided

DOUBLETREE BY HILTON

AAA Benefit: Members save 5% or more!

Address: 1960 Chain Bridge Rd 22102 **Location:** I-495 exit 46A, 0.5 mi s on SR 123, just nw on International Dr, then just sw on Greensboro Dr. Located near shopping malls, business offices and Tysons Corner Metro. 🚇 Tysons Corner, 101. **Facility:** 316 units. 3-9 stories, interior corridors. **Parking:** on-site (fee). **Amenities:** *Some:* safes. **Dining:** 2 restaurants. **Pool:** heated indoor. **Activities:** exercise room. **Guest Services:** valet and coin laundry, area transportation.

SAVE ECO 🍴 🛗 ▼ CALL ♿ 🏊 🛗 BIZ HS
📶 ✕ 🖥 /SOME UNITS 🍳 🛏 🚌

EMBASSY SUITES HOTEL BY HILTON TYSONS CORNER
(703)883-0707   **59**
♥♥♥ Hotel. **Address:** 8517 Leesburg Pike 22182

AAA Benefit: Members save 5% or more!

EXTENDED STAY AMERICA-WASHINGTON, DC-TYSONS CORNER   (703)356-6300   **65**
♥♥ Extended Stay Hotel. **Address:** 8201 Old Courthouse Rd 22182

(See map & index p. 38.)

HILTON MCLEAN TYSONS CORNER

(703)847-5000 **55**

Hotel
$95-$449

 Hilton
HOTELS & RESORTS

AAA Benefit: Members save 5% or more!

Address: 7920 Jones Branch Dr 22102 **Location:** I-495 exit 46A, 0.3 mi sw on SR 123, just nw on Tysons Blvd, 0.4 mi ne on Galleria/Westpark Dr, then just s; I-495 Express Lanes exit Jones Branch Dr. McLean, 100. **Facility:** Near two shopping malls in a business park area, this hotel is ideal if traveling on business or leisure and is well designed for today's technology demands. 458 units. 9 stories, interior corridors. **Terms:** check-in 4 pm, 1-7 night minimum stay, cancellation fee imposed. **Amenities:** safes. **Pool:** heated indoor. **Activities:** exercise room. **Guest Services:** valet laundry, area transportation.

HYATT REGENCY TYSONS CORNER CENTER

(703)893-1234 **62**

Hotel
$99-$459

 HYATT REGENCY

AAA Benefit: Members save 10%!

Address: 7901 Tysons One Pl 22102 **Location:** I-495 exit 46A, just s on SR 123. Connected to Tysons Corner Shopping Mall. Tysons Corner, 101. **Facility:** 300 units. 17 stories, interior corridors. **Parking:** on-site (fee) and valet. **Terms:** 3 day cancellation notice-fee imposed. **Amenities:** safes. **Pool:** heated indoor. **Activities:** exercise room. **Guest Services:** valet laundry, area transportation.

RESIDENCE INN BY MARRIOTT-TYSONS CORNER

(703)893-0120 **57**

Extended Stay Hotel
$63-$294

 Residence Inn Marriott

AAA Benefit: Members save 5% or more!

Address: 8616 Westwood Center Dr 22182 **Location:** I-495 exit 47A, 1.9 mi w on SR 7, then just s. Located in a commercial and business area. Spring Hill, 103. **Facility:** 96 kitchen units, some two bedrooms. 2 stories (no elevator), exterior corridors. **Terms:** check-in 4 pm, cancellation fee imposed. **Pool:** outdoor. **Activities:** hot tub, exercise room. **Guest Services:** valet and coin laundry, area transportation. **Featured Amenity:** full hot breakfast.

RESIDENCE INN BY MARRIOTT TYSONS CORNER MALL

(703)917-0800 **63**

Extended Stay Hotel. **Address:** 8400 Old Courthouse Rd 22182

AAA Benefit: Members save 5% or more!

THE RITZ-CARLTON, TYSONS CORNER

703/506-4300 **58**

Hotel
Rates not provided

 THE RITZ-CARLTON

AAA Benefit: Unequaled service at special member savings!

Address: 1700 Tysons Blvd 22102 **Location:** I-495 exit 46A, 0.3 mi sw on SR 123, then just nw; I-495 Express Lanes exit Jones Branch Dr. Connected to Tysons Galleria. Tysons Corner, 101. **Facility:** Warm wood accents, polished marble, quality artwork and abundant fresh flowers lend an air of opulence to this renowned hotel's public areas. The spa facilities will make anyone feel pampered. 398 units. 24 stories, interior corridors. **Parking:** on-site (fee) and valet. **Amenities:** safes. **Pool:** heated indoor. **Activities:** sauna, hot tub, steamroom, exercise room, spa. **Guest Services:** valet laundry, boarding pass kiosk, area transportation.

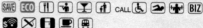

SHERATON TYSONS HOTEL

(703)448-1234 **56**

Hotel
$79-$299

 Sheraton

AAA Benefit: Members save 5% or more!

Address: 8661 Leesburg Pike 22182 **Location:** SR 7, just e of jct SR 267 (Dulles Toll Rd). Located in a commercial area. Spring Hill, 103. **Facility:** 449 units. 3-24 stories, interior corridors. **Parking:** on-site (fee) and valet. **Terms:** cancellation fee imposed. **Amenities:** safes. **Pool:** heated indoor. **Activities:** exercise room. **Guest Services:** valet laundry, rental car service, area transportation.

TYSONS CORNER MARRIOTT HOTEL

(703)734-3200 **64**

Hotel
$71-$529

MARRIOTT

AAA Benefit: Members save 5% or more!

Address: 8028 Leesburg Pike 22182 **Location:** I-495 exit 47B, just w on SR 7. Near Tysons Corner Mall. Tysons Corner, 101. **Facility:** 396 units. 15 stories, interior corridors. **Parking:** on-site (fee). **Terms:** check-in 4 pm, 3 day cancellation notice-fee imposed. **Amenities:** safes. **Pool:** heated indoor. **Activities:** hot tub, exercise room. **Guest Services:** complimentary and valet laundry, rental car service, area transportation.

WHERE TO EAT

BOMBAY TANDOOR   703/734-2202 **36**
Indian. Casual Dining. **Address:** 8603 Westwood Center Dr 22182

BUSARA   703/356-2288
Thai. Casual Dining. **Address:** 8142 Watson St 22102

(See map & index p. 38.)

THE CAPITAL GRILLE   703/448-3900 (48)
♦♦♦ Steak. Fine Dining. **Address:** 1861 International Dr
22182

COASTAL FLATS   703/356-1440 (46)
♦♦ American. Casual Dining. **Address:** 7860-L Tysons
Corner Center 22102

DA DOMENICO   703/790-9000 (45)
♦♦♦ Italian. Fine Dining. **Address:** 1992 Chain Bridge Rd
22102

FLEMING'S PRIME STEAKHOUSE & WINE BAR
                                  703/442-8384 (44)
♦♦♦ Steak. Fine Dining. **Address:** 1960-A Chain Bridge Rd
22102

LA SANDIA MEXICAN KITCHEN & BAR   703/893-2222 (47)
♦♦ Mexican. Casual Dining. **Address:** 7852-L Tysons Corner
Center 22102

LEBANESE TAVERNA   703/847-5244 (39)
♦♦♦ Lebanese. Casual Dining. **Address:** 2001 International
Dr 22102

LEGAL SEA FOODS   703/827-8900 (40)
♦♦♦ Seafood. Casual Dining. **Address:** 2001 International
Dr 22102

MAGGIANO'S LITTLE ITALY   703/356-9000 (42)
♦♦♦ Italian. Fine Dining. **Address:** 2001 International Dr
22102

MCCORMICK & SCHMICK'S   703/848-8000 (43)
♦♦♦ Seafood. Fine Dining. **Address:** 8484 Westpark Dr
22102

NEISHA THAI CUISINE   703/883-3588 (49)
♦♦ Thai. Casual Dining. **Address:** 8027 Leesburg Pike, Suite
110 22182

THE PALM RESTAURANT   703/917-0200 (41)
♦♦♦ American. Fine Dining. **Address:** 1750 Tysons Blvd
22102

P.F. CHANG'S CHINA BISTRO   703/734-8996 (37)
♦♦♦ Chinese. Casual Dining. **Address:** 1716-M
International Dr 22102

RUTH'S CHRIS STEAK HOUSE   703/848-4290 (38)
♦♦♦ Steak. Fine Dining. **Address:** 8521 Leesburg Pike
22182

SILVER DINER   703/821-5666
♦♦ American. Casual Dining. **Address:** 8101 Fletcher Ave
22182

URBANNA pop. 476

SOMETHING DIFFERENT COUNTRY STORE   804/758-8000
♦♦ American. Casual Dining. **Address:** 213 Virginia St 23175

⊘ **From simple to spectacular:**

AAA.com/travelguides/restaurants

VESUVIUS

SUGAR TREE INN   540/377-2197
♦♦♦ Historic Country Inn. **Address:** 145 Lodge Tr 24483

VIENNA (B-12) pop. 15,687, elev. 345'
• Hotels p. 256 • Restaurants p. 256
• Hotels & Restaurants map & index p. 38

WOLF TRAP NATIONAL PARK FOR THE PERFORMING ARTS is off I-495 (Capital Beltway) exit 45, then SR 267 (Dulles Toll Rd.) w. to exit 15. Wolf Trap is the only national park dedicated to the performing arts. Opera, symphony, jazz, folk, musical, country, dance and popular music productions are presented from late May to early September. Guided backstage tours, ranger programs and educational programs are offered October through April.

Situated in a setting of rolling hills and woodland, the Filene Center, the largest of Wolf Trap's several venues, is an open-air pavilion with a sloping lawn that can accommodate an audience of 7,028. Performances are held at the Filene Center from late May to early September. Wolf Trap's Children's Theatre-in-the-Woods is an open-air venue that accommodates an audience of 800 and presents family-friendly performances featuring dance, music, puppetry, storytelling and theater from late June to early August.

Hours: Park open daily 7 a.m.-dusk (may stay open later to accommodate park festivals). Guided backstage tours are given selected days at 11 or 2, Oct.-Apr. Park closes 2 hours prior to and 1 hour following Filene Center performances. Children's Theatre-in-the-Woods performances Tues.-Sat. at 10:30, late June to mid-Aug. Phone ahead to confirm all schedules.

Cost: Park admission free. Ticket prices vary by performance. Children's Theatre-in-the-Woods tickets $8-$10; free (ages 0-2). **Phone:** (703) 255-1900 for the Wolf Trap Foundation for the Performing Arts, (703) 255-1868 for general performance information, (703) 255-1800 for the national park, or (877) 965-3872 daily 10-9 for ticket information. GT 🍴 🎫

The Barns at Wolf Trap is .25 mi. s. of Wolf Trap National Park for the Performing Arts at 1635 Trap Rd. This 382-seat facility, operated by the Wolf Trap Foundation for the Performing Arts, is home to the Wolf Trap Opera, one of the country's outstanding resident training programs for young opera singers. The indoor performance space has superb acoustics created by the wood interior and enhanced by a state-of-the-art sound system. Opera, bluegrass, chamber music, country, folk, jazz, zydeco and other performances take place. **Hours:** Shows are held year-round; phone the Barns box office for event schedule. **Cost:** Ticket prices vary by performance.

(See map & index p. 38.)

Advance ticket purchase encouraged. **Phone:** (703) 255-1900, or (877) 965-3872 daily 10-9 for ticket information.

COURTYARD BY MARRIOTT DUNN LORING FAIRFAX
(703)573-9555 **97**

Hotel
$68-$318

COURTYARD Marriott

AAA Benefit: Members save 5% or more!

Address: 2722 Gallows Rd 22180 **Location:** I-495 exit 50A, just w to SR 650, then 1 mi n; 0.4 mi n of jct US 29. Located in a commercial/residential area with restaurants and shopping nearby. Dunn Loring-Merrifield, 31. **Facility:** 206 units. 10 stories, interior corridors. **Terms:** cancellation fee imposed. **Pool:** heated indoor. **Activities:** exercise room. **Guest Services:** valet and coin laundry, boarding pass kiosk. **Featured Amenity: full hot breakfast.**

WHERE TO EAT

AMPHORA RESTAURANT   703/938-7878 **106**
American. Casual Dining. **Address:** 377 Maple Ave W 22180

ANITA'S   703/255-1001
Mexican. Casual Dining. **Address:** 521 E Maple Ave 22180

CAFE RENAISSANCE   703/938-3311 **104**
Continental. Fine Dining. **Address:** 163 Glyndon St SE 22180

CLARITY   703/539-8400 **109**
American. Casual Dining. **Address:** 442 Maple Ave E 22180

ISTANBUL BLUE   703/938-8948 **107**
Turkish. Casual Dining. **Address:** 523 Maple Ave W 22180

RISTORANTE BONAROTI   703/281-7550 **103**

Northern Italian Fine Dining
$15-$31

AAA Inspector Notes: Pleasing locals since 1982, the restaurant employs servers who display an excellent knowledge of the menu, which includes such offerings as fried calamari, tender veal, fresh fish and homemade pasta. Tastefully decorated, the upscale dining room is a perfect setting for an intimate, relaxed dining experience. **Features:** full bar. **Reservations:** suggested. **Address:** 428 E Maple Ave 22180 **Location:** SR 123, 1.5 mi s of jct SR 7. **L** **D**

SUNFLOWER VEGETARIAN RESTAURANT
703/319-3888 **108**
Vegetarian. Casual Dining. **Address:** 2531 Chain Bridge Rd 22181

TOM YUM THAI   703/255-2467 **105**
Thai. Casual Dining. **Address:** 226 Maple Ave W 22180

VIRGINIA BEACH (I-11) pop. 437,994, elev. 10'
• Hotels p. 259 • Restaurants p. 266
• Hotels & Restaurants map & index p. 134, 140, 144
• Part of Hampton Roads Area — see map p. 124

Although there have been a few additions to the Virginia Beach coastline since the first English settlers stepped ashore here on April 26, 1607, exquisite natural vistas continue to entice explorers to this windswept patch at the mouth of Chesapeake Bay. The vast assortment of must-sees and must-dos involve the great outdoors—after all, this *is* a beach town! You'll encounter bicyclists and inline skaters whizzing along the attractive, resort-strewn oceanfront, creative sand castle builders inspired by speckled shores, and laid-back surfers awaiting a wicked swell.

After relaxing by the seaside, kayak through First Landing State Park *(see attraction listing),* at Cape Henry on US 60, or practice your swing at such challenging links as The Signature at West Neck, 3100 Arnold Palmer Dr.; Red Wing Lake Golf Course, 1144 Prosperity Rd.; and Hell's Point Golf Club, 2700 Atwoodtown Rd.

In addition, pier fishing for Atlantic mackerel, bluefish and sea bass is a popular pastime (local experts proffer more than a few tips at Lynnhaven Pier off Starfish Road), though some prefer stalking larger species, including blue marlin and yellowfin tuna, just offshore. Fishing charters can be arranged at several neighborhood marinas, including Virginia Beach Fishing Center, 200 Winston Salem Ave., and Long Bay Pointe Marina, 2109 W. Great Neck Rd. Anglers summering in the area also will enjoy the 4-day Virginia Beach Billfish Tournament in August.

If worms and hooks aren't your idea of fun, cruise out to see bottlenose dolphins and humpback whales at play in their natural habitat. Seasonal excursions depart from the Virginia Aquarium & Marine Science Center *(see attraction listing).* Landlubbers also will discover a boundless array of wildlife viewing opportunities in Virginia Beach—from exploring the Seashore to Cypress Birding Trail, frequented by migrant shorebirds, songbirds and raptors, to hiking through Back Bay National Wildlife Refuge.

While Virginia Beach's natural beauty is undeniable, the locale is home to a number of alluring manmade attractions as well. Bring lunch—and your skateboard—to Mount Trashmore Park, which features a skate park and picnic shelters as well as two mountains formed out of solid waste and clean soil, an environmentally friendly demonstration garden and a 1.45-mile walking trail. Or, climb to the top of the Old Cape Henry Lighthouse *(see attraction listing),* one of the first public works facilities authorized by Congress, built here in 1792. Its replacement, the 1881 Cape Henry Lighthouse, is one of the tallest cast-iron lighthouses in the United States.

Stroll the 3-mile boardwalk and you'll come across King Neptune—a 34-foot-tall cast bronze statue of the mythological sea god. Holding court at

(See maps & indexes p. 134, 140, 144.)

31st Street and Atlantic Avenue, the commanding figure is the centerpiece of the ⚡ Virginia Beach Neptune Festival, a well-attended September event featuring arts and crafts shows, fireworks and sports competitions. A variety of festivals also take place at BeachStreetUSA (Atlantic Avenue between Fifth and 34th streets), where wacky and talented street performers entertain throngs of sun-kissed tourists daily from Memorial Day through Labor Day.

Virginia Beach Visitor Information Center: 2100 Parks Ave., Virginia Beach, VA 23451. **Phone:** (757) 385-7873 or (800) 822-3224.

Shopping: While most visitors to Virginia Beach come for the sparkling sand and water and assorted beach activities, there's a shopper in every group, and Virginia Beach doesn't disappoint.

There's an unwritten law that says you have to bring back kitschy souvenirs from your beach vacation, and Virginia Beach has plenty to offer. Find that perfect T-shirt, beach towel, seashell necklace, picture frame, pair of flip-flops—you get the idea. And you won't have to venture far from the beach. Atlantic Avenue, just one block removed from the water, has blocks upon blocks of souvenir shops. Caltwater taffy, anyone?

Also on Atlantic Avenue is The Shoppes at 31 Ocean, a decidedly more chic shopping venue. The 31 Ocean part of the name refers to the center's location at Atlantic Avenue and 31st Street. In-vogue fashions, beach-related items, gift shops and several restaurants are the focus here.

Just a few minutes' drive inland from the oceanfront is The Shops at Hilltop at First Colonial and Laskin roads, a large open-air shopping center that is divided into three sections: Hilltop North, East and West. With more than 120 stores, including 27 restaurants, you can shop for hours among the clothing boutiques and gift, jewelry and home accessories shops and then have a nice meal.

Town Center of Virginia Beach, a mixed-use shopping complex with a performing arts center, hotels and residences, covers a 17-block area at Independence and Virginia Beach boulevards and Constitution Drive. Upscale shops and restaurants include Ann Taylor Loft, Brooks Brothers, Cheesecake Factory and Ruth's Chris Steak House.

Visitors also can check out Lynnhaven Mall (701 Lynnhaven Pkwy.), one of the largest malls on the East Coast. The retail giant features a movie theater, three department stores (Dillard's, JCPenney and Macy's), and more than 180 specialty stores and eateries.

Nightlife: You come to Virginia Beach to enjoy the beach and all it has to offer—the sand, the surf, the boardwalk, coastal dining and certainly the nightlife. Lounges and restaurants in numerous beachfront hotels and restaurants have live music during the summer. Just meander the boardwalk until you've found your groove, then join the fun.

Summer evenings the beachfront transforms into BeachStreetUSA. Festive outdoor entertainment (almost always free) extends mostly from 17th through 25th streets on Atlantic Avenue and spills over onto the stages at 7th, 13th 17th, 24th, 25th and 31st streets. Music of all types, street performers, magic shows and fireworks displays take place on select nights throughout the summer; the visitor center can give you information about who's performing when and where.

In the Oceanfront area, you'll find live music nightly at Abbey Road (203 22nd St.). The casual pub, which was named for the Beatles' album and boasts it carries 101 international beers, features mostly acoustic rock groups. Hot Tuna Bar & Grill (2817 Shore Dr.) has a devoted following who come for their signature yellowfin tuna and stay for the high-energy dance music cranked out by local bands and DJs. Phone (757) 425-6330 for Abbey Road or (757) 481-2888 for Hot Tuna Bar & Grill.

The open-air amphitheater Veterans United Home Loans Amphitheater (3550 Cellar Door Way) is the place to go for major concerts. You can sit on the lawn or under a pavilion roof and listen to music's biggest names play under the Virginia stars; phone (757) 368-3000. Presenting dance, music and theater performances is the more intimate Sandler Center for the Performing Arts, at 201 Market St. at the Town Center of Virginia Beach, a 17-block shopping, dining and nightlife area. Phone (757) 385-2787.

CAPT. JACK'S PIRATE SHIP ADVENTURES departs from Inlet Station Marina at 308 Mediterranean Ave. Though the costumed pirate crew of the *Lost Pearl* stays in character throughout the Family Fun Adventure, guests are warmly greeted aboard the ship, which sets sail from Rudee Inlet and motors out on a 75-minute excursion paralleling Virginia Beach's oceanfront resort strip. After kiddos take a pirate oath, deckhands paint fake tattoos, beards and scars onto the pint-size passengers, transforming them into bona fide swashbucklers.

Actors entertain with stories, games and more. Occasionally, Navy jets flying overhead and dolphins can be seen during the high seas adventure. Free parking is available at 2nd Street and Atlantic Avenue; shuttle service to the dock is provided.

Time: Allow 2 hours, 30 minutes minimum. **Hours:** Family Fun Adventure departs Mon.-Sat. at 10, noon and 4, Sun. at noon and 4, mid-June through Aug. 31; Tues. and Thurs. at noon, Sat.-Sun. at noon and 4, mid-May to mid-June and early to late Sept. Phone ahead to confirm schedule. **Cost:** Family Fun Adventure $27; $23 (ages 3-16). Reservations are required. **Phone:** (757) 305-9700. GT 🍴

FIRST LANDING STATE PARK is at 2500 Shore Dr. (US 60). The men of the Virginia Company who went on to establish Jamestown first made landfall here on April 26, 1607. Encompassing 2,888 acres of maritime forest, the park offers about 19 miles of

258 VIRGINIA BEACH, VA

(See maps & indexes p. 134, 140, 144.)

trails for hikers and bicyclists. Additional recreational activities include crabbing, swimming, saltwater fishing and boating. *See Recreation Areas Chart.*

Two visitor centers with exhibits relating the natural and cultural history of the area are on-site. One focuses on the ecology of the swamp; the other features a miniature aquarium and displays about the area's first European settlers and their interactions with Native Americans. Also showcased is a re-created Eastern Woodland Indian village. **Hours:** Park daily 8-dusk. Visitor center daily 8-4:30. **Cost:** Mon.-Fri. $6 (per private out-of-state vehicle); $4 (per private in-state vehicle). Sat.-Sun. and holidays $7-$9 (per private out-of-state vehicle); $5-$7 (per private in-state vehicle). **Phone:** (757) 412-2300.
🅰 🍴 ⊗ 🐾 ⛱

MILITARY AVIATION MUSEUM, 1341 Princess Anne Rd., showcases one of the largest private collections of World War I, World War II and Korean War-era fighters, bombers and trainers. Motorcycles and other vehicles also are on display, as are uniforms, artwork and engines—all of which are housed in large hangars at the Virginia Beach Airport. An English control tower built in 1940 and a German hangar from 1934 can be seen. Flight demonstrations are offered some days. Featuring biplanes and triplanes, the Warbirds Over the Beach World War II Air Show, a World War I-themed event, takes to the skies the weekend before Memorial Day.

Time: Allow 45 minutes minimum. **Hours:** Daily 9-5. Closed Thanksgiving and Christmas. **Cost:** $15; $13 (ages 65+); $12 (active military with ID); $7.50 (ages 6-17); free (ages 0-5 and World War II and Korean War veterans). **Phone:** (757) 721-7767. GT

NAVAL AIR STATION OCEANA TOURS departs from a kiosk at jct. 24th St. and Atlantic Ave. With retired military personnel serving as guides, narrated bus trips afford an insider's look at Naval Air Station Oceana, a military airfield that is home to several squadrons of strike fighter jets.

Along the route are armed forces memorials as well as the base's flight school and hangars; in addition passengers may see jets taking off and landing during a stop at Observation Park. All tours allow visitors to disembark for close-up views of decommissioned F/A-18 Hornets and Super Hornets.

Note: Visitors over age 16 must present a photo ID. Backpacks are not permitted. **Time:** Allow 2 hours, 30 minutes minimum. **Hours:** Tours depart Mon.-Fri. at 11, mid-June through Labor Day (weather permitting). Closed major holidays. Phone ahead to confirm schedule. **Cost:** $16; $12 (ages 3-11 and 60+). **Phone:** (757) 721-7767. GT

OLD CAPE HENRY LIGHTHOUSE is at 583 Atlantic Ave. within Joint Expeditionary Base Little Creek-Fort Story. One of the first public works facilities authorized by Congress, the structure was completed in 1792 and operated until 1881. The top of the lighthouse affords views of the military base, Chesapeake Bay and the Chesapeake Bay Bridge-Tunnel.

Note: To enter the military base, drivers must present vehicle registration and proof of current vehicle insurance. A photo ID also is required for all visitors over age 16. The climb to the top of the lighthouse involves more than 190 steps. Visitors under 42 inches tall are not permitted in the dune area.

Time: Allow 1 hour minimum. **Hours:** Daily 10-5, mid-Mar. through Oct. 31; 10-4, rest of year. Closed Jan. 1-2, Shamrock Marathon (in mid-Mar.), July 4, Thanksgiving, Christmas Eve, Christmas and Dec. 30-31. **Cost:** $8; $7 (ages 60+ and military with ID); $6 (ages 0-12 who are at least 42 inches tall). **Phone:** (757) 422-9421.

THOROUGHGOOD HOUSE, 1636 Parish Rd., is one of the oldest surviving brick houses from the Colonial period. Guided tours of this small residence on the Lynnhaven River highlight the life of colonist Adam Thoroughgood, who came to Virginia in 1621 as an indentured servant. He quickly rose in stature and eventually became a member of the House of Burgesses at Jamestown. The structure, built by Thoroughgood's great grandson Argall in the early 1700s, is furnished with 17th- and 18th-century antiques.

Time: Allow 1 hour minimum. **Hours:** Tours are given Thurs.-Sat. 10-4, Sun. noon-4. Last tour begins 30 minutes before closing. **Cost:** $8; $7 (ages 65+); $5 (students with ID); free (ages 0-5). Combination ticket with Francis Land House and Lynnhaven House $16; $14 (ages 65+); $10 (students with ID). **Phone:** (757) 385-5100. GT

VIRGINIA AQUARIUM & MARINE SCIENCE CENTER is 1 mi. s. of the Rudee Inlet Bridge at 717 General Booth Blvd. More than 10,000 animals that represent some 350 species can be seen in hands-on exhibits and a multitude of aquariums which spotlight Virginia's marine environment. The attraction's two pavilions—the Bay & Ocean Pavilion and the Marsh Pavilion—are separated by a .3-mile nature path.

The Bay & Ocean Pavilion is the center's main building. Here you'll find the immense Norfolk Canyon Aquarium that introduces you to the creatures typically found there, including three types of sharks and several varieties of fish.

The Restless Planet gallery showcases habitats that simulate periods in Virginia's early history, hundreds of millions of years ago. Begin in Indonesia's volcanic Flores Island complete with Komodo dragons and colorful finches. Move on to the Red Sea tunnel aquarium to view tropical fish, spotted eagle rays and a zebra shark. End in the humid Malaysian Peat Swamp where guests can see crocodiles, lizards and turtles.

(See maps & indexes p. 134, 140, 144.)

In addition to a variety of fish, the Chesapeake Light Tower exhibit is home to loggerhead, green and the critically endangered Kemp's ridley sea turtles. Another highlight is a National Geographic 3-D theater presenting educational documentaries and Hollywood film releases.

The Owls Creek Nature Trail skirts the edge of Owls Creek and leads to the Marsh Pavilion. The scenic 10-minute walk showcases plants and fauna native to Virginia and also features a 30-foot observation tower. Also on the path is the Adventure Park at Virginia Aquarium, a zipline and aerial course in the Owls Creek marshlands. The Marsh Pavilion includes a river otter habitat and other marsh animal exhibits as well as a children's play corner.

A 65-foot catamaran, the *Atlantic Explorer*, is located on the property and offers seasonal excursions. Whales & Wildlife, Dolphin Discoveries and Ocean Collections Sea Adventures are manned by educators eager to answer questions and share details about the aquarium's ongoing research and conservation efforts.

Time: Allow 3 hours minimum. **Hours:** Aquarium daily 9-5. Closed Thanksgiving and Christmas. **Cost:** Aquarium $24.05; $22.95 (ages 62+ and active military with ID); $19.95 (ages 3-11). 3-D film $7.95. Adventure Park $55; $47 (ages 7-11); free (one child ages 5-6 per paying adult). Combination tickets are available. **Phone:** (757) 385-3474.

VIRGINIA MUSEUM OF CONTEMPORARY ART, 2200 Parks Ave., offers rotating exhibits by both international and regional artists. Hanging in the museum's Rodriguez Pavilion is a glass chandelier crafted by Dale Chihuly. A regular schedule of educational programming, including films, lectures, classes and family-friendly activities, is offered. **Time:** Allow 30 minutes minimum. **Hours:** Tues. 10-9, Wed.-Fri. 10-5, Sat.-Sun. 10-4. Closed major holidays. **Cost:** $7.70; $5.50 (ages 65+ and students and military with ID); free (ages 0-4). **Phone:** (757) 425-0000.

19 ATLANTIC HOTEL   (757)428-4440   31

Hotel
$69-$229

Address: 203 19th St 23451 **Location:** I-264 terminus, just s; between Pacific and Atlantic aves. **Facility:** 68 units. 3 stories, interior corridors. **Terms:** closed 10/1-2/28, check-in 4 pm, 2 night minimum stay - seasonal and/or weekends, 3 day cancellation notice-fee imposed, resort fee imposed. **Amenities:** safes. **Activities:** beach access. **Guest Services:** coin laundry.

BARCLAY COTTAGE BED & BREAKFAST   757/422-1956   36
Historic Bed & Breakfast. **Address:** 400 16th St 23451

BARCLAY TOWERS   (757)491-2700   41

Extended Stay Hotel
$79-$359

Address: 809 Atlantic Ave 23451 **Location:** Oceanfront. I-264 0.8 mi s of terminus; jct Atlantic Ave and 9th St. **Facility:** 84 kitchen units. 8 stories, interior corridors. **Terms:** 3 day cancellation notice. **Amenities:** safes. **Pool:** heated indoor. **Activities:** hot tub, exercise room. **Guest Services:** coin laundry. **Featured Amenity:** breakfast buffet.

All oceanfront 2-room suites, private balcony, kitchen, indoor pool, breakfast buffet, WIFI.

BEACH QUARTERS RESORT   757/422-3100   46
Hotel. **Address:** 501 Atlantic Ave 23451

BEACH SPA BED AND BREAKFAST   757/578-1008   23

Bed & Breakfast
Rates not provided

Address: 2420 Arctic Ave 23451 **Location:** I-264 terminus, just n to 25th St. **Facility:** This cozy B&B sits just three blocks from the activity of the boardwalk oceanfront in the Old Beach neighborhood. The 1937 cottage has been renovated and expanded to offer eight luxurious rooms. 8 units. 2 stories (no elevator), interior corridors. **Activities:** hot tub, massage. **Guest Services:** complimentary laundry. **Featured Amenity:** full hot breakfast.

BELVEDERE BEACH RESORT   (757)425-0612   3

Motel
$59-$399

Address: 3603 Atlantic Ave 23451 **Location:** Oceanfront. I-264, 1 mi n of terminus; jct Atlantic Ave and 36th St. **Facility:** 50 units, some efficiencies. 5 stories, exterior corridors. **Terms:** closed 11/17-3/18, cancellation fee imposed. **Dining:** The Belvedere Coffee Shop & Diner, see separate listing. **Pool:** heated outdoor. **Activities:** bicycles.

 / SOME UNITS

BEST WESTERN CENTER INN   (757)363-2500   4

Hotel
$65-$259

Best Western.

AAA Benefit: Members save 10% or more & earn 10% bonus points!

Address: 5718 Northampton Blvd 23455 **Location:** I-64 exit 282, 1 mi n on US 13 (Northampton Blvd). **Facility:** 58 units. 2 stories (no elevator), exterior corridors. **Terms:** cancellation fee imposed. **Pool:** outdoor. **Featured Amenity:** full hot breakfast.

(See maps & indexes p. 134, 140, 144.)

BEST WESTERN PLUS SANDCASTLE BEACHFRONT HOTEL
(757)428-2828 **37**

 Hotel $89-$359

 AAA Benefit: Members save 10% or more & earn 10% bonus points!

Address: 1307 Atlantic Ave 23451 **Location:** Oceanfront. I-264, 0.5 mi s of terminus; at 14th St. Adjacent to Lynnhaven Fishing Pier. **Facility:** 147 units. 9 stories, interior corridors. **Terms:** 2-3 night minimum stay - seasonal, 3 day cancellation notice-fee imposed. **Amenities:** safes. **Dining:** 2 restaurants. **Pool:** heated indoor. **Activities:** bicycles, exercise room. **Guest Services:** valet and coin laundry.

GET THE APP

Download today. Connect every day.
AAA.com/mobile
CAA.ca/mobile

BEST WESTERN PLUS VIRGINIA BEACH
(757)428-5370 **14**

 Hotel $73-$300

AAA Benefit: Members save 10% or more & earn 10% bonus points!

Address: 2809 Atlantic Ave 23451 **Location:** Oceanfront. I-264, 0.5 mi n of terminus; jct 28th St. **Facility:** 214 units. 2-8 stories, interior/exterior corridors. **Terms:** check-in 4 pm, 3 night minimum stay - seasonal, 3 day cancellation notice-fee imposed. **Amenities:** safes. **Pool:** outdoor, heated indoor. **Activities:** game room, exercise room. **Guest Services:** valet and coin laundry. *(See ad this page.)*

 Best Western PLUS. Located on the Virginia Beach boardwalk, within walking distance to shops, restaurants and parks!

BOARDWALK RESORT HOTEL AND VILLAS
757/213-3099 **34**
Hotel. **Address:** 1601 Atlantic Ave 23451

THE BREAKERS RESORT INN   757/428-1821 **35**

 Hotel Rates not provided

Address: 1503 Atlantic Ave 23451 **Location:** Oceanfront. I-264, 0.5 mi s of terminus. **Facility:** 56 units, some two bedrooms and efficiencies. 9 stories, interior corridors. **Amenities:** safes. **Pool:** heated outdoor. **Activities:** bicycles. **Guest Services:** coin laundry. *(See ad p. 261.)*

▼ See AAA listing this page ▼

(See maps & indexes p. 134, 140, 144.)

CANDLEWOOD SUITES   757/213-1500 **15**
▼▼▼ Extended Stay Hotel. **Address:** 4437 Bonney Rd 23462

THE CAPES OCEAN RESORT   (757)428-5421 **30**
▼▼▼ Hotel. **Address:** 2001 Atlantic Ave 23451

CLARION INN & SUITES   (757)961-8190 **19**
▼▼▼ Hotel. **Address:** 2604 Atlantic Ave 23451

COMFORT INN & SUITES VIRGINIA BEACH/NORFOLK
                                     (757)965-3503 **5**
▼▼▼ Hotel. **Address:** 5808 Burton Station Rd 23455

COMFORT INN & SUITES VIRGINIA BEACH-OCEANFRONT   (757)425-8200 **29**
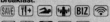
▼▼▼ Hotel $109-$680
Address: 2015 Atlantic Ave 23451 **Location:** Oceanfront. I-264, just s of terminus. **Facility:** 83 units, some two bedrooms. 10 stories, interior corridors. **Terms:** check-in 4 pm, 3 day cancellation notice, resort fee. **Amenities:** safes. **Pool:** heated indoor. **Activities:** hot tub, bicycles, exercise room. **Guest Services:** valet and coin laundry. **Featured Amenity:** full hot breakfast.

Award winning oceanfront hotel on Boardwalk. Balconies, indoor pool, free hot breakfast, suites avail.

COMFORT SUITES BEACHFRONT VIRGINIA BEACH
                                     (757)491-2400 **24**
▼▼▼ Hotel. **Address:** 2321 Atlantic Ave 23451

COUNTRY INN & SUITES BY CARLSON (OCEANFRONT)
                                     757/437-9100 **33**
▼▼▼ Hotel. **Address:** 1801 Atlantic Ave 23451

COURTYARD BY MARRIOTT-OCEANFRONT NORTH
                                     (757)437-0098 **2**

▼▼▼ Hotel $79-$437
COURTYARD Marriott **AAA Benefit:** Members save 5% or more!
Address: 3737 Atlantic Ave 23451 **Location:** Oceanfront. I-264, at terminus, 1 mi n; jct 37th St. **Facility:** 160 units. 10 stories, interior corridors. **Parking:** on-site (fee) and valet. **Terms:** check-in 4 pm, 3 day cancellation notice-fee imposed. **Pool:** outdoor, heated indoor. **Activities:** hot tub, exercise room. **Guest Services:** valet and coin laundry, boarding pass kiosk.

For complete hotel, dining and attraction listings:
AAA.com/travelguides

▼ See AAA listing p. 260 ▼

The Breakers resort inn
1503 Atlantic Ave., Virginia Beach, VA 23451
Toll Free 1-800-237-7532
info@breakersresort.com • www.breakersresort.com
Private Balconies • Cable TV • In-Room Coffee
Free Bicycles • Outdoor Heated Pool • Refrigerator
Microwave • Coffee Shop • Laundry Facilities
Enclosed Corridors • King Room w/Jacuzzi
2-Room Suites w/3 Beds • High-Speed Internet Access

Scan this code with your smartphone.

(See maps & indexes p. 134, 140, 144.)

COURTYARD BY MARRIOTT-OCEANFRONT SOUTH
(757)491-6222 **21**

Hotel
$84-$459

COURTYARD Marriott

AAA Benefit: Members save 5% or more!

Address: 2501 Atlantic Ave 23451 **Location:** Oceanfront. I-264, n of terminus; at 25th St and Atlantic Ave. Adjacent to Norwegian Lady Park. **Facility:** 141 units. 11 stories, interior corridors. **Parking:** on-site (fee). **Terms:** check-in 4 pm, 3 day cancellation notice-fee imposed. **Pool:** heated indoor. **Activities:** hot tub, exercise room. **Guest Services:** valet and coin laundry.

SAVE ECO 🍴 🍸 CALL 🚹 🏊 🛗 BIZ 🛜 ❌ 🛏 🖨 /SOME UNITS 🖼

COURTYARD BY MARRIOTT VIRGINIA BEACH NORFOLK
(757)490-2002 **12**

🔷🔷🔷 Hotel. **Address:** 5700 Greenwich Rd 23462

AAA Benefit: Members save 5% or more!

CROWNE PLAZA VIRGINIA BEACH
757/473-1700 **16**

🔷🔷🔷 Hotel. **Address:** 4453 Bonney Rd 23462

DAYS INN OCEANFRONT
757/425-6920 **22**

Hotel
Rates not provided

Address: 2417 Atlantic Ave 23451 **Location:** Oceanfront. I-264, n of terminus; at 25th St. **Facility:** 105 units. 7 stories, interior corridors. **Terms:** check-in 4 pm. **Amenities:** safes. **Pool:** heated indoor. **Featured Amenity:** continental breakfast.

SAVE 🍴 CALL 🚹 🏊 🛜 ❌ 🛏 🖼 🖨

DOUBLETREE BY HILTON HOTEL VIRGINIA BEACH
(757)422-8900 **7**

Hotel
$119-$309

 DOUBLETREE BY HILTON

AAA Benefit: Members save 5% or more!

Address: 1900 Pavilion Dr 23451 **Location:** I-264 exit 22 (Birdneck Rd), just e. Adjacent to Virginia Beach Convention Center. **Facility:** 292 units. 12 stories, interior corridors. **Terms:** check-in 4 pm, 1-7 night minimum stay, cancellation fee imposed. **Amenities:** safes. **Pool:** heated indoor. **Activities:** exercise room. **Guest Services:** valet laundry, area transportation.

SAVE ECO 🍴 🚹 🍸 CALL 🚹 🏊 🛗 BIZ 🛜 ❌ 🛏 🖨 /SOME UNITS 🐾 🖼

ECONO LODGE OCEANFRONT
(757)428-2403 **27**

Hotel
$119-$309

Address: 2109 Atlantic Ave 23451 **Location:** Oceanfront. I-264, just n of terminus; jct 21st St. **Facility:** 56 units, some efficiencies. 10 stories, interior corridors. **Terms:** 3 day cancellation notice. **Amenities:** safes. **Pool:** heated indoor. **Featured Amenity:** continental breakfast.

SAVE 🔌 🍴 CALL 🚹 🏊 🛜 🛏 🖼 🖨

▼ See AAA listing p. 263 ▼

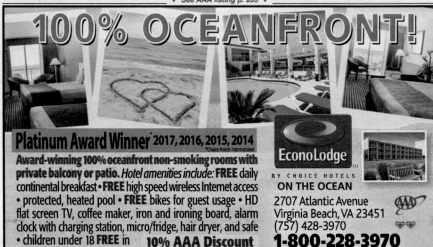

(See maps & indexes p. 134, 140, 144.)

ECONO LODGE ON THE OCEAN (757)428-3970 **16**

Motel
$59-$319

Address: 2707 Atlantic Ave 23451 **Location:** Oceanfront. I-264, just n of terminus. **Facility:** 38 units, some kitchens. 3 stories (no elevator), exterior corridors. 3 day cancellation notice. **Amenities:** safes. **Pool:** heated outdoor. **Featured Amenity: continental breakfast.** (See ad p. 262.)

FAIRFIELD INN & SUITES BY MARRIOTT VIRGINIA BEACH OCEANFRONT (757)422-4885 **32**

Hotel
$78-$447

 AAA Benefit: Members save 5% or more!

Address: 1901 Atlantic Ave 23451 **Location:** Oceanfront. I-264, at terminus, just s. **Facility:** 114 units. 9 stories, interior corridors. **Terms:** check-in 4 pm, 3 day cancellation notice-fee imposed. **Pool:** heated indoor. **Activities:** hot tub, exercise room. **Guest Services:** valet and coin laundry. **Featured Amenity: breakfast buffet.**

THE FOUNDERS INN AND SPA 757/424-5511 **16**
Resort Hotel. **Address:** 5641 Indian River Rd 23464

FOUR POINTS BY SHERATON VIRGINIA BEACH OCEANFRONT (757)428-1183 **38**

Hotel
$79-$409

 FOUR POINTS BY SHERATON

AAA Benefit: Members save 5% or more!

Address: 1211 Atlantic Ave 23451 **Location:** Oceanfront. I-264, 0.5 mi s of terminus; at Atlantic Ave and 12th St. **Facility:** 99 units. 9 stories, interior corridors. **Terms:** check-in 4 pm, 2-3 night minimum stay - seasonal and/or weekends, 3 day cancellation notice-fee imposed. **Amenities:** safes. **Dining:** 2 restaurants. **Pool:** heated indoor. **Activities:** bicycles, exercise room. **Guest Services:** coin laundry. (See ad this page.)

FOUR SAILS RESORT HOTEL (757)491-8100 **9**
Extended Stay Hotel. **Address:** 3301 Atlantic Ave 23451

HAMPTON INN NORFOLK/VIRGINIA BEACH (757)490-9800 **14**
Hotel. **Address:** 5793 Greenwich Rd 23462

AAA Benefit: Members save up to 10%!

(See maps & indexes p. 134, 140, 144.)

HAMPTON INN VIRGINIA BEACH OCEANFRONT NORTH
(757)428-7233 **11**

Hotel
$99-$409

AAA Benefit: Members save up to 10%!

Address: 3107 Atlantic Ave 23451 **Location:** Oceanfront. I-264, 0.8 mi n of terminus; just n of jct Laskin Rd (US 58) at 32nd St. Adjacent to 31st St Park. **Facility:** 120 units. 8 stories, interior corridors. **Terms:** check-in 4 pm, 1-7 night minimum stay, cancellation fee imposed. **Amenities:** safes. **Dining:** North Beach Bar & Grill, see separate listing. **Pool:** heated indoor. **Activities:** hot tub, exercise room. **Guest Services:** valet and coin laundry. **Featured Amenity:** breakfast buffet.

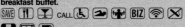

All Oceanfront Rooms. Free Breakfast Buffet. Free WiFi. Free Onsite Parking.

HAMPTON INN VIRGINIA BEACH OCEANFRONT SOUTH
(757)965-2300 **39**

Hotel
$109-$409

AAA Benefit: Members save up to 10%!

Address: 1011 Atlantic Ave 23451 **Location:** Oceanfront. I-64 terminus, 0.6 mi s. **Facility:** 141 units. 10 stories, interior corridors. **Terms:** check-in 4 pm, 1-7 night minimum stay, cancellation fee imposed. **Pool:** heated indoor. **Activities:** exercise room. **Guest Services:** valet and coin laundry. **Featured Amenity:** breakfast buffet.

HILTON GARDEN INN VIRGINIA BEACH OCEANFRONT
757/305-9000 **8**

Hotel. **Address:** 3315 Atlantic Ave 23451

AAA Benefit: Members save up to 10%!

HILTON GARDEN INN VIRGINIA BEACH, TOWN CENTER
(757)326-6200 **8**

Hotel. **Address:** 252 Town Center Dr 23462

AAA Benefit: Members save up to 10%!

HILTON VIRGINIA BEACH OCEANFRONT
(757)213-3001 **12**

Hotel. **Address:** 3001 Atlantic Ave 23451

AAA Benefit: Members save 5% or more!

HOLIDAY INN & SUITES - NORTH BEACH
757/428-1711 **1**

Hotel
Rates not provided

Address: 3900 Atlantic Ave 23451 **Location:** Oceanfront. I-264, 2 mi n of terminus; at 39th St. **Facility:** 238 units. 6-7 stories, interior corridors. **Terms:** check-in 4 pm. **Dining:** 3 restaurants, also, Isle of Capri, see separate listing. **Pool:** outdoor, heated indoor. **Activities:** hot tub, recreation programs in summer, exercise room. **Guest Services:** complimentary and valet laundry.

HOLIDAY INN EXPRESS HOTEL & SUITES VIRGINIA BEACH OCEANFRONT
757/491-6900 **18**

Hotel. **Address:** 2607 Atlantic Ave 23451

HOLIDAY INN OCEANSIDE
757/491-1500 **28**

Hotel. **Address:** 2101 Atlantic Ave 23451

HOLIDAY INN VIRGINIA BEACH/NORFOLK HOTEL & CONFERENCE CENTER
757/499-4400 **13**

Hotel
Rates not provided

Address: 5655 Greenwich Rd 23462 **Location:** I-64 exit 284B (Newtown Rd); jct I-64 and 264. **Facility:** 307 units. 6 stories, interior corridors. **Amenities:** Some: safes. **Pool:** outdoor. **Activities:** exercise room. **Guest Services:** valet and coin laundry.

HOMEWOOD SUITES BY HILTON
(757)552-0080 **11**

Extended Stay Hotel. **Address:** 5733 Cleveland St 23462

AAA Benefit: Members save up to 10%!

HYATT HOUSE VIRGINIA BEACH/OCEANFRONT
(757)428-4200 **17**

Extended Stay Hotel
$89-$459

HYATT house™
AAA Benefit: Members save 10%!

Address: 2705 Atlantic Ave 23451 **Location:** Oceanfront. I-264, n of terminus; at 27th St. **Facility:** 156 units, some efficiencies. 20 stories, interior corridors. **Parking:** on-site (fee) and valet. **Terms:** 3 day cancellation notice-fee imposed. **Amenities:** safes. **Pool:** heated indoor. **Activities:** exercise room. **Guest Services:** valet and coin laundry. **Featured Amenity:** full hot breakfast.

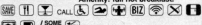

LA QUINTA INN & SUITES VIRGINIA BEACH
(757)428-2203 **15**

Hotel. **Address:** 2800 Pacific Ave 23451

(See maps & indexes p. 134, 140, 144.)

MARJAC SUITES   (757)425-0100 [26]

Motel
$49-$650

Address: 2201 Atlantic Ave 23451 **Location:** Oceanfront. I-264 terminus; just n at 22nd St. **Facility:** 60 efficiencies. 6 stories, exterior corridors. **Terms:** check-in 4 pm, 3 day cancellation notice-fee imposed, resort fee. **Amenities:** safes. **Pool:** outdoor. **Guest Services:** coin laundry.

OCEANAIRE RESORT HOTEL   757/452-6080 [6]
Hotel. **Address:** 3421 Atlantic Ave 23451

OCEAN BEACH CLUB RESORT   757/213-0601 [7]
Hotel. **Address:** 3401 Atlantic Ave 23451

THE OCEANFRONT INN   (757)422-0445 [13]

Hotel
$54-$259

Address: 2901 Atlantic Ave 23451 **Location:** Oceanfront. I-264, n of terminus; at 29th St. **Facility:** 147 units. 7 stories, interior corridors. **Terms:** check-in 4 pm, cancellation fee imposed. **Amenities:** safes. **Pool:** heated indoor.

OCEAN SUITES   (757)428-1111 [25]

Motel
$59-$329

Address: 2315 Atlantic Ave 23451 **Location:** Oceanfront. I-264, just n of terminus. **Facility:** 54 efficiencies. 8 stories, exterior corridors. **Terms:** closed 10/15-3/14, 2-3 night minimum stay - seasonal and/or weekends, 3 day cancellation notice-fee imposed. **Amenities:** safes. **Pool:** outdoor. **Guest Services:** coin laundry. *(See ad p. 263.)*

QUALITY INN   (757)460-5566 [3]

Motel
$72-$149

Address: 5189 Shore Dr 23455 **Location:** Just w of Independence Blvd (SR 225); at Gate 5 of the Naval Amphibious Base. **Facility:** 59 units, some efficiencies. 2 stories (no elevator), exterior corridors. **Amenities:** safes. **Guest Services:** coin laundry. **Featured Amenity:** continental breakfast.

 / SOME UNITS

QUALITY INN & SUITES   (757)428-8935 [42]
Hotel. **Address:** 705 Atlantic Ave 23451

RAMADA ON THE BEACH   757/425-7800 [43]
Hotel. **Address:** 615 Atlantic Ave 23451

RESIDENCE INN BY MARRIOTT VIRGINIA BEACH OCEANFRONT   (757)425-1141 [10]
Extended Stay Hotel. **Address:** 3217 Atlantic Ave 23451

AAA Benefit: Members save 5% or more!

ROYAL CLIPPER INN & SUITES   (757)428-8992 [5]

Motel
$55-$279

Address: 3508 Atlantic Ave 23451 **Location:** I-264 terminus; 1 mi n. **Facility:** 86 units, some two bedrooms and kitchens. 5 stories, exterior corridors. **Terms:** closed 10/15-3/14, 2-3 night minimum stay - seasonal and/or weekends, 3 day cancellation notice-fee imposed. **Amenities:** safes. **Pool:** outdoor. **Activities:** beach access. **Guest Services:** coin laundry. *(See ad p. 263.)*

SCHOONER INN   757/425-5222 [46]

Motel
Rates not provided

Address: 215 Atlantic Ave 23451 **Location:** Oceanfront. I-264, 1.4 mi s of terminus. **Facility:** 89 units, some efficiencies and kitchens. 6 stories, exterior corridors. **Terms:** check-in 4 pm. **Amenities:** safes. **Pool:** heated outdoor. **Guest Services:** coin laundry.

The Schooner Inn has a great location on the southend peninsula of the Virginia Beach Resort.

SEAHAWK MOTEL   (757)428-1296 [20]

Motel
$59-$299

Address: 2525 Atlantic Ave 23451 **Location:** Oceanfront. I-264, n of terminus; at 26th St. **Facility:** 48 units, some efficiencies. 6 stories, interior corridors. **Terms:** closed 11/1-3/1, check-in 4 pm, 2-3 night minimum stay - seasonal and/or weekends, 3 day cancellation notice-fee imposed, resort fee. **Amenities:** safes. **Pool:** heated indoor. **Activities:** hot tub. **Guest Services:** coin laundry.

SHERATON VIRGINIA BEACH OCEANFRONT HOTEL   (757)425-9000 [4]

Hotel
$99-$299

Sheraton

AAA Benefit: Members save 5% or more!

Address: 3501 Atlantic Ave 23451 **Location:** Oceanfront. I-264, 1 mi n of terminus; jct 36th St. **Facility:** 214 units. 11 stories, interior corridors. **Parking:** on-site and valet. **Terms:** check-in 4 pm, cancellation fee imposed. **Amenities:** safes. **Dining:** 2 restaurants. **Pool:** outdoor, heated indoor. **Activities:** hot tub, bicycles, exercise room. **Guest Services:** valet and coin laundry.

/ SOME UNITS

(See maps & indexes p. 134, 140, 144.)

SPRINGHILL SUITES BY MARRIOTT VIRGINIA BEACH OCEANFRONT (757)417-3982 **40**
◈◈◈ Hotel. **Address:** 901 Atlantic Ave 23451

AAA Benefit: Members save 5% or more!

SURFBREAK OCEANFRONT HOTEL - AN ASCEND HOTEL COLLECTION MEMBER 757/422-5000 **47**
◈◈◈ Hotel. **Address:** 1101 Atlantic Ave 23451

TOWNEPLACE SUITES BY MARRIOTT (757)490-9367 **10**

◈◈ Extended Stay Hotel $76-$286

TOWNEPLACE SUITES MARRIOTT

AAA Benefit: Members save 5% or more!

Address: 5757 Cleveland St 23462 **Location:** I-64 exit 284B to I-264 exit Newtown Rd N. **Facility:** 94 kitchen units, some two bedrooms. 3 stories, interior corridors. **Terms:** cancellation fee imposed, resort fee. **Pool:** outdoor. **Activities:** exercise room. **Guest Services:** valet and coin laundry. **Featured Amenity:** continental breakfast.

SAVE ECO [TI] CALL ⟨⟩ ⟲ [wheelchair]
BIZ 🛜 ✕ 🖥 🖨 💻 / SOME UNITS 🐾

TURTLE CAY RESORT 757/437-5565 **44**
◈◈◈◈ Hotel. **Address:** 600 Atlantic Ave 23451

VIRGINIA BEACH RESORT HOTEL & CONFERENCE CENTER 757/481-9000 **1**

◈◈◈ Resort Hotel Rates not provided

Address: 2800 Shore Dr 23451 **Location:** Oceanfront. US 60, 3.5 mi e of US 13 (Northampton Blvd); jct Shore Dr and N Great Neck Rd. **Facility:** This large hotel sits on the beach overlooking the smooth shallow waters of the Chesapeake Bay. Many beach rentals and activities are offered such as kiteboarding, stand-up paddle board, and more. 295 units. 9 stories, interior corridors. **Terms:** check-in 4 pm. **Dining:** Tradewinds, see separate listing. **Pool:** outdoor, heated indoor. **Activities:** sauna, hot tub, fishing, recreation programs in summer, kids club, bicycles, exercise room, massage. **Guest Services:** valet and coin laundry, area transportation.

SAVE [TI] 🍴 [Y] 🛝 CALL ⟨⟩ ⟲ [wheelchair] BIZ 🛜
✕ 🖥 🖨 💻

THE WESTIN VIRGINIA BEACH TOWN CENTER (757)557-0550 **9**

◈◈◈◈ Hotel $109-$399

WESTIN HOTELS & RESORTS

AAA Benefit: Members save 5% or more!

Address: 4535 Commerce St 23462 **Location:** I-264 exit 17B (Independence Blvd), just n, then just e. **Facility:** 236 units. 15 stories, interior corridors. **Parking:** on-site and valet. **Terms:** check-in 4 pm, cancellation fee imposed. **Amenities:** safes. **Pool:** heated indoor. **Activities:** exercise room. **Guest Services:** valet laundry.

SAVE ECO [TI] 🍴 [Y] CALL ⟨⟩
⟲ [wheelchair] BIZ HS 🛜 ✕ 🍽 🖥 💻
/ SOME UNITS 🐾

WINGATE BY WYNDHAM-NORFOLK AIRPORT 757/363-2901 **6**
◈◈◈ Hotel. **Address:** 5800 Burton Station Rd 23455

WYNDHAM VIRGINIA BEACH OCEANFRONT 757/428-7025 **2**
◈◈◈ Hotel. **Address:** 5700 Atlantic Ave 23451

WHERE TO EAT

1608 CRAFTHOUSE 757/965-4510 **24**
◈◈ Southern American. Gastropub. **Address:** 1608 Pleasure House Rd 23455

ABBEY ROAD PUB & RESTAURANT 757/425-6330 **22**
◈◈ American. Casual Dining. **Address:** 203 22nd St 23451

ABERDEEN BARN 757/464-1580 **37**
◈◈ Steak. Casual Dining. **Address:** 5805 Northampton Blvd 23455

ALDO'S RISTORANTE 757/491-1111 **49**
◈◈◈ Italian. Casual Dining. **Address:** 1860 Laskin Rd, Suite 107 23454

ANCHOR ALLIE'S BISTRO 757/961-1880 **18**
◈◈ Breakfast Sandwiches. Casual Dining. **Address:** 4701 Shore Dr, Suite 117 23455

AZAR'S NATURAL FOODS
◈◈ Mediterranean. Casual Dining.
LOCATIONS:
Address: 108 Prescott Ave 23452 **Phone:** 757/486-7778
Address: 1624 Laskin Rd, Suite 727 23451 **Phone:** 757/422-2927

BAKER'S CRUST 757/422-6703
◈◈ American. Casual Dining. **Address:** 704 Hilltop North Shopping Center 23451

BALADI MEDITERRANEAN CAFE 757/425-8877 **44**
◈◈ Mediterranean Natural/Organic. Casual Dining. **Address:** 626 Hilltop West Shopping Center 23451

BANGKOK GARDEN
◈◈ Thai. Casual Dining.
LOCATIONS:
Address: 4000 Virginia Beach Blvd 23452 **Phone:** 757/498-5009
Address: 737 First Colonial Rd 23451 **Phone:** 757/425-4909

BAY LOCAL EATERY 757/227-4389 **6**
◈◈ Breakfast. Casual Dining. **Address:** 2917 Shore Dr 23451

BEACH BULLY BARBEQUE 757/422-4222 **42**
◈ Barbecue. Quick Serve. **Address:** 601 19th St 23451

BEACH PUB 757/422-8817 **32**
◈◈ Seafood. Casual Dining. **Address:** 1001 Laskin Rd 23451

BELLA MONTE RESTAURANT & ENOTECA 757/425-6290 **34**
◈◈◈ Italian. Casual Dining. **Address:** 1201 Laskin Rd, Suite 100 23451

THE BELVEDERE COFFEE SHOP & DINER 757/425-0613 **6**
◈ Breakfast Sandwiches. Casual Dining. **Address:** 3601 Atlantic Ave 23451

BIG ITALY 757/213-0600 **10**
◈ Italian Pizza. Casual Dining. **Address:** 3316 Atlantic Ave 23451

BIG SAM'S INLET CAFE & RAW BAR 757/428-4858 **31**
◈◈ Seafood. Casual Dining. **Address:** 300 Winston Salem Ave 23451

(See maps & indexes p. 134, 140, 144.)

THE BOARDWOK RESTAURANT   757/426-1700
♛♛ Asian. Casual Dining. **Address:** 1993 Sandbridge Rd 23456

BUBBA'S CRABHOUSE & SEAFOOD RESTAURANT
                                 757/481-3513   (14)
♛♛ Seafood. Casual Dining. **Address:** 3323 Shore Dr 23451

BUOY 44 SEAFOOD GRILL   757/965-4413   (9)
♛♛ Seafood. Casual Dining. **Address:** 4536 Ocean View Ave 23455

CACTUS JACK'S SOUTHWEST GRILL   757/802-9898   (18)
♛♛ Southwestern. Casual Dining. **Address:** 2736 Atlantic Ave 23451

CAPTAIN GEORGE'S SEAFOOD RESTAURANT   757/428-3494
♛♛ Seafood. Casual Dining. **Address:** 1956 Laskin Rd 23454

CASBY'S KITCHEN & TAP   757/481-1600   (26)
♛♛ American. Casual Dining. **Address:** 1336 N Great Neck Rd 23454

CATCH 31 FISH HOUSE & BAR   757/213-3472   (16)
♛♛♛ Seafood. Casual Dining. **Address:** 3001 Atlantic Ave 23451

CHICK'S OYSTER BAR   757/481-5757   (15)
♛♛ Seafood. Casual Dining. **Address:** 2143 Vista Cir 23451

CHIX SEA GRILL AND BAR   757/428-2449   (27)
♛♛ American Seafood. Casual Dining. **Address:** 701 Atlantic 23451

CITRUS   757/227-3333   (7)
♛♛ Breakfast. Casual Dining. **Address:** 2265 W Great Neck Rd 23451

CITRUS   757/222-9555   (58)
♛♛ American. Casual Dining. **Address:** 357 N Great Neck Rd 23454

COASTAL GRILL   757/496-3348   (20)
♛♛♛ American. Fine Dining. **Address:** 1440 N Great Neck Rd 23454

COBALT GRILLE   757/333-3334   (38)
♛♛♛ American. Fine Dining. **Address:** 1624 Laskin Rd, Suite 762 23451

COMMUNE   757/373-3219   (25)
♛♛ Vegetarian Natural/Organic. Casual Dining. **Address:** 501 Virginia Beach Blvd 23451

CONFETTI CAFFE & GELATO   757/227-6682   (73)
♛ Sandwiches Desserts. Quick Serve. **Address:** 233 Market St 23462

CP SHUCKERS CAFE & RAW BAR   757/425-8676   (19)
♛♛ Seafood. Casual Dining. **Address:** 2407 Pacific Ave 23451

CROC'S 19TH STREET BISTRO   757/428-5444   (45)
♛♛♛ American. Casual Dining. **Address:** 620 19th St 23451

DANCING TOMATO   757/499-0000   (77)
♛ Soup Sandwiches. Quick Serve. **Address:** 205 Business Park Dr, Suite 108 23462

DISH RESTAURANT   757/496-3474   (5)
♛♛ Scandinavian. Casual Dining. **Address:** 2301 Red Tide Rd 23451

DOC TAYLOR'S   757/425-1960   (21)
♛♛ American. Casual Dining. **Address:** 207 23rd St 23451

DOUGH BOYS CALIFORNIA PIZZA
♛♛ Pizza. Casual Dining.
LOCATIONS:
Address: 2410 Atlantic Ave 23451 **Phone:** 757/425-7108
Address: 1700 Atlantic Ave 23451 **Phone:** 757/422-6111

EAT-AN AMERICAN BISTRO   757/965-2472   (1)
♛♛♛ New American. Casual Dining. **Address:** 4005 Atlantic Ave 23451

EL AZTECA MEXICAN RESTAURANT   757/473-1746   (65)
♛♛ Mexican. Casual Dining. **Address:** 314 Constitution Dr 23462

ESOTERIC CRAFT BEER AND CURATED PROVISIONS
                                 757/822-6008   (32)
♛♛♛ New American Small Plates. Fine Dining. **Address:** 501 Virginia Beach Blvd 23451

EURASIA CAFE & WINE BAR   757/422-0184   (30)
♛♛♛ New American. Fine Dining. **Address:** 960 Laskin Rd 23451

FRUITIVE   757/351-0559   (40)
♛ Natural/Organic Vegan. Quick Serve. **Address:** 1624 Laskin Rd 23451

THE GREEN CAT   757/417-7377   (4)
♛ Vegan Vegetarian. Quick Serve. **Address:** 3801 Pacific Ave 23451

GREEN PARROT GRILLE   757/460-4640   (10)
♛♛ Seafood. Casual Dining. **Address:** 4494 Lookout Rd 23455

GRINGO'S TAQUERIA   757/961-2987   (54)
♛♛ Mexican. Casual Dining. **Address:** 612 Norfolk Ave, Suite 109 23451

GUADS   757/491-1613   (51)
♛♛ Mexican. Casual Dining. **Address:** 509 Hilltop Plaza 23454

HAIR OF THE DOG EATERY   757/321-2200   (80)
♛♛ American. Casual Dining. **Address:** 4000 Virginia Beach Blvd 23452

HAN WOO RI   757/363-3354   (35)
♛♛ Korean. Casual Dining. **Address:** 1209 Baker Rd, Suite 202 23455

HAVANA   757/496-3333   (23)
♛♛ American. Casual Dining. **Address:** 1423 N Great Neck, Suite 101 23454

HEARTH WOOD-FIRED CUISINE & CRAFT BEER
                                 757/582-1727   (78)
♛♛ Pizza. Casual Dining. **Address:** 605 Virginia Beach Blvd 23451

THE HERITAGE NATURAL MARKET & CAFE
                                 757/428-0500   (31)
♛ Vegetarian. Quick Serve. **Address:** 984 Laskin Rd 23451

HOT TUNA BAR & GRILL   757/481-2888   (2)
♛♛♛ Seafood. Casual Dining. **Address:** 2817 Shore Dr 23451

IL GIARDINO   757/422-6464   (26)
♛♛♛ Italian. Fine Dining. **Address:** 910 Atlantic Ave, Suite 200 23451

IL GIARDINO RISTORANTE   757/412-0203   (13)
♛♛♛ Italian. Casual Dining. **Address:** 2105 W Great Neck Rd 23451

ISLE OF CAPRI   757/428-2411   (3)
♛♛♛ Italian. Fine Dining. **Address:** 3900 Atlantic Ave 23451

(See maps & indexes p. 134, 140, 144.)

JADE VILLA CHINESE RESTAURANT   757/473-2228   67
◆◆ Chinese. Casual Dining. **Address:** 353 Independence Blvd 23462

JAVA SURF BEACH CAFE   757/963-6600   43
◆ Coffee/Tea Sandwiches. Quick Serve. **Address:** 1807 Mediterranean Ave 23451

JENNA'S MEDITERRANEAN DELI   757/460-0973   19
◆◆ Mediterranean. Casual Dining. **Address:** 2104-I Pleasure House Rd 23455

JUDY'S SICHUAN CUISINE   757/499-2810   64
◆◆ Chinese. Casual Dining. **Address:** 328 Constitution Dr 23462

KELLY'S TAVERN
◆◆ American. Casual Dining.
LOCATIONS:
Address: 2131 General Booth Blvd, Suite 130 23454
Phone: 757/430-8999
Address: 1936 Laskin Rd, Suite 201 23454
Phone: 757/491-8737

LA BELLA ITALIA TRATTORIA   757/422-8536   33
◆◆ Italian. Casual Dining. **Address:** 1065 Laskin Rd 23451

LEAPING LIZARD CAFE   757/460-5327   17
◆◆◆ American. Casual Dining. **Address:** 4408 Shore Dr 23455

LOS CUATES TIENDA Y TAQUERIA   757/589-7061   70
◆◆ Mexican. Casual Dining. **Address:** 412 Newtown Rd 23462

LUBO WINE BAR & CAFE   757/216-2900   21
◆◆ American. Casual Dining. **Address:** 1658 Pleasure House Rd #101 23455

LYNNHAVEN FISH HOUSE RESTAURANT
757/481-0003   3

◆◆◆◆
Seafood
Fine Dining
$11-$33
AAA Inspector Notes: *Classic.* Perched on the rolling dunes of Chesapeake Bay, this longtime popular spot has big picture windows that overlook the beach and is known for great service. Very fresh local seafood is the hallmark of the menu with such as favorites as she crab soup, oysters Rockefeller, fried-fantail shrimp, crab cakes, crab Norfolk, and the seafood tower. **Features:** full bar. **Reservations:** suggested. **Address:** 2350 Starfish Rd 23451 **Location:** Just n of US 60; 2.8 mi e of jct US 13 (Northampton Blvd). [L] [D] CALL [&]

MAHI MAH'S SEAFOOD RESTAURANT & SUSHI SALOON
757/437-8030   29
◆◆ Seafood Sushi. Casual Dining. **Address:** 615 Atlantic Ave 23451

MANNINO'S ITALIAN BISTRO OCEANFRONT
757/390-2580   8
◆◆ Italian. Casual Dining. **Address:** 3420 Atlantic Ave 23451

MARCHESE ITALIAN MARKET & CAFE   757/460-4720   79
◆ Italian Sandwiches. Quick Serve. **Address:** 1700 Pleasure House Rd, Suite 106 23455

MARY'S RESTAURANT   757/428-1355   48
◆◆ Breakfast Comfort Food. Casual Dining. **Address:** 616 Virginia Beach Blvd 23451

MAYFLOWER CAFE   757/417-0117   9
◆◆ Mediterranean. Casual Dining. **Address:** 209 34th St 23451

MIZUNO JAPANESE RESTAURANT   757/422-1200   50
◆◆◆ Japanese. Fine Dining. **Address:** 1860 Laskin Rd, Suite 115B 23454

NAWAB INDIAN CUISINE   757/491-8600
◆ Indian. Casual Dining. **Address:** 756 First Colonial Rd 23451

NO FRILL BAR & GRILL   757/425-2900
◆◆ American. Casual Dining. **Address:** 1620 Laskin Rd 23451

NORTH BEACH BAR & GRILL   757/491-1800   12
◆◆ American. Casual Dining. **Address:** 3107 Atlantic Ave 23451

ONE FISH TWO FISH   757/496-4350   12
◆◆◆ Seafood. Fine Dining. **Address:** 2109 W Great Neck Rd 23454

PACIFICA LITTLE BAR & BISTRO   757/422-5770   2
◆◆ New Small Plates. Casual Dining. **Address:** 214 40th St 23451

PASTA E PANI   757/301-7488   25
◆◆◆ Italian. Casual Dining. **Address:** 1340 N Great Neck Rd, Suite 1228 23454

PELON'S BAJA GRILL   757/417-3970   7
◆ Mexican. Quick Serve. **Address:** 3619 Pacific Ave 23451

PERKED UP COFFEE CAFE   757/422-0032   11
◆ Coffee/Tea Sandwiches. Quick Serve. **Address:** 3198 Pacific Ave 23451

PETER CHANG - TOWN CENTER   757/963-5051   72
◆ Chinese. Casual Dining. **Address:** 4830 Virginia Beach Blvd 23462

PHO 79   757/687-7844   71
◆◆ Vietnamese. Casual Dining. **Address:** 4816 Virginia Beach Blvd 23462

PHO 79   757/644-6799   52
◆◆ Vietnamese. Casual Dining. **Address:** 507 Hilltop Plaza 23454

PIER CAFE   757/481-5950   4
◆◆ Seafood. Casual Dining. **Address:** 2350 Starfish Rd, Suite B 23451

PLAZA AZTECA MEXICAN RESTAURANT   757/425-1676
◆◆ Mexican. Casual Dining. **Address:** 1824 Laskin Rd 23454

POLLARD'S CHICKEN   757/340-2565   62
◆ American. Quick Serve. **Address:** 100 London Bridge Shopping Center 23454

PULCINELLA   757/222-0081   34
◆◆ Italian. Casual Dining. **Address:** 1255 Fordham Dr 23464

REGINELLA'S ITALIAN RISTORANTE & PIZZERIA
757/498-9770   69
◆◆ Italian. Casual Dining. **Address:** 4000 Virginia Beach Blvd 23452

REPEAL BOURBON & BURGERS   757/321-8885   23
◆◆ Burgers. Gastropub. **Address:** 212 22nd St 23451

ROCKAFELLER'S   757/422-5654   60
◆◆◆
Seafood
Casual Dining
$10-$33
AAA Inspector Notes: Overlooking the sparkling waters and marinas of Rudee Inlet, this is a beautiful spot in which to enjoy local seafood such as crab cakes, flounder, grilled tuna, barbecue shrimp, lump crab-topped steak and even baby back ribs. **Features:** full bar, early bird specials, Sunday brunch. **Reservations:** suggested. **Address:** 308 Mediterranean Ave 23451 **Location:** I-264 terminus, 1.3 mi s to Rudee Inlet. [L] [D] CALL [&]

ROCKFISH BOARDWALK BAR & SEA GRILL
757/213-7625   24
◆◆ Seafood. Casual Dining. **Address:** 1601 Atlantic Ave 23451

(See maps & indexes p. 134, 140, 144.)

THE ROUTE 58 DELICATESSEN   757/227-5868 **68**
♦♦ Deli Sandwiches. Casual Dining. **Address:** 4000 Virginia Beach Blvd, Unit 156 23452

RUDEE'S ON THE INLET   757/425-1777 **61**
♦♦ **AAA Inspector Notes:** This large, popular spot occupies a prime location at the marina and offers a big seasonal
Seafood
Casual Dining
$9-$35
deck and bar famous for its glider tables. The menu offers classic Mid-Atlantic seafood favorites such as steamed shellfish, crab cakes, raw bar items, fried
shrimp and flounder, and hush puppies, as well as burgers, sandwiches and salads. A late-night menu is served in season. Sunsets are beautiful, and you can check out the deck cam on-line for a glimpse of the weather. **Features:** full bar, Sunday brunch. **Address:** 227 Mediterranean Ave 23451 **Location:** I-264 terminus, 1.3 mi s to Rudee Inlet.

[L] [D] [LATE] CALL [♿]

SAFFRON INDIAN BISTRO   757/644-6904 **76**
♦♦ Indian. Casual Dining. **Address:** 4532 Columbus St 23462

SAGE KITCHEN AT ANDERSON'S SHOWPLACE
                              757/599-3510
♦♦ American. Casual Dining. **Address:** 1925 Fisher Arch 23456

SAIGON 1 RESTAURANT   757/518-0307 **66**
♦♦ Vietnamese. Casual Dining. **Address:** 448 Newtown Rd 23462

SAKURA SUSHI BAR   757/428-2899 **5**
♦♦ Japanese Sushi. Casual Dining. **Address:** 3623-3627 Pacific Ave 23451

SAKURA SUSHI BAR & JAPANESE RESTAURANT
                              757/318-9002 **39**
♦♦ Japanese. Casual Dining. **Address:** 5824 Northampton Blvd, Suite 102 23455

SALACIA   757/213-3472 **13**
♦♦♦ Steak. Fine Dining. **Address:** 3001 Atlantic Ave 23451

SHOREBREAK PIZZA, SPORTS AND BILLIARDS
                              757/481-9393 **8**
♦♦ Pizza Wings. Casual Dining. **Address:** 2941 Shore Dr 23451

SIRENA SERIOUS EATALIAN   757/481-1650 **27**
♦♦♦ Italian. Fine Dining. **Address:** 1328 N Great Neck Rd 23454

SONOMA WINE BAR & BISTRO   757/490-9463 **75**
♦♦♦ American. Fine Dining. **Address:** 189 Central Park Ave 23462

SOYA SUSHI BAR & BISTRO   757/417-7692 **14**
♦♦ Japanese. Casual Dining. **Address:** 225 Laskin Rd 23451

STEINHILBER'S RESTAURANT   757/340-1156 **59**
♦♦♦ Seafood. Fine Dining. **Address:** 653 Thalia Rd 23452

THE STOCKPOT   757/995-7197 **47**
♦ Natural/Organic Soup. Casual Dining. **Address:** 700 19th St 23451

SUGAR PLUM BAKERY & CAFE   757/422-3913 **36**
♦ Breads/Pastries Desserts. Quick Serve. **Address:** 1353 Laskin Rd 23451

SURF CLUB OCEAN GRILLE   757/425-5699 **16**
♦♦♦ Seafood. Fine Dining. **Address:** 5700 Atlantic Ave 23451

SURF RIDER GRILL
♦♦ Seafood. Casual Dining.
LOCATIONS:
Address: 2100 Marina Shores Dr 23451 **Phone:** 757/481-5646
Address: 928 Diamond Springs Rd 23455 **Phone:** 757/497-3534

SWAN TERRACE   757/366-5777 **35**
♦♦♦ American. Fine Dining. **Address:** 5641 Indian River Rd 23464

TAD'S DELI   757/422-3577 **53**
♦ Deli. Quick Serve. **Address:** 600 Norfolk Ave 23451

TASTE UNLIMITED   757/464-1566
♦ Sandwiches Deli. Quick Serve. **Address:** 4097 Shore Dr 23455

TASTE UNLIMITED   757/422-3399
♦ Specialty Sandwiches. Quick Serve. **Address:** 3603 Pacific Ave 23451

TASTE UNLIMITED   757/425-1858
♦ Specialty Sandwiches. Quick Serve. **Address:** 1544 Laskin Rd, Suite 110 23451

TAUTOG'S   757/422-0081 **20**
♦♦ Seafood. Casual Dining. **Address:** 205 23rd St 23451

TEMPT RESTAURANT & LOUNGE   757/437-8230 **17**
♦♦ American. Casual Dining. **Address:** 500 Pinewood Rd 23451

TERRAPIN   757/321-6688 **15**
♦♦♦♦ **AAA Inspector Notes:** Expect a menu of contemporary American cuisine that
New
American
Fine Dining
$22-$43
focuses on fresh gourmet ingredients highlighting regional farms and purveyors, seasonal availability, sustainability, and items raised organically. Service is focused and sophisticated, as is the wine list. The setting is chic and
modern including the zebra wood bar that overlooks the gleaming stainless steel kitchen. When the weather is comfortable, seating is also offered on a breezy romantically-lit patio. **Features:** full bar, patio dining. **Reservations:** suggested. **Address:** 3102 Holly Rd, Suite 514 23451 **Location:** I-264 terminus, just n on Baltic Ave to Holly Rd; jct 32nd St; in Pinewood Square.

[D] CALL [♿]

THREE SHIP COFFEE   757/321-9371 **41**
♦ Coffee/Tea Breads/Pastries. Quick Serve. **Address:** 607 19th St 23451

TRADEWINDS   757/481-9000 **1**
♦♦♦♦ **AAA Inspector Notes:** A panoramic view of the Chesapeake Bay is available from the dining room and patio
American
Casual Dining
$7-$27
of this beachside restaurant. Specialties include lump crab cakes, stuffed shrimp, poached salmon and seafood Caesar salad. Gluten-free menu
items are available. Mouthwatering pastries, bread and desserts are baked on the premises. **Features:** full bar, patio dining, Sunday brunch. **Reservations:** suggested, weekends. **Address:** 2800 Shore Dr 23451 **Location:** US 60, 3.5 mi e of US 13 (Northampton Blvd); jct Shore Dr and N Great Neck Rd; in Virginia Beach Resort Hotel & Conference Center. [B] [L] [D] CALL [♿]

Bayfront Dining

VENUTO ITALIAN   757/496-2663 **22**
♦♦♦ Italian. Casual Dining. **Address:** 1427 N Great Neck Rd 23454

VIETNAM GARDEN   757/631-8048 **63**
♦♦ Vietnamese. Casual Dining. **Address:** 2404 Virginia Beach Blvd, Suite 114 23454

(See maps & indexes p. 134, 140, 144.)

VOLCANO SUSHI BAR   757/481-3141 (28)
◆◆ Japanese. Casual Dining. **Address:** 1328 N Great Neck Rd, Suite 106-107 23451

WARRIOR'S GRILL   757/498-0323 (56)
◆ Mongolian. Casual Dining. **Address:** 401 N Great Neck Rd 23454

WATERMAN'S SURFSIDE GRILL   757/428-3644 (30)

◆◆ | **AAA Inspector Notes:** This beach land-mark has been a family-run favorite
Seafood | since 1981 for its boardwalk patio, laid-
Casual Dining | back vibe, upper deck views, and of
$8-$33 | course, the famous Orange Crush cock-tails. Menu specialties include crab cakes, stuffed flounder, she crab soup, baby-back ribs, and spicy Thai mussels. **Features:** full bar, patio dining, Sunday brunch, happy hour. **Address:** 415 Atlantic Ave 23451 **Location:** I-264, 1 mi s of terminus; jct 5th St. **Parking:** on-site and valet. L D CALL ♿

WHEN IN ROME PASTA BAR   757/351-3705 (57)
◆◆ Italian. Casual Dining. **Address:** 401 N Great Neck Rd 23454

YNOT ITALIAN RESTAURANT   757/496-9111 (29)
◆◆ Italian Pizza. Casual Dining. **Address:** 2102 First Colonial Rd 23454

ZEKE'S BEANS & BOWLS   757/963-5155 (55)
◆ Natural/Organic Vegetarian. Casual Dining. **Address:** 616 Norfolk Ave 23451

ZIA MARIE   757/460-0715 (11)
◆◆ Italian. Casual Dining. **Address:** 4497 Lookout Rd 23455

ZOE'S   757/437-3636 (46)

◆◆◆ | **AAA Inspector Notes:** This self-proclaimed fusion steakhouse is a
New | stylish spot near the beach featuring
American | modern and creative dishes with influ-
Fine Dining | ences from Asia to the American South.
$20-$40 | The wine program is extensive with a fabulous selection and various wine din-ners throughout the year choreographed by the chef and the Master Sommelier. The menu changes sea-sonally, but specialties like blue crab mac 'n' cheese, seared scallops, rack of lamb and crab "hushpuppies" are almost al-ways available. **Features:** full bar. **Reservations:** suggested. **Address:** 713 19th St, Suite 102 23451 **Location:** I-264 exit Birdneck Rd, just s to 19th St, then just e; adjacent to Virginia Beach Convention Center. **Parking:** valet only. D CALL ♿

ZUSHI JAPANESE BISTRO   757/321-1495 (74)
◆◆◆ Japanese Sushi. Fine Dining. **Address:** 4540 Main St 23462

WAKEFIELD pop. 927

VIRGINIA DINER   757/899-3106
◆◆ Regional Southern. Casual Dining. **Address:** 408 N County Dr 23888

WARM SPRINGS pop. 123

THE INN AT GRISTMILL SQUARE   540/839-2231
◆◆◆ Historic Country Inn. **Address:** 124 Old Mill Rd 24484

WHERE TO EAT

WATERWHEEL RESTAURANT   540/839-2231
◆◆◆ American. Fine Dining. **Address:** Old Mill Rd (Rt 645) 24484

WARRENTON pop. 9,611

HAMPTON INN WARRENTON   (540)349-4200
◆◆◆ Hotel. **Address:** 501 Blackwell Rd 20186

AAA Benefit: Members save up to 10%!

WHERE TO EAT

BLACK BEAR BISTRO   540/428-1005
◆◆ American. Casual Dining. **Address:** 32 Main St 20186

THE IRON BRIDGE WINE CO.   540/349-9339
◆◆◆ American. Casual Dining. **Address:** 29 Main St 20186

WARSAW pop. 1,512

QUALITY INN WARSAW   (804)333-1700
◆◆◆ Hotel. **Address:** 4522 Richmond Rd 22572

WHERE TO EAT

THE DAILY   804/333-3455
◆◆ Deli Breakfast. Casual Dining. **Address:** 130 Court Cir 22572

WASHINGTON pop. 135

THE INN AT LITTLE WASHINGTON   (540)675-3800

◆◆◆◆◆ | **Address:** Middle and Main Sts 22747
Classic | **Location:** Jct Middle and Main sts. **Fa-**
Country Inn | **cility:** This property features multiple
$525-$945 | buildings. All rooms are appointed differ-ently with rich fabrics; some have balco-nies and some have sitting areas. The walk-in showers are outstanding and amazing. 24 units, some houses and cottages. 3 stories (no elevator), interior corridors. **Parking:** on-site and valet. **Terms:** 7 day cancellation notice-fee im-posed. **Amenities:** safes. **Dining:** The Inn at Little Washington Dining Room, see separate listing. **Activities:** bicycles, massage. **Guest Services:** valet laundry.

SAVE ⊟ ▯⊣ ⧆ ☂ BIZ HS

🛜 ☒ / SOME UNITS 🛏 ▯

MIDDLETON INN   (540)675-2020

◆◆◆ | **Address:** 176 Main St 22747 **Location:**
Historic Bed | 0.5 mi w on US 211 business route. **Fa-**
& Breakfast | **cility:** Afternoon tea and a greeting by
$345-$425 | friendly resident dogs await arrivals to this Federal-style manor house fronted by a winding driveway. Horse stables are nearby. Rooms are appointed with plush beds. 5 units, some cottages. 2 stories (no elevator), interior/exterior cor-ridors. **Terms:** 14 day cancellation notice-fee imposed. **Activities:** mas-sage. **Guest Services:** valet laundry. **Featured Amenity:** full hot breakfast.

SAVE 🛜 ☒

/ SOME UNITS 🛏 🛏 🖼 ▯

WHERE TO EAT

COUNTRY CAFE   540/675-1066
◆ American. Casual Dining. **Address:** 389A Main St 22747

🔵 **Save on travel, shopping and more:**
AAA.com/discounts

THE INN AT LITTLE WASHINGTON DINING ROOM
540/675-3800

Regional American Fine Dining $198-$218

AAA Inspector Notes: Uncompromising cuisine with a prix-fixe menu representing the freshest of premium ingredients artfully prepared and presented is what makes this restaurant shine. The opulent atmosphere, world-class wine list and gracious staff are well orchestrated by chef/owner Patrick O'Connell. Don't miss the opportunity to tour the kitchen and the outside garden area—it's one of a kind. Two- to three-week advance notice for reservations is required. **Features:** full bar. **Reservations:** required. **Address:** Business Rt US 211 22747 **Location:** Jct Middle and Main sts; in The Inn at Little Washington. **Parking:** on-site and valet.

WAVERLY pop. 2,149

COWLINGS BARBEQUE 804/834-3100
 Barbecue. Casual Dining. **Address:** 7019 General Mahone Hwy 23890

WAYNESBORO pop. 21,006, elev. 1,293'
• Part of Shenandoah National Park area — see map p. 241

BELLE HEARTH BED & BREAKFAST (540)943-1910
Historic Bed & Breakfast. **Address:** 320 S Wayne Ave 22980

BEST WESTERN PLUS WAYNESBORO INN & SUITES CONFERENCE CENTER (540)942-1100

Hotel $109-$199

Best Western PLUS

AAA Benefit: Members save 10% or more & earn 10% bonus points!

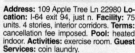

Address: 109 Apple Tree Ln 22980 **Location:** I-64 exit 94, just n. **Facility:** 75 units. 4 stories, interior corridors. **Terms:** cancellation fee imposed. **Pool:** heated indoor. **Activities:** exercise room. **Guest Services:** coin laundry.

COMFORT INN WAYNESBORO (540)932-3060
Hotel. **Address:** 15 Windingrove Dr 22980

DAYS INN WAYNESBORO 540/943-1101

Motel Rates not provided

Address: 2060 Rosser Ave 22980 **Location:** I-64 exit 94, 0.5 mi n on US 340. **Facility:** 97 units. 2 stories (no elevator), exterior corridors. **Pool:** outdoor. **Guest Services:** valet laundry. **Featured Amenity:** continental breakfast.

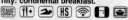

HOLIDAY INN EXPRESS 540/932-7170
 Hotel. **Address:** 20 Windingrove Dr 22980

THE IRIS INN & CABINS (540)943-1991
Bed & Breakfast. **Address:** 191 Chinquapin Dr 22980

QUALITY INN WAYNESBORO (540)942-1171

Motel $70-$135

Address: 640 W Broad St 22980 **Location:** I-64 exit 96, 3 mi w on SR 624; jct US 250 and 340. **Facility:** 75 units. 2 stories (no elevator), interior/exterior corridors. **Pool:** outdoor. **Guest Services:** valet laundry. **Featured Amenity:** continental breakfast.

RESIDENCE INN BY MARRIOTT WAYNESBORO (540)943-7426
Extended Stay Hotel. **Address:** 44 Windigrove Dr 22980

AAA Benefit: Members save 5% or more!

SUPER 8 WAYNESBORO 540/943-3888
Motel. **Address:** 2045 Rosser Ave 22980

WHERE TO EAT

THE FISHIN' PIG 540/943-3474
Barbecue. Casual Dining. **Address:** 117 Apple Tree Ln 22980

GAVIDS STEAK HOUSE FAMILY GRILL 540/949-6353
Steak. Casual Dining. **Address:** 1501 W Broad St 22980

THE GREEN LEAF GRILL 540/949-4416
American. Casual Dining. **Address:** 415 W Main St 22980

HERITAGE ON MAIN STREET 540/946-6166
American. Casual Dining. **Address:** 309 W Main St 22980

JAKE'S BAR & GRILL 540/451-2252
American. Casual Dining. **Address:** 137 N Wayne St 22980

MI RANCHO MEXICAN RESTAURANT 540/941-5980
Mexican. Casual Dining. **Address:** 408 E Main St 22980

THE NEW MING GARDEN 540/942-8800
Chinese. Casual Dining. **Address:** 316 Federal St 22980

PLAZA AZTECA 540/949-4205
Mexican. Casual Dining. **Address:** 23 Windigrove Dr 22980

THE PURPLE FOOT 540/942-9463
American. Casual Dining. **Address:** 1035 W Broad St 22980

SCOTTO'S ITALIAN RESTAURANT 540/942-8715
Italian. Casual Dining. **Address:** 1412 W Broad St 22980

WHITE HALL elev. 722'

THE INN AT SUGAR HOLLOW FARM 434/823-7086
Bed & Breakfast. **Address:** 6051 Sugar Hollow Rd 22905

WHITE MARSH (B-3) elev. 55'
• Part of Hampton Roads Area — see map p. 124

Archeological evidence dates the earliest settlements of coastal Virginia Native Americans to 8,000 B.C. By the time the Jamestown colonists arrived in 1607, some 15,000 Powhatans inhabited the Chesapeake Bay region, led by Wahunsunacock, or

Chief Powhatan. In 2003 researchers announced the discovery of the lost village of Werowocomoco—the chief's home and the first known capital of Virginia—on a farm near White Marsh. Thousands of artifacts have been found on the 50-acre site; excavations are ongoing.

WHITE POST (E-8) elev. 607'

White Post takes its name from the white post erected by surveyor George Washington to mark the route to Lord Thomas Fairfax's wilderness manor, Greenway Court. A white post at the junction of SRs 628 and 658 still points the way to Fairfax's estate, torn down in 1858.

Following his residency at Belvoir with his cousin William Fairfax, Lord Thomas Fairfax moved to White Post in 1748 and built Greenway Court, where he threw lavish parties for his male acquaintances. He lived at Greenway Court until his death at the age of 91. Legend has it that Fairfax, a loyal Tory, took to his bed and died soon after he learned of Gen. Charles Cornwallis' surrender.

DINOSAUR LAND is at 3848 Stonewall Jackson Hwy. More than 50 life-size reproductions of dinosaurs are displayed, including a tyrannosaurus, velociraptor and apatosaurus. Many photo opportunities exist at this family-oriented attraction. **Time:** Allow 1 hour minimum. **Hours:** Daily 9:30-6, Memorial Day-Labor Day; daily 9:30-5:30, Mar. 1-day before Memorial Day and day after Labor Day-Sept. 30; Fri.-Wed. 9:30-5:30, Oct.-Dec. Phone ahead to confirm schedule. **Cost:** $6; $5 (ages 2-10). **Phone:** (540) 869-2222.

L'AUBERGE PROVENCALE FRENCH COUNTRY INN
540/837-1375
▼▼▼ Historic Country Inn. **Address:** 13630 Lord Fairfax Hwy 22663

WHERE TO EAT

L'AUBERGE PROVENCALE
540/837-1375
▼▼▼▼ Regional French. Fine Dining. **Address:** 13630 Lord Fairfax Hwy 22663

WHITE STONE pop. 352

THE SANDPIPER
804/435-6176
▼▼ Seafood. Casual Dining. **Address:** 850 Rappahannock Dr 22578

WILDERNESS (C-11) elev. 247'

The Wilderness, a region of dense thickets south of the Rapidan River, is where Gen. Ulysses S. Grant opened his 1864 campaign. In the Battle of the Wilderness, beginning on May 5, Grant's troops met Gen. Robert E. Lee's Confederates, and fighting raged for 2 days.

Fierce attacks and counterattacks swept through the Wilderness. The woods caught fire, making an inferno in which many of the wounded perished. By the end of the second day neither side had gained the advantage. On May 7 Grant again started his army toward Richmond, but he met Confederate resistance at Spotsylvania Court House *(see Spotsylvania p. 244).*

The Wilderness is now part of Fredericksburg and Spotsylvania National Military Park *(see place listing p. 117).*

WILLIAMSBURG, JAMESTOWN & YORKTOWN

America's history lives in this triangle of sites in southeastern Virginia. A visit to Jamestown, Williamsburg and Yorktown is very much like a history lesson—American History 101, so to speak.

Open the book to the beginning pages. Chapter 1 starts in 1607 when the first English settlers reached these shores, predating the Pilgrims at Plymouth by 13 years. When The Virginia Company of London sent the *Susan Constant, Discovery* and *Godspeed* to this new land, the intent was to establish a permanent British colony in the New World.

After a 5-month journey across the Atlantic, 104 Englishmen landed on the banks of the James River. These colonists were ill-prepared for what awaited them, and disease and a severe drought took a heavy toll. The harsh winter of 1609-10, which came to be known as the "starving time," claimed the lives of two-thirds of the colonists. With the arrival of much-needed supplies, more settlers, and a successful crop (tobacco), the colony of Virginia and its first capital, Jamestown, survived. Thanks to the efforts of such familiar names such as Pocahontas, John Smith and John Rolfe, the seeds of a nation were sown.

After the Colonial capital was moved farther inland to Williamsburg in 1699, the settlement at Jamestown fell to ruins. Diligent work by archeologists at Historic Jamestowne, as it's now called, has unearthed the location of the 1607 fort, and ongoing digs continue to provide insights into the hardships and lives of those earliest settlers. At nearby Jamestown Settlement, costumed historical interpreters at three re-created sites—a palisaded Colonial fort, a Powhatan Indian village and reproductions of the ships that brought the settlers to this continent—bring 17th-century American history to life.

The Williamsburg chapter of American history defines the years when that city was the political, social and cultural center of Virginia. It's easy to return to the 1770s here, to relive those fascinating times when our country's future was being debated and decided. Should the Colonies remain part of Great Britain, or should the rumblings of independence be seriously considered?

Stroll among townsfolk, dressed in clothing appropriate to their status in life, as they go about their daily business. You're just as likely to mingle with an aristocrat in powdered wig, ruffled shirt and knee breeches as a tradesman who might have fashioned that wig or tailored those breeches. Follow a fife and drum parade as it marches down Duke of Gloucester Street. Dodge a horse and carriage as it clip-clops its way along a dusty road. The restoration is so realistic you halfway expect to encounter Thomas Jefferson and Patrick Henry engaged in a discussion about liberty and personal freedom.

Stop in some of those tradesmen's shops and see how gunsmiths, printers, shoemakers, wheelwrights, basketmakers and weavers created their goods. Dine in some of the Colonial taverns and

This map shows cities in Williamsburg, Jamestown & Yorktown where you will find attractions, hotels and restaurants. Cities are listed alphabetically in this book on the following pages.

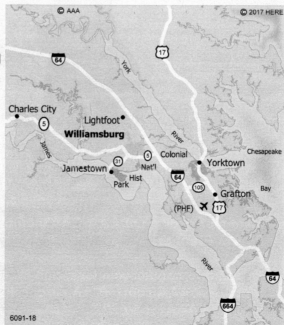

6091-18

sample Brunswick stew, peanut soup, oyster fritters, spoon bread and syllabub. See where justice was meted out at the courthouse. Contrast the lifestyle of the royal governor and his "palace" and the home of a craftsman.

Separation from Great Britain proved to be inevitable, though, and the conclusion to our history lesson involves the final chapter of the Revolutionary War and the third part of Virginia's historic triangle, Yorktown. The long road to independence essentially ended here in 1781 when Gen. Charles Cornwallis, greatly outnumbered by troops led by generals George Washington and Jean Baptiste Donatien de Vimeur, comte de Rochambeau, surrendered.

Those heady days are remembered by two driving tours that trace the progression of the battle and include such important sites as Washington's headquarters and the site of the surrender. And history comes to life here as well, at the American Revolution Museum at Yorktown's Continental Army encampment complete with musket and cannon firing demonstrations and a farmstead typical of the 1780s.

All three sites are linked by the 23-mile-long Colonial Parkway, a scenic, winding road through the Virginia countryside.

After you've immersed yourself in the historic area's trifecta of Colonial experiences, venture out on picturesque SR 5 (also known as the John Tyler Highway) to see some of the James River plantation homes, elaborate 18th-century estates built along the curving river by many of the region's most prominent families.

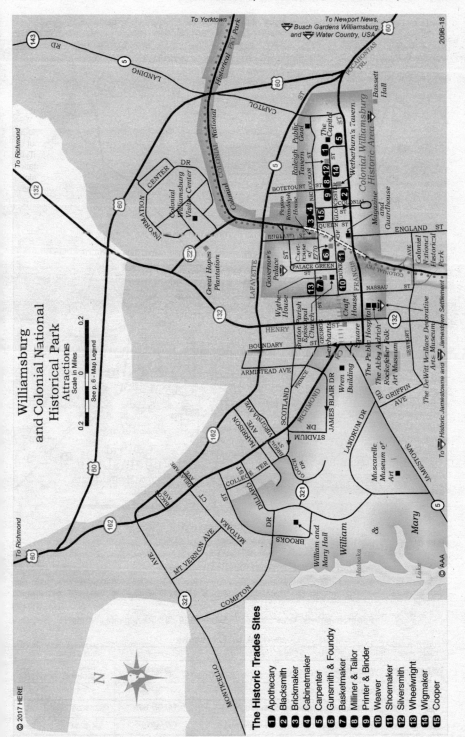

Williamsburg and Colonial National Historical Park Attractions

Scale in Miles

0.2   0   0.2

See p. 6 - Map Legend

The Historic Trades Sites

1. Apothecary
2. Blacksmith
3. Brickmaker
4. Cabinetmaker
5. Carpenter
6. Gunsmith & Foundry
7. Basketmaker
8. Milliner & Tailor
9. Printer & Binder
10. Weaver
11. Shoemaker
12. Silversmith
13. Wheelwright
14. Wigmaker
15. Cooper

© 2017 HERE

© AAA

2096-18

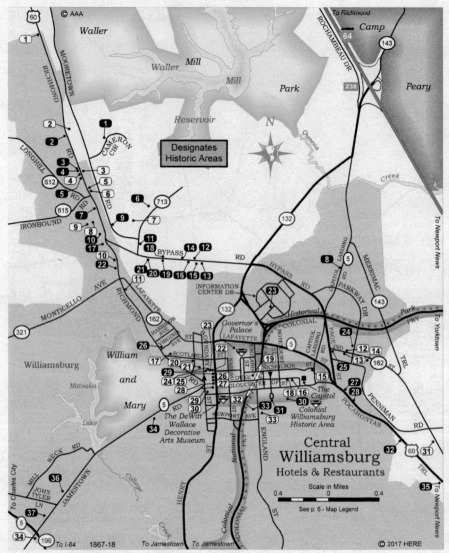

Central Williamsburg

This index helps you "spot" where approved hotels and restaurants are located on the corresponding detailed maps. Hotel daily rate range is for comparison only. Restaurant price range is a combination of lunch and/or dinner. Turn to the listing page for more information and consult display ads for special promotions.

 For more details, rates and reservations: AAA.com/travelguides/hotels

CENTRAL WILLIAMSBURG

Map Page	Hotels	Diamond Rated	Rate Range	Page
1 this page	Wyndham Governor's Green	🔷🔷🔷	Rates not provided	289
2 this page	Hampton Inn & Suites	🔷🔷🔷	$79-$179	288
3 this page	**Residence Inn by Marriott Williamsburg**	🔷🔷🔷	$67-$325 SAVE	289
4 this page	**SpringHill Suites by Marriott Williamsburg**	🔷🔷🔷	$54-$230 SAVE	289

CENTRAL WILLIAMSBURG (cont'd)

Map Page	Hotels (cont'd)	Diamond Rated	Rate Range	Page
5 p. 276	**Hilton Garden Inn**	◆◆◆	$89-$219 [SAVE]	288
6 p. 276	Wyndham Kingsgate Resort	◆◆◆	Rates not provided	290
7 p. 276	**Holiday Inn Express Hotel & Suites**	◆◆◆	$79-$239 [SAVE]	289
8 p. 276	**Hampton Inn & Suites Historic Area**	◆◆◆	$89-$199 [SAVE]	288
9 p. 276	Embassy Suites by Hilton	◆◆◆	$89-$189	288
10 p. 276	**Patriot Inn**	◆◆◆	$117-$157 [SAVE]	289
11 p. 276	**Best Western Plus Historic Area Inn**	◆◆◆	$79-$199 [SAVE]	287
12 p. 276	**Homewood Suites by Hilton**	◆◆◆	Rates not provided [SAVE]	289
13 p. 276	**Hampton Inn & Suites Williamsburg-Central**	◆◆◆	$79-$209 [SAVE]	288
14 p. 276	**Holiday Inn & Suites Gateway**	◆◆◆	Rates not provided [SAVE]	289
15 p. 276	Days Inn Williamsburg Historic Area	◆◆◆	Rates not provided [SAVE]	288
16 p. 276	La Quinta Inn & Suites Williamsburg	◆◆◆	$59-$214 [SAVE]	289
17 p. 276	**Fairfield Inn & Suites by Marriott**	◆◆◆	$60-$235 [SAVE]	288
18 p. 276	**Comfort Inn Williamsburg Gateway**	◆◆◆	$78-$270 [SAVE]	287
19 p. 276	**Country Inn & Suites By Carlson**	◆◆◆	Rates not provided [SAVE]	287
20 p. 276	Comfort Suites	◆◆◆	$85-$350	287
21 p. 276	Sleep Inn	◆◆	$65-$150	289
22 p. 276	Westgate Historic Williamsburg	◆◆◆	$69-$200	289
23 p. 276	Colonial Williamsburg-Woodlands Hotel & Suites	◆◆◆	Rates not provided	287
24 p. 276	Econo Lodge Colonial	◆◆	$55-$115	288
25 p. 276	Rodeway Inn Historic in Williamsburg	◆◆	$65-$140	289
26 p. 276	Colonial Capital Bed & Breakfast	◆◆◆	Rates not provided	287
27 p. 276	Bluegreen Vacations Patrick Henry Square, an Ascend Resort Collection Member	◆◆◆	$109-$799	287
28 p. 276	**Best Western Williamsburg Historic District**	◆◆◆	$59-$199 [SAVE]	287
29 p. 276	The Fife and Drum Inn	◆◆◆	$165-$199	288
30 p. 276	The Griffin Hotel	◆◆◆	$99-$279	288
31 p. 276	Williamsburg Inn	◆◆◆◆	$369-$569	289
32 p. 276	**Fort Magruder Hotel & Conference Center**	◆◆◆	$109-$299 [SAVE]	288
33 p. 276	Williamsburg Lodge, Autograph Collection	◆◆◆	$117-$246	289
34 p. 276	Cedars of Williamsburg Bed & Breakfast	◆◆◆	Rates not provided	287
35 p. 276	**Country Inn & Suites By Carlson Busch Gardens Area**	◆◆◆	Rates not provided [SAVE]	288
36 p. 276	Liberty Rose Bed & Breakfast	◆◆◆◆	Rates not provided	289
37 p. 276	Colonial Gardens Bed & Breakfast	◆◆◆	Rates not provided	287

Map Page	Restaurants	Diamond Rated	Cuisine	Price Range	Page
1 p. 276	La Tolteca	◆◆	Mexican	$6-$15	290
2 p. 276	Fireside Chophouse	◆◆◆	Steak	$10-$30	290
3 p. 276	Food For Thought	◆◆	American	$8-$22	290

Map Page	Restaurants (cont'd)	Diamond Rated	Cuisine	Price Range	Page
④ p. 276	**Seafare of Williamsburg**	◆◆◆	Seafood	$24-$46	291
⑤ p. 276	Kyoto Japanese Steakhouse & Sushi Bar	◆◆	Japanese	$15-$34	290
⑥ p. 276	Aberdeen Barn	◆◆	Steak	$19-$35	290
⑦ p. 276	El Sabroson Traditional Latin Food	◆◆	Latin American	$8-$15	290
⑧ p. 276	Plaza Azteca Mexican Restaurant	◆◆	Mexican	$7-$22	290
⑨ p. 276	Le Yaca French Restaurant	◆◆◆	French	$16-$48	290
⑩ p. 276	Cozy Patio Cafe	◆◆	Cajun	$10-$16	290
⑪ p. 276	Peter Chang China Cafe	◆◆	Chinese	$7-$20	290
⑫ p. 276	Second Street American Bistro	◆◆◆	American	$15-$30	291
⑬ p. 276	La Tolteca Mexican Restaurante	◆◆	Mexican	$5-$13	290
⑭ p. 276	Cochon on 2nd	◆◆◆	American	$13-$29	290
⑮ p. 276	Christiana Campbell's Tavern	◆◆	Seafood	$20-$34	290
⑯ p. 276	Shields Tavern	◆◆	American	$10-$24	291
⑰ p. 276	Culture Cafe	◆◆	Small Plates	$8-$10	290
⑱ p. 276	King's Arms Tavern	◆◆	American	$12-$34	290
⑲ p. 276	Chowning's Tavern	◆◆	American	$6-$30	290
⑳ p. 276	Rick's Cheese Steak Shop	◆	Sandwiches	$5-$11	290
㉑ p. 276	Oishii Japanese Ramen & Hibachi Grill	◆	Japanese	$8-$11	290
㉒ p. 276	Aromas	◆	Coffee/Tea Sandwiches	$7-$15	290
㉓ p. 276	Retro's-Good Eats	◆	Burgers Hot Dogs	$4-$8	290
㉔ p. 276	Lokal	◆	Vegan Vegetarian	$5-$8	290
㉕ p. 276	Blue Talon Bistro	◆◆◆	French	$13-$30	290
㉖ p. 276	DoG Street Pub	◆◆	American	$8-$30	290
㉗ p. 276	The Trellis Restaurant	◆◆◆	Regional American	$7-$32	291
㉘ p. 276	**Fat Canary**	◆◆◆◆	Regional American	$28-$39	290
㉙ p. 276	The Cheese Shop	◆	Specialty	$5-$9	290
㉚ p. 276	Berret's Seafood Restaurant and Taphouse Grill	◆◆◆	Seafood	$8-$30	290
㉛ p. 276	Emily's Donuts & Cafe	◆	Sandwiches Breads/Pastries	$8	290
㉜ p. 276	Traditions	◆◆◆	American	$8-$23	291
㉝ p. 276	Golden Horseshoe Club House Grill	◆◆	American	$8-$12	290
㉞ p. 276	Old Chickahominy House	◆◆	Regional Southern	$6-$9	290

Use the free online TripTik
Travel Planner at AAA.com/maps

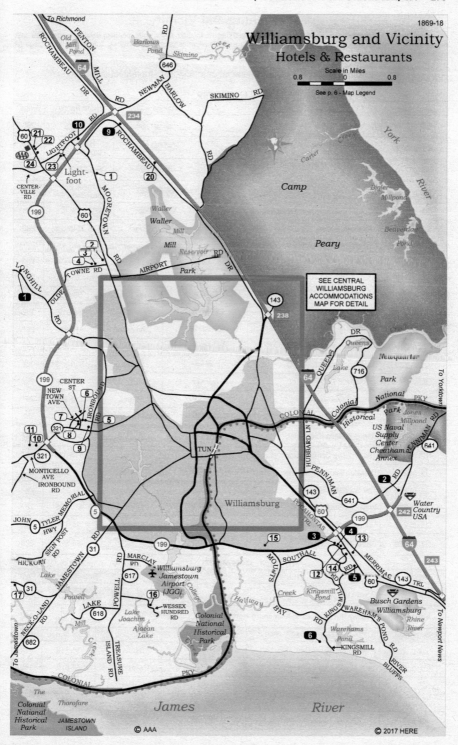

1869-18

Williamsburg and Vicinity
Hotels & Restaurants

Scale in Miles
0.8   0   0.8

See p. 6 - Map Legend

SEE CENTRAL
WILLIAMSBURG
ACCOMMODATIONS
MAP FOR DETAIL

Camp

Peary

York River

Carter Creek

Bigler Millpond

Beaverdam Pond

Newquarter Park

National

Colonial

Historical

Park

US Naval Supply Center Cheatham Annex

Jones Millpond

Water Country USA

Busch Gardens Williamsburg

Rhine River

Williamsburg

Williamsburg Jamestown Airport (JGG)

WESSEX HUNDRED RD

Colonial National Historical Park

Wareham's Pond

KINGSMILL RD

RIVER BLUFFS

To Newport News

To Yorktown

James River

Colonial National Historical Park

JAMESTOWN ISLAND

To Jamestown

To Richmond

© AAA

© 2017 HERE

Williamsburg and Vicinity

This index helps you "spot" where approved hotels and restaurants are located on the corresponding detailed maps. Hotel daily rate range is for comparison only. Restaurant price range is a combination of lunch and/or dinner. Turn to the listing page for more information and consult display ads for special promotions.

 For more details, rates and reservations: AAA.com/travelguides/hotels

WILLIAMSBURG

Map Page	Hotels	Diamond Rated	Rate Range	Page
1 p. 279	War Hill Inn Bed & Breakfast	◈◈◈	Rates not provided	286
2 p. 279	Wyndham Garden Williamsburg Busch Gardens Area	◈◈◈	Rates not provided (SAVE)	286
3 p. 279	Courtyard by Marriott Williamsburg Busch Gardens Area	◈◈◈	$72-$235 (SAVE)	285
4 p. 279	Holiday Inn Express Williamsburg Busch Gardens Area	◈◈◈	Rates not provided (SAVE)	286
5 p. 279	DoubleTree by Hilton Williamsburg	◈◈◈	$79-$179 (SAVE)	285
6 p. 279	Kingsmill Resort	◈◈◈◈	$139-$249 (SAVE)	286

Map Page	Restaurants	Diamond Rated	Cuisine	Price Range	Page
① p. 279	Bellissimo Pizza Cafe	◈	Pizza	$8-$20	286
② p. 279	Edwards Virginia Ham Shoppe	◈	Sandwiches	$5-$9	287
③ p. 279	Oceans & Ale	◈◈	Steak Seafood	$9-$23	287
④ p. 279	Giuseppe's Italian Cafe	◈◈◈	Italian	$8-$19	287
⑤ p. 279	Dudley's Bistro	◈◈◈	American	$10-$30	287
⑥ p. 279	Ichiban	◈◈◈	Chinese	$14-$22	287
⑦ p. 279	Center Street Grill	◈◈◈	American	$10-$23	286
⑧ p. 279	The Corner Pocket	◈◈◈	American	$9-$24	287
⑨ p. 279	Opus 9 Steakhouse	◈◈◈	Steak	$10-$66	287
⑩ p. 279	The Grecian Plate	◈◈	Greek	$8-$11	287
⑪ p. 279	Honey Butter's Kitchen	◈◈	Breakfast Comfort Food	$9-$15	287
⑫ p. 279	The Whaling Company Inc	◈◈	Seafood	$13-$28	287
⑬ p. 279	Doraldo Ristorante Italiano	◈◈	Italian	$9-$22	287
⑭ p. 279	The Sportsmans Grille	◈◈	American	$7-$11	287
⑮ p. 279	Waypoint Seafood & Grill	◈◈◈	American	$10-$35	287
⑯ p. 279	Gabriel Archer Tavern	◈◈	American	$8-$14	287
⑰ p. 279	Carrot Tree Kitchens	◈◈	Southern Breads/Pastries	$8-$17	286

LIGHTFOOT

Map Page	Hotels	Diamond Rated	Rate Range	Page
9 p. 279	Great Wolf Lodge	◈◈◈	Rates not provided	162
10 p. 279	Holiday Inn Express Williamsburg North	◈◈◈	Rates not provided (SAVE)	162

Map Page	Restaurants	Diamond Rated	Cuisine	Price Range	Page
⑳ p. 279	Pierce's Pitt Bar-B-Que	◈	Barbecue	$5-$19	162
㉑ p. 279	Taco Mexicali	◈◈	Mexican	$4-$13	162
㉒ p. 279	New York Deli	◈	Deli	$5-$14	162
㉓ p. 279	La Petite Tea Room	◈◈	Specialty	$8-$14	162
㉔ p. 279	Francesco's Ristorante Italiano	◈◈	Italian	$9-$25	162

WILLIAMSBURG (B-3) pop. 14,068, elev. 78'

- Hotels p. 285 • Restaurants p. 286
- Hotels & Restaurants map & index p. 279
- Part of Williamsburg, Jamestown & Yorktown area — see map p. 273

"That the future may learn from the past" is the theme for the Colonial Williamsburg Foundation, which operates this restoration project. Through extensive research, the 301-acre Colonial area of the city has been restored as nearly as possible to its 18th-century appearance.

Within this historic area are 88 buildings that survived from the 1700s. In addition more than 400 others have been faithfully rebuilt on their original sites.

Stately public buildings and a variety of Colonial homes, shops, taverns and gardens are on or just off historic Duke of Gloucester Street, the main thoroughfare of the city.

Interpreters dressed in 18th-century attire populate the historic area. Fife and drum parades take place April through October. Drum corps and fireworks stir up plenty of patriotic feelings during Williamsburg's ☀ Independence Day celebration. In early December ☀ Grand Illumination Festivities herald the beginning of the Christmas season. Candles light up the regal homes of the historic district as fireworks streak across the night sky.

Greater Williamsburg Chamber & Tourism Alliance: 421 N. Boundary St., Williamsburg, VA 23187. **Phone:** (757) 229-6511 or (800) 368-6511.

Shopping: You won't have far to go to begin your shopping expedition in Williamsburg—the Colonial Williamsburg Historic Area, and Merchant Square in particular, are chockablock with stores selling Colonial inspired items. Find reproduction Williamsburg furniture, linens, soaps, ceramics, baskets, petticoats, three-cornered hats, quill pens, birdhouses, toy drums and wooden tops, all based on 18th-century designs and many hand-crafted by Williamsburg tradespeople. Smithfield country hams and hand-cooked Virginia peanuts are tasty ways to remember your visit.

Speaking of Merchant Square, if you happen to be there on Saturday from April through October, be sure to peruse the fresh produce, flowers and delectable goodies at the Williamsburg Farmers Market (402 W. Duke of Gloucester St.).

Shopaholics will swoon at Williamsburg Premium Outlets on Richmond Road (US 60). The mall directory features 120 stores, including Banana Republic, Chico's, Michael Kors, Reebok and True Religion.

If the 18th-century ambience of Williamsburg has inspired you, check out the Williamsburg Antique Mall (500 Lightfoot Rd.), where more than 400 dealers display antiques and collectibles.

Williamsburg Pottery Factory (6692 Richmond Rd.) started out by making 18th-century saltglaze pottery reproductions in the 1930s. Inspired by traditional European markets, a 2012 renovation project transformed the once no-frills shopping attraction

into a modern 160,000-square-foot retail complex. Today four buildings offer a variety of goods, including silk and dried flowers, crystal, furniture, glassware, rugs, shells, Asian and Christmas items, garden pots and china.

A business park and residential areas in addition to dining, shopping and entertainment options comprise New Town, at the junction of Ironbound Road and Monticello Avenue. More than 170 shops and restaurants are part of an outdoor Main Street-style mall near William & Mary.

INSIDER INFO:
Colonial Williamsburg Visitor Center

Northeast of the Governor's Palace at 101 Visitor Center Dr., the Colonial Williamsburg Visitor Center is open daily 8:45-5. Holiday and seasonal hours may vary. Go to the center first for tickets and information as well as a schedule of children's activities and special programs. Streets in the Historic Area are closed to automobiles. Park at the visitor center; shuttle buses leave for the historic area every 20 minutes.

All Colonial Williamsburg admission tickets include access to the bus system and an orientation film. Excluded are select walking tours, evening programs and special events requiring a separate admission. The Single-day Ticket is $40.99; $20.49 (ages 6-12). The Multiday Ticket (valid for 3 days through the end of the year) is $50.00; $25.49 (ages 6-12). The Sampler Ticket (includes admission to two trade shops, one family home and the Public Gaol) is $25.99; $12.49 (ages 6-12). The Art Museum Single-day Ticket is $12.99; $6.49 (ages 6-12).The annual pass (valid for 1 year from date of purchase) is $66.99; $33.49 (ages 6-12).

Note: It is a good idea to verify hours and admission fees in advance.

Further information about Colonial Williamsburg's points of interest can be obtained by contacting The Colonial Williamsburg Foundation; phone (888) 965-7254.

BUSCH GARDENS WILLIAMSBURG is at 1 Busch Gardens Blvd. This 100-acre adventure park features thrill rides, animal attractions and shows, and shops and eateries set amid various European-themed villages. Sesame Street Forest of Fun is a family-friendly area offering children's rides and playgrounds as well as meet and greets with Sesame Street characters.

The Tempesto roller coaster races into turns at 63 mph and rolls through a complete inversion 154 feet in the air. InvadR, a Viking-themed wood roller coaster, reaches speeds of 48 mph and features a 74-foot plunge. On Verbolten, visitors zip along a German autobahn and then veer into the Black Forest. Griffon thrills riders with two Immelmann loops, dramatic drops and speeds of up to 75 mph as it climbs 205 feet, then dives 90 degrees straight

(See map & index p. 279.)

down. The hypercoaster Apollo's Chariot takes riders over nine camelback humps, while the inverted steel coaster Alpengeist propels riders on a dynamic, high-speed journey. The Loch Ness Monster, named after Scotland's serpent, hurls passengers through interlocking loops.

Seasonal events include the Busch Gardens Food & Wine Festival in the spring, Howl-O-Scream in the fall and Christmas Town: A Busch Gardens Celebration in the winter.

Kennels are available. **Hours:** Open Mar.-Dec.; days and hours vary. Phone ahead to confirm schedule. **Cost:** $90; $80 (ages 3-9). Multiday and combination tickets with Water Country USA are available. **Parking:** $15. **Phone:** (757) 229-4386 or (800) 343-7946. [¶]

COLONIAL WILLIAMSBURG HISTORIC AREA is off I-64 exit 238, following signs. This 301-acre interactive living-history museum recreates the spirit and culture of everyday life in the 18th-century capital of Virginia. Engaging educational programming focusing on guest interaction is introduced seasonally.

After 1780, when Richmond became Virginia's capital, Williamsburg reverted to the status of a quiet college town. Fearing that many of its historic buildings would be lost, a local minister, the Rev. W.A.R. Goodwin, persuaded John D. Rockefeller Jr. to finance the restoration of the Colonial town. In 1926 the two men embarked on an ambitious project with architects, archeologists and historians to preserve some 70 structures.

Colonial Williamsburg is a step back in time to the 18th century, where costumed interpreters—tradespeople, housewives, slaves, freemen, governmental officials and soldiers—go about their everyday duties. Many of the buildings can be visited on self-guiding tours, while others are open for guided tours only.

Live outdoor theater experiences are offered daily re-creating the struggle for American independence 1774-81. The program focuses on the collapse of the royal government and the Colonies at war. Events take place throughout the historic area; hours vary seasonally. Leashed pets are permitted in some outdoor areas.

Hours: Most historic area buildings open daily 9-5. Museums and The Public Hospital open daily at 10. Museums close at 7 p.m. on Fri. and Sat. Various performances depicting aspects of Colonial life take place daily throughout the historic area. Phone ahead to confirm schedule.

Cost: Tickets, which are required to enter buildings and to ride the shuttle, are available at the Colonial Williamsburg Visitor Center *(see Insider Info p. 281)*, the Greenhow Lumber House ticket office on Duke of Gloucester Street and at the Merchants Square Information Station. Single-day Ticket $40.99; $20.49 (ages 6-12). Multiday Ticket (valid for 3 days through the end of the year) $50.99;

$25.49 (ages 6-12). Sampler Ticket (admission to two trade shops, one family home and the Public Gaol) $25.99; $12.49 (ages 6-12). Art Museum Single-day Ticket $12.99; $6.49 (ages 6-12). Discounted tickets are available in advance at participating AAA offices. **Phone:** (888) 965-7254. [GT] [¶] [🐾]

The Abby Aldrich Rockefeller Folk Art Museum is at 326 W. Francis St. adjacent to the Colonial Williamsburg Historic Area, off I-64 exit 238. The institution is dedicated to the collection and preservation of American folk art. Eleven galleries display items from the 18th century to the present. Exhibits include carvings, embroideries, paintings, toys and weather vanes. **Hours:** Daily 10-5 (also Fri.-Sat. 5-7). Phone ahead to confirm schedule. **Cost:** Single-day Colonial Williamsburg admission pass $40.99; $20.49 (ages 6-12). Multiday Colonial Williamsburg admission pass (valid for 3 days through the end of the year) $50.99; $25.49 (ages 6-12). Art museum single-day ticket $12.99; $6.49 (ages 6-12). Other combination passes are available. **Phone:** (888) 965-7254.

Anderson's Blacksmith Shop & Public Armoury is just w. of jct. Duke of Gloucester St. and N. Botetourt St. at the Colonial Williamsburg Historic Area, off I-64 exit 238. Costumed interpreters convey the amount of work necessary here prior to and during the Revolutionary War to supply soldiers with ammunition and other military supplies.

The reconstructed industrial site encompasses the blacksmith shop, where craftsmen continue to forge iron into such implements as swords, guns and everyday 18th-century items; the Anderson kitchen, where cooking demonstrations take place as part of the Historic Foodways Program; and an armory, which has six structures, including a tinsmithing operation.

Time: Allow 15 minutes minimum. **Hours:** Hours vary seasonally; phone ahead. **Cost:** Single-day Colonial Williamsburg admission pass $40.99; $20.49 (ages 6-12). Multiday Colonial Williamsburg admission pass (valid for 3 days through the end of the year) $50.99; $25.49 (ages 6-12). Other combination passes are available. **Phone:** (888) 965-7254.

Bassett Hall is at 522 E. Francis St. at the Colonial Williamsburg Historic Area, off I-64 exit 238. This was the Williamsburg home of John D. and Abby Aldrich Rockefeller. The 18th-century house is named for Martha Washington's nephew, Burwell Bassett, who owned it 1800-39. It is furnished to reflect the Rockefellers' lifestyle during the 1930s when they were instrumental in restoring Colonial Williamsburg. A 10-minute video presentation precedes a tour of the house and grounds.

Time: Allow 30 minutes minimum. **Hours:** Hours vary seasonally; phone ahead. **Cost:** Single-day Colonial Williamsburg admission pass $40.99; $20.49 (ages 6-12). Multiday Colonial Williamsburg

(See map & index p. 279.)

admission pass (valid for 3 days through the end of the year) $50.99; $25.49 (ages 6-12). Other combination passes are available. **Phone:** (888) 965-7254. GT

Bruton Parish Episcopal Church is at 201 W. Duke of Gloucester St. at the Colonial Williamsburg Historic Area, off I-64 exit 238. The Rev. W.A.R. Goodwin, rector of this church in the early 1900s, approached John D. Rockefeller, Jr. with the idea of preserving Colonial Williamsburg. The church itself was erected 1710-15 to replace an earlier building and has been restored. The bell tower was constructed in 1769 and contains a bell that was cast in 1761; it still rings for services. **Hours:** Daily 10-4. Phone ahead to confirm schedule. **Cost:** Donations. **Phone:** (757) 229-2891.

The Capitol is at the e. end of Duke of Gloucester St. at the Colonial Williamsburg Historic Area, off I-64 exit 238. The current structure represents the first capitol, which was built in 1701 and reconstructed during the 1930s. The Capitol was the site of many important political events. The most significant of these took place May 15, 1776, when Virginia's legislators—nearly 2 months before the Continental Congress adopted the Declaration of Independence in Philadelphia—voted for delegates in Philadelphia to introduce a resolution declaring the Colonies independence from England.

Hours: Dancing, entertainment and other evening programs take place on a varying schedule; phone ahead for more information. **Cost:** Single-day Colonial Williamsburg admission pass $40.99; $20.49 (ages 6-12). Multiday Colonial Williamsburg admission pass (valid for 3 days through the end of the year) $50.99; $25.49 (ages 6-12). Other combination passes are available. **Phone:** (888) 965-7254.

Courthouse of 1770 is at 101 W. Duke of Gloucester St. at the Colonial Williamsburg Historic Area, off I-64 exit 238. Costumed interpreters enlist the help of Colonial Williamsburg guests to demonstrate the workings of local 18th-century government and justice, culminating in a re-enactment of a typical courtroom proceeding. A brief background of Colonial law and the building's history also is provided. **Hours:** Hours vary seasonally; phone ahead. **Cost:** Single-day Colonial Williamsburg admission pass $40.99; $20.49 (ages 6-12). Multiday Colonial Williamsburg admission pass (valid for 3 days through the end of the year) $50.99; $25.49 (ages 6-12). Other combination passes are available. **Phone:** (888) 965-7254.

The DeWitt Wallace Decorative Arts Museum is at 326 W. Francis St. at the Colonial Williamsburg Historic Area, off I-64 exit 238. The museum houses British and American decorative arts dating from 1600 through 1830. An impressive assembly of furniture is on display, including what is said to be the world's largest collection of Virginia

furniture. In addition to maps, paintings, prints and textiles, the museum features a fine assortment of English pottery.

Hours: Daily 10-5 (also Fri.-Sat. 5-9). Phone ahead to confirm schedule. **Cost:** Single-day Colonial Williamsburg admission pass $40.99; $20.49 (ages 6-12). Multiday Colonial Williamsburg admission pass (valid for 3 days through the end of the year) $50.99; $25.49 (ages 6-12). Art museum single-day ticket $12.99; $6.49 (ages 6-12). Other combination passes are available. **Phone:** (757) 220-7724 or (888) 965-7254. TI

Geddy Gunsmith is at 117 W. Duke of Gloucester St. at the Colonial Williamsburg Historic Area, off I-64 exit 238, following signs. The house was built in the 1760s. James Geddy Jr. operated a silversmith business here; a foundry and 18th-century furnishings can be seen. At this trade site, skilled artisans cast objects in brass, bronze, pewter and silver. The Gunsmith Shop also is on-site. Children can take part in storytelling activities, dance lessons and games.

Hours: Hours vary seasonally; phone ahead. **Cost:** Single-day Colonial Williamsburg admission pass $40.99; $20.49 (ages 6-12). Multiday Colonial Williamsburg admission pass (valid for 3 days through the end of the year) $50.99; $25.49 (ages 6-12). Other combination passes are available. **Phone:** (888) 965-7254.

Governor's Palace is at 300 Palace Green St. at the Colonial Williamsburg Historic Area, off I-64 exit 238. When it was completed in 1722, the residence of Virginia's royal governor was considered one of the finest structures in British North America. The elegant and imposing residence has been the home of seven royal governors and the commonwealth's first two state governors. The current building faces the Palace Green and was reconstructed on the original foundations; it opened to the public in April 1934.

The palace complex also includes a kitchen, where 18th-century cooking demonstrations are featured, and elaborate gardens with vegetables, flowers, greenery, arbors and a garden maze. **Hours:** Hours vary seasonally; phone ahead. **Cost:** Single-day Colonial Williamsburg admission pass $40.99; $20.49 (ages 6-12). Multiday Colonial Williamsburg admission pass (valid for 3 days through the end of the year) $50.99; $25.49 (ages 6-12). Other combination passes are available. **Phone:** (888) 965-7254.

Great Hopes Plantation is at the Colonial Williamsburg Historic Area off I-64 exit 238. Dedicated to African-American history and rural trades, the site interprets the lives of slaves and middle-class farmers. Costumed re-enactors convey a variety of 18th-century agricultural techniques and activities. Buildings include a smokehouse, slaves' quarters and a carpentry shed; tobacco fields and animal pens also are on the grounds.

(See map & index p. 279.)

Hours: Hours vary seasonally; phone ahead. **Cost:** Single-day Colonial Williamsburg admission pass $40.99; $20.49 (ages 6-12). Multiday Colonial Williamsburg admission pass (valid for 3 days through the end of the year) $50.99; $25.49 (ages 6-12). Other combination passes are available. **Phone:** (888) 965-7254.

The Historic Trades Sites are throughout the Colonial Williamsburg Historic Area, off I-64 exit 238. Collectively, the practiced trades replicate an 18th-century production system. More than 70 artisans—including brickmakers, coopers, milliners and silversmiths—offer insights into early American society and technology. The trades sites produce the materials used in the historic area's reconstructions. Guests can work in the brickyard and learn about the skills and training needed to become a master tradesman.

Hours: Hours vary seasonally. Some trades are demonstrated outdoors (weather permitting). Phone ahead for schedules. **Cost:** Single-day Colonial Williamsburg admission pass $40.99; $20.49 (ages 6-12). Multiday Colonial Williamsburg admission pass (valid for 3 days through the end of the year) $50.99; $25.49 (ages 6-12). Other combination passes are available. **Phone:** (888) 965-7254.

Magazine and Guardhouse is on Market Square at the Colonial Williamsburg Historic Area, off I-64 exit 238. The storehouse for arms and ammunition was built in 1715. The magazine displays firearms and military artifacts. Artillery demonstrations take place regularly. **Hours:** Hours vary seasonally; phone ahead. **Cost:** Single-day Colonial Williamsburg admission pass $40.99; $20.49 (ages 6-12). Multiday Colonial Williamsburg admission pass (valid for 3 days through the end of the year) $50.99; $25.49 (ages 6-12). Other combination passes are available. **Phone:** (888) 965-7254.

Peyton Randolph House is at 101 E. Nicholson St., at the Colonial Williamsburg Historic Area, off I-64 exit 238. The historic building was once the residence of the first president of the Continental Congress. During an interactive tour, guests learn about the lives of Randolph, his wife and the 27 slaves who lived here in the 18th century. Also onsite are various outbuildings, including a kitchen where cooking demonstrations are featured; a granary; storehouses; and a smokehouse.

Hours: Hours vary seasonally; phone ahead. **Cost:** Single-day Colonial Williamsburg admission pass $40.99; $20.49 (ages 6-12). Multiday Colonial Williamsburg admission pass (valid for 3 days through the end of the year) $50.99; $25.49 (ages 6-12). Other combination passes are available. **Phone:** (888) 965-7254. GT

Public Gaol is at 461 E. Nicholson St. at the Colonial Williamsburg Historic Area, off I-64 exit 238. This 1704 jail with later additions is completely restored and includes an early form of indoor plumbing and cells for criminals. Its most infamous occupants were 15 of the pirate Blackbeard's henchmen, caught in 1718, and Henry "Hair Buyer" Hamilton, a British lieutenant governor who allegedly offered bounties for patriots' scalps.

Hours: Hours vary seasonally; phone ahead. **Cost:** Single-day Colonial Williamsburg admission pass $40.99; $20.49 (ages 6-12). Multiday Colonial Williamsburg admission pass (valid for 3 days through the end of the year) $50.99; $25.49 (ages 6-12). Other combination passes are available. **Phone:** (888) 965-7254.

The Public Hospital is at 326 W. Francis St. at the Colonial Williamsburg Historic Area, off I-64 exit 238. This building was reconstructed on the original site of the Public Hospital for Persons of Insane and Disordered Minds. Opened in 1773, it was the first public institution in the English Colonies devoted solely to the treatment of mental illness. An exhibit on the first floor focuses on the history of the hospital.

Other subjects addressed are the underlying reasons for the facility's establishment, its doctors, patients and methods of treatment. **Hours:** Hours vary seasonally; phone ahead. **Cost:** Single-day Colonial Williamsburg admission pass $40.99; $20.49 (ages 6-12). Multiday Colonial Williamsburg admission pass (valid for 3 days through the end of the year) $50.99; $25.49 (ages 6-12). Other combination passes are available. **Phone:** (757) 220-7724 or (888) 965-7254.

Raleigh Tavern is at 413 E. Duke of Gloucester St. at the Colonial Williamsburg Historic Area, off I-64 exit 238. First established around 1717, the tavern became a center of social and political life during the 18th century. George Washington, Thomas Jefferson and Patrick Henry are a few of the patriots who helped make history here. It was in the Apollo Room that students from William & Mary are said to have founded the Phi Beta Kappa Society in 1776.

The building was reconstructed after a fire destroyed it in 1859. Today, it is the setting of comedy skits, dance programs and more. **Hours:** Hours vary seasonally; phone ahead. **Cost:** Single-day Colonial Williamsburg admission pass $40.99; $20.49 (ages 6-12). Multiday Colonial Williamsburg admission pass (valid for 3 days through the end of the year) $50.99; $25.49 (ages 6-12). Other combination passes are available. **Phone:** (888) 965-7254.

R. Charlton's Coffeehouse is on Duke of Gloucester St. at the Colonial Williamsburg Historic Area, off I-64 exit 238. Costumed interpreters serving coffee, hot chocolate and tea welcome visitors to this Colonial coffeehouse. In the 1700s, businessmen, politicians and other townspeople seeking more stimulating conversation than could be found at the local tavern frequented these types of businesses.

Time: Allow 30 minutes minimum. **Hours:** Hours vary seasonally; phone ahead. **Cost:** Single-day

(See map & index p. 279.)

Colonial Williamsburg admission pass $40.99;
$20.49 (ages 6-12). Multiday Colonial Williamsburg
admission pass (valid for 3 days through the end of
the year) $50.99; $25.49 (ages 6-12). Other combination passes are available. **Phone:** (757) 220-7645
or (888) 965-7254. GT

Wetherburn's Tavern is at 406 E. Duke of Gloucester St. at the Colonial Williamsburg Historic Area,
off I-64 exit 238. Owned by Henry Wetherburn, the
establishment figured prominently in the commercial
life of Williamsburg in the 1750s. The tavern is furnished in period. **Hours:** Hours vary seasonally;
phone ahead. **Cost:** Single-day Colonial Williamsburg admission pass $40.99; $20.49 (ages 6-12).
Multiday Colonial Williamsburg admission pass
(valid for 3 days through the end of the year) $50.99;
$25.49 (ages 6-12). Other combination passes are
available. **Phone:** (808) 965 7254.

Wythe House is at 112 Palace Green St. at the Co-
lonial Williamsburg Historic Area, off I-64 exit 238.
Built in the mid-18th century, the attractive
Georgian-style structure was the home of George
Wythe, one of the period's most prominent lawyers.
He was a scholar who mentored Thomas Jefferson,
a signer of the Declaration of Independence and the
first law professor at William & Mary. **Hours:** Hours
vary seasonally; phone ahead. **Cost:** Single-day
Colonial Williamsburg admission pass $40.99;
$20.49 (ages 6-12). Multiday Colonial Williamsburg
admission pass (valid for 3 days through the end of
the year) $50.99; $25.49 (ages 6-12). Other combination passes are available. **Phone:** (888)
965-7254.

**THE ORIGINAL GHOSTS OF WILLIAMSBURG
CANDLELIGHT TOUR** departs from Barnes &
Noble at 345 W. Duke of Gloucester St. Guided 90-
minute tours explore the streets of Williamsburg by
lantern. Based on the works of author L.B. Taylor Jr.,
the tour makes the rounds of the haunted streets of
Colonial Williamsburg. Also offered is the 2-hour Extreme Tour, which departs from Bruton Parish
Church on W. Duke of Gloucester Street and highlights Williamsburg's scariest stories.

Note: General tour tickets can be purchased at
the General Store at 1656 Richmond Rd. Extreme
Tour tickets are available online only. **Time:** Allow 1
hour, 30 minutes minimum. **Hours:** Candlelight
tours depart nightly at 8 (also at 8:45 p.m., June-
Aug.). Extreme Tours depart nightly at 9:15, June-
Aug.; Fri.-Sat. at 9:15, in May. Closed July 4. **Cost:**
Candlelight tour $12; free (ages 0-6). Extreme Tour
$16. Reservations are required. **Phone:** (757)
253-1058 or (877) 624-4678. GT

WATER COUNTRY USA, 176 Water
Country Pkwy., is said to be the Virgin-
ia's largest water park, offering 43 acres of pools,
children's play areas, lazy rivers and water rides.

Celebrating the music of the 1950s and '60s,
Rock 'n' Roll Island features nearly 600 feet of body
slides, a 700-foot lazy river and a 1,000-square-foot
pool. Hubba Hubba Highway is a free-floating interactive river ride where coconuts, cacti and geysers
provide a drenching experience. Colossal Curl is the
water park's newest attraction and features a combination of funnel and wave elements. Vanish Point
is a 75-foot-tall vertical drop slide, and Meltdown
takes riders on a high-speed toboggan race down a
flume full of twists, turns and banks.

Visitors can experience the rush of a thrilling
wipeout on Malibu Pipeline or take a family white-
water rafting ride aboard Aquazoid. Racers can see
who passes the finish line first on Nitro Racer, a
super-speed slide. Other rides include Jet Scream;
Rampage; Surfer's Bay, a wave pool; and a water-
soaked children's area with H2O UFO, Kritter Korral
and Cow-A-Bunga.

Hours: Opens daily at 10, Memorial Day-Labor
Day. Days and closing times vary. Phone ahead to
confirm schedule. **Cost:** $60; $53 (ages 3-9). Multiday and combination tickets with Busch Gardens
Williamsburg are available. Rates may vary; phone
ahead. **Parking:** $15. **Phone:** (800) 343-7946.

**COURTYARD BY MARRIOTT WILLIAMSBURG BUSCH
GARDENS AREA** (757)221-0700 **3**

Hotel
$72-$235

COURTYARD Marriott

AAA Benefit:
Members save 5%
or more!

Address: 470 McLaws Cir 23185 **Location:** I-64 exit 242A, just e of jct SR
199/Humelsine Pkwy on US 60. Located
in Busch Corporate Center. **Facility:** 151
units. 4 stories, interior corridors. **Terms:**
cancellation fee imposed. **Pool:** heated
outdoor, heated indoor. **Activities:** hot
tub, exercise room. **Guest Services:**
valet and coin laundry.

DOUBLETREE BY HILTON WILLIAMSBURG
(757)220-2500 **5**

Hotel
$79-$179

DOUBLETREE BY HILTON

AAA Benefit:
Members save 5% or
more!

Address: 50 Kingsmill Rd 23185 **Location:** I-64 exit 242A, 0.5 mi e on SR 199
to US 60; just w of Busch Gardens. **Facility:** 295 units. 6 stories, interior corridors. **Terms:** check-in 4 pm, 1-7 night
minimum stay, cancellation fee imposed.
Amenities: safes. **Dining:** 2 restaurants. **Pool:** outdoor, heated indoor. **Activities:** tennis, game room, exercise
room. **Guest Services:** valet and coin
laundry, area transportation.

(See map & index p. 279.)

HOLIDAY INN EXPRESS WILLIAMSBURG BUSCH GARDENS AREA
757/220-1100   **4**

Hotel
Rates not provided

Address: 480 McLaws Cir 23185 **Location:** I-64 exit 242A, just e of jct SR 199/Humelsine Pkwy on US 60. **Facility:** 100 units. 3 stories, interior corridors. **Amenities:** safes. **Pool:** outdoor. **Activities:** exercise room. **Guest Services:** valet and coin laundry. **Featured Amenity:** full hot breakfast.

KINGSMILL RESORT
(757)253-1703   **6**

Resort Condominium
$139-$249

Address: 1010 Kingsmill Rd 23185 **Location:** Waterfront. I-64 exit 242A to US 60, 1 mi e, follow signs. **Facility:** This sprawling resort on the banks of the James River offers extensive golf facilities, a full-service spa, a new family pool with lazy river and waterslide, and a beach area with water sports. 410 units, some cottages and condominiums. 3 stories (no elevator), exterior corridors. **Terms:** check-in 4 pm, 3 day cancellation notice-fee imposed. **Amenities:** safes. **Dining:** 3 restaurants. **Pool:** outdoor, heated indoor. **Activities:** sauna, hot tub, motor boats, marina, fishing, regulation golf, tennis, recreation programs, kids club, bicycles, playground, game room, lawn sports, trails, health club, spa. **Guest Services:** valet laundry, area transportation.

WAR HILL INN BED & BREAKFAST
757/565-0248   **1**
Bed & Breakfast. **Address:** 4560 Longhill Rd 23188

WYNDHAM GARDEN WILLIAMSBURG BUSCH GARDENS AREA
757/253-6444   **2**

Hotel
Rates not provided

Address: 201 Water Country Pkwy 23185 **Location:** I-64 exit 242B, just w on SR 199; facing Water Country. **Facility:** 201 units. 8 stories, interior corridors. **Amenities:** safes. **Pool:** outdoor. **Activities:** exercise room. **Guest Services:** valet and coin laundry.

WHERE TO EAT

BAKER'S CRUST   757/253-2787
American. Casual Dining. **Address:** 5234 Monticello Ave, Unit 115 23188

BANGKOK GARDEN   757/565-3939
Thai. Casual Dining. **Address:** 1346 Richmond Rd 23185

BELLISSIMO PIZZA CAFE   757/220-3371   **1**
Pizza. Quick Serve. **Address:** 6614-C Mooretown Rd 23188

CARROT TREE KITCHENS   757/229-0957   **17**
Southern Breads/Pastries. Casual Dining. **Address:** 1782 Jamestown Rd 23185

CENTER STREET GRILL   757/220-4600   **7**
American. Casual Dining. **Address:** 5101 Center St 23188

▼ See AAA listing p. 175 ▼

(See map & index p. 279.)

THE CORNER POCKET 757/220-0808 (8)
 American. Casual Dining. **Address:** 4805 Courthouse St 23188

DORALDO RISTORANTE ITALIANO 757/220-0795 (13)
Italian. Casual Dining. **Address:** 1915 Pocahontas Tr, Suite F1 23185

DUDLEY'S BISTRO 757/566-1157 (5)
American. Fine Dining. **Address:** 4904 Courthouse Ln 23188

EDWARDS VIRGINIA HAM SHOPPE 757/220-6618 (2)
Sandwiches. Quick Serve. **Address:** 5541C Richmond Rd 23185

GABRIEL ARCHER TAVERN 757/229-0999 (16)
American. Casual Dining. **Address:** 5800 Wessex Hundred 23185

GIUSEPPE'S ITALIAN CAFE 757/565-1977 (4)
Italian. Casual Dining. **Address:** 5525 Olde Towne Rd 23188

THE GRECIAN PLATE 757/565-2888 (10)
Greek. Casual Dining. **Address:** 4000 D Monticello Ave 23188

HONEY BUTTER'S KITCHEN 757/221-8038 (11)
Breakfast Comfort Food. Casual Dining. **Address:** 4680 Monticello Ave, Suite 17 23188

ICHIBAN 757/253-8898 (6)
Chinese. Casual Dining. **Address:** 4905 Courthouse St 23188

OCEANS & ALE 757/871-3463 (3)
Steak Seafood. Casual Dining. **Address:** 5601 Richmond Rd 23188

OPUS 9 STEAKHOUSE 757/645-4779 (9)
Steak. Fine Dining. **Address:** 5143 Main St 23188

THE SPORTSMANS GRILLE 757/220-4634 (14)
American. Casual Dining. **Address:** 240 McLaws Cir 23185

WAYPOINT SEAFOOD & GRILL 757/220-2228 (15)
American. Fine Dining. **Address:** 1480 Quarterpath Rd, Suite 4A 23185

THE WHALING COMPANY INC 757/229-0275 (12)
Seafood. Casual Dining. **Address:** 494 McLaws Cir 23185

CENTRAL WILLIAMSBURG
- Restaurants p. 290
- Hotels & Restaurants map & index p. 276

BEST WESTERN PLUS HISTORIC AREA INN
(757)220-0880 (11)

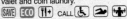
Hotel $79-$199

Best Western PLUS **AAA Benefit:** Members save 10% or more & earn 10% bonus points!

Address: 201 Bypass Rd 23185 **Location:** US 60, just se of jct Richmond Rd. **Facility:** 120 units. 4 stories, interior corridors. **Terms:** check-in 4 pm, cancellation fee imposed, resort fee. **Pool:** heated indoor. **Activities:** hot tub, game room, exercise room. **Guest Services:** valet and coin laundry.

BEST WESTERN WILLIAMSBURG HISTORIC DISTRICT
(757)229-4100 (28)

 Hotel $59-$199
 Best Western. **AAA Benefit:** Members save 10% or more & earn 10% bonus points!

Address: 351 York St 23185 **Location:** US 60 E, 0.3 mi se of jct SR 5 and 31. **Facility:** 140 units. 4 stories, interior corridors. **Terms:** check-in 4 pm, 3 day cancellation notice-fee imposed, resort fee. **Pool:** heated indoor. **Activities:** hot tub, exercise room. **Guest Services:** valet and coin laundry.

BLUEGREEN VACATIONS PATRICK HENRY SQUARE, AN ASCEND RESORT COLLECTION MEMBER (757)229-9540 (27)
Hotel. **Address:** 315 York St 23185

CEDARS OF WILLIAMSBURG BED & BREAKFAST 757/229-8591 (94)
Historic Bed & Breakfast. **Address:** 616 Jamestown Rd 23185

COLONIAL CAPITAL BED & BREAKFAST 757/645-4525 (26)
Historic Bed & Breakfast. **Address:** 501 Richmond Rd 23185

COLONIAL GARDENS BED & BREAKFAST 757/220-8087 (37)
Bed & Breakfast. **Address:** 1109 Jamestown Rd 23185

COLONIAL WILLIAMSBURG-WOODLANDS HOTEL & SUITES 757/220-7960 (23)
Hotel. **Address:** 105 Visitor Center Dr 23185

COMFORT INN WILLIAMSBURG GATEWAY
(757)253-1166 (18)

Hotel $78-$270

Address: 331 Bypass Rd 23185 **Location:** US 60 (Bypass Rd), 0.5 mi w of SR 132. **Facility:** 116 units, some two bedrooms. 4 stories, interior corridors. **Pool:** outdoor. **Activities:** exercise room. **Guest Services:** valet and coin laundry. **Featured Amenity:** breakfast buffet.

COMFORT SUITES (757)645-4646 (20)
Hotel. **Address:** 220 Bypass Rd 23185

COUNTRY INN & SUITES BY CARLSON
757/259-7990 (19)

Hotel Rates not provided

Address: 400 Bypass Rd 23185 **Location:** US 60 Bypass Rd, just e of jct Richmond Rd; 0.7 mi w of jct SR 132. **Facility:** 66 units. 3 stories, interior corridors. **Pool:** heated indoor. **Activities:** hot tub, exercise room. **Guest Services:** valet and coin laundry. **Featured Amenity:** breakfast buffet.

(See map & index p. 276.)

COUNTRY INN & SUITES BY CARLSON BUSCH GARDENS AREA
757/229-6900 **35**

Hotel
Rates not provided

Address: 7135 Pocahontas Tr 23185 **Location:** I-64 exit 242 (SR 199), 0.5 mi w on US 60. **Facility:** 88 units. 5 stories, interior corridors. **Pool:** outdoor. **Activities:** exercise room. **Guest Services:** valet and coin laundry. **Featured Amenity:** full hot breakfast.

DAYS INN WILLIAMSBURG HISTORIC AREA
757/229-9230 **15**

Hotel
Rates not provided

Address: 706 Bypass Rd 23185 **Location:** US 60 Bypass Rd, 0.5 mi w of jct SR 132. **Facility:** 157 units. 3-4 stories, interior/exterior corridors. **Pool:** outdoor, heated indoor. **Activities:** sauna, hot tub. **Guest Services:** valet and coin laundry.

ECONO LODGE COLONIAL
(757)253-6450 **24**
Motel. **Address:** 216 Parkway Dr 23185

EMBASSY SUITES BY HILTON
(757)229-6800 **9**
Hotel. **Address:** 3006 Mooretown Rd 23185

AAA Benefit: Members save 5% or more!

FAIRFIELD INN & SUITES BY MARRIOTT
(757)645-3600 **17**

Hotel
$60-$235

AAA Benefit: Members save 5% or more!

Address: 1402 Richmond Rd 23185 **Location:** US 60, jct Richmond and Bypass rds. **Facility:** 148 units. 4 stories, interior corridors. **Terms:** cancellation fee imposed. **Pool:** heated indoor. **Activities:** exercise room. **Guest Services:** valet and coin laundry, boarding pass kiosk.

THE FIFE AND DRUM INN
(757)345-1776 **29**
Bed & Breakfast. **Address:** 441 Prince George St 23185

FORT MAGRUDER HOTEL & CONFERENCE CENTER
(757)220-2250 **32**

Hotel
$109-$299

Address: 6945 Pocahontas Tr 23185 **Location:** US 60, 0.8 mi e of jct SR 5 and 31. **Facility:** 303 units. 4 stories, interior corridors. **Terms:** check-in 4 pm, cancellation fee imposed. **Pool:** outdoor, heated indoor. **Activities:** hot tub, exercise room. **Guest Services:** valet and coin laundry.

THE GRIFFIN HOTEL
757/565-8440 **30**
Hotel. **Address:** 305 E Francis St 23185

HAMPTON INN & SUITES
(757)229-4900 **2**
Hotel. **Address:** 1880 Richmond Rd 23185

AAA Benefit: Members save up to 10%!

HAMPTON INN & SUITES HISTORIC AREA
(757)941-1777 **8**

Hotel
$89-$199

AAA Benefit: Members save up to 10%!

Address: 911 Capitol Landing Rd 23185 **Location:** I-64 exit 238, 1 mi e on SR 143, then just w on SR 5. **Facility:** 109 units. 4 stories, interior corridors. **Terms:** 1-7 night minimum stay, cancellation fee imposed. **Amenities:** safes. **Pool:** heated indoor. **Activities:** hot tub, exercise room. **Guest Services:** valet and coin laundry. **Featured Amenity:** full hot breakfast.

HAMPTON INN & SUITES WILLIAMSBURG-CENTRAL
(757)229-7330 **13**

Hotel
$79-$209

AAA Benefit: Members save up to 10%!

Address: 718 Bypass Rd 23185 **Location:** I-64 exit 238, on US 60 Bypass Rd, then 0.5 mi w of jct SR 132. **Facility:** 105 units. 5 stories, interior corridors. **Terms:** 1-7 night minimum stay, cancellation fee imposed. **Pool:** outdoor, heated indoor. **Activities:** hot tub, exercise room. **Guest Services:** valet and coin laundry. **Featured Amenity:** breakfast buffet.

HILTON GARDEN INN
(757)253-9400 **5**

Hotel
$89-$219

AAA Benefit: Members save up to 10%!

Address: 1624 Richmond Rd 23185 **Location:** On US 60, w of jct Bypass Rd. **Facility:** 119 units. 4 stories, interior corridors. **Terms:** 1-7 night minimum stay, cancellation fee imposed. **Pool:** heated indoor. **Activities:** hot tub, exercise room. **Guest Services:** valet and coin laundry.

(See map & index p. 276.)

HOLIDAY INN & SUITES GATEWAY 757/229-9990

Hotel
Rates not provided

Address: 515 Bypass Rd 23185 **Location:** US 60 Bypass, 1 mi e of jct Richmond Rd. **Facility:** 96 units, some two bedrooms. 5 stories, interior corridors. **Amenities:** safes. **Pool:** heated indoor. **Activities:** hot tub, exercise room. **Guest Services:** valet and coin laundry. **Featured Amenity:** full hot breakfast.

HOLIDAY INN EXPRESS HOTEL & SUITES
(757)941-1057

Hotel
$79-$239

Address: 1452 Richmond Rd 23185 **Location:** On US 60, just w of jct Bypass Rd. **Facility:** 93 units. 4 stories, interior corridors. **Terms:** cancellation fee imposed. **Pool:** heated indoor. **Activities:** exercise room. **Guest Services:** valet and coin laundry.

HOMEWOOD SUITES BY HILTON 757/259-1199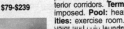

Extended Stay Hotel
Rates not provided

 **AAA Benefit:** Members save up to 10%!

Address: 601 Bypass Rd 23185 **Location:** US 60 Bypass, 0.5 mi w of jct SR 132. **Facility:** 61 efficiencies, some two bedrooms. 5 stories, interior corridors. **Terms:** check-in 4 pm. **Pool:** heated indoor. **Activities:** exercise room. **Guest Services:** valet and coin laundry. **Featured Amenity:** full hot breakfast.

LA QUINTA INN & SUITES WILLIAMSBURG
(757)220-2800

Hotel
$59-$214

Address: 600 Bypass Rd 23185 **Location:** US 60 Bypass Rd, 0.5 mi w of jct SR 132. **Facility:** 135 units, some two bedrooms. 5 stories, interior corridors. **Pool:** outdoor. **Activities:** exercise room. **Guest Services:** valet and coin laundry. **Featured Amenity:** continental breakfast.

LIBERTY ROSE BED & BREAKFAST 757/849-8250
Historic Bed & Breakfast. **Address:** 1022 Jamestown Rd 23185

PATRIOT INN (757)378-2929

Hotel
$117-$157

Address: 1420 Richmond Rd 23185 **Location:** 1.5 mi nw of Colonial Williamsburg on US 60 (Richmond Rd); jct Bypass Rd. **Facility:** 65 kitchen units, some two bedrooms. 4 stories, interior corridors. **Terms:** check-in 4 pm, 2 night minimum stay - seasonal and/or weekends, 3 day cancellation notice-fee imposed, resort fee. **Pool:** outdoor. **Activities:** hot tub, exercise room. **Guest Services:** complimentary laundry.

RESIDENCE INN BY MARRIOTT WILLIAMSBURG
(757)941-2000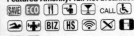

Extended Stay Hotel
$67-$325

Residence Inn Marriott **AAA Benefit:** Members save 5% or more!

Address: 1648 Richmond Rd 23185 **Location:** US 60, just w of jct Bypass Rd. **Facility:** 108 units, some two bedrooms, efficiencies and kitchens, 4 stories, interior corridors. **Terms:** check-in 4 pm, cancellation fee imposed. **Pool:** outdoor. **Activities:** hot tub, exercise room. **Guest Services:** valet and coin laundry. **Featured Amenity:** breakfast buffet.

RODEWAY INN HISTORIC IN WILLIAMSBURG
(757)229-1955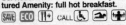
Motel. **Address:** 309 Page St 23185

SLEEP INN (757)259-1700
Hotel. **Address:** 220 Bypass Rd 23185

SPRINGHILL SUITES BY MARRIOTT WILLIAMSBURG
(757)941-3000

Hotel
$54-$230

SPRINGHILL SUITES MARRIOTT **AAA Benefit:** Members save 5% or more!

Address: 1644 Richmond Rd 23185 **Location:** US 60, just w of jct Bypass Rd. **Facility:** 120 units. 4 stories, interior corridors. **Terms:** check-in 4 pm, cancellation fee imposed. **Pool:** heated indoor. **Activities:** hot tub, exercise room. **Guest Services:** valet and coin laundry. **Featured Amenity:** breakfast buffet.

WESTGATE HISTORIC WILLIAMSBURG (757)229-6220
Extended Stay Hotel. **Address:** 1324 Richmond Rd 23185

WILLIAMSBURG INN (757)220-7978
Classic Historic Hotel. **Address:** 136 E Francis St 23185

WILLIAMSBURG LODGE, AUTOGRAPH COLLECTION
(757)220-7976
Hotel. **Address:** 310 S England St 23185

AAA Benefit: Members save 5% or more!

WYNDHAM GOVERNOR'S GREEN 757/564-2420
Condominium. **Address:** 4600 Mooretown Rd 23185

(See map & index p. 276.)

WYNDHAM KINGSGATE RESORT   757/220-5702   **6**
♦♦♦ Resort Condominium. **Address:** 619 Georgetown Crescent 23185

WHERE TO EAT

ABERDEEN BARN   757/229-6661   **6**
♦♦ Steak. Casual Dining. **Address:** 1601 Richmond Rd 23185

AROMAS   757/221-6676   **22**
♦ Coffee/Tea Sandwiches. Quick Serve. **Address:** 431 Prince George St 23185

BERRET'S SEAFOOD RESTAURANT AND TAPHOUSE GRILL
          757/253-1847   **30**
♦♦♦ Seafood. Casual Dining. **Address:** 199 S Boundary St 23185

BLUE TALON BISTRO   757/476-2583   **25**
♦♦♦ French. Casual Dining. **Address:** 420 Prince George St 23185

CAPTAIN GEORGE'S SEAFOOD RESTAURANT   757/565-2323
♦♦ Seafood. Casual Dining. **Address:** 5363 Richmond Rd 23188

THE CHEESE SHOP   757/220-0298   **29**
♦ Specialty. Quick Serve. **Address:** 410 Duke of Glouchester St 23185

CHOWNING'S TAVERN   757/229-2141   **19**
♦♦ American. Casual Dining. **Address:** 109 E Duke of Gloucester St 23185

CHRISTIANA CAMPBELL'S TAVERN   757/229-2141   **15**
♦♦ Seafood. Casual Dining. **Address:** 120 S Waller St 23185

COCHON ON 2ND   757/229-1199   **14**
♦♦♦ American. Fine Dining. **Address:** 311-106 2nd St 23185

COZY PATIO CAFE   757/229-1012   **10**
♦♦ Cajun. Casual Dining. **Address:** 1330 Richmond Rd 23185

CULTURE CAFE   757/378-2556   **17**
♦♦ Small Plates. Casual Dining. **Address:** 747 Scotland St 23185

DOG STREET PUB   757/293-6478   **26**
♦♦ American. Gastropub. **Address:** 401 W Duke of Gloucester St 23185

EL SABROSON TRADITIONAL LATIN FOOD
          757/220-3145   **7**
♦♦ Latin American. Casual Dining. **Address:** 122 Waller Mill Rd, Suite G 23185

EMILY'S DONUTS & CAFE   757/345-3602   **31**
♦ Sandwiches Breads/Pastries. Quick Serve. **Address:** 7123 Merrimac Tr 23185

FAT CANARY   757/229-3333   **28**

Regional American Fine Dining $28-$39

AAA Inspector Notes: This stylish spot overlooks historic Merchants Square but is all modern inside, with crisp lines and creative gourmet fare that changes seasonally to offer fresh regional ingredients. The South is a heavy influence, but one will find the chef has also drawn inspiration from around the world. An excellent complement of wines is offered. Dishes often change but house specialties include house-made mozzarella, rabbit and biscuits, and pan-seared scallops. **Features:** full bar. **Reservations:** suggested. **Address:** 410 W Duke of Gloucester St 23185 **Location:** At Merchants Square. **D**

FIRESIDE CHOPHOUSE   757/229-3310   **2**
♦♦♦ Steak. Casual Dining. **Address:** 1995 Richmond Rd 23185

FOOD FOR THOUGHT   757/645-4665   **3**
♦♦ American. Casual Dining. **Address:** 1647 Richmond Rd 23185

GOLDEN HORSESHOE CLUB HOUSE GRILL
          757/565-8460   **33**
♦♦ American. Casual Dining. **Address:** 401 S England St 23185

KING'S ARMS TAVERN   757/229-2141   **18**
♦♦ American. Casual Dining. **Address:** 416 E Duke of Gloucester St 23185

KYOTO JAPANESE STEAKHOUSE & SUSHI BAR
          757/220-8888   **5**
♦♦ Japanese. Casual Dining. **Address:** 1621 Richmond Rd 23185

LA TOLTECA   757/253-2939   **1**
♦♦♦ Mexican. Casual Dining. **Address:** 3048 Richmond Rd 23185

LA TOLTECA MEXICAN RESTAURANTE   757/259-0598   **13**
♦♦ Mexican. Casual Dining. **Address:** 135 Second St 23185

LE YACA FRENCH RESTAURANT   757/220-3616   **9**
♦♦♦ French. Fine Dining. **Address:** 1430 High St 23185

LOKAL   757/229-1464   **24**
♦♦ Vegan Vegetarian. Casual Dining. **Address:** 445 Prince George St 23185

NAWAB INDIAN CUISINE   757/565-3200
♦♦ Indian. Casual Dining. **Address:** 204 Monticello Ave 23185

OISHII JAPANESE RAMEN & HIBACHI GRILL
          757/220-6880   **21**
♦ Japanese. Quick Serve. **Address:** 515 Prince George St 23185

OLD CHICKAHOMINY HOUSE   757/229-4689   **34**
♦♦ Regional Southern. Casual Dining. **Address:** 1211 Jamestown Rd 23185

PETER CHANG CHINA CAFE   757/345-5829   **11**
♦♦ Chinese. Casual Dining. **Address:** 1203 Richmond Rd 23185

PLAZA AZTECA MEXICAN RESTAURANT   757/345-2901   **8**
♦♦ Mexican. Casual Dining. **Address:** 1430 High St, Suite 901 23185

RETRO'S-GOOD EATS   757/253-8816   **23**
♦ Burgers Hot Dogs. Quick Serve. **Address:** 435 Prince George St 23185

RICK'S CHEESE STEAK SHOP   757/221-9566   **20**
♦ Sandwiches. Quick Serve. **Address:** 603 Prince George St 23185

(See map & index p. 276.)

SEAFARE OF WILLIAMSBURG   757/229-0099   ④

◈◈◈◈

Seafood
Fine Dining
$24-$46

AAA Inspector Notes: Diners who crave Atlantic or Chesapeake Bay seafood and Prime beef are likely to enjoy this nautical spot. Haunting ship portraits with glowing portholes line the walls. There are many seafood dishes from which to choose, in addition to good bread and excellent homemade Caesar salad. Patrons can expect more formal service than is the norm; trained staff members carry out their duties in a polished, unobtrusive way. **Features:** full bar. **Reservations:** suggested. **Address:** 1632 Richmond Rd 23185 **Location:** 2 mi nw on US 60. ⃞D CALL ♿

Serving the highest quality steaks, seafood & veal

SECOND STREET AMERICAN BISTRO   757/220-2286   ⑫
◈◈◈ American. Casual Dining. **Address:** 140 Second St 23185

SHIELDS TAVERN   757/229-2141   ⑯
◈◈ American. Casual Dining. **Address:** 422 E Duke of Gloucester St 23185

TRADITIONS   757/229-2141   ㉜
◈◈◈ American. Fine Dining. **Address:** 310 S England St 23185

THE TRELLIS RESTAURANT   757/229-8610   ㉗
◈◈◈ Regional American. Fine Dining. **Address:** 403 Duke of Gloucester St 23185

WILLIAMSVILLE

FORT LEWIS LODGE   540/925-2314
◈◈◈ Country Inn. **Address:** SR 625 (River Rd) 24460

WILLIS WHARF

THE SEASIDE GRILL AT WILLIS WHARF   757/442-2696
◈◈ American. Casual Dining. **Address:** 4456 Willis Wharf Rd 23486

WINCHESTER (E-8) pop. 26,203, elev. 717'
• Hotels p. 292 • Restaurants p. 293

Established in 1732 by German, Scottish and Irish settlers heading south from Pennsylvania, Winchester played a major part in the French and Indian and Civil wars. It was in Winchester that a young George Washington established his surveying career. He also built Fort Loudoun and had his headquarters in the town as commander on the Virginia frontier 1755-58. In addition Washington was elected in Winchester to the Virginia House of Burgesses in 1758 and 1761.

During the Civil War, the town changed hands at least 72 times, including 13 times in a day. The First, Second and Third battles of Winchester occurred in 1862, 1863 and 1864. The Confederate and National cemeteries contain the bodies of 7,500 Union and Confederate soldiers. The 55-acre Mount Hebron Cemetery, on E. Boscawen Street in the historic district, includes the Stonewall Confederate Cemetery and two original church cemeteries. Among its monuments is one dedicated to 829 unknown Confederate dead.

The Winchester POW/MIA Memorial at Jim Barnett Park was built in 2005 to honor and recognize Virginia soldiers, airmen, sailors and marines who have yet to come home. The Korean War Memorial is dedicated to veterans of "the Forgotten War."

Lower Shenandoah Valley history is preserved in books, manuscripts and archives at the Handley Regional Library, an elaborate 1908 beaux-arts structure at the corner of Braddock and Piccadilly streets; phone (540) 662-9041.

An early landlord in the Shenandoah Valley, George Washington required each tenant to plant 4 acres of apples. As a result extensive orchards surround Winchester. For 10 days from late April to early May the ❧ Shenandoah Apple Blossom Festival features dances, live music, parades and various competitions.

Winchester-Frederick County Visitor Center: 1400 S. Pleasant Valley Rd., Winchester, VA 22601. **Phone:** (540) 542-1326 or (877) 871-1326.

Self-guiding tours: The convention and visitor bureau serves as a Civil War orientation center for the Shenandoah Valley Battlefields Foundation. It offers brochures detailing walking and driving tours as well as video presentations about the area.

❧ ⃞SAVE **MUSEUM OF THE SHENANDOAH VALLEY** is at 901 Amherst St. (SR 50W). Anchoring a 214-acre cultural site, the 50,000-square-foot regional history museum contains four galleries that document the history of the Shenandoah Valley. Changing exhibits are displayed, as is a collection of miniature houses.

The property's 7 acres of manicured grounds include formal Chinese, water, rose, parterre, herb and vegetable gardens showcasing shady passages made from flowering crab apple trees, fountains and statues. The complex also features the Glen Burnie House, built in 1794 by Robert Wood, son of Winchester founder Col. James Wood.

Time: Allow 2 hours minimum. **Hours:** Museum Tues. and Thurs.-Sun. 10-4, Wed. 10-8, Memorial Day-Labor Day; Tues.-Sun. 10-4, Apr. 1-day before Memorial Day and day after Labor day-Dec. 31; Tues.-Sun. 11-4, rest of year. House and gardens Tues.-Sun. 10-4, Apr.-Dec. Closed Jan. 1, Thanksgiving, Christmas Eve and Christmas. **Cost:** $10; $8 (ages 13-18 and 60+); free (ages 0-12 and to all Wed.). **Phone:** (540) 662-1473, ext. 235, or (888) 556-5799, ext. 235. ⃞¶

SHENANDOAH VALLEY DISCOVERY MUSEUM is at 19 W. Cork St. Appealing to all ages are exhibits based on science, math and art. Highlights include a Native American longhouse, an art area, a vertical maze, HealthWorks and a collection of brain teasers. Changing exhibits also are featured. **Time:**

Allow 1 hour minimum. **Hours:** Tues.-Sat. 9-5 (also first Fri. of the month 5-7:30), Sun. 1-5. **Cost:** $8; free (ages 0-1). **Phone:** (540) 722-2020.

STONEWALL JACKSON'S HEADQUARTERS is s. on US 11 at 415 N. Braddock St. The 1854 Gothic Revival house served as Gen. Thomas J. "Stonewall" Jackson's headquarters from November 1861 to March 1862. The house contains many of Jackson's possessions, along with prints, pictures and artifacts of the Civil War. Also displayed are items that belonged to topographer Jed Hotchkiss and cavalry general Turner Ashby.

　Time: Allow 30 minutes minimum. **Hours:** Mon.-Sat. 10-4, Sun. noon-4, Apr.-Oct. **Cost:** $5; $4.50 (ages 60+); $2.50 (ages 7-18). A combination ticket with Abram's Delight Museum and George Washington's Office Museum is available. **Phone:** (540) 667-5505 or (540) 662-6550.

BEST WESTERN LEE-JACKSON INN & CONFERENCE CENTER　　　　　　　　(540)662-4154

Hotel
$73-$89

BW Best Western. AAA Benefit: Members save 10% or more & earn 10% bonus points!

Address: 711 Millwood Ave 22601 **Location:** I-81 exit 313B, just nw on US 17/50/522. **Facility:** 139 units. 2 stories (no elevator), exterior corridors. **Terms:** cancellation fee imposed. **Pool:** outdoor. **Activities:** exercise room. **Guest Services:** valet and coin laundry, area transportation.

CANDLEWOOD SUITES　　　　　　　540/667-8323
Extended Stay Hotel. **Address:** 1135 Millwood Pike 22602

COUNTRY INN & SUITES BY CARLSON　540/869-7657
Hotel. **Address:** 141 Kernstown Commons Blvd 22602

COURTYARD BY MARRIOTT WINCHESTER MEDICAL CENTER　　　　　　　　(540)678-8822
Hotel. **Address:** 300 Marriott Dr 22603

AAA Benefit: Members save 5% or more!

ECONO LODGE NORTH　　　　　　(540)662-4700

Motel
$67-$100

Address: 1593 Martinsburg Pike 22603 **Location:** I-81 exit 317, 0.3 mi sw on US 11. **Facility:** 49 units. 2 stories (no elevator), interior corridors. **Guest Services:** valet laundry. **Featured Amenity: continental breakfast.**

FAIRFIELD INN & SUITES BY MARRIOTT IN WINCHESTER
　　　　　　　　　　　　　　　　　(540)665-8881
Hotel. **Address:** 250 Front Royal Pike 22602

AAA Benefit: Members save 5% or more!

THE GEORGE WASHINGTON HOTEL, A WYNDHAM GRAND HOTEL　　　　　　　　540/678-4700
Historic Hotel. **Address:** 103 E Piccadilly St 22601

HAMPTON INN NORTH　　　　　　(540)678-4000
Hotel. **Address:** 1204 Berryville Ave 22601

AAA Benefit: Members save up to 10%!

HAMPTON INN WINCHESTER UNIVERSITY MALL
　　　　　　　　　　　　　　　　　(540)667-8011
Hotel. **Address:** 1655 Apple Blossom Dr 22601

AAA Benefit: Members save up to 10%!

HILTON GARDEN INN-WINCHESTER　(540)722-8881
Hotel. **Address:** 120 Wingate Dr 22601

AAA Benefit: Members save up to 10%!

HOLIDAY INN EXPRESS & SUITES WINCHESTER
　　　　　　　　　　　　　　　　　540/667-7050
Hotel. **Address:** 142 Fox Ridge Ln 22603

HOLIDAY INN WINCHESTER HISTORIC GATEWAY
　　　　　　　　　　　　　　　　　(540)667-3300

Hotel
$99-$299

Address: 333 Front Royal Pike 22602 **Location:** I-81 exit 313, just e. **Facility:** 130 units. 5 stories, interior corridors. **Pool:** heated indoor. **Activities:** exercise room. **Guest Services:** coin laundry.

THE HOTEL MODERN　　　　　　(540)678-8899
Hotel. **Address:** 1055 Millwood Pike 22602

RED ROOF INN - WINCHESTER   (540)667-5000

Motel
$50-$80

Address: 991 Millwood Pike 22602 **Location:** I-81 exit 313 northbound; exit 313A southbound, just se on US 50/17. **Facility:** 113 units. 2 stories (no elevator), exterior corridors. **Guest Services:** coin laundry. **Featured Amenity: continental breakfast.**

SLEEP INN & SUITES   (540)667-7636

Hotel
$75-$164

Address: 140 Costello Dr 22602 **Location:** I-81 exit 313, s on US 522, then just left. **Facility:** 72 units. 4 stories, interior corridors. **Amenities:** *Some:* safes. **Pool:** heated indoor. **Activities:** exercise room. **Guest Services:** valet and coin laundry. **Featured Amenity: continental breakfast.**

TOWNEPLACE SUITES BY MARRIOTT WINCHESTER   (540)722-2722

Extended Stay Hotel. **Address:** 170 Getty Ln 22602

| AAA Benefit: Members save 5% or more! |

WINGATE BY WYNDHAM   540/670-4283

Hotel
Rates not provided

Address: 150 Wingate Dr 22601 **Location:** I-81 exit 313 northbound; exit 313B southbound, 0.6 mi nw, then just s. **Facility:** 84 units. 4 stories, interior corridors. **Amenities:** safes. **Pool:** indoor. **Activities:** exercise room. **Guest Services:** valet and coin laundry. **Featured Amenity:** breakfast buffet.

WHERE TO EAT

CASTIGLIA'S ITALIAN EATERY   540/723-4650
Italian. Casual Dining. **Address:** 212 Grocery Ave 22602

CORK STREET TAVERN   540/667-3777
American. Casual Dining. **Address:** 8 W Cork St 22601

EL CENTRO   540/313-4583
Mexican. Casual Dining. **Address:** 1 N Loudoun St 22601

GEORGE'S FOOD & SPIRITS   540/678-4700
American. Fine Dining. **Address:** 103 E Piccadilly St 22601

GLORY DAYS GRILL   540/662-9922
American. Casual Dining. **Address:** 130 Featherbed Ln 22601

Where Diamonds make the difference:

AAA.com/travelguides/hotels

VENICE ITALIAN RESTAURANT   540/722-0992
Italian. Casual Dining. **Address:** 1490 N Frederick Pike 22601

VIOLINO RISTORANTE ITALIANO   540/667-8006
Northern Italian. Casual Dining. **Address:** 181 N Loudoun St 22601

WINTERGREEN pop. 165, elev. 3,084'

WINTERGREEN RESORT   434/325-2200
Resort Hotel. **Address:** 39 Mountain Inn Loop 22958

WISE pop. 3,286

BEST WESTERN OF WISE   (276)328-3500

Hotel
$82-$125

AAA Benefit: Members save 10% or more & earn 10% bonus points!

Address: 124 Woodland Dr SW 24293 **Location:** 1 mi n on US 23, just e. **Facility:** 60 units. 3 stories, interior corridors. **Terms:** cancellation fee imposed. **Pool:** heated indoor. **Activities:** exercise room. **Guest Services:** coin laundry.

WOODBRIDGE (B-12) pop. 4,055, elev. 75'
• Restaurants p. 294

Woodbridge, a census-designated place, is home to the Potomac Nationals, an affiliate of the Washington Nationals. The minor league baseball team plays at G. Richard Pfitzner Stadium at 7 County Complex Ct.; phone (703) 590-2311. If you'd rather play than watch, recreational activities such as hiking, fishing and boating can be enjoyed at 543-acre Leocylvania State Park *(see Recreation Areas Chart)*, on the Potomac River at 2001 Daniel K. Ludwig Dr. Phone (703) 730-8205.

Shopping: Potomac Mills (2700 Potomac Mills Cir.) has more than 225 factory outlet stores, including Coach, IKEA, Nordstrom Rack, Polo Ralph Lauren, Sears Appliance and Tommy Hilfiger.

BEST WESTERN POTOMAC MILLS   703/494-4433

Hotel
Rates not provided

AAA Benefit: Members save 10% or more & earn 10% bonus points!

Address: 14619 Potomac Mills Rd 22192 **Location:** I-95 exit 156B, 0.5 mi w. **Facility:** 172 units. 9 stories, interior corridors. **Pool:** outdoor. **Activities:** exercise room. **Guest Services:** valet and coin laundry.

COMFORT SUITES NEAR POTOMAC MILLS   (703)490-4100
Hotel. **Address:** 14525 Gideon Dr 22192

COUNTRY INN & SUITES BY CARLSON, POTOMAC MILLS/WOODBRIDGE   703/492-6868
Hotel. **Address:** 2621 Prince William Pkwy 22192

COURTYARD BY MARRIOTT POTOMAC MILLS/WOODBRIDGE
(703)491-4525
◈◈◈ Hotel. **Address:** 14300 Crossing Pl 22192

AAA Benefit:
Members save 5% or more!

FAIRFIELD INN & SUITES BY MARRIOTT POTOMAC MILLS
(703)497-4000
◈◈ Hotel. **Address:** 2610 Prince William Pkwy 22192

AAA Benefit:
Members save 5% or more!

HAMPTON INN BY HILTON POTOMAC MILLS/WOODBRIDGE
(703)490-2300
◈◈◈ Hotel. **Address:** 1240 Annapolis Way 22191

AAA Benefit:
Members save up to 10%!

HILTON GARDEN INN WOODBRIDGE
703/590-2500
◈◈◈ Hotel. **Address:** 2500 Neabsco Common Pl 22191

AAA Benefit:
Members save up to 10%!

HOLIDAY INN EXPRESS & SUITES-WOODBRIDGE
(703)576-1600
◈◈ Hotel. **Address:** 14030 Telegraph Rd 22192

HOMEWOOD SUITES BY HILTON WOODBRIDGE
703/590-0100
◈◈◈ Extended Stay Hotel. **Address:** 2650 Neabsco Common Pl 22191

AAA Benefit:
Members save up to 10%!

RESIDENCE INN BY MARRIOTT POTOMAC MILLS
(703)490-4020
◈◈◈ Extended Stay Hotel. **Address:** 14301 Crossing Pl 22192

AAA Benefit:
Members save 5% or more!

SLEEP INN WOODBRIDGE   (703)730-5508

◈◈ Hotel $79-$219

Address: 14080 Shoppers Best Way 22192 **Location:** I-95 exit 158B (Prince William Pkwy), 1.2 mi w. **Facility:** 61 units. 2 stories, interior corridors. *Bath:* shower only. **Activities:** exercise room. **Guest Services:** coin laundry. **Featured Amenity: continental breakfast.**

   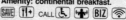

SPRINGHILL SUITES BY MARRIOTT POTOMAC MILLS/WOODBRIDGE
(703)576-9000
◈◈◈ Hotel. **Address:** 14325 Crossing Pl 22192

AAA Benefit:
Members save 5% or more!

WHERE TO EAT

AL-ZAYTOUN KABOB & GRILL   703/730-0410
◈ Afghan. Quick Serve. **Address:** 13871 Smoketown Rd 22192

BISTRO L'HERMITAGE   703/499-9550
◈◈◈ French. Fine Dining. **Address:** 12724 Occoquan Rd 22192

SILVER DINER   703/643-2363
◈◈ American. Casual Dining. **Address:** 14375 Smoketown Rd 22192

TASTE OF TANDOOR   703/897-7200
◈◈ Indian. Casual Dining. **Address:** 13836 Smoketown Rd 22192

WOODSTOCK pop. 5,097

COMFORT INN WOODSTOCK   (540)459-7600
◈◈◈ Hotel. **Address:** 1011 Motel Dr 22664

HAMPTON INN & SUITES BY HILTON WOODSTOCK
(540)459-7111

◈◈◈ Hotel $109-$179

AAA Benefit:
Members save up to 10%!

Address: 1150 Motel Dr 22664 **Location:** I-81 exit 283, just e. **Facility:** 92 units. 4 stories, interior corridors. **Terms:** 1-7 night minimum stay, cancellation fee imposed. **Amenities:** video games. **Pool:** heated indoor. **Activities:** hot tub, exercise room. **Guest Services:** coin laundry. **Featured Amenity: full hot breakfast.**

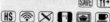

HOLIDAY INN EXPRESS WOODSTOCK   (540)459-5000
◈◈◈ Hotel. **Address:** 1130 Motel Dr 22664

THE INN AT NARROW PASSAGE   (540)459-8000
◈◈◈ Historic Bed & Breakfast. **Address:** 30 Chapman Landing Rd 22664

WHERE TO EAT

JOE'S STEAKHOUSE   540/459-5637
◈◈ Steak. Casual Dining. **Address:** 124 S Main St 22664

PAISANO'S   540/459-8756
◈◈ Italian. Casual Dining. **Address:** 483 W Reservoir Rd 22664

SPRING HOUSE TAVERN   540/459-4755
◈◈ American. Casual Dining. **Address:** 325 S Main St 22664

WOODSTOCK CAFE   540/459-8888
◈ American. Quick Serve. **Address:** 117 S Main St 22664

WOOLWINE

THE MOUNTAIN ROSE INN   (276)930-1057
◈◈◈ Historic Bed & Breakfast. **Address:** 1787 Charity Hwy 24185

WYTHEVILLE (H-5) pop. 8,211, elev. 2,230'

At the crossroads of early pioneer routes, Wytheville (WITH-vill) was a 19th-century transportation center. Two federal highways, I-77 and I-81, make it a modern-day junction.

Founded in 1790, Wythe County was named for Virginia's first signer of the Declaration of Independence, George Wythe. The town was the site of several Civil War skirmishes, including a July 1863 attack by Union forces under Col. John Toland. The mountain town in the Blue Ridge Highlands later became a summer resort due to its cool climate and "healing waters." The second wife of President Woodrow Wilson, Edith Bolling, was born in Wytheville, the daughter of a local judge.

The surrounding Jefferson National Forest *(see place listing p. 119)*, Big Walker Mountain Scenic Byway and the historic New River offer vast recreational opportunities including hiking, bicycling, fishing, camping, boating and picnicking. A 100-foot observation tower on top of Big Walker Mountain offers a panoramic view of the surrounding mountains. Numerous sites on Virginia's Birding Trails and Virginia's Civil War Trails can also be explored. The Claw of the Dragon Motorcycle Trail offers more than 200 miles of scenic routes to explore.

Wytheville Convention & Visitors Bureau: 975 Tazewell St., Wytheville, VA 24382. **Phone:** (276) 223-3355 or (877) 347-8307.

Self-guiding tours: Walking tours of the town showcase more than 100 historic structures, beginning downtown at Wytheville's Heritage Preservation Center at 115 W. Spiller St. Tours are divided into several themed loops allowing for both short and long walks. Both printed brochures and audio versions of the tours are available from the heritage center and from the convention and visitors bureau. A mobile website also is available, as is a brochure describing a driving tour of local African-American historical sites.

Shopping: Along East Lee Highway off I-81/I-77, three antique malls collectively feature more than 300 dealers.

BEST WESTERN WYTHEVILLE INN   (270)228-7300

Hotel
$70-$131

AAA Benefit: Members save 10% or more & earn 10% bonus points!

Address: 355 Nye Rd 24382 **Location:** I-77 exit 41, just e. **Facility:** 99 units. 2 stories (no elevator), interior corridors. **Terms:** cancellation fee imposed. **Amenities:** safes. **Pool:** outdoor. **Activities:** exercise room. **Featured Amenity:** full hot breakfast.

BUDGET HOST INN   (276)228-8618
Motel. **Address:** 705 Chapman Rd 24382

COMFORT INN   (276)228-4488
Hotel
$90-$135
Address: 315 Holston Rd 24382 **Location:** I-81 exit 70, just w. **Facility:** 78 units. 2 stories (no elevator), interior corridors. **Pool:** outdoor. **Activities:** exercise room. **Guest Services:** valet laundry. **Featured Amenity:** full hot breakfast.

COMFORT INN   (276)637-4281
Hotel. **Address:** 2594 E Lee Hwy 24382

COMFORT SUITES   (276)228-1234
Hotel. **Address:** 695 Peppers Ferry Rd 24382

COUNTRY INN & SUITES BY CARLSON   (276)223-1058
Hotel. **Address:** 697 Peppers Ferry Rd 24382

DAYS INN   276/228-5500
Motel. **Address:** 150 Malin Dr 24382

FAIRFIELD INN & SUITES BY MARRIOTT   (276)228-8080
Hotel. **Address:** 200 Marriott Way 24382   **AAA Benefit:** Members save 5% or more!

HAMPTON INN   (276)228-6090
Hotel. **Address:** 950 Peppers Ferry Rd 24382   **AAA Benefit:** Members save up to 10%!

LA QUINTA INN WYTHEVILLE   (276)228-7400
Hotel. **Address:** 1800 E Main 24382

QUALITY INN & SUITES   (276)228-4241
Motel. **Address:** 2015 E Main St 24382

RED ROOF INN & SUITES- WYTHEVILLE   (276)223-1700
Motel. **Address:** 1900 E Main St 24382

SLEEP INN   (276)625-0667

Hotel
$70-$180
Address: 135 Nye Cir 24382 **Location:** I-77 exit 41, just e. **Facility:** 72 units. 3 stories, interior corridors. **Activities:** exercise room. **Featured Amenity:** breakfast buffet.

WHERE TO EAT

1776 LOG HOUSE   276/228-4139
American. Fine Dining. **Address:** 520 E Main St 24382

PEKING RESTAURANT   276/228-5515
Chinese. Casual Dining. **Address:** 105 Malin Dr 24382

SAGEBRUSH STEAKHOUSE   276/228-7103
Steak. Casual Dining. **Address:** 170 Nye Cir 24382

SKEETERS   276/228-2611
American. Quick Serve. **Address:** 165 E Main St 24382

YORKTOWN (B-3) pop. 195, elev. 12'
- **Hotels p. 297** • **Restaurants p. 298**
- **Hotels & Restaurants map & index p. 128**
- **Part of Williamsburg, Jamestown & Yorktown area — see map p. 273**

Yorktown, founded in 1691, was a busy 18th-century tobacco port. The town is best remembered for the Siege of Yorktown, which effectively ended the Revolutionary War. Less than 100 years later, Yorktown was embroiled in another major battle when Union general George McClellan landed his

(See map & index p. 128.)

troops at Fort Monroe in 1862 and opened the Peninsular Campaign.

Gen. John Magruder, commanding the Confederate forces, fortified Yorktown and threw a line of trenches from town to the James River. Magruder marched his outnumbered forces back and forth behind the fortifications and convinced McClellan that he was facing a force twice the size of his own.

So convincing was Magruder's charade that the Union forces slowed their advance and began to besiege the town. Rather than face the Union artillery amassing in Yorktown, Gen. Joseph Johnston, replacing Magruder, moved his troops toward Williamsburg. The Union forces moved into Yorktown and retained control throughout the rest of the war.

Ten 18th-century buildings survived the 1781 Battle of Yorktown and can still be seen. While most are private, several are open to the public, including Nelson House and Moore House; phone (757) 898-2410. The restored Somerwell House, at Main and Church streets, was once an 18th-century inn and is now a retail establishment that sells 17th- and 18th-century reproductions of ceramics, glassware, furniture and prints. The free Yorktown Trolley, which operates spring through fall, stops approximately every 20-25 minutes at nine locations in the historic area.

The headquarters and the Yorktown Battlefield Visitor Center of Colonial National Historical Park *(see place listing p. 97)* are on the northeast edge of town at the end of the Colonial Parkway. For further information about the park and homes phone (757) 898-2410.

Yorktown Information Center/Gallery at York Hall: 301 Main St., P.O. Box 226, Yorktown, VA 23690. **Phone:** (757) 890-4490.

Self-guiding tours: Brochures detailing a self-guiding walking tour of Historic Yorktown are available from the information center/gallery. The route begins at York Hall, 301 Main St., and showcases more than 50 noteworthy sites, structures and museums.

Shopping: The streets of Historic Yorktown are lined with art galleries, antique shops and boutiques. Specialty stores designed in the spirit of Colonial architecture offer patriotic items, artwork, home decor, jewelry, clothing, beach sundries and more. Retailers are mainly clustered along Main Street, Ballard Street and along the waterfront on Water Street.

AMERICAN REVOLUTION MUSEUM AT YORKTOWN is off I-64 exit 247 on SR 1020 near the Colonial Pkwy. and US 17. The indoor and outdoor exhibits at this museum of the American Revolution, tell the story of the founding of the United States and the complexity of the country's Revolutionary heritage. Permanent exhibition galleries include period artifacts, immersive environments, dioramas, short films and an experiential theater with wind, smoke and cannon-fire special effects.

Living-history takes place outdoors where visitors learn about daily life in a re-created Continental Army encampment. Soldiers at a 250-person amphitheater demonstrate how to fire a musket and recruit and train "volunteers" for positions on an artillery crew. Rows of tents include an adjutant's office, captain's quarters and an earthen kitchen.

A different perspective can be seen at a middle-class Revolution-era farm complete with a house, a tobacco barn, a kitchen, fields and a garden. Visitors can help the costumed interpreters tend crops and lend a hand with daily chores. Recently reconstructed slave quarters reflect the lives of enslaved African-Americans during the Revolution.

(See map & index p. 128.)

Time: Allow 2 hours minimum. **Hours:** Daily 9-6, June 15-Aug. 15; 9-5, rest of year. Closed Jan. 1 and Christmas. **Cost:** $15; $7.50 (ages 6-12). Combination ticket with Jamestown Settlement (see attraction listing p. 157) $25.50; $12.25 (ages 6-12). Combination tickets with other area attractions also are available. **Phone:** (757) 253-4838 or (888) 593-4682.

SCHOONERS *ALLIANCE* AND *SERENITY* depart Riverwalk Landing Pier at the corner of Ballard and Water sts. on the downtown waterfront. Two-hour sightseeing cruises are available aboard the schooners, which sail along the York River, past Yorktown Battlefield and other historic sites. Two-hour sunset sails and science cruises also are offered. Family-friendly pirate adventure cruises are offered.

Hours: Sightseeing cruises depart daily at 11 and 2, Apr.-Oct. Sunset cruises depart daily; departure times vary seasonally. Pirate cruises depart at 11, May-Sept. Phone ahead to confirm schedule. **Cost:** Sightseeing cruise $37; $22 (ages 0-12). Sunset cruise $37. Reservations are recommended. **Phone:** (757) 639-1233 or (844) 724-5956. [GT] [T]

WATERMEN'S MUSEUM is e. on SR 238 to 309 Water Ct. Both indoor galleries and outdoor exhibits portray the history of Virginia's civilian and military watermen, from pre-Colonial to modern times, who worked on or along the Chesapeake Bay and its tributaries. Exhibits include boats, ship models, paintings, dioramas, photographs and tools. A full-size replica Colonial windmill is on the property. On the beach, a 40-foot, gondola-style replica of a 1775 gunboat. Re-enactors can be seen firing cannons and performing seaside duties on a regular basis.

A variety of special events and activities, including Friday concerts, dances and lectures, are offered; phone ahead for more information. **Hours:** Tues.-Sat. 10-5, Sun. 1-5, Apr. 1-Christmas; hours vary rest of year. **Cost:** $5; $4 (students with ID); free (ages 0-12 and active military with ID). **Phone:** (757) 887-2641. [T]

YORKTOWN BATTLEFIELD is on the eastern end of the Colonial Pkwy. The last major battle of the Revolutionary War was fought here in 1781, when Gen. Charles Cornwallis sought to establish a British naval port at Yorktown with 8,300 soldiers. Gen. George Washington moved his American army into Virginia to reinforce the Marquis de Lafayette's allied forces; the French fleet blockaded Chesapeake Bay. Under siege by 17,600 Continental troops, Cornwallis surrendered.

The battlefield is administered by Colonial National Historical Park (see place listing p. 97). Two driving tours begin at the visitor center. The 7-mile Battlefield Tour Road includes earthworks, siege lines and the site of the British surrender. At Moore House, officers met to negotiate the capitulation. The 9-mile Encampment Tour Road passes allied camps, Washington's Headquarters and the French Cemetery.

Hours: Roads open daily 8-dusk. Closed Jan. 1, Thanksgiving and Christmas. **Cost:** Admission, valid for 7 days, $7; free (ages 0-15). Battlefield Tour Road driving tour CD $4.95. **Phone:** (757) 898-2410.

Yorktown Battlefield Visitor Center is on the s. edge of Yorktown at 1000 Colonial Pkwy. The center includes a museum housing the tents used by Gen. George Washington, a reconstructed section of a gun deck and a British frigate captain's cabin. A 15-minute film relates the events of the siege. Driving tours begin at this point; self-guiding tour leaflets and audio tours of the battlefield are available.

Hours: Daily 9-5. Closed Jan. 1, Thanksgiving and Christmas. **Cost:** Admission, valid for 7 days, $7; free (ages 0-15). Battlefield Tour Road driving tour CD $4.95. **Phone:** (757) 898-2410.

CANDLEWOOD SUITES-YORKTOWN   757/952-1120 **15**
♦♦♦ Extended Stay Hotel. **Address:** 320 Commonwealth Dr 23693

COURTYARD BY MARRIOTT   (757)874-9000 **13**
♦♦♦ Hotel. **Address:** 105 Cybernetics Way 23693

AAA Benefit: Members save 5% or more!

DUKE OF YORK HOTEL   757/898-3232

Hotel
Rates not provided

Address: 508 Water St 23690. **Location:** Waterfront. SR 238; downtown. **Facility:** 57 units. 2-3 stories, interior/exterior corridors. **Terms:** check-in 4 pm. **Pool:** outdoor. **Activities:** beach access.

RED ROOF INN YORKTOWN   (757)283-1111 **19**
♦♦ Hotel. **Address:** 4531 George Washington Memorial Hwy 23692

STAYBRIDGE SUITES   757/251-6644 **16**
♦♦♦ Extended Stay Hotel. **Address:** 401 Commonwealth Dr 23693

TOWNEPLACE SUITES BY MARRIOTT
(757)874-8884 **14**

♦♦♦
Extended Stay Hotel
$67-$211

TOWNEPLACE SUITES MARRIOTT
AAA Benefit: Members save 5% or more!

Address: 200 Cybernetics Way 23693 **Location:** I-64 exit 256B, e to Kiln Creek Pkwy. **Facility:** 94 kitchen units, some two bedrooms. 3 stories, interior corridors. **Terms:** cancellation fee imposed. **Pool:** outdoor. **Activities:** exercise room. **Guest Services:** valet and coin laundry.

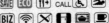

/ SOME UNITS

(See map & index p. 128.)

WHERE TO EAT

BEACH DELLY   757/886-5890

♦♦
American
Casual Dining
$10-$24

AAA Inspector Notes: This simple spot offers panoramic views of the riverfront from its beachside perch. The simple menu offers local favorites such as she-crab soup, local scallops, subs, burgers, pizzas with a wide variety of gourmet toppings and boardwalk fries. **Features:** beer & wine. **Address:** 524 Water St 23690 **Location:** Downtown. [L] [D]

THE CARROT TREE   757/988-1999

♦ Sandwiches Soup. Casual Dining. **Address:** 323 Water St 23690

COUNTY GRILL & SMOKEHOUSE   757/591-0600   [22]

♦♦ Barbecue. Casual Dining. **Address:** 1215 George Washington Pkwy, Suite A 23693

FOOD CRAFT KITCHEN & BAR   757/234-6940   [21]

♦♦ Breakfast Comfort Food. Casual Dining. **Address:** 5005 Victory Blvd, Suite A1 23693

SMOKIN' JOE'S BARBEQUE   757/875-7774

♦ Barbecue. Casual Dining. **Address:** 5619 George Washington Memorial Hwy 23692

ZION CROSSROADS

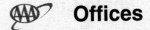 **Offices**

Main office listings are shown in **BOLD TYPE** and toll-free member service numbers appear in *ITALIC TYPE*.
All are closed Saturdays, Sundays and holidays unless otherwise indicated.
The addresses, phone numbers and hours for any AAA/CAA office are subject to change.
The type of service provided is designated below the name of the city where the office is located:

✦ Auto travel services, including books and maps, and on-demand TripTik® routings.
● Auto travel services, including selected books and maps, and on-demand TripTik® routings.
■ Books/maps only, no marked maps or on-demand TripTik® routings.
▲ Travel Agency Services, cruise, tour, air, car and rail reservations; domestic and international hotel reservations; passport photo services; international and domestic travel guides and maps; travel money products; and International Driving Permits. In addition, assistance with travel related insurance products including trip cancellation, travel accident, lost luggage, trip delay and assistance products.
✪ Insurance services provided. If only this icon appears, only insurance services are provided at that office.
🜚 Car Care Plus Facility provides car care services.
🔌 Electric vehicle charging station on premises.

AAA NATIONAL OFFICE: 1000 AAA DRIVE, HEATHROW, FLORIDA 32746-5063, (407) 444-7000

VIRGINIA

ALEXANDRIA—AAA MID-ATLANTIC, 2231 EISENHOWER AVE, 22314. WEEKDAYS (M-F) 9:00-5:30, SAT 9:00-3:00. (703) 549-1080 ✦▲✪

BLUEFIELD—AAA ALLIED GROUP INC, 4003A COLLEGE AVE, 24605. WEEKDAYS (M-F) 9:00-6:00, SAT 9:00-3:00. (276) 988-6800, *(800) 642-5878.* ✦▲✪

CHARLOTTESVILLE—AAA MID-ATLANTIC, 616 ALBEMARLE SQ, 22901. WEEKDAYS (M-F) 9:00-5:30, SAT 9:00-3:00. (434) 017 5930 ✦▲✪

CHESAPEAKE—AAA TIDEWATER VIRGINIA, 1023 S BATTLEFIELD BLVD, 23322. WEEKDAYS (M-F) 8:00-6:00, SAT 8:00-4:00. (757) 963-1222 🔌

CHESAPEAKE—AAA TIDEWATER VIRGINIA, 111 KEMPSVILLE RD, 23320. WEEKDAYS (M-F) 8:30-5:30, SAT 8:30-12:30. (757) 547-9741 ✦▲✪

COLONIAL HEIGHTS—AAA MID-ATLANTIC, 707 SOUTHPARK BLVD #7, 23834. WEEKDAYS (M-F) 9:00-5:30, SAT 9:00-3:00. (804) 520-7388 ✦▲✪

DANVILLE—AAA MID-ATLANTIC, 165 HOLT GARRISON PK 530B, 24540. WEEKDAYS (M-F) 8:30-5:00. (434) 797-2493 ✪

FAIRFAX—AAA MID-ATLANTIC, 4100 MONUMENT CORNER DR, 22030. WEEKDAYS (M-F) 9:00-5:30, SAT 9:00-3:00. (703) 222-4200 ✦▲✪

FAIRFAX—AAA MID-ATLANTIC, 9400 MAIN ST, 22031. WEEKDAYS (M-F) 7:00-7:00, SAT 8:00-5:00, SUN 10:00-4:00. (703) 995-3970 ✦▲✪

FALLS CHURCH—AAA MID-ATLANTIC, 6290 ARLINGTON BLVD, 22044. WEEKDAYS (M-F) 7:00-7:00, SAT 8:00-5:00, SUN 10:00-4:00. (703) 269-4040 ■▲✪🔌

FREDERICKSBURG—AAA MID-ATLANTIC, 2871 PLANK RD, 22401. WEEKDAYS (M-F) 7:00-7:00, SAT 8:00-5:00, SUN 10:00-4:00. (540) 785-0282 ✦▲✪🔌

HAMPTON—AAA TIDEWATER VIRGINIA, 1520 ABERDEEN RD, 23666. WEEKDAYS (M-F) 8:00-6:00, SAT 8:00-4:00. (757) 963-1222 🔌

HAMPTON—AAA TIDEWATER VIRGINIA, 1520 ABERDEEN RD, 23666. WEEKDAYS (M-F) 8:30-5:30, SAT 8:30-12:30. (757) 826-1061 ✦▲✪

LYNCHBURG—AAA MID-ATLANTIC, 717-C WARDS FERRY RD, 24502. WEEKDAYS (M-F) 9:00-5:30, SAT 9:00-1:00. (434) 385-0091 ✦▲✪

MANASSAS—AAA MID-ATLANTIC, 7865 SUDLEY RD, 20109. WEEKDAYS (M-F) 7:00-7:00, SAT 8:00-5:00, SUN 10:00-4:00. (571) 383-3790 ■▲✪🔌

MIDLOTHIAN—AAA MID-ATLANTIC, 13732 HULL STREET RD, 23112. WEEKDAYS (M-F) 7:00-7:00, SAT 8:00-5:00, SUN 10:00-4:00 (804) 744-1513 ✦▲✪🔌

NEWPORT NEWS—AAA TIDEWATER VIRGINIA, 733 J CLYDE MORRIS BLVD, 23601. WEEKDAYS (M-F) 8:30-5:30, SAT 8:30-12:30. (757) 246-4746 ✦▲

NORFOLK—AAA TIDEWATER VIRGINIA, 330 W 22ND ST STE 101, 23517. WEEKDAYS (M-F) 9:00-5:30, SAT 9:00-1:00. (757) 622-5634 ✦▲

NORFOLK—AAA TIDEWATER VIRGINIA, 5732 E VIRGINIA BCH BLVD, 23502. WEEKDAYS (M-F) 8:00-6:00, SAT 8:00-4:00. (757) 963-1222 🔌

RICHMOND—AAA MID-ATLANTIC, 1201 MALL DR, 23235. WEEKDAYS (M-F) 9:00-5:30, SAT 9:00-3:00. (804) 379-4487 ✦▲✪

RICHMOND—AAA MID-ATLANTIC, 7009 WEST BROAD STR, 23294. WEEKDAYS (M-F) 7:00-7:00, SAT 8:00-5:00, SUN 10:00-4:00. (804) 281-7100 ✦▲✪🔌

ROANOKE—AAA MID-ATLANTIC, 1376 TOWNE SQUARE BLVD NW, 24012. WEEKDAYS (M-F) 9:00-5:30, SAT 9:00-3:00. (540) 344-0943 ✦▲✪

SUFFOLK—AAA TIDEWATER VIRGINIA, 3529 BRIDGE RD, 23435. WEEKDAYS (M-F) 8:00-6:00, SAT 8:00-4:00. (757) 963-1222 🔌

SUFFOLK—AAA TIDEWATER VIRGINIA, 3529 BRIDGE RD, 23435. WEEKDAYS (M-F) 8:30-5:30, SAT 8:30-12:30. (757) 397-5941 ✦▲✪

VIENNA—AAA MID-ATLANTIC, 8300 OLD COURTHSE RD #110, 22182. WEEKDAYS (M-F) 9:00-5:30, SAT 9:00-3:00. (703) 790-2600 ✦▲✪

VIRGINIA BEACH—AAA TIDEWATER VIRGINIA, 1424 N GREAT NECK RD, 23454. WEEKDAYS (M-F) 8:00-6:00, SAT 8:00-4:00. (757) 963-1222 🔌

VIRGINIA BEACH—AAA TIDEWATER VIRGINIA, 296 KINGS GRANT RD, 23452. WEEKDAYS (M-F) 8:30-5:30, SAT 8:30-12:30. (757) 340-7271 ✦▲✪

VIRGINIA BEACH—AAA TIDEWATER VIRGINIA, 5366 VIRGINIA BEACH BLVD, 23462. WEEKDAYS (M-F) 8:30-5:30, SAT 8:30-12:30. (757) 233-3800 ✦▲✪

WILLIAMSBURG—AAA TIDEWATER VIRGINIA, 6517 RICHMOND RD, 23188. WEEKDAYS (M-F) 8:00-6:00, SAT 8:00-4:00. (757) 963-1222 🔌

WILLIAMSBURG—AAA TIDEWATER VIRGINIA, 6517 RICHMOND RD, 23188. WEEKDAYS (M-F) 8:30-5:30, SAT 8:30-12:30. (757) 564-7711 ✦▲✪

Photo Credits

Page numbers are in bold type. Picture credit abbreviations are as follows:
■ (i) numeric sequence from top to bottom, left to right ■ (AAA) AAA Travel library.

A REWARDING PARTNERSHIP.

DRIVING EXCLUSIVE SAVINGS AND BENEFITS FOR AAA MEMBERS.

- Save up to 20%* on base rate for car rentals
- Earn Hertz Gold Plus Rewards® points
- No charge for additional driver if AAA member
- Free use of one child seat
- Special daily rate of $6.99/ for NeverLost® navigation system

For discounts and reservations, visit AAA.com/hertz.

*Taxes, fees and options excluded. Terms apply.